ENCYCLOPEDIA OF 20TH-CENTURY ARCHITECTURE

ENCYCLOPEDIA OF 20TH-CENTURY ARCHITECTURE

GENERAL EDITOR:
VITTORIO MAGNAGO LAMPUGNANI

HARRY N. ABRAMS, INC., PUBLISHERS, NEW YORK

Translated from the German and edited by Barry Bergdoll

Library of Congress Cataloging in Publication Data

Hatje-Lexikon der Architektur des 20. Jahrhunderts.
English.
Encyclopedia of 20th century architecture.

Translation of: Hatje-Lexikon der Architektur des 20. Jahrhunderts/translated from the German and edited by Barry Bergdoll.
"Originally published in 1964 as Encyclopedia of modern Architecture. Translated and adapted from Knaurs Lexikon der modernen Architektur"—
Includes index.
I. Architecture, Modern—20th century—Dictionaries.
I. Lampugnani, Vittorio Magnago, 1951-
II. Bergdoll, Barry. III. Title.
NA680.H3913 1985 724.9'I'0321 84-24166
ISBN 0-8109-0860-3
ISBN 0-8109-2335-1 (pbk.)

Published in Great Britain under the title *The Thames and Hudson Encyclopedia of 20th-Century Architecture*

Printed and bound in Japan

General Editor's Preface

The predecessor of this work, the *Encyclopaedia of Modern Architecture*, was first published in 1963. Now, after an interval of twenty years, a new, expanded and completely revised version is available.

Any attempt at an overview of architectural development, such as that presented in an encyclopaedia, is inevitably rooted in the assumptions and historical perspectives of the period in which it is compiled. It comes as no surprise, therefore, that in the early 1960s an over-riding concern was to present an extensive panorama of architectural modernism, with the result that concepts and movements like contemporary historicism or Art Deco were – despite their wide implications – omitted. Similarly, important figures such as Heinrich Tessenow, then not the subject of much discussion, were not accorded individual entries alongside a Mies van der Rohe or a Terragni; even Erich Mendelsohn was included primarily for his bold use of modern materials, rather than for the expressive and sculptural qualities of his work; and, in the context of building materials, glass, steel and reinforced concrete – viewed as primary stimuli in the evolution of a new architecture – were accorded their own entries.

In short, after more than twenty years, the preparation of a new edition could not be restricted to bringing existing entries up to date and introducing new names and concepts. Rather, the entire work had to be revised and given a broader historical basis. It is thus not a matter of chance that this latest edition appears under a different title, one in which the emotive and subjective concept of the Modern Movement has been replaced by a neutral designation based on the period covered.

The scope of this encyclopaedia is, then, the architecture and urban planning of the 20th century seen in an overall spectrum and presented in three different general categories of subject-matter: biographies of individual architects; surveys of architectural developments in individual countries; and overviews of movements, groups and stylistic trends.

The number of individual biographical entries which can be included in an encyclopaedia of this type is of necessity limited, but an index of proper names is also included for the reader's convenience. In each case the decision for or against inclusion has to be based on a variety of criteria, and many an omission may well seem unjust. The same holds true in the case of those individual countries whose significant architectural output is the subject of closer scrutiny; as with the biographical entries, the choice has had to be severely restricted and the coverage general. The situation is no different, either, in the case of movements, groups and trends; their inclusion brings with it an involvement in the questionable game of philological classification and labelling – something which inevitably tends to categorize in crude terms the complex and multifarious elements that interact with each other in a cultural context.

The era in which an encyclopaedia could lay claim to being a tool for 'knowing everything' is past. Denis Diderot and Jean-Baptiste d'Alembert could still put forth a thoroughly unified and complete system of human knowledge as a manifesto of the Enlightenment. Today, when knowledge presents itself as fragmentary and contradictory, it is no longer possible to produce encyclopaedias in which a great deal of varied information is juxtaposed with equal weighting. Thus, our aim here is to offer a handbook which contains an overview, and even more a book to provide the reader with a sense of orientation within a larger context, rather than to present a definitive and complete compilation of facts. The latter is better achieved in works devoted to specific topics.

Jorge Luis Borges' statement that 'to possess an encyclopaedia is to possess all books' can only be valid if the general work directs the reader to the specific. The present encyclopaedia seeks to achieve this by means of bibliographical citations at the end of individual entries, as well as by its overall structure: by taking a middle course in being as exact and complete as necessary, but at the same time as lucid and as far-reaching as possible. Thus, the architects selected are those who first formulated or advocated independent and clearly stated positions (and in some cases themselves embodied shifts in entirely new directions); the countries are those which have witnessed important and influential architectural developments; and the movements those which have had a decisive influence on the entire architectural panorama.

Even if the final responsibility for the selection and the balancing of the entries lies with the editor, there is certainly no other type of book in which one relies more on the help of others than is the case with an encyclopaedia. The present work is the result of the collective efforts of a group of colleagues, almost without exception well-acquainted and often close friends, who, despite holding varying viewpoints, united in this common purpose. These contributors cannot all be suitably thanked here, and least of all Axel Menges, who was the most closely involved with the book as a relentless reader and a most competent contributor, as well as bearing the brunt of the task of co-ordination; and Gerd Hatje, who was naturally also closely involved as a contributor, friend, critic, adviser and publisher.

Finally, mention must be made of the fact that a significant part of my own work on this book was done at Columbia University, New York, especially on those articles which directly concern the USA. This would not have been possible without the generous support of the American Council of Learned Societies and, in particular, the personal and friendly interest of Richard Downar, Director of the American Studies Program.

VML

List of contributors

FA	Friedrich Achleitner
RB	Reyner Banham
BB	Barry Bergdoll
MB	Moritz Besser
PB	Peter Blake
CB	Christian Borngräber
RBr	Robert Bruegmann
MC	Max Cetto
AC-P	Alexandre Cirici-Pellicer
JLC	Jean Louis Cohen
RLD	Robert L. Delevoy
PD	Philip Drew
TF	Tobias Faber
KF	Kenneth Frampton
JG	Jorge Glusberg
VG	Vittorio Gregotti
OWG	Oswald W. Grube
IH	Ids Haagsma
HdH	Hilde de Haan
HH	Horst Hartung
GHa	Gerd Hatje
GHe	Gilbert Herbert
AH	Antonio Hernandez
TH	Thomas Herzog
JMJ	John M. Jacobus, Jr
FJ	Falk Jaeger
JJ	Jürgen Joedicke
WHJ	William H. Jordy
WK	Walter Kieß
BL	Björn Linn
DM	David Mackay
VML	Vittorio Magnago Lampugnani
CM	Carolina Mang
KM	Karl Mang
RM	Robert Maxwell
HM	Harold Meek
AM	Axel Menges
NM	Norbert Meßler
RMi	Robin Middleton
KM	Kirmo Mikkola
HEM	Henrique E. Mindlin
LM	Leonardo Mosso
CFO	Christian F. Otto
JPa	Jürgen Paul
WP	Wolfgang Pehnt
JPo	Julius Posener
CR	Christopher Riopelle
PR	Peter Rumpf
JR	Joseph Rykwert
PCvS	Peter C. von Seidlein
MS	Margit Staber
GS	Gavin Stamp
PS	Pekka Suhonen
JS	Julia Szabó
BT	Barbara Tilson
GV	Giulia Veronesi
JJV	Jacobus Johannes Vriend
FW	Frank Werner
AW	Arnold Whittick
IBW	Iain Boyd Whyte
AWi	Alfred Willis
HY	Hajime Yatsuka

Dating

In references to individual buildings, the dates cited are presented in accordance with the information available. If specific, distinct dates are known for the original design and for subsequent construction, both are given (e.g. '1937, 1939–42'); in many instances, however, only the overall period from design to completion or of the period of construction alone may be known, and in such cases a simple span of years is indicated (e.g., '1939–42'); in other instances it has only been possible to state the year of completion.

Cross-references

Further information in related entries is indicated by means of an asterisk preceding the title of the entry to be consulted.

A

Aalto, (Hugo) Alvar (Henrik), b. Kuortane, Finland 1898, d. Helsinki 1976. Studied at the Polytechnic in Helsinki from 1916, graduating in 1921; he was a pupil of Armas Lindgren and Lars Sonck. In the following years he travelled widely in Scandinavia, Central Europe and Italy and was probably active for a short time in the Planning Office of the Gothenburg Fair of 1923. His career began officially with the Tampere Industrial Exhibition of 1922, although various minor works dating from his student years are known.

In 1923 A. opened his first office in Jyväskylä, and in 1925 he married the architect Aino Marsio, who was to be his most important collaborator until her death in 1949, above all in handling the production and direction of the firm of Artek Wooden Furniture, which was first conceived in 1928 in conjunction with the construction of the Sanatorium at Paimio.

In 1927 A. left Jyväskylä, where he had designed several important buildings including the Workers' Club of 1923–5 and the building for the Patriots' Associations, 1927–9 – works which belong to his pre-functional, neo-classical period. He settled in Turku, then Finland's most artistically receptive city. These were key years in his development as an architect, a period in which his works attest to the same direction and the same level of quality as the most advanced contemporary work in Central Europe. The standardized block of flats of 1927–8 in Turku, with its prefabricated concrete elements, is comparable with the contemporary experiments of *Mies van der Rohe and *Gropius in Stuttgart.

In 1929 A. worked in collaboration with *Bryggman on the exhibition held to celebrate the 700th anniversary of the city of Turku; staged one year before the better-known Stockholm Exhibition designed by *Asplund, it was, together with the house A. built in Turku, the first complete and public expression of modern architecture in Scandinavia. In the same year A. was drawn into the international architectural avant garde as the result of Sigfried Giedion's praise and through his participation at the meeting of *CIAM. This year also marks the beginning of his relationship with artists such as Fernand Léger, Constantin Brancusi, László Moholy-Nagy, Georges Braque and Alexander Calder. A. and his family moved to Helsinki in 1931, an event which signalled his complete integration into Finnish cultural life.

The highly important Turku period closed with the shift of A.'s work and of Finnish architecture in general towards modernism. At the same time his work in Turku anticipated the later, fully developed Aalto style. Thus, the works of this period already encapsulated the outstanding characteristic of A.'s architecture: its capacity to be both of its time and essentially timeless. Examples are the Headquarters of the *Turun Sanomat* newspaper in Turku (1927–8, 1928–9), the Library in Viipuri (1927, 1930–5) and the Sanatorium of Southwest Finland in Paimio (1928, 1929–33). Numerous other works date from this period, many of which were soon to become classics of modern architecture: A.'s own house in Helsinki (1934, 1935–6); the Finnish Pavilion at the Paris Exposition Universelle (1935, 1936–7); the complex for the Cellulose Factory in Sunila (1935–7, 1936–9); the Villa Mairea, near Noormakku (1937–8); the Finnish Pavilion at the New York World's Fair (1937, 1938–9), and the Terrace House in Kauttua (1937, 1938–40). Moreover, several unexecuted designs of this period are essential to an understanding of the complex themes of A.'s work. These include: the Blomberg Cinema in Helsinki (1938); the competition design for the extension of the University Library in Helsinki

Aalto. Municipal Library, Viipuri (1930–5)

Aalto. Cellulose Factory, Sunila (1935–7, 1936–9)

Aalto. Town Hall, Säynätsalo (1949, 1950–2)

(1938); the competition entry for the Haka district in Helsinki (1940); the 'Experimental City' (1941); and the development plan for the Kokemäki valley (1941–2).

The war years, during which A. served on the front, and the period immediately after the war, in which he was actively engaged in reconstruction work in Finland (including the development plan for the ruined capital of Finnish Lapland, Rovaniemi, which he drew up in 1944–5), interrupted the architect's creative development; around 1950, however, his fertile mind was directed towards even more complex problems, considering simultaneously the fundamental physical, psychological, social and cultural needs of the era. From this period date: the Senior Students' Dormitory (Baker House) at the Massachusetts Institute of Technology in Cambridge, Mass. (1947–8); and the Town Hall in Säynätsalo (1949, 1950–2), a timeless masterpiece in which a love of materials and a romantic sense of space are rediscovered as a means to enhance the social and political values of the community. The unrealized design for the cemetery chapel in Malm in north Helsinki (1950) reflects a psychological sensitivity to human fragility and a respect for the pain experienced by those having to face the fact of another person's death; here Aalto achieved the profundity and tenderness of high poetry, for which no parallel exists in the architecture of this period. Likewise unrealized, the cemetery project for Kongens Lyngby, near Copenhagen (1951), succeeded more than any other design in encapsulating A.'s relationship to Nature as a logical collaborator in the creative process. Finally, the project for the Vogelweidplatz in Vienna (1953) expresses another recurrent and complex theme in A.'s work – the effect on the individual of being handled as part of the greater mass.

A. achieved at this point an absolute control in the handling of technique and space, based on his thirty years' experience and enriched by his continual involvement with human and psychological needs. This was also the period of his urban involvement, culminating in his different plans for the centre of the Finnish capital (1959–73). His most important buildings in Helsinki include: the National Pensions Institution (1948, 1952–6); the Rautatalo Office Building (1952, 1953–5); the Cultural Centre (1955–8); the Administration Building of the Enso-

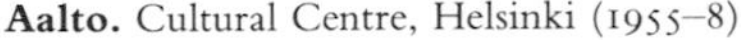

Aalto. Cultural Centre, Helsinki (1955–8)

Aalto. Vuoksenniska Church, Imatra (1957–9)

Gutzeit Company (1959, 1960–2); the Scandinavian Bank Building (1962, 1962–4); the University Bookshop (1962, 1966–9); the Concert and Congress Hall (1962, 1967–71); and finally the 'Finlandia' conference centre and concert hall (1970, 1973–5).

The architect Elissa Mäkiniemi, whom A. had married in 1952, collaborated increasingly in his later works, and particularly on the extension to the Polytechnic in Otaniemi and the Lappia Cultural Centre in Rovaniemi, the latter built 1970–5 as part of the administrative and cultural centre originally projected in 1963. Since 1976 Elissa Aalto has continued the work of A.'s office, having finished work left incomplete or still at the planning stages at the time of the master's death, including the Essen Opera House (1959ff.), the Civic Centre in Jyväskylä (1964ff.), and the church at Lahti (competition project 1950, realized 1970ff.).

In addition to work in Helsinki, a whole series of buildings, development plans and projects outside the capital bear witness to the high quality of A.'s design capabilities and to the profundity of his thought, deeply rooted in the historical, cultural, and geographical traditions of his country. For example: the programme and the prototype houses for the reconstruction after the war (1941); the master-plan for Imatra (1947–53); the regional plan for Lapland (1950–5); the campus of the College of Education, Jyväskylä (1950, 1953–6); the centre of Seinäjoki with the Protestant Church (1952, 1958–60), the Town Hall (1960, 1962–5), Library (1963, 1964–5) and Parish Community House (1963, 1964–6); A.'s own summer house in Muuratsalo (1953); his own studio in Munkkiniemi (1953–5); the main building of the Polytechnic in Imatra (1956, 1957–9); the Vuoksenniska church, Imatra (1956, 1957–9); the Museum of Central Finland in Jyväskylä (1959, 1960–2); the Library of the Polytechnic in Otaniemi (1964, 1965–9); the Sports Institute of the College of Education, Jyväskylä (1967–8, 1968–70); and the Alvar Aalto Museum in Jyväskylä (1971, 1971–3).

A. was also responsible for a series of buildings and projects outside Finland. These include, in addition to those already mentioned: the apartment building for 'Interbau' in Berlin's Hansaviertel (1955–7); the Finnish Pavilion at the Venice Biennale (1956); the Maison Carré at Bazoches-sur-Guyonne (1956–9); the North Jutland Museum in Ålborg, Denmark (1958,

Aalto. Maison Carré, Bazoches-sur-Guyonne, France (1956–9)

Aalto. Church at Riola di Vergato (1966–78)

1969–73); the apartment block in Bremen's Neue Vahr development (1958, 1959–62); the cultural centre (1958, 1959–62) and the parish community centre (1959, 1960–2) in Wolfsburg; the Västmanland-Dala Students' Association headquarters in Uppsala (1961, 1963–5); Scandinavia House in Reykjavik (1962–3, 1965–8); the interior design of the Institute of International Education, New York (1963, 1964–5); the Schönbühl apartment house, Lucerne, (1965, 1966–8), the Library of Mount Angel Benedictine College, Mount Angel, Oregon (1965–6, 1967–70); and the parish community centre in Riola di Vergato, near Bologna (1966–78). Among A.'s unrealized projects were those for town halls in Gothenburg (1955–7), Marl (1957) and Castrop-Rauxel (1965), for a cultural centre in Leverkusen (1962), and for museums in Baghdad (1958) and Shiraz (1970).

The furniture, lighting fixtures and other useful objects designed by A. in conjunction with his individual building projects from 1928 on, and produced under his supervision, reflected the same development stages as are seen in his architecture. These interior fittings were always conceived as 'detached parts' of the particular building for which they were intended – they should not be regarded simply as instruments of, but rather as one aspect of an all-encompassing architectonic vision. LM

□ Aalto, Alvar, 'Rationalism and Man', *The Architectural Forum* (New York), September 1935; ——, 'Zwischen Humanismus und Materialismus', *Der Bau* (Vienna), nos. 7/8, 1955; ——, 'Problemi di architettura', *Quaderni ACI* (Turin), November 1956; Labò, Giorgio, *Alvar Aalto*, Milan 1948; Gutheim, Frederick, *Alvar Aalto*, New York 1960; Mosso, Leonardo, *L'opera di Alvar Aalto*, Milan 1965: *Alvar Aalto, I: 1922–62*, Zurich 1963; *Alvar Aalto, II: 1963–70*, Zurich 1971; *Alvar Aalto, III: Projekte und letzte Zeichnungen*, Zurich 1978;

Pearson, P. D., *Alvar Aalto*, New York 1978, 1980; Mosso, Leonardo, *Alvar Aalto* (exhibition catalogue), Turin 1981; Quantill, Malcolm, *Alvar Aalto: a critical study*, London 1983.

Abramovitz, Max, b. Chicago, 1908. Studied at the University of Illinois at Champaign-Urbana, Columbia University in New York, and at the *Ecole des Beaux-Arts in Paris. In 1941 he entered the office of Wallace K. *Harrison and Jacques André Fouilhoux; from 1945 to 1976 he was Harrison's partner.
☐ *The Architecture of Max Abramovitz*, Champaign-Urbana, Ill. 1963.

Adler, Dankmar, b. Stadt Lengsfeld, near Weimar, Germany 1844, d. Chicago 1900. The son of a cantor, A. began his drawing studies at fifteen. Emigrated to Detroit, 1854. Worked in association with A. J. Kinney, 1869–71; Edward Burling, 1871–9; Louis H. Sullivan, 1881–95. (*USA; *Chicago School).

With Burling, he collaborated on numerous designs during the building boom in Chicago which followed the great fire of 1871. In 1879, he set up independent practice and was joined two years later by Sullivan. His most important work was the Central Music Hall in Chicago (later demolished to provide space for the present retail store of Marshall Field and Co.), which was entirely A.'s work except for Sullivan's decorative organ grilles. Finished in 1879, it was the prototype for a subsequent series of theatres by the firm, notably the Auditorium Building. The planning, layout and lighting were noteworthy in these buildings, although A. was praised primarily for his instinctive mastery of acoustics. Sullivan rose rapidly to the position of chief draughtsman. During his later years, A. managed the engineering and business aspects of the firm and was active in various architectural organizations, introducing many progressive reforms and attempting to improve the position of architecture in American society. Among his works were a series of interesting synagogues, one, Anshe Ma'arev, for his father's congregation.
☐ Salzstein, Joan; 'Dankmar Adler: the Man, the Architect, the Author', *Wisconsin Architect* 38.

Aida, Takefumi, b. Tokyo 1937. A member of the *Architext group, he represents an architecture of 'concealment', be it the concealment of the building itself, as in his PL Institute Kindergarten in Osaka (1974), or a conscious restraint in architectural expression, as in the Nirvana House in Fujisawa (1972) or in the Annihilation House in Mutsuura (also 1972). AM
☐ *The Japan Architect* (Tokyo), 232, vol. 51 (1976), no. 6, pp. 29–38; op. cit., 247, vol. 52 (1977), nos. 10/11, pp. 51–4.

Aillaud, Emile, b. Mexico 1902. The housing estates which A. built after World War II in France, such as Les Courtilières in Pantin (1955–56, 1957–60), Wiesberg at Forbach (1959, 1961 ff.) and La Grande Borne at Grigny (1964–71), are representative of the attempts to compensate for the uniformity which resulted from extensively industrialized constructional methods (principally heavy construction employing prefabricated reinforced-concrete panels) by adopting more individualizing urban planning strategies. This is chiefly achieved in the overall arrangement of the building masses, reduced to smooth abstract forms, in curved serpentine compositions; through the integration of works of art; and finally through the careful handling of public spaces, at times eccentrically shaped and colourfully treated. The residents are thereby given an impetus to identify with their environment. AM
☐ Dhuys, Jean-François, *L'Architecture selon Emile Aillaud*, Paris 1983.

Aillaud. Les Courtillières housing estate, Pantin (1955–6, 1957–60)

Albini, Franco, b. Robbiate, Como, 1905, d. Milan 1977. Studied at Milan Politecnico; diploma 1925. From 1930 he practised alone and after 1952 with Franca Helg; in 1962 Antonio Piva joined the practice, followed in 1965 by A.'s son Marco. He was a professor at Milan Politecnico, 1963–77, and a member of *CIAM.

The Pavilion for the Istituto Nazionale delle Assicurazione (INA) at the Milan Congress of 1935, A.'s first executed work, exhibits already in unmistakable fashion his straightforward reductivist style, which is not uninfluenced by the architectural vocabulary of *Mies van der Rohe. His style is characterized by formal restraint, geometric order, technical perfection and the careful attention to detail.

A. applied these principles in the totality of his artistic activity. Important stages in his strictly-defined architectural work are: the Favio Filzi workers' housing in Milan (1936; with Renato Camus and Giancarlo Palanti); the Villa Pestarini, also in Milan (1938); the INA Building in Parma (1951); and the department store La Rinascente in Rome (1957–62; with Franca Helg), in which the mat black steel construction takes up the moulding patterns of Roman Renaissance palaces, while the infill panels harmonize with the existing urban environment through their reddish colour and granular texture. Representative of his interior schemes and restorations, principally of museums, is the Museo del Palazzo Bianco at Genoa (1951), where the metaphysical spatial effects of clear geometries and transparent or intersecting glass surfaces became prototypical; the Museo del Tesoro di San Lorenzo (1954–6), also in Genoa, with its crystalline dovetailed ground-plan and dramatic lighting effects; and the restoration of the Chiostro degli Eremitani for the municipal museum in Padua (1969–74). A.'s industrial design work extends from his role in the team-designed metal chair for the 1936 Triennale to the circular 'Margherita' armchair of Spanish cane and bamboo (with Franca Helg) for the 1960 Triennale. Among his town-planning activities, the plan for Reggio Emilia (1947–8) is noteworthy; Giancarlo *De Carlo and other architects collaborated on this project.

Albini. La Rinascente department store, Rome (with Franca Helg; 1957–62)

A's. architectural work, in which the identification of form and structure is a constant theme, in practice went – in its attention to the historical urban context – beyond the limits of dogmatic *Rationalism, though without abandoning its fundamental principles. VML

☐ Argan, Giulio Carlo, *Franco Albini*, Milan 1962; Moschini, F., *Franco Albini*, London 1979.

Alexander, Christopher, b. Vienna 1936 (the son of English parents). Studied architecture and mathematics. In 1970 he became Professor of Architecture at the University of California in Berkeley. His contribution to contemporary architecture lies foremost in the realm of planning theory, which he attempts to establish on a more solid basis by the application of scientific principles. A. started from the observation that original native cultures, because of their gradual organic development, unconsciously produce forms in complete harmony with their environment. He then developed complex mathematical formulae, as equivalents of this type of 'unconscious' form-creation process, by which design and planning problems are decomposed into a series of components and then by reversal recomposed into fundamental 'patterns' to synthesize form. The experimental results achieved at the Center for Environmental Structures (CES) founded in 1967 at Berkeley led to a greater emphasis on empirical investigation of the needs and demands of users. The first major practical testing of A.'s theories was his contribution to the competition for a residential quarter with 1,500 units in Lima (1969). AM

☐ Alexander, C., *Notes on the Synthesis of Form*, Cambridge, Mass. 1964; ——, *The Oregon Experiment*, London 1975; ——, *A Pattern Language*, London 1977; ——, *The Timeless Way of Building*, London 1979.

Almqvist, Osvald, b. Trankil, near Karlstad 1884, d. Stockholm 1950. Studied first at the Technical College and then at the Academy of Fine Arts in Stockholm, which he left in 1910 to establish, along with six fellow-students including Sigurd *Lewerentz, the short-lived Free Architectural School. There – under the professors Carl Bergsten, Ragnar Östberg, Ivar Tengbom and Carl Westman – Gunnar *Asplund was to study. In opposition to the academic *neo-classicism which was taught at the time in Sweden, A. and his associates embraced a re-evaluation of the Swedish vernacular tradition, a sort of 'national realism'. With his designs for standardized kitchen components (1922) and his hydro-electric power plants near Hammarsfors and Krångfors (both 1925–8), in which all ties to the past are cut, A. became one of the pioneers of modernism in Sweden. GHa

☐ Linn, Björn, *Osvald Almqvist: En Arkitekt och Hans Arbete*, Stockholm 1967.

Alvarez, Mario Roberto, b. Buenos Aires 1913. Immediately upon completing his studies in Buenos Aires in 1937, he opened his own office (since 1947 Mario Roberto Alvarez y Asociados). He was Architect to the Ministry for Public Works in Buenos Aires, 1937–42, and City Architect of Avellaneda, 1942–7; he acted as Advisor to the Secretary of Public Works of his native city, 1958–62. A. became one of the leading architects of Argentina and an important advocate of the Modern Movement, to which he remained consistently faithful. Interested in the shaping of all aspects of the physical environment, he has been active not only in conventional architectural matters, but also, for instance, in dealing with issues of engineering construction and the problems of prefabrication in relation to prevailing conditions in Argentina. An example of his more recent work is the headquarters of the Somisa firm in Buenos Aires (1966), the country's first building made entirely of steel. AM

☐ Trabuco, Marcelo A., *Mario Roberto Alvarez*, Buenos Aires 1975.

Amsterdam, School of. Group of architects whose analysis of the works of *Berlage and the young Frank Lloyd *Wright served as a point of departure for their own work, and who represented a local 'vernacular' parallel to German *Expressionism, particularly as it had been manifested in the early works of Erich *Mendelsohn. Their mouthpiece was the magazine *Wendingen* (1918–36), edited by Hendricus Theodorus Wijdeveld. Their sculpturally-conceived, picturesquely-composed brick buildings stand in abrupt contrast to the spare rationalist buildings of the contemporary De *Stijl group. The most eminent exponents of the Amsterdam School were J. M. van der *Mey, P. L. *Kramer and Michel de *Klerk.

☐ Pehnt, Wolfgang, *Expressionist Architecture*, London and New York 1980; Searing, Helen, 'Berlage or Cuypers? The Father of them all' in Searing, H. (ed.), *In Search of Modern Architecture*, Cambridge, Mass. 1983, pp. 226–44.

Andrews, John, b. Sydney 1933. Studied at the University of Sydney and at Harvard University under J. L. *Sert. In 1962 he opened his own office in Toronto and in 1973 one in Sydney. He taught at the University of Toronto 1962–9. His debut on the international architectural scene came with Scarborough College, Ontario (1st phase 1963; 2nd phase 1969), a late masterpiece of New Brutalism. In addition to the emphasis

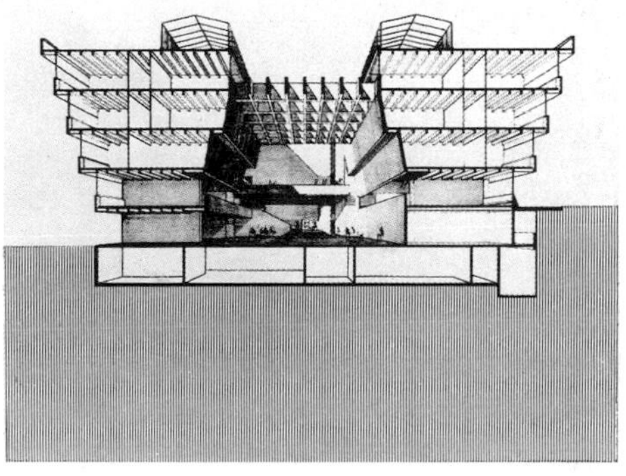

Andrews. Scarborough College, Ontario: section through Humanities Wing (1964–5)

on raw materials and monumental forms, an essential characteristic of the building is the internal street (a concession to the cold Canadian winter) which serves to unite all the college functions one to another. A.'s other important buildings include the Seaport Passenger Terminal in the Port of Miami, Florida (1967), the Graduate School of Design at Harvard University (1968), and the Cameron Office Block at Belconnen, Canberra, Australia. AM

☐ Drew, Philip, *The Third Generation, the Changing Meaning of Architecture*, New York 1972; 'Conversations with the John Andrews Architects', *Progressive Architecture*, no. 54 (Feb. 1972), pp. 62–75.

Arbeitsrat für Kunst. Group of German architects and artists founded in December 1918 under the leadership of Bruno *Taut; it rapidly gained a large membership, which included the architects Otto *Bartning, Walter *Gropius, Erich *Mendelsohn and Max *Taut, the painters César Klein, Erich Heckel, Ludwig Meidner, Max Pechstein, Karl Schmidt-Rottluff and Lyonel Feininger, and the sculptors Rudolf Belling, Oswald Herzog and Gerhard Marcks. It was Taut's original intention that the Arbeitsrat – unlike the *Novembergruppe – should exercise political influence in the post-revolutionary government as an artistic equivalent to the workers' and soldiers' councils which briefly held power in November and December 1918. The founding manifesto demanded: 'Art and the people must form a unity .... From now on the artist alone, as moulder of the sensibilities of the people, will be responsible for the visible fabric of the new state.' No political power was gained, however, and Taut resigned from the leadership at the end of February 1919, to be replaced by Gropius.

Dismissing any direct political aspirations, Gropius suggested that the Arbeitsrat should be reorganized into a community of radical architects, painters and sculptors who would work together on a symbolic building task, the 'Bauprojekt'. This would provide the means of achieving the group's main artistic aim, which was defined as 'the fusion of the arts under the wing of a great architecture'. However, the combination of political instability, inflation and material shortages precluded any concrete progress on this project.

In April 1919, Gropius took up his post at the newly-established *Bauhaus at Weimar, whose first programme closely reflected the ideals of the Arbeitstrat. Although the 'Bauprojekt' was retained as an ultimate goal, the group increasingly devoted its attention to publications and exhibitions. In addition to its own programmes and the 'Architektur-Programm' of Bruno Taut, the group also published two books, *Ja! Stimmen des Arbeitsrates für Kunst in Berlin* (1919), and *Ruf zum Bauen* (1920). Among the exhibitions organized by the Arbeitsrat were the 'Ausstellung für unbekannte Architekten' (April 1919), another devoted to workers' and children's art (January 1920), and 'Neues Bauen' (May 1920). The group also arranged exhibitions of contemporary German art in Antwerp and Amsterdam. Although the exhibitions attracted considerable public attention, the finances of the group became increasingly strained during 1920 and the Arbeitstrat was formally dissolved on 30 May 1921. IBW

☐ *Arbeistrat für Kunst* (exhibition catalogue), Berlin 1980; Whyte, Iain Boyd, *Bruno Taut and the Architecture of Activism*, Cambridge 1982.

Archigram. The Archigram group was formed through the collaboration of six young architects who came together in 1960 while working for Taylor Woodrow Construction Co. on the redevelopment of Euston Station, London, under the direction of Theo Crosby: Warren Chalk (b. 1927), Peter *Cook, Dennis Crompton (b. 1935), David Greene (b. 1937), Ron Herron (b. 1930) and Michael Webb (b. 1937). The first number of *Archigram* appeared in 1961, and the name of the publication soon became the name of the group and a statement of their method: architecture by drawing. They were identified publicly after their first exhibition – 'Living City' in 1963 at the Institute of Contemporary Arts in London.

Their ideas were initially directed against formal conventions and towards all kinds of loose and free associations. This led towards expendables, towards pop culture and its optimistic assimilation of new technology, and the idea that the most advanced space hardware should be available as an everyday enabling system to generate more personal choices and to break down the tyranny of the traditional city. As architects, they were able to project their ideas graphically with great verisimilitude and knowledge of technical gadgetry.

The group found a strong supporter in the critic Reyner Banham, whose writings, in

Archigram. Walking City project (Ron Herron; 1964)

addition to their own prolific talents, spread their ideas worldwide. It could be said that the group did for architecture something akin to what the Beatles did for music in the 1960s. Their concepts of expendability were also adopted by the *Metabolism school in Japan.

Their most influential utopian projects were Fulham Study (1963), Plug-in City (Cook, 1964–6), Walking City (Herron, 1964), Cushicle (Webb, 1966/7), Instant City (Cook, 1968) and Inflatable suit-Home (Greene, 1968); among their realized or realizable designs were the Archigram Capsule at Expo '70 in Osaka, the project for a summer casino at Monte Carlo (1971), a review of contemporary British design at the Louvre in Paris (1971) and the still extant Malaysian Exhibition at the Commonwealth Institute in London (1973). RM

□ *Archigram* (London), 1961–70; Cook, Peter, *Architecture. Action and Plan*, London and New York 1967; ——, *Experimental Architecture*, London and New York 1970; ——, *Archigram*, London and New York 1974.

Architects' Co-Partnership. Practice originally founded in 1939 by eight former students of the Architectural Association, London, and reformed in 1945 by C. K. Capon, P. L. Cocke, M. H. Cooke-Yarborough, L. M. de Syllas, J. M. Grice and M. A. R. Powers. Their rubber factory at Brynmawr, South Wales (1949), with its repetition of simple but powerful shapes, gave the first indication of the feeling for sculptural effect which characterizes the firm's style and announced their pragmatic, modernist-intoned approach to design. This was subsequently displayed in a series of educational buildings, including schools in London, Warwickshire, Hertfordshire and Dorset, and university premises at Leicester, Carmarthen and Cambridge. Their early use of industrialized building materials and their preference for an 'anonymous' team approach to architecture, legacies of the European continental Modern Movement, were developed into the current sophisticated consultant engineering firm. HM

Architext. An informal group of architects, centred on the periodical of the same name, founded in 1971 by Takefumi *Aida, Takamitsu *Azuma, Mayumi Miyawaki, Makoto Suzuki, and Minoru Takeyama. The various members subscribe to no complete doctrine, as was the case with *Archigram in England or the representatives of *Metabolism in Japan, but rather the rejection of such doctrines, which they consider to be expressions of the totalitarian pretensions of modernism. Convinced individualists, they argue for pluralism, discontinuity and contradiction. AM

□ *Architext* (Tokyo); 'Architext', *The Japan Architect* (Tokyo), 232, vol. 51 (1976), no. 6, pp. 19–80.

Art Deco, which borrowed its name from the 'Exposition Internationale des arts décoratifs et industriels modernes' held in Paris in 1925, developed rapidly from being a uniquely French phenomenon to become an international fashion in design, interior decoration and architecture. As a synthetic form of stylization, mediating between the avant garde and tradition, it absorbed impulses from *Cubism, *Futurism, *Expressionism and other movements.

In French architecture Art Deco appeared in the most varied guises: pseudo-purist in *Mallet-Stevens' residential complex in the Rue Mallet-Stevens in Paris (1926–7), a style-conscious offspring of Cubist thought which draws markedly on *Le Corbusier's formal vocabulary; opulent, luxuriant, and frankly ornamental in Pierre Patout's Pavillon du Collectionneur at the Paris exhibition of 1925, where the pyramidal massing predominates over structural expression; decidedly arid in Patout's house in the Avenue Jean-Baptiste Clément at Boulogne-sur-Seine (1929), which is articulated by clear cubic forms; and, finally, idealistic-technological in *Chareau and Bijvoet's Maison de Verre in Paris (1928–32), which points clearly beyond Art Deco as the expression of a bourgeois fashion for the avant garde in the radical nature of its machine metaphor.

Elsewhere in Europe, Art Deco was integrated with existing architectural traditions such as the School of *Amsterdam in Holland (Bijenkorf department store in The Hague by *Kramer, 1924–5), as well as with the legacy of Frank Lloyd *Wright, or with Expressionism in Germany (Paula Modersohn-Becker House in the Böttchergasse, Bremen, by Bernhard Hoetger, 1926).

Art Deco's stylistic flourishing is to be found in the *USA, where a scenographic architecture of highly decorative façades was launched through the use of polychromy and ornamentation (modernistic as well as historicizing). There, Art Deco mediated between the tradition of the French *Ecole des Beaux-Arts and modern constructional techniques in its distinction between skeleton and cladding. It combined influences derived from skyscraper Gothic (Cass Gilbert), Art Nouveau ornament (*Sullivan), traditionalism (Eliel *Saarinen) and the emerging *International Style, a melange best exemplified by Art Deco's American icon, William van Alen's Chrysler Building in New York (1928–30). NM

☐ Hillier, Bevis, *Art Déco*, Minneapolis 1971; Robinson, Cervin, and Bletter, Rosemarie Haag, *Skyscraper Style*, New York 1975.

Art Deco. Residential complex by Rob Mallet-Stevens in the Rue Mallet-Stevens, Paris (1926–7)

Art Deco. The Chrysler Building, New York, by William van Alen (1928–30)

Art Nouveau. An individualist and highly romantic reaction to the currents of *eclecticism and academic classicism (*Ecole des Beaux-Arts) in late 19th-century architecture, Art Nouveau was a diverse phenomenon which affected most of Europe and, some historians argue, even North America between 1890 and 1910. Known at the time under a variety of rubrics which reflect its sources in the investigations of individual architects and the specific contexts of various national traditions. It was known for instance in England at the time as the 'modern style'; in *Belgium as the *coup de fouet* (whiplash) or *paling* (eel) style (from the flexible line introduced by *Horta), or the *style des Vingt* (in view of the important part played by the group Les Vingt led by Octave Maus); in Germany it was called the *Jugendstil*, from the Munich periodical *Jugend*; in France it was known variously as the *style nouille* (noodle style), *style Guimard* (after the architect Henri *Guimard, who designed the decorative entrances to the Paris Métro stations in 1899), or *Art Nouveau*. The Austrians named it the *Secessionsstil* (after the Viennese Secession group, led from 1897 on by the painter Gustav Klimt and the architects *Hoffmann and *Olbrich); in Italy it was the *stile Liberty* or *stile floreale*; and in Spain *modernisme*. The anti-historicist (*historicism) polemic often obscured a considerable debt to ornamental and structural research which had been initially conducted within the context of the revival styles, as for instance in the case of the various theories of finding the geometric or organic principles underlying all historical styles so as to use those principles in turn as the starting point for defining a new, 'modern' style.

Often referred to simply as the *style 1900*, Art Nouveau expresses an essentially decorative trend that aims to highlight the ornamental value of the curved line, which may be floral in origin (Belgium, France) or geometric (Scotland, Austria). This line gives rise to two-dimensional, slender, sinuous, undulating and invariably asymmetrical forms. The applied arts were the first to be affected (textiles by William Morris, 1880; wood-engraved title page to *Wren's City Churches* by Arthur H. Mackmurdo, 1883; vases by Emile Gallé, 1884; ornamental lettering by Fernand Khnopff and Georges Lemmen, 1890–1; mural tapestry *The Angels' Vigil* by Henry *van de Velde, 1893; furniture by Gustave Serrurier-Bovy, 1891; title page for *Dominical* by van de Velde, 1892).

Next came architecture, represented by the house which Victor Horta built in Brussels in 1892–3 for the engineer Tassel, a key work of the new style, which was to find a dazzling counterpart a few years later in the Elvira studio in Munich by August *Endell (1897–8, destroyed). Among the most characteristic architectural products of Art Nouveau, albeit widely differing in purpose and plastic expression, were: the houses built by Paul Hankar in Brussels (1893–1900); the works of Willem Kromhout (1864–1940), Th. Sluyterman (1863–1931) and L. A. H. Wolf in the *Netherlands; Guimard's Castel Béranger (1897–8), entrances to Métro stations and the auditorium

Art Nouveau. The Elvira Photo Studio, Munich (1897–8), by August Endell: façade and staircase

Art Nouveau. Hôtel Solvay, Brussels (1895–1900), by Victor Horta

Art Nouveau. Karlsplatz Station of the Vienna Stadtbahn (1897) by Otto Wagner

of the Humbert de Romans building (1902, destroyed) in Paris; Horta's Maison du Peuple (1896–9, destroyed) and the former Hôtel Solvay (1895–1900) in Brussels; the overhead Stadtbahn station in the Karlsplatz, Vienna (1897) by Otto *Wagner; and the Museum Folkwang, with interior design by van de Velde, at Hagen (1900–2).

All these works are the result of a deliberate attempt to put an end to imitations of past styles; in its place is offered a florid type of architecture which exploits craft skills, using coloured materials (faience cabochons, stoneware, terracotta panels, stained glass), exotic veneers, moulded stonework, grilles, balconies, and tapered brackets in wrought iron; and burgeoning with asymmetrical door- and window-frames, bow and horseshoe windows, etc. The common denominator of these diverse works is then more a new conception of the relationship between surface and ornament, rather than a change in spatial expression of plan. An exception to this may, however, be found in buildings designed in the tradition of the English country house (*Voysey, *Mackintosh), with their principle of building from inside to out; and the Continental examples based on them (Olbrich's houses on the Mathildenhöhe at Darmstadt). In the later phases of Art Nouveau, façade decoration was accompanied by a powerful plastic treatment of the whole building, either by the dramatic accentuation of individual parts of the structure (Glasgow Art School, 1898–1909, by Mackintosh) or by the sculptural modelling of the whole building mass (Werkbundtheater, Cologne, 1914 by van de Velde; Casa Milà, Barcelona, 1905–10, by *Gaudí).

Art Nouveau was first and foremost an aesthetic undertaking, based on social theories and inspired by aesthetes such as Ruskin, Morris and Oscar Wilde. It was born of a reaction to the rise of industrialism, and from a determination to create a new style, in view of the belief that the 19th century had been stylistically impotent. Its proponents sought a style which would affect the design of objects of everyday use as well as architecture and leave its mark ultimately on the décor and surroundings of daily life. In terms of its theory, from the ethical and political point of view Art Nouveau appears as an attempt to integrate art with social life; in practice, and from the cultural point of view, however, it quietly assumes the manner of a reactionary bourgeois movement. Art Nou-

Art Nouveau. Casa Milà, Barcelona (1905–10), by Antonio Gaudí

veau tried, in effect, to relieve man from the pressures of a technological milieu. Faced with the machine, which it regarded as the work of the devil, it aimed at renewing contact with nature and rehabilitating the tool in its role of the 'lengthener of the hand': by the same token, it obliged the artist to express himself in the margin of the living forces of technology. On the other hand, it claimed to be able to fashion a three-dimensional universe, independent of the fundamental support of the true creators of the epoch (Cézanne, Gauguin, Van Gogh, Munch) or rather, only borrowing the most external trappings of their inspiration. The point may thus be seen at which Art Nouveau (in the midst of its romantic, sentimental and social outbursts) posed in contradictory terms the problem of the social relations of art. It may also be seen how it produced, in all fields, a real severance between life and thought, and partially destroyed the 'relation between plant and soil'.

Art Nouveau may thus be compared to an electrical short circuit; by confounding style and surface ornament, and by basing all its efforts on theories of decoration, it was a stylistic recuperation with relatively few repercussions in subsequent architectural developments. Distinguished architects of the Art Nouveau style, such as Mackintosh, *Behrens and the Viennese masters became pioneers of modern architecture, it is true, but with their forward-looking buildings they overstepped the frontiers which the style had imposed upon its adherents. RLD/BB

□ Schmalenbach, F., *Jugendstil. Ein Beitrag zu Theorie und Geschichte der Flächenkunst*, Würzburg 1934; Madsen, Stephan Tschudi, *Sources of Art Nouveau*, New York 1956; Seling, Helmut (ed.), *Jugendstil. Der Weg ins 20. Jahrhundert*, Heidelberg 1959; Selz, Peter, and Constantine, Mildred (eds.), *Art Nouveau. Art and Design at the Turn of the Century*, New York 1959; Gans, Louis, *Nieuwe Kunst. De Nederlandse Bijdrage tot de 'Art Nouveau'*, Utrecht 1960; Cassou, Jean, Langui, Emil, and Pevsner, Nikolaus, *Durchbruch zum 20. Jahrhundert. Kunst und Kultur der Jahrhundertwende*, Munich 1962; Schmutzler, Robert, *Jugendstil–Art Nouveau*, Stuttgart 1962; Russell, Frank (ed.), *Art Nouveau Architecture*, London 1979.

Arts and Crafts. Movement which developed in reaction to the cheap, machine-produced kitsch which inundated the furnishing and architecture market of the mid-19th century in the wake of the Industrial Revolution. Much inspired by the writings of Pugin and especially of Ruskin, the English architect and social reformer William *Morris was one of the first to strive for a revival of handicraft. The symbolical start was the Red House (1859) at Bexley Heath, Kent, which Morris commissioned after his marriage from his friend Philip *Webb. Seen as an escape from the tasteless and 'false' *eclecticism of contemporary design, the Red House represented the first and most important attempt to renew domestic architecture within the Gothic Revival.

However, this individualistic response was not sufficient for the socially-engaged Morris (he was a member of Engel's Social Democratic Federation and later, in 1891, wrote the socialist utopian novel, *News from Nowhere*). In 1861, on the model of Henry Cole's Art Manufactures, Morris founded, together with a group of painters and architects, the firm of Morris, Marshall, Faulkner and Co., to produce high-quality wallpapers, woven and printed fabrics, tapestries, and stained glass. Subsequently Morris ran the company alone as Morris & Co. The products of the Morris workshops, as successful as they were exclusive, were oriented towards medieval models, as well as more exotic patterns drawn from that very same *Grammar of Ornament* by Owen Jones which was subsequently to provide a source of inspiration to *Sullivan and *Wright in America. With this undertaking, Morris laid the foundations for a far-reaching movement, which aimed at the renewal of handicraft and was characterized by moralizing undertones. In place of the 'ugly' and 'decadent' domination of the machine, he advocated an anachronistic anti-machine stance. In spite of all their social claims and intentions, however, the adherents of the Arts and Crafts philosophy were not prepared to confront the dilemma that handicraft was far more costly than machine production and that their handsome products were indeed largely beyond the means of the wide spectrum of the very public for whom they were originally intended.

This was equally the case for the associations of architects and artists that grew up within Morris's circle: from the Century Guild of Artists, founded in 1882 by Ruskin's pupil Arthur Heygate Mackmurdo and a small group of friends; to St George's Art Society, which was started by five students of *Shaw, including *Lethaby and Edward S. Prior, in 1883 and established one year later as the Art Workers' Guild. From this group there developed in 1888 a parallel organization, the Arts and Crafts Exhibition Society, which also represented Morris's workshops; it was here for the first time that the term 'Arts and Crafts' was introduced. Also in 1888, the Guild and School of Handicraft was founded by C. R. *Ashbee, an independent disciple of Ruskin. This was to represent a highpoint of the movement and would continue to flourish until 1905.

Arts and Crafts. Red House, Bexley Heath, Kent (1859), by Philip Webb

In the meantime the much-hated phenomenon of industrial production had become a reality that could no longer be ignored. Ashbee came to terms with it, if only faint-heartedly, and accepted at least in theory the notion of collaboration with the machine. He thus introduced the methods of industrial design, which had seemed, since the Crystal Palace of 1851, predetermined for the Machine era.

The Arts and Crafts Society maintained a far more conservative position. Its first president, Walter Crane, who was personally allied with the romantic-regressive aesthetic of the Pre-Raphaelites, was at first opposed to any opening-up of the movement. Thus the young C. R. *Mackintosh and the entire Glasgow School (*Art Nouveau) were categorically excluded from their exhibitions. In any case, numerous architects figured among the first members and exhibitors, including Ashbee, Prior, ⋆Voysey, George Walton, ⋆Lutyens and W. R. Lethaby, the leading promoter and, in 1894, the first Director of the Central School of Arts and Crafts in London.

The effects of the Arts and Crafts movement were, for all its contradictions, as profound as they were lasting and far-reaching. In ⋆Great Britain a notably high professional standard was established in its circles, which was characterized by an intensive reformatory involvement with the problem of the house. It was here that the concept of the house as a 'total work of art' was developed. It was also out of the theoretical principles and architectural statements of the Domestic Revival that the Garden City movement developed. This was launched in 1898 by Ebenezer ⋆Howard with his book *Tomorrow, A Peaceful Path to Social Reform* (retitled in the second edition of 1902 *Garden Cities of Tomorrow*). The battle against the stylistic revivals of the 19th century, the rejection of illusionistic representation in decorative design and the preference for closed form provided the basis for that break with the aesthetic of the 19th century that was advocated by artists at the turn of the century. Finally, the idea of a reunion of art, handicraft and architecture was introduced in Germany, through the agency of ⋆Muthesius, into the circle of the ⋆Deutscher Werkbund. GV/VML

☐ Pevsner, N., *The Sources of Modern Architecture and Design*, London and New York 1968; ——, *Pioneers of Modern Design from William Morris to Walter Gropius*, Harmondsworth 1974; Davey, P., *The Arts and Crafts Movement in Architecture*, London 1980.

Arup, Ove (Nyquist), b. Newcastle-upon-Tyne 1895. A. studied at first philosophy and mathematics and then civil engineering. From 1934 to 1938 he was Director and Chief Engineer of the English engineering firm J. L. Kier and Company. Then, in 1938 he founded, together with his cousin, the engineering and consulting firm Arup and Arup, which he left in 1946 to open an independent engineering office, active since 1949 under the name Ove Arup and Partners. Finally in 1963 he launched, together with the architect Philip Dowson and others, the interdisciplinary planning firm Arup Associates, which today employs a staff of over 1,600 in Great Britain and a further 1,000 worldwide. From early on, A. was inclined to architectural modernism. He was one of the founding members in 1933 of the Modern Architecture Research Group (⋆MARS), and subsequently was active as a consultant to ⋆Lubetkin and his ⋆Tecton group. Other examples of his engineering activities are the school at Hunstanton, Norfolk (1949, 1952–4) by Alison and Peter ⋆Smithson, the Sydney Opera House (1956–74) by ⋆Utzon, the multifunctional Hall for the 1975 Bundesgartenschau (Federal Garden Show) in Mannheim (1973–4, 1974–5) by Carlfried Muttschler, Joachim Langner and Frei ⋆Otto, as well as the Centre Pompidou in Paris (1971–7) by ⋆Piano and ⋆Rogers. Not only as engineers, but also as architects, Arup Associates have undertaken numerous university buildings. The pedestrian bridge over the River Wear in Durham (1963) is an example of A.'s personal design work. AM

☐ *Arup Journal* (London); 'Arup's First Ten Years', *Architecture Plus* (New York), November–December 1974; 'Arup Associates', *Architecture and Urbanism* (Tokyo), December 1977; Brawne, Michael, *Arup Associates*, London 1983.

Ashbee, Charles Robert, b. London 1863, d. London 1942. Strongly influenced by the ideas of Ruskin and ⋆Morris, A. founded the Guild and School of Handicraft in 1888, a highpoint in the ⋆Arts and Crafts movement. His own works included several houses in Cheyne Walk, London (1897–1904), and Norman Chapel

Ashbee. Houses in Cheyne Walk (nos. 39 and 38), London (1904)

House, Broad Campden, Glos. (1906). His influence was especially felt through his elegant design for craft objects. He was active as an urban planner in Egypt during World War I and later in Jerusalem (*Israel). In 1924 he returned to Kent. VML

☐ Ashbee, C. R., *A Book of Cottages and Little Houses*, London 1906; Service, Alistair, *Edwardian Architecture*, London 1978; *C. R. Ashbee and the Guild of Handicraft* (exhibition catalogue), Cheltenham 1981.

Aslin, Charles Herbert, b. Sheffield 1893, d. 1959. Studied at Sheffield University Department of Architecture. After a career in various local authority offices, A. became County Architect for Hertfordshire in 1945, where he stayed till his retirement in 1958.

At the end of World War II, an acute shortage of school places in Hertfordshire, together with lack of manpower and craftsmen in the building trade, moved A. to tackle the problem as a quasi-military 'planned operation'. Taking advantage of the production potential of light industry, built up during the war, he organized a system of school prefabrication from factory-made parts, but with sufficient flexibility to allow each school to be treated individually.

The prototype was Cheshunt Primary School, built in 1946 on an 8 ft 3 in. (2·52 m) grid. In 1947, eleven schools were projected on a serial production basis, with flat roofs, solid floors, and standardized stanchions and beam connections; in 1948/9, development proceeded on twenty-one primary schools, while the 1947 schools were being completed. The hundredth school of this type was opened in 1955 (*Great Britain). HM

☐ Aslin, C. H., 'Specialized developments in school construction', *JRIBA*, November 1950; Twist, K. C., Redpath, J. T. and Evans, K. C., 'Hertfordshire Schools Development', *Architects' Journal* (London), 12 and 26 May 1955, 19 April and 2 August 1956.

Asplund, (Erik) Gunnar, b. Stockholm 1885, d. Stockholm 1940. Asplund was one of the most prominent Swedish architects of the first half of the 20th century; his work is of historical significance for its combining of traditional and modern architecture. He received his architectural training at the Technical College in Stockholm and at the Free Architectural Academy founded there in 1910 by *Almqvist, *Lewerentz and others. From 1931 to 1940 he was a professor at the Technical College.

Asplund. Restaurant building at the Stockholm Exhibition (1930)

Asplund. Stockholm South Cemetery: Crematorium (1935–40)

In 1914 A., in collaboration with Lewerentz, won the competition for the layout of Stockholm South Cemetery, where he later built the Woodland Chapel (1918–20). Other works of these years include the Snellman villa in Djursholm (1917–8), the Skandia Cinema (1922–3) and the Stockholm City Library (1924–7). The Skandia Cinema, much admired at the time of its construction, is rectangular in shape, with side balconies; it depends for aesthetic effect on a balance of verticals and horizontals and a restrained use of classical decoration. The City Library is symmetrical in plan with a large central cylindrical lending area enclosed on three sides by rectangular volumes containing reading and study rooms and offices. The work is classicist in conception, recalling ultimately the ageless theme of the merging of cube and cylinder; the accent on simplicity and severity was a trend of the time. However, had A. continued designing in the style of the cinema and library, he might have been regarded simply as just another competent traditionalist. With the buildings for the Stockholm Exhibition of 1930, he revealed himself as a modernist, skilfully handling glass and steel expressively to achieve a great lightness of effect. This is seen especially in the Paradise Restaurant, with its slender supports, glass walls, circular glass tower and large coloured sunblinds, elements which were to be basic to 'the new architecture' in Europe.

After this exhibition A. designed the Bredenberg store in Stockholm (1933–5), which has something of the lightness of the exhibition buildings; the State Bacteriological Laboratory, Stockholm (1933–7); the Gothenburg City Hall Extension (1934–7), the design of which is modern in spirit yet harmonizes in scale with the original building in the classical style; and lastly the Crematorium, Stockholm South Cemetery (1935–40). The group of buildings consists of three chapels, the crematorium and the columbarium; at the main entrance is a large portico with numerous plain shafts. Simple, dramatic and original as is the design for a purpose of this kind, it is essentially Greek in conception, the feeling of repose that it creates depending on the relationship of verticals and horizontals; it demonstrates clearly Asplund's conviction that the classical Greek architectural sense can harmonize with the modern spirit. AW

☐ Zevi, Bruno, *E. Gunnar Asplund*, Milan 1948; Holmdahl, Gustav, Lind, Sven Ivar, and Odeen, Kjell (eds.), *Gunnar Asplund, Architect, 1885–1940*, Stockholm 1950; de Maré, Eric, *Gunnar Asplund, A Great Modern Architect*, London 1955; Wrede, S., *The Architecture of Erik Gunnar Asplund*, Boston, Mass. 1980.

Atelier 5. Group of architects founded in Berne in 1955 by Erwin Fritz, Samuel Gerber, Rolf Hesterberg, Hans Hostettler and Alfredo Pini. In 1983 Atelier 5 included twelve partners: Jacques Blumer, Christian Flückiger, Anatole du Fresne, Ralph Gentner, Christiane Heimgartner, Rolf Hesterberg, Hans Hostettler, Pier Lanini, Alfredo Pini, Denis Roy, Bernard Stebler and Fritz Thormann. The strong influence of *Le Corbusier on the group's early work is evident in the Halen housing estate near Berne (1955–61), which is based on the master's unrealized project for a housing estate at La Sainte-Baume (1948), in which rows of terrace houses were rolled out almost like a carpet on the landscape. Their early style, dominated by a unified formal vocabulary derived from *New Brutalism, gave way increasingly in the early 1970s to a tendency to derive formal expression from the particular demands of the commission and the local context. Examples of this are the Thalmatt housing estate at Herrenschwanden, near Berne (1967–72), and the Stuttgart University Dining Hall (1970–6) at Stuttgart-Vaihingen. AM

☐ Bezzola, Leonardo, Thormann-Wirz, Esther, and Thormann, Fritz, *Wohnort Halen. Eine Architekturreportage*, Teufen 1964; 'Atelier 5 – Terrace Houses: Flamatt, Halen & Brugge', *Global Architecture* (Tokyo), no. 23, 1973; 'Atelier 5', *Bauen + Wohnen* (Munich), 35, nos. 7/8, 1980, pp. 14–77.

Atelier 5. Halen housing estate, near Berne (1955–61)

Athens Charter. At its fourth congress, held in 1933 on a cruise between Marseilles and Athens aboard the *Patris II*, the *CIAM organization undertook a systematic investigation of thirty-three major cities; the result was the 'Principles of the Fourth Congress'. These were concerned with the 'functional city' (as it had been defined two years earlier at a meeting in Berlin) and were based principally on *Le Corbusier's ideas (which he revised in 1941 and published anonymously in 1943 as a book under the title *La Charte d'Athènes*. One of the six basic principles was the distribution and ordering of the four primary functions of the city (residential, work, free-time and traffic), which established the urban planning of modernism on a simple formula at once concise and, arguably, ill-conceived. VML

☐ [Le Corbusier], *Urbanisme des CIAM, La Charte d'Athènes*, Paris 1943 (English ed.: *The Athens Charter*, New York 1973).

Austria. As the capital of a multi-nation state, Vienna had, by the late 19th century, developed, even in architecture, that polyglot character and that emphatic consciousness of language, which have remained typical of the cultural life of the city to this day. This social pluralism was reflected in the multiplicity of architectural schools and trends. Otto *Wagner, the executor of Gottfried *Semper's will and the last architect of the epoch of the Viennese Ringstraße, introduced the new approaches of the Secession (*Art Nouveau) and the seeds of architectural modernism into the broad current of Viennese classicism. Wagner's empirical positivism, got up in the slogan-like doctrine of a 'Nutzstil' (functionalist style) and united with a solid artistic training, endowed his school with the legendary reputation that it still enjoys. To cite his most important pupils is to

Austria. Palm House in the Burggarten, Vienna (1902–4), by Friedrich Ohmann

Austria. Project for the XXIInd District, Vienna (1910–11), by Otto Wagner

Austria. Sanatorium at Purkersdorf (1902) by Josef Hoffmann

Austria. Steiner House, Vienna (1910), by Adolf Loos

demonstrate the geographical extent of his influence: active in Vienna were Hermann Aichinger, Leopold Bauer, Karl *Ehn, Max Fellerer, Franz and Hubert Geßner, Josef *Hoffmann, Emil Hoppe, Marcel Kammerer, Oskar Laske, Ernst Lichtblau, Rudolf Perco, Josef Plečnik (later in Prague and Laibach [now Ljubljana]), Heinrich Schmid and Otto Schöntal; in the provinces Mauriz Balzarek (Linz) and Wunibald Deininger (Salzburg). Working in Prague were Josef Chochol, Bohumil Hübschmann, Pavel Janák and Jan Kotěra – the central figures of Czech *Cubism. Similarly, István Benkó-Medgyaszay (Budapest), Viktor Kovačić (Zagreb) and Giorgio Zaninovich (Trieste) were to be major influential figures in their native countries. Rudolph *Schindler's work in California is well known. In addition, although they were not Wagner's pupils, Max Fabiani (Vienna and Görz) and J. M. *Olbrich (Vienna, Darmstadt and Düsseldorf) were strongly influenced by him.

Wagner's opposite number was Friedrich Ohmann, a native of Prague and director of the second 'special class' at the Akademie der bildenden Künste. Today, his romanticizing, atmospheric and emotionally charged architecture seems a more direct reflection of the Viennese fin-de-siècle, than does the optimistic forward-looking ethos of Wagner. The conservative schools (such as that of Karl König) at the Technische Hochschule also had a particular significance for later developments. From these schools emerged the critical intellectuals of Viennese architecture, such as Josef Frank and Oskar Strnad, who later, as teachers at the Kunstgewerbeschule (today Hochschule für angewandte Kunst) along with Hoffmann and Heinrich *Tessenow, were to exercise a great influence on the Viennese scene, and in particular within the Werkbund.

Adolf *Loos was naturally a focal point of the architectural debate, especially after 1897 through his writings. Loos was at once an innovator and a traditionalist, a critical voice within his medium, as were his friends Karl Kraus and Arnold Schönberg. He discussed architecture as a cultural phenomenon and in relation to society. His thinking, as contradictory and fascinating as the city which he both hated and loved, still provides the stimulus for any Viennese architectural discussion.

The architecture of the 1920s, almost exclusively determined by the housing programmes of the Viennese municipal authorities, was unquestionably dominated by the School of Otto Wagner. The architecture of the 'Superblocks' derived from a strong typology of the apartments, a labour-intensive building technology (to counteract unemployment), from the expression of planned urban form and from a pluralistic language of detail. The revolutionaries of the Wagner School became pragmatists who understood how to clothe the new politically provocative building types so as to convey an appropriate sense of architectural continuity. In opposition, Loos, Josef Frank, Franz Schuster and others involved themselves in the residents' movement. The Viennese Werkbundssiedlung (under the general direction of Frank, 1932) once again united all progressive forces with a programme to provide for the workers housing that combined the maximum of 'bourgeois culture' with a minimum of building costs.

A new school began to exercise its influence in Vienna after World War I (*Behrens, *Holzmeister, Tessenow, as well as Strnad and Frank). At the same time Vienna witnessed a loosening of its hold over the regions, accelerated by the political opposition ('Red Vienna'). In the Tyrol, under the influence of Munich, there developed a regional modernism (Franz Baumann, Theodor and Wilhelm Nikolaus Prachensky, Lois Welzenbacher); Wunibald Deininger and Clemens Holzmeister dominated in Salzburg, Mauriz Balzarek, Julius Schulte, Kurt Kühne and Hans Steineder in Upper Austria. A small but effective opposition was formed in Styria by Hubert Eicholzer, Max Lukas and Rambald von Steinbüchel-Rheinwall. Finally in Vienna after 1934 the progressive forces went over to the defensive. After Josef Frank's emigration and the dissolution of the Werkbund (1934), only Ernst A. Plischke was able to maintain a firm position in the face of regionalism and a new national romanticism.

With the exception of several industrial enterprises and numerous 'Südtiroler Siedlungen' (South Tyrolean housing estates), the architecture of National Socialist Austria dating from the period of the 'Austrofascist' Assembly (1934–8) established by the Hitler regime represents a questionable legacy. After World War II many architects tried to pick up lost threads; among these were Clemens Holzmeister, who returned from exile in Ankara, Oswald Haerdtl, Max Fellerer, Eugen Wörle, Franz Schuster and Lois Welzenbacher. In contrast to this, Roland *Rainer deliberately sought, on the one hand, to consolidate the 'consequences and perceptions of modernism' and, on the other, to adapt the urban planning ideas of the English Garden City movement (*Howard) to new conditions. The architectural scene began to change in the wake both of Rainer's work as Vienna's city planner (1958–63) and of the contemporary buildings of Karl Schwanzer. Above all, the Arbeitsgruppe 4 (consisting of Wilhelm *Holzbauer, Friedrich Kurrent, Johannes Spalt and – for a short time – Otto Leitner) began in the 1950s to revive architectural debate through exemplary designs, exhi-

Austria. Parish Community Centre, Puchenau, near Linz (1973–6), by Roland Rainer

Austria. Interior of the branch bank of the Zentralsparkasse der Gemeinde Wien at Floridsdorf (1970–4), by Friedrich Kurrent and Johannes Spalt

Austria. Vorarlberg Provincial Government Building, Bregenz (1973–82), by Wilhelm Holzbauer and others

bitions and writings. At the same time they began to mine Vienna's own architectural history, from Otto Wagner to Josef Frank. Thus the lessons of history were introduced early on in Vienna among a younger generation of architects and came to play a major role in architectural theory. Even today, this view of history continues to be the link between the diversified work of such architects as Johann Georg Gsteu, Wilhelm Holzbauer, Viktor Hufnagl, Gustav *Peichl, Hans Puchhammer, Anton Schweighofer, Günther Wawrik, Ottokar Uhl and others. While most of the members of this group were strongly influenced by Konrad *Wachsmann's Summer Seminars at Salzburg, in 1963 Hans *Hollein and Walter Pichler launched the Viennese functionalist critique. Far from Vienna, Pichler is building his 'Cult Places', a testimony to the fact that a 'universal meaning' is still possible in architecture.

In the early 1960s Günther Feuerstein's Club-Seminar was a hothouse for architectural theory which gave birth to the activist and utopian groups *Haus-Rucker-Co, *Coop Himmelblau, Zünd up–Salz der Erde, and Missing Link.

The 'wild' 1960s also spurred fundamental changes in Graz. On the one hand, teachers such as Friedrich Zotter, Karl Raimund Lorenz, Hubert Hoffmann and Ferdinand Schuster guaranteed a continuity of development on which architectural co-operatives like the Werkgruppe Graz (Eugen Groß, Friedrich Groß-Rannsbach, Werner Hollomey, Hermann Pichler) and Team A Graz (Franz Cziharz, Dietrich Ecker, Herbert Missoni, Jörg Wallmüller) could build. On the other hand, there was the 'Graz School' in the stricter sense, with its expressive formal language, and also such architects as Günther Domenig, Eilfried Huth, Klaus Kada, Karla Kowalski, Michael Szyszkowitz, Heidulf Gerngroß and Helmut Richter who emerged from the studios of the Technische Hochschule in Graz. The contemporary spectrum in Styria is further enriched by a broad movement for participatory construction (Huth) and a new form of regionalism. There are independent developments in other provinces, led in Upper Austria by Roland Ertl, August Kürmayr, Klaus Nötzberger, Karl Odorizzi, Franz Riepl and the Werkgruppe Linz (Helmut Frohnwieser, Heinz Pammer, Edgar Telesko and Helmut Werthgarner; in Salzburg by Gerhard Garstenauer; in the Tyrol by Othmar Barth, Ekkehard Hörmann, Josef Lackner, Günther Norer and Horst Parson; in

Austria. The Favoriten branch in Vienna of the Zentralsparkasse der Gemeinde Wien (1975–9), by Günther Domenig

Austria. Head Sales Office of the Austrian Travel Bureau, Vienna (1976–8), by Hans Hollein

Carinthia by Karl Hack, Manfred Kovatsch, Gernot Kulterer and Felix Orsini-Rosenberg; and finally in the Vorarlberg region by a homogeneous 'Bauschule' represented by Hans Purin, Rudolf Wäger, Günther Wratzfeld and the younger architects Dieter Eberle and Markus Koch. All of these regional developments already bear witness to a strong self-dynamism.

In Vienna a vibrant scene of 'minor architecture', which is especially bound up with the Viennese tradition of Loos and Frank, has developed in opposition to the commercial architecture of large office blocks. The new generation which has grown up in the charged field that lies between Arbeitsgruppe 4 and Hans Hollein has shown a particularly high level of architectural awareness. Luigi Blau, Hermann Czech, Igirien (Werner Appelt, Eberhard E. Kneissel, Elsa Prochaszka), Missing Link (Otto Kapfinger, Adolf Krischanitz) and Heinz Tesar, together with an even wider circle, will assure both the multiplicity of the architectural continuity that has been so typical of the capital and above all a critical approach to architecture seen as a social art. FA

☐ Schwanzer, Karl (ed.), *Wiener Bauten. 1900 bis heute*, Vienna 1964; Uhl, Ottokar, *Moderne Architektur in Wien. Von Otto Wagner bis heute*, Vienna 1969; Graf, Otto Antonia, *Die vergessene Wagnerschule*, Vienna 1969; *Neue Architektur in Österreich 1945–70*, Vienna 1970; *Sechs Architekten vom Schillerplatz* (exhibition catalogue), Vienna 1977; Bode, Peter M., and Peichl, Gustav, *Architektur aus Österreich seit 1960*, Salzburg 1980; Achleitner, Friedrich, *Österreichische Architektur im 20. Jahrhundert*, 3 vols., Salzburg 1980–5; *Architektur aus Graz*, Graz 1981.

Aymonino, Carlo, b. Rome 1926. Studied at the University of Rome; diploma 1950. He was an editor of *Casabella-continuità*, 1959–64, and became a professor at the Istituto Universitario di Architettura in Venice in 1968. Since 1981 he has been an architectural consultant to the city authorities in Rome.

In 1950, in the construction of the populist INA-Casa in the Tiburtino quarter of Rome, he shared the experience of Italian architectural neo-realism with members of the 'Rome School', such as Lodovico Quaroni and Marco *Ridolfi. Later he designed the residential complex 'Gallaratese 2' in Milan (built 1967–73; in collaboration with his son Maurizio, as well as with Giorgio Ciucci, Vittorio De Feo,

Aymonino. Gallaratese 2 residential complex, Milan (Aymonino and others; 1967–73)

Alessandro De Rossi, Mario Manieri-Elia and Sachin Messaré). The rows of houses – one by Aldo *Rossi – are mostly seven storeys high and are arranged geometrically and urbanistically around an amphitheatre-shaped centre. The architects sought thus to recapture urban qualities in this desolate suburban area through a simultaneously strong and expressive multiplicity of formal elements and types. In the G. Marconi Technical School in Pesaro, built in 1970, the fundamental principles of *Rationalist architecture are independently worked out.

Through his role in city-centre planning schemes – Turin, Bologna (both 1962), Reggio Emilia (1971; with Constantino Dardi) and Florence (1978; with Aldo Rossi) – and his numerous publications, A.'s work has greatly influenced recent architecture, particularly through his view of the city as a functionally integrated and historically created form. VML

☐ Aymonino, C., *La formazione del concetto di tipologia edilizia*, Venice 1965; ——, *Origine e sviluppo della città moderna*, Padua 1965; ——, *Il significato della città*, Bari 1975; ——, *Lo studio dei fenomeni urbani*, Rome 1977; 'Carlo Aymonino', *Architecture and Urbanism* (Tokyo), February 1978.

Azuma, Takamitsu, b. Osaka 1933. Before opening his own office in Tokyo, A. was for many years head designer in Junzo Sakakura's office. He was a founding member of the *Architext group in 1971. A. seeks 'oppositional harmonies' in his architecture, that is the harmonic juxtaposition of opposites which he does not seek to resolve, but rather to stress in order to engender tension. A telling example of his design philosophy is his own house in Tokyo (1967), a tall narrow concrete tower deliberately contrasted with the traditional single-storey buildings that surround it. In the Satsuki Kindergarten in Osaka (1969–73) the relationship between courtyard and street spaces is endowed with a degree of tension by the inclusion of wide openings in the smooth façade. AM

☐ *The Japan Architect* (Tokyo), 232, vol. 51 (1976), no. 6, pp. 39–48; ibid., 247, vol. 52 (1977), nos. 10/11, pp. 72, 73.

Azuma. Satsuki Kindergarten, Osaka (1969–73)

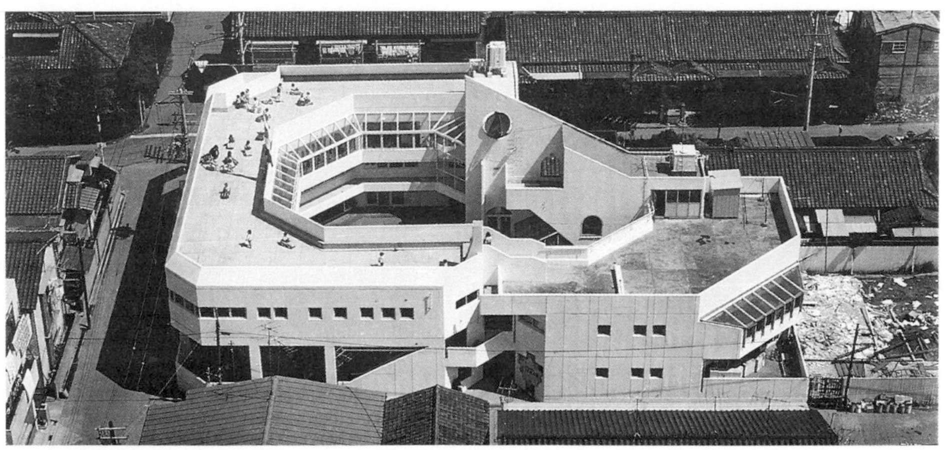

B

Bakema, Jacob Berend, b. Groningen 1914, d. Rotterdam 1981. Studied at the Technikum in Groningen, the Architectural Academy in Amsterdam and the Technical College in Delft. While still a student, B. worked under Cor van *Eesteren, then under Willem van Tijen and H. A. Maaskant, as well as for the municipal architectural office in Rotterdam. In 1948 he entered into partnership with J. H. van den *Broek, and they soon became an influential force in Dutch architecture. In 1947 B. became a member of *CIAM and in 1963 of Team X; he was co-editor, 1959–64, of the journal *Forum*, which helped at that time to prepare the ground for Dutch *Structuralism. From 1965 B. was a professor at the Staatliche Hochschule für Bildende Künste in Hamburg.

Van den Broek and Bakema's architecture has remained indebted to the formal and philosophical ideals of De *Stijl and the *International Style. The Lijnbaan shopping street (1952–4) in the centre of Rotterdam, an area destroyed in World War II, features a clearly articulated and partially covered urban environment; flanked by low, unobtrusive buildings, the street is a pedestrian zone. The sculpturally expressive town hall in Terneuzen (1968) and the psychiatric hospital in Middelharnis (1973–4) display an optimism ultimately derived from *Constructivism. GHa

□ Bakema, Jacob, *Towards an Architecture for Society*, Delft 1963; ——, *Städtebauliche Architektur*, Salzburg 1965; Joedicke, Jürgen (ed.), *Architektur und Städtebau. Das Werk der Architekten van den Broek und Bakema*, Stuttgart 1963; —— (ed.), *Architectengemeenschap van den Broek en Bakema. Architektur + Urbanismus*, Stuttgart 1976.

Baldessari, Luciano, b. Rovereto 1896, d. Milan 1982. Studied at the Politecnico in Milan; diploma 1922. Baldessari began his career in the 1920s as a stage designer and painter. In 1929–32, together with Luigi *Figini and Gino *Pollini, he undertook the elegant rationalist building of the De Angeli Frua Press in Milan. In 1932–3 he built, with Gino *Ponti, the Cima chocolate factory, also in Milan. Of his varied

Bakema. Psychiatric Hospital, Middelharnis (Bakema and van den Broek; 1973–4)

work in the field of exhibition architecture, two examples stand out: the Vesta Pavilion for the Milan Fair of 1933, a strong, formalistic structure with an elegantly proportioned and mullioned glass façade; and the Brida Pavilion at the Milan Fair of 1951, with a bold free-form roof of thin concrete. B. is one of the least conventional exponents of Italian *Rationalism: very early in his career he abandoned unthinking *Functionalism in order to create spaces endowed with a more pronounced abstract clarity. VML

□ *Contraspazio*, 10 (1978), special issue; Veronesi, Giulia, *Luciano Baldessari architetto*, Trent 1957.

Banfi, Gianluigi, b. Milan 1910, d. in the Mauthausen concentration camp 1945. Studied at the Milan Politecnico. In 1932 he was a founding member of the firm *BBPR in Milan.

Barnes, Edward Larrabee, b. Chicago 1922. Studied under *Gropius and *Breuer at Harvard. Since 1949 he has had his own office in New York. Strongly influenced through his teachers by the *Bauhaus, B. has favoured abstract compositions of clear geometric form with smooth, unornamented surfaces, which are designed with notable sensitivity for the specific situation. The Student Center of Monterey Peninsula College in Monterey, Cal. (1973), the Walker Art Center in Minneapolis (1974) and the IBM World Trade Americas/Far East Corporation Headquarters in Mount Plea-

Barragán. San Cristobal estate, Mexico City (1967–8)

sant, N.Y. (1977), and the Visual Arts Center of Bowdoin College in Brunswick, Maine (1978), are among his best works. AM

☐ Robinson, Cervin, 'Edward Larrabee Barnes: Profile of Firm and Work', *American Institute of Architects Journal*, April 1980, pp. 52–71.

Barragán, Luis, b. Guadalajara, Mexico 1902. Trained as an engineer, B. is self-taught as an architect. After travel in Spain and France, he established himself in Guadalajara in 1927, but since 1936 he has worked and lived in Mexico City. His earliest work was characterized by the adaptation of indigenous vernacular forms of Mexican architecture, as well as by elements drawn from Islamic architecture, particularly that of Morocco, which he had studied in books. His move to Mexico City coincided with a shift to the *International Style and especially to *Le Corbusier. Around 1940 and under the influence of the French painter and landscape architect Ferdinand Bac and the German-born Mexican sculptor Mathias Goeritz, B. finally developed a personal form of artistic expression. Vegetation, water and a simple architecture of primary geometric forms are combined in his composition of surrealistic retreats. In his later works this effect is heightened by magically oscillating colours. Among the most important milestones in this last phase, which translated Mexican building tradition into an abstract architectural language, are the architect's own house in Tacubaya (1947) and, in Mexico City: the towers of the Ciudad Satélite (1957, with Goeritz); the overall planning and several public spaces for the Las Arboledas residential quarter (1957–61); and a house and stud-farm stables for the San Cristobal estate (1967–8). AM

Ambasz, Emilio, *The Architecture of Luis Barragán*, New York 1976; 'Luis Barragán. House for Luis Barragán & San Cristobal', *Global Architecture* (Tokyo), no. 48, 1979.

Bartning, Otto, b. Karlsruhe 1883, d. Darmstadt 1959. Studied at the Technische Hochschulen in Berlin and Karlsruhe. He was Director of the Hochschule für Handwerk und Baukunst in Weimar, 1926–30. B.'s work consists of industrial, administrative, residential and hospital buildings, but above all Protestant

Bartning. Star Church project (1921–2)

churches, mostly planned around a central altar. His early country house designs are part of architectural *Expressionism, as is the project for a Sternkirche (Star Church; 1921–2) in which the structural idea of the Gothic was to be realized with modern building methods. The steel church for the 'Pressa' exhibition in Cologne (1928) and the Church of the Resurrection, with a circular ground-plan, in Essen (1930) seem closer to the *Rationalism of those years in German architecture. After the war, he was involved with the emergency programme to provide churches of prefabricated timber construction, sponsored by the German Evangelical Relief Organization (designed 1946).

☐ Bartning, O., *Vom neuen Kirchenbau*, Berlin 1919; Mayer, Hans K. F., *Der Baumeister Otto Bartning und die Wiederentdeckung des Raumes*, Heidelberg 1951.

Basile, Ernesto, b. Palermo 1857, d. Palermo 1932. Studied at the University of Palermo, moved to Rome in 1881, where he taught after 1883 at the University. In 1892 he was appointed a professor at the University of Palermo. After several early eclectic works (project for the Parliament Building in Rome, 1883–4; Villino Florio in Palermo, 1899), B. adopted the Italian version of *Art Nouveau around the turn of the century (Villino Basile, Palermo, 1903). Later, his architecture adapted classicist-traditional traits (Istituto Provinciale Antitubercolare, Palermo, 1920–5; Albergo Diurno, Palermo, 1925) and thereby came into opposition with the *Rationalism of the 1920s in Italy. VML

☐ *Ernesto Basile architetto* (exhibition catalogue), Venice 1980.

Baudot, Anatole de, b. Sarrebourg 1834, d. Paris 1915. Pupil of Henri Labrouste and the favoured disciple of Viollet-le-Duc, he was active as a restorer of medieval buildings in *France and a propagandist of Viollet-le-Duc's rationalized gothic point of view. After the master's death, his attention turned increasingly to experiments with reinforced concrete and brickwork, culminating in his church of St Jean-de-Montmartre in Paris (1894–1904), where reinforced concrete is combined with a metal roof structure. B.'s attempts to incorpo-

Baudot. St Jean-de-Montmartre, Paris (1894–1904)

rate his experiments into Viollet-le-Duc's historical schema are reflected also in his numerous writings, notably *L'Architecture et le béton armé* (1905). BB

☐ Françoise Boudon, 'Recherche sur la pensée et l'œuvre d'Anatole de Baudot 1834–1905'. *Architecture, mouvement, continuité*, March 1973.

Bauhaus. In the fourteen years of its existence the Bauhaus showed itself to be not just an important school of art, design and (belatedly) architecture, but much more importantly it was a crucible of European modernism, an organization which took up numerous reform ideas of the epoch and helped to ensure that they were pursued to the greatest possible effect. Although its director and teachers always eschewed the notion of a Bauhaus style, its teaching and artistic successes made the Institute and its production an oft-imitated model. Not without some part in this was the Bauhaus's own self-dramatization, which arose from its continual sense of a need to legitimize itself. Like the Weimar Republic itself, the Bauhaus was founded in the city of Goethe and Nietzsche, lasted from 1919 until 1933 and experienced heated political confrontation to which it finally fell victim. Its fate was, for better or for worse, tied to that of Germany's first democratic government. This parallel as well, lent the Bauhaus an exemplary role.

The involvement of the Grand Duchy of Saxe-Weimar with Walter *Gropius went back as far as 1915. Henry *van de Velde had suggested Gropius as his successor at Weimar's Kunstgewerbeschule (Arts and Crafts School), while lecturers of the Hochschule für Bildende Kunst had declared their interest in Gropius as director of a new architecture section. In spring 1919, Gropius was charged with the direction of both schools, now to be united, to which he gave the name 'Staatliches Bauhaus in Weimar'. This background history attests to his intention of creating a comprehensive art institution: 'The Bauhaus strives to collect all artistic creativity into a unity, to reunite all artistic disciplines – sculpture, painting, design and handicraft – into a new architecture', as it was formulated in the prospectus of April 1919. In this celebration of handicraft, of teaching workshops, of a communal collaboration of teachers and students, and the synthesis of all the arts, the early Bauhaus took up notions which had circulated in expressionist artistic circles in the months immediately after World War I (*Expressionism), but which go back ultimately to the *Arts and Crafts movement of the 19th century.

In the first years this union of art and craft was achieved in communal teaching activity directed by 'Formmeistern' (masters of design) and 'Werkmeistern' (work masters), that is of artists and trained craftsmen. Studies were conducted in workshops (sculpture, theatre, stained glass, photography, metalwork, woodwork, ceramics, typography/advertising/exhibition design, mural painting, weaving), and this provided the opportunity for individuals to earn money for themselves. At the end of the course, examinations were held for associates' or masters' diplomas.

Gropius' skill in the selection of his collaborators explains, in the end, the fact that a typical school of the period could succeed in becoming an artistic and intellectual centre of the republic. Artists were engaged as masters, including the painters Lyonel Feininger, Oskar Schlemmer, Georg Muche, Paul Klee and Vassily Kandinsky, and the sculptor Gerhard Marcks. Johannes Itten, who developed the 'Vorkurs' (introductory course), was especially influential in the early phase. This elementary instruction, compulsory for all beginners at the Bauhaus, introduced the student to the principles of form, taught him to work with materials and colours, directed him to an analytical study of pictorial works of art and sought above all to stimulate a free creativity independent of all preconceived notions or models.

The orientation of the Bauhaus was modified by the influence of De *Stijl, whose leading spokesman Theo van *Doesburg gave independent courses in Weimar, and by Russian *Constructivism. The esoteric and romantic was replaced by active involvement in the contemporary scene, active concern with the environment, and a realistic assessment of the needs of an industrial society. Gropius devised the motto 'Art and Technology, a new unity' ('Kunst und Technik, eine neue Einheit'). When Itten left the Bauhaus in 1932, his responsibilities were taken over by László Moholy-Nagy and Josef Albers. The resulting change in direction manifested itself for the first time in the Bauhaus's involvement in the exhibition organized by the Thuringian provincial government in 1923. Even an architectural experiment, the 'Haus am Horn' designed by Muche, was shown, although the Bauhaus, despite its

Bauhaus. The experimental Haus am Horn by Georg Muche (exhibited 1923)

Bauhaus. Views of the Dessau buildings by Walter Gropius (1925–6)

name, did not have an architectural department until 1927 when Hannes *Meyer arrived.

While the early Bauhaus had startled the Weimar populace with its utopian social ideas and numerous flirtations with mystical and esoteric doctrines and life-styles, the opposition, especially in Thuringian handicraft circles, increased after the students began to take an interest in design prototypes for industrial serial production; the production of its workshops began to seem to be in competition with local workshops. Especially attacked was the link between a state-subsidized teaching institution and workshops run by private enterprise. The provincial elections of 1924 gave the political right wing a majority, a development which led to the masters' decision at the end of the year to disband the school.

In Weimar, the Hochschule für Handwerk und Baukunst, of which Otto *Bartning was director, became successor to the Bauhaus. Gropius and most of the teachers and students of the Bauhaus took up an offer of the city of Dessau to continue their work in that small provincial capital. Thus Dessau not only took over the school, but made possible the construction of a new complex of Bauhaus buildings as well as residences for the masters. Gropius' new Bauhaus complex was occupied by 1926. Its freely disposed layout with three extending wings, a two-storey bridge spanning the street, and the great curtain wall of the workshop building were to serve as practical demonstrations of a modern architecture.

With the new home came a thoroughgoing consolidation. Former associates such as Josef Albers, Herbert Bayer, Marcel *Breuer, Hinnerk Scheper, Joost Schmidt and Gunta Stölzl, who dominated both theoretical and practical principles, took over the workshops and rendered superfluous the former distinction between 'Formmeistern' and 'Werkmeistern'. The production of the Bauhaus – itself now linked, via numerous international connections, with the other centres of European modernism – was determined by functionality, economy, a preference for primary stereometric forms and the crisp elegance of machine-produced objects. Through commissions such as that of 1926 for the experimental housing estate at Dessau-Törten, which was built using industrialized techniques, the Bauhaus was given opportunities to acquire practical experience in the field of mass housing. Not least in its festivals, for which the Bauhaus was renowned, was the new ideal life-style highlighted: unburdened by history, spontaneous, creative, of one mind and uncompromisingly of its own time. It was thus a matter for general astonishment when, in 1928,

Gropius gave up his relatively assured position as director of the school he had founded and justified his action by reference to the renewal of political difficulties.

Gropius himself selected as his successor Hannes Meyer, who sought to emphasize the social aspect of the Bauhaus's work. Meyer expounded the notion of 'the needs of the people instead of the needs of luxury' ('Volksbedarf statt Luxusbedarf'), engaged the city planner Ludwig *Hilberseimer for the architecture department (in which Meyer's professional partner Hans Wittwer was also active), increased the output of the workshops and pressed for the development of inexpensive furniture, textiles, carpets and lamps that could be afforded by the working classes. He unequivocally opposed both the open and the latent aestheticism of the Bauhaus: 'Everything in the world is a product of the formula: function times economy . . . Building is a biological procedure. Building is not an aesthetic process . . . Architecture as the "artist's realization of effects" is without justification.' This stance led to internal conflicts among the artists at the Bauhaus. Meyer's political leanings became increasingly leftist, and he was attacked from outside by the right, increasingly more influential. Finally, the liberal mayor of Dessau, Fritz Hesse, an active supporter of the Bauhaus, was forced to dismiss Meyer.

In its last director, Ludwig *Mies van der Rohe, the Bauhaus gained a leader devoted to absolute standards of quality and a relentless work ethic. This work was especially concentrated on those skills related to 'Bau und Ausbau' ('Building and Development'), so that the conflict with the advocates of an independent art which had begun under Meyer's directorship was continued, even if now under different banners, under Mies van der Rohe. In 1932 the right-radical faction of the Dessau municipal council put down a motion to close the Bauhaus, and this was adopted with the support of the Social Democrats. For over six months Mies van der Rohe carried on the work of the Bauhaus as a private institute, housed in an abandoned telephone factory in Berlin-Steglitz. However, after the enforced closure of the school by the Gestapo and the S.A., the Bauhaus's board voted on 20 July 1933 to disband for good.

According to the estimate of its chronicler Hans M. Wingler, the Bauhaus had scarcely more than 1,250 pupils in total. Its influence stands in inverse proportion to this limited number. The enforced emigration of many Bauhaus members dispersed its principles throughout the world. Its work was continued in the *USA, by Gropius and Breuer at Harvard University, by Moholy-Nagy at the New Bauhaus in Chicago, by Mies van der Rohe, Hilberseimar and Walter Peterhans at the Armour Institute (today Illinois Institute of Technology), also in Chicago, and by Albers at Black Mountain College in North Carolina. Exhibitions, such as that at the Museum of Modern Art in New York in the winter of 1938–9, and numerous publications spread the fame of the school worldwide. The Bauhaus became a legend of modernism and thus attracted much of the criticism voiced in the 1960s in connection with the discussion of *functionalism. Both in its reputation and as a target, the Bauhaus assumed in later history, and for the first time, a monolithic character that it had never possessed during its brief career – a career characterized rather by contradiction, controversy, and lively artistic discussion. WP

☐ *Staatliches Bauhaus Weimar 1919–1923*, Munich and Weimar 1923; Gropius, Walter, *Idee und Aufbau des Staatlichen Bauhauses*, Munich and Weimar 1923; Bayer, Herbert, and Gropius, Walter and Ise (eds.), *Bauhaus 1919–1928*, New York 1938; Wingler, Hans M., *Das Bauhaus 1919–1933 Weimar Dessau Berlin*, Cologne 1962; *50 Jahre Bauhaus* (exhibition catalogue), Stuttgart 1968; Franciscono, Marcel, *Walter Gropius and the creation of the Bauhaus in Weimar*, Urbana, Ill. 1971; Hüter, Karl-Heinz, *Das Bauhaus in Weimar*, Berlin 1976.

BBPR. Partnership founded in Milan in 1932 by Gianluigi *Banfi, Lodovico *Belgiojoso, Enrico *Peressutti and Ernesto Nathan *Rogers. BBPR was launched in the overheated atmosphere of the Italian Rationalist debate, creating its first masterpiece in the late 1930s, the Sanatorium at Legnano (1937–8). The 'objectivity' manifested there was continued in the reductivist geometries of their Memorial to the victims of the concentration camps, erected in Milan in 1946. With the Torre Velasca in Milan (1954–8) they created a building which reacted against the polemic of the *International Style, treating its machine aesthetic as an isolated and unique episode in modern architecture. With its abstracted medieval reminiscences, the design

BBPR. Torre Velasca, Milan (1954–8)

of the tower responds to its prestigious location, near Milan's Gothic cathedral. This rejection of dogmatic modernism, which was vigorously criticized by many at the time, anticipated by a decade the later international reorientation of architecture. It was not, however, an isolated incident in BBPR's development. Already in the restoration of the Monastery of San Simpliciano in Milan (1940; with E. Radice Fossati), they demonstrated an unusual awareness of traditional values, which recurs in the same city both in the equally elegant and clear museum installation in the Castello Sforzesco (1952–6) and in the offices of the Chase Manhattan Bank (1969), notable for an expressive steel façade sensitively harmonized with its urban surroundings. VML

☐ Paci, Enzo, 'Continuità e coerenze dei BBPR', *Zodiac* (Milan), no. 4, 1959, pp. 82–115; Bonfanti, E., and Porta, M., *Città, museo e architettura: Il gruppo BBPR nella cultura architettonica italiana 1932–70*, Florence 1973; Pavia, Antonio, *BBPR a Milano*, Milan 1982.

Beaudouin, Eugène, b. Paris 1898. Studied at the *Ecole des Beaux-Arts in Paris and the Académie de France in Rome. One of the leading exponents of the Modern Movement in France, he designed, in collaboration with Marcel *Lods, the Cité de la Muette at Drancy, near Paris (1932–4), a mixed-development estate where prefabricated reinforced-concrete units were used (developed in collaboration with Eugène *Freyssinet), the Pavilion School at Suresnes (1932–5); and the Maison du Peuple at Clichy (1937–9), in which the engineer Jean *Prouvé played an important part. He drew up the plans for the Cité Rotterdam suburb at Strasbourg (1951–3) and built (with *Nervi and Alberto Camenzind) the extension to the Palace of the League of Nations in Geneva (1967–73).

Behnisch, Günter, b. Lockwitz, near Dresden, 1922. Studied at the Technische Hochschule in Stuttgart, where in 1952 he founded an office with Bruno Lambart. After their partnership was dissolved in 1956, he continued alone until 1966 when the firm of Behnisch and Partners was formed, consisting of Fritz Auer (left 1981),

Behnisch. Study Centre of the Lutheran Church, Stuttgart-Birkach (1977–9)

Winfried Büxel, Manfred Sabatke, Erhard Tränkner and Karlheinz Weber (left 1981). Since 1967 he has served as a professor at the Technische Hochschule in Darmstadt.

Undoubtedly the best-known works of the Behnisch office are the sports buildings of the Olympiapark, Munich (1967–72), built for the 1972 Olympic Games. The tent-roof construction (designed in collaboration with Frei *Otto) over the stadium, sports hall and swimming pool seems at first glance uncharacteristic of the work of B. and his partners in its virtuoso engineering. Yet the concept expresses very clearly their understanding of the architectural requirement to create an adaptable artificial environment, and was notable for its reflection of the festive character of the games.

Initially, B. was active almost exclusively in school building, in which field he made several important pioneering contributions in the use of prefabrication. Important stages were the Hohenstaufen-Gymnasium in Göppingen (1956–9), the Staatliche Fachhochschule für Technik in Ulm (1959–63), the Mittelpunktschule in Oppelsbohm (1966–9) and the Progymnasium in Lorch, Württemberg (1972–3). The strong circular form of the school in Oppelsbohm is further developed in Lorch into a free framework of a classroom core and attached wings for special uses. The graceful looseness of this composition established the pattern for the firm's work. Among their most important recent designs are: the Old People's and Convalescent Home at Reutlingen (1973–6); various projects for the governmental quarter of Bonn (1973–81); the replanning of the Königstraße and the Schloßplatz in Stuttgart (1973–80); the Sports Hall in Sindelfingen (1976–7); and the Study Centre of the Lutheran Church in Stuttgart-Birkach (1977–9). FJ

☐ *Behnisch & Partner, Bauten und Entwürfe*, Stuttgart 1975; Klotz, Heinrich, conversation with Günter Behnisch, in: *Architektur in der Bundesrepublik. Gespräche mit sechs Architekten*, Frankfurt am Main, Berlin and Vienna 1977, pp. 13–63; 'Behnisch + Partner', *Das Kunstwerk* (Stuttgart), 32 (1979), nos. 2/3, pp. 22–29; 'Offenheit und Vielfalt. Behnisch & Partner, Stuttgart', *Deutsche Bauzeitung* (Stuttgart), 116 (1982), no. 3, pp. 12–42.

Behrens, Peter, b. Hamburg 1868, d. Berlin 1940. In a society torn between archaic mental attitudes and a blind faith in the rapid progress of technology, B. was one of the first architects of the 20th century to develop a form of architectural thought that would answer to the demands of an industrialized civilization. At a period when the moral and social demands put forward by the Expressionist painters of Dresden (Die Brücke) were leading to new directions in the graphic arts, he was in at the birth of modern architecture in Germany, where he exerted a leading influence between 1900 and 1914. Furthermore, the sidelines derived from architecture in which he engaged inaugurated (1907) a form of specialization that has become widely known in our times under the name of Industrial Design. Here, too, he deeply influenced the development of technology and style at a time when the propagation of craft-derived forms by the exponents of *Art Nouveau was threatening to undermine any attempts to formulate design principles in conformity with new ways of living.

B. did not discover his true vocation from the first. Like *van de Velde and *Le Corbusier, he began as a painter and came to architecture via the so-called applied arts. From 1886 to 1889 he attended painting classes at the art schools of Karlsruhe and Düsseldorf. In 1890 he was impressed by the work of the *luministes* (Josef Israels) in Holland, and the work of painters such as Leibl in Munich; he was a founder-member of the Münchner Sezession in 1893. Already interested in the graphic arts, his early compositions (coloured woodcuts, frontis-

Behrens. The architect's house on the Mathildenhöhe, Darmstadt (1901)

Behrens. AEG high-tension plant, Berlin (1910)

pieces for books, etc.) are still permeated by the decorative influence of Art Nouveau.

After travelling in Italy (1896), B. turned in 1898 to problems of industrial production and designed a number of prototype flasks for mass production by a large glass works; these are already notable for their plain, straightforward shapes. In 1899 the Grand Duke Ernst Ludwig invited him to stay at Darmstadt and join a group of young artists (the architect J. M. *Olbrich, the interior decorators P. Huber and P. Bürck, the painter H. Christiansen, and the sculptors L. Habich and R. Bosselt) who under the name of 'Die Sieben' (The Seven) had as their aim the establishment of effective relationships between all the plastic arts. It was then that B. took up architecture and, as van de Velde had done at Uccle five years before, built his own house and fitted it out completely in a unitary style that betrayed the influence of both van de Velde and *Mackintosh. At the instance of *Muthesius, he was appointed head of the Düsseldorf School of Art in 1903, a post he held until 1907. From this period onwards his classical temperament led him to design sober, powerful and massive works, strongly functionalist in style. The Obenauer House (Saarbrücken, 1905–6), as well as the Cuno and Schroeder Houses (Eppenhausen, near Hagen, 1908–10) express this rationalistic tendency, that was ultimately to distinguish the work of Behrens from the plastic dynamism and lyricism of *Poelzig and *Mendelsohn.

In 1907 (the year the *Deutscher Werkbund was founded), B. was summoned to Berlin by the AEG (the German General Electrical Company). His duties comprised the design not only of electrical appliances (cookers, radiators, ventilators, lamps, etc.), but also of the firm's packaging, catalogues, leaflets, posters, letterheads, showrooms, shops, and, to boot, factories and workshops. This marks for the first time, in a large industrial context, the emergence of a desire to humanize technology. By employing an architect to ensure a good visual appearance for their products, the AEG was bringing objects into daily life that were not only functionally efficient, but were harmoniously and sensitively designed as well, permeated as they were by an authentic creative style which, in the last analysis, projected the brand image of a major industrial company. At

Behrens. Technical administration building of the Hoechst Dyeworks, Frankfurt (1920–5)

the same time, B. introduced a new expression of monumentality to European architecture with his turbine factory for AEG (1908–9) – the first German building in glass and steel – the high-tension plant (1910) and the factory for small motors (1910–11), etc. B. also built a complete district of flats for AEG workers at Henningsdorf, near Berlin (1910/11). Apart from numerous factories erected at various times throughout his career, mention should be made of certain other major works designed in a neo-classic style that expressed the clients' need for prestige. These include the Mannesmann AG offices at Düsseldorf (1911–12), those for the Continental Rubber Company at Hanover (1913–20), and the German Embassy in St Petersburg (now Leningrad; 1911–12).

In 1922 B. was appointed director of the School of Architecture at the Vienna Akademie der bildenden Künste; some of the buildings he designed in the following years may be considered as examples of German *Expressionism (Hoechst Dyeworks, 1920–5). In 1936 he became head of the department of architecture at the Prussian Academy of Arts, Berlin. Among B.'s most outstanding pupils are: Le Corbusier, who worked in his Berlin office from 1910 to 1911; *Gropius, from 1907 to 1910; and *Mies van der Rohe, from 1908 to 1911. RD

☐ Behrens, Peter, *Feste des Lebens und der Kunst*, Jena 1900; Hoeber, Fritz, *Peter Behrens*, Munich 1913; Cremers, Paul Joseph, *Peter Behrens, Sein Werk von 1909 bis zur Gegenwart*, Essen 1928, Grimme, K. M., *Peter Behrens und seine Wiener akademische Meisterschule*, Vienna 1930; Buddensieg, Tilman, et al., *Industriekultur. Peter Behrens und die AEG; 1907–1914*, Berlin 1979; Windsor, Alan, *Peter Behrens, Architect and Designer, 1868–1940*, London 1981.

Belgiojoso, Lodovico (Barbiano di), b. Milan 1909. Studied at the Milan Politecnico. He was a professor at the Istituto Universitario di Architettura in Venice, 1955–63, and from 1963 at the Politecnico in Milan. He was a founder-member of the firm *BBPR, established in Milan in 1932.

Belgium. Brussels was the leading European centre for advanced architectural production during the Art Nouveau phase in the 1890s. The influence of Belgian Art Nouveau in its many guises was widely felt, particularly in *France and *Germany; the principal features were the

distinctive personal styles of Victor *Horta and Paul Hankar, both based in Brussels and credited with independently achieving a non-historicizing architecture as early as 1893. Horta went further than any other architect of his time in dissolving traditional interior volumes into unified flowing space. Hankar superimposed and interlocked interior volumes just as he did the structural and graphic elements that defined them, so as to express their special integrity as discrete components of a whole. Henry *van de Velde, interior designer, craftsman, and artist, as well as architect and theoretician, was invited in 1902 to teach at the design school in Weimar, whence he exerted a great influence on German *Jugendstil*.

The determining sources of Belgian Art Nouveau lay in the ferment of architectural ideas in Brussels during the 1880s, catalyzed by the completion there of Joseph Poelaert's overwhelming Palace of Justice (1866–83) and tempered by the contributions of such eclectic architects as Alphonse Balat, Henri Beyaert, and Jean Baes. The theories of Viollet-le-Duc permeated the scene not only during that decade but also during those that preceded and followed it. Another major influence on the efflorescence of Belgian Art Nouveau was the English *Arts and Crafts movement. Beginning in 1888, Gustave Serrurier-Bovy, a Liège cabinet-maker and the leading Belgian exponent of Art Nouveau outside Brussels, imported the products of Liberty and Company of London.

The various Art Nouveau styles attained immense popularity throughout Belgium around the turn of the century. Some of the considerable production in these modes was of unquestionable originality, but the mass of it was derivative, based on the successes of the style's leading practitioners. Among the more original minor masters of Art Nouveau were Octave van Rijsselberghe and Gustave Strauven in Brussels; Paul Jaspar in Liège; and Emile van Averbeke in Antwerp.

Even as Art Nouveau enjoyed its greatest vogue in the design of residential buildings, gaining an enviable reputation abroad, revival styles remained in extensive use for all building types. Not infrequently, Art Nouveau motifs

Belgium. Hôtel Tassel, Brussels (1892–3), by Victor Horta: façade and internal staircase

were eclectically mingled with stylistic elements of neo-Gothic and neo-Renaissance derivation. French academic classicism (*Ecole des Beaux-Arts) was favoured by King Leopold II personally and particularly for large-scale secular work; ecclesiastical commissions were usually executed in neo-Gothic style. By *c.* 1910, Art Nouveau was losing its prominence, even in the domestic sector, to the very historicizing styles whose hegemony it had originally challenged. Designers such as Horta and Antoine Pompe switched from primarily fluid geometries to more rigid, mainly orthogonal ones, responding to conservative trends in taste and also to the tone set by early 20th-century Viennese work (introduced directly into Brussels by Josef *Hoffmann's Palais Stoclet, 1904–11), and prefiguring *Art Deco. Meanwhile, a desire for a quaint regional character in new buildings informed much Belgian architecture from *c.*1900 onwards. Bruges, perhaps, was the major centre for regionalist ideology in Flanders, with Liège playing this role in Wallonia.

After World War I, most of the reconstruction work in such devastated cities as Louvain and Ypres was carried out in the conservative regionalist vein that had set in well before 1914. Advanced Belgian architecture of the 1920s, such as that of Huibrecht Hoste, often reflected contemporary Dutch building as well as the rationalist tradition, ultimately deriving from Viollet-le-Duc, carried on in Belgium by Louis Cloquet of Ghent. Garden-city housing estates planned along English lines were occasionally the setting for progressive domestic architecture of Cubist character (*Cubism).

In the late 1920s and 1930s, Art Deco and streamlined styles were widely employed, notably in Ghent and Charleroi and their suburbs. Albert van Huffel stunningly exploited an Art Deco manner in his modified design for the unfinished national memorial basilica, Koekelberg, Brussels (1921; completed 1970).

The *International Style, on the other hand, made less of an impact in Belgium – although not for any lack of talented and dedicated representatives there: *Le Corbusier himself built the Guiette studio-house (1925–7) in an Antwerp suburb, and he had many Belgian followers, including Renaat Braem, L. H. De Koninck, and Victor *Bourgeois. Belgians were present at La Sarraz and subsequent *CIAM meetings, as well as at the Weißenhof housing exhibition in Stuttgart in 1927. The New Objectivity (*Neue Sachlichkeit), brought to Belgium principally via the Netherlands, appealed mainly to Flemish architects like Braem and Leon Stijnen. The Brussels design school of La Cambre, opened in 1928 with van de Velde as director, was a veritable Belgian *Bauhaus. Belgium was to be a crossroads of various modern tendencies without ever making an original contribution of importance to developments outside the country. Conservative public taste between the wars was the major factor in limiting the opportunities available to Belgian architects to experiment fruitfully. None of the ambitious modernist projects, including one by Le Corbusier and Hoste entered in the IMALSO competition for the development of the left bank of the Scheldt river opposite Antwerp (1933), was executed.

After World War II, the new international political and economic order made a preponderant American influence on Belgian architecture and planning inevitable. The application of pseudo-CIAM principles, in conjunction with American-inspired traffic-flow models, to the development not only of certain suburban areas but also the central areas of such cities as Brussels and Liège benefited the narrow interests of developers more than society at large, and in many places resulted in a serious erosion of the historic urban fabric. Through the 1950s and 1960s, talented architects such as Braem and Stijnen continued to produce designs of quality, but their contributions were obscured by the enormous quantity of undistinguished curtain-wall structures that increasingly dominated many Belgian cities. The Brussels Exposition of 1958 provided an occasion for demonstrating many new building materials to an international audience; but many of its pavilions seemed to caricature the Functionalist aesthetic (*Functionalism). Such pavilions did even less than the prize-winning design by *Skidmore, Owings and Merrill, erected in Brussels for the Banque Lambert (1960), to inspire significant improvement in the declining standards of Belgian urban design, but rather encouraged the multiplication of bizarre formalist exercises in the 1960s. The finest examples of Belgian architecture from the 1950s and 1960s were to be found in the private residential sector and in rural or semi-rural contexts.

Beginning *c.* 1970, local councils and planning groups, such as the Atelier de Recherche et d'Action Urbaines in Brussels, were able to

Belgium. Students' Residence, Université Catholique de Louvain, Woluvé Saint-Lambert (1970–7), by Lucien Kroll

organize popular opposition to grandiose planning schemes and the banal architecture that accompanied them. The rehabilitation of disused structures, the preservation of significant older buildings, and the rights of squatters became issues with which municipal authorities have been forced to reckon. Widespread disillusionment with late Modern architecture, such as that seen in the Quartier Nord in Brussels (1960–ongoing), favoured the development in Belgium of a nexus of fertile Post-Modernist alternatives (*Post-Modernism). Belgium's leading Post-Modernist, Lucien *Kroll, has had a profound influence on many members of a younger generation of architects, including Rudy Vael of Sint-Niklaas. In Liège, Charles Vandenhove has rationalized local vernacular styles and deployed them sensitively in a variety of different situations. An interest in pure geometry and proportioning systems in architectural design runs strong in the Belgian Post-Modernist milieu, which includes such notable figures as Bob Van Reeth, Marc Van Bortel, and Georges Baines of Antwerp; Paul Robbrecht and Ilde Daem of Ghent; and Philippe Caucheteux of Mons. AWi

Belluschi, Pietro, b. Ancona 1899. Studied at the University of Rome and at Cornell University. He was chief designer in the office of A. E. Doyle and Associates in Portland, Oregon, 1927–42. In 1943 he founded his own office there, which was taken over by *Skidmore, Owings & Merrill in 1950. He was Dean of the School of Architecture and Planning at the Massachusetts Institute of Technology in Cambridge, 1951–65. From 1965 he again had his own office in Portland. B. first came to public attention with his Equitable Savings Building in Portland (1948), an early example of a curtain wall in which all the façade elements are composed in the same plane. The Juilliard School of Music in New York's Lincoln Center (1970), with its incorporation of various functions within a large single structure, is evidence of B.'s continued devotion to the ideal of a late *International Style container architecture. GHa

☐ Gubitosi, C., and Izzo, A. (eds.), *Pietro Belluschi: Edifici e progetti, 1932–1973*, Rome 1974.

Berg, Max, b. Stettin 1870, d. Baden-Baden 1947. Studied at the Technische Hochschule in Berlin-Charlottenburg. Later he was Municipal Architect in Breslau. His Jahrhunderthalle (Century Hall) in Breslau (1912–13), a huge cupola with exposed ribs, was one of the boldest reinforced-concrete buildings of its time. Its expressionistic (*Expressionism) feeling is derived purely from the formal pattern of its structural skeleton.

Berlage, Hendrik Petrus, b. Amsterdam 1856, d. The Hague 1934. Studied in Zurich, and had his own practice in Amsterdam from 1889 onwards; he figures among the great innovators of architecture around the turn of the century. Reacting against 19th-century *eclecticism, he aimed at an 'honest awareness of the problems of architecture' and a craftsmanlike approach to materials and construction. B. revealed once more to his contemporaries the meaning and magic of brickwork. Plastering a wall was in his view tantamount to falsification, and he eschewed the practice even in the rooms of private houses. His 'moral' outlook was in harmony with the social climate of the times, which since *c.* 1895 was strongly influenced by the rising labour movement.

B. felt attracted by the massive gravity of the Romanesque, which is reflected in his semicircular arches and his large unbroken wall surfaces. These features also recall the work of the American architects H. H. Richardson, Louis *Sullivan and Frank Lloyd *Wright, whose work he had seen on his 1911 trip to the *USA. Characteristic works of his own include the Diamond-Workers' House, Amsterdam (1899–1900), Holland House, London (1914), and above all the Amsterdam Stock Exchange, completed in 1903. The Stock Exchange was the outcome of a competition held in 1897; B.'s winning design was subsequently altered by him in many details. In this monumental work, he used a light-coloured stone for special features, in addition to brick. The steel roof structure over the main hall is left exposed.

As an architectural writer, B. exerted great influence (notably bringing the work of Frank Lloyd Wright to public notice in Europe) through his numerous publications and lectures. Many buildings, especially in the *Netherlands, are in fact based on B.'s work, even though they differ formally from it. The poetry of smooth surfaces had considerable influence on the Modern Movement in Holland (De *Stijl), while his expressive use of historic forms influenced the development of Dutch *Expressionism (*Amsterdam, School of). In 1928 he attended the first congress of *CIAM at La Sarraz, but felt himself to be too committed to a

Berg. Jahrhunderthalle, Breslau (1912–13)

Berlage. Stock Exchange, Amsterdam (1903): exterior and interior views

more traditional conception of architecture to be able to join CIAM. JJV/GHa

☐ Berlage, Hendrik Petrus, *Gedanken über den Stil in der Baukunst*, Leipzig 1905; ——, *Grundlagen und Entwicklung der Architektur*, Berlin and Rotterdam 1908; ——, *Studies over Bouwkunst, Stijl en Samenleving*, Rotterdam 1910; Gratama, Jan, *Dr. H. P. Berlage Bouwmeester*, Rotterdam 1925; Havelaar, J., *Dr H. P. Berlage*, Amsterdam 1930; Singelenberg, Pieter, *H.P. Berlage*, Amsterdam 1969.

Bill, Max, b. Winterthur 1908. Painter, sculptor, exhibition designer, architect. Studied at the Kunstgewerbeschule in Zurich and from

Bill. Hochschule für Gestaltung, Ulm (1953–5)

1927 to 1929 at the *Bauhaus in Dessau. From 1944 he was involved in industrial design. From 1951 to 1956 he was Rector of the Hochschule für Gestaltung at Ulm, as well as being in charge of the departments of architecture and industrial design. He taught at the Hochschule für Bildende Kunst, Hamburg, 1967–74. His best-known architectural work, the Hochschule für Gestaltung in Ulm (1953–5), embodies a complex scheme in an open, easily grasped layout, which harmonizes well with its setting (*Switzerland).

☐ Maldonado, Tomás, *Max Bill*, Buenos Aires 1955; Staber, Margit, *Max Bill*, St Gallen 1971; Huttinger, Eduard, *Max Bill*, Zurich 1977.

Block, Der (The Block). Association of traditionally-oriented German architects, founded in Berlin in 1928 principally as a counter-movement to the avant-gardist *Ring group. The impetus was the dispute over the Weißenhofsiedlung in Stuttgart, in which both Paul *Bonatz and Paul Schmitthenner were meant to have participated. At the behest of the *Deutscher Werkbund, Bonatz prepared a site-plan which proposed an overall scheme for building pitched-roof houses – a plan which soon met with resistance. Ludwig *Mies van der Rohe was then called in, and his 'modernist' solution won favour. In protest, Bonatz and Schmitthenner withdrew from the undertaking; a year later they were joined by German Bestelmeyer, Paul Schultze-Naumburg and other conservative architects to form the 'Block', whose members were united to create an architecture 'which takes account of the life-styles and views of a people and the conditions and nature of the country.' VML

Blom, Piet (Pieter), b. Amsterdam 1934. Studied under Aldo van *Eyck at the Architectural Academy in Amsterdam. In 1962 he was awarded the Rome Prize for a project for a Pestalozzi Village. Since 1967 he has had his office in Monnickendam. Alongside van Eyck, Herman *Hertzberger, and Frank van Klingeren, B. is one of the most important exponents of Dutch *Structuralism, the pursuit of which has sometimes given rise in his work to extremely provocative forms. The 'Kasbah' housing estate at Hengelo (1965–73) is a manifesto of structuralist urban planning: the houses were densely packed and the ground level was kept free and open with the intention of creating an unobstructed circulation zone, which, however, was not achieved. B. built 't Speelhuis community centre and its surround-

Blom. 'Kasbah' housing estate, Hengelo (1965–73)

ing ring of houses at Helmond, 1975–8. Here the dominant theme was that of a cube set on one corner; the housing units are stacked on hexagonal shafts, resulting in a kind of 'forest' formed of a series of 'tree' dwellings. AM

☐ Lüchinger, Arnulf, *Strukturalismus in der Architektur*, Stuttgart 1981.

Bofill (Levi), Ricardo, b. Barcelona 1939. Studied at the Escuela Tecnica Superior de Arquitectura in Barcelona and at the University of Geneva. In 1962 he founded Taller de Arquitectura, an interdisciplinary team of artists, writers, musicians and architects. With the Taller de Arquitectura team B. realized, among other projects: the Calle J. S. Bach flats in Barcelona (1964–5); the Barrio Gaudí residential quarter in Reus (1964–7); the La Muralla Roja holiday complex in Calpe (1968–73); the 'Walden 7' flats at Sant Just Desvern, near Barcelona (1970–5); and, in France, the housing complex Les Arcades du Lac at Saint-Quentin-en-Yvelines. After his neo-realist and *New Brutalist experiments in the 'Barcelona school' of the 1960s, B. turned decisively in the mid-1970s to historical prototypes. He developed, most prominently at Saint-Quentin-en-Yvelines, a monumental neo-classical architectural language which, he claims, reconstructs the collective consciousness. FW

☐ Bofill, Ricardo, *L'Architecture d'un homme*, Paris 1978; Goytisolo, José Augustin, *Taller de Arquitectura*, Barcelona 1977; *Taller de Arquitectura. Ricardo Bofill* (exhibition catalogue), London 1981.

Bohigas (Guardiola), Oriol, b. Barcelona 1925. Studied at the Escuela Tecnica Superior de Arquitectura in Barcelona. In 1951 he formed a partnership with Joseph *Martorell, which was joined in 1962 by David *Mackay. He became a professor at the Architecture School in Barcelona in 1971 and its director in 1977. Since 1981 he has served as architectural adviser to the City of Barcelona. B. has achieved prominence not only as a practising architect but also as a theorist. AM

☐ Bohigas, Oriol, *Arquitectura modernista*, Barcelona 1968; ——, *Contra una arquitectura adjetivada*, Barcelona 1969; ——, *La arquitectura española de la Segunda Republica*, Barcelona 1970; ——, *Proceso y erotica del diseño*, Barcelona 1972; ——, *Catalunya: Arquitectura y urbanisme durant la Republica*, Barcelona 1978.

Böhm, Dominikus. Frielingsdorf parish church, near Cologne (1926–7)

Böhm, Dominikus, b. Jettingen, Bavaria 1880, d. Cologne 1955. Studied under Theodor *Fischer at the Technische Hochschule in Stuttgart. In 1902 he opened his own office in Cologne, which he directed from 1952 on, in collaboration with his son Gottfried *Böhm. He was a professor at the Kunstgewerbeschule in Offenbach, 1914–26, and at the Cologne Werkschule, 1926–35. From the 1920s on, B. advocated a reform in ecclesiastical architecture in Germany, by the abandonment of the historical formal vocabulary as well as by the bringing together of congregation and altar. A strong sensory-emotional element pervades his work, whether it be that which depends ultimately on *Expressionism, as in the Circumstantes project (1922), the Christkönigskirche in Mainz-Bischofsheim (1926) or the parish church in Frielingsdorf, near Cologne (1926–7), with their dematerialized, abstractly gothicizing white folds, or whether it be churches of his late period, which are more influenced by European modernism, such as St Engelbert at Cologne-Riehl (1932) and St Maria Königin at Cologne-Marienburg (1954). GHa

☐ Hoff, August, *Dominikus Böhm*, Berlin 1930; Hoff, A., Muck, H., and Thoma, R., *Dominikus Böhm; Leben und Werk*, Munich and Zurich 1962; Stalling, Gesine, *Studien zu Dominikus Böhm*, Berne and Frankfurt 1974.

Böhm, Gottfried. Pilgrimage church at Neviges (1963–8)

Böhm, Gottfried, b. Offenbach am Main 1920. In Munich he studied architecture at the Technische Hochschule and sculpture at the Akademie der bildenden Künste. In 1952 he entered the office of his father Dominikus *Böhm, which he took over upon the latter's death in 1955. Since 1963 he has been Professor for Regional Planning and Public Works at the Technische Hochschule in Aachen. Following his father, B. initially was primarily a church designer, his work being characterized by a highly expressive formal language derived from *Expressionism. A highpoint was the pilgrimage church in Neviges (1963–8), where crystalline forms are composed into a towering rugged mountain of concrete. The same sculptural approach also endows the town hall in Bernsberg (1962–7) with a powerful shape. In this case, B. enlarged the existing ruins of a medieval castle to produce an impressive ensemble in a harmonious architectural style. The Old People's Home in Düsseldorf-Garath (1962–7) and the residential quarter in Cologne-Chorweiler (1969–75) reveal a sensitivity to patterns of social relationships, as well as to the nature of specific sites. The last few years have witnessed entirely new types of commissions, as well as a marked tendency towards an architectural language more influenced by *Rationalism; examples are the – often metal – skeletal structures such as in the Landesamt für Datenverarbeitung und Statistik (Provincial Administration for Data Processing and Statistics) in Düsseldorf (1969–76) and the pilgrimage church in Wigratzbad (1972). FJ

□ 'Gottfried Böhm', *Architecture and Urbanism* (Tokyo), March 1978; 'Böhm, *Das Kunstwerk* (Stuttgart), 32 (1979), nos. 2/3, pp. 30–7; Raev, Svetlozar, *Gottfried Böhm. Bauten und Projekte 1950–1980*, Cologne 1982.

Bonatz, Paul, b. Solgne, Lorraine 1877, d. Stuttgart 1956. Studied at the Technische Hochschule in Munich 1896–1900. Worked as Theodor *Fischer's assistant at the Technische Hochschule in Stuttgart, 1902–6, and was appointed a professor there in 1908. He was in partnership with Friedrich Eugen Scholer, 1913–27, and served as adviser to Fritz Todt for the construction of the German Autobahn system, 1935–40. After a period as consulting architect to the City of Ankara, 1943–6, and as a professor at the Technical University in Istanbul, 1949–53, he returned to Stuttgart in 1954.

The forcefully expressed monumentality of the Central Station in Stuttgart (1911–27; with Scholer) recalls the contemporary industrial buildings of Peter *Behrens. In its union of functionalist articulation and reduced *historicism, it is related to Eliel *Saarinen's Helsinki Station, which actually served as a model. In residential architecture B. purveyed a tasteful and definite traditionalism, while in transportation and industrial structures he tended to a rationalist 'objectivity' (*Neue Sachlichkeit) which was only superficially disguised under the Third Reich. From the 1930s he adopted a conservative architectural stance in his theoretical writings. GHa

□ Bonatz, P., *Leben and Bauen*, Stuttgart 1950; Graubner, G. (ed.), *Paul Bonatz und seine Schüler*, Stuttgart 1930; Tamms, Friedrich (ed.), *Paul Bonatz: Arbeiten aus den Jahren 1907 bis 1937*, Stuttgart 1937; Bongartz, N., Dübbers, P., and Werner, F., *Paul Bonatz 1877–1956*, Stuttgart 1977.

Botta, Mario, b. Mendrisio, Ticino (Switzerland) 1943. Trained as a technical draughtsman, 1958–61, and studied at the Istituto Universitario di Architettura in Venice, 1964–9. In 1976 he was a visiting professor at the Ecole Polytechnique Fédérale, Lausanne. He worked in *Le Corbusier's office in 1965 and with Louis *Kahn in 1969, and is one of the most important members of the 'Ticenese School' (*Switzerland). Already in his first building, the clergy house in Genestretta, built in 1961–3 (thus before his architectural studies), the principal lines of his later work were encapsulated: attention to topographical conditions, regionalist sensibility, preference for clear architectural types, desire for geometric order and emphasis on craftsmanship. These maxims reach a poetic synthesis in the school at Morbio Inferiore (1972–7) – a straight, three-storeyed series of concrete units, additively composed of slightly varied elements. Although carved out of the landscape as an artificial ordered feature, it reflects the visual impulses of its very natural setting. B.'s legible formalistic attitude is expressed above all in a series of refined single-family houses, from the house in Stabio (1965–7), still strongly reminiscent of Le Corbusier, to the independent buildings at Cadenazzo (1970–1) and Riva San Vitale (1972–3) and the mannered, elegantly striped house at Ligornetto (1975–6). The house at Riva San Vitale renders the relationship between building and landscape problematic: as a tower constructed on a slope, it is built on a rectangular group plan, but at its uppermost level – a separate entrance is reached by a wire-mesh gangway. With the administration building for the Staatsbank in Fribourg (1977–82), B. began his involvement with the problems of integrating a new building with an existing urban fabric. VML

Bonatz. Central Station, Stuttgart (with F. E. Scholer; 1911–27)

Botta. School at Morbio Inferiore (1972–7)

□ Rota, Italo (ed.), *Mario Botta. Architetture e progetti negli anni '70. Architecture and projects in the '70*, Milan 1979; *Mario Botta; Bâtiments et projets, 1978–1982*, Paris 1982.

Bourgeois, Victor, b. Charleroi 1897, d. Brussels 1962. Studied at the Académie Royale des Beaux-Arts in Brussels, 1914–19. Active as an architect in Brussels from 1920, he also became a professor at the Ecole Nationale Supérieure d'Architecture, Brussels. He was editor of various technical periodicals, and was vice-president of *CIAM, 1928–40. The most important advocate of modernism in Belgium, he realized his masterpiece early in his career: the Cité Moderne at Berchem-Sainte-Agathe, near Brussels (1922–5). Influenced in its formal expression by Tony *Garnier's Cité Industrielle as well as by Frank Lloyd *Wright's early works, the architecture of the estate is distinguished by differentiated articulation of the housing terraces, numerous squares and courtyards, and by an elegant and classically enlivened façade composition. It was to influence *May's first work in Frankfurt am Main, the flats in the Bruchfeldstraße (1925; with C. H. Rudloff). B.'s other works include his own house in Brussels (1925), a house at the Weißenhofsiedlung in Stuttgart (1927), and the house for the sculptor O. Jaspers in Brussels (1928). □ Flouquet, Pierre-Louis, *Victor Bourgeois: Architecture 1922–1952*, Brussels 1952; Linze, Georges, *Victor Bourgeois*, Brussels 1959; *Victor Bourgeois 1897–1962* (exhibition catalogue), Brussels 1971.

Brazil. When in 1943 the Museum of Modern Art in New York presented its exhibition on old and new architecture in Brazil, the world was suddenly made aware that here the *International Style of the 1920s had blossomed into a tropical version. Characterized by its daring formal expression, its lyrical content, and its regional connotations, it also had strong spiritual links with the country's colonial past. In fact, it had sprung up in the wake of two rebel movements, the Modern Art Week in São Paulo, 1922, and the Regionalist movement in Recife, 1926, led by Gilberto Freyre, which aimed at giving new shape to Brazilian intellectual and artistic life, not only by introducing a truly modern outlook rooted in the most genuine sources of Brazilian life, but also by attempting to destroy the alien influences which had dominated the country since the arrival in 1806 of the King of Portugal, who fled the Napoleonic invasion and transferred his court to Rio de Janeiro. In 1816 Dom João VI invited a French mission of painters, sculptors, and architects to 'civilize' the country, with the result that the organic development of a local architecture, brought about throughout the colonial period by an ecological assimilation of the Portuguese Baroque style, was disrupted, and all kinds of foreign pseudo-styles were introduced, turning the 19th century into an uncharacteristic interval, chiefly notable for the copying of whatever might be done abroad – not only in architecture but in all the arts.

A few years before these two new movements, scientific studies of the effect of sunlight in relation to buildings had been started by Alexandre Albuquerque, who in 1916 succeeded in incorporating into the Building Code of the city of São Paulo precise requirements as to the minimum provision of sunlight in a new building. Thus, there existed in the 1920s not only an intellectual atmosphere receptive to new ideas in architecture but also a sound regional approach to the basic problem of the exposure of buildings, both in order to assure a minimum of sunlight and also to control any excess. In 1927 in São Paulo, Gregori *Warchavchik, a newcomer from Russia, presented his first cube-like houses to the public, and was later joined in partnership by Lúcio *Costa. When the Revolution of 1930 upset all the conventional political and cultural values of the country and launched a programme of important new public works, the younger architects were already prepared for the decisive, if paradoxical, episode of the new building for the Ministry of Education and Health. A competition was held for the design of this building, and all the modern projects were disqualified by a conservative jury. But the Minister of Education, Gustavo Capanema, who was surrounded by a group of far-seeing collaborators, was bold enough – after the paying the prizes awarded by the jury – to invite Lúcio Costa, one of the unsuccessful competitors, to design the final project. Costa insisted on the formation of a team to include all the other rejected candidates, and this was done. Thus Costa, Oscar *Niemeyer, Jorge Machado Moreira, Affonso Eduardo *Reidy, Ernani Vasconcelos and Carlos Leão were jointly responsible for the development of the final design, with landscaping by Roberto *Burle Marx. In 1936, *Le Corbusier was invited to act as a consultant on this project, as well as on one for the New University City. He stayed in Brazil only three weeks, but during this short stay the turning-point was reached and modern architecture was irrevocably established. Le Corbusier's main ideas fell on fertile ground. The use of *pilotis* was especially appropriate for the Brazilian climate, the *brise-soleil* was in many cases an absolute necessity, and his basically lyrical formal approach was thoroughly suited to the Brazilian spirit. A local version of the International Style thus emerged.

The high quality of modern architecture achieved in Brazil from 1936 on can be seen in an impressive number of buildings, including: Rino Levi's Art Palacio Cinema in São Paulo (1936), Oscar Niemeyer's Day Nursery in Rio de Janeiro (1937), his Ouro Preto Hotel (1940), his Casino, Yacht Club and Restaurant (1943) and the São Francisco Chapel (1944) at Pampúlha; Luiz Nunes's (with Fernando Saturnio de Brito) Water Tower at Olinda (1937); Attilio Corrêo Lima's Santos Dumont de Hidros Airport in Rio de Janeiro (1938), with Jorge Ferreira, Thomaz Estrella, Renato Mesquita dos Santos and Renato Soeiro; Lúcio Costa's and Oscar Niemeyer's (with Paul Lester Wiener) Brazilian Pavilion at the New York World's Fair (1939); Marcelo and Milton Roberto's ABI (Brazilian Press Association Building; 1938), the Instituto de Resseguros Building (1942), and the Santos Dumont Airport Building (1944), all in Rio de Janeiro; Alvaro Vital Brasil's Edificio Esther apartment building (with Adhemar Marinho) in São Paulo (1938); Olavo Redig de Campos's Social Centre in Rio (1942); Firmino Saldanha's Mississippi (1938) and Mossoró (1940) apartment buildings in Rio, not to mention the Ministry of Education and Health itself, started in 1937 and finished in 1943.

After the war years the country entered a phase of rapid industrialization which helped to raise standards of construction, as well as a period of tremendous real-estate speculation, which naturally gave rise to various mediocre

Brazil. Ministry of Education and Health, Rio de Janeiro (1936–43), by Lúcio Costa, with Le Corbusier and others

Brazil. São Francisco Chapel, Pampúlha (1944), by Oscar Niemeyer

Brazil. Museum of Modern Art, Rio de Janeiro (1954–9), by Affonso Eduardo Reidy

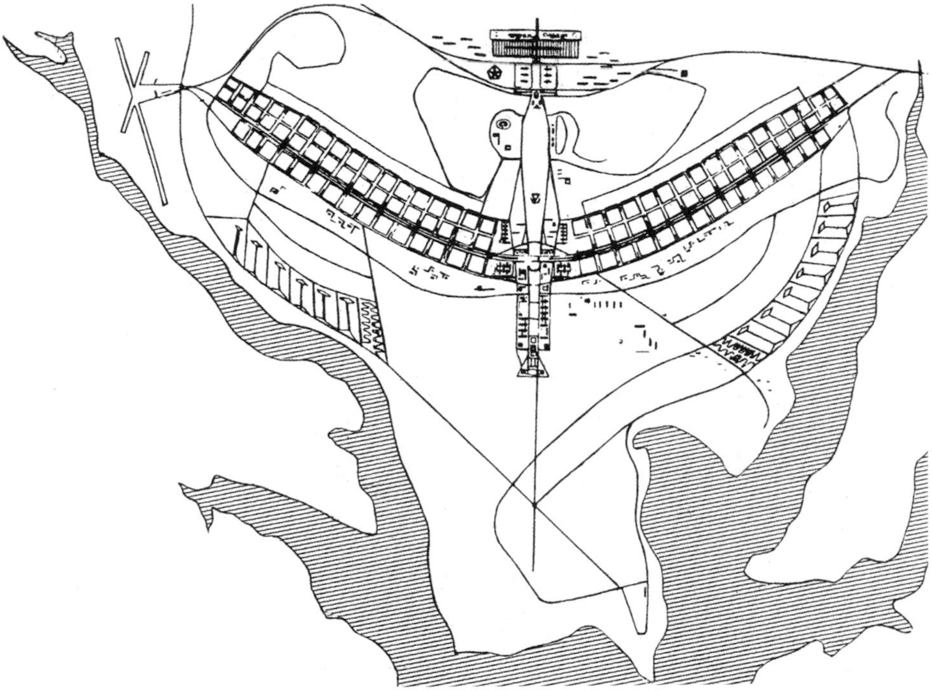

Brazil. General plan for Brasilia (1957) by Lúcio Costa

Brazil. Presidential Palace, Brasilia (1958), by Oscar Niemeyer

buildings alongside those of genuine quality. Architects whose work has become better known abroad include Paulo Antunes Ribeiro, João Vilanova Artigas, Sergio Bernardes, Francisco Bolonha, Oswaldo Bratke, Icaro de Castro Mello, Ary García Roza, Henrique E. Mindlin and Giancarlo Palanti. The most important examples of Brazilian architecture since 1950 are Oscar Niemeyer's Ibirapuéra Exhibition Pavilions in São Paulo (1951–4); in Rio, Lúcio Costa's Parque Guinle apartment buildings (1948, 1950 and 1954); Affonso Eduardo Reidy's Pedregulho Housing Estate (1947–52) and Museum of Modern Art (1954–9), both in Rio de Janeiro; Jorge Machado Moreira's University City, Rio de Janeiro (1949–62); and, of course, Niemeyer's buildings in Brasilia.

Brasilia, the new capital for the country, was founded some 1,000 km (600 miles) from the Atlantic coast, in hitherto virgin territory. Located on gently sloping highlands, half surrounded by a huge artificial lake, this new city, planned for 600,000 inhabitants, was formally inaugurated as the new seat of the Federal Government on 21 April 1960, only three years after an international jury had selected Lúcio Costa's plan in an open competition among Brazilian architects. In a general outline reminiscent of an aeroplane, the wings are devoted to the super-blocks of apartment dwellings; the main axis, along what would correspond to the fuselage of the plane, to the monumental distribution of the Ministries and the Plaza of the Three Powers (Presidential Palace, Supreme Court, and Congress), with the business and entertainment districts at the intersection, which is emphasized by the bus depot, arranged on several levels. Thoroughly planned with deep human concern, yet deliberately aiming at a clear symbolic expression of the city's unique function, Brasilia has carried to the man-in-the-street the concept of urban planning to an unsurpassed degree. The unity and integrated character of Brasilia derive not only from Costa's lucid plan but also from Oscar Niemeyer's striking designs for the public buildings.

Building Brasilia was not only the highest peak of Brazilian architecture, as a mere function of the sheer magnitude of the task and the architectural postulates formulated there. It also implied a certain break with rationalist modernism. Although buildings continued to be built according to International Style principles and in keeping with its utilitarian and technical as well as economic guidelines, it is important to stress the significance of new trends. One, the improvement of the 'quality of life', argued for an ecologically minded point of view, while the other sought explicit references to Brazil's traditions and life-style.

The deaths of Rino Levi and Marcello Roberto in 1965 and of Mindlin in 1971 coincided with the coming of age of a new generation of Brazilian architects. One of the most brilliant among these is Joaquim Guedes. Critical of Le Corbusier, whose influence in Brazil was indeed considerable, Guedes rejected formalism in favour of an architecture based on environmental, and even more significantly, on economic conditions. He objected to a transposition to Brazil of architectural models originally created for societies with high purchasing power. Guedes is predominantly concerned with housing, particularly for low-income groups. A demonstration of his ideals is to be found in the new city of Caraiba (1976 ff.).

Another architect who seeks expression in themes identifiable with the environment is Carlos Nelson Ferreira dos Santos, who worked extensively on Brazil's shanty towns or *favelas*. Furthermore, the process of change has evidently brought about a new, locally inspired, use of materials. In this context it is appropriate to mention Zanino Caldas and his simple building techniques. The 'new' generation of architects also includes Fabio Penteado (although his professional beginnings date from 1950), Filgueiras Lima (creator of the exceptional Bahia Administrative Centre) and Paulo Mendes da Rocha. HEM/JG

☐ Goodwin, Philip L., *Brazil Builds*, New York 1943; Hitchcock, Henry-Russell, *Latin American Architecture since 1945*, New York 1955; Mindlin, Henrique E., *Modern Architecture in Brazil*, Rio de Janeiro and Amsterdam 1956; Bracco, S., *L'architettura moderna in Brasile*, Bologna 1967; Bullrich, F., *New Directions in Latin American Architecture*, New York 1969.

Brazil. Anna Moreau Residence, Ibiuna, São Paulo (1978), by Joaquim Guedes

Breuer, Marcel (Laiko), b. Pecs, Hungary 1902, d. New York 1981. In 1920, B. entered the Akademie der bildenden Künste in Vienna, intending to become a painter and sculptor. After a brief attendance there he became disillusioned with its 'tired eclecticism' and looked around for a practical apprenticeship in one of the crafts. Before long, he heard of Walter *Gropius and the *Bauhaus, and, late in 1920, he left Vienna for Weimar to become one of the youngest members of the first generation of Bauhaus students. B.'s principal interest, at that time, was in the area of furniture design, and by 1924, at the age of twenty-two, he took over the direction of the Bauhaus's furniture department. Before long, his preoccupation with standardized, modular unit furniture led him to interior design and standardized, modular unit housing – and thus to architecture.

B.'s most notable contribution to contemporary design in the 1920s was in the field of furniture, for he had invented, as early as 1925, a

Breuer. Multiple housing in the Doldertal, Zurich (1935–6)

Breuer. The architect's own house, New Canaan, Conn. (1947)

series of systems that employed continuously bent steel tubes (painted or chromium-plated) to form the structural frames of stools, chairs, and tables. Much of this important experimental work in furniture design was made possible by the move, in 1925, of the Bauhaus to Dessau, and the construction of the new Bauhaus by Gropius. B. was commissioned to design all the furniture needed in the new buildings, and this commission provided an important stimulus to his work in this field. In later years he maintained his interest in furniture design and produced some of the first bent and moulded plywood chairs, as well as some of the first chairs using aluminium as a structural supporting frame.

He left the Bauhaus in 1928 to practise as an architect and interior designer in Berlin, and during the next half-dozen years built several houses and apartments quite as radical as – and often more practical than – the contemporary work of *Le Corbusier and others. Moreover, he entered a number of competitions and prepared theoretical projects for cities, theatres, factories, etc. In 1935 B. moved to England and soon entered into partnership with F. R. S. *Yorke in London. The partnership lasted until 1937, when Walter Gropius, who had been appointed Chairman of the Department of Architecture at Harvard, invited B. to join him there as Associate Professor. At the same time, the two men formed an architectural partnership in Cambridge, Mass.

While it is difficult, if not impossible, to separate the individual contributions of Gropius and Breuer both to the teaching at Harvard and to the houses designed in their office, it is fair to say that B.'s contact with individual Harvard students was especially close (he was closer to them in age, and he tended to be extremely practical in his approaches to design problems); and it is fair, also, to say that much of B.'s attention to detail is evident in the work completed by the Gropius and Breuer partnership. In any event, both B.'s teaching and his completed buildings left a profound impression on a new generation of American architects. Among his students, for example, were Philip *Johnson, Paul *Rudolph, John *Johansen, and Edward L. *Barnes.

In 1941 B. set up an independent practice in Cambridge, and in 1946 he moved to New York City. For the first few years, his work was limited largely to houses and relatively small-scale institutional buildings; but in 1952 he was selected (with *Nervi and *Zehrfuss) to be one of the three architects for the new Headquarters for UNESCO in Paris (built 1953–8). Among his other buildings were St John's Abbey and University in Collegeville, Minn. (1953–61), the former New York University campus at University Heights, N.Y. (1956–61), the IBM Research Centre at La Gaude, France (1960–9), the Winter Sports Centre at Flaine, France (1960–9), the Whitney Museum of American Art in New York (1963–6), as well as the IBM complex in Boca Raton, Fla. (1967–77).

Breuer. Whitney Museum of American Art, New York (Marcel Breuer and Associates; 1963–6)

A characteristic feature of Breuer's architecture, which reflects the decisive influence of the *Constructivist movement in Russia and Western Europe on his early career, is his sense of strong articulation. All his designs were highly articulated: a Breuer chair would express every element separately, both in form and in material; a Breuer house would express different areas of activity in different and separate forms (his H-plans for houses, which separate the day-time areas from the night-time areas, are especially well known); in his construction details, every element of the structure was always clearly defined and separately articulated; and even in his large buildings, such as the UNESCO Headquarters, there was always a clear distinction and separation of functionally different elements – whether different kinds of building or different parts of the same building. Already in his early American houses B. had abandoned the rigid formulae of the *International Style and had adopted a style in which regional characteristics were given new life by the generous use of texturally rich materials, such as wood and rubble masonry, and by close attention to the nature of the topography and specific landscape. The large buildings of the early 1950s signalled a shift towards strongly expressive forms, whether in detail, such as the façade elements of the IBM Research Centre in La Gaude, or in overall form, as in the belfry of the church of St John's Abbey in Collegeville. In the face of the exhaustion of *Rationalism, B. can be counted among the first to turn to the search for new principles of architectural creation. PB/AM

☐ Blake, Peter, *Marcel Breuer: Architect and Designer*, New York 1949; —— (ed.), *Marcel Breuer: Sun and Shadow. The Philosophy of an Architect*, London, New York and Toronto 1956; Argan, Giulio Carlo, *Marcel Breuer. Disegno industriale e architettura*, Milan 1957;

Brinkman. Van Nelle Tobacco Factory, Rotterdam (with J. H. van den Broek; 1926–30)

Jones, Cranston (ed.), *Marcel Breuer, 1921–1961, Buildings and Projects*, London 1962; Papachristou, Tician, *Marcel Breuer. Neue Bauten und Projekte*, Stuttgart 1970; Wiek, Christopher, *Marcel Breuer: Furniture and Interiors* (exhibition catalogue), New York 1981.

Brinkman, Johannes Andreas, b. Rotterdam 1902, d. Rotterdam 1949. From 1925 he was in partnership with L. C. van der *Vlugt; later, 1937–48, with J. H. van den *Broek. The Van Nelle Tobacco Factory in Rotterdam (1926–30), to whose design Mart *Stam contributed substantially, is, with its transparent façade and exposed structure, one of the most important industrial buildings of the 20th century and an elegant manifesto of the modern movement. The slab-shaped Bergpolder block in Rotterdam, built in 1933–4 (Brinkman, van der Vlugt and Willem van Tijen), was an early example of a domestic building elevated on stilts.

Broek, Johannes Hendrik van den, b. Rotterdam 1898, d. The Hague 1978. Studied at Delft Technical College, from which he graduated in 1924. He started his own practice in 1927 at Rotterdam, entering into partnership with J. A. *Brinkman in 1937, and with J. B. *Bakema in 1948. JJV

☐ Broek, J. H. van den, *Creative Krachten in de architectonische conceptie*, Delft 1948.

Bryggman, Erik, b. Turku 1891, d. Turku 1955. Studied at the Helsinki Polytechnic, where he graduated in architecture in 1916. After collaborating on a variety of projects, he opened his own office in 1923 in the old capital, where he always lived, and where he was joined a few years later by Aino and Alvar *Aalto. This collaboration did not last long, however, as the Aaltos moved on to Helsinki; but it came during the most critical period in the development of their architectural thought and resulted in a unique work of collaboration, of great importance in the history of Finnish architecture: the design for the Exhibition commemorating the 700th anniversary of the City of Turku, which took place in 1929.

B. had carried out a good many works before the Turku Exhibition; they mark the most important stages in that process leading to a modernism which was silently developing in Finnish architecture. Amongst them may be noted: a block of flats for employees of the Finnish Sugar Company at Turku (1923–4); some houses in Turku and elsewhere; and two hotels in Turku – the Seurahuone, with very sophisticated décor (1928), and the Hospits Betel (1927–9). His finest work, characterized by a very pure Rationalist style, was carried out, however, between 1930 and 1940, starting with the Parainen Cemetery Chapel and the Finnish Pavilion at the Antwerp International Exhibition, both dating from 1930; the Vierumäki Sports Club (1931–6); and the Library of Öbo Academy in Turku (1935). The tower of the Library rises in a district of the old city, over which the dark mass of the Cathedral looms in the distance. It is remarkable for the balance of its openings in the large white walls, and for the perfect way it fits in with its surroundings, by means of subtle handling of proportions and a complete understanding of the *genius loci*. Turku Cemetery Chapel (1938–41) is B.'s best-known work, and is undoubtedly very fine, especially in the magical lightness of its internal space, but taken as a whole it reveals the intrusion of romanticism into the serene rationalism of the architect's previous work.

Bryggman. Cemetery Chapel, Turku (1938–41)

B.'s notable post-war works, in the decade from 1945 to 1955 – a period of romantic decline – include a housing estate at Pansio, near Turku (1946), the Students' Union and the chemistry laboratory of Öbo Academy, Turku (1950), and Riihimäki Water Tower (1952). These later works show a tendency towards more complex forms, at times pointing toward *organic architecture, with the careful siting of buildings in the landscape, at others revealing a more strictly 'national' inspiration. LM

☐ Mosso, Leonardo, 'L'opera di Erik Bryggman nella storia dell'architettura finlandese', *Atti S.J.A.* (Turin), December 1958; Stigell, Anna-Lisa, *Erik · Bryggman*, Ekenäs 1965; Piironen, Esa, *Erik Bryggman* (exhibition catalogue), Turku 1967.

Burle Marx, Roberto, b. São Paulo 1909. After a long stay in Berlin, where he attended a private art school and was inspired by the Botanical Gardens in Dahlem to take a close interest in the world of plants, he studied for a time at the Escola Nacional de Belas Artes in Rio de Janeiro. In 1934 he established himself as a landscape architect. Although he had had no professional training in garden design, he soon gained a reputation throughout Brazil. A profound knowledge of tropical flora, developed on extensive trips throughout the country, is the basis of his art. Spacious, rhythmically articulated forms, which often seem an abstraction of the landscape itself, are typical of his gardens and parks. His involvement with painting is especially evident in his conscious manipulation of the colours in different plants. Among the highpoints of his extensive œuvre are: the garden of the former Education Ministry in Rio de Janeiro, a building designed by Lúcio *Costa, Oscar *Niemeyer and others, with *Le Corbusier as consultant (1938); the garden setting of the Yacht Club and Restaurant in Pampúlha by Niemeyer (1943); the grounds of Botafogo in Rio de Janeiro (1954); and the Del-Este Park in Caracas (1956). AM

☐ Bardi, Pietro Maria, *The Tropical Gardens of Burle Marx*, New York 1964; *Roberto Burle Marx* (exhibition catalogue), Paris n.d.

C

Canada. A country formerly subject to colonial rule, and now to economic domination by its neighbour, the United States (*USA), Canada reflects its colonial past in the essential features of its national architecture imported from abroad. At the time of Confederation in 1867, Gothic Revival dominated public building. Frederick William Cumberland followed his friend John Ruskin's precepts when he built University College at the University of Toronto (1856), while Thomas Fuller initiated a long line of government facilities in Gothic style with the Centre Block and Library of the Dominion Parliament Buildings, Ottawa (1859–67), a powerful symbol of British authority, crowning a cliff on what was then the edge of wilderness. (Destroyed by fire in 1916, the Centre Block was rebuilt to the more severe design of John A. Pearson and J. Omar Marchand.) The national railways saw tourist potential in this confrontation of picturesque architecture and dramatic natural sites, and built imposing château-style hotels, all turrets and pinnacles, of which an impressive example is the Château Frontenac in Quebec City (begun by Bruce Price in 1892; additions by Edward and E. S. Maxwell, 1920–4). While Collegiate Gothic played an important role well into the 20th century (Henry Sproatt & E. R. Rolph, Hart House and Soldiers Tower, University of Toronto, 1912–25), architects explored the full range of historical styles current at the turn of the century. Trained at the Ecole des Beaux-Arts in Paris, Edward Maxwell was as adept at mixing Romanesque and Italianate elements (Henry Birks & Sons Store, Montreal, 1893) as he was with pure classical forms (Montreal Art Association Gallery, now Musée des Beaux-Arts, 1910–12). Edward J. Lennox frankly imitated H. H. Richardson's Allegheny County Courthouse, Pittsburgh, when he built the Toronto Municipal Building and Courthouse in 1887–9, and F. M. Rattenbury won the 1893 competition for the British Columbia Legislature, Victoria, with a design combining English Renaissance and Richardsonian Romanesque elements. Frank Darling and John A. Pearson provided the financial world with elegant Beaux-Arts banking halls and office towers (Bank of Commerce Main Branch, Winnipeg, Man., 1910–11), while John Lyle, who with Hugh Jones designed Toronto's cavernous Union Station (1912), 'nationalized' the foreign-born styles with architectural ornament based on Canadian flora and fauna.

Although the influence came first from the United States, French-speaking architects in Quebec, sympathetic to emerging nationalism in the province, saw in the Second Empire style a way to proclaim their commitment to French culture (*France). Henry Maurice Perrault's Bureau de Poste (1872) and Hôtel de Ville (1875) in Montreal, both destroyed, and E. E. Taché's Assemblée Nationale in Quebec City (1878), which translates the High Victorian plan of Fuller's Parliament into a French idiom, are all carried out in the Second Empire style, while Taché's Manège militaire (1888) in the same city is a rare North American example of Gothic Revival influenced by Viollet-le-Duc.

Among domestic architects, Samuel Maclure provided the sedate ascendancy of Victoria, B.C., with residences such as the Biggerstaff-Wilson House (1905–6) characterized by the use of natural materials, sensitive siting in a rugged landscape, and compact cross-axial plans focusing on stairways or large, open entertainment spaces. Francis C. Sullivan, a student of Frank Lloyd *Wright, introduced a version of the Prairie Style house (Connors House, Ottawa, 1915), while at a later date Robert Blatter (Bourdon House, Sillery, Que., 1935) and Ernest Cormier (his own house, Montreal, 1934–5) were influenced by the asymmetrical, planar forms of European modernism.

Canada. Supreme Court Building, Ottawa (1938–50), by Ernest Cormier

Cormier (1885–1980) must be accounted the leading architect of the half-century. Trained at the *Ecole des Beaux-Arts and in Rome, he combined rare gifts for rational planning, rich ornament and the creation of ceremonial spaces with a mastery of new technology and materials. His masterpiece is the *Art Deco building for the Université de Montréal (1928–55). The Supreme Court, Ottawa (1938–50), shows that he was alive to the 17th-century French classical tradition, while the curtain-wall National Printing Bureau, Hull, Que. (1950–8), places Cormier among technical innovators.

After World War II the *International Style gained ground, first in Vancouver where the innovative firm of Sharp & Thompson, Berwick, Pratt built the sleek Vocational Institute in 1948–9 and the BC Hydro Building, an early curtain-wall skyscraper, in 1955–7. John C. Parkin, whose masters were Walter *Gropius and Ludwig *Mies van der Rohe, provided Toronto with a manifesto of the new functionalism in the steel-and-glass office he built for his firm (1954; demolished). Parkin deftly solved complicated transportation problems at Malton International Airport, Toronto (1964) and at Ottawa Railway Station (1967). In the 1960s banks and corporations imported prestigious architects such as Mies van der Rohe and I. M. *Pei to design their office towers and it was only later that Canadian firms received major corporate commissions; unfortunately the results were often over-wrought imitations of the latest American angularities. Notable, however, are Arthur *Erickson's 'Doric' MacMillan-Bloedel Building, Vancouver (1968–9), and the NOVA Building, Calgary, Alta. (1982), by J. H. Cook. Mention should be made of the speculative building activities of the huge Canadian real-estate development corporations, which have employed teams of architects to transform city skylines across the country and are finding a ready market for their efficient expertise in the USA.

In an inhospitable climate architects have proved skilful in the design of large, technologically sophisticated, multi-use structures, often incorporating interior circulation spines and atria, such as Place Bonaventure in Montreal (1964–7) by Affleck, Desbarats, Dimakopoulos, Lebensold & Sise; Simon Fraser University, Burnaby, B.C. (1964–5), and the Provincial Government Offices and Law Courts, Vancouver (1974–9), both by Erickson; and the University of Alberta Students' Union, Edmonton (1974), by Jack Diamond and Barton Myers. Although in plan a variation on the suburban shopping mall, Eberhard Zeidler's immense and immensely popular Eaton Centre in downtown Toronto (1973–81; with Bregman & Hamann) recaptures the urban animation of the 19th-century European *galleria*.

Moshe *Safdie's much remarked experiment in modular mass housing, 'Habitat' (Montreal, 1967) built at the time of Expo '67, has had little direct influence in Canada. Nonetheless, as Canadian cities attempt to ensure that large, heterogeneous sectors of the population live in the city cores, mass housing remains a lively

Canada. Concordia Hall, Place Bonaventure, Montreal (1964–7), by Affleck, Desbarats, Dimakopoulos, Lebensold & Sise

Canada. Students' Union, University of Alberta, Edmonton (1974), by Jack Diamond and Barton Myers

Canada. Scarborough College, Ontario (1966), by John Andrews

architectural concern. The 'towers-in-the-park' concept has been abandoned in favour of communities integral to the urban fabric, such as the co-operative St Lawrence Neighbourhood, Toronto (by various architects), and False Creek Development, Vancouver (Thompson, Berwick, Pratt & Partners, co-ordinating architects), both projects adjacent to the respective city centres. At his own house in Toronto (1972) Barton Myers offered a prototype of the small, efficient single-family home, easily replicated, and sensitively adapted to the existing urban fabric. Where no recognizable urban centre existed, Raymond Moriyama (Scarborough, Ont., Civic Centre, 1975), Phillip H. Carter (Markham, Ont., Village Green and Community Library, 1981), and J. Michael Kirkland, winner of the 1982 competition for Mississauga, Ont., City Hall are providing them. Historical areas are being preserved in St John's, Newfoundland, Halifax, N.S., Montreal and, most remarkably, at Granville Island, Vancouver, where 20th-century industrial buildings and warehouses are being wittily recycled under the direction of Norman Hotson.

Mention should be made, finally, of the Australian architect John *Andrews, whose Canadian works include Scarborough College (1966) and the eerily beautiful CN Tower (1975), both in Toronto; of Paul Cardinal's sinuous St Mary's Church, Red Deer, Alta. (1977), a vivid focus of attention in a flat prairie landscape; of Arthur *Erickson's Museum of Anthropology, University of British Columbia, Vancouver (1971–7); and of Peter Rose's private residences near Montreal, subtle evocations of Shingle Style vacation homes. CR

□ Gowans, Alan, *Building Canada: An Architectural History of Canadian Life*, Toronto 1966; Ritchie, Thomas, *Building Canada 1867–1967*, Toronto 1967; Noppen, Luc, and others, *Québec: Trois Siècles d'architecture*, Quebec 1979; *Architectural Review*, special Canada issue, May 1980; Bernstein, William, and Cawker, Ruth, *Building with Words: Canadian Architects on Architecture*, Toronto 1981.

Candela, Félix, b. Madrid 1910. Studied at the Escuela Superior de Arquitectura and at the Academia de Bellas Artes de San Fernando, Madrid. Towards the end of his studies, C. had the opportunity of watching two of the best-known structures by *Torroja, the roof of the spectators' stand at the La Zarzuela racecourse and the roof of the Frontón Recoletos, being built. The double barrel-vault of the latter, spanning an area of 60 × 36m (197 × 118 ft), and other works by Torroja probably awakened C.'s interest in shell vaulting, a construction method which combines, to an almost unparalleled degree, inspiration and precise calculation. After fighting in the Spanish Civil War on the Republican side, C. arrived in *Mexico in the summer of 1939 via the refugee camps at Perpignan. After twelve years in his adopted country, during which time he, and later his brother Antonio, made their living as architects and builders, he began advocating the use of shell vaulting, at first in articles and lectures. The building of the University City in Mexico City gave him an opportunity to construct the first hyperbolic paraboloids, which enabled him to reduce the roof of the Cosmic Ray Building (1951) to a thickness of 15 mm. ($\frac{5}{8}$ in.).

A special advantage of hyperbolic paraboloids (as compared with the sphere or other types of vault) is that the shuttering required can be made from straight boards. Due to the relative simplicity of this process, and the great saving in material, C.'s constructions are more economical than other rigid roofs, and this fact alone won his firm numerous industrial commissions. His spans increased with every project and he became increasingly bolder in the exploitation of shell vaulting. When he maintains that he has been guided less by exact calculation than by an intuitive feeling 'in the manner of the old master-builders of cathedrals', we must recall that his intuition has a very firm foundation in his knowledge of materials and stresses, which has grown with each new building.

Candela. Church of Santa Maria Miraculosa, Mexico City (with Enrique de la Mora; 1954–5)

As an architect and designer, C. has distinguished himself with his Church of Santa Maria Miraculosa in Mexico City (1954–5, with Enrique de la Mora) which shows the unmistakable influence of *Gaudí. Later buildings of a non-industrial nature, such as several churches and pavilions in Mexico City and Cuernavaca, the Los Manantiales restaurant in Xochimilco (1958), and the Olympic Stadium in Mexico City (1968), were executed in collaboration with different architects, who were glad to avail themselves of the free outlines of his structures in their search for organic or baroque shapes.

From 1953 to 1970 C. was a professor at the National University of Mexico, and from 1971 to 1978 in the USA at the University of Illinois, Chicago, where he has also worked as an architect. MC/GHa

□ Faber, Colin, *Candela: The Shell Builder*, New York and London, 1963; Smith, Clive B., *Builders in the Sun: Five Mexican Architects*, New York, 1967; 'Candela: Recent Works', *Zodiac* (Milan), no. 22, 1973, pp. 70–87.

Candilis, Georges, b. Baku, Russia 1913. Studied at the Polytechnikum in Athens where, at the 1933 *CIAM Congress, he first encountered *Le Corbusier. He emigrated to Paris in 1945 to join Le Corbusier's office and he remained until 1950 (from 1948 as site architect of the Unité d'Habitation, Marseilles). He worked in partnership with Vladimir Bodiansky and Shadrach *Woods in the African office of ATBAT (Atelier des Bâtisseurs) in Casablanca, 1951–5. In 1955 he founded in Paris, with Alexis *Josic and Woods, the firm Candilis/Josic/Woods, which he continued with Woods alone after Josic's departure in 1963. Since 1967 he has had his own office in Paris.

In collaboration with Josic and Woods, he planned the new towns Bagnols-sur-Cèze (1956) and Toulouse le Mirail (competition 1962, realization 1964–77), in which the firm sought to create differentiated urban spaces through a system of spatially identifiable 'nuclear' unities. In keeping with the propositions of the Team X critique (*CIAM) and the *Athens Charter, urban functions were integrated as fully as possible in order to favour a

Candilis. Plan for Toulouse le Mirail (Candilis/Josic/Woods; 1962)

more organic surface distribution. In the complex of Institute buildings for the Free University in Berlin-Dahlem (1963, 1967–79; also with Josic and Woods, together with Manfred Schiedhelm), Jean *Prouvé served as consultant on the façade construction. The individual buildings are freely inserted in an orthogonal transportation network. GHa

☐ *Candilis/Josic/Woods. Ein Jahrzehnt Architektur und Stadtplanung*, Stuttgart 1968; *Toulouse le Mirail. Geburt einer neuen Stadt. Candilis/Josic/Woods*, Stuttgart 1975; Candilis, Georges, *Recherches sur l'architecture des loisirs*, Paris 1973; ——, *Bâtir la Vie: Un architecte témoin de son temps*, Paris 1977.

Casson, Sir Hugh (Maxwell), b. London 1910. Studied at Cambridge; the British School at

Candilis. Free University, Berlin-Dahlem (Candilis/Josic/Woods, with Manfred Schiedhelm; 1967–79)

Athens; and the Bartlett School of Architecture, University of London. In private practice from 1937 with the late C. Nicholson; resumed 1946, after war service, latterly with Neville Conder. He has been senior partner of Casson, Conder and Partners since 1953, and was Professor of Interior Design, Royal College of Art, 1953–75. His directorship of architecture at the *Festival of Britain, 1948–51, ensured its remarkable triumph as a piece of organized townscape; the same powers of urbanistic control are evident in his schemes for Cambridge University (with N. Conder). His Youth Hostel in Holland Park, London, blends sympathetically with the remains of Holland House (17th century).

He has exercised considerable influence over the British art establishment, especially during his period of office as President of the Royal Academy of Arts (1971–84).

☐ Casson, H., *Homes by the Million*, London, 1946; Murray, Peter, 'Looking Back', *Building Design*, January 1975.

Chamberlin, Powell and Bon. Firm established in 1952 by Peter Chamberlin, Geoffrey Powell and Christof Bon. In the same year they first attracted attention for their prize-winning scheme for high-density housing at Golden Lane, London (1953–7), a controversial layout with interesting treatment of multiple ground levels, a preoccupation later (1957) developed in their plan for the Barbican district of London, with separate routes for traffic and pedestrians; a concern for urban mise-en-scène and the large-scale design characterizes all the firm's work. Their Bousfield Primary School, with its exteriors in the manner of *Mies van der Rohe, was awarded the London Bronze Medal for Architecture in 1956. Among their other schemes mention may be made of the Sports Centre for Birmingham University, with sculpturesque buildings atop a large podium, and the development plan for Leeds University, which closely integrates the academic layout with the city centre. HM

☐ 'Detailed Proposals for the Barbican Redevelopment', in *Architects' Journal* (London), 4 June 1959; 'Barbican Metropolitan Neighbourhood', *Bauen und Wohnen* (Zurich), April 1974.

Chamberlin, Powell and Bon. New Hall, Cambridge University (1966)

Chareau. Maison de Verre, Paris (with Bernard Bijvoet; 1928–32)

Chareau, Pierre, b. Bordeaux 1883, d. East Hampton, N.Y., 1950. After studies at the *Ecole des Beaux-Arts in Paris and a period of apprenticeship with the Paris office of an English furniture firm, he established a practice as a private architect and furniture designer in 1918. He first came to public attention at the 1919 Salon d'Automne in Paris, when he exhibited furniture designed for the Dalsace apartment. Dr Dalsace and his wife also commissioned the Maison de Verre in Paris (1928–32), at once one of the most thoroughgoing realizations of the idea of the 'Machine for Living in' (first postulated by *Le Corbusier in his description of the Maison Citrohan design) and probably the most poetic example of architecture inspired by the world of modern technology. The Maison de Verre was realized, as were several other buildings of those years, in collaboration with Bernard Bijvoet who, as Johannes *Duiker's partner, had also worked on the Zonnestraal Sanatorium at Hilversum (1926–8). C. was a founding member of the Union des Artistes Modernes, launched in Paris in 1929. In 1940 he emigrated to the USA where he built, notably, a house for the painter Robert Motherwell at East Hampton, N.Y. AM

☐ Herbst, René, *Un inventeur, l'architecte Pierre Chareau*, Paris 1954; Frampton, Kenneth, 'Maison de Verre', *Perspecta* (New Haven), no. 12 (1969), pp. 77–126; 'Pierre Chareau with Bernard Bijvoet. Maison Dalsace ("Maison de Verre")', *Global Architecture* (Tokyo), no. 46 (1977).

Chermayeff, Serge, b. 1900 in Russia. A leading British Modernist in the late 1920s and 1930s, C. achieved prominence in interior design as Modern Art Department director at Waring and Gillow, London, 1928–31, and with his interiors for the Exhibition of Modern Furnishings (1928–9) and the Cambridge Theatre, London (1929–30). As a freelance designer, he worked on BBC studios (1931) in London and Birmingham, but principally on domestic interiors. By 1935, his work embraced furniture, rugs, textiles, exhibitions, clocks and radios.

In 1932 C. entered the field of architecture proper, designing his own house in Rugby (built 1933). He was in partnership with Erich Mendelsohn, 1933–6. This phase dominated his career and resulted in prominent British Modern Movement buildings (using Samuely's structural engineering), including: Shrubs Wood (1933–4); De La Warr Pavilion, Bexhill-on-Sea (1933–5); House in Chelsea (1934–6); Gilbey offices (1935–7) and ICI Manchester (1936–8). The architect's own house, Bentley Wood (1937–8), anticipated his American period and his experiments with wood-frame structures.

After emigration to the *USA in 1940, he distinguished himself as a teacher, promoting curriculum planning, urban organization, and research into the multivalent discipline of 'environmental design'. He was successively Director, Department of Art, Brooklyn College, 1942–6; President, Chicago Institute of Design, 1946–51; Professor of Architecture, Harvard University, 1952–62; and Professor, Yale University, 1962–9. Collaboration with other architects and several key students was an important force in crystallizing his architectural theories. He was in partnership with Heywood Cutting (ex-Chicago Institute), 1952–7; at Harvard he collaborated with Christopher Alexander, and at Yale with Alexander Tzonis. Executed works include fabrics, paintings, interiors and exhibitions, while his domestic architectural projects include: houses in Piedmont (with Clarence Mayhew) and in Redwood (both 1942); extensions to his own house at Truro (1945–72); a house in Portland and his own studio in Truro (both 1952); houses in Truro (1954, 1956); and his own house in New Haven, Conn. (1962–3). BT

☐ Chermayeff, S., and Alexander, C., *Community and Privacy*, London 1963; Chermayeff, S., and Tzonis, A., *Shape of Community*, London 1971; Plunz, Richard (ed.), *Design and the Public Good*, Cambridge, Mass. 1983.

Chiattone, Mario, b. Bergamo 1891, d. Lugano 1957. Studied architecture and painting at the Accademia di Brera in Milan. In 1914, in Milan, he exhibited, together with his fellow-student *Sant'Elia, a group of drawings with the titles 'Structures for a modern Metropolis', 'Factory' and 'Forms'; these were among the most important formulations of *Futurist architecture. In his later work, however, C. approached increasingly the harmonic monumentality of the Novecento Italiano group (*Italy).

☐ Veronesi, Giulia, and Regoli, Gigetta Dalli, *L'opera di Chiattone* (exhibition catalogue), Pisa 1965.

Chicago School. Designation for a group of architects active in the last quarter of the 19th century, above all in Chicago, or rather for a group of commercial and office buildings constructed in Chicago between 1875 and 1910. These buildings have two principal characteristic features: a steel-skeleton supporting structure, and a clear expression of the static and functional structure in the building's form, whereby a straightforward and often novel architectural vocabulary, which anticipated modernism, was employed.

After the great fire of 1871 and the worldwide depression two years later, Chicago witnessed a tremendous expansion within a very brief period. This resulted from the shift in

Chiattone. Structures for a modern metropolis (project, 1914)

agricultural production from hand labour to industrialization; Chicago benefited tremendously due to its position as the market place for the region. Buildings began to grow like mushrooms, and as sites were expensive and scarce, the new structures rose to a great height and were in close juxtaposition. Single multi-storey high-rise buildings had already been constructed in the *USA. One of the first was the Jayne Building in Philadelphia, built in 1849–50 by William Johnston; among the most impressive was the Tribune Building in New York by Richard Morris Hunt (1873–5). Nonetheless, as a new constructive, functional and aesthetic creation built in significant numbers, the skyscraper type was born in Chicago. One of the two prerequisites for multi-storey residential, commercial and office buildings had been available since the mid-19th-century: Elisha Graves Otis had invented the elevator and in 1853 demonstrated it in spectacular style in New York. The second prerequisite was an appropriate construction system which would at once allow construction to great height and be fireproof; this was still lacking.

The credit for having discovered a structural solution able to carry loads for tall fireproof buildings largely erected by assembly fell to William Le Baron Jenney. He used a steel skeleton, in contrast to the cast-iron type which the inventor and architect James Bogardus had already tested in a five-storey factory building in New York in 1848. This proved not only reliable under stress but also under strain and thus formed a completely rigid structural system, which he clad with masonry to make it more heat-resistant. The first Leiter Building (later Morris Building, today 208 West Monroe Street) was erected in Chicago in 1879; although it still had a cast-iron skeleton, the structure already suggested the lightness of later works. It was followed by the Home Insurance Building in 1883–5 (subsequently extended); the Manhattan Building in 1889–90, together with D. H. Burnham and J. W. Root's contemporary Rand McNally Building, one of the first skyscrapers entirely of steel-skeleton construction; and the second Leiter Building (today Sears, Roebuck & Co.) in 1889–91, a classic of the Chicago 'commercial style'. With his new mode of construction, Jenney overcame the height restrictions associated with conventional load-bearing masonry construction.

Jenney's technologically pioneering ten-storey Home Insurance Building did not, in terms of external articulation, free itself any more from the *historicism of the Victorian period than did the 16-storey Manhattan Building; both were out of step with the innovative structural type on account of their conventional additive façade articulation. In fact, as far as a formal vocabulary was concerned, it was not Jenney who provided the most important impulses for the Chicago School (nor by any means only for it), but H. H. Richardson. Richardson studied in Paris at the *Ecole des Beaux-Arts, worked in the atelier of Henri Labrouste and, after his return to America, designed numerous buildings in a purified and powerful neo-Romanesque style. He completed the Marshall Field Wholesale Store in Chicago (1885–7), a massive, rationally designed masonry building, the effect of which derived principally from the expressiveness of its rusticated façade. This straightforward monumentaility, whose closed character was softened by the great round-arched windows, was to be imitated by, among others, Dankmar *Adler and Louis *Sullivan, in the architectural language of the Auditorium Building (1887–9; today Roosevelt University), as traditional in its architectural language as it was technologically progressive.

Richardson's model was also taken over and reduced by Burnham and Root in the powerful

Chicago School. The Marshall Field Wholesale Store, Chicago (1885–7), by H. H. Richardson

Rookery Building (1885–6) and in the Monadnock Building (1889–91) – the last tall building in this group with load-bearing outer walls – all ornament is avoided: instead the exterior of the 16-storey building is enlivened by simple, canted bow-windows which elegantly subdivide the façade. The corner of the building from ground level to the upper window ledge is sharply angled, and the projecting cornice as well as its upward tapered base are reduced to simple curves. The steel frame for skyscrapers received a significant exterior form for the first time in D. H. Burnham & Co.'s Reliance Building (today 32 North State Street), erected in Chicago in 1894–5 (design by Charles B. Atwood). The light, almost floating skeletal structure, with its overwhelmingly vertically-articulated façade, anticipated the aesthetic of the glass-and-steel buildings of the mid-20th century.

William Holabird and Martin Roche likewise followed in the tracks of Richardson, with the Tacoma Building (1887–9), and the reserved and elegant Marquette Building (1893–4), both in Chicago. Their unpretentious and well-balanced aesthetic reached a highpoint, as unobtrusive as it was noteworthy, in the McClurg Building (today Crown Building) of 1899–1900.

The most important protagonist of the Chicago School and its formative head was, however, Louis Sullivan. He studied briefly at the Massachusetts Institute of Technology and later, like Richardson, in Paris; he worked in Philadelphia under Frank Furness and in Chicago under Jenney, then in 1881 formed a partnership with Dankmar Adler in which he

Chicago School. The Monadnock Building, Chicago (1889–91), by Burnham and Root

Chicago School. The Reliance Building, Chicago (1894–5), by D. H. Burnham & Co.

Chicago School. The Gage Building, Chicago (1898–9), by Holabird & Roche, with (right) the façade designed by Sullivan

took responsibility for the form of the building. In his works, the elegant neo-Romanesque style of Richardson was transformed into a rugged rigorism with classic handling of masses and oriental-gothicist decoration. The Wainwright Building in St Louis, a bold upward-soaring steel-skeleton structure, dates from 1890–1; it already manifests Sullivan's typical tripartite division into a massive lower storey with a mezzanine, a vertically articulated office section, as well as a tall attic for mechanical services. It marked the moment of birth for the skyscraper as an independent and significant building type. In 1898–9, Sullivan designed one part of the façade of Holabird & Roche's Gage Building in Chicago; while respecting the existing grid of the construction, he created a fully independent work. The diverse qualities of the Chicago School are clearly seen in this façade: the directness and simplicity of Holabird and Roche's work formed a revealing contrast to Sullivan's refined, complicated, but nonetheless uncommonly clear design.

Sullivan built the Schlesinger and Mayer Department Store (today Carson Pirie Scott & Co.) in two phases (1899 and 1903–4); he created there one of the most significant buildings of the Chicago School. The interior space, with its continuous surfaces, was of the conventional department store type. The particular achievement lay in the façade: the tautly organized network of horizontal and vertical lines give expression to the underlying steel-skeleton construction, displaying a strength at once rational and legible. The wide, horizontally arranged Chicago windows (each divided into a broad fixed central part with a narrower sash window at either side) are framed by metal casements; those of the lower storey are united by a narrow band of terracotta ornament in order to emphasize the dominant horizontals. In conscious contrast to this restraint, the two floors of the display windows are clad in a lively organic ornamentation of filigree cast iron.

The World's Columbian Exposition in Chicago (1893), whose layout was originally projected by Root in a romantic way nearly in the manner of Richardson (1891) but subsequently realized in the calmer Beaux-Arts manner of Burnham's plan, marked the end of the Chicago School's heyday. This opting in favour of the neo-classicist 'White City' was no coincidence. After the grand episode of noble, but mainly disparate individuals, with each reaching separately for the sky, it was necessary for architecture to turn again to the traditional concept of the city as a coherent continuum. Thus, by *c.* 1900 the period of the proto-modernist commercial buildings of Chicago was over. Isolated later instances are to be found in such works as the Chaplin and Gore Building (1901–4; later Nepeenauk Building, today 63 East Adams Street) by Richard Schmidt; the Montgomery Ward and Co. Warehouse (1906–8) by Schmidt, Garden & Martin; and, in an especially challenging way, in the Larkin Building in Buffalo, N.Y. (1904–5), built by Sullivan's most independently minded pupil – Frank Lloyd *Wright. Nearly thirty years were to pass before Raymond *Hood and John Mead Howells, under the influence of European *Rationalism, would erect the *Daily News* Building in New York (1929–30), and thus introduce a new era for the modern American skyscraper. VML

□ *Early Modern Architecture: Chicago 1870–1910*, New York 1930, 2nd ed. 1940; Tallmadge, Thomas E., *Architecture in Old Chicago*, Chicago 1941; Randall, F. A., *A History of the Development of Building Construction in Chicago*, Urbana, Ill. 1949; Condit, Carl W., *The Rise of the Skyscraper*, Chicago 1952; ——, *The Chicago School of Architecture*, Chicago 1964.

CIAM (Congrès Internationaux d'Architecture Moderne). The foundation of CIAM in 1928 has been called the beginning of the 'academic' phase of modern architecture: the time certainly appeared propitious for the introduction of some kind of international order into the scattered and independent essays towards a new architecture whose international unity of intention and style had been demonstrated at the Weißenhof exhibition of the previous year.

The effective impetus towards the foundation of CIAM came from Hélène de Mandrot, a sincere and intelligent woman who had aspirations towards being a patroness of the arts. She proposed in the first place a reunion of creative spirits at her château at La Sarraz, Switzerland, but this romantic project was turned to something more purposeful after consultation with Sigfried Giedion and *Le Corbusier. The preparatory document, issued to intending delegates, stated: 'This first congress is convened with the aim of establishing a programme of action to drag architecture from the academic impasse and to place it in its proper social and economic milieu. This congress should . . . determine the limits of the studies and discussions shortly to be undertaken by further congresses.' Although a distinction was thus made between the preparatory congress and later meetings, the date of 26, 27, and 28 June 1928 at La Sarraz is remembered and recorded as CIAM I, in spite of the fact that the properly constituted series of congresses did not begin until the following year.

The contents of the declaration of 28 June embodied most of the best aspirations as well as the most fashionable fetishes of the architecture of the time. Sample statements read: 'It is only from the present that our architectural work should be derived', and 'The intention that brings us together is that of attaining a harmony of existing elements – a harmony indispensable to the present – BY PUTTING ARCHITECTURE BACK ON ITS REAL PLANE, THE ECONOMIC AND SOCIAL PLANE; therefore architecture should be freed of the sterile influence of the Academies and of antiquated formulas', and again, 'The most efficacious production is derived from rationalization and standardization.'

The historical irony of these repeated invectives against the Academies is underlined by the dry, formalistic statement of aims that appears as the preamble to the statutes drawn up at Frankfurt-am-Main in 1929 (CIAM II). The Frankfurt Statutes also gave CIAM three operative organs; (1) the *Congrès* or general assembly of the members; (2) CIRPAC (Comité Internationale pour la Résolution des Problèmes de l'Architecture Contemporaine), to be elected by the *Congrès*; and (3) working groups, to apply themselves to specific subjects in collaboration with non-architectural specialists. At the same time the hierarchy of membership was stabilized in the form of national member-groups, to which individuals belonged.

The Frankfurt Congress had been called under the auspices of Ernst *May, the city architect and Europe's greatest expert on low-cost housing, and its outcome was a serious report, *Die Wohnung für das Existenzminimum*. CIAM III was held in Brussels in 1930, through the good offices of Victor *Bourgeois, and applied itself to basic problems of land-organization for housing, publishing an equally important report, *Rationelle Bebauungsweisen*.

By 1930 it was already becoming apparent that CIAM was neither intellectually nor organizationally prepared for the problem to which the logic of its discussions had driven it – town planning. In order to deal with this situation CIAM set to work to standardize the graphic techniques, scales, and methods of presentation used by its members (an enterprise that was not really completed until the adoption of the *Grille-CIAM* after 1949). The Dutch national group, under Cor van *Eesteren, became the working group entrusted with the evolution of an effective symbol language for town planning. These labours, conducted against a background of growing political tensions and disintegrating international relations, proved to be protracted, and CIRPAC met three times (Berlin, 1931, Barcelona, 1932, and Paris, 1933) before it was felt that work was sufficiently advanced for another plenary *Congrès* to be called.

CIAM IV – theme 'The Functional City' – took place in July and August aboard the S.S. *Patris*, between Marseilles and Athens. It was the first of the 'romantic' congresses, set against a background of scenic splendour, not the reality of industrial Europe, and it was the first *Congrès* to be dominated by *Le Corbusier and the French, rather than the tough German realists. The Mediterranean cruise was clearly a welcome relief from the worsening situation of Europe, and in this brief respite from reality the delegates produced the most Olympian, rhetorical, and ultimately most misapplied document to come out of CIAM: the *Athens Charter.

Its tone remained dogmatic, but was generalized and less specifically related to immediate practical problems than the Frankfurt and Brussels reports had been. The generalization had its virtues, where it brought with it a greater breadth of vision and insisted that cities could be considered only in relation to their surrounding regions, but this persuasive generality which gave the Athens Charter its air of universal applicability concealed a very narrow conception of both architecture and town planning and committed CIAM unequivocally to: (*a*) rigid functional zoning of city plans, with green belts between the areas reserved to the different functions, and (*b*) a single type of urban housing, expressed in the words of the Charter as 'high, widely-spaced apartment blocks wherever the necessity of housing high densities of population exists'. With the benefit of hindsight, we recognize this as merely the expression of an aesthetic preference, but at the time it had the power of a Mosaic commandment and effectively paralysed research into other forms of housing. The Paris *Congrès* of 1937 (CIAM V) did little more than make marginal annotations to the Charter.

After World War II, the next meeting, CIAM VI, was held in 1947 at Bridgwater, England; this was a joyous reunion of the heroes of Weißenhof and the followers they had collected in the 1930s, and its outcome was a review of buildings erected since CIAM V by the members, edited by Giedion and published under the title of *A Decade of New Architecture*. But at CIAM VII, held at Bergamo in 1949, a new pattern was beginning to emerge, with the growing importance of the Italian delegation and the gathering of numbers of war-toughened students on the fringes of the *Congrès* in order to sit at the feet of those, to them, legendary figures, the makers of modern architecture.

At CIAM VIII, held at Hoddesdon in England, in honour of the *Festival of Britain, 1951, the new pattern of CIAM was becoming plain – increasing numbers of students, and official recognition of the inadequacy of the Charter, since the theme was 'The Urban Core'. For this theme the delegates were as unprepared intellectually as they had been for town planning in 1930, and the Congress report was little more than a compendium of fashionable clichés, such as the need to integrate painting and sculpture into architecture.

It was not long before the failure of CIAM VIII was recognized, but in the meantime CIAM IX at Aix-en-Provence had taken place; its theme was officially 'Habitat', but the *Congrès* will be chiefly remembered as a mass rally of Le Corbusier's student fan-club and the proceedings, culminating in an impromptu striptease performance on the roof of the Unité at Marseilles, were marked by adolescent *bonhomie* rather than mature celebration. Yet it was to be the young who undertook to deliver CIAM from the new 'academic impasse' into which it had lapsed. The group who were entrusted with the preparation of CIAM X (who were therefore known as Team X) took up a position that, though it drew to some extent on the programme documents for CIAM IX, nevertheless represented a clean break with both the mood and the content of the Athens Charter. Against the large-scale diagrammatic generalizations of the Athenian tradition, Team X set up the personal, the particular, and the precise: 'Each architect is asked to appear with his project under his arm, ready to commit himself. Today we recognize the existence of a new spirit. It is manifest in our revolt from mechanical concepts of order . . . CIAM X must make it clear that we, as architects, accept the responsibility for the creation of order through form . . . the responsibility for each act of creation, however small.'

Though the theme of CIAM X was still nominally 'Habitat', the real business of the *Congrès*, which took place in Dubrovnik in 1956, was the direct challenge presented to the established members by the young radicals of Team X, *Bakema, *Candilis, the *Smithsons, and van *Eyck. By the end of the congress, CIAM was in ruins and Team X stood upon the wreckage of something that they had joined with enthusiasm, and – with equal enthusiasm – destroyed. The sense of the end of an epoch was so strong that the *Congrès* accepted the fact of death with comparative calm; the national groups were instructed to wind up their affairs, and the project of a memorial volume covering twenty-five years of work was seriously discussed. But there were national groups, notably the Italian, who felt that CIAM could still be of service. In addition, Team X were not averse to international meetings as such, and the combination of these two parties produced, in 1959, a further congress in Otterlo, Holland. In content this was to be similar to what Team X had intended for CIAM X, and particular projects were indeed discussed, individual responsibility was accepted, and the results, edited by Oscar Newman, were published as *CIAM '59 in Otterlo*. These published documents reveal that close discussion of the particular could often be as trivial as broad discussion of generalities, while the title of the report conceals a bitter dispute among the delegates who, in fact, voted to dissociate their activities from the label 'CIAM'.

This was neither a productive nor a dignified outcome to thirty years of international activity, and the blame for the final collapse of CIAM must be laid chiefly on the inability of the founder-members to resist the temptation to *faire école*. They failed to guard against the academic tendencies in their midst, and became the victims of what van Eesteren termed 'a too formal structure' to which work-programmes had to be subordinated. Nevertheless, in two vital periods – 1930–4 and 1950–5 – CIAM was the major instrument through which the ideas of modern architecture and town planning were made known to the world, while it performed an equally vital function during the war years in maintaining the nucleus of an international network of communications between progressive-minded architects. It is quite possible that these achievements may ultimately prove to be of greater historical importance than any of the documents that CIAM produced, even the Athens Charter. RB

□ *Die Wohnung für das Existenzminimum*, Stuttgart 1930; *Rationelle Bebauungsweisen*, Stuttgart 1931; *Logis et loisirs*, Paris 1938; Sert, J. L., and CIAM, *Can Our Cities Survive?*, Cambridge, Mass., and London 1942; [Le Corbusier], *Urbanisme des CIAM. La Charte d' Athènes*, Paris 1943; Giedion, Sigfried, *A Decade of New Architecture*, Zurich 1951; Rogers, E. N., Sert, J. L., and Tyrwhitt, J. (eds.), *The Heart of the City*, New York and London 1952; Newman, Oscar (ed.), *CIAM '59 in Otterlo*, Stuttgart 1961.

CLASP (acronym for Consortium of Local Authorities Special Programme). In 1957, a group of local education authorities in England banded together to exploit a system of prefabricating schools, originally devised in Nottingham under Donald Gibson to counteract subsidence in mining areas and later extended, as in C. H. *Aslin's Hertfordshire schools, to allow buildings to be erected rapidly from mass-produced prefabricated units at low cost and with a small labour force. Consortium components accounted for about half the cost of CLASP schools; £7 million worth of work was built in 1961–2, and a second consortium was formed by other authorities (SCOLA).

A 3 ft 4 in. (1·01 m) planning grid was used, with external walls that can change direction at 6 ft 8 in. (2·02 m) or 10 ft (3·05 m) intervals. An organic grouping of elements with carefully controlled relationships between the spaces creates a deceptive, though usually successful feeling of informality. The same informality,

CLASP. Croxley Green Junior School, Hertfordshire (1947–9) by C. H. Aslin

however, when evoked in the choice of external cladding components often appears arbitrary and visually confused, lessening the effect of the carefully related spaces. HM

Coates, Wells (Windemut), b. Tokyo 1895 of Canadian parents, d. London 1958. After engineering studies in Vancouver and London, C. first worked for a number of years as a journalist for the *Daily Express* (London) and then for a short time as an engineering and architectural consultant. In 1929 he opened his own architectural office in London which he continued until his death, with the exception of periods during World War II and during several years involvement in urban planning affairs in *Canada. He was a founder-member in 1933 of the *MARS group and one of the leading English exponents of modernism before the war. His Lawn Road Flats in Hampstead, London (1933), a slender concrete building with continuous balcony fronts, is one of the earliest expressions of the *International Style in *Great Britain. C. was particularly active in industrial design, designing notably a radio set which can be considered a classic of its time. AM
☐ Cantacuzino, Sherban, *Wells Coates*, London 1978.

Coates. Lawn Road Flats, Hampstead, London (1933)

Constructivism. As Le Corbusier once remarked, Constructivism is a term whose connotations are vague, for, unlike *Purism or Italian *Rationalism, its boundaries were never clearly defined. It is possible, however, to assign an identifiable profile to Constructivism since it strove to eliminate the traditional distinctions separating art from life, or as the Productivists put it in their slogans of the early 1920s: 'Down with Art! Long live technology! . . . Long live the Constructivist Technician!'

In *Russia, Constructivism passed through two distinct phases. The first was a period of *agitprop* timber construction which was employed for exhibitions or for revolutionary forms of street art. The second was a professional phase in which buildings were conceived as a genre lying somewhere between machine form and biological structures. The scientific ideology of this second phase accounts, in part, for the invention of complex sections such as interlocking dwelling units, and for the expression of access systems such as ramps and elevators. This drive also accounts for the introduction of extra-architectural elements such as searchlights, electrical sky-signs, radio aerials and cinematographic equipment. Such a rhetoric of machine expression subsequently alienated more formalist artists like the Suprematist-Elementarist, El *Lissitzky, or the leader of Dutch *Neo-plasticism, Theo van *Doesburg, or certain Russians who were seemingly closer to the radical impulse, such as the VKHUTEMAS architect Nikolai Ladovsky, who founded the formalist ASNOVA group (New Association of Architects) in 1923.

The canonical Constructivist work was Vladimir *Tatlin's project for a gigantic Monument to the Third International, first exhibited in 1920. This design, projected as a distorted frustum (logarithmically diminishing in a spiral vortex towards the summit), was inspired, like all Constructivism, by the triumphs of modern technology. And yet, while the precedent for this project was clearly the Eiffel Tower of 1889, the science-fiction aura of its form derived from Alexei Kruchenikh's Futurist opera *Victory over the Sun*. Naum Gabo's public criticism of Tatlin's proposal – 'Either build functional houses and bridges or create pure art, not both. Don't confuse one with the other.' (made within the Moscow VKHUTEMAS) – was instrumental in persuading a number of artists to abandon fine art to work as industrial designers; figures such as Alexei Gan, Liubov Popova, Alexander Rodchenko, Varvara Stepanova and Vladimir Tatlin claimed for themselves the description Productivist rather than Constructivist.

As far as architecture is concerned, Russian Constructivism was never more 'production'-oriented than in the early timber structures designed by Konstantin *Melnikov, whose Mahorka pavilion at the All-Russia Agricultural and Craft Exhibition in Moscow of 1923 was a non-folkloric reinterpretation of traditional Russian agrarian construction. This vivacious method of building was to be repeated in Melnikov's Sucharev Market, built in Moscow in 1923, and in his Russian Pavilion (1925) erected in Paris for the 'Exposition internationale des arts décoratifs et industriels modernes'. Articulated pre-cut, standard timber members, wood-block stencils, interlocking mono-pitched roofs and rhetorical stairways are the salient features of Melnikov's early style. Melnikov's manner changed, however, when he started to use sophisticated technology in a series of workers' clubs, of which the Rusakov Club in Moscow (1927–8), with its cantilevered concrete lecture halls, is the most characteristic example.

Constructivism. Monument to the Third International (1920), project by Vladimir Tatlin

The post-Revolutionary attempt to evolve a totally new architectural expression, one which would be based on the direct revelation of structural and technical form, gave rise within

Constructivism. The Rusakov Club, Moscow (1927–8), by Konstantin Melnikov

Constructivism. Project for the *Leningradskaya Pravda* building, Moscow (1923), by Alexander Vesnin

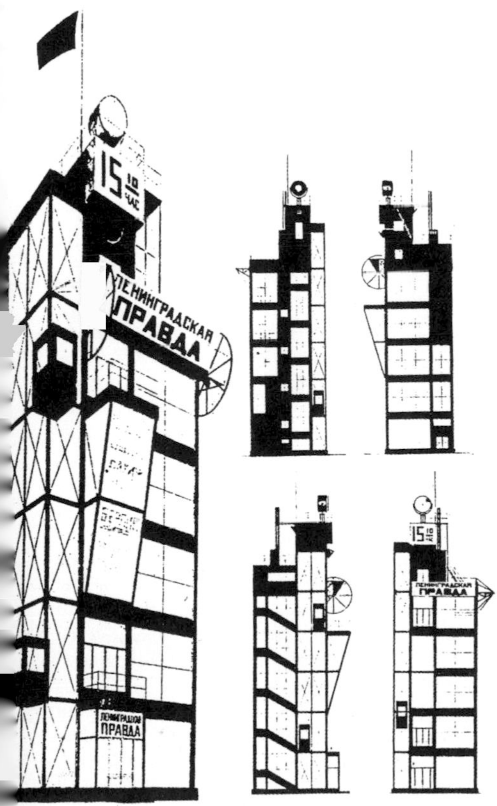

the VKHUTEMAS to a number of rival factions. The most prominent of these, the functionally-oriented OSA group (Association of Contemporary Architects), was founded in 1925 by Alexander Vesnin. Vesnin, who taught in the VKHUTEMAS from 1921 onwards, was one of the first to formulate the architectural syntax of Constructivism in his project for the *Leningradskaya Pravda* Building in Moscow (1923), of which Lissitzky wrote in 1929: 'All accessories . . . such as signs, advertising, clocks, loud-speakers and even the elevators inside, have been incorporated as integral elements of the design and combined into a unified whole. This is the aesthetic of Constructivism.'

However, the method for determining form varied from one faction to the next. There was a wide divergence between the functionalist ideology of Vesnin's OSA group and the more formal *gestalt* theories advanced by ASNOVA, the latter ultimately seeking a lexicon of pure forms which could be seen as inducing certain psychological states.

In programmatic terms, Russian Constructivist architects focused on two primary themes. In the first place, they attempted to invent the form of the ideal socialist town – an endeavour which attained its apotheosis in N. A. Miliutin's model for a 'six-banded' linear city (1930). In the second place, they tried to postulate the new 'social condensers' of the society at both an architectural and institutional level. This accounts for the prevalence of workers' clubs in the late 1920s and for Soviet research into communal housing prototypes under the leadership of the OSA architect, Moisei Ginzburg. Ginzburg realized one such *dom-kommund* prototype in his Narkomfin housing block in Moscow (1929). The dwelling unit employed in this block was derived from the OSA housing competition of 1927, and from an inquiry which was conducted by the OSA magazine.

Given the priorities of the Soviet Union, Russian Constructivism came to be devoted in the main to meeting the infra-structural needs of society, most of the realized works being such structures as offices, department stores, sanatoria, printing plants, research stations, factories, workers' clubs and, last but not least, hydro-electric installations. Among this last category was the largest Russian civil-engineering undertaking of the inter-war period, the famous Dnieperstroi Dam, completed to the designs of Victor Vesnin in 1932.

It was in the late 1920s that Constructivism began to exert an influence outside the Soviet Union in countries as diverse as France, Sweden, Switzerland, Czechoslovakia, England and even the United States (Philadelphia Saving Fund Society Building in Philadelphia by *Howe and *Lescaze). Constructivism at its most authentic, however, was largely restricted to the Netherlands and Germany, where such architects as Mart *Stam and Johannes *Duiker, or in Germany Hannes *Meyer and Walter *Gropius, realized works which consisted of little more than translucent envelopes, stretched over exposed structural frames, with directly expressed systems of access and circulation. The most purely Constructivist work of this era seems to have been in the Van Nelle factory in Rotterdam (1926–30) by Johannes Andreas *Brinkman and Leendert Cornelius Van der Vlugt, on which job Stam also worked. Close in spirit to Hannes Meyer and Hans Wittwer's Constructivist entry for the League of Nations competition of 1926–7, the Van Nelle factory still stands today as a *tour de force* in curtain-walled, mushroom-column, reinforced-concrete construction. What finally confirms it as a Constructivist work, however, is the use of continuously moving conveyor belts, crossing back and forth in transparent elevated tubes, between the factory slab and the canal-side warehouse. With the work of Duiker and his partner Bernard Bijvoet, however, we are confronted with a Constructivism which is more formalist in its intentions. This much is clear from Duiker's symmetrically planned Zonnestraal Sanatorium in Hilversum (1926–8) and from his equally symmetrical Open Air School built in Amsterdam in 1928–30. A higher-level synthesis between these two aspects of International Constructivism – that is, between the asymmetrical Functionalism of Stam on the one hand, and the symmetrical formalism of Duiker on the other – was possibly attained in Pierre *Chareau's Maison de Verre (designed in collaboration with Bijvoet), Paris (1928–32). It says something for the continuation of the Constructivist tradition that Richard *Rogers – the co-designer with Renzo *Piano of the Centre Pompidou in Paris (1972–7) – was to make a study of this machine-house in the early 1960s. KF

□ Kopp, Anatole, *Ville et révolution*, Paris 1967; Quilici, Vieri, *L'architettura del costruttivismo*, Bari 1969; Shvidkovsky, O. A. (ed.), *Building in the USSR, 1917–1932*, London and New York 1971; Lissitzky, El, *Russia: An Architecture for World Revolution*, Cambridge, Mass. 1970.

Cook, Peter, b. 1936 Southend, Essex. Received his architectural education first at the Bournemouth College of Art, and then at the Architectural Association in London. His love for seaside suburbia (where he grew up) and the fantasy of holiday resorts has imbued his whole production with a sense of play and enjoyment. His free-ranging imagination was equally at home in the technologically super-heated 1960s and the regressive '70s. As a founder-member of the *Archigram group, in 1960, his reputation has been both enhanced and obscured by the success of that group. His own peculiar brand of eclecticism has become more apparent in his more recent work, particularly in the Green, Yellow, Red and Blue Houses he designed with Christine Hawley in 1979, where a kind of Californian *Art Deco spirit emerges: as these houses were designed to be built, they are more important as concrete indications of his specifically architectural talent than are the more wayward and fantastical drawings such as the Arcadia sequence of 1977–9, which exist primarily as art works. They blend a reflection of the aspirations of the high technology era with a kind of intense hedonism, indeed eroticism, which may well provide evidence for future generations of the fantasy inherent in technological dreams. RM

□ Cook, Peter, *Architecture, Action and Plan*, London and New York 1967; ——, *Experimental Architecture*, London and New York 1970; ——, *Archigram*, London and New York 1974; ——, *The Arcadian City*, London 1978.

Coop Himmelblau. Group of architects founded in Vienna in 1968 by Wolf D. Prix, Helmut Swiczinsky and Rainer Michael Holzer (dissolved in 1971). Under the influence of Hans *Hollein and contemporary experimental teams such as *Haus-Rucker-Co, the group was at first concerned with pneumatic space structures. It was, however, pyschological and aesthetic matters rather than technological concerns which engaged their interest. With their 'Wiener Supersommer' (Viennese Super Summer) of 1976, Coop Himmelblau for the first time made strong play with their alternatives to currently accepted modes of urban design. This

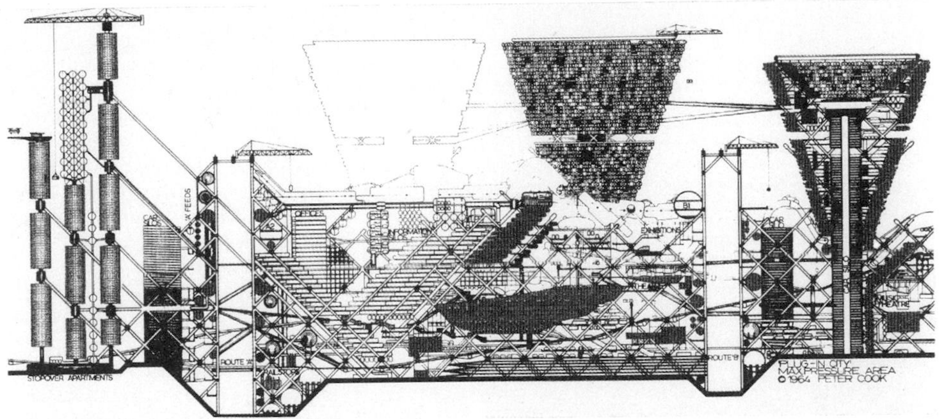

Cook. Plug-in City, project (Archigram; 1964–6)

form of confrontation became a hallmark of the group. Architecture should not mollify or reconcile, but rather represent in a visually heightened way the contemporary tensions of a particular place. Thus they conceived architectural projects that were evocative of terror, harmful, or even aflame. The group produced such poetically aggressive 'demonstration objects' as the Reiss Bar in Vienna (1977), the branches of 'Humanic' in Mistelbach (1979) and Vienna (1980), and the Flammenflügel (Flamewing; 1980), as well as the 'Roter Engel' (Red Angel) Music Bar in Vienna (1981). FW
☐ Coop Himmelblau, *Architektur muß brennen*, Graz 1980.

Coop Himmelblau. Cloud project (1968)

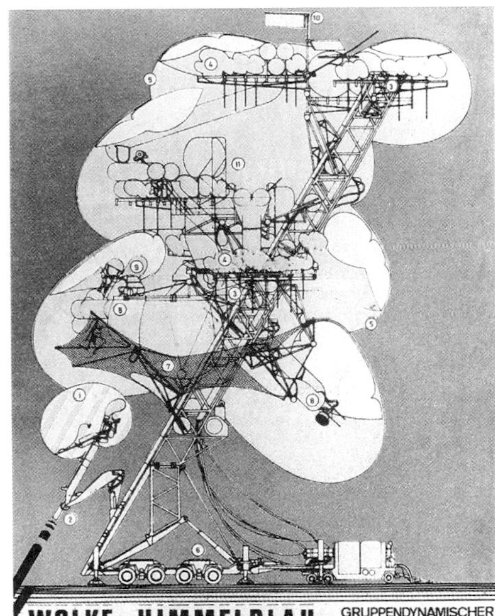

Costa, Lúcio, b. Toulon 1902. After graduating in 1924 from the Escola Nacional de Belas Artes in Rio de Janeiro, he entered into an early partnership with Gregori *Warchavchik. In 1931 he was appointed to the directorship of the School of Fine Arts in Rio de Janeiro, which included the School of Architecture, and adopted new teaching methods, through which a generation of young architects were given a grounding in the principles of the European avant garde of the 1920s and '30s. Between 1936 and 1943 the Ministry of Education and Health (now Palace of Culture) in Rio de Janeiro – for which *Le Corbusier was consulting architect and C. was for a time the leader of the team of architects, which included *Niemeyer and *Reidy – was under construction; this proved to be the most important building in *Brazil in terms of spreading Modern Movement ideas there. With Niemeyer, C. designed the Brazilian Pavilion at the New York World's Fair (1939). Subsequently he was actively involved in city planning, culminating in his master-plan for Brasilia (1956); in this plan the principles of the *Athens Charter found their greatest expression, providing a superb framework for Niemeyer's public buildings. HEM/VML
☐ Gazenco, J. O., and Scarone, M. M., *Lúcio Costa*, Buenos Aires 1959; Costa, Lúcio, *Sobre Arquitectura*, Porto Alegre 1962.

Cubism. Movement in European painting in the early 20th century which developed the new 'way of seeing' which Paul Cézanne had already introduced around the turn of the century, whereby the representation of objects is reduced to compositions of elemental forms. The Cubist movement arose in Paris between 1905 and 1910 from parallel developments in which, above all, Georges Braque and Pablo Picasso played decisive roles. The essence of their experiments, which drew their formal inspiration from a variety of sources including African art, was the depiction of three-dimensional space without recourse to illusionistic perspective devices. Among the most important characteristics of the Cubist formal language were: composition of pictures with simple geometric structures; sculptural reproductions of objects in their spatial entirety, in which they separated the component surfaces and either placed them next to one another or represented them as penetrating one another by transparent effects; simulation of the simultaneous perception of the diverse aspects of an object, in which no single aspect is given priority. All of these techniques gave expression to their principal aim: to represent not only what can be seen but, above all, what is known about an object.

The direct application of Cubism to architecture remained problematic. The project for a 'Villa Cubiste' by the sculptor Raymond Duchamp-Villon (1912) was nothing more than a conventional neo-classical house with applied Cubist decoration. The situation was not greatly different in the case of the Prague or Czech architectural Cubist group, which coalesced after 1911 around the magazine *Umělecký Měsíčník*. Yet, even in their work the Cubist elements were confined to ornament, or at best a sculptural handling of façades, which did not affect either the ground-plan or the 'type' of the buildings. In any case the relatively short-lived episode produced bizarre architectural sculpture often close in spirit to contemporary *Expressionism. The principal protagonists of Cubist architecture were Josef Čapek, Josef Chochol, Josef Gočár, Vlastislav Hofman, Pavel Janák and Otokar Novotny.

A less rushed and immediate investigation of the application of Cubist principles to architecture was reserved for the masters of the Modern Movement; but with their work the fundamental experiences of Cubism – asymmetry, transparency, volumetric interpenetration and the simultaneity of perception – were adapted to a more comprehensive view of architecture as an independent discipline. VML

□ Barr, Alfred H., Jr, *Cubism and abstract art*, New York 1936; Sting, H., *Der Kubismus und seine Einwirkung auf die Wegbereiter der modernen Architektur*, Aachen 1965; Burkhardt, François, and Lamarova, Milena, *Cubismo cecoslovacco, architetture e interni*, Milan 1982.

Cuypers, Petrus Josephus Hubertus, b. Roermond 1827, d. Roermond 1921. Studied at the Antwerp Academy; a follower of the theories of Viollet-le-Duc, and like him an admirer of the Gothic style, C. stood at the watershed between *historicism and the Modern Movement in the *Netherlands. He designed numerous Roman Catholic churches in a freely adapted Gothic manner. The Rijksmuseum (1877–85) and Central Station in Amsterdam (1881–9), both with strongly symmetrical plans, display lively, monumental silhouettes. They are examples of a picturesque architecture whose principles of truth to materials and expressivity were to be important impetuses for the School of *Amsterdam.

□ *Het Werk van Dr. Petrus Josephus Hubertus Cuypers, 1827–1917*, Amsterdam 1917.

Cuypers. Rijksmuseum, Amsterdam (1877–85)

D

D'Aronco, Raimondo, b. Gemona, Udine 1857, d. Naples 1932. After receiving a diploma from the Accademia delle Belli Arte in Venice, he was active in Italy and Turkey. With Ernesto *Basile and Giuseppe *Sommaruga, he was one of the leading exponents of Italian *Art Nouveau. He designed the entrance pavilions and the main building for the Turin Arts and Crafts Exhibition of 1902 – a stylistically bizarre mixture revealing the most varied influences: especially apparent was that of the Viennese School centred on Otto *Wagner and that of Joseph Maria *Olbrich's buildings in Darmstadt. Later, however – like *Horta and *Behrens – he turned to a more classically oriented architectural style, as in the town hall at Udine (1909).
□ Nicoletti, Manfredi, *Raimondo D'Aronco*, Milan 1955.

De Carlo, Giancarlo, b. Genoa 1919. After studying engineering at the Milan Politecnico and architecture at the Istituto Universitario d'Architettura in Venice, he established himself in 1950 as an architect in Milan. He was appointed Professor of Town Planning at the architecture school in Venice in 1955. As a member of Team X (*CIAM), he was at the heart of the movement seeking an ethical and formal renewal within modernism during the 1950s. His first important work was the Students' Residence in Urbino (1962–6), in which are convincingly united the vocabulary of *New Brutalism, responses to particular historic and geographic conditions, as well as the specific programmatic solutions. Urbino has remained the centre of his activity, and his work has continued to display the virtues of the Students' Residence. In collaboration with Fausto Colombo and Valeria Fossati, he built the Matteotti workers' housing in Terni (1st phase 1970–4). The scheme was planned in close co-operation with the inhabitants and forms a dense complex of three-storey houses with differentiated floor-plans and with a garden or garden terrace for each dwelling. AM
□ De Carlo, G., *Questioni di architettura e urbanistica*, Urbino 1965; Colombo, C., *Giancarlo De Carlo*, Milan 1964; 'G. De Carlo. La réconciliation de l'architecture et de la politique', *L'Architecture d'aujourd'hui* (Paris), no. 177, January–February 1975, pp. 32–43.

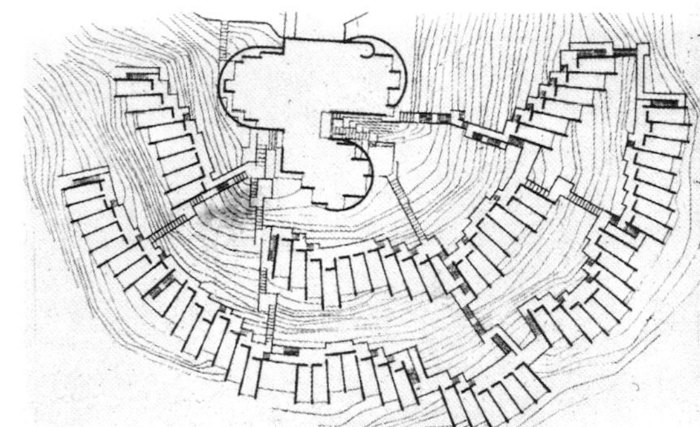

De Carlo. Students' Residence, Urbino (1962–6): site plan

Denmark. The Danes have always drawn inspiration from the major centres of world culture, but have shown a critical and cautious approach when adapting borrowed ideas to Danish landscape and climate, customs and building practices. Thus the process whereby Danish architecture acquired its own character was markedly evolutionary. Securely anchored in their own tradition of craftsmanship, the Danes developed a sense for simple order, natural proportions and rhythm, first through half-timbered work and afterwards through the brick buildings of the Empire period. Emotionalism in architecture was distrusted, and thus the worst excesses of *eclecticism were avoided; on the other hand, avant-garde tendencies were slow to make themselves felt.

A functional tradition runs through Danish architecture, from the simple brick housing of the Empire period, via Michael Gottlieb Bindesbøll onward to 20th-century *neo-classicism and to Ivar Bentsen and Kay Fisker. Bindesbøll's Medical Association houses and Oringe Hospital (*c.* 1850) are simple buildings of yellow brick serving a clear functional purpose. Daniel Herholdt's work *c.* 1860 has a more pronounced stylistic expression, but maintains the same respect for simple structures and truthful expression of materials. Herholdt was the first to use cast iron in a major building – Copenhagen University Library (1861). The architect of Copenhagen's City Hall, Martin

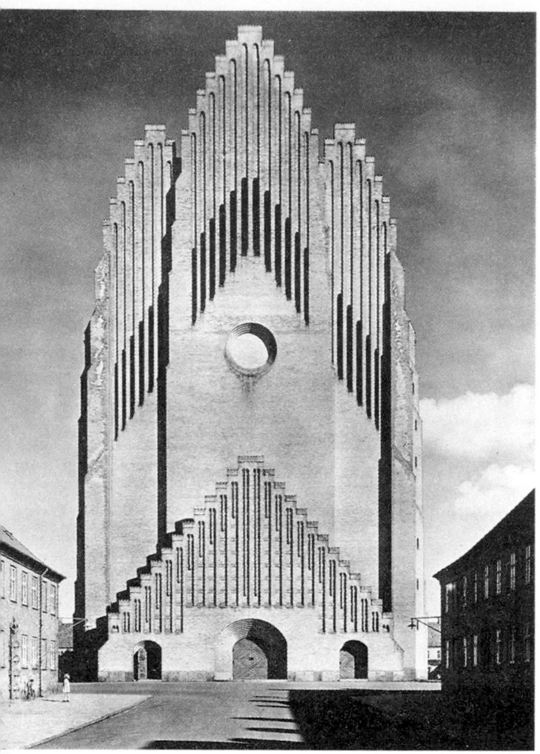

Denmark. Grundtvig Church, Copenhagen (1913, 1921–40), by Jensen Klint

Nyrop, developed this materialist approach to architecture further, while Jensen *Klint, who also took the Danish brick-building tradition as his point of departure, achieved an architecture of expressive effects in the Grundtvig Church (1913, 1921–1940) in Copenhagen, a gigantic paraphrase of the Danish village church type. The *Art Nouveau period left only a few notable traces in Denmark; its most important exponents were Anton Rosen and Thorvald Bindesbøll.

The chief monuments of the neo-classicism which predominated immediately before World War I are: Carl Petersen's Fåborg Museum (designed 1912); and, in Copenhagen, the Police Station (1918–22) by Hack Kampmann, his two sons, and Åge Rafn. In terms of future developments, the chief significance of this neo-classicism was that it led to a more severe artistic discipline and a heightened feeling for the qualities of craftsmanship and material.

Denmark. Århus University: main building (1942–6) by C. F. Møller

From the 1920s Kay Fisker was the leading exponent of traditionalism, playing a leading part in the efforts to improve the quality of housing. The most important product of traditionalism is Århus University (begun 1931), the first part of which was designed by Fisker in collaboration with Christian Frederik Møller and Povl Stegmann. Its many separate buildings stand skilfully related to one another in a park-like campus. Møller later continued work on the University alone, without sacrificing the unity projected in the original design. Fisker's strong personality shows to advantage in Copenhagen's Voldparkens School and the Maternity Care Building of the mid-1950s. Kaare Klint carried on the ideas of his father Jensen Klint in the Bethlehem Church (1937) in Copenhagen, and also became the leading figure in Danish furniture design, with traditional work of the highest craftsmanship. Characteristic of such traditionalist housing of the post-war years as Søndergårdsparken in Bagsvaerd (1950) by Povl Ernst Hoff and Bennet Windinge is a harmonic relationship of buildings to the terrain and its landscaping. The traditionalist-oriented school architecture of the 1950s consisted principally of one-and two-storey buildings intended to provide a milieu on an intimate scale for the pupils. One of the finest examples is the Hansstedt School in Copenhagen (1954–8) by Frederik Christian Lund and Hans Christian Hansen.

The *International Style first made itself seriously felt after the Stockholm Exhibition of 1930, which was a revelation for young Danish architects. Vilhelm Lauritzen became an outstanding exponent in projects such as Copenhagen Airport at Kastrup (1939) and Broadcasting House (1938–45). Mogens Lassen built the first *Le Corbusier-inspired villas and Fritz Schleget became the Danish exponent of a freedom from aesthetic preconceptions established by *Perret with his use of reinforced concrete (Mariebjaerg Crematorium at Lyngby, near Copenhagen, 1937). The young Arne *Jacobsen also belonged to this pioneering group, with the Bellavista residential development at Bellevue, near Copenhagen, and later (in collaboration with Møller and Lassen) with the Århus and Søllerød town halls. These represented the climax of avant-garde building in the 1930s, before the material shortages during the war and in subsequent years brought a return to the cultivation of traditional qualities.

The post-war years have been marked especially by inspiration from the USA, first by Frank Lloyd *Wright's houses and their adaptation to the landscape, later by *Mies van der Rohe's disciplined steel structures. Again Jacobsen was the leading figure, with large administration buildings and hotels, like Rødovre Town Hall (1955), and the SAS Building (1958–60) and the National Bank (1965–71), both in the capital. In his schools and housing Jacobsen convincingly combined foreign inspiration with Danish tradition. Jørn *Utzon is the country's most important representative of a dynamic and expressive architecture. In Denmark he has built noteworthy single-family and terrace houses and his only public building, the church at Bagsvaerd (1974–6). In the Sydney Opera House in Australia he realized a building of great expressive power. Halldor Gunnløgsson is a fine exponent of a severe classicist architecture (Kastrup town hall, 1957–60, with Jørn Nielsen). Vilhelm Wohlert and Jørgen Bo have created a delightful setting for contemporary art in Louisiana Museum at Humlebaek, near Copenhagen (1958).

Through the 1960s the country enjoyed economic growth, with plentiful building activity. Industrialized building methods now began to dominate the scene to such an extent that they accounted for the greater part of new housing. Building projects have increasingly involved larger units. One of the first big

Denmark. Broadcasting House, Copenhagen (1938–45), by Vilhelm Lauritzen

Denmark. National Bank, Copenhagen (1965–71), by Arne Jacobsen

Denmark. Kingo houses, Helsingor (1956–60), by Jørn Utzon

Denmark. Louisiana Museum, Humlebaek (1958), by Jørgen Bo and Vilhelm Wohlert

Denmark. Odense University (1966–76) by Krohn, Rasmussen and Holscher

housing developments carried out entirely in prefabrication was Høje Gladsaxe near Copenhagen (1960–4). The concept of 'open architecture' offering the highest degree of flexibility has been realized in such institutional buildings as Odense University (1966–76) by Gunnar Krohn, Hartvig Rasmussen and Knud Holscher, and in the Copenhagen Country Hospital at Herlev (1960–76) by Gehrdt Bornebusch, Max Brüel and Jørgen Selchau. Between 1968 and 1974 Knud Friis and Elmar Moltke Nielsen, with their secondary schools at Riiskov, Skanderborg and Viborg, created some of the finest works of the period.

Most recently, architecture has been characterized by a strong reaction against huge residential developments such as those of the 1960s. Smaller units of high-density low-rise developments, providing greater opportunities for community life and with variations in design, are now more frequent. A fine example is Galgebakken at Herstederne (1969–74) by J. P. Storgård, J. Ørum-Nielsen, H. Marcussen and A. Ørum-Nielsen. In recent years a growing general interest in historical buildings and cityscapes has also led to a series of well-executed examples of conservation. TF

□ Fisker, Kay, and Millech, Knut, *Danske Arkitektur strømninger 1850–1950*, Copenhagen 1951; Faber, Tobias, *Neue dänische Architektur*, Stuttgart 1968; ——, *Danske Arkitektur*, Copenhagen 1977.

Deutscher Werkbund. Founded in Munich on 9 October 1907 as an association of architects, craftsmen, industrialists, teachers and publicists, its aim was the 'ennobling of German work'. Its members conceived of work as embracing both handiwork and industrial work, which constituted the major difference between the Werkbund and the English *Arts and Crafts movement, which had served as the basis for the German group. The Arts and Crafts embodied the protestations of men such as William *Morris against the flood of flimsy, ugly, characterless objects produced by industrial methods. Morris considered the machine inappropriate for producing objects intended for everyday use. Such objects should be reserved for handiwork, so that the quality of products and of work might be re-established. The Werkbund took up this protest against an environment lacking in quality, but its founders – Hermann *Muthesius, Fritz Schumacher and Peter *Behrens – saw in the machine an improved tool which must, and could, be used to ensure that its products were also of high quality. The Werkbund took as a starting point the idea that industrial development could not be reversed.

Their efforts had a strong echo immediately, and the effect of their movement extended throughout the cultivated middle classes who suffered from the general lack of culture during this period. Industrialists and businessmen recognized the advantage that tasteful modern products could afford. In the very year of the Werkbund's foundation, 1907, Emil Rathenau, the founder of the AEG (Allgemeine Elektricitäts-Gesellschaft, or General Electric Company), chose the painter-architect Peter Behrens

Deutscher Werkbund. Model factory building by Gropius and Glass Pavilion by Bruno Taut at the Cologne exhibition (1914)

as designer for his factories, workers' estates, company graphics, and even for certain of the company's products, such as the lamps which have, justly, been considered early examples of Industrial Design. The Werkbund was also considered good for the standing of German work in the world. Friedrich Naumann, who can be considered the chief ideologue of the Werkbund in the early years, never tired of pointing this out.

Between 1907 and 1914 new developments included: factories by Behrens, *Poelzig and *Gropius; country houses by Muthesius; furniture made by the Deutsche Werkstätte für Handwerkkunst (German handicraft workshops) in Hellerau, near Dresden, as well as the Garden City of Hellerau itself (*Riemerschmid, Muthesius and *Tessenow). Also produced were railway coaches designed by Gropius, automobiles styled by Ernst Neumann and steamships with interiors by Bruno Paul. These were presented annually (from 1912) in the Werkbund's *Jahrbücher*. Their influence was immediately felt: in keeping with the activity of the Werkbund, which comprised handicraft, art and industry, the annuals also illustrated silver designs, painted glass, applied sculpture and even painting.

In July 1914, on the occasion of the first Werkbund exhibition held in Cologne, at which *van de Velde's Werkbund Theatre, Gropius's model factory and Bruno *Taut's Glass Pavilion were shown, Muthesius put out a suggestion which he hoped would overcome the duality of the Werkbund: 'Die Werkbundarbeit der Zukunft' (The Werkbund's work of the future) – the title of his discourse — should serve as the typical object, not as an individual work of art or handicraft. This suggestion provoked considerable and lively opposition within the Werkbund. Van de Velde protested in the name of free art 'against any suggestion of a canon or a standardization' and the younger members, Taut and Gropius, supported him. But the advent of World War I prevented the immediate collapse of the Werkbund. With the end of the war in 1918 came the victory of the majority in 1914 – the victory of handicraft over industrial production. In 1919 Poelzig delivered a campaigning speech in Stuttgart in which he renounced the tendency towards big business advocated by Naumann and Muthesius, and proclaimed handicraft as the goal of the Werkbund. It seemed as though the movement might be reverting to the ideology of William Morris.

Deutscher Werkbund. Weißenhofsiedlung, Stuttgart (1927)

But German industry was not devastated and the Werkbund again took up the question of industrial work; now it was essentially the social aspect which interested them, and housing and advice for the 'Existenzminimum' (minimal existence) in particular. Walter Gropius, who had founded the *Bauhaus in Weimar – the name was meant to call to mind the workshops or 'Bauhütte' of medieval cathedrals – claimed in 1926 that all men's needs were the same and that they could be better and less expensively satisfied by machine than by the hand. 'A violation of the individual through standardization is not to be feared'; Gropius and his Bauhaus were again on the path towards industry after 1922.

The Weißenhofsiedlung (housing estate) in Stuttgart in 1927 was the great accomplishment of the Werkbund in that year. Designed under the supervision of *Mies van der Rohe, it was the first of the Werkbundsiedlungen (Werkbund housing estates): that in Breslau came two years later, that in Vienna in 1932. Foreign architects were heavily involved in the Weißenhof estate: *Le Corbusier from Paris, Victor *Bourgeois from Brussels, J. J. P. *Oud from Rotterdam, Mart *Stam from Amsterdam, Josef Frank from Vienna. Even before the war, Werkbünde had been founded in *Austria and in *Switzerland, and in 1915, in the midst of the war, the Design Association was founded in *Great Britain, intended as an English counterpart of the Werkbund.

The Werkbund exhibition in Paris in 1930, which Gropius designed, had rather horrific results in terms of both doctrine and discipline. It was more an exhibition of the Bauhaus than of the Werkbund. It should not be forgotten that men like Adloph Schneck worked in the Werkbund, and that their clear and straightforward furniture designs were not indebted to the machine aesthetic of the Bauhaus. Nor should it be forgotten that others, such as Paul *Bonatz and Paul Schmitthenner, also belonged to the Werkbund.

The political transition from Republic to Third Reich witnessed a situation in which several members sought to assure their position by a cautious strategy – Mies van der Rohe belonged to this group, along with several committed National Socialists and others, such as Winfried Wendland, who joined the Party. There were also those such as Walter Riezler, who remained unswerving. The National Socialists adopted catchwords of the Werkbund, such as 'quality', 'value of work', 'meaning', 'accomplishment', but these were always qualified by the adjective 'German'. The dissolution of the Werkbund as an essentially organizational entity can be dated to 1934, although the National Socialists sought to preserve its principles in an 'Amt Schönheit der Arbeit' (Office for the beauty of work).

The Werkbund was refounded in 1947. In the first ten years of the new Werkbund, it seemed as though the old union with industry would again find validity. The German section at the Brussels World's Fair of 1957 was created by the Werkbund and revealed to an astonished world that German work had won back its high quality: this was equally true of the exhibition buildings (by Egon *Eiermann and Sep Ruf), the gardens (Walter Rassow) and the objects exhibited.

However, it also served as proof that in its campaign for 'good form' the Werkbund had been too successful. Industry thought it no longer needed the Werkbund, and the Werkbund was more severely critical of it in the context of a world faced with new requirements and new problems. This was in keeping with Werkbund tradition, and it had been the desire to re-establish the Werkbund on the basis of a simple design – or overseeing – function. But the Werkbund had in fact never been satisfied with 'good form'. In the 1960s the expression 'Tassenwerkbund' (coffee-cup Werkbund) was coined to indicate a Werkbund which could be satisfied with 'good form'. The Werkbund had never been such an organization and now it desired less than ever to become such a Tassenwerkbund. Certainly the Werkbund both before and after the war has concerned itself with our immediate environment: that of the table, bed, lamp and, by extension, the street, garden and greenery. But it is also concerned with threats to the environment, to the status quo which it wishes to maintain, with its form, its tradition and its substance. The title would now have to be changed for an essay on the activities of the Werkbund, but the essence has remained the same: it has always striven to be broader in scope than the narrow concept of an industrial culture.

The theme of the Werkbund is, in the broadest sense, that of a cultural critique. It has never been anything else. That the Werkbund should find it less simple today than in the 1920s and 1930s to imagine and define its relationship to economic forces is evident. JPo

☐ *Jahrbücher des Deutschen Werkbundes*, 1912, 1913, 1914, 1915, 1917, 1920; *Die Form*, monthly publication, 1922, 1925–34; *Werk und Zeit*, monthly publication, since 1952; *Zwischen Kunst und Industrie. Der Deutsche Werkbund* (exhibition catalogue), Munich 1975, also Berlin and Hamburg 1976; Burckhardt, Lucius (ed.), *Werkbund. Germania, Austria, Svizzera*, Venice 1977; Campbell, Joan, *The German Werkbund. The policy of reform in the applied arts*, Princeton, N.J. 1978; Junghanns, Kurt, *Der Deutsche Werkbund. Sein erstes Jahrzehnt*, Berlin (East) 1982.

Dinkeloo, John (Gerard), b. Holland, Mich. 1918, d. Fredericksburg, Va. 1981. After studies at the University of Michigan at Ann Arbor, he joined the Chicago office of *Skidmore, Owings & Merrill, where he was head of project planning, 1946–50. He began his collaboration with Eero *Saarinen in 1950 in the same capacity and was promoted to partnership in 1956. After Saarinen's death in 1961, D. took over the office, together with Kevin *Roche, and moved it from Bloomfield Hills and Birmingham, Mich., to Hamden, Conn., where, until D.'s death, it was known as Kevin Roche John Dinkeloo and Associates. In his collaboration with Roche, D. was especially responsible for the high formal value of the structural aspect of the firm's work. He was the technical innovator to whom can be attributed the introduction of synethetic rubber mouldings, metallic smoked glass and weatherproof steel in an architectural context. AM

☐ See under Roche.

Doesburg, Theo van, b. Utrecht 1883, d. Davos 1931; real name Christiaan Emil Marie Küpper. He began his career as a painter and, after conventional beginnings, broke away *c.* 1912 and investigated the formal language of Kandinsky. His contacts with Mondrian, with whom he planned as early as 1915 a journal to propagate the new ideas of *Neo-plasticism, resulted in his first neo-plasticist pictures. In collaboration with the architects *Oud and Jan Wils, he endeavoured to transfer his painting from the two-dimensional into something spatial and to connect it organically with architecture. In 1916, together with Oud, he founded the Sphinx group in Leiden, but it did not last long. One year later, he joined a group of artists and architects in De *Stijl, a movement set up to achieve a 'radical renewal of art'; he became the spokesman of the group, whose ideology was rationalist-inclined and advocated a geometric, sculptural architecture in opposition to the picturesque effects of *Expressionism and the School of *Amsterdam.

In 1917, with Oud, he designed the hall of Oud's house at Noordwijkerhout, near Leiden, in which he sought to reinforce and stress the

Doesburg. Café L'Aubette, Strasbourg (1926–8)

architecture through the medium of painting. His use of primary colours, tiled flooring and geometrical leading on the windows is in harmony with De Stijl methods. In the following years, D. was invited to lecture on the movement's activities at the *Bauhaus in Dessau and Berlin. The Bauhaus published his book on the fundamental principles of art (originally published in Dutch, Amsterdam, 1919) as the sixth of the series of *Bauhausbücher*, entitled *Grundbegriffe der bildenden Kunst* (Munich, 1924).

When the Café L'Aubette in Strasbourg was renovated in 1926–8, D. was able to realize his ideas of space and colour on a larger scale, in collaboration with Hans Arp. Moving to Paris, he built a house and studio for himself at Meudon-Val-Fleury (1929–30), which soon became the focal point of De Stijl. He renewed his collaboration with Cor van *Eesteren, with whom he had worked in the early 1920s, and turned his attention to applying the principles of De Stijl to town planning.

D.'s death in 1931 marked the end of De Stijl as a group. Although his emphasis on the primacy of the fine arts over architecture had already come under critical attack in the 1920s and had resulted in his break with Oud, the concepts of space which he helped to define remain a living issue today. JJV

□ Doesburg, Theo van, *De Nieuwe Beweging in de Schilderkunst*, Delft 1917; ——, *Drie voordrachten over de nieuwe bildende Kunst*, Amsterdam 1919; ——, *Grondbegrippen der beeldenden Kunst*, Amsterdam 1919; ——, *Klassiek, barok, modern*, The Hague 1920; ——, *L'Architecture vivante*, Paris 1925; *Theo van Doesburg 1883–1931* (exhibition catalogue), Eindhoven 1968; Balieu, Joost, *Theo van Doesburg*, London 1974.

Drew, Jane Beverley, b. 1911. Studied at the Architectural Association School, London. In partnership with J. T. Allison, 1934–9. Independent practice, 1939–45. In partnership with Maxwell *Fry (whom she married in 1942) from 1945. Early work in Kenya led to specialization in tropical architecture. She was Assistant Town Planning Adviser, West Africa, 1944–5. As well as being responsible for schools, housing and colleges in Ghana, she undertook joint work with Fry on the University of Ibadan, Nigeria. Other projects were in: Kuwait (1,000-bed hospital); India (hospitals, housing, and a large school; senior architect at Chandigarh in collaboration with *Le Corbusier); Singapore; Sri Lanka; south Persia (housing, town planning, hospital extensions, cinemas); and Mauritius (hospitals and housing). She was Beamis Professor at the Massachusetts Institute of Technology in 1961, and has lectured widely elsewhere. She retired from practice in 1974.

□ Drew, Jane, *Kitchen Planning*, London 1945; Fry, E., and Drew, J., *Tropical Architecture in the Dry and Humid Zones*, London 1966; Brockman, H. A. N., *Fry, Drew, Knight, Cramer. Architecture*, London 1978.

Dudok, Willem Marinus, b. Amsterdam 1884, d. Hilversum 1974. Trained as an engineer at the Royal Military Academy, Breda. In 1913–14 he had his own office in Leiden, and from 1915 in Hilversum, where he was also director of municipal works, 1915–27, and municipal architect from 1927. Although deriving something from both the School of *Amsterdam and De *Stijl, D. evolved an independent position of his own. The contrast of solid and void areas, horizontals and verticals, recalls De Stijl, but D.'s brick buildings nearly always retain that quality of mass and weight which also characterizes the work of Michel de *Klerk. His formal solutions also reveal the influence of Frank Lloyd *Wright. D.'s most important buildings are at Hilversum, including the Vondel School (1928–9) and the Town Hall (1928–30). He also designed Netherlands House at the

Cité Universitaire, Paris (1927–8), and the Bijenkorf department store in Rotterdam (1929–30, destroyed in World War II).
☐ Stuiveling, G., Bakker-Schut, F., et al., *Willem M. Dudok*, Amsterdam 1954.

Duiker, Johannes, b. The Hague 1890, d. Amsterdam 1935. Studied at the Technical College in Delft. From 1916 he was in partnership with Bernard Bijvoet in Amsterdam, and was editor of the journal *De 8 en Opbouw*, 1932–5. D. was an independently minded figure of the Modern Movement in Holland. In his Zonnestraal Sanatorium at Hilversum (1926–8, with Bijvoet) the geometrical strength of ★Neo-plasticism is softened by combining it with curved volumetric forms. Its generous glazing and powerfully projecting terraced roofs are not without some influence on Alvar ★Aalto's Sanatorium at Paimio (1929–33). The Open Air School in the Cliostraat in Amsterdam (1928–30), a five-storey complex with terraces for outdoor classes, is a highly transparent structure that makes free display of its concrete skeleton. The Handelsblad-Cineac Cinema in Amsterdam, completed in 1934, the year before D.'s early death, is an elegant composition of white surfaces, glass and a light metal structure, in which the influences of ★Le Corbusier and above all of Russian ★Constructivism are evident. VML
☐ Duiker, Johannes, *Hoogbouw*, Rotterdam 1930; 'Duiker 1' and 'Duiker 2', in *Forum* (Amsterdam), November 1971 and January 1972.

Duiker. Zonnestraal Sanatorium, Hilversum (with Bijvoet; 1926–8)

E

Eames, Charles, b. St Louis, Missouri 1907, d. St Louis 1978. Architect and designer. Together with his wife Ray, E. was active in almost every domain of design from toys and furniture (including the Eames Chair, 1956), to films and exhibitions. His own house at Pacific Palisades, Cal. (1949), a steel-frame building constructed from prefabricated units, is reminiscent – in its proportions and light appearance — of an old Japanese house.
☐ Drexler, Arthur, *Charles Eames* (exhibition catalogue), New York 1973.

eclecticism. The free use of elements of various styles, even within a single building. The highpoint of eclecticism was reached as an expression of ★historicism in the architecture of the second half of the 19th century. It has also played a major role in ★Post-Modernism.

Eames. The architect's own house, Pacific Palisades, Cal. (1949)

Ecole des Beaux-Arts. The Ecole des Beaux-Arts in Paris, which dates back ultimately to Colbert's organization of the Académie d'Architecture in 1671, was reorganized in 1816 and quickly became not only the most important school of architecture in *France, but by the third quarter of the 19th century the most influential such institution in the world. Although various reforms were effected, notably in 1863, the methods and philosophy of the Ecole des Beaux-Arts displayed an overall unity for some 150 years. The same teaching methods were employed until the student revolts of 1968, which led *inter alia* to the separation of the architecture section from the fine arts divisions of the Ecole des Beaux-Arts. Thus, despite often virulent internal conflicts, the Ecole came to represent a bastion of official taste and to serve as the symbol of the architectural establishment. Earlier, in the 19th century, Viollet-le-Duc had taken a polemical stance in refusing its instruction, although his own critique was sharpened after his ill-fated lectures there in 1863. Architectural manifestos and treatises – from Viollet-le-Duc to Le Corbusier – have used the Ecole as a negative postulate in defining a rational modern architecture.

If as an institution the school defended the classical tradition – and especially that of the French 'grand siècle' and the late International Baroque which had been the formative influences in its nascent period – its method was more one of abstract design principles than stylistic representation. While the classical ideal was upheld, it was subjected to considerable reinterpretation and renewal at the hands of 'rebels' turned masters from the generation of Henri Labrouste and Félix Duban in the 1830s to Charles Garnier in the 1860s and finally Tony *Garnier in the 1920s. The unifying method – belatedly codified in Julien Guadet's great four-volume *Eléments et théorie de l'architecture* (1903–5) – was the basis of design in composition, i.e. in the abstraction of the building programme into a balance between expression and formal pattern. Students were taught to conceptualize the essence of an assigned programme and then according to the rules of proportion, symmetry, axial organization, and *convenance* or typology, to find an appropriate compositional expression (*parti*).

Technically speaking, the Ecole itself did not provide practical instruction in design. It offered lectures in mathematics, perspective, stereotomy, construction, and history of architecture. Design and drafting however were taught in independent *ateliers* (studios), run by practising architects, many of whom also served as professors within the Ecole. In the *ateliers* students were prepared to compete in the monthly *concours* (competitions) set by the Académie and administered by the faculty of the school. These culminated in the renowned Grand Prix (Prix de Rome) which permitted one student a year to continue his study for several years (the number varied from three to five over the century) at the French Academy in Rome (Villa Medici) and later in Athens as well. This system, formalized by the regulations of 1819, was designed to cultivate architects to fill the prestigious governmental architectural posts which dominated the hierarchy of the profession in France.

By the late 19th century, the Ecole des Beaux-Arts counted numerous foreign students in its various *ateliers* (there were three large 'official' *ateliers* after 1863), including the Americans Louis *Sullivan and C. F. McKim (*McKim, Mead & White), as well as numerous English and German students. Even more importantly, the French Ecole served as a prototype for architectural education either by emulation – as in the earliest American architectural schools at MIT in Cambridge, Mass., or Columbia University in New York – or by critique.

If the Ecole des Beaux-Arts system came increasingly under attack at the hands of the masters of the Modern Movement, its influence remained nonetheless strong until World War II. The *Art Deco style, for instance, was in many respects a streamlined image for established compositional principles whose relation to Beaux-Arts teaching was especially evident in American examples. Even the most vehement critics of the Ecole, such as *Le Corbusier, were not totally free from its influence or methods.

A re-evaluation of the Ecole, that *bête noire* of the avant garde, might be said to have begun in the 1950s, and notably in the work of Louis *Kahn and his disciples. Kahn's formalized composition, hierarchy of spaces, and preference for sequential articulation of volumes draw heavily on the Beaux-Arts element in his own training under Paul Cret at the University of Pennsylvania. Through Kahn and Robert *Venturi the Ecole was to be re-examined not only for its formal principles, but as a particular approach to the problem of style, raised again in the context of the growing disillusionment with the *International Style in America.

A 1975 exhibition of Beaux-Arts student drawings held at the Museum of Modern Art in New York marked a watershed in historical study and architectural taste. 'Beaux-Arts' once again became a household word in Anglo-American architectural circles and its imagery and approach to representation were quickly assimilated in the eclectic catalogue of *Post-Modernism. Contemporary appreciation of the French tradition is, however, highly inflected according to architectural position and philosophy, from the self-styled defenders of an eternal classicism to the most independently spirited proponents of an imagistic and metaphorical architectural language. BB

☐ Drexler, Arthur (ed.), *The Architecture of the Ecole des Beaux-Arts*, New York and London 1975; Lipstadt, Hélène, *Architecte et Ingénieur dans la Presse; Débat-Conflit-Polémique*, Paris 1980; Egbert, Donald Drew, *The Beaux-Arts Tradition in Architecture*, Princeton, N.J. 1981; Middleton, Robin (ed.), *The Beaux-Arts and French Nineteenth-Century Architecture*, London and Cambridge, Mass. 1982 (paperback edition, London 1984).

Eesteren, Cor (Cornelius) van, b. Kinderdijk (Alblasserdam), 1897. He worked with Willem Kromhout in Rotterdam, 1914, and gained his Architectural Diploma at the Academie van Beeldende Kunsten en Technische Wetenschappen, Rotterdam, in 1917. He studied at the Hoger Bouwkunstonderwijs in Amsterdam, 1919–22; he won the Prix de Rome and spent some time at the *Bauhaus. He belonged to De *Stijl, and in 1922 met Theo van *Doesburg, with whom he formulated the architectonic principles of *Neo-plasticism. He worked under Jan Wils, 1924–7. As Architect of the Town Planning Office of Amsterdam (1929–59, after 1952 Director), he co-ordinated the city's expansion, basing his work on a plan prepared by *Berlage in 1917, which he substantially revised and enlarged. For many years he was president of *CIAM.

☐ Jaffé, Hans L. C., 'Prof. C. van Eesteren 4. juli 70 jaar', *Bouwkundig Weekblad* (Amsterdam), no. 85, 1967, pp. 213 ff.

Ehn, Karl, b. Vienna 1884, d. Vienna 1957. After attending the Staatsgewerbeschule and studying at the Akademie der bildenden Künste (under Otto *Wagner) in Vienna, he worked as official City Architect in Vienna.

In the 1920s and early 1930s he was responsible for the public housing projects in which he established prototypes for Viennese architecture of the inter-war years. His Hermeswiese (1923) was still oriented towards the English Garden City movement, while in the Lindenhof (1924) he focused more on social needs, looking especially to such Dutch examples as Michel de *Klerk's block of flats on the Vrijheidslaan (1921–2) in Amsterdam. Of E.'s subsequent buildings, the Bebelhof (1925), Karl-Marx-Hof (1927) and the Adelheid-Popp-Hof (1932) deserve special mention. In formal terms, his work bears witness to a progression

Ehn. The Lindenhof, Vienna (1924)

Ehn. The Karl-Marx-Hof, Vienna (1927)

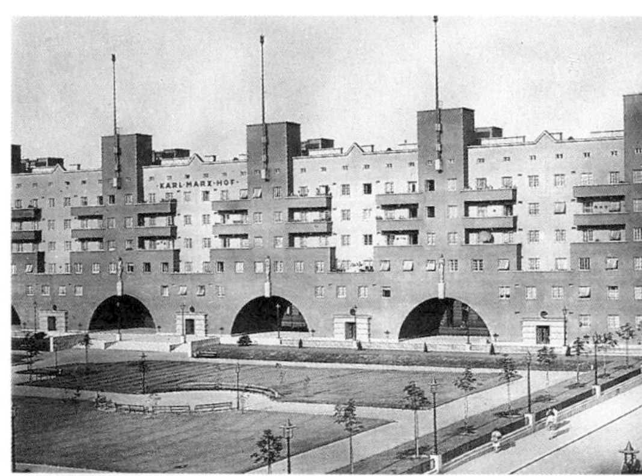

from Biedermeier-inspired stylistic elements (Hermeswiese) via a monumental *Expressionism (Karl-Marx-Hof) to a smooth cubistic compositional mode (Adelheid-Popp-Hof). After the Civil War in 1934 and to the end of the Social Democratic era in the Viennese city administration, E. found himself unable to realize anything more than a few smaller private houses. CM/KM

□ Mang, Karl, *Kommunaler Wohnungsbau in Wien. Aufbruch, 1923–1934, Ausstrahlung* (exhibition catalogue), Vienna 1977; Hautmann, H. and R., *Die Gemeindebauten des Roten Wien 1919–1934*, Vienna 1980.

Eiermann, Egon, b. Neuendorf near Berlin 1904, d. Baden-Baden 1970. In the post-war period E. became the dominant figure among architects in West *Germany during the first quarter century of the Federal Republic's existence. The example of his buildings, as well as his teaching career at the Technische Hochschule in Karlsruhe (1947–70) and his membership of numerous competition juries, assured him a degree of influence in Germany in his own lifetime comparable only to that exercised by Hans *Scharoun. E., who preferred the resilient precision of steel to the sculptural possibilities of reinforced concrete, attached tremendous importance to pronounced articulation, logical expression of the skeletal structure and clarity of detail. His buildings evoke impressions of exceptional clarity and rigid organization. For E., who also designed furnishings, the requirements of architecture were 'to make visible the order of urban planning down to the smallest structure.' Components of circulation or technology, such as stair or lift towers, heating equipment or machine shops for industrial installations (handkerchief factory in Blumberg, 1949–51), are treated as aesthetically enlivening architectural elements. In his later work, E. tended to establish a secondary outer skin of steel railings, balconies and sun screens placed in front of the building volume. Thus, even large building masses, such as the Neckermann Export Company in Frankfurt am Main (1958–61), the tower of the Bundestag (Parliament) in Bonn (1965–9) or the IBM Administration Building in Stuttgart (1967–72) were given a light, elegant, indeed cheerful character.

E. Studied at the Technische Hochschule in Berlin-Charlottenburg, 1923–7, where he was a pupil of Hans *Poelzig. He wrote a diploma

Eiermann. Handkerchief factory, Blumberg (1949–51)

Eiermann. Neckermann Export Company building, Frankfurt am Main (1958–61)

thesis on department stores and worked first in the building office of the Karstadt department store chain; from 1920 he had his own practice. Decorative screens were used in his post-war department stores for the Horten chains (Heilbronn, Stuttgart and Heidelberg), as well as in several churches, most notably the Matthäuskirche in Pforzheim and the Kaiser-Wilhelm-Gedächtnis-Kirche in Berlin (1959–63), whose existing war-damaged tower is contrasted with the simple geometry of the new building. In these church buildings, he employed coloured glazing which produces an unreal lighting effect in the interior. The dramatic contrast between old and new in the Gedächtnis-Kirche was symbolic of the post-war rebuilding of West Berlin. In his later works E. also sought to create striking architectural images through the

Eiffel. The Eiffel Tower, Paris (1887–9) with part of the site of the Exposition Universelle (1937), showing the German Pavilion (left) and, facing it, the Russian Pavilion

structure itself; the towers of the Olivetti headquarters in Frankfurt-Niederrad (1968–72) are raised on gradually widening concrete supports.

After his pavilion group at the Brussels World's Fair (1958, with Sep Ruf) E. received numerous government commissions. The new German Embassy in Washington (1959–64), an act of architectural diplomacy in its contextual discretion, won him a certain international success. WP

☐ Rosenthal, H. Werner, 'Egon Eiermann 1904–1970', *JRIBA*, January 1971.

Eiffel, Gustave, b. Dijon 1832, d. Paris 1923. After training as a chemist, he became a structural engineer almost by chance. Several years as a consultant to building firms and later as an independent consulting engineer immersed him in the problems confronting bridge designers as railway construction extended into ever more difficult territory. In his much acclaimed wide-span railway bridges, such as the Douro bridge near Oporto (1877–8) and the Truyère bridge near Garabit in the Massif Central (1880–4), E. was able to exploit the advantages of rolled steel for large-scale structures. He used this material, itself much more resistant to stress than cast iron, in the construction of three-dimensional space-frames built up from small individual members and riveted together. His structures were of fundamental significance for the modern aesthetic of reduced use of materials (as exemplified in *Mies van der Rohe's dictum 'Less is more'). His most renowned structure, the Eiffel Tower in Paris (1887–9), was built for the Exposition Universelle in 1889; the enthusiasm for the tower shown by such artists as Robert Delaunay and Fernand Léger became a reality in 20th-century architecture only in the 1930s, through the work of Le Ricolais and Konrad *Wachsmann on space structures. GHa

☐ Besset, Maurice, *Gustave Eiffel*, Milan 1957 and Paris 1959; Harris, Joseph, *The Tallest Tower; Eiffel and the Belle Epoque*, Boston, Mass. 1975; *Gustave Eiffel et son temps* (exhibition catalogue), Paris 1982.

Eisenman, Peter, b. Newark, N.J. 1932. Studied at Cornell and Columbia Universities and then in England at Cambridge University. In 1957–58 a collaborator of the *TAC team.

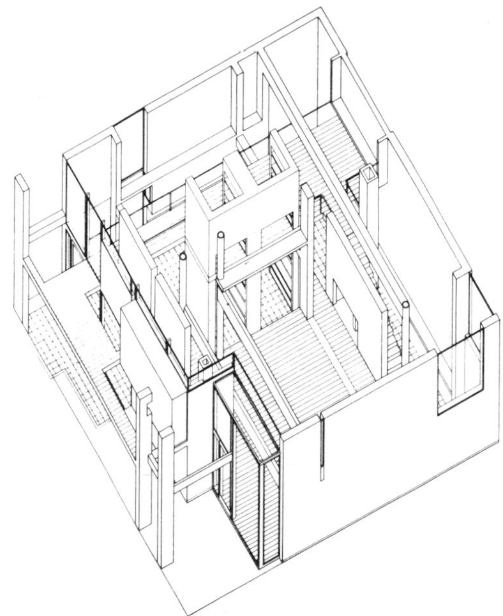

Eisenman. House I (Barenholtz Pavilion), Princeton, N.J. (1967–8)

Taught at Cambridge and Princeton Universities and, from 1967, at the Cooper Union in New York. Until 1982 he was Director of the Institute for Architecture and Urban Studies in New York, which he founded in 1967, and co-editor of the architectural review *Oppositions*. E., whose work draws especially on the Italian ★Rationalism associated with Giuseppe ★Terragni, has closely bound theory and practice in his investigation of the relationship of form and function or the meaning of form '*an sich*' (form *qua* form). His realized œuvre consists of houses which are at the same time architectural experiments and products which he numbers like abstract sculptural works or paintings, including: House I (Barenholtz Pavilion) in Princeton, N.J. (1967–8); House II (Falk House) in Hardwick, Conn. (1969–70); House III (Miller House) in Lakeville, Conn. (1969–70). A high-point in his disdain for function was achieved in House VI, built in 1972, the Frank Residence in Cornwall, Conn., with its red staircase which cannot be climbed and leads to a floor which does not exist. These constructions of complex geometrical systems are not meant to fulfil any needs; E.'s aesthetic mannerism brushes aside the client's expectations in order to criticize them. In the El Even Odd House of 1978, an 'Axonometric object' based on a background play with the representation and the reality of architecture, E. carried to its limits his radical plea for an autonomous architecture (★New York Five). VML

☐ *Five Architects*, New York 1972; Eisenman, P., *House of Cards*, New York 1978.

Ellwood, Craig, b. Clarendon, Texas 1922. He first worked for several years as an accountant and manager for a contracting firm before opening his own architectural office in Los Angeles in 1948. In order to deepen the practical knowledge he had gained, he enrolled in evening courses in civil engineering at the University of California in Los Angeles, 1949–54. Since 1976 has been active as a painter and sculptor and spends part of each year in Tuscany. E., who has built almost exclusively in steel, is known chiefly for the houses he realized from 1951 on in the context of the Case-Study programme of the journal *Arts and Architecture*. In his dependence on ★Mies van der Rohe, as well as in his structural sense and spatial organization, his work displays an uncommon elegance and reductivist discipline. Among his most important works – all in California – are the Case Study House No. 18 in Beverly Hills (1955, 1957–8), the Hunt House in Malibu (1955, 1956–7), the Scientific Data Systems Building (today Xerox Building) in El Segundo (1965, 1966), and the bridge-like Arts Center of the College of Design which spans a street in Pasadena. AM

☐ McCoy, Esther, *Craig Ellwood*, New York 1968.

Endell, August, b. Berlin 1871, d. Breslau 1925. Self-taught craftsman and architect of the German *Jugendstil* (★Art Nouveau). Member of the Munich group and art journal *Jugend* (Youth); from 1900 he was director of the Kunstgewerbeschule in Breslau. His most important works, the Elvira Photo Studio in Munich (1897–8) and the decoration of the Buntes Theater (Multi-coloured theatre) in Berlin (1901), are characterized by lively ornamentation attached to flat surfaces. In 1912 the Trabrennbahn in Berlin-Mariendorf was built to his designs.

☐ Weiss, Peg (ed.), *Kandinsky in Munich: the formative years*, Princeton, N.J. 1979, pp. 34–40; Killy, H. E., Pfankuch, P., and Scheper, D.,

Erskine. Byker housing development, Newcastle-upon-Tyne (1969–80)

Poelzig-Endell-Moll und die Breslauer Kunstakademie: 1911–32 (exhibition catalogue), Berlin 1965.

England. *Great Britain.

Erickson, Arthur (Charles), b. Vancouver 1924. Studied at the University of British Columbia in Vancouver and McGill University in Montreal, 1942–50. Active in various partnerships from 1953, and since 1977 as principal of the firm Arthur Erickson Associates, with offices in Vancouver, Toronto, Kuwait and Jeddah. Simon Fraser University at Burnaby near Vancouver (begun 1963) assumes a key position in E.'s work: it reveals the influence of *Le Corbusier, *Kahn, *Rudolph and *New Brutalism, all independently reworked and further developed in this building. The setting of the campus is particularly striking. It assumes the image of a mountain peak with its futuristic autonomous forms. With his paradigmatic use of axes, symmetries, linear rows of arcades and iconographic feeling, E. embraced theoretic positions which would only later be reclaimed by the practitioners of the *International Style. A tremendous interest in the iconographic aspect of architecture is also evident in such works as the Canadian Pavilion at Expo '70 in Osaka, the Museum of Anthropology of the University of British Columbia in Vancouver (1971–7) and the great urban-block structure of the new Justice Building in Vancouver (1973–80). In addition to large-scale public projects, E. has developed a number of simple wooden houses in the structuralist tradition of *Mies van der Rohe, in which he has not been afraid to adopt regionalist characteristics. The frequent comparison of E.'s work with that of Philip *Johnson is valid at least insofar as he has exercised as considerable an influence on the post-war Canadian (*Canada) scene as Johnson has on the American (*USA). FW

☐ *The Architecture of Arthur Erickson*, Montreal 1975.

Erskine, Ralph, b. London 1914. After study at the Quaker school in Saffron Walden, Essex (which had a lasting influence on his development) and architectural studies at the Regent Street Polytechnic in London, he moved in 1939 to Sweden, which seemed to him the promised land in which society was the leader and modern architecture was understood to be its servant. In 1944–5 he completed further studies at the Stockholm Art Academy and in the following year opened his own office in Drottningholm, which he now supervises in partnership with the Danish architect Aage Rosenvold. The determinant factors in E.'s architecture are, on the one hand, a pronounced social consciousness, and, on the other, the extreme climatic conditions of his adopted homeland. The challenge of the climate led E. to a specifically Scandinavian regionalism free from historical models. This prompted his adherence in 1959 to the precepts of Team X (*CIAM). His first important work was the Ski Hotel, Borgafjäll, Lapland (1948–50), in which the roof grows out of the ground so that under the winter snow the building is at one with the ground below. Further examples of this climatically inspired architecture are the paper factory at Fors (1950–3), the housing estates in Kiruna (1961–2) and Svappavara (1963), as well as the new town on Resolute Bay in *Canada, on which work began in 1973. E. was to receive the greatest international acclaim for his planning of the new housing development at Byker in Newcastle-upon-Tyne (1969–80), the form of which was developed in close dialogue with the residents. Drawing on his earlier concepts, he designed an immense housing scheme, up to eight storeys in height, stretching for over 1 km ($\frac{5}{8}$ mile); it features few and small window openings on the outer wall, thus protecting an inner zone of two-storey terrace houses (some 80% of the programme) from the noise of traffic on the adjacent expressway. AM

□ Egelius, Mats, 'Ralph Erskine: the humane architect', *Architectural Design* (London), 47 (1977), nos. 11/12 (special number); Collymore, Peter, *The Architecture of Ralph Erskine*, London, Toronto, Sydney and New York 1982.

Ervi, Aarne (Adrian), b. Forssa, Finland 1910, d. Helsinki 1977. Studied architecture at the Helsinki Technical Institute, and in 1935 collaborated with *Aalto; from 1938 he had his own practice. E. drew up the master-plan (1952) for the garden city of Tapiola, near Helsinki, for which he also designed and executed a number of projects (city centre and terraced housing, 1952–64; swimming hall, 1962; Tapiola Garden Hotel, 1974). Tapiola is one of the most successful of the 20th century's new towns, not least because its city centre and three residential quarters are separated one from the other by a green belt and ideally combined with the natural conditions of the site. E. also realized buildings for the University of Turku (1952–6). GHa

□ Solla, Pentti, *Aarne Ervi arkkitehturia*, Helsinki 1970.

Expressionism. Expressionist architects, like Expressionist painters, had no cultural groupings, with unified programmes and activities, and most architects who came within the ambit of Expressionism did so only for a short period of their development, although this often proved to be the zenith of their artistic careers. In the work of the best of them, the most varied outlooks and artistic influences must be recognized. It was principally a German phenomenon.

In *Germany, during the years immediately prior to 1914, the architectural avant garde consisted of men who owed their allegiance to *Art Nouveau, with its considerable inheritance from the historical styles and its general picturesqueness and a taste for organic forms, and hence we shall readily perceive the numerous connecting links with avant-garde German Expressionist movements such as Die Brücke and Der Blaue Reiter. In this context one thinks of the work of Otto Eckmann, Bernhard Pankok, Hermann Obrist, August *Endell, Joseph Maria *Olbrich, who played a key role at this period with his activities at Darmstadt, and above all of Richard *Riemerschmid with his Hellerau factory (1910) and Henry *van de Velde, for their direct influence on the architects of Expressionism.

It was Peter *Behrens who achieved the transition to Expressionism with his buildings for the AEG in Berlin (1908–13). We are not concerned here with those elements which clearly anticipated the Rationalist style. Behrens' factories were not designed with the kind of utilitarian character associated with the functional tradition, but rather as the representation of a new power, and they took on an almost representational character which, as it were, apologised for their actual function.

Apart from Behrens, only two architects before World War I were clearly distinguishable as Expressionists: Hans *Poelzig and Max *Berg. The conventional exterior of Berg's reinforced-concrete Centenary Hall in Breslau (1912–13) gives no indication of the exciting three-dimensional treatment inside the enormous dome 65 m (213 ft) in diameter. No other early reinforced-concrete building was as compelling or had as little of the schematic about it in comparison with the rich spatial treatment of this hall. Of these three architects, however, it was Poelzig who adhered most consciously to Expressionism. His large industrial complex at Luban (1911–12) seems even more unprejudiced in design than the best works of Behrens at this period. His volumes are built up of asymmetrical blocks, whose organic unity seems to underline the peculiar individuality of the design. Three years previously, Poelzig had built a large house near Breslau, where the plastic fusion of all the elements towards a volumetric continuity recalls some of van de Velde's villas of the same epoch.

Thanks to the absence of preconceived types, it was industrial architecture that offered the path of least resistance to progressive experiments at the time. This may be seen in the great structure built by Poelzig at Posen (1911), with a water-tower above and an exhibition hall below; brick is used here to clad a steel framework. The bold handling of volumes makes it one of the most significant German buildings of its day – the 'total transposition of a personal idea into a work' which Kirchner demanded as the basis for art. A series of sketches dating from this period are clearly influenced in conception by certain drawings of Oskar Kokoschka, and show a desire to model a building with an aggressive immediacy that leaves no part of its surface unmarked by its author's will.

Expressionism. Water-tower and exhibition hall, Posen (now Poznan; 1911), by Poelzig

German culture in the years after World War I became progessively more political in character. The Socialist revolution accompanied Expressionism as a form of protest for at least ten years, in an ideologically hybrid identification between cultural avant-gardism and progressive politics. Examples of this tendency may be seen in the *Arbeitsrat für Kunst and the *Novembergruppe. The latter group attracted all the foremost representatives of German artistic life in the years 1918–20; many architects were members, including *Gropius, *Mendelsohn and Bruno *Taut. Its programme accorded particular importance to architecture, regarded as a direct instrument for raising social standards. The group was dissolved after the bloody suppression of the Spartacist rising, and the ensuing disillusion among the progressive spirits of the Weimar Republic contributed decisively to the emergence of *Neue Sachlichkeit, which took up the essential ideas of Expressionism.

The *Bauhaus, too, especially during its Weimar period, absorbed many features of Expressionism: the crude pragmatism; the stark expressive simplicity; a tenacious grip on reality combined with an ethical sense of human obligation; all accord well with the School's methodological programme as also with a type of design that was a frequent outcome of Expressionist theory. It is in this light that some of the works of the protagonists of Rationalism designed at this period may be clearly explained – works carried out in a style with close affinities to Expressionism. They include *Mies van der Rohe's project for an office building in the Friedrichstraße, Berlin (1919), and his memorial to Rosa Luxemburg and Karl Liebknecht in Berlin (1926; demolished), as well as Gropius' War Memorial at Weimar (1922) and his theatre at Jena (1923).

Among the most important Expressionist buildings in Germany in the first years after the war were: in Hamburg the Chilehaus by Fritz Höger (1923–4), the Ballinhaus by the brothers Hans and Oskar Gerson (1922–4) and their Sprinkenhof (1926–8), all influenced by Fritz Schumacher; at Potsdam, the Einstein

Expressionism. Einstein Tower, Potsdam (1917–21), by Mendelsohn

Tower by Erich Mendelsohn (1917–21); and in Frankfurt the administration building of the Hoechst Dyeworks by Peter Behrens (1920–5). In the entrance hall of Behrens' building, the wall-surface features continuous punctuation by varying textures and materials, which emphasizes a feeling of unrest and instability that seems to lurk beneath the severe overall design. The brickwork is in shades which range from blue to orange and yellow, a palette which recalls the watercolours of Nolde or Kirchner. Mendelsohn, on the other hand, was influenced by the movement Der Blaue Reiter – he knew Franz Marc and Vassily Kandinsky when a student at Munich in 1911 – and his Jugendstil reminiscences derive from that source. His sketches, executed between 1914 and 1920, display the same stylistic idioms, and that character of cosmic and stylistic search and lyric effusion as an act of liberation, and at the same time the mystical union with the world that is typical of Der Blaue Reiter's spiritual posture. His use of sketches to work out his approach to a theme, without reference to structure, is typically Expressionist.

Two other architects deserve special notice: Hugo *Häring and Otto *Bartning. For Häring adherence to the Expressionist aesthetic was tantamount to a recognition of German Gothic as an anti-illuminist culture that shunned the laws of geometry and was hence organic in form (farm buildings, Garkau, 1924–5). For Bartning, however, architecture was growth and activity, the force of nature itself (Star church project, 1921–2). Poelzig's development between 1919 and 1930 is in two phases. The Großes Schauspielhaus in Berlin (1918–19) and the designs for the Salzburg Festival Theatre (1920–2) carry the process of dissolving not only

Expressionism. Office building in the Friedrichstraße, Berlin (project, 1919), by Mies van der Rohe

Expressionism. Chilehaus, Hamburg (1922–3), by Fritz Höger

Expressionism. Salzburg Festival Theatre, project (3rd version, 1921), by Poelzig

Expressionisn. The second Goetheanum, Dornach (1924–8), by Rudolf Steiner

the classic rules of composition but the very constituent elements of the structure itself to extraordinary lengths. A second phase witnesses the reassertion of volumetric values, with a severer and more monumental style, as exemplified by his designs for the IG-Farben offices at Frankfurt (1928–31) and his broadcasting studios in Berlin. Rudolf Steiner's second Goetheanum at Dornach (1924–8) is linked to Expressionism by its picturesque treatment, but occupies a place apart, as it was designed in accordance with the principles of Anthroposophy.

Under the stress of the menacing political situation in the early 1930s, the artistic forces of the time tended to crystallize into groups centring around the democratic opposition or the Nazi party. The sharpening of this crisis betokened the end of Expressionism, which by its intrinsic nature could not tolerate extreme ideological conditions, although it tended to promote and educe them. The 'white' architecture of Rationalism became a symbol of the democratic opposition, while Expressionism began to acquire pan-Germanic and nationalist traits, and in its ideological uncertainty was relegated to a position of cultural insignificance.

The School of *Amsterdam, too, whose mouthpiece was the journal *Wendingen*, displayed in its buildings parallels to German Expressionism, but was more concerned with the development of low-cost housing estates in South Amsterdam. The Expressionist character of these buildings derives from a peculiar ability to evolve an endless variety of forms, in a three-dimensional treatment that often achieves almost fairy-tale effects. VG

☐ Borsi, Franco, and König, Giovanni Klaus, *Architettura dell'espressionismo*, Genoa n.d. [1967]; Sharp, Dennis, *Modern Architecture and Expressionism*, London 1966; Pehnt, Wolfgang, *Expressionist Architecture*, London 1973.

Eyck, Aldo van, b. Driebergen, Holland, 1918. Studied at the Eidgenössische Technische Hochschule, Zurich. He was a professor at Delft Technical College (from 1967) and has held numerous guest lectureships in Europe and the USA. A member of Team X (*CIAM) from 1953, he came to an adherence to *Structuralism through his studies of the Dogon, the African tribe of the upper Niger region (Mali), where he spent the winter of 1959–60, as well as through his involvement with the archetype of the House. As co-editor of the periodical *Forum*, he became one of the movement's most influential spokesmen. In the Municipal Orphanage in Amsterdam, built 1957–60, small and large forms are developed on a quadratic frame to produce the effect of a small city. Important later buildings are the sculpture pavilion in Arnhem (1966) and the Pastoor van Arskerk church in The Hague (1970), GHa

☐ 'Aldo van Eyck. En quête d'une clarté labyrinthienne', *L'Architecture d'aujourd'hui* (Paris), no. 177. January–February 1975, pp. 14–30.

F

Fahrenkamp, Emil, b. Aachen 1885, d. Düsseldorf 1966. Received his training at the Technische Hochschule in Aachen and at the Kunstgewerbeschule in Düsseldorf under Wilhelm *Kreis. In 1919 he became a professor at the Düsseldorf Kunstakademie, and in 1939 its director. As architect to the Rheinstahl AG (Rhine Steel Corporation), 1921–3, he designed various factory and administration buildings. In 1927 he won, with A. Denecke, a first prize in the competition for the League of Nations Building for Geneva. His most elegant work is 'Shell House' (today Bewag-Administration Building, Berlin Gas & Electric Co.) on the Landwehr canal in Berlin (1930–2), a steel-frame building clad in travertine with strip front, and gently curved step-backs in both plan and elevation. FJ

☐ Hoff, A., *Emil Fahrenkamp*, Stuttgart 1928.

Fathy, Hassan, b. Alexandria 1900. Practises in Cairo, where he is head of the Architecture Faculty of the University. His attempt to reinvigorate the nearly forgotten traditional local building methods of the underdeveloped rural areas of Egypt began early on. He has employed expensive, imported techniques only when they have permitted a more effective use of existing local resources. He thus set an example, since adopted worldwide for building in a manner that is in its context at once socially, ecologically, economically, and not least aesthetically appropriate. His best-known work is the New Gourna village near Luxor, built of traditional sun-dried bricks; entangled in countless quarrels between the residents and the bureaucrats, this has not, unfortunately, proved to be an unqualified success. AM

☐ Fathy, Hassan, *Gourna: A Tale of Two Villages*, Cairo 1969; (expanded edition: *Architecture for the Poor*, Chicago and London 1973); ——, *The Arab House in the Urban Setting. Past, Present, Future*, London 1972; 'Hassan Fathy', *L'Architecture d'aujourd'hui* (Paris), no. 195, February 1978, pp. 42–78.

Fehling, Hermann, b. Hyères, France 1909. Received his training at the Baugewerkschule in Hamburg and established himself as an independent architect in Berlin in 1945. Since 1953 he has directed his office in collaboration with Daniel *Gogel, and in their own way they continue the work of Hans *Scharoun. Their architecture, which disdains right-angles in either plan or elevation, is developed anew from the ground up in each commission; the dynamic of form grows out of the almost scholastic graphic indications of functions and their interrelationships. Among their most important buildings are the Max-Planck-Institut für Bildungsforschung (Educational Research) in Berlin-Dahlem (1965–74) and the Max-Planck-Institut for Astrophysics (1975–80) and the European Southern Observatory (1976–80) at Garching, near Munich. FJ

Fehling. European Southern Observatory, Garching, near Munich (with Daniel Gogel; 1976–80)

☐ Conrads, U., and Sack, M. (eds.), *Fehling + Gogel*, Berlin and Brunswick 1981.

Festival of Britain. A national manifestation organized throughout *Great Britain in 1951, at the original suggestion of Sir Gerald Barry, to mark the centenary of the Great Exhibition of 1851. Its most important architectural expression was the exhibition laid out on the South

Bank of the Thames in London (Director of Architecture: Hugh *Casson). This was significant not only for the opportunity it afforded millions of people to see stimulating modern architecture of an almost uniformly high level of design, but because it provided an occasion for displaying the principles of townscape which had been developing and clarifying themselves over the previous years. Eschewing the formal layouts that had been usual in earlier major exhibitions, recourse was had to a subtly planned disposition of buildings and features, an exploitation of changes of level, progressively evolving views and the dramatic long-distance backdrop of the north bank of the Thames to give an exciting complexity and size that was quite extraordinary for so small a site. Of the various buildings on the South Bank site only the Royal Festival Hall by Sir Leslie *Martin remains.

Notable contributions were made by Ralph Tubbs (Dome of Discovery), Arcon (Transport), Maxwell *Fry and Jane *Drew, Edward *Mills (administration building), R. Y. Goodden and R. D. Russell (Lion and Unicorn), H. T. Cadbury-Brown (Land of Britain), Brian O'Rorke and F. H. K. Henrion (The Natural Scene and the Country), *Architects' Co-Partnership (Minerals of the Land), G. Grenfell Baines and H. J. Reifenberg (Power and Production) and Basil *Spence (Sea and Ships).

☐ Casson, H., 'The 1951 Exhibition', *JRIBA*, April 1950; Banham, Mary, and Hillier, Bevis (eds.), *A Tonic for the Nation*, London 1976.

Festival of Britain. The Royal Festival Hall (1951) by Sir Leslie Martin

Figini, Luigi, b. Milan 1903. Studied at the Milan Politecnico. Founding member of *Gruppo 7 and of the *M.I.A.R. movement. From 1929 he worked in collaboration with Gino *Pollini; their residential and industrial buildings for Olivetti at Ivrea (1934–57) figure among the masterpieces of Italian *Rationalism. However, the Church of the Madonna dei Poveri in Milan (1952–6), built on a basilican plan, seeks to evoke a mystical atmosphere of faith by way of its visible concrete frame, narrow slits lighting the nave, and the desired appearance of being raw and unfinished (*New Brutalism), thereby leading away from the principles they had earlier advocated.

☐ Gentile, Eugenio, *Figini e Pollini*, Milan 1959; Blasi, Cesare, *Figini e Pollini*, Milan 1963.

Finland. The origins of modern architecture in Finland lie in the stylistic revolution that occurred around the turn of the century. Both national and international in character, National Romanticism – further encouraged by the political pressure of neighbouring Russia on Finnish autonomy – influenced all the arts. It inspired architects also to seek the native and popular roots of Finnish architecture, which they felt lay partly in the birthplace of the Finnish national epic poem, *Kalevala*, the Karelian border country scoured by Finnish artists and architects in the 1890s, and partly in the country's medieval stone churches and castles. The resulting so-called Karelian wooden architecture found its best expressions in the Helsinki area with the Kallela studio house of the painter Akseli Gallén-Kallela in Ruovesi (1895), the house of the architect Lars Sonck on Åland (also 1895) and the Hvitträsk studio house near Helsinki (1903) by the architects Hermann Gesellius, Armas Lindgren and Eliel *Saarinen. Sonck, Gesellius, Lindgren and Saarinen were also the creators of a National Romantic architectural style using stone; the last three designed the Finnish Pavilion at the Paris Exposition Universelle of 1900, which proved to be especially important symbolically as an intellectual focal point. In the Pohjola Insurance Company Building (1899–1901) and the Finnish National Museum (1904–10) in Helsinki, both likewise by Gesellius, Lindgren and Saarinen, National Romantic motifs were manifested chiefly in details, while the overall composition drew on international movements, and especially on H. H. Richardson's style. Richardson's neo-Romanesque formal language also plays a considerable role in Tampere Cathedral (1902–7) and the Telephone Company Building in Helsinki (1905) by Lars Sonck.

Further international influence was exerted by England and by Vienna. The ideas of the English *Arts and Crafts reform movement were adopted, including a new concept of domestic life which permitted a much looser arrangement of internal spaces. Typical examples are the villas of the trio Gesellius, Lindgren and Saarinen, as well as Sonck's Eira Hospital (1905). The influence of early Viennese modernism is especially evident in the Takaharju Sanatorium (1903) by Onni Tarjanne, as well as the Suvilahti Power Plant in Helsinki (1908–13) and in the Villa Ensi (1911), both by Selim A. Lindqvist, the latter building being strongly reminscent of *Hoffmann's Palais Stoclet in Brussels.

In 1904, as a response to the competition for Helsinki Central Station, Sigurd Frosterus and Gustaf Strengell published a polemical pamphlet in which they called for an international approach and for rationalist design principles. About this time the National Romantic vocabulary lost its hold on Finnish architecture, to be replaced by an archaicizing monumentality often with a strongly symmetrical emphasis, a reflection of the country's economic prosperity in the period before World War I. Characteristic works of this period are the Hypotheque Bank (1908) and the Stock Exchange (1911) in Helsinki, both by Sonck, as well as the buildings of the Suomi (1911) and Kaleva (1913) Insurance Companies in Helsinki by Lindgren. A more modern tendency can be detected in the Wuorio Company Building in Helsinki (1908) by Gesellius, and especially in Eliel Saarinen's Helsinki Central Station (1904, 1910–14). Saarinen's large city planning projects – that for Munkkiniemi-Haaga (1910–15) and the general plan for Greater Helsinki (1917–18) – also anticipated future developments in their very modern approach to considerations of structure, traffic circulation and demography. World War I and the subsequent period of economic stagnation hindered, however, the realization of these grand schemes, and in 1923 and now unemployed Saarinen emigrated to the *USA, where he had already won second prize in the *Chicago Tribune* Tower competition.

Finland. Tampere Cathedral (1902–7) by Lars Sonck

Finland. Suvilahti Power Plant, Helsinki (1908–13), by Selim A. Lindqvist

A massive *neo-classicism was typical of Finnish architecture of the 1920s; this trend reflected, on one hand, the tight economic conditions and, on the other hand, increased Scandinavian influence, especially that of the Swede Gunnar *Asplund. Public housing was the dominant concern until the new economic

upswing at the end of the decade; the most successful projects were Käpylä Garden City in Helsinki (1920–5) by Martti Välikangas, as well as Gunnar Taucher's designs for blocks of flats in Helsinki (1926). The most important public buildings of the time were *Aalto's church in Muurame (1927), Hilding Ekelund's Art Museum in Helsinki (1928), Erik *Bryggman's Hospits Betel Hotel in Turku (1927–9), and especially the monumental Parliament Building in Helsinki (1924–31) by Johan Sigfrid Sirén.

Modernism began to penetrate Finland in 1928. As the leading architects of the time, Aalto, Bryggman, P. E. Blomstedt and Ekelund had all worked already in a reductivist neoclassical style; they thus made the transfer to a modernist camp with little difficulty. Even public opinion offered no noteworthy resistance to the new style. Because of the economic position, however, the accent of Finnish modernism – unlike the situation on the Continent and in Sweden, where prototypes were especially sought by Finnish architects – was directed not so much to housing, but rather was regarded, more than anywhere else, as a style for public buildings, which underlined the modernity of the young Republic.

Alvar Aalto immediately assumed the leading position among the modernists; his Sanatorium in Paimio (1928–33) and Municipal Lib-

Finland. Helsinki Central Station (1910–14), by Eliel Saarinen

Finland. Olympic Stadium, Helsinki (1940–52), by Lindegren and Jäntti

rary in Viipuri (1927–35; now in the USSR) are classic monuments of the Modern Movement. Other important buildings included: Erkki Huttunen's Mills in Viipuri (1931, destroyed in World War II) and church in Nakkila (1937); P. E. Blomstedt's Pohjanhovi Hotel, Rovaniemi (1935, destroyed in World War II); and Yrjö Lindegren and Toivo Jäntti's Olympic Stadium in Helsinki (1940–52). Aalto, who had from the outset been critical of the mechanistic thinking of the Modern Movement, developed a personal form of expression around the mid-1930s which led him towards *organic architecture. Great curved forms were already introduced in the auditorium ceiling of the Viipuri library as well as in the great exhibition wall of the Finnish Pavilion at the New York World's Fair of 1939. In the Cellulose Factory complex at Sunila (1935–9) he employed red brick for the first time, while in the accompanying workers' housing estate the housing groups blended harmoniously with the sloping terrain. The Finnish Pavilion at the Paris Exposition Universelle of 1937 heralded the beginning of a predominance of wood as a building material, and the Villa Mairea near Noormarkku (1937–9) represents a synthesis of all these themes.

Psychological and regionalist factors were introduced in his work at the end of the 1930s, and these were to expand considerably the vocabulary of modern architecture. A parallel line of development, which corresponded roughly to Swedish neo-empiricism, was chiefly represented by Bryggman and the Neo-romanticism of the 1940s. There was a cultural and philosophical basis for the former, while in the case of the latter the paucity of available building materials also contributed to a revival of traditional methods.

At the beginning of the 1950s there was a return to the modernist tradition, the lead being taken by Viljo *Revell in particular; an example is the industrial centre in Helsinki (1952) by Revell and Keijo Petäjä. On the other hand, Aalto introduced in the Senior Students' Dormitory at the Massachusetts Institute of Technology in Cambridge (1947–8) his 'red' period (so called for the predominant use of red brick), of which the masterpieces were the Town Hall in Säynätsalo (1949–52) and the administration building of the National Pensions Institution in Helsinki (1948–56). At the same time both Aulis Blomstedt and Kaija and Heikki *Sirén created sensitively conceived housing; the Siréns also realized notably the chapel in Otaniemi (1957), imbued with a pantheistic spirit. Aarne *Ervi came closest to Revell, and like Revell was especially interested in industrial building (Porthania Institute at the University of Helsinki, 1957).

Finland. National Pensions Institution, Helsinki (1948–50), by Aalto

The ideal experimental field for Finnish town planning in the post-war years was Tapiola Garden City, where construction began in 1953. Tapiola is the only community in which the structural principles of Saarinen's Greater Helsinki Plan of 1917–18 have been realized. As Finnish town planning had not advanced in social terms beyond the workers' housing at Sunila and the Olympic Village in Helsinki (1940) by Hilding Ekelund and Martti Välikangas, Tapiola was an important testing ground. At the same time it is the most representative application in Finland of the 'Wooded City' ideal, where the town is embedded in natural surroundings. The urban milieu of Tapiola is to a certain degree heterogeneous; but careful environmental planning eliminated this shortcoming to a large extent. The centre of Tapiola (1954–69) by Ervi is an important

Finland. Municipal Theatre, Helsinki (1964–7), by Timo Penttilä

realization of the town-planning principles of *Le Corbusier; later additions have, however, adversely affected its expressive character.

Towards the end of the 1950s the profile of Finnish architecture began to diversify. Aalto entered his white 'Baroque' period, Revell embraced geometric formalism, spiritually related to *Niemeyer's architecture; while Blomstedt remained the most prominent adherent to modernist *Rationalism. Aarno Ruusuvuori, Pekka Pitkänen and Osmo Lappo were the principal upholders of the modernist legacy in the 1960s. Although Aalto never created a 'school' in Finland, his spirit is nevertheless present in the works of Timo Penttilä (Municipal Theatre in Helsinki, 1964–7) and Reima *Pietilä (Kaleva Church in Tampere, 1966; Dipoli Students' Residence in Otaniemi, 1967). Pietilä's individualist solutions fired a lively discussion between Pietilä himself and the younger generation who had studied under Blomstedt. This touched on – among other things – the dispute which flared up in the 1960s between informal and constructive art. Out of this dispute developed a sort of constructivism in the 1970s; as the dominant strain in Finnish architecture, its goal was the creation of an anonymous and flexible architecture. It was hoped to resolve the social problems of the day, which had been aggravated by the trend towards urbanization prevalent in the 1960s. This architectural aesthetic was based on the beauty of construction and materials and on the harmony of proportions, as well as on the careful handling of details. Although several small house projects, such as the Modular System (1970–4) by Kristian Gullichsen and Juhani Pallasmaa achieved this goal, they were unable to make an impact on a building industry that relied on its own crude prefabrication systems. Several industrial buildings which were manifestations of new technologies can be seen as successful examples of this constructivism, notably the Marimekko factory (1972) by Erkki Kairamo and Reijo Lahtinen, but on the whole the architectural achievements of this constructivist period were few. One of the principal reasons was no doubt the alien nature of industrialized building methods in the context of Finnish architectural tradition.

*Post-Modernism instigated a lively architectural debate in Finland, which had an influence on architectural practice. Post-Modernism's own characteristic *historicism and its individualistic formal experiments are hardly represented in Finland, although *Pietilä's buildings might be cited in this context. Characteristic instead is a striving to enrich the prosaic and technological nature of modernism through a partial return to manual production and by the use of a wider range of materials and forms. Examples of this 'softened' modernism are the churches by Juha Leiviskä. On the other hand, noteworthy examples of the application of the most recent technology are to be found in the Training Centre for the Metalworkers'

Finland. Training Centre for the Metalworkers' Union, Teisko (1976), by Pekka Helin and Tuomo Siitonen

Finland. Valio Dairy Company administration building, Helsinki (1979), by Matti K. Mäkinen and Karina Löfström

Union in Teisko (1976), by Pekka Helin and Tuomo Siitonen, as well as in the administration building for the Valio Dairy Company in Helsinki (1979), by Matti K. Mäkinen and Kaarina Löfström. KM

☐ Wickberg, Nils Erik, *Byggnadskonsti Finland*, Stockholm 1959; Becker, Hans J., and Schlote, Wolfram, *Neuer Wohnbau in Finnland*, Stuttgart 1964; Suhonen, Pekka, *Uuta suomalaista arkkitehtuuria*, Helsinki 1967; Tempel, Egon, *Finnish Architecture Today*, Helsinki 1968; Richards, J. M., *800 Years of Finnish Architecture*, Newton Abbot 1978; Suhonen, Pekka (ed.), *Finnish architects and their work since 1949*, Helsinki 1980.

Finsterlin, Hermann, b. Munich 1887, d. Stuttgart 1973. He first studied medicine, physics and chemistry, and then philosophy and painting. He participated in the 'Exhibition of unknown architects' arranged by *Gropius in Berlin in 1919, was a member of the *Arbeitsrat für Kunst and of Die *Gläserne Kette. Close to the theosophists, he designed unreal sculptural

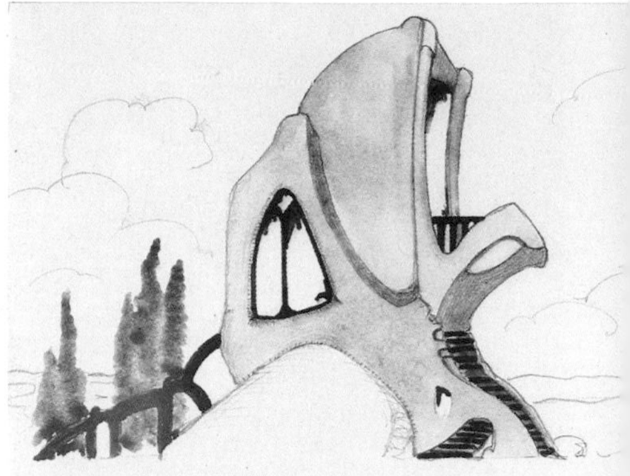

Finsterlin. Villa on the lake (project, 1918)

architecture, biomorphic form fantasies, in line with Darwin's evolutionary teachings, harbingers of a new great cultural level which would supersede the contemporary 'geometric epoch'. As a theoretician and dreamer F. was spared the conflicts with reality which his own expressionistic departures stimulated within the *Rationalist camp. After 1922 he was little concerned with architecture. Moving to Stuttgart in 1926, he subsequently worked principally as a painter and writer. FJ

☐ Finsterlin, Hermann, 'Die Genesis der Weltarchitektur oder die Deszendenz der Dome als Stilbeispiel', *Frühlicht*, no. 3, spring 1922, pp. 73 ff.; Borsi, Franco (ed.), *Hermann Finsterlin. Idea dell'architettura. Architektur in seiner Idee*, Florence 1969; Lienemann, Knut, and Weidner, H. P. C., *Hermann Finsterlin. Architekturen. 1917–24*, Stuttgart n.d.

Fischer, Theodor, b. Schweinfurt 1862, d. Munich 1938. Collaborated with Paul Wallot on the Reichstag Building, Berlin. He was active as teacher and architect in Stuttgart, Munich and elsewhere, and was a signatory of the foundation manifesto of the *Deutscher Werkbund. His work is characterized by a personal combination of classicist and regionalist formal elements, controlled restraint in decoration and the use of new building materials, such as reinforced concrete. He designed the Pfullinger Hallen in Pfullingen (1904–7), the Evangelical Garrison Church at Ulm (1911), numerous offices, schools and museums.

☐ Karlinger, Hans, *Theodor Fischer. Ein deutscher Baumeister*, Munich 1932; Pfister, Rudolf,

Theodor Fischer. Leben und Wirken eines deutschen Baumeister, Munich 1968.

Förderer, Walter Maria, b. Laufen-Uhwiesen (Canton Zurich) 1928. After working as a sculptor, he became an apprentice to the Basle architect Hermann Baur, 1954–6. Since 1966 he has held a professorship in the discipline 'Art in Construction' at the Staatliche Akademie der bildenden Künste in Karlsruhe. As a planner F. is a proponent of the attempt to achieve functionally indeterminant spaces which permit the accommodation of a variety of activities. In formal terms, his buildings are closest to *New Brutalism in their use of emphatic compositional elements and in the cubistic, sculptural development of the building mass as a response to the variegated internal spatial articulation. His architectural career began with the Hochschule für Wirtschafts- und Sozialwissenschaften in St Gallen (1957–63, with Rolf Georg Otto and Hans Zwimpfer). Subsequently his work focused principally on church design, such as St Nicholas in Hérémence, Canton Wallis (1963–71), the Church of the Holy Cross in Chur (1963–9) and the St Konrad multi-purpose centre, Schaffhausen (1968–71). In the 1970s urban renewal schemes came to the fore, and he has recently revived his interest in sculpture. AM

☐ Förderer, Walter Maria, *Kirchenbauten von heute für morgen?*, Würzburg 1964; Burckhardt, Lucius, and Förderer, Walter Maria, *Bauen ein Prozess*, Teufen 1968; *Walter Maria Förderer, Architektur und Skulptur*, Neuchâtel 1975.

Foster, Norman, b. Manchester 1935. After study at the University of Manchester and at Yale University, he founded, in collaboration with his wife Wendy and Su and Richard *Rogers, the office 'Team 4' in London, which since 1967 has practised under the name of Foster Associates. This includes eight partners in addition to Norman and Wendy Foster (Loren Butt, Chubby S. Chhabra, Spencer de Gray, Roy Fleetwood, Birkin Haward, James Meller, Graham Phillips and Mark Robertson). Along with his early partner Rogers, F. is one of the most important representatives of an architecture based on modern technology ('High Tech'). The dominating building type in his work is the great neutral space envelope, whose interior can adjust to the most differentiated functions. In contrast to *Mies van der Rohe's essential classicism, F. does not strive to elevate the mundane functional requirements into commemorative monuments; his overall forms and details refer much more consciously to the world of machinery. Their beauty arises from precise engineering calculations, as in aircraft or industrial design. Among his most important works are the passenger terminal and administration building of Fred Olsen Lines in London (1971), the headquarters of the Willis Faber & Dumas insurance company in Ipswich (1975), whose curved glass façade harmonizes with the urban environment, the Sainsbury Centre for

Foster Associates. Willis, Faber & Dumas administration building, Ipswich (1975)

Foster Associates. Sainsbury Centre for Visual Arts, Norwich (1978)

Visual Arts at the University of East Anglia, near Norwich (1978), as well as the headquarters of the Hongkong and Shanghai Banking Corporation in Hong Kong. AM

☐ 'Foster Associates', *Architectural Design* (London), vol. 47 (1977), nos. 9/10, pp. 614–25; *Foster Associates*, London 1979; 'Recent Works of Foster Associates', *Architecture and Urbanism* (Tokyo), February 1981, pp. 43–112.

France. In a country which saw the beginnings of the Industrial Revolution several decades later than in England, the use of iron and glass in building further spurred efforts towards a classification of types and systems in architecture, a process already initiated by such methodical thinkers as Jean-Nicolas-Louis Durand and Jean-Baptiste Rondelet at the dawn of the 19th century. It was the combination of this classifying approach and newly learned lessons based on recent archaeological excavations in Greece carried out in accordance with new guiding principles – great interest was shown in polychromy and antique construction – which opened the way for works such as those of Henri Labrouste, and which led to a crisis in the *Ecole des Beaux-Arts. The Ecole was especially shaken by the reform efforts which coincided with the short-lived period of teaching by Viollet-le-Duc in 1863–4. Away from the hostile outcries of the students, this theorist persisted in his efforts to confront new technical possibilities and historical lessons, notably in the *parti pris* of 'absolute sincerity' evoked in his influential *Entretiens sur l'architecture* (Discourses on Architecture, 1863 and 1872).

The contradictions inherent in Viollet-le-Duc's doctrines were made manifest in the temporary constructions built for the Expositions Universelles of 1878, 1889 and 1900, held in Paris; in these the decorative envelopes of the buildings were ever more in open contradiction with their metal skeletons. This state of conflict was also echoed in the domestic architecture which followed the great building boom under Haussmann. Although French architects rarely attained the acuity of a *Horta in Belgium or an Otto *Wagner in Austria, in the buildings of *Guimard such as the Castel Béranger in Paris (1897–8) or in the works of the Ecole de Nancy (*Sauvage) a typological renewal was combined with a new aesthetic freed from strict adherence to historic styles.

Despite the contributions of theorists such as Auguste Choisy, whose analyses introduced a rational ordering of all architectural history (1899), and Julien Guadet, whose four-volume *Eléments et théorie de l'architecture* (1902–4) is the most complete expression of the compositional doctrines of the Ecole des Beaux-Arts, it was in fact reinforced concrete which was, at this very moment, to provide the basis for new ideas in architecture. The technical innovations of contractors such as François Hennebique, who had developed earlier contributions by men such as Joseph Monier, were soon carried further in the work of architects like Anatole de *Baudot. His church of Saint-Jean-de-Montmartre in Paris (1894–1902) and his projects for public buildings extended the spatial and technical possibili-

France. Bibliothèque Sainte-Geneviève, Paris (1843–50), by Henri Labrouste.

France. Cité Industrielle (project, 1901–4) by Garnier: harbour area and residential quarter

ties of this new material well beyond the suggestions of Viollet-le-Duc. At the same time these researches received a new impetus in the hands of engineers, including *Freyssinet, whose works became emblematic of concrete's role in modern architecture, and architects such as *Perret, whose apartment house in the Rue Franklin (1903) and garage in the Rue de Ponthieu (1906), Paris, both had concrete frames. It was, however, on an entirely different plane that young architects were to break with the educational establishment.

Unlike in *Germany, where the border area between architecture and the decorative arts provided an experimental testing ground for new ideas, the graducates of the Ecole des Beaux-Arts turned to urbanism where they sought to apply the techniques of monumental composition taught by Guadet. The generation which succeeded Tony *Garnier in Rome had the same intense curiosity for urban organization. This was true in the case of Léon Jaussely, who won the 1904 competition for the extension of Barcelona, and of Henry Prost who won second prize in the 1910 competition for the replanning of the former ring of fortifications in Antwerp. Their efforts to define the governing principles of the replanning and expansion of large cities complemented those of Alfred Agache and especially the metropolitan visions of Eugène Hénard's *Etudes sur les transformations de Paris* (1903–9), in which he sought to reconcile the new traffic requirements with the urban legacy of Haussmann's major schemes. It was at such institutions as the Musée Social, which gave birth in 1913 to the Société Française des Architectes Urbanistes, that these architects first met the partisans of housing for the working classes, who were to join in their efforts to create a convincing approach to urban planning.

In Paris, Henri *Sauvage's 'habitations à bon marché hygiéniques' in the Rue de Trétaigne (1903) and the housing which A. Augustin-Rey built in the Rue de Prague as a result of the important competition organized in 1905 by the Rothschild Foundation reflect the often difficult relations between the new social policies and a modern architecture still somewhat unsure of itself. At the same time the Association Française des Cités-Jardins, created in 1903 by Georges Benoit-Lévy, achieved little else besides a few modest suburban schemes. In addition to novel public buildings such as the Central Telephone Office in the Rue Bergère by François Le Cœur (1912) and the swimming pool on the Butte-aux-Cailles by Louis Bonnier (1912–24), the features of the new urban architecture of Paris were clarified before 1914 with Sauvage's apartment building in the Rue Vavin (1912) and with the Théâtre des Champs-Elysées (1911–13), where Perret snatched Henry *van de Velde's commission on the basis of his dual role as architect and contractor.

The effects of World War I were so rapidly felt that *Le Corbusier, who had only recently arrived in Paris, seized the opportunity offered by a still hypothetical reconstruction to propose, beginning in 1914–15, his 'Dom-ino' housing prototypes. The 'Reconstructed City' exhibition in 1916 marked the launching of a regionalist architecture which predominated during the entire inter-war period, appearing notably in the garden cities such as those at Tergnier, Longueau, Lille and Rheims, and on the outskirts of Paris, as at Draincy or Stains. With these garden cities the hygienic ideals of the pre-war years, which had won the political support of the Conseil Général de la Seine in the person of the socialist mayor of Suresnes, Henri Sellier, were continually discussed and kept alive until, having received state funding for the construction of housing under the Loi Loucheur of 1928, these ideas encountered the themes of modernism.

The principles of the new architecture were formed by the integration of the structural researches launched by *Perret and the explorations of form which set out to establish the new aesthetic 'après le cubisme', to borrow the title of the manifesto published by Le Corbusier and Amédée Ozenfant in 1918. This architecture was disseminated through the pages of the periodical *L'Esprit nouveau* ('The New Spirit'), founded in 1920, as well as in juxtaposition with foreign work in the plates of Jean Badovici's journal *L'Architecture vivante*, first published in 1923. At the 1925 Exposition Internationale des Arts Décoratifs et Industriels Modernes in Paris – where the presence of the Soviet Union's spectacular pavilion should not make one forget the absence of a Germany still subject to postwar mistrust – the only manifestos of a new architectural approach were Le Corbusier's Pavillon de l'Esprit Nouveau and *Mallet-Stevens' Pavillon du Tourisme. Their radiance was reflected elsewhere mainly in the private houses by these same two architects and by André *Lurçat and Gabriel Guévrékian, to which should be added the Maison de Verre in Paris by Pierre *Chareau and Bernard Bijvoet (1928–32) and the Villa at Roquebrune (1927–9) by Eileen Bray and Jean Badovici.

Complexes of public housing designed by modernist architects were in fact the exception. At the Cité du Champ des Oiseaux at Bagneux (1932) and the Cité de la Muette at Drancy (1934) Eugène *Beaudouin and Marcel Lods made extensive use of prefabrication. Morice Leroux's proposal for a 'skyscraper' zone at Villeurbanne, at the gates of Lyons, where Tony *Garnier realized the Quartier des Etats-Unis (1924–35), is more monumental even if bearing the stamp of a modernist idiom. It was especially the rise of tourism in the south of France which spurred the wide diffusion of modernist architecture, from Lurçat's Hotel Nord-Sud at Calvi (1930) to Chareau's Golf Club at Beauvallon (1927), or especially to Georges-Henri Pingusson's Hôtel Latitude 43 at Saint-Tropez (1933). The most important, unfettered opportunities were to be found,

France. Pavillon de l'Esprit Nouveau, Paris (1925), by Le Corbusier

France. Karl-Marx School, Villejuif (1931–3), by Lurçat

France. Maison du Peuple, Clichy (1937–9), by Beaudouin, Lods and Prouvé

France. Residential buildings on the Place de l'Hôtel de Ville, Le Havre (begun 1947), by Perret

however, in municipal patronage, the only sector where building activity was unaffected by the economic crisis. This margin of freedom was exploited by Lurçat in his Karl–Marx School at Villejuif (1931–3) and especially by Beaudouin and Lods in the Open Air School at Suresnes (1932–5) and the Maison du Peuple at Clichy (1937–9), in which Jean *Prouvé collaborated. However, as the architectural debate which was occasioned by the Exposition Universelle of 1937 demonstrated, the climate in France was more susceptible to compromise than to conflict in forms or doctrines. The appearance in the 1930s of a 'third way' between classicism and modernism, marked by the launching of the journal *L'Architecture d'aujourd'hui*, is particularly evident in the architecture of Michel Roux-Spitz.

The preparations for post-war reconstruction begun by the Vichy government (1940–4) resulted in a triumph, as clear as it was short-lived, for a more sober form of modernism and especially for regionalism. After the war, however, the decisive factor was the direct intervention of the authoritarian state in urbanism and architectural patronage. The reconstructions of Le Havre by Perret, of Maubeuge by Lurçat, of Sotteville-les-Rouen by Lods, by Pingusson in the Saarland, and Le Corbusier's wanderings from La Rochelle-Pallice to Saint-Dié and from Marseilles to Strasbourg – all these are examples of that centralized state patronage which fostered the widest dispersal of prototypes of functionalist buildings and urban forms. As a result of these immense undertakings, which were continued from the mid-1950s in the 'Grands Ensembles' and the 'Zones à Urbaniser en Priorité', industrialized construction reached a level in France unparalleled elsewhere. Yet the success of Modern Movement architects did not in practice open the doors of the *Ecole des Beaux-Arts to new ideas. This deficiency in architectural education, which was made worse by the paralysis of the architectural press, accounts for the feeble success of the following generations to develop a doctrinal debate. It was rather in the open fields of opportunity in Tunisia, Morocco and Algeria that *Zehrfuss, Michel Ecochard, Pierre-André Emery, Roland Simounet, Louis Miquel and Georges *Candilis set about renewing modernist orthodoxy. Candilis was a leading light in France of Team X – born of the crisis within *CIAM – whose ideas were developed by him, together with Alexis *Josic and Shadrach *Woods, in the new town project for Toulouse le Mirail (1962, 1964–77). In such individual approaches as those of Jean Dubuisson, André Wogenscky, Edouard Albert, Raymond Lopez or Emile *Aillaud, formal researches and curiosity in technology exist side by side without ever being integrated. Le Corbusier continued his series of Unités d'habitation and forged an influential change in style with Notre-Dame-du-Haut at Ronchamp (1950–4) and Sainte-Marie-de-la-Tourette at Eveux-sur-l'Arbresle (1957–60), while Jean Prouvé pursued his researches into a light-metal architecture, and Paul Bossard explored industrialization in an entirely personal manner at Créteil (1959–60, 1961–2).

In the 1960s, the urban utopias of Paul Maymont and Yona *Friedman bore witness to an escapist desire entirely foreign to the more prosaic adventures of the generation involved in the 'multi-disciplinary teams' such as the Atelier de Montrouge (Pierre Riboulet, G. Thurnauer, Jean-Louis Véret and Jean Renaudie) or the Atelier d'Urbanisme et Architecture (A.U.A.; Paul Chemetov, Maria Deroche, Georges Loiseau, Jean Perrottet, Jean Tribel, Valentin Fabre, Jacques Allégret). These teams produced the finest buildings of French *New Brutalism for municipal clients in the suburbs of Paris. The launching of the Villes nouvelles in

France. Notre-Dame-du-Haut, Ronchamp (1950–4), by Le Corbusier

France. Town centre, Ivry (1970–8), by Jean Renaudie

France. Housing development at Saint-Ouen (1980) by Paul Chemetov

the Paris region in 1965 marked the re-animation of that state building policy which had been inaugurated earlier in a series of Prefectures, with notably mediocre results. It is nonetheless here that one must seek the anchoring point of the new themes which emerged from the crisis of 1968.

The real turning point in the debate and in architectural culture in general was indeed marked by a crisis in education and in the architectural profession; the principal consequence of this was the reconstitution of the intellectual fundamentals of training and practice and a greater receptiveness in France to the international architectural debate. The works of the A.U.A. – from the urban plan for the satellite town of Grenoble (1968) to the housing built in the Paris region – and Jean Renaudie's work at Ivry (1970–8) coincided with new efforts on the part of the state and numerous architects to create cities formed of the simple multiplication of industrialized cells. These 'innovative' schemes were soon widely applied in the Villes nouvelles. Towards the mid-1970s, this spurred a reaction, much influenced by Italian ideas, amongst such architects as Bernard Huet or Antoine Grumbach, who advocated an architecture based on urban values. At the same time the debate over industrialization was relaunched with the propositions of Alain Sarfati and Bernard Hamburger, while the cunning and patience of Paul Chemetov succeeded in by-passing some of the closed systems which dominated the housing market.

Despite the success of Renzo *Piano and Richard *Rogers in the competition for the Centre National d'Art et de Culture Georges Pompidou in Paris (1971–7), the role of foreign architects in France remained marginal, as it had done throughout the century, if one excepts several isolated works such as those of Adolf *Loos (Tzara House, Paris, 1926), Theo van *Doesburg (Van Doesburg House, Meudon-Val-Fleury, 1929–30), Alvar *Aalto (Maison Carré, Bazoches-sur-Guyonne, 1956–9), Marcel *Breuer and Pier Luigi *Nervi (UNESCO Headquarters, Paris, 1953–8), or Josep Lluis *Sert (Fondation Maeght, Saint-Paul-de-Vence, 1959–64).

While architectural politics provided foreigners with few openings – the *succès de scandale* of Ricardo *Bofill remains a spectacular exception – it has, under the cultural pressure of the 1970s, given rise to a new generation – notably Henri Ciriani, Henri Guadin, Yves Lion and Christian de Portzamparc – who, despite stylistic divergences, share the same concern for maintaining cultural values and an interest in the existing urban fabric into which an individual building is to be inserted. JLC

☐ Giedion, Sigfried, *Bauen in Frankreich. Eisen und Eisenbeton*, Leipzig 1929; Ginsburger, Roger, *Frankreich*, Vienna 1930; Dormoy, Marie, *L'Architecture française*, Paris 1938; 'La Contribution française à l'évolution de l'architecture', *L'Architecture d'aujourd'hui* (Paris), nos. 46/47, 1953; Piccinato, Giorgio, *L'architettura contemporanea in Francia*, Bologna 1965; Besset, Maurice, *Neue französische Architektur*, Stuttgart 1967; Evenson, Norma, *Paris. A Century of Change, 1878–1978*, Berkeley, Cal. 1979; *Architectures en France. Modernité, post-modernité* (exhibition catalogue), Paris 1981; Roncaylo, Marcel (ed.), *La Ville d'Aujourd'hui. Croissance urbaine et crise de la cité*, Paris 1983; Architecture d'Aujourd'hui (ed.), *Guide d'Architecture en France, 1945–1983*, Paris 1983.

Freyssinet, Eugène, b. Objat, Corrèze, 1879, d. Saint-Martin-Vésubie, Alpes-Maritimes, 1962. Pursuing his technical studies, F. graduated from both the Ecole Polytechnique and the Ecole des Ponts et Chaussées in Paris, where Charles Rabut, one of the pioneers in the use of reinforced concrete, first directed his attention to this new building technique. He worked in public administration in Moulins, 1907–13, and from 1918 to 1928 was Director of the Société des Entreprises Limousin in Paris, in which city he opened his own engineering office in 1928.

F. was one of the most important pioneering advocates of pre-stressed concrete. The fact that this process requires smaller cross-sectional surfaces for the installation of the spanning cables than is required in loosely-stretched reinforced-concrete construction led – in both bridges and buildings – to lighter, more economic constructions and thus to the slender and elegant forms of modern engineering constructions. As both constructor and designer, F. relied much more on his own instinct than on mathematical calculations. In this regard he should be grouped with the other reinforced-concrete designers: *Maillart, *Nervi, and *Torroja. He himself claimed as the basis of his work a perception of facts and an intuition controlled by experience which was enhanced by a sense of responsibility and daring.

Already in his early bridges of the Moulins period (bridges over the Allier near Le Veurdre and near Boutiron) he had begun to move away from conventional techniques; although still built of compressed concrete, the bridges were boldly conceived and executed.

Later, F. built several reinforced-concrete aircraft hangars, as at Istres, Bouches-du-Rhône (1914) and at Avord, Cher (1916). The experience gained there prepared him for the two dirigible hangars built at Orly (1916–24, destroyed 1944). Here he used reinforced-concrete arches – only 9 cm ($3\frac{1}{2}$ in.) thick – with a profile determined by the stress lines of a catenary arch. These were joined in a regular

Freyssinet. Airship hangar at Orly (1916–24)

Freyssinet. Bridge near Plougastel (1925–30)

corrugated pattern to lend them longitudinal rigidity. Thus the supporting construction and the form-giving infill created an architectonic unity. Although the very large hangars were devoid of artistic ambitions, they expressed harmony, stability and clarity simply by their size. In the locomotive depot at Bagneux (1929) F. perfected the technique of thin shell construction to an even greater degree. From 1933 on, he was involved with large-scale applications of pre-stressed concrete: he built the substructure of the Gare Maritime at Le Havre (1935), the Beni-Bahdel Dam in Algeria (1935–40), the runway of Orly airfield (1946), the rectangular water tower (capacity 7,000 m^3) at Orléans (1948), and the subterranean Basilica of St Pius X at Lourdes (1958; with Pierre Vago). In addition to the earlier bridges, F. was responsible for, among others, those at Tonneins-sur-Garonne (1922), Saint-Pierre-du-Vauvray (1922–3), Plougastel (1925–30), Luzancy (1941–5) and Esbly (1946–50), as well as the Saint-Michel bridge in Toulouse (1959), all most impressive in formal appearance.

Incessant research, practical adjustment, a consistent handling of materials and a rare ability as a designer enabled F. to achieve in his œuvre a complete unity of structural needs and aesthetic expression. WK

☐ Freyssinet, E., *Une Révolution dans les techniques du béton*, Paris 1926; ——, 'Une Révolution dans l'art de bâtir. Les constructions précontraintes', *Travaux*, November 1941; Günschel, Günter, *Große Konstrukteure. 1. Freyssinet – Maillart – Dischinger – Finsterwalder*, Berlin, Frankfurt am Main and Vienna 1966; Fernandez Ordoñez, José, *Eugène Freyssinet*, Barcelona 1978.

Friedman, Yona, b. Budapest 1923. After studying in Budapest and Haifa (Israel), he worked as an independent architect before going to Paris in 1957 in order to devote himself entirely to research on urban planning. In 1958 he founded the Groupe d'Etude d'Architecture Mobile (GEAM) which also included Frei *Otto, Werner Ruhnau and Eckhard Schulze-Fielitz, among others. Since 1956 F. has pursued the idea, highly influential on the utopian urbanism of the 1960s, of dissecting the city into a permanent primary structure – the infrastructure – and a changeable secondary structure. He imagines the primary element as a spatial supporting structure suspended above the ground, the secondary features being the inserted infill elements whose development would more than ever before involve the users in the shaping of their environment. The generalized 'Ville Spatiale' (1959), which F. designed to demonstrate his 'mobile architecture', was soon followed by more concrete projects such as 'Paris Spatial' and 'Tunis Spatial' (both 1960), as well as Bridge-City over the Ärmel Canal (1963). Since the 1970s he has been chiefly concerned with build-it-yourself methods and simple technologies. AM

☐ Friedman, Yona, *L'Architecture mobile*, Brussels 1968; ——, *Les Mécanismes urbains*, Brussels 1968; ——, *Pour une architecture scientifique*, Paris 1971; ——, *Alternatives énergétiques*, Saint-Jean-de-Bray 1982.

Fry, Edwin Maxwell, b. London 1899. Studied at the Liverpool School of Architecture. Worked 1924–34 in the firm of Adams & Thompson; was in partnership with *Gropius 1934–6, and with Jane *Drew 1945–50; practised as Fry, Drew, Drake and Lasdun, 1951–8, and subsequently as Fry, Drew and Partners. He retired from practice in 1973. A pioneer of modernism in Great Britain, he shows – in his Sun House, Frognal, Hampstead, London (1934–5) – his debt to *Mies van der Rohe, while his Kensal House housing scheme at Ladbroke Grove, London (1937; in collaboration) was the nearest British pre-war approach to a Continental *Siedlung*. In 1936 he collaborated with Gropius on the design for the progressive Impington Village College, Cambs., and in the following year collaborated on the *MARS plan for London. From 1942, with his wife Jane Drew, he worked extensively in West Africa and specialized in tropical architecture and design problems. He worked as a town planner in West Africa 1943–5, and was a senior architect at Chandigarh in collaboration with *Le Corbusier, 1951–4.

☐ See under Drew.

Fuller, Richard Buckminster, b. Milton, Mass. 1895, d. Los Angeles 1983. Not an architect in the usual sense of the word, but instead a unique reflection of those 20th-century concepts related to the machine aesthetic. His formal education was sketchy and did not progress much beyond two years at Harvard, 1913–15. In 1927 he perfected a kind of 'machine for living in' which he called the 'Dymaxion [dynamic plus maximum efficiency] House'. In contrast to the poetic expressions of the machine age which were so frequently manifested in the buildings of the 1920s in Europe, and especially in *Le Corbusier's Villa Savoye (1929–31), F.'s product was a machine for living in in a literal rather than in a metaphorical sense. Unlike the contemporary masterpieces of European *Rationalism, the Dymaxion House was not in any consequential way an object for aesthetic contemplation, but is more correctly viewed as an assemblage of mechanical services in conjunction with living areas. In 1933 F. developed a motorized version of this idea in his 'Dymaxion Three-Wheeled Auto'.

Subsequently, he devoted much time and effort to the art of structures, and these studies led to his Geodesic Domes, structures of metal, plastic, or even of cardboard based upon octahedrons or tetrahedrons. He came to use the domical shape not for a traditional, architectural reason – not for instance, because it was an 'ideal' form – but because of its natural efficiency in providing the greatest space enclosed in relation to the surface area of the enclosing form. In their use of standardized parts, these Geodesic Domes are, in a sense, the most recent descendants of the assembly techniques that were first employed by Sir Joseph Paxton in the Crystal Palace, London, 1851. The largest of these domes to be erected was the repair shop for the Union Tank Car Co., Baton Rouge, La. (1958), with a diameter of 117 m (384 ft), a span that exceeds those of the mammoth 19th-century exhibition halls. F.'s best-known dome is without doubt the one for the U.S. Pavilion at the World's Fair in Montreal (1967).

He also produced a structural system known as Tensegrity Structures (a contraction of Tension Integrity), spatial skeletal structures utilizing distinct elements in compression and tension rods, whereby the tension rods are joined together only via elements in compression.

Understandably more popular with students than with the established elements in the architectural profession, F. enjoyed notable success as a visiting lecturer in various architectural schools in the USA, among them Cornell, Massachusetts Institute of Technology, Princeton University and Yale University. He held a professorship at Southern Illinois Institute of Technology, 1949–75, and was an indefatigable author and promoter of his ideas. JMJ

☐ Marks, Robert W., and Fuller, R. B., *The Dymaxion World of Buckminster Fuller*, Garden City, N.Y. 1973 (first pub. 1960); McHale, John, *R. Buckminster Fuller*, New York 1962; Rosen, Sidney, *Wizard of the Dome. R. Buckminster Fuller, Designer for the Future*, Boston 1969; Meller, James (ed), *The Buckminster Fuller Reader*, London 1970; Robertson, Donald W., *Mind's Eye of Buckminster Fuller*, New York 1974.

Fuller. Dymaxion House (project, 1927)

Fuller. U.S. Pavilion at Expo '67, Montreal (1967)

Functionalism. Architectural principle according to which the form of a building is to be derived from the function it is intended to fulfill; the schematic and technological aspect of architectural modernism (*Rationalism), whose wider theoretical stance comprises also philosophical, political, social, economic, stylistic and symbolical questions.

Functionalism in architecture remains in part the essence of the modern as opposed to the traditional. Therefore there is hardly an architectural principle which occurs with greater persistence in the history of architecture, nor one which is less appropriate to characterize any particular chronologically delimited movement. Even in palaeolithic cave dwellings and in neolithic lake dwellings form was determined by function; in Roman fortifications and aqueducts, in medieval castles, in Renaissance palaces and Baroque country houses, in 18th-century warehouses, in residential architecture of the 19th century and office skyscrapers of the 20th, there is a close relationship between form and function. Functionalism is as old as building itself.

Parallel to that, the theoretical basis of Functionalism also goes back to the beginnings of architectural theory: thus, Vitruvius insisted that the form of a structure must be derived from its intended use. Functionalist postulates reappear from then on, above all in the rationalist treatises of the 18th century by Carlo Lodoli, Marc-Antoine Laugier and Francesco Milizia. In the 19th century it was above all Viollet-le-Duc, Gottfried Semper, Henri Labrouste and Julien Guadet who advocated a close and realizable relationship between form and function in architecture.

Louis *Sullivan is considered the founder of 'modern' functionalism. In his 1896 essay 'The tall office building, artistically considered', he coined the maxim 'form follows function'. He was building on the thoughts of the sculptor Horatio Greenough, who had introduced the notion of a dialectic between form and function in objects such as a frigate, in which design considerations were dictated by exposure to extreme physical conditions. Although Sullivan drew parallels with 'circling eagles' and open apple blossom, his expression was soon restricted in meaning to scarcely more than 'naked functionality' in the view of Functionalism.

Thus restricted, the concept of Functionalism was to be used as the slogan for the most varied directions in avant-garde architecture during the first half of the 20th century: from the romantic *organic architecture of *Wright to the classicist *Rationalism of *Mies van der Rohe, from the lively *Expressionism of *Mendelsohn to the severe monumentalism of *Terragni, from the independent formal play of *Häring to the strong geometries of *Le Corbusier. Sharper contrasts are hardly imaginable, and the bitter dispute between Häring and Le Corbusier alone makes evident the inappropriateness of such generalizing classification.

The matter is further complicated by the fact that in the architectural discussion of the 1920s, Rationalism and Functionalism were highly disputed as to both meaning and relationship. However, after Alberto Sartoris was persuaded by Le Corbusier to change the title of the book he had originally planned in 1932 to call *Architettura razionale*, it was published instead as *Gli Elementi dell'architettura funzionale*; thus, the concept of Functionalism entered everyday parlance as a synonym of or even a replacement for Rationalism. Hence, his meaning was restricted, and he thus aligned himself with that very architectural movement that was least functionalist. If the term can still be used justly to describe the 'organic' houses by Häring, which tried to attribute to each function its own specially formed corner, it is hardly also appropriate in relation to a building by *Gropius or Mies van der Rohe. Indeed, function is practically the last factor which determined the eminently symbolic form of the Fagus Factory or the Barcelona Pavilion. Their implications are far more complex and the first aspect to be sacrificed is precisely that usefulness on which their reputation had been founded. With regard to the inadmissible conflation of Rationalism and Functionalism, the words of Le Corbusier, that great apologist of engineers, and admirer of the Blériots, the *Aquitania* and the Bugattis, should not be forgotten: 'Architecture is the masterly, correct and magnificent play of masses brought together in light . . . cubes, cones, spheres, cylinders or pyramids are the great primary forms which light reveals to advantage . . . [they] are *beautiful forms, the most beautiful forms.*' (*Vers une architecture*). PB/VML

☐ Zurko, E. R. de, *Origins of Functionalist Theory*, New York 1957; Banham, Reyner, *Theory and Design in the First Machine Age*, London 1960; Posener, Julius, *Anfänge des Funktionalismus. Von Arts and Crafts zum Deutschen Werkbund*, Berlin, Frankfurt am Main and Vienna 1964; ——, 'Kritik der Kritik des

Funktionalismus', *Arch* + (Berlin), vol. 27 (1975).

Futurism. In 1909 the Italian writer Filippo Tommaso Marinetti published the 'Manifeste du futurisme' in the Paris newspaper *Figaro* and announced 'We affirm that the world's magnificence has been enriched by a new beauty: the beauty of speed.' With that the central concern of Futurism was formulated as a reaction to the decadent and symbolic bourgeois art of the fin-de-siècle. To this was joined a polemically advanced break with the past, an emotionally intoned machine culture, activism, and a fascination with world-scale war. Futurism remained almost entirely confined to *Italy, and soon dried up after entering the service of Fascism. The ideas it propagated, however – often in a bombastic, spectacular, and propagandistic way – were to bear fruit throughout the international avant garde.

The Futurist movement, which counted writers, painters, sculptors, architects, stage designers, musicians, and film-makers among its members, had already put forth elements of an individual architectural theory with the publication of Umberto Boccioni's 'Manifesto tecnico della scultura futurista' (1912) and with Marinetti's essay 'Lo splendore geometrico e meccanico nelle parole in libertà' which appeared in early 1914 in the periodical *Lacerba*. With Antonio *Sant'Elia's entry into the movement and the publication of the manifesto 'L'architettura futurista' in *Lacerba* (1 August 1914), Futurism also became officially established in the field of architecture.

The manifesto was nothing other than a version, slightly lengthened, by Marinetti of a text which had appeared several weeks earlier under Sant'Elia's name (and with his thoughts) in a catalogue of an exhibition held in Milan of the young non-futurist group of artists 'Nuove Tendenze', although it had been originally written by Ugo Nebbia (who had edited the catalogue) and was later entitled 'Messaggio' (as opposed to 'Manifesto'). Next to the furious rejection of all past norms, an architecture was advocated which would employ new materials; which was expressive and artistic; which gave preference to diagonal and elliptical lines (these were supposed to be more emotionally charged); which renounced ornament; which found its inspiration in the world of machines; which accepted no preconceived design maxims; which would bring the environment into harmony with the new man; which would be light, perishable and dynamic so that every generation can, and must, build its own city. These propositions took account of new scientific and technological developments and accorded extensively with the Futurists' demands for the other arts: the 'preference for lightness, usefulness, ephemeralness and speed' is evidently derived from Boccioni's theory of 'dinamismo plastico'. Thus an unresolved contradiction was introduced into the movement's architecture, which is confirmed by comparing the texts with Futurist architectural drawings: if the first encouraged a simultaneity, speed, and temporariness, the latter displayed a monumental architecture which radiated most effectively, for all its innovative potential, an expressive modernist classicism.

Futurism. Città Nuova (project, 1913–14) by Sant-Elia

In reality the manifesto served as a courageous theoretic document which engaged Italy in the European architectural discussion; otherwise it remained, simply, potent rhetoric. Along with Sant'Elia, Mario *Chiattone, his lifelong friend, entered the Futurist movement. Somewhat later, they were joined by the architect Virgilio Marchi. But in 1915 Italy entered World War I – thanks in part to the interventionism of, among others, the Futurists, of all people – and the following year Sant'Elia lost his life on the front. No important Futurist work was ever built. Apart from the manifestos – to which were added: Marchi's 'Manifesto dell'architettura futurista; dinamico, stato d'animo drammatica' (1920, in the avant-garde publication *Roma futuristà*); *Architettura Futurista*, published only in 1924 although written for the most part in 1919; and somewhat later *Italia nuova, architettura nuova* (1931) – it was only the virtuoso drawings of these three men which bear architectural witness to this short episode.

Fourteen years passed before Futurist architecture again became a live issue in the context of the search for an artistic identity for young Italian fascism. In 1928, in Turin, the painter and journalist Fillía (Luigi Colombo), one of the most convinced followers of Futurist ideas, mounted the first (and last) 'Mostra di architettura futurista'. The work of artists of very different origins was exhibited. Architecture was represented by Sant'Elia, Chiattone, Alberto Sartoris, Virgilio Marchi, Enrico Prampolini, Nicola Diulgheroff and Fortunato Depero. The only architecture, apart from the exhibition building itself, actually to be built, was by Sartoris; it was in any case a classic example of Italian *Rationalism and had nothing to do with Futurist principles. But Fillía retained his faith in the possibility of a Futurist architecture as an official state style and pursued his goal in the various publications which he edited or launched to this end (*La Città futurista*; *La città nuova*), in articles and books (*Arte fascista*, 1928; *La nuova architettura*, 1931). The Futurist aesthetic witnessed both its coronation and its conclusion in the 'Mostra della rivoluzione fascista' (Exhibition of the Fascist Revolution) in Rome in 1932. Largely organized by architects, painters and graphic artists, who for the most part had their origins in Futurism, this exhibition was the only artistic manifestation under fascism, which demonstrated a historical connection with the rest of Europe, but Futurist sentiment was already merged with Rationalist, Expressionist or even neo-classicist notions.

Likewise the few buildings which appeared under the banner of Futurism in the 1920s were scarcely to be distinguished in their formal language from those of Rationalism or the Novecento Italiano. This is as true for Duilgheroff's 'futurist villas' in Turin and Albisola as for Depero's Bestetti-e-Tumminelli pavilion at the Biennale in Monza of 1927 or Prampolini's pavilion for the 'Mostra di architettura futurista' in the Parco del Valentino, Turin (1928). In fact the significance of Futurism resides less in its direct production than in its deep influence. Its principles influenced nearly the entire European and American avant garde of the early 20th century. It was Italian Futurism which served as a starting point for Soviet *Constructivism; even an individualist talent such as *Le Corbusier's was in no small measure indebted to Sant'Elia and Chiattone, and even to such little-known Futurists as Guido Fiorini and his 'grattacielo in tensistruttura' (1933). Finally, even to this day the entire 'Internationale' of technological Utopia, from R. Buckminster *Fuller via *Archigram to *Piano, *Rogers, and *Foster, continues to feed on the bold visions of Futurism. GV/VML

□ [Sant'Elia, A.], 'L'architettura futurista', *Lacerba* (Florence), 1 August 1914; Arata, Giulio Ulisse, 'L'architettura futurista', *Pagine d'arte* (Milan), II, 1914; Marchi, Virgilio, *Architettura futurista*, Foligno 1924; Marinetti, F. T., Prampolini, E., and Escodamé, *Sant'Elia e l'architettura futurista mondiale*, Milan 1931; Sartoris, A., *Sant'Elia e l'architettura futurista*, Rome 1944; Banham, Reyner, 'Futurismo and Modern Architecture', *JRIBA*, Feb. 1957; Gambillo, D., and Fiori, T., *Archivi del futurismo*, Rome 1958; Taylor, Joshua C., *Futurism*, New York 1961; Clough, Rosa, *Futurism: the Story of a Modern Art Movement*, New York 1961; Apollonio, Umbro (ed.), *Futurist Manifestos*, London and New York 1973.

G

Gardella, Ignazio, b. Milan 1905. Studied at the Politecnico in Milan and at the Istituto Universitario di Architettura, Venice, where he later taught. In contrast to the other architects of his generation, he did not have recourse to any social or aesthetic ideologies for the genuine *Rationalism displayed in his first works. His designs were characterized by elegance and purity of composition, in a lyric vein which he used to provide magisterially free and simple solutions to the most complex problems.

He began his career with interior decoration and rebuilding schemes, notably the renovation of the theatre at Busto Arsizio (1934) and an extension of the Villa Borletti in Milan (1935), which established his reputation. Soon afterwards came his finest work to that date, 'an outstanding example of Italian rationalism' (Mazzariol): the Anti-tuberculosis Dispensary at Alessandria (1936–8). In this building the most interesting lines of G.'s architecture are defined: clarity in the handling of plane surfaces and a judicious use of materials as a means of expression. In this connection, the extensive employment of brick to face a reinforced-concrete building shows G.'s tendency to respect local traditions – and this at a time when such respect was hardly common.

The Dispensary was the first and most significant of G.'s many architectural activities in Alessandria, where his most important works were built, including the Provincial Laboratory for Hygiene and Prophylaxis (1937–9), and a block of flats for employees of the Borsalino company (1951–3), in which he tried, by an interesting play of movement on the elevation and the emphatic use of projecting eaves, to go beyond a purely 'rationalist' scheme. In 1946, in a block of flats he designed at Castana, particular emphasis was laid on an attempt to reinterpret regional and traditional elements in a modern idiom. Little by little, this characteristic was to lead G. a long way from his initial standpoint, with his architecture diverging from the tenets of strict Rationalism. He returned to the 'rationalist' manner with the annexe for the Museum of Modern Art in Milan (1953).

Gardella. Flats for employees of the Borsalino Company, Alessandria (1951–3)

Thereafter, however, he achieved – as in the Casa alle Zattere, Venice (1957) – a light, playful synthesis of sensible, functional forms and regional traditions. GV/GHa

☐ Argan, G. C., *Ignazio Gardella*, Milan 1959; Rossi, Aldo, 'Ignazio Gardella', *Architecture and Urbanism* (Tokyo), December 1976.

Garnier, Tony, b. Lyons 1869, d. La Bédoule 1948. Studied at the Ecole Nationale des Beaux-Arts in Lyons and in Paris at the *Ecole des Beaux-Arts and in the atelier of Julien Guadet. Awarded the Prix de Rome, he spent the years 1899–1904 in Rome; he was city architect of Lyons, 1905–19, and continued there afterwards in private practice.

During his years in Paris, he moved in the socialist circles of Jean Jaurès and Emile Zola, increasingly radicalized by the Dreyfus affair. Subsequently, his studies at the Villa Medici in Rome were focused less on historical buildings than on the preparation of one of the most important projects of 20th-century architecture: the Cité Industrielle. He addressed himself to the theme of an industrial city because he was convinced that such was to be overwhelmingly the trend for new cities in the new century. He selected a terrain half-flat and half-hilly in a river valley, which setting, although hypothetical, was in practice similar to that of his home town, Lyons; he even included a medieval settlement in his planning. For a population of 35,000 (scarcely greater than in *Howard's Garden City), G. envisaged a residential quarter, city centre, industry, a railway station and all the requisite public buildings; he omitted, however, barracks, police stations, prisons and churches, all of which he considered would be unnecessary in the new socialist society. He decided that the buildings would be primarily in reinforced concrete, even though at the time only a handful of experimental structures had been built by this method. He thus presented a revolutionary urban vision, which already contained in essence the fundamental planning principles of the Modern Movement: clear distinction between various functions – residence, work, recreation, and transportation; division of vehicular and pedestrian traffic, with a further distinction between through and local traffic corridors; decentralized layout, though based on an urban grid system to guarantee orientation and still permit expansion; 'residential islands', each 30 × 150 m (approx. 100 × 500 ft), without interior courtyards but surrounded by green space equal to at least 50 per cent of their area. In addition, he projected traffic-free, generously planted pedestrian paths; a community centre which not only anticipated in its programme the social centres of modern housing estates, but bore on its façade – and not by chance – two quotations from Zola's utopian socialist novel *Travail*; a completely equipped sports ground with a stadium for 20,000 spectators; and finally, a novel canal system.

Taking this global vision as a starting point, G. immersed himself with equal profundity and creativity in the architectonic, constructive and technological detail of his plan. He developed formal elements which took the greatest advantage of the possibilities of reinforced concrete: strip windows, glass walls, *pilotis*, projecting canopies, open ground-plans, and roof terraces. With these means he projected: a modernistic railway station with subterranean platforms and tracks; clearly disposed factories and workshops; a single-level, practically organized school on an open site; a hospital composed of easily surveyed pavilions; small residential blocks and loosely divided single-family houses of elegant cubic simplicity and with well-organized plans. Everything, even down to technical innovations such as electric heating systems and temperature controls (for the economy of the Cité Industrielle was to be based on the availability of inexpensive electricity), was precisely set out in the accompanying texts.

For all his innovative powers, G. did not conceive his project in a vacuum. Not only was he influenced by the Rationalism of his teacher Guadet, but he also drew on the experiments of the pioneer of reinforced concrete, François Hennebique, as well as on the progressive urban planning ideas of his contemporaries Léon Jaussely and Eugène Hénard. He by no means rejected tradition, which he had imbibed during his Beaux-Arts training and on a trip to Greece in 1903. In fact, the residential quarter of the Cité Industrielle is represented as an arcadian-meridional garden city with clear classical formal reminiscences; and the community centre is nothing but a modern interpretation of a roofed agora, under whose reinforced-concrete peristyle people in Biedermeier-like dress stroll about like ancient Greek citizens.

The Cité Industrielle, of which the plans were exhibited in 1904 and published in 1917, was, despite limited public response, rapidly taken up in progressive architectural circles. Both its overall planning concept and the architectonic types influenced the entire Modern Movement. Its influence on *Le Corbusier, for instance, was substantial; he published parts of the Cité Industrielle in the journal *L'Esprit nouveau* in 1920 and later in his book *Vers une architecture* (1923). G.'s planning principles were reworked theoretically by *CIAM and accord with the later *Athens Charter.

Almost immediately after completing the plans of the Cité Industrielle, G. was given an opportunity to realize some of the ideas embodied there. In 1905 the newly elected reform-minded mayor of Lyons, Edouard Herriot, appointed him city architect, with a brief to take over the 'Grands Travaux de la Ville de Lyon'. Between 1909 and 1913 he built the Abattoirs de la Mouche, a slaughterhouse complex centred around a huge open hall, the interior of which, with its exposed steel struts and glazed roof, recalls the Galerie des Machines in Paris (1899) by Ferdinand Dutert and Victor Contamin; the smoke stacks were formed as simplified columns which narrowed towards the top. The Olympic Stadium was built in 1913–16, the Grange-Blanche Hospital with its 22 pavilions in 1915–30, and the 'Les Etats-Unis' residential quarter between 1924 and 1935. In all of these executed works G. needed to look no further for ideas than the solutions already worked out in the Cité Industrielle. VML

□ Garnier, Tony, *Une Cité industrielle. Etude pour la construction des villes*, Paris 1917, 1932;

Garnier. Abattoirs de la Mouche, Lyons (1909–13)

Badovici, Jean, and Morance, A., *L'Oeuvre de Tony Garnier*, Paris 1938; Veronesi, Giulia, *Tony Garnier*, Milan 1948; Pawlowski, Christophe, *Tony Garnier et les débuts de l'urbanisme fonctionnel en France*, Paris 1967; Wiebenson, D., *Tony Garnier. The Cité Industrielle*, New York 1969.

Gaudí, Antoni, b. Reus, Catalonia 1852, d. Barcelona 1926. Coming from a family of coppersmiths, G. began his architectural studies in Barcelona at the age of seventeen and graduated in 1878. He felt little attraction for the official courses, whereas, during his years as a student, he was an assiduous frequenter of the philosophy classes of Llorens i Barba and the lectures on aesthetics by Pau Milà i Fontanals. In his youth Milà i Fontanals had lived in Rome during its romantic period, where he had moved in the circle of the Nazarenes, Friedrich Overbeck and his fraternity. As in many places in Europe, there was in Catalonia – which had always maintained a certain degree of cultural and political independence in Spanish history – a romantic movement, the Renaixença; this was concerned with Catalan language and poetry, as well as the medieval history and architecture of the region. The Spanish *Modernisme which developed from this movement towards the end of the 19th century had a decisive influence on G.'s imagination, and led him to a veneration of craftwork and the honesty of medieval art; to a mechanistic logic inspired by Viollet-le-Duc's conception of medieval architecture; and to nature as a source of inspiration, not only for decorative details but for structures as well. In this context he also concerned himself with the ideas of the *Arts and Crafts movement, with which he came into contact through the agency of his patron, the textile manufacturer Güell.

In 1878, shortly after graduating, he designed the Casa Vicens, in Barcelona, a building suggestive of Islamic prototypes with its stepped prismatic blocks, its alternations of stone and brick, and its brilliant decoration in polychrome tiles. Constructed as it was at a period when revivalism was in full flood, it had the merit of belonging to no known style. An important feature of the interior was the modulation of indirect light, something that was to be as much part and parcel of his architecture as was his use of mosaics and of polychromy. A milestone in G.'s artistic development was the Palau Güell, Barcelona (1885–9), where his structural experiments – the use of parabolic arches is the most evident one – create a personal style, which formed the basis of his complete liberation from *historicism.

Gaudí. Palau Güell, Barcelona (1885–9)

In 1883 G. was commissioned to continue the work on the Church of the Sagrada Familia in Barcelona, a building of great size that was progressively to monopolize his activities, but which remains unfinished even today. A neo-Gothic design by Villar was already in existence; this G. abandoned, but the lines of the apse, the first part he built, still contain many Gothic reminiscences, although the mouldings and decorative details are drawn much more closely from nature.

Work on the Sagrada Familia continued with the Nativity façade of the east transept. This consists of three open portals between four interpenetrating square-based towers, set diagonally, which rise to a height of 107 m. (350 ft) and terminate in thin, curved, circular features crowned by a piece of capricious play with intersecting surfaces, covered in mosaic. A complex and lively world, modelled for the most part by G. himself and comprising an

Gaudí. Church of the Sagrada Familia, Barcelona (1883–1926)

immense variety of plants and animals, throngs the great concavities below the gables.

Henceforth, as in the Casa Batlló in the Paseo de Gracia, Barcelona (1905 7), natural and organic forms no longer simply comprise a kind of ornament superimposed on the building, but go on to constitute essential structural elements, as in the case of the bone-shaped columns, the undulating façade covered with polychrome mosaics like a sheet of sea-water set on end, and the imbricated roof like an armadillo's back. This type of effect is a transitional one between the sculptural plasticity of G.'s earlier years (1878–91), and the structural type characteristic of his later period.

This structural plasticity has as one of its chief features the system of design used by G. for the Colonia Güell Church at Santa Coloma de Cervelló, near Barcelona (1898–1914), which was planned by means of a string model representing the structural ribs of the building, from which were hung weights proportional to the loads which each member would have to carry. The catenaries formed by these strings gave the inverted shape of the building's columns. It permitted a type of vaulted structure without buttresses of any kind, since all thrusts are taken up by suitably inclined pillars. This method was later used in designing the naves of the Sagrada Familia.

In the Güell Park, Barcelona (1900–14), G. made systematic use of inclined supports for retaining walls and bridges. An important feature in this park is the abundant employment of ceramic and glass mosaic, which presents an extraordinary ensemble of powerfully expressive abstract compositions.

The Casa Milà (1905–10), called *la Pedrera* (the quarry), is perhaps G.'s most original work. Plastically speaking, it constitutes a great stone structure of organic shape, with a rhythm of undulating horizontal edges, comparable to eyebrows or lips; an affinity between G.'s work and Surrealism is especially evident here. His structural masterpiece is the Sagrada Familia schools (1909), walled and roofed by undulating membranes of thin brick.

Towards the end of his career, G. asserted that the straight line belonged to men, the curved one to God. Shortly before his death he invented a system of well-nigh universal application, based on hyperboloids and paraboloids, though his designs were never purely geometrical. They always preserved a close tie with familiar living shapes: bones, muscles, wings and petals, and at other times with caves and even stars and clouds.

Because of its increasingly accentuated individualism, G.'s architecture could not serve as the nucleus of a school or following, and with the growing adherence to Modernism in the

Gaudí. Casa Batlló, Barcelona (1905–7)

first half of the century, appreciation was long postponed. Indicative of this reappraisal are two comments of Sir Nikolaus Pevsner: while he wrote in 1949 that 'Gaudí's Church of the Sagrada Familia will without a doubt be judged the most anachronistic example of the eternal southern Baroque', he concluded finally in 1957, 'He was the only genius produced by the Art Nouveau'. AC-P/GHa

☐ Collins, George, *Antonio Gaudí*, New York 1960; Brunet, César Martinelli y, *Gaudí. Su vida, su teoria, su obra*, Barcelona 1967; Sweeney, J. J., and Sert, J. L., *Antoni Gaudí*, New York 1970; Mower, D., *Gaudí*, London 1977; Collins, G., and Bassegoda, N., *The Designs and Drawings of Antonio Gaudí*, Princeton, N.J. 1982.

Gehry, Frank O., b. Toronto 1929. Studied at the University of Southern California in Los Angeles and at Harvard University. From 1953 he worked under Victor Gruen, Hideo Sasaki and William Pereira, among others, before establishing an independent office in Los Angeles in 1962. G.'s limited œuvre, comprising largely unrealized works, is neither theoretically nor formally aligned with any specific trend. After a series of interiors and shops, he built in the early 1970s a considerable number of single-family houses in which, increasingly, traditional forms are eliminated. His own house in Santa Monica (1977, 1978–9) represents a synthesis of the experiments pursued in such buildings as the Davis House in Malibu, Cal. (1970–2), the De Mesnil Residence in New York and the Spiller Residence in Venice, Cal. (both 1978–9). His house, in principle only the renovation of an existing complex, breaks out of existing tight structures and spatial boundaries in order to restructure them in multi-layered, overlapping and antithetical ways; the result evokes a comparison with the spatial stratifications of a Guarino Guarini. Evidence of G.'s ability to master large-scale composition is provided in Santa Monica Place, a complex of shops and parking facilities in Santa Monica (1979–81) which, in its relatively straightforward construction, recalls older, traditionally structured buildings. FW

☐ Nairn, Janet, 'Frank Gehry: the search for a "no rules" architecture', *Architectural Record*, June 1976, pp. 95–102.

Gehry. The architect's own house, Santa Monica, Cal. (1978–9)

Germany. In the closing years of the 19th century and beginning of the 20th the German Empire was successful in catching up with countries such as *Great Britain where industrialization had begun much earlier. This was achieved through the development of commercial trade relations, the acquisition of colonial possessions and the sudden acceleration of industrial production (steel, chemicals and electrical industries). Both public architecture and that commissioned by the growing industrial concerns reflected this ambition to count among the leading nations. A steady upward trend, even if interrupted by the Depression, freed capital to an unprecedented extent for construction, at the same time as a policy of cultivating national prestige provided the necessary aesthetic incentives. While Great Britain remained the only real economic rival, it was Paris, despite the French defeat in 1870–1, which retained unblemished its glittering role as cultural 'Capital of the Nineteenth Century' (Walter Benjamin) and thus provided the stimulus for official architectural policy. In particular the development of Wilhelminian Berlin looked to the French capital as a model. The aspirations of Schinkel and Semper to foster a new indigenous architectural style from the 'harmonious melding of the best of all periods' (Schinkel) and the incorporation of new needs, materials, and construction methods were not abandoned but, with the new interest in the associational values of certain historic styles, merely retreated into the background.

For nationalistic representation, the Gothic, which had been given a great impetus through the completion of Cologne Cathedral, as well as the 'German Renaissance' movement and finally – because of its abundant representation in German architecture – the Baroque, were all called into service. On the other hand *neoclassicism, which was stamped with reminiscences of the Wars of Liberation in 1813 and (thanks to Schinkel's pupils) had long dominated in Prussia, was still a viable alternative in the early 20th century. Architects maintained various rapports to this stylistic repertoire in accordance with the nature of building tasks. Thus, for civic buildings the Renaissance style of the bourgeois city-states seemed most appropriate, while for large official buildings, such as Parliament buildings, Law Courts, or administration buildings, Baroque prototypes were often chosen; this was also functionally appropriate, for the axially-ordered monastic and castle complexes of the 18th century had already united a variety of administrative functions. For ecclesiastical architecture the so-called 'Germanic' Style, i.e. Romanesque and Gothic, was codified for the Protestant part of Germany in the ten theses of the Eisenach Regulations of 1861. These relationships were either negated or enhanced by regional traditions and landscapes. Thus, 19th-century *historicism had at its disposal rather differentiated architectural means whose complicated rules in the end came increasingly to compromise the very understanding they were meant to engender. The tendency of the late 19th century towards richness, exuberance, and encrusting of forms resulted in an *eclecticism which increasingly obscured the possibilities for entirely new demands: there were in fact no historical prototypes for factories, modern transport facilities and large-scale apartment houses.

The entire social structure was also transformed by advancing industrialization. Between 1882 and 1907 the proportion of the population employed in agriculture and forestry dropped from 43 to 29 per cent, while the percentage employed as labourers and in services rose accordingly. As a result, the rapid growth of population was almost exclusively in the cities and the new industrial regions along the Rhine and in the Ruhr, in Central Germany and Upper Silesia. An unprecedented rise in the demand for inexpensive housing and the liberalization of the property market caused the price of land to rise rapidly and led to densely populated 'Miethaus' (barracks) quarters, in contrast to the prevailing type of artisans' dwelling in England, the terrace house. The catastrophic living conditions that resulted were hardly improved through the first reform efforts of co-operative or cottage housing. The problem of housing continued until well into the 20th century to be an unresolved preoccupation of politicians, architects and that new breed which was itself born in the late 19th century: urban planners. These unmastered problems stood in great contrast with the tremendous organizational efforts and investments that went into tramways and railway construction, sewers and electrification, and even into the beautification of public streets and squares.

While Paris offered the model for the grandeur of a capital city, the impetus for a practical approach to achieving more comfortable housing and reasonable living conditions came from England. In 1902 the German Garden Cities Association was founded on the British model, and realized its first noteworthy scheme at Hellerau, near Dresden. Hermann *Muthesius, who had worked as an attaché in the German Embassy in London, studied the English country house and sought to introduce some of its qualities in Germany. Both Richard *Riemerschmid and Peter *Behrens launched their architectural careers with their own houses. This narrowness was not intended as a denial of the problem, since the residential reform was not to be determined by popular taste, but rather, as Henry *van de Velde expressed it, from the 'ethos of the most intimate of man's possessions', i.e. the ethos of his own home. The Exhibitions on the Mathildenhöhe in Darmstadt (from 1901), which consisted mainly of such individual homes, were thus by no means private, but rather public events of considerable significance.

Unlike the situation in *France or *Belgium, *Art Nouveau (*Jugendstil* in Germany) was dominated, at least in architecture, by a sense of proven solidty and of honesty in the expression of materials and functions. The inner convictions of the *Jugendstil* continued thus to flourish even when the outward signs of the new style had withered. Enterprises such as the Vereinigten Werkstätten (United Workshops) in Munich, the Werkstätten für Handwerkskunst (Workshops for Handicraft) in Dresden, and above all the *Deutscher Werkbund – founded in 1907 and to which the most important *Jugendstil* artists belonged – carried these ideas

Germany. The Buntes Theater, Berlin (1901), by August Endell

further. The departure from the *Jugendstil* was indeed much easier in Germany, for no German architect had so thoroughly subscribed to the aims of the style as had *Horta in Brussels, *Mackintosh in Glasgow, *Gaudí in Barcelona, or *Guimard in Paris. August *Endell's buildings, the most ingenious creations of German *Jugendstil* in architecture, remain principally decorative art, in which three-dimensional architectural elements are subordinate to attached two-dimensional surfaces. The Belgian van de Velde built too late in Germany to have any significant influence on architectural developments there. Already *c.* 1910 other models, such as the Empire and Biedermeier styles, were adopted, as the *Jugendstil* had been, to help counteract historicism. They inspired a 'bürgerliche Sachkunst' (Muthesius: a bourgeois matter-of-fact art) in housing and interior design, while Behrens and other designers of industrial buildings employed a monumentalized neo-classicism for their great factory and administration building commissions.

These various tendencies were summarized, on the eve of World War I, at the Werkbund Exhibition of 1914 in Cologne. Beside the representative festival buildings by Behrens and *Hoffmann and the theatre endowed by van de Velde with the most generous flowing lines of late Art Nouveau, two buildings pointed to the future: Bruno *Taut's pavilion for the German glass industry and the model factory by Walter *Gropius. Both buildings featured an expressively exaggerated use of materials, glass and steel, and reinforced concrete, respectively. Thus the comparatively new materials were now translated from utilitarian buildings to public architecture. The firm Wayss and Freytag, having acquired patents from Joseph Monier, developed reinforced concrete into an innovative undertaking. Germany witnessed technical novelties of international importance with the reinforced-concrete dome of Max *Berg's Jahrhunderthalle (Century Hall) in Breslau (1912–13) and the shell structures of the 1920s and 1930s.

World War I and its unfortunate consequences for the countries of Central Europe caused stylistic discussions as well as experimentation with new materials and technologies to be pushed into the background for the duration. Shortages of building materials, spiralling building costs and the high cost of credit combined to hinder the building trades from taking advantage of the inflationary conditions of the first post-war years. The housing shortage inherited from the 19th century became even more critical. Architecture was synonymous with the administration of shortages. In this situation of urgency, which was at the same time a period of political hope, the avant garde dreamed of utopias, which ran the gamut from new schemes for town and country to cosmic visions. Nearly all the architects who played an important role in the 1920s went through an Expressionist phase: Bruno Taut, around whom a whole circle of younger artists and architects assembled (*Gläserne Kette), his brother Max *Taut, Erich Mendelsohn, Hans *Poelzig, Ludwig *Mies van der Rohe (in his glass-tower designs and the memorial to Karl Liebknecht and Rosa Luxemburg in Berlin; 1926), and Walter Gropius (in the War Memorial in Weimar; 1922).

For the *Neues Bauen group the *Bauhaus became a kind of high school, first in Weimar, later at Dessau, which was accompanied by a series of other important schools in Frankfurt, Berlin, Breslau, and at Burg Giebichenstein. Although the educational principles were established at the Bauhaus and although its school buildings in Dessau became exemplary models for *Rationalism in Europe, the real test of the Modern Movement took place in the major cities, with Berlin at the centre. Since the new zonal plan which Martin Mächler had presented in 1920, and due to the activities of the *Novembergruppe and the *Arbeitsrat für Kunst, a sense of creative activity prevailed in

Germany. Glass tower (project, 1921–2) by Mies van der Rohe

Germany. Memorial to Karl Liebknecht and Rosa Luxemburg, Berlin (1926), by Mies van der Rohe

Berlin; this was not confined to the individual buildings, but encompassed a town-planning concept. Berlin's housing estates, with their rows of buildings set in green surroundings, still bear witness to this spirit even today. The Weißenhofsiedlung (1927) at Stuttgart was in large measure disputed by Berlin architects, who, despite stylistic and conceptual differences, had formed the association known as the *Ring. Their secretary was Hugo *Häring, who, together with *Scharoun, represented the organic version of the new architecture.

The new architecture spread its tendrils from Berlin. Its principal outposts were represented by Bruno Taut, who for a while served as City Architect in Magdeburg; Ernst *May, who built the 'Vororttrabanten' ('suburban satellites') in Frankfurt and advocated the industrialization of building; and Otto *Haesler in Celle and Kassel. Contacts with the *Netherlands and with *France strengthend the avant garde. Mies van der Rohe's German Pavilion at the World's Fair in Barcelona (1928–9), a subtle composition of flat, space-creating planes, as well as numerous buildings of the Prussian state, reveal that this architecture was also beginning to be recognized as representative of the young Republic.

The position of the new 'objective' architecture was by no means undisputed. In North Germany, where Fritz Schumacher created the foundations for a regional plan that went beyond the limits of civic design, architects felt at home with an architecture that was based on the local tradition of building in brick and preserved its expressive character somewhat longer. Just as this was characterized in the North as a sort of de-sentimentalized local art, so in the South similar efforts to preserve local features were launched by the Stuttgart school around Paul *Bonatz and Paul Schmitthenner and in Munich by the liberal Theodor *Fischer and the conservative German Bestelmeyer. Politically, these architects were more receptive to the ideology of National Socialism than were the adherents of the 'Neues Bauen', who found their success in the middle-left governments of certain cities and provinces.

The coming to power of the National Socialists marked a sudden end for the new architecture. The Bauhaus was disbanded, and architects such as Gropius, *Hilberseimer, *Breuer, Martin *Wagner, Mies van der Rohe, Mendelsohn, May and *Meyer emigrated. In contrast to Italian Fascism, National Socialism would tolerate virtually no modern architecture. The official style would be modernized neo-classicism, the formulation of which was largely the work of the Führer's 'erster Baumeister', Paul Ludwig Troost. He was succeeded by the young Albert *Speer, a pupil of the respected Heinrich *Tessenow. Speer's plans and the colleagues he installed in the 'Führerstädten' and regional 'Gauhauptstädten' foresaw a monumental remodelling of the most important German cities, a process in which Hitler personally played a part. Aside from official state and party buildings, a regionalism was purveyed which looked back to the conservative architecture of the Weimar Republic and even further to its antecedents before 1914. Only in industrial buildings was a functional, prefabricated architecture still possible; this gave rise to a sort of internal emigration.

The *tabula rasa* after 1945 was complete. German architecture of the 1920s had been able to look back to pioneer work done before World War I; after World War II there was no tradition that could be immediately resumed or revived. It was a necessary but laborious process to investigate the accomplishments of the 1920s, without ever reaching the formal and social qualities of that decade. Up to that point, the upper hand had been held by conservative elements, whose representatives had made great compromises in order to co-operate with the Third Reich. Now, the emergency situation was far worse than that of 1918: the need for housing in West Germany alone was estimated in 1948 at 6·5 million units and in 1960 still stood at 1·3 million. Building production in the 1960s and early 1970s, impressive in quantitative terms, showed a yearly average of more than 500,000 units, in peak years over 600,000 housing units. At first the tendency was to concentrate on the hasty, and often bad, rebuilding of the cities and on the state-sponsored estates of single-family homes. When problems of traffic circulation and building maintenance became evident, attention was turned to more concentrated satellite towns, at first extending horizontally, as in the case of the Neue Vahr in Bremen (1957–62), then in chains of apartment towers such as the problematic 'Gropiusstadt' (1960, 1964–75) and the Märkisches Viertel (1962, 1963–74), both in Berlin. Nearly every major German city would in time have a Märkisches Viertel of its own.

In the meantime, growing prosperity fostered the massive renovation of inner-city areas. Administration and other service functions acquired the most expensive sites and forced increasing numbers of residents into the outer neighbourhoods. Attempts were made to set aside compact areas for offices, such as in Hamburg (City Nord) and in Frankfurt (Niederrad), but as single-function areas they remained unhappy solutions and even in these

Germany. The Märkisches Viertel, Berlin (1962–72), by Hans Müller, Georg Heinrichs and Werner Düttmann

cities they were not successful in counteracting the pressure of change which was exerted on the inner cities. With the change of direction from wholesale redevelopment to smaller-scale, fragmentary renewal schemes and construction in the context of the existing urban fabric – a trend which developed in the late 1970s – a different kind of expulsion process arose: cheap inner-city housing was now replaced by expensive property.

Since 1960 the legal basis of construction in the Federal Republic has been the Bundesbaugesetz (Federal Building Code); this replaced the reconstruction laws of the various *Länder* with their sometimes more favourable planning provisions. The scandal of profits arising from land speculation and planning decisions persisted. The social responsibility of property ownership established by the constitution (section 14 of the Basic Law) was as haphazardly respected in reality as the more far-reaching provisions of the Weimar Imperial Constitution of 1919 had been. Indeed, in the case of the cities, one must wonder whether the paucity of planning instruments has not proven for the worst.

The architecture of the German Democratic Republic (East Germany), which accorded much greater powers to its planners, of whom the most important was Hermann Henselmann, provides the negative response to this question. Monotony and an absence of standards were even more dominant in the East through the absolute priority accorded to industrialized building production which after *c.* 1955 succeeded an academic formalist phase. The second segment of the Stalinallee (later Karl-Marx Allee) in East Berlin – the first had been begun in 1952–8 as a closed urban space – was continued in 1959–65 with prefabricated elements and in a series of independent building blocks. This was a prelude to the compulsory industrialization of construction in order to achieve economic housing throughout the country. Neither in the East nor in the West did an intelligent and useful simplification of the procedure result; rather, a rigid and flat building technique continued to dominate.

With the advent of international competitions in West Germany in the 1950s, architects began to orient themselves to the architectural standards of the *USA, which in turn had been decisively shaped by the German émigré architects. Both Gropius and Mies van der Rohe

Germany. Phoenix-Rheinrohr A.G. administration building (Thyssenhaus), Düsseldorf (1957–60), by Hentrich, Petschnigg and Partners

received German commissions. For the 'Interbau' exhibition in Berlin of 1957 leading architects of the Western world were invited to design a model inner-city quarter. In keeping with the then reigning doctrines, this merely resulted in a collection of individual buildings set in green surroundings. Rectilinear steel-and-glass cubes, such as the North American office buildings which *SOM had developed under the influence of Mies van der Rohe, were seen as testimony to a regained respectability both in the West and – although slightly later – in the East. Important public buildings in East Berlin, such as the Staatsratsgebäude (1962–4) or the Palast der Republik (1973–6) by Heinz Graffunder and others, were no longer in the prevailing reinforced-concrete idiom, but were built rather as slender steel-skeleton structures.

In West Germany this architecture of crisply cut profiles and hung façades was purveyed by Otto Apel, Helmut Hentrich and Hubert Petschnigg, Friedrich Wilhelm Kraemer, Egon *Eiermann and many others. In contrast, Hans Scharoun and his school, especially in Berlin, represented an architecture of free groundplans and individualistic forms. Characteristic of Scharoun's work are the Philharmonic Hall (1960–3) and the Staatsbibliothek Preußischer Kulturbesitz (Prussian State Library; 1967–78), situated in the cultural complex on the southern edge of the Tiergarten; as clear evidence of the achievements of the free world, they are symbolic rivals to communist East Berlin's Stalinallee and city centre. Scharoun's lead has been followed by a narrow faction with Hermann *Fehling and Daniel *Gogel at the head.

In the field of ecclesiastical architecture, Dominikus *Böhm, Rudolf *Schwarz, Emil *Steffan, Dieter Oesterlen and others continued into the 1960s to produce works of calculated simplicity and sculptural directness. It was precisely in this area that a triumph of emotion could seek to compensate for the pervading sadness of the environment by means of strongly expressed individuality in church design. Gottfried *Böhm's great space-creating sculptures in reinforced concrete demonstrate just how much freedom ecclesiastical and official patrons were prepared to grant architects in extreme cases.

Among the relatively small group of internationally recognized successes in German postwar architecture are the sports buildings in the Olympic Park in Munich (1967–72), in which Günter *Behnisch and his partners adopted the tent principle developed by Frei *Otto. The contemporary scene is no more unified in Germany than in other countries. Megalomaniac projects and Brutalist (*New Brutalism) megastructures no longer command respect; instead a respect for urban preservation ('urban repair') has gained support, and conservation issues can be relied upon to produce a surprisingly large public response. At the level at which prestigious new commissions are awarded, the liberal, open buildings of Behnisch and his partners stand in contrast to the severely ornamented historicism of Alexander von Branca; Ludwig Leo's designs derive from particular functional requirements of any situation and contrast with the projects of an architect such as Josef Paul *Kleihues, who works largely within the Prussian tradition.

O. M. *Ungers has achieved an international reputation, his reputation being founded almost entirely on his teaching activity and his morphological studies; only recently – after a break of nearly ten years – has he attracted commissions again. History as a source of architectural inspiration has gained a new prestige, be it as a signpost to the archetype or as a source – especially for a whole group of younger architects – for a wide variety of quotations.

Germany. Church of St Bonifatius, Aachen (1962–4), by Rudolf Schwarz

Germany. The DLRG Building, Berlin-Spandau (1969–71), by Ludwig Leo

Germany. Lightweight umbrellas by Frei Otto at the Bundesgartenschau, Cologne (1970–1)

Amidst this contradictory panorama, a number of structures primarily determined by technological considerations serve as examples for the minimizing of expense and the continuity of research: Fritz Leonhard's television tower (1956) in Stuttgart, with an elegance unequalled by any of its successors; bridges, including the inclined cable types, a German speciality; halls and other large enclosed spaces using lightweight construction, in which Frei Otto has been a pioneer. The economy of means is a lesson of which architecture will have increasing need in a period of dwindling resources. WP

□ Müller-Wulckow, W., *Deutsche Baukunst der Gegenwart* (3 vols.), Leipzig 1925–8; Herrmann, Wolfgang, *Deutsche Baukunst des 19. und 20. Jahrhunderts*, (pt I) Breslau 1932, (pts I and II) Basle and Stuttgart 1977; Schumacher, Fritz, *Strömungen in deutscher Baukunst seit 1800*, Leipzig 1935; Hatje, G., Hoffmann, H., and Kaspar, K., *New German Architecture*, London 1956; *Planen und Bauen im neuen Deutschland*, Cologne 1960; *Neue deutsche Architektur 2*, Stuttgart 1962; Pehnt, Wolfgang, *Neue deutsche Architektur 3*, Stuttgart 1970; Huse, Norbert, *'Neues Bauen' 1918 bis 1933*, Munich 1975; Nestler, P., and Bode, Peter M., *Deutsche Kunst seit 1960, Architektur*, Munich 1976; Petsch, Joachim, *Baukunst und Stadtplanung im Dritten Reich*, Munich 1976; Klotz, Heinrich, *Architektur in der Bundesrepublik*, Frankfurt and Berlin 1977; Pehnt, Wolfgang, 'Architektur', in: Erich Steingräber (ed.), *Deutsche Kunst der 20er und 30er Jahre*, Munich 1979; Bofinger, Helge and Margret (eds.), 'Architektur in Deutschland', *Das Kunstwerk* (Stuttgart), 32 (1979), nos. 2/3.

Gibberd. Liverpool Cathedral (R.C.; 1960–7)

Gibberd, Sir Frederick, b. Kenilworth, near Coventry 1908, d. 1984. Studied at Birmingham School of Architecture, where he met F. R. S. *Yorke; in private practice from 1930. Planning consultant to several borough councils and architect and planner of Harlow New Town, G. was responsible for a wide range of buildings, including flats, housing schemes and hospitals. Notable post-war buildings were: Scunthorpe steelworks and power house (1947–9); Heathrow Airport, London (1950–69); National Dock Labour Board Offices, London (1956); Didcot Power Station, Berkshire (1964–8); Ulster Hospital, Belfast (1953–61). His prize-winning 'Crown of Thorns' design for the Roman Catholic Cathedral at Liverpool (1960–7) shows the influence of *Niemeyer's Brasilia Cathedral. His more recent work in the capital included the Inter-Continental Hotel, Hyde Park Corner (1975), and the Central London Mosque (1977) in Regent's Park.

Gill, Irving John, b. Syracuse, N.Y. 1870, d. Carlsbad, Cal. 1936. First worked in the office of *Adler and *Sullivan in Chicago; after 1896 in San Diego on his own. His early buildings are in a unified style, followed after *c.* 1906 by work in which simple geometric elements assume importance: 'the straight line, the arc, the cube and the circle, the mightiest of all lines' (Wilson Acton Hotel at La Jolla, 1908; Dodge House, Los Angeles, 1916). His whitewashed, flat-roofed asymmetrically disposed reinforced-concrete buildings, which often display no mouldings of any kind and are presented as abstract stereometric compositions, were inspired by Spanish missions in California and are markedly similar to the Cubist architecture of Adolf *Loos.

□ *Irving Gill 1870–1936* (exhibition catalogue), Los Angeles 1958; McCoy, Esther, *Five California Architects*, New York 1960; Kamerling, Bruce, *Irving Gill: The Artist as Architect*, San Diego, Cal. 1979.

Gisel, Ernst, b. Adliswill, near Zurich 1922. After training as an architectural draughtsman and studying at the Kunstgewerbeschule in Zurich, he worked under Alfred Roth, the principal proponent of the Modern Movement in *Switzerland. In 1945 he entered into partnership with Ernst Schär; since 1947 he has had his own office in Zurich. Characteristic of G.'s architecture, which is a distant reflection of *New Brutalism, are the lively collision of cubic and circular geometric forms; large, calm surfaces; and natural materials or those handled as if natural, including stone, brick, concrete and wood. Among G.'s most important works figure, besides the relatively atypical Park Theatre in Grenchen (1949–55): the Bergkirche in Rigi-Kaltbad (1962–4); the Protestant Community Centre in Stuttgart-Sonnenberg (1964–6); a residential complex with 1,800 units in the 'Märkisches Viertel' of Berlin (1965ff).); and the Gymnasium and Realschule in Vaduz, Liechtenstein (1968–73). FJ

Gisel. Gymnasium and Realschule, Vaduz (1968–73)

□ Maurer, F., and Kimmig, E., *Ernst Gisel. Bauten und Projekte*, pamphlet on the exhibition of the Württemberg section of the Association of German Architects (Bund Deutscher Architekten), Stuttgart 1966; 'Ernst Gisel', *Architecture and Urbanism* (Tokyo), August 1977; 'Ernst Gisel', *Werk, Bauen + Wohnen* (Munich), vol. 69, nos. 7/8, pp. 18–71, Munich 1982.

Gläserne Kette. In November 1919, Bruno *Taut wrote to thirteen German architects, artists and critics, suggesting that they should band themselves into a private forum for the exchange of architectural ideas, drawings and fantasies. With one exception – the critic Adolf Behne – all agreed. The group was made up of Wilhelm Brückmann, Hermann *Finsterlin, Paul Goesch, Jakobus Göttel, Walter *Gropius, Wenzel August Hablik, Hans Hansen, Carl Krayl, Hans *Luckhardt, Wassili *Luckhardt, Hans *Scharoun, Bruno Taut and Max *Taut. These thirteen were later joined by the playwright Alfred Brust, who also coined the title 'Die gläserne Kette'. At Bruno Taut's instigation, pseudonyms were used in the correspondence.

The common factor shared by the members of the group was a desire to break away from the norms of academic architecture, and many had exhibited at the 'Ausstellung für unbekannte Architekten' organized by the *Arbeitsrat für Kunst in April 1919. There was no group style, but rather a tendency to look for fundamental constructional forms taken from nature: crystals, shells, amoebae and plant forms were favoured as models for future architecture. For structural purposes, glass, steel and concrete were the favoured materials, reflecting the influence of Bruno Taut and his mentor, the glass fantasist Paul Scheerbart. Also from Scheerbart, reinforced by the Berlin Dadaists, came the wilful nihilism and infantilism which appeared particularly in the contributions of Goesch, Krayl and Bruno Taut. Most of the work of the members of the group was published by Taut in the journal *Frühlicht*.

The correspondence ran until December 1920. Several members of the group later joined the ★Ring, whose aims were more in accord with the new spirit of ★Functionalism and ★Neue Sachlichkeit. IBW

□ *Die gläserne Kette. Visionäre Architekturen aus dem Kreis um Bruno Taut* (exhibition catalogue), Leverkusen and Berlin 1963; Whyte, Iain Boyd, *Bruno Taut and the Architecture of Activism*, Cambridge 1982.

Goff, Bruce, b. Alton, Kansas 1904, d. Tyler, Texas 1982. He had his first independent office in Chicago, 1935–42, and later practised in Berkeley, Cal., 1945–6, Bartlesville, Okla., 1956–64, Kansas City, 1964–9, and Tyler 1970–82. He was a professor at the School of Architecture of the University of Oklahoma at Norman, 1947–55, and from 1948 also Dean of the school. His built work consisted mostly of houses, in which the influence of Frank Lloyd ★Wright is especially evident in the early years. G.'s ebullient individualism resulted in designs of an expressionist eccentricity. Technical calculations and emotional improvisations are often the mutually contradictory sources of his inspiration. In the Bavinger House in Norman, Okla. (1950–5), a logarithmic spiral of space is contained externally by a wall of raw sandstone, while the irregular roof, the stairs, the access bridges and the living quarters are all suspended from a central mast by steel cables. GHa

Goff. Bavinger House, Norman, Okla. (1950–5)

□ DeLong, David, *The Architecture of Bruce Goff: Buildings and Projects, 1916–1977* (2 vols.), New York 1977; *Architectural Design*, AD Profiles 16: *Bruce Goff*, London 1978; Cook, Jeffrey, *The Architecture of Bruce Goff*, London and New York 1978.

Gogel, Daniel, b. Berlin 1927. After study at the Hochschule für bildende Künste in Berlin, G. established himself as an independent architect in his native city, and since 1953 he has worked in partnership with Hermann ★Fehling.

Gollins, Melvin, Ward Partnership. Partnership established in 1947 by Frank Gollins, James Melvin and Edmund Fisher Ward. Extensive practice initially involved largely with post-war rehabilitation work, distinguished for ability to handle large masses and exploit the results of careful research work. Extensive work for schools and universities and for the National Health Service, as well as numerous offices. Their offices in New Cavendish Street, London (1957), represented a pioneering use of the curtain-wall glass façade. The firm, which now has some 150 employees, enjoys an international clientèle.

□ *Architecture of the Gollins Melvin Ward Partnership*, London 1974

Grassi, Giorgio, b. Milan 1935. Studied at the Milan Politecnico; diploma 1960. From 1961 to 1964 he worked for the periodical *Casabella-continuità*. In 1965 he was appointed a professor at Milan Politecnico, and 1965–78 also at the University in Pescara. Even more radically than Aldo ★Rossi, G. attacks individualism and fashionable experimentation in architecture. He considers that architectural history already makes abundantly available the archetypes which can be applied to the entire spectrum of possible architectural tasks. Not coincidentally, the rigorous work of Heinrich ★Tessenow is, alongside the traditional architecture of the large, strongly articulated farm buildings of Lombardy, one of his principal models. The house in Vello di Marone on the Lago d'Iseo, built in 1962 in collaboration with G. Favazzeni, already demonstrates G.'s reductivist impulse. In his project for the conversion of the Castello Visconteo at Abbiategrasso into a Town Hall (1970) he contrasts historical forms with a neutral monumentality. In 1976 he collaborated with Antonio Monestiroli on the design of the Students' Residence in Chieti, under construction from 1979. The heart of the composition is a straight agora-style street which, in its tall colonnades of slender square pilasters flanking the street, also recalls Friedrich Weinbrenner's unrealized design for the Lange Straße in Karlsruhe (1808). G.'s own quest for a collective, maximally objective, formal language, represents the limits of *Rational architecture, in that economic factors and reason alone determine design. VML

☐ Grassi, G., *La costruzione logica dell'architettura*, Venice 1967; ——, *L'architettura come mestiere e altri scritti*, Milan 1980 (originally published as *La arquitectura como oficio y otros escritos*, Barcelona 1979); *Giorgio Grassi. Progetti e disegni 1965–1980* (exhibition catalogue), Mantua 1982.

Graves, Michael, b. Indianapolis 1934. Studied at the University of Cincinnati, Ohio, and at Harvard University, after which he was a Fellow at the American Academy in Rome for two years. In 1964, he opened his own office in Princeton, N.J., where he was appointed professor at the University in 1972. G.'s name first came to wide public attention in 1972 through the inclusion of his work in *Five Architects*, alongside that of *Eisenman, *Gwathmey and Siegel, *Hejduk and *Meier (*New York Five). His work at that point – such as the Hanselmann House in Fort Wayne, Ind. (1967), and the addition to the Benacerraf House in Princeton (1969), both illustrated in the book – shared with that of the other four architects a formal, often radical, return to the style of *Le Corbusier's work of the 1920s. The primacy of architectural form soon led G. to some far-reaching excursions into history, first to Boullée and Ledoux and finally to the antique and thus continually further from a rationalistic white architecture to a more colourful one of delicate pastel tones. As earlier with his neo-modernism, this neo-historicism (*historicism) also moved towards a highly abstract level which eliminated direct borrowings from early styles. Characteristic examples of his most recent creative phase are the Fargo-Moorhead Cultural Center Bridge between Fargo, N.D., and Moorhead, Minn. (designed 1977), the Kalko House in Green Brook, N.J. (designed 1978), and the Public Services Building in Portland, Oregon (1980–2). AM

Graves. Public Services Building, Portland, Oregon (1980–2)

☐ *Five Architects*, New York 1972; Colquhoun, Alan, and Carl, Peter, *Michael Graves*, London 1979.

Great Britain. At the turn of the century British architecture seemed in some respects to be the most advanced. In the second half of the 19th century, the movement for the reform of design teaching and patronage led by Sir Henry Cole was centred on the South Kensington (later Victoria and Albert) Museum, and the Royal College of Art produced several generations of well-trained designers. Art schools were influenced by the preaching of John Ruskin, as well as by the teaching and example of William *Morris, who contributed to a powerful revival of crafts and opposed the spread of mechanization in everyday life. Attempts were made to bridge the contradiction by architect-designers of the *Arts and Crafts movement such as C. R. *Ashbee and C. F. A. *Voysey, as well as by other leading architects of the time, notably Richard Norman *Shaw. Perhaps the most important attempt in this direction was the creation of the Garden City movement through the teaching of Ebenezer *Howard. While England remained virtually untouched by *Art Nouveau, Scotland had in Charles Rennie *Mackintosh a one-man protagonist of this movement. In England the Arts and Crafts designers produced a successful simplification of Continental excesses in the decorative arts, and this was re-exported to the Continent by the early exponents of the *Neue Sachlichkeit, notably Hermann *Muthesius.

However, in the years before World War I and for some time after, British architecture was dominated by a revival of 18th-century monumentalism, strongly influenced by French academic teaching. Shaw became the most important protagonist of this tendency, followed by his principal disciples Reginald Blomfield (Piccadilly Hotel, the Regent Street Quadrant and the layout of Piccadilly Circus in London, 1904–23) and Sir Edwin *Lutyens, who presided over the maximum extension of British architecture in the heyday of the Empire. Its climax was the building of the government city of New Delhi in *India (1912–31), though the manner was also exported to Canada, Australia and South Africa. At home, it dominated new commercial building in the City of London, as in Britannic House (1920–4) and the Midland Bank (1924–39) by Lutyens.

Meanwhile, a modified 19th-century style (Neo-Georgian) was taken up by the Garden Cities (Letchworth, Welwyn) and by the newly constituted architectural offices of local government authorities, notably the London County Council (LCC). The new (1918 and after) London Underground authority, amalgamated with others in 1933 to become the London Passenger Transport Board, patronized an overall standard of design which extended from lettering and trains (1922) to the actual buildings; their architects, C. Percy Adams, Charles Holden and J. L. Pearson, achieved a remarkable amalgam of imported Dutch (*Amsterdam, School of) and native elements, creating a homogeneous and impressive style.

The 1920s were also a time when Britain was infected with an enthusiasm for the *Art Deco fashion from Paris. This was fused with certain Swedish and German Expressionist features

Great Britain. Arnos Grove Underground Station, London (1922), by C. Percy Adams, Charles Holden and J. L. Pearson

(*Expressionism) into a persuasive interior manner, often in conjunction with Dutch-influenced exteriors, which was used in the many town halls, cinemas, hotels and restaurant chains (particularly, of this last type, those done for J. Lyons & Co. by Oliver P. Bernard). The post-war period was dominated by the academic 'pompier' architects; besides Lutyens and Blomfield, Sir Giles Gilbert Scott, Sir Edwin Cooper (Marylebone Town Hall; Port of London Authority) and Sir Herbert Baker (Offices and Assembly in New Delhi; rebuilding of the Bank of England in London) deserve mention. The younger generation was represented by three remarkable architect-teachers, who were inclined to entertain both new ideas and new

Great Britain. Peter Jones department store, London (1934), by C. H. Reilly with Crabtree, Slater and Moberley

materials: Albert Richardson, Howard Robertson and C. H. Reilly. Richardson (Financial Times Building in London) represented the extreme academic position; Robertson (Royal Horticultural Society Hall in London, 1923, with Murray Easton; British Pavilions in Paris, 1925; Brussels, 1935; New York, 1939) dominated the Architectural Association; and Reilly (Dorset House in Piccadilly, 1923, with Carrère & Hastings of New York; the Peter Jones department store in Sloane Square, London, 1934, with his ex-pupils Crabtree, Slater and Moberley – a showpiece of the new *Functionalism) made the Liverpool University Architectural School the leading one in Britain. Thomas J. Tait, who worked through the established practice of the Scot, Sir John Burnet (extension of the British Museum, London), introduced a daring Dutch strain into their later work such as the Royal Masonic Hospital in Hammersmith (1930–4), the Mount Royal Hotel in Oxford Street, London (1932–3), and St Andrew's House, the monumental Scottish government centre in Edinburgh (1933–9). Joseph Emberton had been an assistant of Tait's, and began his career with the vast concrete Expressionist Olympia Exhibition Halls (1929–30). The Royal Corinthian Yacht Club at Burnham-on-Crouch was a much more sober concrete-and-glass pavilion in the water. Of his later buildings, the stores for Simpson's in Piccadilly (1933–4) and His Master's Voice in Oxford Street, London (1938–9), both variants on the horizontal articulation of the street façade, are the best known.

However, the most showy innovator of the period was not an architect: Owen *Williams had worked on the design of railways and aircraft. He became a specialist in reinforced-concrete construction. His first major building was the mushroom-columned and continuously glazed factory for Boots at Beeston, near Nottingham (1930–2), the next was the Wembley swimming pool (1933–4), while at the same time he worked on the Pioneer Health Centre in Peckham, another concrete-frame building, largely faced with glass. The office building for the *Daily Express* in London was an early experiment in the use of opaque glass as a facing material. In the area of domestic building the scene was dominated by the expansion of transport, which was co-ordinated with suburban developments on a large scale; this happened particularly around London. The Garden

Great Britain. Boots Factory, Beeston, near Nottingham (1930–2), by Owen Williams

Great Britain. 'High and Over', Amersham, Bucks. (1929–30), by Amyas Connell

Cities grew only moderately, and did not multiply, though the new LCC office did attempt to experiment with relatively high-rise building (Somerstown, 1922–32).

Meanwhile a new generation of architects had matured. Amyas Connell built 'High and Over' at Amersham, Bucks. (1929–30), for the archaeologist Bernard Ashmole; but his best work was done in collaboration with Basil Ward (after 1931) and Colin Lucas (after 1933), a partnership which lasted until 1939. Apart from some film studios, their work consisted entirely of houses and apartments which, despite their modest scale, revealed a daring formal attack, and among British architects this group comes nearest to a Constructivist approach (*Constructivism). E. Maxwell *Fry had been a pupil of Reilly, and his first major independent building was the Sun House in Frognal, Hampstead, London (1934–5), a remarkably accomplished exercise in concrete and glass. Fry was to work in partnership with Walter *Gropius during the latter's first exile in Britain in 1935. The partnership's only important non-domestic building, Impington Village College, Cambs. (1930–40), became the prototype for much English scholastic architecture after the war. Fry at this time also completed his pioneering housing scheme, Kensal House, London. Marcel *Breuer entered into a similar partnership with F. R. S *Yorke, as did Erich *Mendelsohn with Serge *Chermayeff, an anglicized Russian, with whom he built a number of houses and De La Warr Pavilion, a seaside concert hall and restaurant complex, in Bexhill, Sussex. After Mendelsohn's departure for Palestine, Chermayeff designed a large warehouse in Camden Town, London, and was working on an industrial complex for ICI Ltd in Manchester, and meanwhile had also built a remarkable all-timber house at Bentley, Sussex, for himself. However, at the beginning of World War II he left for the United States. Another Russian, Berthold *Lubetkin, had arrived in London from Paris (where he had worked for Auguste *Perret) in 1931. The group of younger architects which formed around him, *Tecton, did some work at the London Zoo, including a virtuoso exercise in reinforced concrete for the penguin pool; and in the very important blocks of flats, Highpoint I (1933–5) and Highpoint II (1936–8), in Highgate, north London, the new architecture was treated with a brio and elegance unrivalled in

Great Britain. The De La Warr Pavilion, Bexhill-on-Sea, Sussex (1934), by Mendelsohn and Chermayeff

Great Britain. Penguin pool at the London Zoo (1934) by Tecton

Britain. After the war Lubetkin worked primarily on the New Town of Peterlee, near Durham.

Peterlee was one of the many New Towns conceived and designated after the war. The most important group of them was sited to the north of London. This policy was the implementation at government level of some Garden City ideas. The last of the New Towns, Milton Keynes, was not designated until 1967, and is still under construction. The war period was devoted to temporary construction (various types of prefabricated housing) and to the setting of town-planning exercises of some ambition, of which the Abercrombie plan for the LCC is best known. Post-war reconstruction inevitably started with emergency housing, though from the outset planning ideas were being implemented. The 1944 educational reforms required the building of many new schools, and some local authorities (notably Hertfordshire under Charles Herbert *Aslin) experimented with various methods of prefabrication. The methods used were taken over and developed by the Ministry of Education into the metal-frame and concrete system which came to be known as *CLASP.

By way of contrast with the rather restrictive nature of the reconstruction programmes and the earnest atmosphere of post-war austerity, the *Festival of Britain took place in 1951, the centenary of the Great Exhibition, with the participation of established architects who had been active before the war, as well as many newcomers. The most important feature was the complex of exhibition buildings on the South Bank of the Thames, of which only one remains, the Royal Festival Hall, a major concert hall designed by a team in the LCC architects' office led by Sir Leslie *Martin. It has since become a major feature of the South Bank cultural complex which now includes two smaller concert halls and a large exhibition gallery (LCC, 1968–9), the National Film Theatre, and the National Theatre (Denys *Lasdun, 1967–76).

In the 1950s a new generation of architects was already making its mark. Peter and Alison *Smithson had won the competition for a

Great Britain. The National Theatre, London (1967–76), by Denys Lasdun

school at Hunstanton, Norfolk, which they designed in a manner scaled down from the work of *Mies van der Rohe; their attack on the rather happy-go-lucky formal attitudes in Britain and their attempt to form a Brutalist movement (*New Brutalism) seemed in contradiction. In any case, attention was still very much focused on the work coming out of the local authorities' design offices, and the LCC office assumed the characteristics of a school. The most famous of its products was the housing estate at Roehampton, London, which clearly showed the debate between the 'empiricists', or Swedish-oriented group that designed the first section consisting of tower blocks (1952), and the 'formalist', *Le Corbusier-oriented group responsible for the later (1955) point blocks and slabs set in the undulating park site.

The forecasts of a rapid population rise led to an expansion of the educational system, especially of the universities in the 1950s and '60s. A number of new universities were founded, and their new buildings were the only large-scale institutional commissions in the country. The first, and one of the most successful, was the University of Sussex in Brighton (begun 1952) by Sir Basil *Spence, which institutionalized Le Corbusier's Maisons Jaoul; York University was built by Sir Robert Matthew (who had headed the LCC office at the height of its activity) and S. Johnson-Marshall, using a modified version of the CLASP prefabrication system; the University of East Anglia at Norwich (1962–8) was planned by Lasdun as a continuous spatial structure. At this time the first public authority mega-structure was conceived by Geoffrey Copcutt as part of Cumbernauld New Town near Glasgow, a concrete shopping and civic centre begun in 1960. An analogous housing scheme in London was the Brunswick Centre in Bloomsbury (1962–8) by Patrick Hodgkinson (with Sir Leslie Martin).

Great Britain. Housing estate at Roehampton, London (1952–5), by the London County Council architects' office (Hubert Bennett)

Great Britain. University of Sussex, near Brighton (1964), by Sir Basil Spence

In the late 1950s and '60s there developed a local brand of science-fiction fantasy projects associated with the *Archigram group, most notably their scheme for a Plug-in City (1964–6). Although the group had little direct influence on architecture, its indirect impact was considerable: Richard *Rogers (with Renzo *Piano) monumentalized the High-Tech manner popularized by Archigram in the

Great Britain. Brunswick Centre, Bloomsbury, London (1962–8), by Patrick Hodgkinson

design of the Centre Pompidou in Paris (1971–7). The intense commercial building activity being undertaken in city centres had produced no architecture of great distinction, but did, in the mid-1970s, produce a government-sponsored movement for urban renewal. The principal innovations are still to be seen in the field of academic buildings: the Leicester University Engineering Building (1959–63) by *Stirling and Gowan became perhaps the most-publicized new British building. University buildings by Stirling included those in Oxford (at Queen's College, 1966–71) and Cambridge (History Faculty Building, 1964–7), as well as in Scotland at St Andrews (student housing, 1964–8). Among his other works are a large housing development in Runcorn New Town (1967–74), as well as the extension of the Tate Gallery in London. JR

☐ Ellis, C. W., and Summerson, J., *Architecture Here and Now*, London 1934; Royal Institute of British Architects, *One Hundred Years of British Architecture, 1851–1951*, London 1951; Mills, Edward D., *The New Architecture in Great Britain, 1946–1953*, London 1953; Summerson, J., *Ten Years of British Architecture*, London 1956; 'Great Britain', *Zodiac* (Milan), no. 18 (1968); Landau, Royston, *New Directions in British Architecture* London and New York 1968; Pevsner, N., *Pioneers of Modern Design*, Harmondsworth 1972; Maxwell, Robert, *New British Architecture*, London 1972 and New York 1973; *Thirties: British Art and Design before the War* (exhibition catalogue), London 1979; Lyall, Sutherland, *The State of British Architecture*, London 1980; Architectural Design (ed.), *British Architecture*, London and New York 1982.

Greene, Charles Sumner, b. Brighton, Ohio 1868, d. Carmel, Cal. 1957. Studied at the Massachusetts Institute of Technology in Cambridge. He was in joint practice with his brother Henry Mather *Greene in Pasadena and Los Angeles, 1894–1922, then independently in Carmel, Cal. The houses of Greene & Greene were from the beginning stamped with the handicraft ideal of the *Arts & Crafts movement. At the highpoint of their extensive œuvre stand the Blacker House (1907) and the Gamble House (1908–9), both in Pasadena, which, with their interpenetration of interior and exterior space, their projecting roofs, their flat gables, their warm materials (wood, shingle-clad walls, stained-glass windows) and highly elaborated details, are among the best examples of a Californian version of *Art Nouveau, inspired by the *japonisme* of the epoch.

☐ McCoy, Esther, *Five California Architects*, New York 1960; Current, William, *Greene and Greene: Architecture in the Residential Style*, Dobbs Ferry, N.Y. 1974; Strand, Janann, *A Greene and Greene Guide*, Pasadena 1974; Makinson, Randell L., *Greene and Greene* (2 vols.), Salt Lake City 1977/9.

Greene, Charles S. and Henry M. The Gamble House, Pasadena, Cal. (1908–9)

Greene, Henry Mather, b. Brighton, Ohio 1870, d. Altadena, Cal. 1954. Studied at the Massachusetts Institute of Technology in Cambridge. Worked in partnership with his brother Charles Sumner *Greene in Pasadena and Los Angeles, 1894–1922, then independently in Pasadena.

Gregotti, Vittorio, b. Novara 1927. Studied at the Milan Politecnico; diploma 1952. From 1952 to 1967 he was in partnership in Milan with Lodovico Meneghetti and Giotto Stoppino as Architetti Associati; since 1974 with Pierluigi Cerri and Hiromichi Matsui as Gregotti Associati. He was an editor of *Casabella-continuità*, 1952–60, of *Edilizia Moderna*, 1962–4, and of *Il Verri*, 1963–5; Director of *La Rassegna italiana* since 1980 and, since 1982 of *Casabella*. He has been a professor, first at the Milan Politecnico, 1964–78, and, since 1978, at the Istituto Universitario di Architettura in Venice.

G., who during the years he spent with E. N. *Rogers on the editorial staff of *Casabella-continuità* had been an apologist for Italian Neoliberty (block of flats for the Bossi company in Cameri, near Novara, 1956–7), developed in the course of his work a progressively more detached, rationally controlled formal language. His interest in topographical factors as a basis for determining a design – already evident in his urban plan for Novara (executed 1962–7) – reached spectacular heights in the grand projects for Palermo University (from 1970), the Quartiere Zen in Palermo (from 1970), and the University of Calabria (from 1972), near Cosenza. The last (designed with Emilio Battisti, Hiromichi Matsui, Pierluigi Nicolin, Franco Purini, Carlo R. Clerici, Bruno Viganò) is an extensive, bridge-like structure set in the landscape at right-angles to the nearby parallel mountain ranges. Communal services and public plazas are clustered at the point where the two-storey 'bridge' (for vehicles and pedestrians) adjoins the old streets of the town, while the University services – housed in buildings attached to the bridge-like spine – serve to 'fill up' the valley. G.'s constant concern to base his own artistic positions on rational ideas and to express them in theoretical terms, lends his work a particular weight. This, together with his undogmatic openness, has placed him in a middle position in the contemporary architectural scene, one which is at once individual and fruitful. VML

□ Gregotti, Vittorio, *Il territorio dell'architettura*, Milan 1966; ——, *New Directions in Italian Architecture*, London 1968 and New York 1969; 'Vittorio Gregotti', *Architecture and Urbanism* (Tokyo), July 1977; Tafuri, Manfredo, *Vittorio Gregotti. Buildings and Projects*, New York 1982.

Gregotti. Residence for employees of a textile factory, Cameri, near Novara (Architetti Associati; 1956–7)

Gropius, Walter, b. Berlin 1883, d. Boston, Mass., 1969. One of the outstanding architects and teachers of the 20th century, G. was the son of an architect who occupied an important official position in Berlin. His great-uncle, Martin Gropius, himself an architect of some

repute, served as Principal of the Kunst- und Gewerbeschule (Arts and Crafts School) in Berlin and Director of art education in Prussia.

G. received his training in architecture at the Technische Hochschule, first in Munich and then Berlin. In 1907, he entered the office of Peter *Behrens, where so many young architects later to become famous had also worked, among them *Mies van der Rohe and *Le Corbusier. After three years in Behrens' office G. started on his own in 1910 as an industrial designer and architect. His designing covered a wide range and included interior-decoration schemes, wall-fabrics, models for mass-produced furniture, motor-car bodies, and a diesel locomotive. His first important building was the Fagus Factory at Alfeld an der Leine, built in 1911 in collaboration with Adolf *Meyer. This building marked a step forward in steel-and-glass construction. It is three-storeyed, the steel frame supports the floors, and the walls have become glass screens, the non-structural character of which is emphasized by the absence of vertical supports at the corners. At the famous *Deutscher Werkbund Exhibition at Cologne in 1914, G. and Meyer designed the Administrative Office Building which proved to be a very notable contribution to modern architecture. The circular glass towers enclosing the staircases represent the first use of an architectural motif that was to become an important feature in many modern buildings, especially department stores. It was often used by Erich *Mendelsohn to fine effect.

From 1914 to 1918 came a break while G. served in the Germany Army. In 1915 he was appointed by the Grand Duke of Saxe-Weimar to succeed Henry *van de Velde as Director of the Großherzoglich-Sächsische Kunstgewerbeschule and of the Großherzoglich-Sächsische Hochschule für Bildende Kunst at Weimar, and in 1919 he combined the two schools under the name of Das Staatliche Bauhaus Weimar (*Bauhaus), an expression of his own belief in the unity of design and craft, of art and technics. He was Director first at Weimar from 1919 to 1925 and then at Dessau from 1925 to 1928, in which year he resigned in order to devote his energies more wholeheartedly to architecture untrammelled by official duties.

While Director of the Bauhaus, G. designed the school's buildings at Dessau, completed in 1926. The complex consists of a classroom building, a workshop building, a students' hostel, a building with community facilities and a covered bridge between the first two buildings, which, besides administrative rooms and clubrooms, contained a private atelier for G. himself. In the workshops' wing reinforced-concrete floor-slabs and supporting mushroom posts were employed, with the supports set well back to allow a large uninterrupted glass screen on the façade extending for three storeys. This was probably the first time so ambitious a use of the glass screen was adopted in an industrial building, and it paved the way for similar constructions throughout Europe and America.

Among other works was the rebuilding of the Municipal Theatre at Jena (1923), designed in collaboration with Meyer, and two very interesting projects, one a building for an international academy of philosophical studies in Erlangen (1924) and the other the Totaltheater, a design made in 1927 in collaboration with Erwin Piscator, the Berlin theatrical producer. The purpose was to design a theatre that could be adapted to suit the type of play to be performed, from the Greek theatre with semi-circular orchestra, to the circus with central arena, and to a modern proscenium-arch type. The tiers of seats could be revolved in sections to enable the change from one form to another to be effected quickly. A model was exhibited at the 1930 Paris Exhibition, but it was never built.

G. was not only an architect and industrial designer, but a sociologist who wanted to build on the basis of a rational interpretation of the needs of people. During the latter part of his directorship of the Bauhaus, he studied the problem of obtaining the best living conditions in cities while preserving their urban character. He aimed to produce city dwellings in which the inhabitants obtained as much sunlight and open space with trees and lawns as possible at very much the same density as then existed. To achieve this he evolved the tall slab-like apartment block of about ten storeys, sited to gain the maximum of sunshine, with cross-ventilation and with broad stretches of garden between the blocks and open at both ends. He showed that higher blocks housing people at the same overall density would allow far more space at ground-level and greater advantage to be taken of natural light.

G. was able to realize his ideas partially in the Dammerstock housing scheme in Karlsruhe (1927–8); there he not only designed some of the five-storey blocks but acted as a coordinator for eight other architects. In this scheme several blocks are arranged in parallel lines transversely with the streets. A more ambitious scheme was the large Siemensstadt estate in Berlin (1929–30), in which G. acted as supervising architect with several others collaborating, while he was himself responsible for two of the blocks. The general layout consists of long five-storey blocks, orientated north-south so as to receive the maximum sunlight, widely spaced with stretches of grass and tall trees with light delicate foliage between. The blocks have pale plain walls with large windows, and they are planned with two flats per landing. These Siemensstadt flats exerted a wide influence and have been much imitated.

With the accession to power of the National Socialists in 1933, conditions became difficult for liberal and modern-minded architects, so in 1934 G. left Germany for England. He settled in London and entered into partnership with E. Maxwell *Fry, one of the most successful of the younger British architects. Together they designed film laboratories for London Film Productions at Denham (1936); two houses, one in Sussex (1936) and one in Old Church Street, Chelsea (1935); and Impington Village College, Cambridgeshire (1936), one of four village colleges erected by the County Council. This was G.'s most important contribution to architecture in England. It is a one-storey building with single-depth classrooms, fan-shaped hall, and club amenities, sited amongst lawns and trees to serve the dual purpose of a secondary school and community centre for adults. Early in 1937, G. accepted an invitation to become a professor at Harvard University and left for the United States; the following year, he became Chairman of the Department of Architecture at Harvard. One year later, he built his own house in Lincoln, Mass., which has much of the classic restraint of the houses that he had designed for himself and the Bauhaus leaders in 1926. This was followed by a large number of private residences built in collaboration with other architects in America. In the year of his arrival he entered into a partnership with Marcel *Breuer, a former student and master at the Bauhaus. In the years of their partnership, in addition to several houses, including one for Breuer himself, they designed the Pennsylvania Pavilion at New York World's Fair in 1939, and an interesting housing scheme at New Kensington near Pittsburgh for workers in an aluminium factory (1941); the buildings were irregularly sited, following the contours of the hills, and reached by winding paths. The partnership with Breuer ended in 1941.

Gropius. Apartment block in the Siemensstadt estate, Berlin (1929–30)

Already in Germany, in 1932, G. had begun experiments with standarized building elements for mass-produced housing, and he resumed these experiments during the war years 1943–5. While the earlier ideas were concerned with the use of copper-sheet cladding, these later developments employed timber panels based on a module – both horizontally and vertically – of 40 in. (101·6 cm). After experiments made in collaboration with Konrad *Wachsmann on Long Island, N.Y., these houses were erected in considerable numbers in California.

In 1945 G. went into partnership with several architects of the younger generation, forming a team of eight under the name of 'The Architects Collaborative' (*TAC). In this enterprise he was the guide and leading spirit. That he was able to enter with enthusiasm into so large a group demonstrates his great belief in the value of teamwork – something he had always felt to be necessary in modern building. The work of the team includes the Graduate Center, Harvard University, Cambridge (1949–50), which consists of a group of seven dormitory blocks, all sited around the social centre.

Much of G.'s activity in the last years of his life, from *c.* 1957 to 1969, was in West Berlin. In 1957 he built a handsome ten-storey apartment

Gropius. Harvard Graduate Center, Cambridge, Mass. (TAC; 1949–50)

Gropius. Apartment block in the Hansaviertel, Berlin (with Wils Ebert; 1957)

block as part of the Interbau Exhibition in the Hansa district. It has a concave balconied front facing south, with an open ground floor and free-standing piers – a work very much in the late modern idiom. In the 1960s the New Town of Britz-Buckow-Rudow was built to an overall urban plan formulated by G. The Bauhaus Archive in the Berlin Tiergarten was built long after G.'s death, in 1976–8. Originally planned for Darmstadt, it was adjusted to its new site by Alexander Cvijanović.

G.'s buildings are distinguished by an adventurous use of modern materials – steel, concrete and glass – while he may be regarded as perhaps the principal innovator in the use of the glass screen in forming the entire outer shell of a building, thus admitting the maximum of light. Architecturally, his work is always distinguished by a classic restraint and excellence of proportion, of which the houses for the staff at the Bauhaus in Dessau are an example. But important as G. was as an architect, he was possibly even more influential as a teacher. He was a great believer in the intelligent application of standardization and prefabrication, but above all he wanted a building to be the product of teamwork in which each member of the team appreciated fully how his contribution related to the whole design. G. regarded this as a symbol of community living and the intelligent integration of society. AW

□ Gropius, W., *Idee und Aufbau des Staatlichen Bauhauses*, Munich and Weimar 1923; ——, *The New Architecture and the Bauhaus*, London and New York 1936; ——, *Scope of total architecture*, New York 1943; ——, *Apollo in der Demokratie*, Mainz 1967; Giedion, S., *Walter Gropius. Mensch und Werk*, Stuttgart 1954; Fitch, James Marston, *Walter Gropius*, New York and London 1960; Franciscono, Marcel, *Walter Gropius and the creation of the Bauhaus in Weimar*, Urbana, Ill., 1971.

Gruen, Victor, b. Vienna (as Viktor Grünbaum) 1903. Studied in Vienna under Peter *Behrens (1924–5). Emigrated to the USA in 1938. Mainly known for his town and country planning projects (e.g. plan for Fort Worth, Texas 1955). His conception of 'shopping centres' was epoch-making; sited out of town and catering for the needs of a car-owning society (Northland Shopping Center, Detroit, 1952), they became prototypes for the American post-war suburban expansion, although he himself advocated striking a balance between private and mass transit. These ideas were developed in his Fort Worth plan and expounded in his *Heart of our Cities* (New York 1964).
☐ Tunnard, Christopher, *Man-Made America*, New Haven, Conn. 1963.

Gruppo 7. Alliance of seven Milanese architects (from the Scuola Superiore di Architettura del Politecnico di Milano): Ubaldo Castagnoli, Luigi *Figini, Guido Frette, Sebastiano Larco, Gino *Pollini, Carlo Enrico Rava and Giuseppe *Terragni. The group was founded in 1926, but Castagnoli left after several months and was replaced by Adalberto *Libera. They first came to public attention in 1927 with their exhibition at the Biennale in Monza. In a four-part manifesto, published in 1926–7 in the magazine *La Rassegna Italiana*, the members declared their withdrawal from a much too 'romantic' dependence on the past, as the Italian Futurists (*Futurism) had already demanded twelve years earlier, and proposed an 'Italian' version of rationalist modernism. Their work was characterized by a balance between a reverence for *Le Corbusier's machine aesthetic on the one hand, and the classical monumentality of Greek temples on the other; the group laid the theoretical groundwork for Italian *Rationalism. In 1928 the M.A.R. (Movimento Architettura Razionale) grew out of the group. This gave birth two years later to the *M.I.A.R. (Movimento Italiano per l'Architettura Razionale). VML
☐ Articles in *La Rassegna Italiana*, December 1926–May 1927; Kruft, Hanno-Walter, 'Rationalismus in der Architektur – eine Begriffsklärung', *Architectura*, vol. 9, 1979.

Guimard, Hector, b. Paris 1867, d. New York 1942. Studied in Paris at the Ecole des Arts Décoratifs and at the *Ecole des Beaux-Arts. He was influenced by *Horta, the most brilliant and important architect of *Art Nouveau. Among his principal works are the still eclectically composed Castel Béranger in Paris (1897–8), the entrances to the Paris Métro stations (1899–1900), virtuoso pieces of organic design evocative of forms in nature, as well as the Humbert-de-Romans building in Paris (1902), a large auditorium of iron construction. G.'s originality lay principally in ornamental design. He transformed railings, balustrades, furniture, and even the structural elements of his buildings into charged images of highly individual associational richness and refinement.
☐ Graham, F. L., *Hector Guimard*, New York 1970; Naylor, G., and Brunhammer, Y., *Hector Guimard*, London 1978.

Guimard. Entrance to a Paris Métro station (1899–1900)

Gwathmey, Charles, b. Charlotte, N.C. 1938. Studied at the University of Pennsylvania in Philadelphia (under *Kahn and *Venturi) and at Yale University (under *Rudolph, *Stirling and *Woods). He was Professor of Design at the Pratt Institute, New York, 1964–6. Subsequently, he taught at Yale, Princeton, and Harvard Universities and at the University of California in Los Angeles. In 1966 he opened, together with Richard Henderson, his own practice in New York, which he has continued since 1971 in partnership with Robert Siegel, who had joined the firm in the previous year. G. belonged, along with *Eisenman, *Graves, *Hejduk and *Meier, to the *New York Five, who were much discussed in the mid-1970s for their formal, indeed overtly radical, return to early modernism, especially *Le Corbusier's work of the early 1920s. In addition to numerous interiors, G. has for the most part designed private houses, such as his own house at Amagansett, N.Y. (1965–7), the Steel and Orly Houses in Bridgehampton, N.Y. (1969–71; with Siegel), as well as the Cogan House in East Hampton, N.Y. (1971–2; with Siegel). Of the large-scale projects of recent years, the East Campus Complex of Columbia University in New York (1981; with Emery Roth & Sons) is especially to be noted. AM

☐ *Five Architects*, New York 1972; 'Other spatial realms', *Progressive Architecture*, Feb. 1977, pp. 72–83; Breslow, Kay and Paul (eds.), *Charles Gwathmey & Robert Siegel. Wohnbauten 1966–1977*, Fribourg 1979; Marlin, William, 'A section through the thinking of Gwathmey Siegel Architects', *Architectural Record*, Sep. 1979, pp. 91–102; Abercrombie, S., *Gwathmey Siegel*, New York and London 1981.

H

Haesler, Otto, b. Munich 1880, d. Wilhelmshorst, near Potsdam, 1962. After studying at the Baugewerkschulen of Augsburg and Nuremberg and working for a time as a mason, he worked for a time in collaboration with Ludwig Bernoully in Frankfurt am Main before starting his own office in Celle in 1906. He was an advocate of the maximum possible industrialization of housing construction. Such sympathies were, he felt, in harmony with the aims of the architectural association Der *Ring, which he joined in 1926. Among H.'s individual buildings of this period the best known is the Dammerstock estate in Karlsruhe (1927–8, built under the direction of *Gropius). Of his contemporary public work, the 'Italienischer Garten' (Italian garden) in Celle (1924) – isolated portions of which still survive – as well as the Georgsgarten estate in Celle (1925), the Rothenberg estate in Kassel (1929–31) and the Blumenlagerfeld estate in Celle (1931), all of which adhere strongly to the strip-building principle, should be noted. With the rise of National Socialism, H. withdrew in 1934 to Eutin, where he was active as a garden designer. In 1946 he went to Rathenow to rebuild the historic town centre, and from 1953 he lived in Wilhelmshorst. FJ

☐ Haesler, Otto, *Zum Problem des Wohnungsbaues*, Berlin 1930; ——, *Mein Lebenswerk als Architekt*, Berlin (East) 1957; Lane, Barbara Miller, *Architecture and Politics in Germany, 1918–1945*, Cambridge, Mass. 1968

Haller, Fritz, b. Solothurn, Switzerland 1924. After apprenticeship and collaboration with various Swiss architects, as well as with Willem van Tijen and H. A. Maaskant in Rotterdam, H. established his own practice in his home town in 1949. From 1966 to 1971 he was guest professor at the University of Southern California in Los Angeles, where he worked with Konrad *Wachsmann on pioneering studies on movement patterns in space. Since 1977 he has been a professor at the Technische Universität in Karlsruhe.

H. made his name above all with his steel building system, which is one of the finest achievements in industrialized building. In 1960 he was given the task of erecting a fabrication building for the metal constructions firm USM in Münsingen. This was the impetus for his development of a universally applicable system for spanning great distances in building (Maxi system). Several years later, for an administration building to be erected next to the factory, he developed a system involving shorter spans for smaller buildings with appended extension spaces (Mini system). A third building system, likewise developed for the Münsingen-based firm, was the USM Haller office furniture system, which he developed in 1964–70 and which has since become a classic of modern furniture design. Finally, in the early 1970s, H. developed a system for highly systematized construction of buildings with medium spanning distances (Midi system). This was used for the first time on a large scale in the Swiss Railways Training Centre at Murten (1980–2, with Alfons Barth and Hans Zaugg). Among H.'s other buildings, the best known are: those for USM in Münsingen (1960–4); the Wagsenring School in Basle (1st phase 1951–5; 2nd phase 1958–62); the Canton School in Baden (1958–64); and the Höhere Technische Lehranstalt (Higher Technical Training Centre) in Brugg-Windisch (1961–6).

H., who with Franz Füeg is the most prominent representative of the 'Solothurn School' (*Switzerland), has never sought originality, but rather has always aimed at the generally valid solution. His primary concern is the

Haller. Swiss Railways Training Centre, Murten (with Alfons Barth and Hans Zaugg; 1980–2)

Hardy. Olmsted Theater, Adelphi University, Garden City, N.Y. (HHPA; 1974)

mastery of a given task on an abstract level. Just as in architecture – which he considers as based in construction – his approach led him to develop building systems, so in town planning, on which he has written two basic works, he develops ideal plans which exclude any element of chance. TH

☐ Haller, Fritz, *Totale Stadt. Ein Modell*, Olten 1968; ——, *Totale Stadt. Ein globales Modell*, Olten 1975; 'Die Solothurner Schule', *Bauen + Wohnen* (Munich), 36 (1981), nos. 7/8.

Hardy, Hugh (Gelston), b. Majorca 1932 (the son of American parents). Studied at Princeton University and then worked for several years as assistant to the New York stage designer Jo Mielziner. In 1962, he established his own architectural office in New York, and in 1967 entered into a partnership with his earlier collaborators Malcolm Holzman and Norman Pfeiffer as Hardy Holzman Pfeiffer Associates (HHPA). Their work is one of the most convincing examples of the 'third way' in American architecture, between the radicalization of the abstract formal language of modernism on the one hand (*New York Five) and a no less formally obsessed *Post-Modernism on the other. Their work takes up the imagery of everyday culture from that of modern technology, with its prefabricated constructional and installation elements, via that of 'roadway culture' to that of vernacular construction, which at times are combined into an astounding syncretism. A major part of their production falls into the category of 'cultural' buildings, for example the Orchestra Hall in Minneapolis (1974; in collaboration with Hammel Green & Abrahamson), the Olmsted Theater at Adelphi University in Garden City, N.Y. (also 1974), the renovation of the 1904 buildings of the City Art Museum in St Louis, Mo. (1977), as well as the Boettcher Concert Hall in Denver, Col. (1978). A typical example of their residential work is the Cloisters Condominium in Cincinnati, Ohio (1970). AM

☐ 'HHPA's USA', *Progressive Architecture*, February 1975, pp. 42–59; 'Hardy Holzman Pfeiffer Associates', *Architecture and Urbanism* (Tokyo), March 1976; Sorkin, Michael, *Hardy Holzman Pfeiffer*, New York and London 1981.

Häring, Hugo, b. Biberach 1882, d. Göppingen 1958. Studied at the Stuttgart Technische Hochschule (under Theodor *Fischer) and in Dresden. In 1921, he established his own architectural practice in Berlin. In 1924 the Zehnerring was founded to fight the tendencies propagated by Berlin's city architect, Ludwig Hoffmann, and this group was later enlarged to become Der *Ring. The élite of the avant-garde architects of Germany belonged to it, and H., as its secretary, was the leader of the association, and in 1928 he participated in the first *CIAM meeting at La Sarraz. In 1933 the Ring was dissolved by the Nazis. Though *Gropius and *Mies van der Rohe emigrated, H. remained in Germany, where he was the head of a private art school in Berlin from 1935 to 1943. In 1943 he returned to his native town of Biberach.

H. was responsible for a number of important works, of which the Garkau farm buildings (1924–5) and the housing project in Berlin-Siemensstadt (1929–31) became widely known; his real importance, however, lies in the theoretical field. He expounded his views on organic building in numerous articles and lectures (*Organic architecture). He maintained that the work of rejuvenating architecture had to proceed in two stages. The first is concerned with research into changing needs, and aims at fitness for purpose and the 'organism'; the second, on the other hand, deals with 'design'. While in rationalist thinking architectural forms were determined by using geometric forms accepted as *a priori* beautiful, H. attempted to develop designs solely in line with their fitness for a purpose, without preconceived aesthetic ideas. The decisive criterion in organic building is the determination of form from an object's identity. A building derives its shape from the function which it has to discharge as the tool (or 'organ' as H. called it) of man. The house as the tool of its inhabitants is the starting point of his thinking.

H.'s ideas, which in the 1920s were limited to a small circle, became increasingly important with the new phase of modern architecture that started *c.* 1930. Later, architects as different as Alvar *Aalto, Louis *Kahn and Hans *Scharoun adopted similar views. JJ

☐ Häring, H., 'Wege zur Form', *Die Form*, vol. 1, 1925; ——, 'Geometrie und Organik', *Baukunst und Werkform*, vol. 9, 1951; ——, *Die Ausbildung des Geistes zur Arbeit an der Gestalt*, Berlin 1968; Lauterbach, H., and Joedicke, J. (eds.), *Hugo Häring. Schriften, Entwürfe, Bauten*, Stuttgart 1965; Joedicke, J., (ed.), *Das andere Bauen – Gedanken und Zeichnungen von Hugo Häring*, Stuttgart 1982.

Häring. Garkau farm buildings, near Lübeck (1924–5)

Harrison, Wallace K(irkman), b. Worcester, Mass. 1895, d. New York 1981. Studied briefly at the *Ecole des Beaux-Arts in Paris. He worked in association with Harvey Wiley Corbett and William H. MacMurray, 1929–34; together, they formed one of the three architectural teams for the planning of Rockefeller Center in New York (1931–40). In 1934 he formed a partnership with Jacques André Fouilhoux, Raymond *Hood's former partner, which was joined in 1941 by Max *Abramovitz. After Fouilhoux's death, H continued to work with Abramovitz (1945–70); their firm was one of the most successful in post-war America and played a major role in the planning of the United Nations Complex (1947–50) and Lincoln Center (1962–8) in New York, as well as the Albany Mall state administrative and plaza complex in Albany, N.Y. (1972–8). AM

Haus-Rucker-Co. Architectural group founded by Laurids Ortner, Günter Zamp Kelp and Manfred Ortner in Vienna in 1967, and also active in Düsseldorf since 1970, as well as in New York since 1971. The work of Haus-Rucker-Co, which occupies a middle-ground between art and architecture, is to be understood as a 'School of Astonishment', that is as a means to set learning and self-experience processes in motion. They seek to propagate a 'provisional', disposable architecture, a concept which anticipates changes in the environment.

Among the group's best-known achievements are: Balloon for Two, Vienna (1967); the shell around the Haus Lange Museum, Krefeld (1971); and the Oasis Number 5 at 'Documenta 5' in Kassel (1972). In addition, a considerable

Harrison. View over Lincoln Center Plaza, New York (overall plan by Harrison & Abramovitz), showing: (left) the New York State Theater (1964) by Philip Johnson, (right) Philharmonic Hall (1962) by Max Abramovitz, and (centre) the arches of the new Metropolitan Opera House (1966) by Harrison

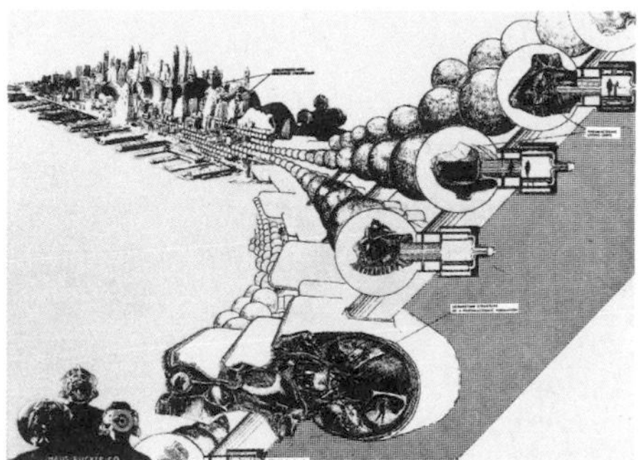

Haus-Rucker Co. Pneumacosm (project, 1967)

number of 'paper projects' have been undertaken. These include: the Pneumacosm (1967), an expansion proposal for New York using pneumatic cells; and the Big Piano (1972), composed of a resounding artificial cloud with a gigantic ladder leading up into it. FW

☐ Ortner, Laurids, *Provisorische Architektur – Medium der Stadtgestaltung*, Düsseldorf 1976.

Havlíček, Josef, b. Prague 1899, d. Prague 1961. Studied at the Technical University and the Fine Arts Academy in Prague (1916–26). Influenced by the cubic architecture of Josef *Hoffmann, he became in the 1920s one of the leading advocates of modernism in Czechoslovakia.

Among his most important works was the headquarters of the State Pensions Office in Prague (1929–33, with Karel Honzik), a complex consisting of a cruciform office tower of 14 and 9 storeys and attached wings with shops, apartments for the employees, etc. It is one of

the most significant buildings of the 1930s in Europe. AM
□ Havlíček, J., *Návrhy a stavby: 1925–1960*, Prague 1964.

Hejduk, John, b. New York 1929. Studied at the Cooper Union in New York, the University of Cincinnati in Ohio and at Harvard University. After working in various offices, including that of I. M. *Pei, he established an independent practice in New York in 1965. Since 1964 he has been professor at the Cooper Union. International interest in H. is based not so much on his limited built work – which includes the Demlin House in Locust Valley, Long Island (1960), the Hommel Apartment in New York (1969) and the restoration of the Foundation Building of the Cooper Union (1975) – but rather much more on his theoretic-didactic engagement with architecture in which he strives to drive space and scale to their absolute limits. His experimental, abstract approach to spatial and formal conflicts made H., together with *Eisenman, the leading theoretician in the *New York Five. FW
□ *Five Architects*, New York 1972; *John Hejduk, Architect* (exhibition catalogue), Zurich 1973

Hertzberger, Herman, b. Amsterdam 1932. Immediately after completing his studies at the Technical College in Delft in 1958, he established his own office in Amsterdam. He taught at the Academy of Architecture in Amsterdam, 1965–70, and since 1970 has been a professor at the Technical College in Delft. Together with *Bakema, van *Eyck and others, he edited the architectural review, *Forum*, 1959–63; this journal helped prepare the way for the Structuralist (*Structuralism) movement in the *Netherlands, with H. and van Eyck as its leaders. For H. the architect's task does not consist of offering ready-made solutions, but rather in providing a spatial framework to be filled in eventually by its users. In keeping with structuralist thought, this spatial framework is conceived as a regular system based on 'Archeforms' which are continually reinterpreted in new ways. The system not only provides for individual expression, but creates the very conditions to make that expression possible. Among H.'s most important buildings are: the Montessori School in Delft (1966–70); the 'Diagoon' houses in Delft (1971); the administration building of the Centraal Beheer Insurance Company in Apeldoorn (1970–2); De Drie Hoven Old People's Home in Amsterdam-Slotervaart (1972–4); and the Vredenburg Music Centre in Utrecht (1976–8). AM
□ Hertzberger, Herman, 'Huiswerk voor meer herbergzame vorm', *Forum* (Amsterdam), 3/1973; Lüchinger, Arnulf, *Strukturalismus in der Architektur*, Stuttgart 1981.

Hertzberger. Centraal Beheer Insurance Co., Apeldoorn (1970–2): exterior and interior

Hilberseimer, Ludwig, b. Karlsruhe 1885, d. Chicago 1967. Studied at the Technische Hochschule in Karlsruhe, 1906–10, and principally active in Berlin as an architect, 1910–28. He taught at the *Bauhaus, 1929–33, and later became Director of the Seminar for Housing and Urban Planning there. He was again in practice as an independent architect in Berlin, 1933–8. He held the post of Professor of City and Regional Planning at the Armour Institute (from 1940 Illinois Institute) of Technology in Chicago, 1938–55, and was Director of the Department of City and Regional Planning there, 1955–7.

From the beginning H. moved in the most advanced of avant-garde circles in German architecture: in 1919 he shared in the experiences of the *Arbeitsrat für Kunst and the *Novembergruppe; in 1925 he was a member of the Expressionist-oriented group of artists known as Der Sturm (*Expressionism) and was the first architect to exhibit with them; in 1927 he joined the *Ring and in 1928 *CIAM; in 1931 he was a director of the *Deutscher Werkbund. His involvement in city planning, begun in 1919 for the 'Existenzminimum', culminated in his 1924 project for a 'skyscraper city', which developed *Le Corbusier's revolutionary notions of 1922 for a 'Ville contemporaine'. Enormous uniform slabs form two superimposed cities; below, the city of business activity and automobile traffic; above it, the residential city with its pedestrian paths. This was intended to minimize the distance between home and work and thus reduce traffic circulation. Apart from meagre roof gardens, no tree and no lawn interrupted the prismatic artificiality of this anti-nature attitude determined by reason. H. applied these theoretical studies in a 1929 plan for central Berlin.

Hilberseimer. Skyscraper city (project, 1924)

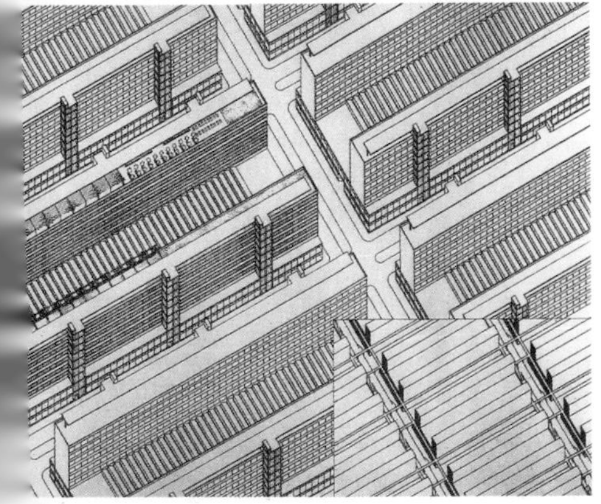

With his few, but programmatic buildings (house at the Weißenhofsiedlung in Stuttgart, 1927; house on the Rupenhorn, Berlin, 1935), his city-planning projects and schemes (among others that for Chicago, 1937–8, reworked 1950) and his writings, H. represented an extreme reductivist position within German *Rationalism. He was thus close to the position of *Mies van der Rohe, whose friend he had been since the time of the magazine *G* and with whom he also collaborated in Chicago. The strong geometric ordering and conscious formal restraint which characterize his obsessively repetitive works are kept alive in the most radical wing of *Rational architecture. VML

☐ Hilberseimer, Ludwig, *Großstadtbauten*, Hanover 1925; —— (ed.), *Internationale neue Baukunst*, Stuttgart 1927; ——, *Großstadtarchitektur*, Stuttgart 1928; ——, *The New City*, Chicago 1944; ——, *The New Regional Pattern*, Chicago 1949; ——. *Entfaltung einer Planungsidee*, Berlin, Frankfurt am Main and Vienna 1963; ——, *Contemporary Architecture: Its Roots and Trends*, Chicago 1963; ——, *The Nature of Cities*, Chicago 1965; Malcolmson, Reginald F., 'Elementos de la nueva ciudad: La obra de Ludwig Hilberseimer', *Hogar y Arquitectura* (Madrid), May–June 1968.

historicism. The concept of historicism in historical science, and particularly in the German philosophical tradition, has been used to designate a consciousness of historical genesis and relativity in not only the material but also the intellectual realm. This view arose in reaction to earlier forms of historical determinism. In a critical sense historicism designated the progression from a 'critique of historical reason' (Wilhelm Dilthey) to an 'irresolute relativism' (Friedrich Meinecke) and the often culturally pessimistic retreat from the present into the past. The first scholar to replace such negative terms as revivalism and (even more unambiguously scornful) *eclecticism as evaluations of 19th-century architecture as a whole, and in particular the stylistic mixtures of the last decades of the century, was the German art historian Hermann Beenken, and in 1928 he introduced the purely historiographical term 'historicism' (with the intent of a positive re-evaluation of the architecture of the 'romantic' period in Germany) into architectural history. With his work the term was accorded a neutral meaning as a time period, although implicitly a fundamental qualitative difference was maintained between the stylistic borrowings of the 19th century and comparable phenomena in the Renaissance. With Beenken the term became standard among German art historians, but even today it has found only limited application in Anglo-American or French art-historical studies, as a term which imparts a structural unity to the salient historical approach which is the common ground in the formally and iconographically diverse architectural solutions adopted in the 19th century. Recent Anglo-American usage has tended, following Mandelbaum's suggestions, to distinguish clearly between eclecticism, as one particular architectural strategy, and historicism as the more general description of an architecture highly self-conscious of its position in a larger chain of development, the structure of which can be assessed by historical analysis. Thus historicism describes a wide variety of architectural theories and doctrines in the 19th century, all of which conceived what Götz has labelled 'a programmatic relationship to history'. These include the social utopian-inspired architectural philosophies of Labrouste, Vaudoyer and their French contemporaries, the structurally analytical and democratic theories of Viollet-le-Duc and Gottfried Semper's approach to the development of types on materialist bases, as well as the clearly historicist notion of 'development' purveyed particularly by the architects of the English High Victorian movement.

From art history the concept of historicism has recently entered into contemporary architectural criticism, where it is often used as an ill-defined and undifferentiated evaluation of the most varied phenomena of 20th-century architecture. The point of departure of the historicist critique is, broadly speaking, the premise that the present century's cultural achievement resides precisely in the emancipation of architecture from historical links and traditions and in the conviction that 'modern' architecture created a 'true' unity of form and function and thereby an ideal unity of art and function, theory and practice, which could indeed be linked to history through common principles, but not by formal analogy.

The adoption of a stylistic concept – devised in the context of an idealist-intoned German approach to art history – to serve as the symbol of the intellectual and cultural unity of an entire epoch and to evoke the theory of an artistic avant garde, opened the way for the postulate of an aesthetic of 'pure' abstract (technical) form. This was asserted as the fulfilment of the old search for a 'new style' and, indeed, the only 'style' of the 20th century. This intellectualized cultural and artistic model, however, denied that historicism remained alive with varying intensity in the artistic consciousness of the 20th century. The by now well-known portrait of a straightforward development of the *International Style out of the revolution of modern architecture against historicism *c.* 1910 is but a myth of architectural history. Throughout the 20th century historicism has continued to play a role in architecture which cannot be understood simply in terms of the characterized antithesis of the *Neues Bauen or *Rationalism and tradition. This requires rather a differentiating analysis of cultural definitions, ideological content and use of historical forms. The rejection of stylistic eclecticism of the late 19 century did not come about by a radical denial of all historical relationships. It was much more a fundamentalist return – after the brief aestheticist episode of the pure decorative freedom and stylistic invention known as *Art Nouveau – to 'genuine' historical principles, that is to the typological and formal paradigms of 'true' monumentality and 'native' traditionalism. The unpretentious *neo-classicism on the model of the 'Prussian style' (Artur Moeller van den Bruck, 1916) seen in the architecture of *c.* 1800 (as in the works of Peter *Behrens. Heinrich Tessenow or Wilhelm *Kreis), the timeless rusticated monumentality of the Stuttgart Central Station (Paul *Bonatz), or the simplified Baroque forms applied to late medieval or Biedermeier types (as in the works of Theodor *Fischer, Paul Schmitthenner or German Bestelmeyer) were, as expressions of conservative bourgeois attitudes, quantitatively much more important in the architecture of the 1920s in *Germany than were the examples of *Neue Sachlichkeit. Even Expressionist architecture (*Expressionism) displayed strong historicist traits, especially in those gothic abstractions based on *gestalt* and cultural psychology (Wilhelm Worringer); and moreover not exclusively in church architecture (Dominikus *Böhm, Peter Vilhelm Jensen

*Klint). This is also true of the brick architectural styles with their ethos of materials and consciousness of tradition (Fritz Schumacher, Fritz *Höger, *Amsterdam, School of), in which the border with anthropological and natural analogies was fluid (Bernhard Hoetger, Anthroposophical architecture). The cultural ideological 'racist' conservatism (Paul Schultze-Naumburg) on the one hand, and the social-utopian futurist pathos (Bruno *Taut) on the other, represent only the extremes of these historicist positions.

The opposition between 'traditionalist' and 'modern' architecture – especially in Germany – was first polarized towards the end of the 1920s (controversy over the Weißenhofsiedlung, Stuttgart), in which more general social conflicts underlay the artistic issues (small town and rural interests *v.* metropolitan societal structures, handicraft *v.* industrial culture, individual *v* standardized form). Thus the monumental building programme and the 'Blut und Boden' (Blood and Earth) Housing Estates of National Socialism represented less an interruption of a modern line of architectural development than a canonization of existing conservative tendencies, albeit now with a strengthened emphasis on historical character and above all the ideological content of a building. In contrast, both of these aspects were less strongly intoned in the official architecture of Fascist *Italy. The League of Nations Competition (1927–8) for Geneva and the governmental and cultural buildings of the 1940s in Washington, D.C., demonstrate, however, that

historicism. Pfullinger Hallen community centre, Pfullingen (1904–7), by Theodor Fischer

historicism. League of Nations Palace, Geneva (project, 1927), by Marcello Piacentini, Gaetano Rapisardi and Angelo Mazzoni

even in countries with democratic institutions the notion of a representative architecture was still strongly tied to historical models. The similar, more strongly eclectic, historicism which held sway in *Russia from the time of the competition for the Palace of the Soviets (1931) into the 1950s, and which after 1945 was a dominant influence also in the Soviet satellite states, was intended to convey the idea of a national architecture, increasingly imbued with a cultural propagandistic significance.

The general label 'historicism' encompasses also the more or less preservation-conscious post-war reconstruction of historic city centres destroyed in World War II. The strong need for a tangible sense of historical continuity is manifested not only in the imitative reconstruction, as in Poland (with its desire for a national historical identity), but also in the restoration of West German cityscapes, in which nearly everywhere a sympathetic-restorative reconstruction found favour, rather than radical suggestions for new construction.

The various strains of *Post-Modernism have developed in a rather contradictory context. These include a historicizing architecture of luxury in the *USA (Philip *Johnson, Minoru *Yamasaki), which continues the implicit protest against the abstract aesthetic rigour of Rationalism first formulated theoretically by Robert *Venturi in 1966, as well as more recently in architecture in which – through intellectual distance – historical elements are used playfully, ironically, or merely aesthetically as a pictorial 'book of quota-

historicism. New Play House Theater, Cleveland, Ohio (1981–4), by Philip Johnson and John Burgee

tions' (Charles W. *Moore), and finally that architecture in which the structural formal canon of classic modernism is reworked aesthetically through historical distancing (*New York Five). In Europe, historicism is manifested in *Rational architecture which harks back to classical architectural theory and the autonomous character of art (Aldo *Rossi) as well as in emphatic formal eclecticism (James *Stirling) and even in more or less conservationist-minded 'architecture in a historical context' approaches (Alexander von Branca).

Despite numerous parallels, these contemporary trends are comparable neither in intent nor in formal character with 19th-century historicism. They are indeed sceptical of progress, but are in no way generally escapist or culturally pessimistic reactions to the ahistorical cultural utopia of an identity of theory and practice, through which the Modern Movement thought to triumph over history. JPa/BB

☐ Götz, Wolfgang, 'Historismus', *Zeitschrift des Deutschen Vereins für Kunstwissenschaft*, 24, 1970; Mandelbaum, Maurice, *History, Man, and Reason. A Study in Nineteenth Century Thought*, Baltimore, Md 1972; Pehnt, Wolfgang, *Die Architektur des Expressionismus*, Stuttgart 1973; Tafuri, M., and Dal Co, F. *Modern Architecture*, New York, 1980; Moos, S. von, 'Schwierigkeiten mit dem Historismus', *Archithese*, 2 (special number), 1972.

Hoffmann, Josef, b. Pirnitz, Moravia 1870, d. Vienna 1956. He completed his architectural studies in Vienna under Otto *Wagner, whose most faithful and convinced disciple he remained. The rationalistic theories that underlay Wagner's teaching and the influence of *Mackintosh, who was represented at the 1900 exhibition of the Wiener Secession, had a decisive influence on the course steered by H. himself. However, his elegance and refinement of taste was far removed from the severity of *Loos. He did not, in fact, despise ornament and this led him to show particular interest in the production of craft objects. He taught at the Kunstgewerbeschule in Vienna from 1899 onwards, and in 1903, together with Koloman Moser, set up a group of studios and workshops, which under the name of Wiener Werkstätte enjoyed widespread success and fame for thirty years.

In 1897 he had joined with other young artists, including Joseph *Olbrich, in founding the Wiener Secession. Under the influence of the Glasgow School and of Belgian and French *Art Nouveau, its aims were more radically modernist than those of Wagner's school. In the opening years of the 20th century H. designed exhibition pavilions, decorative schemes for interiors, and four houses (Moser, Moll, Henneberg and Spitzer). With the Purkersdorf Sanatorium (1903) he became one of the foremost exponents of the early Modern Movement: here the various elements of the external wall were combined in a surface which served to emphasize the abstract quality of the building's volumes. His Palais Stoclet, Brussels (1905), is an architectural masterpiece that evokes the exquisite poetry of Post-Impressionism and Symbolism. Although completely based on modernist theories, it is rich and refined to the point of decadence, a monument of the late bourgeois age which represents a milestone in H.'s own career, and in the history of European architecture.

In the years that followed, he built dozens of villas in Vienna with few essential variations. At the 1914 *Deutscher Werkbund Exhibition in Cologne, for which he designed the Austrian Pavilion in an elegant style of vaguely neo-classic derivation, he encountered in the work of *Gropius and Bruno *Taut a new and more vigorous form of architectural modernity, which gained ever greater influence in conjunction with De *Stijl, the *Bauhaus and *Le Corbusier's circle in Europe; it was also not without its effects on H.'s subsequent work. Thus, the public housing schemes he carried out in 1924 and 1925 in Vienna, and in particular his terrace houses for the 'Internationale Werkbundsiedlung' of 1932, are built in a style of extreme architectural purity that recalls the houses of *Neutra, *Loos, *Rietveld and *Lurçat. The results bear witness to H.'s conscious and deliberate 'presence' at a time of revolutionary development in architecture. H. designed the Austrian Pavilion for the 1934 Venice Biennale and, after World War II, a series of dwellings. GV/GHa

□ Kleiner, Leopold, *Josef Hoffmann*, Berlin, Leipzig and Vienna 1927; Weiser, Armand, *Josef Hoffmann*, Geneva 1930; Rochowanski, L. W., *Josef Hoffmann*, Vienna 1950; Veronesi, Giulia, *Josef Hoffmann*, Milan 1956; Sekler, Eduard F., *Josef Hoffmann*, Salzburg 1982.

Höger, Fritz (Johann Friedrich), b. Beckenreihe, Holstein 1877, d. Bad Segeberg 1949. Trained in the Baugewerkeschule in Hamburg, in which city he opened his own office in 1907. After numerous small houses, showing clearly the influence of Hermann *Muthesius, he designed a number of office buildings in Hamburg, whose clinker-brick façades introduced a renaissance of north German brick architecture. The best known is his Chilehaus (1922–3) whose sharply angled eastern corner recalls the prow of a great ship. With its dynamic crystalline form, the building is one of the masterpieces of north German *Expressionism. H.'s other important works include the *Anzeiger* Tower in Hanover (1927–8) and the Town Hall in Rüstringen (1929). FJ

Hoffmann. Palais Stoclet, Brussels (1905)

□ Westphal, Carl J. H. (ed.), *Fritz Höger. Der niederdeutsche Backstein-Baumeister*, Wolfshagen-Scharbeutz 1938; Gebhard, J., *Fritz Höger, Baumeister in Hamburg*, Hamburg 1952; Kamphausen, A., 'Der Baumeister Höger', *Studien zur Schleswig-Holsteinischen Kunstgeschichte* (Münster), vol. 12, 1972.

Holford, William, b. Johannesburg 1907, d. London 1975. Studied under Charles Reilly at Liverpool University School of Architecture. He became Professor of Civic Design at Liverpool University, 1937; active in formulating framework of English town-planning legislation, he was appointed Professor of Town Planning, University College, London, 1948. He designed houses, factories and public buildings. Planning proposals for the County of Cambridge, 1950; design for St Paul's Cathedral precinct, 1956; three-level plan for Piccadilly. He also developed plans for many universities. He was chiefly active as a consultant and planner, but his fourteen-storey block of flats at Kensal, London (1958), has been called the first large-scale modular building.

Holland. *Netherlands.

Hollein, Hans, b. Vienna 1934. Studied at the Akademie der bildenden Künste in Vienna (under Clemens *Holzmeister), as well as at the Illinois Institute of Technology in Chicago and the University of California at Berkeley. In 1976–7 he conducted a class in architecture at the Staatliche Kunstakademie in Düsseldorf; since 1976 he has been a professor at the Hochschule für angewandte Kunst in Vienna.

H. is one of the most important and gifted intermediaries between art, design, and architecture. With his first commission, the renovation of the Retti Candle Company in Vienna (1964–5), he came to international attention and attracted many further commissions for renovations. Especially notable among these are: the Richard Feigen Gallery in New York (1967–9); the interior design for Siemens AG in Munich (1970–5); the Schullin jewellery store

Hollein. Schullin jewellery store, Vienna (1972–4)

in Vienna (1972–4); and the head sales office of the Austrian Travel Bureau in Vienna (1976–8). All these works are characterized by the use of expensive materials (predominantly marble, brass, and chrome) and by elegant staging, as well as an all but insurpassable attention to details. H.'s imaginative and ironic pleasure in allusions is especially called into play in the Travel Office, where alien accessories or props are meant to evoke associations of travel.

No less do his graphic and environmental works participate in this credo that everything is architecture. Through alienation, cult-worship suggestion and symbolic architectural rituals, H. seeks to foster new ways of seeing and to provoke subconscious associations: Stadtstruktur (City Structure, 1962), Aircraft-carrier City (1963), 'Austriennale' at the XIVth Triennale in Milan (1968), the Exhibition 'Tod' ('Death') in the Städtisches Museum of Mönchengladbach (1970), 'Media-Linien' in the Olympic Village in Munich (1971–2). The building of the Abteiberg Museum in Mönchengladbach (1972–82) bears witness to H.'s total independence even when dealing with large building volumes: smooth cubes, organic volumes and petrified architectural settings produce an artificial landscape at once influential and penetrating in effect, and form a self-conscious accompaniment to the 'art' on display. PR

☐ *Hans Hollein/Walter Pichler, Architektur* (exhibition catalogue), Vienna 1963; *Dortmunder Architekturausstellung 1976* (exhibition catalogue), Dortmund 1976.

Holzbauer, Wilhelm, b. Salzburg 1930. After preliminary training at the Technikum in Salzburg, he studied under Clemens *Holzmeister at the Akademie der bildenden Künste in Vienna. In 1953 he founded, together with Friedrich Kurrent, Otto Leitner and Johannes Spalt, the Arbeitsgruppe 4 (Work Group 4) which played an important role in Austrian post-war architecture. There followed a break of several years during which, among other things, he undertook further studies at the Massachusetts Institute of Technology in Cambridge, and his collaboration with Kurrent and Spalt was resumed only after he opened his own office in Vienna in 1964. After several guest professorships, he was appointed a professor at the Akademie für angewandte Kunst in Vienna in 1970. H.'s architecture cannot be classified under any current trend or theory. While in his St Joseph College in Salzburg-Aigen (1960–4, with Kurrent and Spalt) the influence of Konrad *Wachsmann (who taught at the Salzburg Summer Academy) can be detected in the determination of form entirely through construction, H.'s later works – like, for example, the St Virgil School in Salzburg-Aigen (1966–76), the De Bijenkorf department store in Utrecht (1978–82) or the Amsterdam City Hall (1978 ff.) – reveal his concern to develop each building in terms of its particular context. AM

☐ Hübl, Heinrich, *Wilhelm Holzbauer, Porträt eines Architekten*, Vienna 1977; *Sechs Architekten vom Schillerplatz*, Vienna 1977.

Holzmeister, Clemens, b. Fulpmes, Tyrol 1886, d. Hallein 1983. Studied at the Technische Hochschule in Vienna, where he was later active as an architect, 1914–38, and again (after a period in Turkey), 1954–7. An influential teacher, he was active notably at the Akademie

der bildenden Künste in Vienna (1924–38, 1954–7) and at the Technical College in Istanbul (1940–9); many important Austrian architects were his pupils, including *Hollein, *Holzbauer and *Peichl. Strongly stamped with a basic 'scenographic' sensualism which can be traced back ultimately to the Baroque, H. remained faithful to tradition throughout his career, even when outwardly he drew close to contemporary trends, such as *Expressionism. Among his most important works, in addition to various government buildings in Istanbul and Ankara (1931–2, are the church of St Adalbert in Berlin (1933) and the various renovations and additions to the Festspielhaus (Festival Concert Hall) in Salzburg (from 1926). AM

☐ Gregor, J., *Clemens Holzmeister. Das architektonische Werk*, Vienna 1953; *Clemens Holzmeister* (exhibition catalogue) Vienna 1982.

Hood, Raymond (Mathewson), b. Pawtucket, R.I. 1881, d. Stamford, Conn. 1934. Studied at the Massachusetts Institute of Technology in Cambridge and afterwards at the *Ecole des Beaux-Arts in Paris. He worked in partnership with Frederick A. Godley and Jacques André Fouilhoux, 1924–31, after 1931 with Fouilhoux alone. In 1922, in collaboration with John Mead Howells, he won the competition for the *Chicago Tribune* Tower (finished 1925) with a neo-Gothic design; the other entrants included Eliel *Saarinen, *Gropius, and *Loos. H.'s further evolution brought an abandonment of *historicism and a turning towards a restrained rationalist formal language, with borrowings from the *Art Deco style. Nearly all external

Holzbauer. St Virgil School, Salzburg-Aigen (1966–76)

decoration is avoided in the *Daily News* Building in New York (1929–30). The simple façade, consisting of vertical bands of stone and glass, lends the exterior a pronounced verticality of monumental effect, as is also to be found in the buildings of Rockefeller Center in New York, where H. and Fouilhoux formed one of three

Hood. McGraw-Hill Building, New York (1930)

architectural teams responsible for planning. The McGraw-Hill Building in New York (1930), with its horizontal bands of terracotta panels and glass, introduced the curtain-wall façades of the *International Style. GHa

☐ Schwartzman, John B., *Raymond Hood: The Unheralded Architect*, Charlottesville, Va. 1962; Kilham, Walter H., *Raymond Hood, Architect*, New York 1973; *Raymond M. Hood* (exhibition catalogue), New York 1982.

Horta, Victor, b. Ghent 1861, d. Brussels 1947. A leading figure of Continental *Art Nouveau and the creator of an original vocabulary of ornament, H. helped to open up new paths to 20th-century architecture by doing away with the traditional plan of the private house and providing an architectural expression for the new building programmes set in train by the social and cultural developments of his time. He was also instrumental in devising a number of subtle structural forms that drew on the resources of iron and glass, and was a keen disciple of Viollet-le-Duc.

He began his architectural studies at Ghent Academy (1876) and continued them at the Académie des Beaux-Arts at Brussels. After spending some time in the office of Alphonse Balat, a neo-classical architect of repute, he built a group of three little houses in Ghent (1886) in which his special architectural ability was already obvious despite the modest scale of the project. However, the building which revealed H. as an architect of great creative maturity was the Hôtel Tassel, Brussels (1892-3). This house, a veritable manifesto of Art Nouveau, is revolutionary in form and structure and is regarded today as one of the classic monuments in the history of architecture. It was the product of a country with an expanding middle-class economy, strong craft traditions and a high degree of industrialization. Above all, the Hôtel Tassel is remarkable for the novelty of its plan: instead of the corridor usual in *Belgium, H. substituted an octagonal hall, from which a broad staircase departs, giving access to the various rooms at different levels. The arrangement broke with the practice of uniform layout floor by floor, foreshadowing the 'plan of volumes' conceived by *Loos in 1910 and *Le Corbusier's two-storey system of 1930.

The Hôtel Tassel is also remarkable as being the first private house in which iron is used extensively, both as a structural material (a huge winter garden on the ground floor is carried on an exposed iron frame, while an elegant iron column supports the staircase) and to supply decorative elements in a flexible linear style, exemplified by the wrought-iron handrails of the staircase and balconies. It is in this building, too, that an impressive repertoire of two-dimensional forms was initiated, based on a close study of plants and flowers: the 'whiplash line' or 'Horta line' literally covers the floors, walls and ceilings; it is in evidence everywhere, coiling, interlacing, flying loose, climbing across glazing bars, encircling the feet of furniture, branching out in chandeliers and outstripping, often to excess, every structural requirement.

One year later, in the Hôtel Solvay, Brussels (1895-1900), Art Nouveau can be seen in its fullest maturity: it is an astonishing symbiosis, of Baroque and classical, sentiment and reason, craftsmanship and industry, colour and form, with aesthetics dominating technology. This building, wholly fitted out and furnished by H., is undoubtedly the most significant and complete example of its period. H. built numerous houses in Brussels before World War I in the same style (Autrique, 1893; Winssinger, 1895-6; Van Eetvelde, 1897-1900; Aubecq, 1900).

The Maison du Peuple, designed for the Brussels branch of the Socialist Party (1896–9), and the department store 'A l'Innovation' (Brussels, 1901) both employed the structural resources of iron in the service of a new programme. The large glazed façades of these buildings prefigure the light transparent curtain walls that took the place of the load-bearing wall.

Horta. Maison du Peuple, Brussels (1896–9)

After his appointment (1912) as a professor at the Acádemie des Beaux-Arts, and a stay in the USA (1916–19), H.'s architecture assumed an austere, classical direction; the picturesque and calligraphic tendencies of Art Nouveau were conclusively superseded by the straight line. The Palais des Beaux-Arts in Brussels (1922–8) was the principal work of this period; well laid-out and designed in concrete, it was the first cultural centre of a type that was to gain wider diffusion after World War II. RLD

☐ Delevoy, Robert L., *Victor Horta*, Brussels 1958; Paolo Ortoghesi, *Victor Horta*, Rome 1969; Hoppenbrouwers, A., Vandenbreden, J., and Bruggemans, J., *Victor Horta architectonographie*, Brussels 1975.

Howard, Sir Ebenezer, b. London 1850, d. Welwyn Garden City 1928. Began as a clerk and then as a successful stenographer. While visiting America 1872–7, he met Walt Whitman and Ralph Waldo Emerson, who first stimulated him to contemplate the possibility of a better life than that of the overcrowded and filthy industrial city. Subsequent influences came from the anarchist theories of Peter Kropotkin, the economic ideas of Henry George, John Ruskin's St George's Guild (*Arts and Crafts) and above all from Edward Bellamy's utopian *Looking Backward*. All of these trends have echoes in H.'s book of 1898, *Tomorrow: A Peaceful Path to Social Reform* (entitled *Garden Cities of Tomorrow* in the second edition of 1902). In it, he described his reforming vision of an ideal type of settlement: a self-sufficient Garden City for some 32,000 inhabitants, consisting of rural-like residential neighbourhoods, extensive cultivable terrains (which were to be arranged as a green belt to exclude any urban extension), shopping areas, cultural facilities, a central park for community and recreational activities enclosed in a crystal palace. This organic whole was intended to be related to a large town of no more than 58,000 inhabitants; neither railways nor highways were to pass through the Garden City area.

H.'s ideas were by no means conceived in a void. He relied, on the one hand, on the notions of the utopian socialists such as Robert Owen and Charles Fourier, and on the other hand, on private endeavours such as the company towns of Saltaire and Port Sunlight. With English pragmatism, he sought to find a'middle ground on co-operative principles, with help from

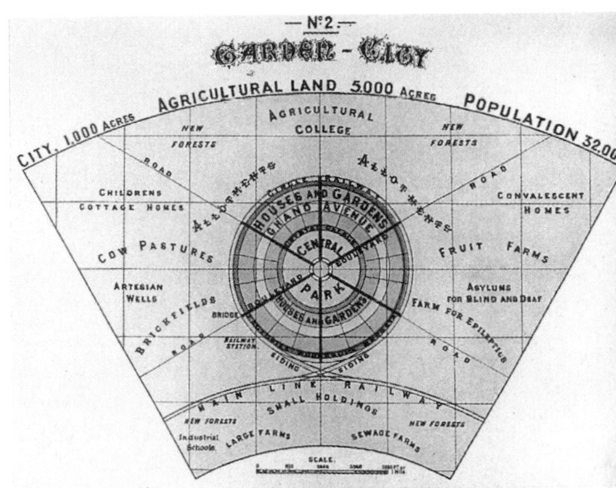

Howard. Garden city scheme: 'Rurisville' (from *Tomorrow*, 1898)

private initiatives, but assured against speculation. The basic idea of his concentrically disposed plan – which he developed only as a diagram – had already been proposed in the Renaissance. The English architect J. B. Papworth had worked on proposals for 'rural towns' as early as 1827 (Hygeia). In addition, James Silk Buckingham's Ideal City of Victoria of 1849 and Joseph Paxton's Great Victorian Way proposals of 1855 were precursors of H.'s formal scheme.

H. campaigned actively in numerous publications, assembled many sympathetic collaborators, and organized the financing of the project. The Garden City Association was launched in 1899. The first Garden City was begun on the plans of Barry Parker and Raymond Unwin in 1903 at Letchworth near London; however, it diverged considerably from H.'s ideal conception. It was to serve as the prototype for *Riemerschmid's design of Hellerau Garden City near Dresden (built 1909 onwards). A second Garden City near London, Welwyn, was begun in 1919; in this instance the plans were drawn up by Louis de Soissons. Countless further new garden cities were subsequently launched throughout the world.

Although most of the garden cities developed into viable residential towns, they remained isolated and weak palliatives against the explosion of city populations in the early 20th century. It was only in *Great Britain, with the New Towns policy of the 1950s, that the garden city idea was developed into an effective, if not unproblematic, means to limit the expansion of the great metropolises. VML

□ Howard, E., *Tomorrow: A Peaceful Path to Social Reform,* London 1898 (2nd ed.: *Garden Cities of Tomorrow*, London 1902); MacFadyen, Dugald, *Sir Ebenezer Howard and the Town Planning Movement*, Cambridge, Mass., 1970; Fishman, Robert, *Urban Utopias in the 20th Century*, New York 1977.

Howe, George, b. Worcester, Mass. 1886, d. Cambridge, Mass. 1955. Studied at Harvard, 1904, and *Ecole des Beaux-Arts, 1907. He was a partner in various firms: Mellor, Meigs & Howe, 1913–16; Howe and *Lescaze, 1929–34; Howe and Bel Geddes, 1935; Howe and *Kahn (Louis) 1941; Howe, Stonorov and Kahn, 1942–3; Howe and Brown, 1950–5. Howe's major work, with William Lescaze, was the Philadelphia Saving Fund Society (PSFS) Building, built 1929–32. One of the first major buildings of the early *International Style in the *USA, PSFS is noteworthy for its strong expression of horizontal and vertical structuring and its T-shaped plan, packaging the services separately from the office spaces. Elements such as the curved corner of the banking room set a trend for skyscraper clichés of the later 1930s. The PSFS Building marked a transition from the first European phase of the International Style to the second American phase. Indeed, H.'s own original, basically Beaux-Arts scheme had been modified to conform to International Style concepts.

Other notable works by H. are: High Hollow, his own house in Chestnut Hill, Pa. (1914–16); the Newbold Farm, Laverock, Pa. (1922–8, since destroyed); the Oakland School, Croton-on-Hudson, N.Y. (1929), the first International Style building on the East Coast of the USA; Carver Court Housing, Coatesville, Pa. (1942–4); the *Philadelphia Evening Bulletin* Building (1954). Square Shadows, in Whitemarch Valley, Pa. (1934), marked a departure from the stuccoed boxes of European modernism by its use of local materials, further developed in his Fortune Rock House (1938–9) on Soames Sound, Maine.

In the 1940s H. was Supervising Architect for the Public Buildings Administration and, later, Deputy Commissioner for Design and Construction. He was Chairman of the Department of Architecture at Yale, 1950–4.

Howe. Philadelphia Saving Fund Society Building, Philadelphia, Pa. (with William Lescaze; 1929–32)

□ Jordy, W. H., 'PSFS: Its Development and its Significance in Modern Architecture', *Journal of the Society of Architectural Historians*, 21 (1962), pp. 47-83. West, Helen Howe, *George Howe, Architect, 1886–1955*, Philadelphia 1973; Stern, Robert A. M., *George Howe*, New Haven, Conn. 1975.

Howell, Killick, Partridge and Amis. Practice established in 1959 by William Gough Howell, John Alexander Wentzel Killick, John Albert Partridge and Stanley Frederick Amis, all of whom had worked for the London County Council. Their style is characterized by a powerful striving after plastic originality. The project for the Department of Commerce and Social Science at Birmingham University features *Gaudí-like façades of precast-concrete balcony units; a redevelopment plan for St Anne's College, Oxford, consists of a series of curved blocks with highly modelled surface treatment, set in a wide oval round the college garden.

Strongly influenced by the principles of the *Smithsons, one of their most important projects while with the LCC was the Roehampton housing estate (1952–5) in south London.

Hungarian Activism was neither a school of modern architecture, nor an association of architects, but a literary and artistic movement which had much in common with the principles of *Constructivism and of the *Bauhaus in the second period of its history. The first circle of Activist artists, writers, poets, painters and sculptors formed around the fortnightly *A TETT* ('Action'), edited by Lajos Kassák in 1915–16 and banned by the Austro-Hungarian authorities because of its anti-war stance. A second periodical with the title *MA* ('today' or 'present age'), issued in 1916–19 in Budapest, was characterized by an Expressive-Cubistic tendency (*Cubism) in literature and in graphic art and influenced also by the dynamism of the Futurists. Great technical achievements in architecture were admired in the poems of Lajos Kassák, Erzsi Ujváry and other poets of the group. After the failure of the 1918–19 revolutions and the Hungarian Republic of Councils, all the members of the MA group were forced to emigrate. *MA* was published in Vienna from 1920 to 1925, during which time the Activist movement became more closely related to the theoretical problems of contemporary architecture. The Dadaist Merz-building of Kurt Schwitters, the Constructivist architecture and art of Theo van Doesburg, J. J. P. *Oud and Pamo en Hardeveld appeared in *MA*, together with the 'engineer's architecture' of Viktor Servrankx, the utopianism of Raoul Hausmann and the constructions of Naum Gabo, Vladimir *Tatlin and the 'Prouns' of El *Lissitzky.

In 1922 Lajos Kassák and László Moholy-Nagy published in Vienna their *Buch neuer Künstler*, a picture-book of new art and architecture where industrial buildings, such as *Bonatz's railway station at Stuttgart and *Poelzig's water-tower at Poznan, were reproduced along with buildings of Hardeweld, Oud, Kurt Schwitters, Tatlin and Huszár. Of the architects at the Bauhaus, Walter *Gropius was included in *MA* and his Hungarian companion Farkas Molnár published some woodcuts of his house-design, although his utopistic Red Cube House (1921) was to be published in the Activist paper *Novi Sad* (Yugoslavia) under the title *Az UT* ('the way'), along with the manifesto 'KURI' ('constructive, utilitarian, rational, international') which was signed by a great number of the younger members of the Bauhaus.

Hungarian Activism. Red Cube House design (1921) by Farkas Molnár

In 1921 László Moholy-Nagy edited a special issue of *MA*, in which his 'railway pictures' and graphics were published (together with an article by Peter Mátyás, which was the very first published interpretation of Moholy's art.) On 1 May 1922 his 'Glass architecture' appeared on *MA*'s cover, a coloured woodcut variant of his pellucid paintings with the same title. These were based on the Expressionist ideas of Scheerbart and the *Taut brothers. Moholy published his first article on modern architecture in the Dadaist *Akasztott Ember* ('Hanged Man'), where Ernst Kállai also published in 1922. Both men declared a deep belief in the functional and aesthetical values of a new constructive architecture which might create a new social harmony. Taking up the pictorial and theoretical approach to the principles of modern architecture, Lajos Kassák himself became a founder of a new trend in graphic art, painting and plastic art, labelled *Bildarchitektur* (pictorial architecture), in 1921. He published a manifesto under the same title in Vienna in which he declared: 'The artist of today . . . again bears his art with him as a manifesto. Not his view of the world, but the essence of the world. Architecture. – The synthesis of the new order . . . Construction is architecture. The absolute picture is *Bildarchitektur*. Art transforms us and we become capable of transforming our surroundings.' Kassák's *Bildarchitektur* took the form either of painted watercolours of a collage or of linocuts composed of geometrical elements. Among the members of the MA group László Moholy-Nagy and László Péri dealt with a special type of sculpto-architecture in graphic art (Moholy-Nagy's Kinetic-constructive system, 1922–8; and Péri's *Linolschnitte* published by *Der Sturm*, Berlin 1922). In March 1923 there was published a statement of Alfred Kemény, Ernst Kállai, László Moholy-Nagy and László Péri, which appeared in the periodical of the Hungarian leftists separated from the MA group. This periodical was called *Egység* ('Unity') and the statement of 1923 proposed a synthesizing of ideological and functional goals. In his series of *Bauhausbücher* Moholy-Nagy continued the Activist-Constructivist urge to transform the face of the whole world into a visual revolution, summarized in his *Von Material zu Architektur* (1929).

The reproductions and articles published in *MA* had a deep influence on such architects as Farkas Molnár, Marcel *Breuer, Alfred Forbát and Andor Weininger, and on such artists as Moholy-Nagy and Péri. Its editor, Lajos Kassák, attempted a Constructivist *Gesamtkunstwerk* in his programmes and publications. JS

□ *The Hungarian Avant Garde, The Eight and the Activists* (exhibition catalogue), London, Hayward Gallery 1980; Szabó, Julia, *A magyar aktivizmus müvészete* ('Art of Hungarian Activism'), Budapest 1981.

I

India. Before independence and the partition of India in 1947, architecture in the sub-continent was dominated by European styles and British architects. Although, in the 19th century, traditional building crafts survived in domestic architecture, public buildings, churches and even the palaces of native princes became the responsibility of British architects and engineers. At first, engineers directed the construction of public buildings but, in the mid-19th century, the first trained architects came out from Britain or buildings were executed locally from designs prepared in London. The results thus reflected architectural developments in Britain: Bombay became dominated by the Gothic Revival while Calcutta remained loyal to the Classical tradition. In both cities, talented local architects were in practice by the 1860s: Walter Granville in Calcutta and F. W. Stevens in Bombay.

By the 1870s, however, a number of British architects began to have doubts about the wisdom of imposing Western styles on an Asian culture. Inspired by the ideals of Ruskin and *Morris, Lockwood Kipling encouraged the employment of native craftsmen and sculptors in new building works, while a number of architects, notably Robert Chisholm, William Emerson, Swinton Jacob and Major Mant, grafted Mughal features onto Gothic Revival compositions, producing the picturesque and adaptable style known as 'Indo-Saracenic'.

By the early 20th century, however, the reaction against Victorian eclecticism also affected India, and the revived Classicism of 'Edwardian Baroque' manifested itself in such buildings as the vast Victoria Memorial in Calcutta, designed by Emerson. The appointment of the first Consulting Architect to the Government of India in 1902 (James Ransome, who was succeeded by John Begg in 1908) brought a new professionalism and sophistication, but the most significant event was the decision to move the capital from Calcutta to Delhi in 1911.

The building of New Delhi between 1912 and 1931 and the appointment of Edwin *Lutyens and Herbert Baker as its architects brought European architecture to India into the avant garde for the first time. New Delhi was important both as an English garden city carried out on a grand, imperial scale, and for the development of Lutyens' monumental Classical manner, fused with Mughal and Buddhist elements. Viceroy's House, now Rashtrapati Bhavan, is both one of Lutyens' finest achievements and the climax of British architectural enterprise in India . *Le Corbusier later praised New Delhi for being built 'with extreme care, great talent and true success'.

Lutyens dominated the remaining years of British architecture in India. Although princes and maharajahs sometimes employed 'Art Deco' and other *moderne* styles for their palaces, most official commissions were strongly influenced by the Lutyens style. This is particularly evident in the work of the last two Chief Architects to the Government of India, R. T.

India. Viceroy's House (now Rashtrapati Bhavan), New Delhi (1912–30), by Sir Edwin Lutyens

Russell and N. A. N. Medd. One building designed by Lutyens' assistant, A. G. Shoosmith, St Martin's Church, New Delhi (1928–30), is remarkable as an essay in abstract geometry in brick, the Lutyens manner of composition being fused with both the modern industrial aesthetic and the resonances of tradition. This single church is one of the finest British buildings of the 20th century.

Another Lutyens assistant, Walter George, carried the legacy of Lutyens past independence in 1947 and his influence and importance resulted in his twice becoming President of the Indian Institute of Architects. However, the British imperial tradition inevitably waned in potency although, ironically, when a new regional capital at Chandigarh was planned by the Indian government in 1950, a European architect was chosen, Le Corbusier, assisted by an Englishman, Maxwell *Fry. India has continued to be dominated by Western cultural imperialism by its acceptance of the *International Style, regardless of the fact that it requires sophisticated services and continuous energy consumption in order to function in a

India. High Court Building, Chandigarh (1950–6), by Le Corbusier

hot climate. Only in recent years has a more basic modern architecture, more appropriate to Indian conditions, been promoted by Indian architects such as Charles Correa, recipient of the RIBA's Gold Medal in 1984 GMS

□ Nilsson, Sten, *European Architecture in India 1750–1850*, London 1968; ——, *The New Capitals of India, Pakistan and Bangladesh*, Lund 1973; Tarapor, Mahrukh, 'John Lockwood Kipling and British Art Education in India', *Victorian*

Studies (Indiana University), xxiv, no. 1, Autumn 1980; George, Walter, 'Indian Architecture: The Prospect before Us', *Journal of the Indian Institute of Architects*, January-March 1951; Shoosmith, A. G., 'Present-Day Architecture in India', *The 19th Century and After*, cxx, London 1938; Stamp, Gavin, 'British Architecture in India, 1857–1947', *JRSA*, cxxix, May 1981; ——, 'India: The end of the Classical Tradition', *Lotus International* (Milan), 34, 1982.

International Style. The phrase 'International Style' was one among many terms used in the 1920s to denote modern architecture. Introduced by an American in order to characterize a particular kind of European architecture (*Rationalism), the term became generally applied in later decades to a broad range of contemporary buildings.

In his book *Modern Architecture, Romanticism and Reintegration* (1929), Henry-Russell Hitchcock argued that 'the international style of Le Corbusier, Oud, Gropius, of Lurçat, Rietveld and Mies van der Rohe' was a separate strain of modern architecture. (Hitchcock had first written about the international style the year before in the magazine *Hound and Horn*; but the more widely circulated book thoroughly discussed the architecture, placing it in a line of historical development.) Basing his analysis on formal characteristics, Hitchcock claimed that a moderately modern architecture of the 'New Tradition', as he designated it, was distinguished by a historical continuity with earlier work, simplified mass, emphasis on surface texture, and reduced and abstracted ornament. On the other hand, the 'New Pioneers' – for him the European practitioners of the International Style, influenced by the aesthetic vision of Cubist and Neo-Plasticist painting – deleted all reference to past architecture, emphasized volume and plane rather than mass, and avoided ornament, employing the machine as an 'art-tool'. The latest advances in engineering that made this work possible lent it a 'technical beauty', although advanced technology was not of primary importance in these structures.

By 1931, the enthusiastic advocacy of Philip *Johnson – then a recent graduate in classics and philosophy who, though not yet an architect, had voluntarily taken up the cause of the new architecture – led him, and other critics following his lead, to define this architecture as the International Style, thereby capitalizing on Hitchcock's generic designation. The term was used more assertively and was given slightly wider application in 1932. In that year, the first show of architecture at the Museum of Modern Art, New York – 'Modern Architecture: International Exhibition' – and a book published in conjunction with it, *The International Style: Architecture since 1922*, both by Hitchcock and Johnson, presented an International Style architecture based on a specific set of 'aesthetic principles': volume (space enclosed by thin planes) rather than mass; regularity as opposed to symmetry; elegant materials; technical perfection and fine proportions in place of applied ornament. Related to these principles was the precept of flexibility, especially in plan.

The notion of an architecture as international was in all likelihood derived from Germany, where the term had been used from the mid-1920s on. In 1925, Walter *Gropius published *Internationale Architektur*, the first in a series of *Bauhausbücher*; two years later, Ludwig *Hilberseimer brought out his *Internationale neue Baukunst*; and in 1927, in conjunction with the Weißenhof housing exhibition, an 'Internationale Plan- und Modell-Ausstellung neuer Baukunst' was held. All illustrated an architecture that Hitchcock had initially considered the 'International Style'. However, in this European context, international meant architecture that expressed the spirit of the times, one that, like the burgeoning technological culture of the 20th century, would spread throughout the West: the machine was international and to the Europeans this architecture was derived from the processes and products of the machine. In addition, the designation was infused with social and political ideology: international alluded to the socialist and Bolshevik Internationals, and an international architecture was seen as a catalyst in the transformation of society – as *Mies van der Rohe put it in 1927 in relation to new efforts at housing, '. . . the struggle for the new dwelling is but part of the larger struggle for a new social order.'

None of this technical or social import was associated with the American use of the phrase International Style. Here the emphasis on formal properties overwhelmed concern for functional considerations that were crucial to European practitioners. Hitchcock and Johnson claimed that it was 'nearly impossible to organize and execute a complicated building without making some choices not wholly determined by technics and economics. One may therefore refuse to admit that intentionally functionalist building [*Functionalism] is quite without a potential aesthetic element.' And by employing the adjective 'international' the socio-political content of the term as used in Europe was drained away, and 'International Style' became another art-historical category, similar to a rubric such as 'International Gothic Style'.

The Museum of Modern Art exhibition travelled to eleven other cities in the United States, and a more portable version of it circulated for six years. While the latter was still making the rounds, three popular and influential statements on the new architecture heightened its meaning. In his *Pioneers of the Modern Movement from William Morris to Walter Gropius* (1936), Nikolaus Pevsner examined English 19th-century reform efforts in the arts and architecture (*Arts and Crafts), and saw them as leading to the Modern Movement, initiated by 1914 in Germany on the basis of Gropius's Fagus Factory and through the agency of the *Deutscher Werkbund; this suggested that the new architecture was the main stream of historical development. The following year, Walter Curt Behrendt – in *Modern Building, Its Nature, Problems, and Forms* – equated European modern architecture with the work of the Modern Movement, as the architecture of the times. Then in 1938–9, Sigfried Giedion delivered the Norton Lectures at Harvard, subsequently published as *Space, Time and Architecture. The Growth of a New Tradition* (1941), in which the new architecture was depicted as inevitably of the time and as a development of progressive design. The cumulative effect of this activity was to establish International Style as the cutting edge of contemporary building. When *Time* magazine, in its issue of 8 February 1937, greeted the arrival of Gropius in the United States, he was celebrated as 'one of the founders of the concrete-pipe-and-plate-glass school of architectural modernism known as the International Style.'

According to Hitchcock and Johnson's restrictive definition, almost none of the architecture in the United States up to 1932 was International Style, and of the little that existed most was on a small scale, and virtually none was by Americans. William *Lescaze, trained in Zurich by the first-generation modernist Karl *Moser, and settled in America since the early 1920s, submitted a modern design in the League of Nations competition (1927–8), published another modern project as 'The Future American Country House' (in *Architectural Record*, 1928), and built the nursery at Oak Lane Country Day School near Philadelphia (1928). Rudolph *Schindler, trained by Otto *Wagner and an émigré from Austria in 1914, lent a heroic appearance to his beach house for the Lovells (Newport Beach, Cal.; 1925–6) by using assertive, reinforced-concrete cantilevers, strip windows, and flat roof. Richard *Neutra, compatriot of Schindler and in America from 1923, began the Lovell House in Los Angeles in 1927; in this a thin steel frame, window walls, flat strips of stucco wall, flat roof, and open plan were arranged with the intention of providing a healthy living environment. Several other émigrés were also building in America, such as Albert Frey, Frederick Kiesler, and Oscar Stonorov.

More visible (and more specifically associated with America) were skyscrapers, of which two or three were drawn into the International Style orbit. Raymond *Hood's *Daily News* Building in New York City was a tall block composed of asymmetrical setbacks, and ornament played no role in larger views of the structure; but in other ways the building was 'less pure in expression', according to Hitchcock and Johnson. A different attitude was displayed in Hood's McGraw-Hill Building:

International Style. Lovell Beach House, Newport Beach, Cal. (1925–6), by Rudolph Schindler

the horizontal, volumetric quality of the exterior was the result of considering each floor a continuous open space. On the other hand, the symmetrical arrangement of setbacks suggested traditional methods of composing a tall building. A third high-rise related to the International Style of these years was the Philadelphia Saving Fund Society by Howe and Lescaze, for which designing began in 1929. Smooth, hard, machined surfaces were used inside and out, and the floors of offices were vertically stacked as a single slab without setbacks. But in other ways the building was more complex and structural: piers were placed outside the slab, a narrower slab was set at right-angles to it for stairs and elevators, and recessed mechanical floors at the base separated it from the larger volumetric ground floors that contained retail stores and public banking spaces. The result was a complex design emphasizing function and structure, quite different from the contained volumes illustrated in Hitchcock and Johnson.

The tightness of definition created other problems when International Style was applied to America. The towering figure of Frank Lloyd *Wright was largely excluded. His work confirmed aspects of the International Style: he replaced enclosing, solid walls with freely arranged planes, his plans explored open, continuous space, he advocated the use of advanced building technologies. Yet he maintained a separate and unique position in regard to International Style architecture, attacking the 'ready-made culture' of the 'internationalists', and employing warm materials and earth-hugging designs that had little to do with the weightless, machined perfection promoted by other exponents of modernism.

Also excluded from this definition were the plentitude of 'modernistic' skyscrapers erected in American cities throughout the 1920s and 1930s by the likes of William Van Alen; Harvey Wiley Corbett; John Mead Howells; Jacques Ely-Kahn; Miller and Pflueger; Morgan, Walls and Clements; and Vorhees, Gmelin and Walker. These buildings were based on vertically composed mass, symmetrical setbacks, and ornament (which, however, was selectively used and abstracted, because it was considered to be both for and about a modern, technological society). Other work, for which a strong International Style argument could have been made, was passed over by Hitchcock and Johnson, such as the glazed and volumetric projects by Norman Bel Geddes, like that for the Toledo Scale Company factory (1929) or Albert *Kahn's factories, beginning even before World War I with the Packard Motor Car Company Forge Shop, Detroit (1911), and fully realized by the time of the Ford Glass Plant, Rouge River (1922), where steel frame, sheets of glass, and precise detail were used in a manner that was similar to International Style design.

Despite the severe economic conditions of the 1930s, some architecture that could be seen as International Style continued to be built throughout the United States. Several architects maintained their practices for a time, such as Neutra and Howe & Lescaze, and others for a time brought theirs into being: Gregory Ain, Philip L. Goodwin, Vincent G. Kling, Edward Stone, William Wilson Wurster, Franklin and Kump, Keck & Keck, A. Lawrence Kocher and Albert Frey.

Also during the 1930s, however, a broad range of issues started to emerge within the American architectural profession, shifting the complexion of modern design. Vernacular architecture began to be assessed for its direct use of materials and sensitive adaptation to climate and site; fifty years of redwood architecture in California was examined for similar lessons. The impact of different climates on design was seen as an issue to be explored. Interest grew in the nature of materials used in construction: laminates and plywood as stressed skin, plywood and plastics and metals in moulded shapes. Prefabrication was evaluated afresh as a means 'to set a depressed economy on its feet'. More varied types of construction opened the possibilities for new forms – the 'free curve', the diagonal, the hexagon – and for a new freedom in comprising roofline and wall arrangement. Standardized equipment introduced the potential of greater design flexibility. It was felt that the open plan had not grappled with the individual's needs for privacy and quiet, so that assumptions about plan arrangements were challenged. Issues of city and neighbourhood planning grew in importance, and the question of monumentality was raised, the ability to achieve an architecture that would 'symbolize social ideals and aspirations'.

These deliberations were given unexpected confirmation in the late 1920s. The rise of National Socialism in Germany prompted major designers and theorists to emigrate to the United States, where many assumed teaching positions and eventually established careers, among them Behrendt, *Breuer, Gropius, Hilberseimer, László Moholy-Nagy, Mies van der Rohe, and Martin *Wagner. In their teaching, through publications and exhibitions, and by means of their architecture, they advanced a set of propositions about the built domain that were similar to the issues already being broached in America. Thus they confirmed changes underway in architectural education, and the discipline that emerged was the one under which many architects practising into the late 1970s were trained.

After World War II, when the explosively expanding American economy provided unequalled opportunities to build, International Style was given new prominence by being generally associated with buildings that were composed of right-angles and parallel lines in machine-like, unornamented precision, using technical materials and glass walls, and favouring open interiors. In a 1947 exhibition at the Museum of Modern Art devoted to Mies van der Rohe's work, and in the accompanying monograph by Johnson, the tenets of the International Style were reiterated; Johnson, now an influential architect and critic, would continue to refer to these principles in various statements, but by the mid-1960s he had modified the definition of the International Style to: 'structural honesty; repetitive modular rhythms; clarity, expressed by oceans of glass; flat roof; box as perfect container; no ornament.' The change was indicative of the popular but simplified use of the term that had by this time come into general use.

The shift was already underway by the early 1950s. When Hitchcock wrote about 'The International Style Twenty Years After' (*Architectural Record*, 1951), he could claim that 'the establishment of a fixed body of discipline in architecture', i.e. the International Style, had been 'successful' in America, and that this work was 'probably the major achievement of the 20th century'. Now generally associated with notions of an industrial, technological society, new building in steel and glass became, as Colin Rowe noted, '. . . a suitable veneer for the corporate activities of an "enlightened" capitalism.' The early phases of this connection can be seen in Pietro *Belluschi's Equitable Life Assurance Building (1944–7), a twelve-storey, glass-and-steel slab in Portland, Oregon; Wallace *Harrison's WFY broadcasting studios, Schenectady, N.Y.; New York University-Bellevue Medical Center, New York City, by *Skidmore, Owings & Merrill (SOM; begun 1945), and Nathaniel Owings' Office Building Project for the Building Managers Association (1947). But it was Mies van der Rohe's Lake Shore Drive Apartments in Chicago (1948–51) that provided the model for the steel-framed high-rise that was to proliferate throughout American cities during the next decades: a rectangular tower or slab sheathed in sheets of glass that in turn were held in place by thin metal frames set in a reticulated pattern, the whole sparsely elegant and conveying the impression of being the product of a highly technical society. Simultaneously, Harrison, as Director of Planning of an international Board of Design Consultants, produced a similar proposal for

International Style. Lake Shore Drive Apartments, Chicago (1948–51), by Mies van der Rohe

International Style. Lever House, New York (1951–2), by Skidmore, Owings & Merrill

the United Nations Secretariat Building, New York City (1947–50). The rapidly expanding firm of SOM, chiefly under the impetus of Gordon Bunshaft as head designer, began to apply the concept to a series of corporate structures: Lever House (1951–2) and Manufacturers Hanover Trust (1953–4), both in New York, and Inland Steel, Chicago (1956–8), are notable instances. Mies van der Rohe himself created the 'impeccable image of power and prestige' (Frampton) in the genre with the bronze-clad Seagram Building, New York (1954–8).

Mies van der Rohe also worked on an analagous design strategy in low, horizontal buildings, whether in an academic (Illinois Institute of Technology, Chicago, 1939 on) or domestic (Farnsworth House, Plano, Ill., 1946–50) context. Eero *Saarinen matched these efforts for the corporate client with his vast General Motors Technical Center, Warren, Mich. (1946–55); and for more than two decades, other corporate centres – located on park-like suburban tracts or in generous, landscaped plots along urban outer ring roads – were constructed along these lines, such as the Connecticut General Life Insurance Company, Bloomfield, Conn. (1954–7), by SOM. Other architects used the steel-and-glass box in smaller, domestic designs: Gregory Ain, Edward Larrabee *Barnes, John *Johansen, Philip Johnson. The importance of this type of dwelling at the time is shown in the West Coast 'Case-Study' houses: Charles *Eames pieced his together in 1949 using standard, factory-produced elements in order to achieve maximum enclosure with minimal means; Raphael Soriano's project, sponsored by *Arts and Architecture*, was developed from Mies's work, but on the basis of available building techniques and hand-crafted components. Gropius, together with Breuer, built several houses in the Boston suburbs in a manner reminiscent of the volumetric, stucco-surfaced houses at the 1927 Weißenhofsiedlung, Stuttgart, and both adapted enlarged versions of these designs to academic buildings: Harkness Commons dormitories, Harvard (1949) by Gropius; and Ferry House dormitory, Vassar (1948–51) by Breuer.

In this setting, the term International Style had come to assume a double meaning. On the one hand, it was compressed to refer to a select architectural repertoire of the 1920s, on the other expanded as the implied basis for any of the innumerable corporate or institutional buildings that were transforming American cities everywhere in the 1950s. Yet in both instances, the historical circumstances of the 1920s that had lent meaning to the architecture in Europe were left aside, and the International Style came to designate an approach to design in formal terms, a European theme and its American variations. CFO

☐ Power, Richard (ed.), 'Revising Modernist History', *Art Journal* (USA), Summer 1983 (special number); see also works cited above.

Isozaki, Arata, b. Oita, Kyushu 1931. Studied under Kenzo *Tange's at the University of Tokyo (1950–4) and later joined Tange's team (1954–63) prior to leaving to establish his own practice in Tokyo in 1963. During the ten-year period with Tange. spanning what must be considered Tange's most creative phase, I. actively contributed to the design of the Ka-

Isozaki. Fujimi Country Clubhouse, Oita (1972–4)

gawa Prefectural Offices in Takamatsu (1955–8), the Imabari City Hall (1957–8) and the Tokyo Plan (1959–60). Even after I. had left his office, Tange continued to employ him on such projects as the reconstruction plan for Skopje, Yugoslavia (1965–6), and the Festival Plaza at Expo '70 in Osaka (1966–70). In the 1960s I. was identified with the *Metabolism movement, even though he eschewed any direct commitment to its principles. In 1973 he married the prominent Japanese sculptor Aiko Miyaki and this led to an extension of his interests in Dadaism. An increasingly historicist (*historicism) emphasis in I.'s architecture during the 1970s led to the assimilation of motifs derived from such architects as Giulio Romano, Andrea Palladio, Etienne-Louis Boullée and Claude-Nicolas Ledoux.

In the 1960s, the period of his first manner, I.'s architecture took on an exaggerated trabeated expression of reinforced-concrete members not dissimilar in style to Tange, but with a stronger conceptual bias and gigantism of scale. The Festival Plaza for the Osaka Expo '70 marked a stylistic crisis in his architecture that heralded the beginning of his second manner: in this his work shows a much greater reliance on European and American models and is typified by highly abstract compositions using additive constructions of cubes or arbitrarily bent semi-cylindrical vaults.

This new style grew from his determination to break away from the rationalistic principles of modern architecture which he sought to replace with a neo-mannerist aesthetic that abrogated the tenets of orthodox modernism. His mannerist approach emphasized fragmentation, dissonance, debasement of the skeleton and compositions based on a heterogeneous assemblage of parts accompanied by an extensive use of metaphor. The most outstanding of his cubic compositions are: the Gunma Prefectural Museum of Modern Art in Takasaki (1971–4); the Kitakyushu City Museum of Art (1972–4); and the Shukosha Building in Fukuoka (1975). Notable examples of the semi-cylindrical vault type are the Fujimi Country Clubhouse in Oita (1972–4) and the Kitakyushu Central Library (1972–5).

Towards the end of the decade there was a further shift in emphasis in I.'s taste towards a more austere neo-classical form in such projects as the Tsukuba Civic Centre (1979–82) and his competition project for a recreation and residential complex by Lake Tegel in West Berlin (1980). PD

☐ Drew, Philip, *The Architecture of Arata Isozaki*, London and New York 1982.

Israel. At the beginning of this century the architecture of the land of Israel, then part of the Ottoman Empire, consisted of the monuments of the successive masters of the Holy Land, set in a context compounded of European *eclecticism and a prevailing Arab vernacular. In a seemingly timeless landscape, the only obtrusions of the machine age were the railway, the brickworks outside Jerusalem, and those monuments to the functional tradition, the wineries in the newly established Jewish settlements of Zichron Yaakov and Rishon Lezion. Only a few architects, such as Alexander Baerwald, in

Israel. Technion, Haifa (1912–24), by Alexander Baerwald

the Technion building at Haifa (1912–24), sought an indigenous style in a synthesis of East and West. After World War I, in what was now the British-mandated territory of Palestine, the foundations were laid for orderly urban planning and a civic architecture of considerable quality, by visiting consultants such as Patrick Geddes and, later, Patrick Abercrombie, and resident British architects and planners of the professional calibre of Charles Robert *Ashbee, Austen St Barbe Harrison and Clifford Holliday. By the 1920s Erich *Mendelsohn had paid his first visit to Palestine, and left, in his unrealized but influential projects, an important legacy. His vision of a regional mutation of the *International Style, responsive to the climate and culture of the Middle East, was realized, not only in his later work in the country, but by other European architects, most notably by Richard Kaufmann, who was also to make his mark as a planner of Israel's pioneer communal settlements, the 'kibbutz' and the 'moshav'. With the exodus of progressive architects from Nazi Germany in the 1930s, the group of architects in Palestine imbued with the spirit of the Modern Movement were strongly reinforced. Of this group some, such as Arieh Sharon and Munio Weinraub, were direct products of the *Bauhaus. Others, like Dov Carmi and Ze'ev Rechter, who had studied in Europe, reflected the new spirit more indirectly. They, together with talented architects such as L. Krakauer, J. Neufeld, G. Averbuch, Max Loeb, to name just a few, constituted a cadre of modern architects. They were joined by architects of international repute: by Mendelsohn, who set up office in Jerusalem, to build several outstanding houses (Schocken, 1936; Weizmann, 1935/36) and hospitals (Mt Scopus, 1936; Haifa, 1936); Alexander Klein, who taught at the Technion in Haifa; Johanan Ratner; and Adolf Rading, practising in Haifa, who later joined the Haifa Municipality. These architects and many others transformed entire areas of Tel Aviv and Haifa into unique homogeneous zones of 'Bauhaus vernacular', unrivalled except by the *Siedlungen* (estates) of Berlin or Frankfurt. The outbreak of war brought a halt to construction, which was not significantly to recommence until the establishment of the State of Israel in 1948, Then, with the flood of immigrants, first priority was given to housing, and mass-housing projects ('shikunim') sprang up across the country. There already existed, of course, a tradition of social housing, in co-operative workers' housing schemes, by Sharon and others, in the 1930s. In the new housing, quantity, speed, economy, were the prime considerations, uniformity and austerity the result. By the 1960s standards were to improve. Apartments were larger, construction techniques more sophisticated; with extensive use of prefabrication, house types were diversified; and the approach to neighbourhood planning became more comprehensive, with an enhanced sensitivity to locality. From the model neighbourhood of Beersheva in the 1960s to the Jerusalem satellite communities East Talpiot, Giloh and Ramot in the 1970s, there is a whole range of interesting experiments in housing form. On a larger scale of regional planning, it should be noted, pioneering work was done, especially by Arthur Glikson. In addition to housing peripheral to existing cities, there was also a bold New Towns programme, from Carmiel in Galilee to Arad in the Negev. At the same time, more venerable, history-laden, and picturesque centres – Jaffa, Safed, and, after 1967, the Old City of Jerusalem (and especially the ravaged Jewish Quarter) – underwent a process of restoration and creative renewal. It was in, or adjacent to the old city, that some of Moshe *Safdie's most exciting projects were located. The centres of the cities developed in Israel, as elsewhere: comprehensive shopping centres, high-rise office towers, many luxurious hotels. These buildings are generally of a high standard of architectural competence, but are stylistically cosmopolitan. It is in the field of institutional buildings that the more significant contributions lie. There are several fine university campuses, of which those at Beersheva and Jerusalem – both in its old

Israel. Apartment-buildings, Tel Aviv (1939), by Arieh Sharon

Israel. Israel Museum, Jerusalem (1959), by Al Mansfeld and Dora Gat

Israel. Convalescent home, Zichron Yaakov (1969), by Yacov Rechter

campus at Givat Ram, and its new and highly controversial megastructure on its original Mt Scopus site – are architecturally the most challenging. A new round of major hospitals, ranging from the Carmel Hospital (1969–75), compact and monumental, on Haifa's skyline, to the giant organism that is the new Tel Hashomer hospital in the making: the former by Yacov Rechter and Moshe Zarhi, the latter by Zarhi alone. Of all the concert halls, the older Mann Auditorium in Tel Aviv (1953–7) by Dov Carmi and Ze'ev Rechter still dominates: serene, monumental, functional. Two fine museums, different in concept and expression, are Al Mansfeld and Dora Gat's Israel Museum in Jerusalem (1959), whose elegant pavilions predicate a cellular plan capable of growth, and the Tel Aviv Museum by Dan Eitan and Itzhak Yashar (1971), an exciting spatial exercise, but in more finite terms. Israel is rich in museums and memorials because, for the Jewish people, memory, a human and national resource, is thus appropriately institutionalized. Arieh Elhanani's Yad Vashem in Jerusalem (1959–64) is both a container of historical documentation and a powerful evocation of the tragedy of the Holocaust. These institutionalized buildings are usually in *béton brut* (exposed concrete), a material handled with great virtuosity and skill by Israeli architects. Its inherent qualities – strength, utility, directness – are particularly appropriate for a pioneering nation trying to make a place for itself in the sun. GHe

☐ 'Architecture en Palestine', *L'Architecture d'aujourd'hui* (Paris), Sept. 1937; Canaan, Gershon, *Rebuilding the Land of Israel*, New York 1954; 'Planen und Bauen in Israel', *Baumeister* (Munich), January 1962; 'Architektur, Planung and Kunst in Israel', *Werk* (St Gallen), 60 (1973), no. 1; Harlap, Amiram, *New Israeli Architecture*, East Brunswick, N.J. 1981.

Italy. Although an Arts and Crafts exhibition was organized in 1902 in Turin, which marked the official entry of Italy into the international *Art Nouveau movement ('stile Liberty' is the name usually employed in Italy), in reality the crisis of *historicism had its beginnings more than thirty years earlier in the works of Camillo Boito and Alessandro Antonelli. In the quest for a rational architecture Boito's contribution was above all in critical and theoretical speculation, while Antonelli was given to structural reflection.

Certainly the most important Milanese architects before 1914 were two pupils of Boito: Gaetano Moretti and Giuseppe *Sommaruga. In Moretti's finest work, the Central Electricity Station of Trezzo d'Adda, the influence of Art Nouveau is indirect, and it is more a naturalist-romantic simplification which characterizes the formal language. Sommaruga interpreted Art Nouveau decoration in strongly sculptural terms, intermingled with Neo-Renaissance influences, as seen in his Palazzo Castiglioni in Milan (1900–3) and numerous other houses in Bergamo, Milan and Piedmont from the same period.

The other two important representatives of Italian Art Nouveau, Ernesto *Basile and Raimondo *D'Aronco, had different origins. Basile, who was the son of Gian Battista Basile, the most important Sicilian architect of the second half of the 19th century, combined with extraordinary refinement an Art Nouveau taste with his Neo-Norman formal approach. D'Aronco was Venetian and directly influenced by Otto *Wagner. He was the protagonist of the Turin Exhibition of 1902 and afterwards built various buildings of unusually modern conception in Turkey, including the Santoro House in Istanbul (1908).

Ulisse Stacchini (designer of the Milan Central Station, won in competition in 1906), Ernesto Pirovano, Giovanni Michelazzi, Pietro Fenoglio and Annibale Rigatti were, in addition, the most important exponents of the widespread renewal movement in which the most important personality of architectural

Italy. Main building at the Turin Exhibition (1902) by Raimondo D'Aronco

Italy. Electricity generating station (project, 1914) by Antonio Sant'Elia

*Futurism, Antonio *Sant'Elia, had his roots.

In contrast to North Italy, Rome's most important architects, such as Guglielmo Calderini or Cesare Bazzani (the creator of the

Museo d'Arte Moderna built for the major exhibition of 1911) remained firmly historicist in approach. The activity of Gino Coppede, who was one of the most imaginative exponents of late *eclecticism, also deserves mention.

The Futurist episode was, at least in architecture, rather more diverse and long-lived than legend would have it. Between 1909, the year of Marinetti's 'Manifeste du futurisme' and 1914, when the manifesto 'L'architettura futurista' appeared, lie not only five years, but also numerous important events, including the establishment of the friendship of Sant'Elia and *Chiattone, both of whom were represented in the 1914 'Nuove Tendenze' (New Tendencies) exhibition. Architectural Futurism had an influence, after this first explosive inroad, on every exhibition through the 1930s. One should cite in this regard Fillía (Luigi Colombo), Virgilio Marchi, Enrico Prampolini, and Fortunato Depero (who created the 'futurist' pavilion at the Monza Biennale of 1927), Nicolà Diulgheroff and Ottorino Aloisio, as well as the extraordinary Interno futurista of Ivo Pannaggi of 1925.

The Futurist strain continued as an impetus to an authentic avant garde which ran parallel to the concept of a 'return to order' which was a common attitude after World War I, even among the Italian modernists. Between 1919 and 1926 (the year of the foundation of the modernist association *Gruppo 7), Italian culture in general – from the literary journal *La Ronda* to *Valori Plastici*, the magazine of the new visual culture – revealed a tendency to regard the romantic avant garde of the pre-war years as obsolete and to rally behind a new nationalistic *neo-classicism.

The Milan architects Giovanni Muzio, Arpago Novello, Giuseppe de Finetti and Gio *Ponti especially worked in this direction, although with different accents. In 1923 Muzio built the Ca'brütta in the Via Moscova in Milan, a building which in formal terms paid homage to Giorgio de Chirico's 'Pittura metafisica'. Also in Milan, in 1925 Finetti designed the Casa della Meridiana, a building rich in reminiscenees of *Loos.

In the same period in Rome, Pietro Aschieri, Alessandro Limongelli and Gino Capponi sought the way to a hesitant renewal. In 1928, Adalberto *Libera and Gaetano Minucci organized in Rome the first 'Esposizione dell' architettura razionale', through which medium the young Rationalists entered into competition with academic architects for the official favour of the Fascist regime. A decision was, in any case, not to be reached until ten years later; although the academicians, with *Piacentini at their head, always enjoyed institutional support, the regime did not adopt a repressive stance towards the Rationalists until 1937 (*M.I.A.R.).

Likewise in 1928, an exhibition held in Turin to mark the tenth anniversary of victory in World War I provided experimental possibilities for young architects, including Giuseppe Pagano and Levi Montalcini (who built the Gualino office building in 1929), Alberto Sartoris and Lavinia Perona. They all joined together to form the Group of Six, led by Edoardo Persico. Moreover, 1928 was also the year of Terragni's Novocomum in Como, the first significant Rationalist building in Italy.

Until 1936 the cultural scene was tense, due to the rivalry of the moderately modern Novecento Italiano and Rationalism. The 1930 exhibition in Monza was dominated by the Novecento, but the Rationalists were represented by the Casa Elettrica of *Figini, *Pollini, and Bottoni. In Milan in 1933, the First Triennale was held in a building designed by Muzio, in which the Rationalists and the 'Novecentists' were equally represented. Especially to be noted are the graphic arts hall by Muzio and Sironi and the Press Pavilion by the Rationalist *Baldessari. In 1932, the Roman 'Mostra della rivoluzione fascista' was put on in an exceptional pavilion by Sironi and Terragni,

Italy. Press Pavilion at the First Milan Triennale (1933) by Luciano Baldessari

and in 1934 the Salon of Air Travel presented one of the most brilliant products of Rationalism: the Hall of the Gold Medals by Persico and Nizzoli. The Second Milan Triennale of 1936, directed by Ponti and Pagano, was the great Triennale of Rationalism.

Between 1932 and 1936 the most important buildings of Italian Rationalism were erected: the buildings for Olivetti by Figini and Pollini (who, along with Terragni and Libera, were the only members of Gruppo 7 to remain true to the principles of modernist architecture); the Parker Company by Persico and Nizzoli; the first of *Albini's refined buildings; the works of the Como group (Pietro Longeri, Cesare Cattaneo and Gianni Mantero); and above all the important works of Terragni. In 1934, *Michelucci's group won the competition for the Santa Maria Novella Station in Florence.

Only a few noteworthy Rationalist buildings were realized in Rome before 1936: the Post Office in the Quartiere Nomentano (1932) and the House in the Via Valentino by *Ridolfi, as well as the Justice Building by Quaroni and Muratori; in addition there were the urban planning projects for the new towns of Pontinia (1933) by Piccinato and Sabaudia (1936) by Quaroni.

The general atmosphere worsened after 1936 and the academicians (of whom many were members of the exhausted Novecento movement) again gained the upper hand.

In the Rationalist camp the *BBPR group (*Banfi, *Belgiojoso, *Peressutti and *Rogers), as well as *Gardella and Mollino, effected a sort of critical Rationalism which showed a great sensitivity to problems of history and local tradition. In 1937, Adriano Olivetti (the clear-sighted industrialist of great importance in the history of Italian architecture, design and urbanism) entrusted the BBPR group, together with Bolloni, Figini and Pollini, with the planning of the Aosta valley. In 1938, the Milan Rationalists prepared the plan for the model quarter Milano Verde. Muzio built the Bonaiti and Malugani houses in Milan (1935–6) in which he introduced Italy to the taste of *Bonatz and *Fahrenkamp, while in his building for the Montecatini Company in Milan, Ponti turned to a moderate Rationalism. The airline terminals at Orbetello were realized by *Nervi in 1940–3.

After the government ordered the journal *Casabella-continuità* – the most important organ of Italian Rationalism – to cease publication, nearly the entire group of Rationalists joned the political underground. Raffaello Giolli, Gian Luigi Banfi and Giuseppe Pagano were arrested and deported to German camps, where they died in 1945: what had seemed a 'question of style' became a question of freedom and death.

The reconstruction after World War II united the Rationalists around a policy of strong continuity with pre-war tradition. In Milan, BBPR built the memorial for the victims of the concentration camps (1946). The Seventh Milan Triennale and the experimental

Italy. Santa Maria Novella Station, Florence (1933–6), by Giovanni Michelucci and others

Italy. Aircraft hangar, Orbetello (1940–3), by Pier Luigi Nervi

residential quarter QT8, built in conjunction with it, are representative of the hopes of those years, and the inclination to a new relationship between Italy's architectural culture and the realities of the day. The architectonic neo-realism of the following years developed in reaction to the disappointment of the left's defeat in the provincial elections of 1948 and the cultural bureaucratization of the Italian Communist Party, which screened itself from contemporary avant-garde culture. This found expression in the work of Mario Ridolfi in Rome, the ideology of the 'commune' and the new interest in spontaneous architecture, in Scandinavian neo-empiricism and in the contradictions of the 'milieu'.

The INA-Casa Tiburtino quarter in Rome (a sort of manifesto of architectural neo-realism), the 'Case a torre' in the Viale Etiopia, also in Rome, by Ridolfi, the village of La Martella near Matera by Quaroni, and the Borsalino houses in Alessandria by Gardella were all realized in the 1950s. In addition to his beautiful

Italy. INA-Casa Tiburtino quarter, Rome (1950), by Mario Ridolfi and others

Italy. Museo del Tesoro di San Lorenzo, Turin: interior design (1954–6) by Franco Albini

museums (Palazzo Bianco in Genoa, 1951), Franco Albini built the INA Building in Parma (likewise 1951) which for twenty years served as a model for the architecture of the region.

The discussion of the internal conflicts of Rationalism, and especially its relationship to tradition, was opened in the second half of the 1950s, first by young architects (Roberto Gabetti, Vittorio *Gregotti, Aimaro Oreglia D'Isola, Giuseppe Raineri), then also by Gardella (Casa alle Zattere in Venice, 1957), Albini (Museo del Tesoro di San Lorenzo in Genoa, 1954–6; and La Rinascente Department Store in Rome, 1957–62) and finally by the BBPR group (the Torre Velasca in Milan, 1954–8).

At the same time a middle generation (Marco Zanuso, Vico Magistretti, Gigi Chessa, Vittoriano Viganò, Ezio Segrelli, Marcello D'Olivo, Angelo *Mangiarotti) developed an interest in industrial production and its ideological and practical implications for buildings. Luigi Cosenza built a noteworthy industrial complex for Olivetti (1955) in Naples. *Nervi, *Morandi and Zorzi also offered interesting constructional experiments. The Pirelli skyscraper in Milan by Gio Ponti and others, built in 1956–8, was typical of a modernistic formalism which had become rather widespread.

The end of the 1950s was characterized by a double crisis. On the one hand a new interest in urban problems developed, especially with the book *L'urbanistica e l'avvenire della città* ('Urbanism and the future of the city', 1959) by *Samonà (the founder of the architectural school in Florence). On the other hand there was a shift in the relationship between ideological obligation and language in favour of a greater concentration on questions specific to architectural discipline.

The competition for the San Giuliano quarter across from Venice was held in 1959, and Quaroni submitted a project based on the problem of hierarchies in the planning of the city. The 1961 competition for the administrative centre of the city of Turin elicited many architecturally important and engaged contributions, as did the later competition (1967) for

Italy. City centre, Turin (project, 1963), by Lodovico Quaroni

the extension of the Chamber of Deputies in Rome.

The important protagonists of the 1960s were Leonardo Ricci, who worked with the theme of informality, Maurizio Sacripanti with his interest in the expressive means of advanced technologies, Giovanni *Michelucci, who built the Church of San Giovanni Battista (1960–3) on the Autostrada del Sole (motorway) near Florence, and not least Carlo *Scarpa, who had already realized his famous pavilion at the Venice Biennale in 1956 and now continued with his exceptional remodelling of museums (Palermo, Verona, Venice). Several younger architects were also confirmed in the 1960s: Gino *Valle, who created a series of industrial buildings in Pordenone (1961), *Aymonino, Vittorio Gregotti, Gae Aulenti, *Rossi and Guido Canella.

The Triennale of Free Time, held in Milan in 1964, once again took up problems of architecture after three successive Triennales had focused on questions of design.

In 1966 two books were published which were to have considerable influence: *Il territorio dell'architettura* by Vittorio Gregotti and *L'Architettura della città* by Aldo Rossi (*Rational architecture).

Italy. Zanussi administration building, Pordenone (1961), by Gino Valle

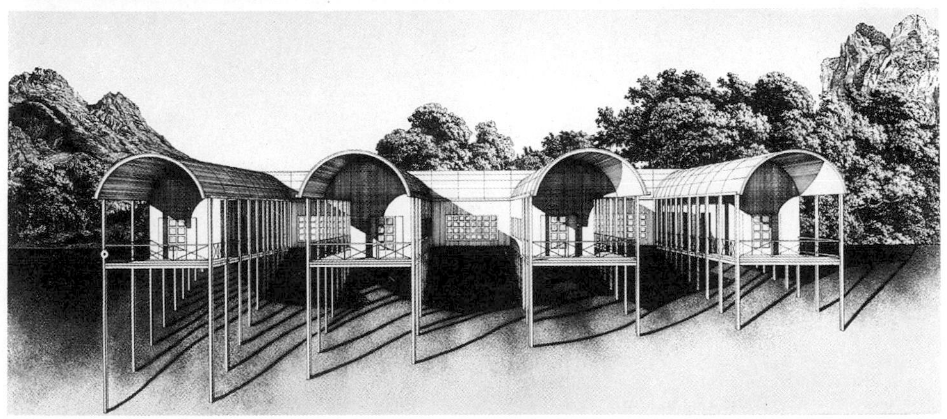

Italy. House at Borgo, Ticino (1973), by Aldo Rossi and Gianni Braghieri

Earlier confidence in a limitless progress ended with the onset of the world-wide economic crisis of the late 1960s and with the crisis of ideals which culminated in the movements of 1968.

The architecture of the 1970s sought to provide a series of answers to this deep crisis. On the one hand there developed a new avant garde (*Superstudio, Archizoom, Ettore Sottsass) which rejected Rationalism and advocated a new creativity, while on the other hand a group of young architects in the circle of the Istituto Universitario di Architettura in Venice proposed a reconsideration of the traditional principles of urban form. Aymonino, Rossi, Polesello, and Semerani were its most important proponents. A further group maintained a strong urban planning position which concentrated essentially on the management and conservation of the existing urban fabric.

Important testing grounds for these various tendencies were offered in the great competitions for new university complexes which were held in the early 1970s (Florence, 1971; Cagliari, 1972; Cosenza, 1973).

Giancarlo *De Carlo has assumed a special position in recent Italian architecture. He has concentrated his efforts principally on the city of Urbino, whose development he has determined not only as a planner but also with built work of a noteworthy standard of architectural quality.

Among the youngest architects one should cite Emilio Battisti, Franco Purini, Pierluigi Nicolin and Emilio Puglielli, whose grounding is the school of Gregotti, as well as Massimo Scolari, Giorgio *Grassi, Umberto Siola and Salvatore Bisogni, who take Rossi's work as a starting point. VG

□ Kidder Smith, G. E., *Italy Builds*, London 1955; Pagano, Carlo, *Architettura italiana oggi/Italy's Architecture Today*, Milan 1955; Meeks, Carroll L. V., *Italian Architecture, 1750–1914*, New Haven, Conn., and London 1966; Galardi, Alberto, *Neue italienische Architekture*, Stuttgart 1967; Fanelli, G., *Architettura moderna in Italia 1900–1940*, Florence 1968; 'Italia', *Zodiac* (Milan), no. 20, 1970; Cresti, Carlo, *Appunti storici e critici sull'architettura italiana dall 1900 ad oggi*, Florence 1971; Patetta, Luciano, *L'architettura in Italia 1919–1943. Le polemiche*, Milan 1972; Patetta, L., and Danesi, S., *Il razionalismo e l'architettura in Italia durante il fascismo*, Venice 1976; Conforto, C., De Giorgi, G., Muntoni, A., and Pazzaglini, M., *Il dibattito architettonico in Italia 1945–1975*, Rome 1977.

J

Jacobsen, Arne, b. Copenhagen 1902, d. Copenhagen 1971. In his work J. was to a notable degree open to new impulses without losing his attachment to the Danish architectural tradition. The same sense of order, modular rhythms and natural proportions characterizes J.'s architecture. When he was a student, *neoclassicism was still dominant in *Denmark and the architecture of the period around 1800 was greatly admired, in particular those buildings by Nicolai Abildgard. However, J.'s first encounter with the architecture of *Le Corbusier and *Mies van der Rohe in exhibitions in Paris (1925) and Berlin (1927–8) was important both for himself and for the whole development of Danish architecture.

Trained in the architectural school of the Academy of Arts, Copenhagen, from which he graduated in 1928, J. later taught there (1956–71). While still a student, he built the first of a long series of single-family houses, reminiscent externally, with its yellow bricks and tiled roof, of the period around 1800. The flexibility of his talent enabled him, however, at the same time to try his hand at the cuboid forms of the

Jacobsen. Bellavista estate, Copenhagen (1934)

modernist style. Together with Flemming Lassen, he created a sensation at an exhibition in 1929 with a circular 'house of the future', complete with helicopter landing-pad on the roof. In 1930–5 he created a harmonious group of buildings in the Bellevue beach area near Copenhagen, beginning with the baths, whose cabins and kiosks were designed with elegance. These were followed by the three-storey Bellavista housing development, with staggered façade features. Finally came the Bellevue Theatre, which was thought of primarily as a summer theatre and therefore given a sliding ceiling to allow the night sky to serve as a roof.

It was through his close friendship with the Swedish architect Gunnar *Asplund that J. learned to work at a building, both technically and architecturally, and to respect detail. Asplund's influence shows clearly in the Stelling House in Copenhagen (1937) and the town halls of Århus (1937) and Søllerød (1940–2), designed in collaboration with Erik Møller and Flemming Lassen respectively.

After a period of enforced isolation during World War II, J. regained his position among the leaders of Danish architecture with his Søholm housing scheme (1950–5). In the Munkegård School at Gentofte (1952–6), a single-storey construction with numerous bays and courtyards, he combined a sense of total unity of design and quality with an atmosphere of intimacy. In a series of buildings he adopted the largely American-developed principle of construction with internal supporting columns and curtain-wall façades, to which he brought a high degree of refinement, as in the Jespersen office building in Copenhagen (1955); Rødovre town hall (1955); and the SAS Building in Copenhagen (1958–60).

Among his industrial buildings, special mention must be made of: the Massey-Harris exhibition and works building, Glostrup (1952); and the Carl Christensen factory in Ålborg (1956). In his later years J. also designed a number of buildings abroad, including: St Catherine's College, Oxford (1960–4); the main administration building of the Hamburgische Electricitäts-Werke, Hamburg (1962–70); and the City Hall, Mainz (1970–3; completed by his colleagues Hans Dissing and Otto Weitling).

At home J.'s last major work was his design for the Danish National Bank in Copenhagen

Jacobsen. Jespersen office building, Copenhagen (1955)

Jacobsen. City Hall, Mainz (1970–3; completed by Hans Dissing and Otto Weitling)

(1961–71). Here, the simple, monumental mass of the building and reflective surfaces were conceived to blend well with the old warehouses near the harbour. J. in fact never wanted to be a specialist. In addition to being an architect he also was an influential designer of silverware, furniture and fabric patterns. Although these were mostly undertaken for particular buildings, they were never of such an individual nature that they could not be put to general use, and many were in fact subsequently mass-produced. TF

☐ Faber, Tobias, *Arne Jacobsen*, Stuttgart 1964; Shriver, Poul Erik, *Arne Jacobsen*, Copenhagen 1972.

Japan. Japan has a long tradition of expanding its own culture by absorbing elements of foreign cultures and then modifying them in its own idiom. Even Japanese traditional architecture was a mixture of older indigenous building methods and the Buddhist temple style imported from China and Korea. Likewise, the 'modernization' of Japanese architecture was essentially synonymous with 'westernization'; in practice, this phenomenon occurred not only in architecture but in the whole of Japanese civilization after the downfall of the feudal system of the Tokugawa Shogunate (1603–1867) and the emergence of the new Meiji era (1868–1912). Even prior to this era of westernization, a few instances of the transplantation of Western domestic architectural styles had occurred. However, after the Meiji restoration, this transplantation process became one of the most important components of the national policy for the modernization of the whole nation. In accordance with this policy, the Meiji government invited many specialists of the building industry to expedite the task of construction of public buildings and to establish a modern system of architectural education. The British architect Josiah Condor, who was among these foreign specialists, made a great contribution to Japanese architecture as a lecturer at the Tokyo Imperial University.

Since the architecture of the Meiji period was patronized by the government and the academic establishment, acting as motivating forces, its development reflected a definite commitment to technocracy and attached greater importance to structural engineering and building economy than to the creativity of the individual architect.

This kind of literal 'functionalism' derived from the concept of 'architecture for the nation', combined with the eclectic style chiefly derived from Victorian architecture in *Great Britain, gradually came to be regarded in the eyes of young students as oppressive. The Taisho period (1912–26), immediately following the Meiji era, was marked by the pursuit of new architecture by the younger generation. In 1920, several students of Tokyo Imperial University formed the 'Japanese Secession', declaring their detachment from the architecture of the past and generating stimulative manifestos and exhibitions of their 'fantastic' projects which were undoubtedly affected by the architecture of German *Expressionism. Among the founding members of the Secessionist movement were Sutemi Horiguchi, Mayumi Takizawa, Mamoru Yamada and Kikuji Ishimoto. As the Meiji 'modernization' was a specifically Japanese phenomenon and its architectural style was in fact nothing new by Western standards, this new movement was virtually the first expression of modern architecture in Japan. In the ensuing years came a number of examples of 'new' architecture, competing with the eclectic works of the older generation of architects. If the first buildings, like the early projects of the Secessionists, still showed Expressionist features – for example, the Central Telegraph Office by Yamada (1926) and the Asahi News Press Building (1927) by Ishimoto, both in Tokyo – there was soon a movement towards the purer *International Style. Of particular interest is the fact that this revolutionary change in the 'architectural language' was reflected in the work not only of independent architects but also of those working for official organs such as the Building Department of the Tokyo Metropolitan Office (which produced several notable school buildings), the Dojunkan Housing Corporation and the Teishin-sho (Communications Services Corporation). In particular, the Teishin-sho staff included a number of talented architects such as Roku Iwamoto, Mamoru Yamada (former Secessionist), Tetsuo Yoshida and Hideo Kosaka. Yamada's Teishin hospitals in Tokyo (1937) and Osaka (1941) and Yoshida's General Post Office in Tokyo (1931) could be counted among the most successful examples of the Modern Movement in pre-war Japan.

Although Japanese architects had already demonstrated in this period that their abilities

Japan. Central Telegraph Office, Tokyo (1926), by Mamoru Yamada

Japan. General Post Office, Tokyo (1931), by Tetsuo Yoshida

Japan. Asahi News Press Building, Tokyo (1927), by Kikuji Ishimoto

were not inferior to those of most Western architects (a typical example is 28-year-old Renshichiro Kawakita's project which won fourth prize in the competition for the theatre of Kharkov, USSR), some noted Western masters exerted a profound influence of the architects of Japan. Two of these masters, Frank Lloyd *Wright and Bruno *Taut, were active there for several years. Wright built the Imperial Hotel (1915–22) as well as the Jiyugakuen Kindergarten (1921), both in Tokyo, and some residences. Taut's most significant works were writings on Japanese architecture and culture in general. Ultimately, however, Taut's works proved to have a greater direct influence on Japanese architects than did Wright's buildings. Wright's works, in spite of their prominence, were too individualistic and unique to serve as models for Japanese architects who were just beginning to establish their own modern idiom. For this reason, aside from several imitative works by such architects as Shin and Endo, the influence of the American master remained rather peripheral, excepting the fact that some of his collaborators contributed much to the future development of Japanese architecture. Antonin Raymond, a Czech architect who came to Japan together with Wright, remained in Japan until his death (except during the war years) and produced a number of excellent and genuinely modernist buildings such as the Tokyo Golf Club (1932) and the Akaboshi residence (1935). Kameki Tsuchiura, who had earlier been one of Wright's assistants, designed his own house (1935), a notable work having a special place in the history of Japanese residential architecture. But neither of their styles contained any important features reminiscent of Wright.

The lessons of the 'New Architecture' were also introduced into Japan by young Japanese architects who had gone to Europe to study under the leading figures of the Modern Movement. Kunio *Mayekawa and Junzo Sakakura worked under *Le Corbusier in Paris, and Bunzo Yagamuchi worked under *Gropius in Berlin. Yamaguchi's remarkable Constructivist annexe to the Tokyo Dental School (1934) and Sakakura's Japanese Pavilion at the World's Fair of 1937 in Paris exhibited the skill of the younger generation of Japanese architects.

In the late 1930s and early '40s, however, this new international language had to confront a new situation, a call for a 'national style'. This problem had already been discussed in the Japanese Architectural Academy as early as 1920, a fact which revealed the Japanese architects' awareness of their own national identity. This issue had been raised during the long planning process for the National Parliament Building, which was ultimately completed in 1936 in a classic *Art Deco style. The rise of Japanese militarism accelerated this call for a 'national style' and gave birth to a strange stylistic mixture of European Fascist architecture, which became known as the 'Imperial-Crown Style'. Hitoshi Watanabe's winning project in the competition for the Tokyo Imperial Museum (1931, built in 1938), which was chosen in preference to Mayekawa's entry in the manner of Le Corbusier, was among the earliest typical examples of this hybrid style.

Kenzo *Tange's sensational début in two competitions was also marked by a definite tendency toward the nationalistic style. In this difficult period, Japanese architects who were opposed to vulgar nationalism formed the Kosaku Bunka Renmei (based on the idea of the *Deutscher Werkbund) to defend the ideals of modern architecture, but the movement soon lost its momentum. During the years of economic recovery after World War II, Japanese architects advocated 'architecture for democracy', as represented in Ryuichi Hamaguchi's book *Architecture of Humanism*, and the N.A.U. (New Japan Architects Union) was formed in 1947 to further this goal. Mayekawa, Sakakura and other modernists held the leadership in this movement for the next two decades. And in 1949, Tange reappeared as a champion of the younger architects after winning the competition for the Hiroshima Peace Centre. After a short period of optimistic belief in Functionalism, a theory of Socialist Realism was introduced to re-evaluate the problem of a national or regional architectural language. During the 1950s, Mayekawa and Tange, among others, showed their ability to synthesize modern technology and 'Japanese character' strongly influenced by the late work of Le Corbusier. In the 1960s the major concern of Japanese architects lay in developing a systematic planning methodology applicable both to building design and construction and to urbanism. Tange,

Japan. Tokyo Imperial Museum (1938) by Hitoshi Watanabe

Japan. Plan for Tokyo (1959–60) by Kenzo Tange

with his Tokyo Plan (1959–60), became once again the leader in this phase, and younger architects formed the Metabolist movement under his influence (*Metabolism). Typical works of this period included several of Tange's public buildings, such as the Kagawa Prefectural Office Building, Takamatsu (1955–8), and the Tokyo National High School (1961–4), as well as Kiyonori *Kikutake's Tokoen Hotel, Yonago (1964), Fumihiko Maki's buildings for Rissho University in Kumagaya (1967–8) and Sachio Ohtani's Kyoto International Conference Hall (1966). Concurrently with the growth of the movement of Metabolism, a number of architects (including some of the older generation) produced highly individual works, as if in reaction against the rigidly systematic designs of the Metabolist mainstream. Togo Murano's Nissei Insurance Building (1964) and Martin Luther Theological School (1970) and Seiichi Shirai's Shinwa Bank, Sasebo (1968–77), were among these works.

The Osaka World's Fair of 1970 represented the culmination of the Metabolist mainstream movement after a decade of growth supported by the great Japanese economic boom of the 1960s. Among the works presented at Expo '70 were Tange's huge space-frame, the novel metabolic capsules of Kikutake and *Kurokawa, and various pneumatic structures. In the wake of this Metabolist 'orgy', optimism about the future value of Metabolism evaporated, and the architectural profession was polarized between the 'professionalist' majority and the 'conceptualist' minority. Arata *Isozaki, with his neo-platonic aesthetic, and Kazuo

★Shinohara, with his intensive symbolism, became the new leaders of the 'conceptualists' in the 1970s and continue in these roles. Young Japanese architects today are even more radical and more individualistic, as young artists have tended to be. HY

☐ Kulterman, Udo, *New Japanese Architecture*, London 1960; Boyd, Robin, *New Directions of the Japanese Architecture*, New York 1968; Tafuri, Manfred, *L'architettura moderna in Giappone*, Rome 1964; Ross, Michael Franklin, *Beyond Metabolism*, New York 1978; Yatsuka, Hajime, 'Architecture in Urban Desert', *Oppositions* (Cambridge, Mass., and London), 23

Japan. International Conference Hall, Kyoto (1966), by Sachio Ohtani

Japan. Gunma Prefectural Museum of Fine Arts, Tagasaki (1971–4), by Arata Isozaki

Johansen, John M(acLane), b. New York 1916. Studied at Harvard University under Walter ★Gropius and Marcel ★Breuer and worked in the offices of Breuer and ★Skidmore, Owings & Merrill. From 1948 to 1970 he had his own office in New Canaan, Conn.; in 1970 he entered a partnership in New York with Ashok M. Bhavnani. In 1976 he became a professor at the Pratt Institute in New York. J. is keenly interested in structural experiments: designs for a holiday house with a reinforced-concrete shell and a 'streamlined house' with walls of sprayed reinforced concrete. His design for the U.S. Embassy in Dublin (1964), a rotunda with circular courtyard and a façade of prefabricated, reinforced-concrete frames, is based on the Irish round-tower tradition.

In the Oklahoma Theater Center in Oklahoma City (1966–70) the various elements – building volumes, services, pedestrian ramps – are expressively articulated and combined in a composition of dynamic movement. This is at once a revival of the approach of Russian ★Constructivism and an attempt to realize a 'kinetic' architecture for the electronic era. G Ha

□Heyer, Paul, *Architects on Architecture*, New York 1966; Johansen, John M., *The New Urban Aesthetic*, New York 1972.

Johansen. Oklahoma Theater Center, Oklahoma City (1966–70)

Johnson, Philip, b. Cleveland 1906. Studied philology at Harvard University, 1923–30, and was the first director of the Architecture Department of the Museum of Modern Art in New York (MOMA), 1930–6. He later returned to Harvard to study architecture under ★Gropius and ★Breuer, 1940–3, and had his own architectural office in Cambridge, Mass., 1942–6. In 1946 he again became Director of the Architecture Department of the Museum of Modern Art, and since 1954 has practised as an architect in New York (1964–7 in partnership with Richard Foster; since 1967 with John Burgee).

His attention was first directed to European avant-garde architecture as early as 1927 by an essay by the architectural historian Henry-Russell Hitchcock, and J. became one of the most influential American propagandists for the style in the 1930s. He arranged for ★Mies van der Rohe's first trip to New York (where the latter redesigned J.'s apartment), as well as that of ★Le Corbusier, and in 1932 published with Hitchcock that most influential book, *The International Style*, which defined the Modern Movement as a formally determined stylistic tendency with no reference to ideological or sociological principles and thereby coined the widely used term ★'International Style' (the suggestion originally came from Alfred Barr, then director of MOMA).

In the 1940s J., inspired by his own activity as a publicist, himself turned to active architectural practice. His first work, realized in 1942, was his own house in Cambridge, Mass. In 1949 he built, also for himself, the 'Glass House' in New Canaan, Conn.; for all the unmistakable influence of Mies van der Rohe's Farnsworth House in Plano, Ill. (designed 1945), J.'s elegant glass prism is a decidedly independent work. Its placement in a park-like landscape and its relationship to the neighbouring guest house and the ornamental pond set before it bear witness to an individual sensibility. The circular bathroom core reveals a new interest in elementary geometrical forms and Mies van der Rohe's striving to make the constructive frame of a building legible takes on a formal-decorative aspect in J.'s equal concern for perfection of details. He drew not only on the German master of ★Rationalism, but also on those architects whom Hitchcock had labelled 'romantic classicists', such as Ledoux and Schinkel. A whole series of smooth and tasteful buildings was to

Johnson. Glass House, New Canaan, Conn. (1949): exterior and interior

follow, including the Hodgson House in New Canaan and the Oneto House in Irvington, N.Y. (both 1951, built in collaboration with Landes Gores), as well as the delicately composed garden of the MOMA (1953).

With the Kneses Tifereth Israel Synagogue in Port Chester, N.Y. (1954–6), J. widened radically the spectrum of his *eclecticism and announced an entire sequence of ever more audacious experiments, notable for displaying a hedonistic nonchalance in a context of equally refined and fickle *historicism. The experiments included the Roofless Church in New Harmony, Indiana (1960), the Sheldon Memorial Art Gallery of the University of Nebraska at Lincoln (1963), as well as the New York State Theater (1960–4), one of the components in *Harrison and *Abramovitz's Lincoln Center complex, which fits easily within the tradition of the *Ecole des Beaux-Arts in American architecture. The fact that J. could also collaborate at the same time with Mies van der Rohe on the puritan-spirited Seagram Building in New York (1954–8) is symptomatic of his lack of rigid aesthetic convictions.

This whimsical changeability is also evident in J.'s subsequent work. The Kline Geology Laboratory Tower at Yale University, a heavy, monumental tower whose historical solemnity recalls Louis *Kahn, was built in 1962–4; the Art Museum of South Texas at Corpus Christi, completed in 1972, is a white complex composed of elementary stereometric volumes. The IDS (Investors Diversified Services) Center in Minneapolis, completed in 1973, was one of the first combined hotel/office buildings with an extensive public lobby, a type developed on an even larger scale by John *Portman. The Pennzoil Place complex in Houston was real-

Johnson. Pennzoil Place, Houston, Texas (1970–6)

ized in 1970–6, and comprises two crisply-cut, dark mirror-glass clad administration towers with an immense public glass hall slipped in between as a unifying element.

In the 1980s J.'s frivolity combined with his craving for the spectacular reached a highpoint. In 1980 he built the 'Crystal Cathedral' in Garden Grove near Los Angeles, an immense glass-enclosed space with breathtaking light effects. The AT&T Building in New York (1978–83) is a skyscraper which sports a mélange of Gothic, Renaissance, neo-classical, and *Art Deco elements. Also under construction is the PPG (Pittsburgh Plate Glass) Building in Pittsburgh, a filigreed complex, which draws on the neo-Gothic of Sir Charles Barry and A. W. N. Pugin and refers with light ironic reverence to the old (Gothic-inspired) University buildings in Pittsburgh.

J. has had and continues to have a probably unequalled influence on American architecture. With the same élan with which he eased the penetration of European modernism into the USA in the 1930s and 1940s, he became subsequently a precursor of *Post-Modernism. However, most of his epigones lack his sure aesthetic sense and cultivated-cynical refinement; they are only able to imitate the hollow masks of his forms in order to make architecture attractive for patrons who are concerned only with appearances and to satisfy a novelty-craving public. VML

☐ Hitchcock, Henry-Russell, and Johnson, Philip, *The International Style*, New York 1932; Johnson Philip, *Machine Art*, New York 1934; ——, *Mies van der Rohe*, New York 1947; Jacobus, John, Jr, *Philip Johnson*, New York 1962; Hitchcock, Henry-Russell, *Philip Johnson: Architecture 1949–1965*, New York and London 1966; Noble, Charles, *Philip Johnson*, London 1972; 'Philip Johnson', *The Architectural Forum* (New York), vol. 138 (1973), no. 1, pp. 26–74; Miller, Nory, *Johnson/Burgee: Architecture*, New York 1979; Stern, Robert A. M. (ed.), *Philip Johnson, Writings*, New York 1979.

Josic, Alexis. b. Stari Becej, Yugoslavia 1921. Studied painting and was active as a film scenographer before turning to architecture. In 1953 he went to Paris where he joined the ATBAT office (Atelier des Bâtisseurs). In 1955 a partnership was formed with *Candilis and *Woods; since 1963 J. has maintained his own office in Sèvres, near Paris. Like Candilis and Woods, he made his name principally for his role in the collaborative planning of the new town of Toulouse le Mirail (competition 1962, realization 1964–77). His designs are generally based on a three-dimensional modular system which permits an orderly growth without compromising the original concept. An example is the new town of Lille-Est (1972–8, with François Calsat). AM

☐ See under Candilis.

K

Kahn, Albert, b. Rhaunen, Westphalia 1869, d. Detroit 1942. Emigrated to the *USA in 1880. He spent the years 1928–32 in *Russia, working on an industrial building programme. Early on, K. paved the way for the precise and finely delineated cubic forms of the 1950s and 1960s (*Mies van der Rohe; Eero *Saarinen). Among the most successful examples of a functionalist architecture in the best sense – one in which the restrained architectural language harmonizes

Kahn, Albert. Rouge River Glass Plant, Ford Motor Company, Dearborn, Mich. (1924)

with industrial requirements – is his Rouge River Glass Plant of the Ford Motor Company in Dearborn, Mich. (1924).

☐ Detroit Institute of Arts, *The Legacy of Albert Kahn* (exhibition catalogue), Detroit, 1970; Hildebrand, Grant, *Designing for Industry: The Architecture of Albert Kahn*, Cambridge, Mass. 1974.

Kahn, Louis I (sadore), b. on the Island of Ösel, Estonia 1901, d. New York 1974. Studied at the University of Pennsylvania in Philadelphia, 1920–4, within the tradition of the French ⋆Ecole des Beaux-Arts. After work in various professional offices (among them that of the academically oriented architect Paul Cret), as well as several extended visits to Europe, K. opened his own office in Philadelphia in 1937. In 1941 he formed a partnership with George ⋆Howe, one of the pioneers of modernism in the ⋆USA; in 1942 Oscar Stonorov joined the partnership, and continued his collaboration with K. until 1948, although Howe left in 1943. K. taught at various institutions, including Yale University, the Massachusetts Institute of Technology and the University of Pennsylvania. He was a member of Team X (⋆CIAM).

In 1941–3 Kahn, Howe and Stonorov realized the much-acclaimed Carver Court Housing estate in Coatesville, Pa. In the late 1940s K. came under the influence of Frederick ⋆Kiesler and especially of R. Buckminster ⋆Fuller. Fuller's impact is especially strong in the various projects based on geodesic principles which K.

Kahn, Louis. City Tower Municipal Building, Philadelphia, Pa. (with Anne Tyng; project, 1957)

drew up between 1952–7 for the City Tower Municipal Building in Philadelphia, in collaboration with Anne Tyng, an ardent disciple of Fuller. Such experiments with utopian megastructures led in 1956–7 to the project for the Midtown City Center Forum in Philadelphia, which drew on his earlier project for a Rational City, which had in turn been inspired by ⋆Le Corbusier's Ville Radieuse (Radiant City) and in which the geometric-technological euphoria is seen to give way to a heavy, historical monumentality.

In 1951–3, in collaboration with Douglas Orr, he realized the extension to the Yale Art

Gallery in New Haven. At a time when the majority of avant-garde American architects, in the wake of an extreme faith in prosperity and growth, advocated that elegant technical perfection which had been introduced by *Mies van der Rohe, K. – although starting from the aesthetic of the master of German Rationalism – presented a bold and skilful ruggedness. He clad the architecture of 'beinahe nichts' (almost nothing) in an expressive, massive monumentality, thereby creating one of the most important buildings in the sphere of *New Brutalism.

Yet the Yale Art Gallery was much more than just that: the strong geometric plan, the simple, clear, prismatic volumes, the visible frame construction, the smooth brick façades and the ceiling of concrete tetrahedra were early evidence of K.'s deep interest in the elementary and in archetypes in architecture. This interest would continue through his entire work, and influence an entire generation.

K.'s preference for stringent adherence to Beaux-Arts typology received full expression in the bathhouse for the Jewish Community Center in Trenton, N.J.: five square rooms rise on a cruciform ground-plan, each roofed with cut-off pyramids except the middle element. In the context of the revivified academicism of the 1950s, the bathhouse is an emblem of classic simplicity and rational strength.

What had been articulated – still with some hesitation – in New Haven and Trenton was brought to a synthesis and a highpoint in the Alfred Newton Richards Medical Research Building at the University of Pennsylvania in Philadelphia (1957–60). The three laboratory blocks, to which the two towers of the Biology Building were added in 1961–4, are all joined by connecting elements to an open block and are 'served' by appended towers in which the staircase and ventilation systems are housed. Thus the laboratory spaces, square in plan, are entirely free and unencumbered. The aggressive towers are axially arranged in relation to the likewise axially composed laboratory blocks; but while the first are entirely closed, the latter are extensively glazed. Rationalistic, futuristic and medieval-romantic elements are here melded into an independent poetic architectural language.

In this building K. had given expression to the principal elements of his future architectural development: his preference for elementary geometric forms and compositions; the overheightened emphasis on function and construction tending towards formalistic autonomy; the hierarchical, and often dramatically treated, differentiation between 'served' and 'servant'

Kahn, Louis. Alfred Newton Richards Medical Research Building, University of Pennsylvania, Philadelphia (1957–60)

Kahn, Louis. Jonas Salk Institute laboratory building, La Jolla, Cal. (1959–65)

spaces, a feature adopted from *Wright's Larkin Building; the monumentalization of secondary elements, typical of *New Brutalism; the involvement with the dualism of 'silence and light' by no means free of mythic connotations; and finally the return to the past, which is manifested partly in abstract terms and partly (particularly in late works) explicitly.

In the laboratory buildings of the Jonas Salk Institute at La Jolla, Cal., built 1959–65, the 'serving' mezzanine floor below each laboratory level (in which both the supporting structure and the technical/mechanical installations are housed) permitted an entirely free and functional organization of work spaces as in the Medical Research Building. In the (unbuilt) reception centre, K. developed for the first time that 'House-within-a-house' principle which he had already sketched out in 1959 (American Consulate in Luanda, Angola) and which was later to become a principal theme of O. M. *Ungers' work. The Unitarian Church in Rochester, N.Y., built 1959–67, was as much a restrained as an elegantly controlled complex. The additively conceived Erdman Hall Dormitories at Bryn Mawr College in Bryn Mawr, Pa., were built in 1960–5. Among his later important works in the USA is the Kimbell Art Museum in Fort Worth, Texas (1966–72, in collaboration with Preston M. Gerne and Associates), and the Yale Center for British Art, New Haven, Conn. (1969–74).

It was the Third World that finally afforded K. the opportunity to put his urban planning and architectural notions into practice on a large scale: the planning for the government centre of Dacca began in 1962 and building was undertaken in 1973–6, thus largely after K.'s death. Like the Indian Institute of Management in Ahmedabad, India (1962–7, in collaboration with B. V. Doshi and A. D. Raje), the fortress-like closed buildings display numerous geometric-decorative types, principally derived from antique Roman models. The 'House-within-a-house' principle is masterfully demonstrated in the Central Building of the Assembly: the supporting brick walls, into which reinforced-concrete elements are set and in which round and arched elements are cut, evoke traditional precedents. The formal language attests to an abstracted *historicism, which seems to strive to fulfil with monumental solemnity the – deeply American – craving for history.

K. is the figurehead of an important transition in architectural culture, in which the late *International Style of the post-war years was dissolved, via *New Brutalism, into a new formalism, the most extreme manifestations of which are, on the one hand, *Post-Modernism and, on the other, *Rational architecture. Supported by a sometimes decidedly cryptic and metaphysically imbued architectural philosophy, K.'s projects as well as his executed buildings have influenced the architects of the succeeding generation in a most decisive manner. His exacting search for architectural form was for him, in the first place, a spiritual, indeed mythical, act; it is no coincidence that his most successful buildings are those of a religious or symbolic nature. Through his creative involvement with the past, which simultaneously provided a restraint and an impulse for his imagination, K. anticipated one of the central problems of the architecture of the 1970s and 1980s and thus prepared the way for personalities as diverse as Aldo *Rossi, James *Stirling, and Mario *Botta. VML

☐ Kahn, Louis I., 'Architecture Is the Thoughtful Making of Spaces', *Perspecta* (New Haven), 4 (1957); ——, 'Remarks', *Perspecta*, 9/10 (1965); Wurman, R. S., and Feldman, E. (eds.), *The Notebooks and Drawings of Louis I. Kahn*, Philadelphia 1962; Scully, Vincent, Jr., *Louis I. Kahn*, New York 1962; 'Louis I. Kahn', *L'Architecture d'aujourd'hui* (Paris), no. 142 (February/March 1969); Giurgola, R., and Mehta, J., *Louis I. Kahn*, Zurich and Boulder, Col. 1975; Ronner, H., Jhaveri, S., and Vesella, A., *Louis I. Kahn: The Complete Works 1935–1974*, Basle, Stuttgart and Boulder, Col. 1977; Lobel, John, *Between Silence and Light: Spirit in the Architecture of Louis I. Kahn*, 1979.

Kiesler, Frederick, b. Vienna 1890, d. New York 1965. Studied at the Akademie der bildenden Künste and the Technische Hochschule in Vienna. After a brief collaboration with *Loos in 1920, he was active notably as a stage designer. In 1923 he joined the artistic group De Stijl, and in 1925 he directed the Austrian section of the 'Exposition internationale des arts décoratifs et industriels modernes' in Paris (*Art Deco). In 1926 he went to New York, where in the same year he formed a partnership with Harvey Wiley Corbett which lasted until 1928. He was Director of Stage Design at the Juilliard School of

Music in New York, 1934–47, and Director of the Laboratory for Design Correlation of the School of Architecture at Columbia University, 1936–42. In 1957 he formed a partnership with Armand Bartos, which continued until K.'s death. His fundamental concern was with the 'endless', with continuous space, which in various guises informs his entire work, beginning with the Endless House (1923, revised repeatedly until 1960), via stage sets – such as that for the Berlin production of Karel Čapek's *R.U.R.* (also 1923) – and the Endless Theatre (1924) to the Universal Theater project for the Ford Foundation (1961). The Endless Theater exercised an influence on Walter ★Gropius's Totaltheater of 1927. AM

☐ *Frederick Kiesler: Environmental Sculpture* (exhibition catalogue), New York 1964; 'Kiesler by Kiesler', *Architectural Forum* (New York), September 1965; Kiesler, Frederick, *Inside the Endless House*, New York 1966; 'Frederick Kiesler 1923–1964', *Zodiac* (Milan), no. 19 (1969), pp. 18–49; *Frederick Kiesler* (exhibition catalogue), Vienna 1975.

Kikutake, Kiyonori, b. Kurume 1928. Studied at the Waseda University in Tokyo, where he has had his own office since 1953. His career is closely tied to Japanese ★Metabolism, in which he played an important formulating role through his projects for cities in the sea, such as the Tower Shaped Community (1958) and the various Marine Cities (1958, 1960, 1963), as well as the Sky House built for himself in Tokyo (1959). In the Sky House the interior service accessories are not united in a central core but rather disposed on the periphery of the open living space. Similarly, in the Pacific Hotel in Chigasaki (1966) the bathrooms are prefabricated units hung on the exterior walls of the bedroom tower. In both cases the underlying principle is that the elements most subject to change should be so arranged that they can easily be replaced, an expression of the Metabolist conception of life as a continual developing stream that architecture must follow. This idea was manifested differently in the Shimane Prefectural Museum in Matsue (1959) with the division of the building into a strongly expressed fixed part in the lower two storeys and an open exhibition hall above, and in the Miyakonoyo Civic Hall (1966) where a light, collapsible roof is raised over a fixed platform. The ties between Metabolism and Japanese

Kikutake. Miyakonoyo Civic Hall (1966)

tradition found architectural expression in the Administration Building of the great shrine in Izumo (1963) and in the Tokoen Hotel in Yonago (1964). K.'s early conceptions of an extension of civilization into the sea was in part realized in the Aquapolis at Okinawa (1975). AM

☐ Kawazoe, N., Kikutake, K., and Kurokawa, K., *Metabolism 1960. Proposals for New Urbanism*, Tokyo 1960; Kikutake, K., *Taisha Kenchikuran* (Metabolic Architecture), Tokyo 1968; Drew, Philip, *The Third Generation: the changing meaning of architecture*, New York 1972; *Kiyonori Kikutake. Works and Methods 1956–1970*, Tokyo 1973; *Kiyonori Kikutake. Concepts and Planning*, Tokyo 1978.

Kleihues, Josef Paul, b. Rheine 1933. Studied first at the Technische Hochschule in Stuttgart and then in Berlin, as well as at the ★Ecole des Beaux-Arts in Paris. He worked in the office of Peter Poelzig (as project director for the new Kopfklinik Westend building in Berlin-Charlottenburg), 1960–2, and since 1962 has had his own office in Berlin (until 1967 in partnership with Hans Heinrich Moldenschardt). He became a professor at the University in Dortmund in 1973 and was appointed Planning Director of the 'Internationale Bauausstellung 1984' (IBA) in 1979. While his early works reflect a continued involvement with ★New Brutalism and ★Structuralism, K. developed at the end of the 1960s an independent architectural language which, on the one hand, has a certain affinity with Italian Rationalism and, on the other

Kleihues. Workshops of the Berlin Sanitation Service, Berlin-Tempelhof (1970–83)

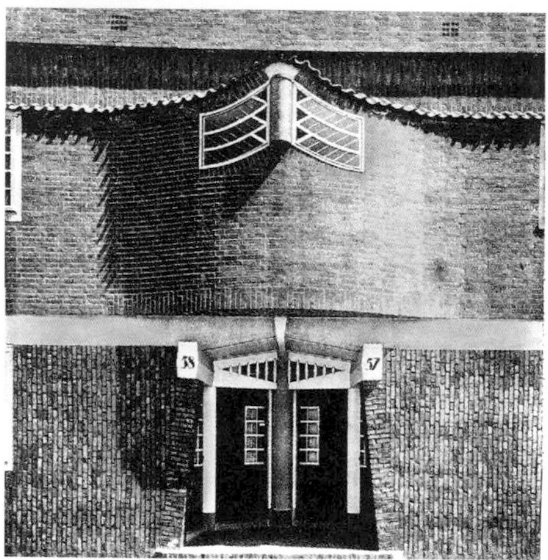

Klerk. Spaarndammerbuurt housing, Amsterdam West (1913–19)

hand, stands clearly in the tradition of Prussian neo-classicism. In addition to the Kopfklinik Westend building (1960–4, 1962–8), K.'s most important works include: the Altenclub (Senior Citizens' Club) in Berlin-Reinickendorf (1966–7); the main workshops of the Berlin Sanitation Service in Berlin-Tempelhof (1969–76, 1970–83); the apartment block 270 in Berlin-Wedding (1969–80); and the Hospital in Berlin-Neukölln (1973, 1976ff). Of his unrealized works, especially noteworthy projects are those for: the University in Bielefeld (1968–9); the Sprengel-Museum in Hanover (1972); the Landesgalerie Nordrhein-Westfalen in Düsseldorf (1975); and the Park Lenné Quarter in Berlin (1976-7). FW

□ 'Kleihues', *Das Kunstwerk* (Stuttgart), 32 (1979), nos. 2/3, pp. 80–9.

Klerk, Michel de, b. Amsterdam 1884, d. Amsterdam 1923. A leading member of the School of *Amsterdam, he created, in his Spaarndammerbuurt housing in Amsterdam West (1913–19), a fascinating and in part decidedly eccentric type of stage architecture notable for its almost complete disregard for constructional and functional considerations. In the Amstellaan housing in Amsterdam South (1920–2), however, he reverted to closed, flat forms in the tradition of *Berlage. GHa

□ Frank, Suzanne, 'Michel de Klerk's Design for Amsterdam's Spaarndammerbuurt', *Nederlands Kunsthistorik Jaarboek*, 22 (1971), pp. 175–213; Searing, Helen, 'With Red Flags Flying: Politics and Architecture in Amsterdam', in: Millon, H., and Nochlin, L. (eds.), *Art and Architecture in the Service of Politics*, Cambridge, Mass. 1978.

Klint, Peter Vilhelm Jensen, b. near Skelskør, Denmark 1853, d. 1930. Worked first as an engineer, then as a painter and from 1896 as an architect. He strove in his buildings to achieve a synthesis of the brick style of northern European Gothic churches and contemporary architectural *Expressionism. His best-known work is the Grundtvig Church in Copenhagen (1913, 1921–40, completed by his son), with its expressive vertical emphasis on the west front at once reminiscent of Gothic types and of a great pipe organ. G Ha

☐ Fisker, Kay, 'Den Klintske Skole', *Arkitektur*, 7 (1963), special number.

Koolhaas, Rem, b. Rotterdam 1944. After a brief career as a copywriter, he left Holland in 1965 to study at the Architectural Association School in London, where he worked with Elia Zenghelis, who later became his partner when the Office for Metropolitan Architecture (OMA) was formed in 1975. K. and Zenghelis were joined by the painters Zoe Zenghelis and Madelon Vriesendorp, these two artists being responsible thereafter for many of the renderings produced by OMA. The first joint work of K. and Zenghelis occurred while the former was still a student. This was a phantasmagoric collage based on the theme of the Berlin Wall and entitled *Exodus* (1972). With the formation of OMA, the work of K. and Zenghelis assumed a more professional stance, as in their 1975 competition entry for a housing complex on Roosevelt Island, New York City. Around the same time, K. designed (in collaboration with Laurinda Spear) the Spear House in Miami Beach, Florida, a work which was finally realized in 1979 by the firm of Arquitectonica. At the same time K. published his manifesto on Manhattanism, entitled *Delirious New York* (1978), a study which, aside from its documentation, was to reflect the evolving sensibility of OMA, through a series of fantasy projects for Manhattan.

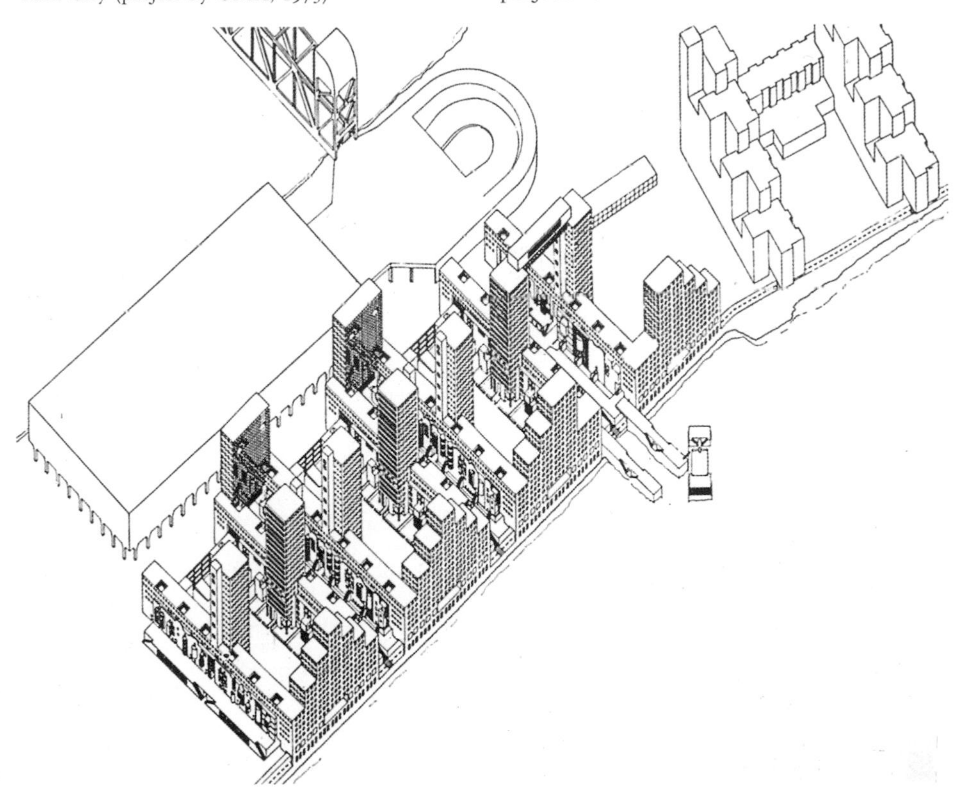

Koolhaas. Housing on Roosevelt Island, New York City (project by OMA, 1975)

In the formation of their highly chromatic style, K. and the OMA team have been affected by a number of influences, ranging from the neo-Suprematist architecture of Ivan *Leonidov, to the Continuous Monument, projected in the 1960s by Adolfo Natalini and *Superstudio.

In almost all of their subsequent work, from their Parliament extension in The Hague (1978, with Zahar Hadid) to the various designs they submitted in 1981 for the Internationale Bauausstellung 1984 in Berlin, OMA have demonstrated a form of unsentimental contextualism, in which the architectural syntax remains unrelentingly modern, while responding to the specific context. KF

☐ Koolhaas, Rem, *Delirious New York. A Retroactive Manifesto for Manhattan*, New York and London 1978; 'OMA', *Architectural Design* (London), vol. 47 (1977), no. 5; *OMA Projects 1978–1981* (exhibition catalogue), London 1981.

Kramer, Pieter Lodewijk, b. Amsterdam 1881, d. Amsterdam 1961. With van der *Mey and de *Klerk, he was one of the triumvirate whose virtuosity lay behind the School of *Amsterdam's reputation as a stringent opponent of 'objective' modernism (*Neue Sachlichkeit). Like his friend de Klerk, K. had enjoyed no formal architectural education, but had acquired the essential professional skills through working in Eduard Cuyper's office. After collaborating with van der Mey on the latter's Scheepvaarthuis in Amsterdam (1911–16), K. concentrated on housing (terrace houses in Park Meerwijk, Bergen, 1915–16; communal housing in Amsterdam). Despite their highly cultivated individuality, his buildings are nonetheless developed from their particular urban situation and architectonic context, especially in the case of the Amsterdam bridges (1918–37). After de Klerk's early death, none of the Amsterdam Expressionists built with the degree of fantasy he had incorporated in his designs. None of the characteristically softly modelled wall planes of K.'s works surpassed the corner solution achieved in his housing complex in Amsterdam South (1921–3) for De Dageraad housing corporation. In the De Bijenkorf department store in The Hague (1924–5), he applied his treatment to a completely different building type. In his later housing (Amsterdam West, on the Hoofdweg, 1923–5), K. adopted a more restrained style. WP

☐ Retera, W., *P. Kramer*, Amsterdam 1927.

Kramer. Housing in Amsterdam South (1921–3)

Kreis, Wilhelm, b. Eltville, Germany 1873, d. Bad Honnef, Germany 1955. After studies at the Technische Hochschulen of Munich, Brunswick, Berlin and Karlsruhe, he became Paul Wallot's assistant and collaborator. Twice, 1902–8 and 1926–41, he was active as a teacher in Dresden, and 1909–26 in Düsseldorf. K.'s career opened with his first prize in the competition for the Battle of Leipzig Memorial (1895) and with his Burschenschaft Monument in Eisenach (1899); over fifty Bismarck Towers throughout Germany were erected to his designs. His first large commissions were the bridge over the Rhine at Düsseldorf-Neuss (1904) and the Augustus Bridge in Dresden (1908). In the numerous department stores which he completed between 1910 and 1914, e.g. those in Elberfeld, Cologne, Chemnitz, Essen and Dortmund, K. – in contrast to his contemporary Alfred Messel – remained largely tied to historical canons and forms. After World War I, however, a tendency towards *Expressionism appears in his work, as in the Rheinhalle at Düsseldorf (1925) built on the occasion of the 'Gesolei' exhibition; but it was finally a more abstract *neo-classicism which gained the upper hand. Under the National

Socialists K. was much favoured, designing notably the buildings intended for the army High Command headquarters, situated on the proposed Berlin 'North-South Axis' planned by *Speer. He also designed a number of memorials ('Totenburgen' or Castles of the Dead), which were intended to be erected on former battle sites after the war. FJ

☐ Kreis, Wilhelm, *Soldatengräber und Gedenkstätten*, Munich 1944; Stephan, Hans, *Deutsche Künstler unserer Zeit. Wilhelm Kreis*, Oldenburg 1944; Rehder, G., *Wilhelm Kreis, Architekt in dieser Zeit, Leben und Werk*, Essen 1953.

Krier, Leon, b. Luxembourg 1946. After a short period at the Technische Hochschule in Stuttgart, he worked under James *Stirling (1968–70) and then under J. P. *Kleihues (1971–2). In 1974 he opened an office in London, where he has also taught, 1973–6, at the Architectural Association School and in 1977 at the Royal College of Art. Like his older brother Rob *Krier, but more radically, he seeks a restoration of the pre-industrial European city through the conceptual tools of *rational architecture. He has seized upon early 19th-century neo-classicism as a valid timeless style, exemplified architectonically with tremendous graphic virtuosity in such polemically intended ideal plans as that for the Lycée Classique at Echternach, Luxembourg (1970), the Royal Mint Square Project for London (1974), the La Villette quarter in Paris (1976), and the centre of Luxembourg City (1978). AM

☐ Krier, L., 'La reconstruction de la ville', *Rational Architecture/Architecture Rationelle*, Brussels 1978, pp. 33–42: ——, *Leon Krier. Drawings 1967–1980*, Brussels 1981.

Krier, Leon. Reconstruction project for Luxembourg City (1978)

Krier, Rob. Dickes House, Bridel, Luxembourg (1974–6)

Krier, Rob(ert), b. Grevenmacher, Luxembourg 1938. After study at the Technische Hochschule in Munich, he worked under O. M. *Ungers in Cologne and under Frei *Otto in Berlin and Stuttgart. Since 1975 he has been a professor at the Technical University in Vienna. Like his brother Leon *Krier and the Brussels-based Maurice Culot, with whom he forms the Belgian-Luxembourgeois line of *Rational architecture, K. has above all been interested in re-investing the contemporary city with the order and form it possessed before the Industrial Revolution. His reconstruction proposals, such as that for inner-city Stuttgart (1975), are based on Camillo Sitte's theses which see urban fabric as the product of the handling of negative spaces. In line with this theory, he extracts a typology of strongly-defined urban spaces from historical prototypes which in turn he implants in existing urban contexts. During his Stuttgart years, K. built the Siemer House at Warmbronn, near Stuttgart (1968), which draws heavily on *Stirling's work; and the Dickes House at Bridel, Luxembourg (1974–6), entirely enclosed in a dominating cubic form. His most recent building is the block of flats in the Ritterstraße, Berlin (1978–80), reminiscent of Karl *Ehn's Karl-Marx-Hof in Vienna. FJ

☐ Krier, R., *Stadtraum in Theorie und Praxis*, Stuttgart 1975; ——, 'The Work of Rob Krier', *Architecture and Urbanism* (Tokyo), June 1977.

Kroll, Lucien, b. Brussels 1927. Studied at the Ecole Nationale Supérieure de la Cambre, at the Institut Supérieur de la Cambre, and at the Institut Supérieur d'Urbanisme in Brussels. He was in partnership with the architect Charles Vandenhove in Brussels from 1951 until 1957, when he opened the Atelier Lucien Kroll in Brussels. Since 1970 he has been a professor at the Ecole Saint-Luc de Saint-Gilles in Brussels. K. is among the most prominent advocates of 'creative participation' in building, a liberation of the victims of 'paramilitary' regimentation and their direction towards the most thoroughgoing self-determination. His most important work is the Student Centre of the faculty of medicine at the Université Catholique de Louvain in Woluwe Saint-Lambert, Brussels (1970–7). Future users will to a considerable degree participate in the continuing elaboration of the design. Similarly, in the realization of the project, the architect's formal vision defers in large measure to that of those who execute the work. The result is a living formal environment of 'controlled anarchy'. AM

□ Hunziger, Christian, 'Portrait de Lucien Kroll', *L'Architecture d'aujourd'hui* (Paris), no. 183, Jan.–Feb. 1976, pp. 69–80; Williams, Stephanie, 'Ecological Architecture of Lucien Kroll', *Architectural Review*, clxv, no. 984, February 1979, pp. 94–101.

Kurokawa. Nagakin Capsule Tower, Tokyo (1972)

Kurokawa. Hawaii Dreamland, Yamagata (1966–7)

Kurokawa, Kisho, b. Nagoya, 1934. Studied at Kyoto and Tokyo Universities. After working under Kenzo *Tange he opened his own office in Tokyo in 1961. A key figure of Japanese *Metabolism, he has played an essential role in this movement, not only through projects and buildings but also through theoretical writings. After putting forward his projects for the Wall Cluster (1960), the Helix City (1961) and his proposal for a house of prefabricated concrete components (1962), K. realized for the first time his notions of an adaptable architecture of high technology on a large scale in the factory building for the Nitto-Sukushin Company at Sagae (1964). Expo '70 in Osaka offered an unrestricted field of activity on which to demonstrate his theories. He designed several exhibition buildings, including the Takara Beautilion and the Living Capsule. These ideas were carried further in the Nagakin Capsule Tower Building in Tokyo (1972) and again in the Sony Tower in Osaka (1976). Reminiscences of traditional Japanese architecture are also manifested in his work, for example the central building of the National Children's Land in Yokohama (1964–5) and the Hawaii Dreamland in Yamagata (1966–7). AM

□ Kurokawa, Kisho, and others, *Metabolism 1960. Proposals for New Urbanism*, Tokyo 1960; Kurokawa, Kisho, *The Concept of Metabolism*, Tokyo 1972; *Works of Kisho Kurokawa*, Tokyo

1970; Drew, Philip, *The Third Generation: the changing meaning of architecture*, New York 1972; *The World of Kisho Kurokawa*, Tokyo 1975.

L

Lasdun, Sir Denys, b. London 1914. Studied at the Architectural Association School, London. Worked under Wells *Coates, 1935–7, before joining the *Tecton group where he was active, with interruptions during the war, until its dissolution in 1948 (from 1946 he was a partner). In 1949–50 he ran an office with Lindsey Drake in London, where in 1960 he founded Denys Lasdun and Partners, which has worked since 1978 under the name Denys Lasdun, Redhouse and Softley. L.'s own architectural style is characterized by his emphasis on horizontal lines, either through the disposition of the building mass itself, as in the block of flats in Bethnal Green, London (1955), or by means of platforms, terraces or bridges which serve to create a sort of built landscape. Particularly expressive examples of this are the University of East Anglia at Norwich (1962–8) and the National Theatre in London (1967–76). AM

☐ Curtis, William J. R., *A Language and a Theme: the Work of Denys Lasdun and Partners*, London 1976

Le Corbusier (pseudonym of Charles-Edouard Jeanneret), b. La Chaux-de-Fonds, Switzerland 1887, d. Roquebrune on Cap Martin, South of France 1965. Le Corbusier (who used this pseudonym from 1920 on as an author, from 1922 as an architect and in everyday affairs, and from 1928 as a painter) was the dominant figure internationally in modern architecture from 1920 to 1960.

In the absence of an academic education, he developed his practical and artistic skills at the arts and crafts school in La Chaux-de-Fonds (training as a metal engraver under Charles L'Eplattenier), on study trips (Italy, Balkans, Istanbul, Mt Athos, the Athenian Acropolis), through his acquaintanceship with Josef *Hoffmann in Vienna (1908) and Henri *Sauvage in Paris (1908), by apprenticeship with Auguste *Perret in Paris (winter 1908–9) and Peter *Behrens in Berlin (1910–11), as well as by encounters with the leaders of the German arts and crafts reform movement and the *Deutscher Werkbund (Hermann *Muthesius, Karl Ernst Osthaus, Heinrich *Tessenow), on which subject he prepared a report for the school administration of his native town. He became acquainted early on with the work of Frank Lloyd *Wright through publications. Of the commonly used textbooks of the period it was, in addition to Charles Blanc's *Grammaire des arts*, above all Auguste Choisy's *Histoire de l'architecture* (Paris, 1899) that influenced him.

Of his early buildings in La Chaux-de-Fonds it was especially the Villa Schwob (1916) – one of the first reinforced-concrete houses – which reflects the impressions of these formative years of travel and the work of Hoffmann and Perret. Here the *Art Nouveau style of his engraver's training gave way to an individualist and classicist reformatory art, although still imprinted with the ideal of handicraft. But in those same years Le Corbusier had already worked out a building type adapted to industrial production. As was to be typical throughout his career, this was endowed with a slogan-like name: the Maison Dom-ino. The prototype for series production, it comprised floor platforms with recessed supports and no load-bearing walls, and individual units could be joined to one another in any direction (1914–15).

When he settled (following a sense of mission nourished by Nietschze) in Paris in 1917 to make his career, one of his aspirations was precisely the fabrication of cinderblocks for use in filling out skeleton constructions. This undertaking was thwarted, however, as were his other plans, by the needs of the post-war

Le Corbusier. Villa Schwob, La Chaux-de-Fonds (1916)

reconstruction and by increasing industrial mechanization.

However, he rose astoundingly quickly to the fore among the avant garde of Parisian painters. The order of the day was ⋆Cubism and the 'return to order'. Together with Amédée Ozenfant, he published the manifesto *Après le cubisme* (1918) – this was followed in 1925 by *La Peinture moderne* – coined the new artistic movement ⋆Purism and edited the successful reforming art journal *L'Esprit nouveau* (1920–5; the programmatic title came from a formulation of Guillaume Apollinaire). The themes of his purist paintings were everyday objects and musical instruments in clear views and analyses, often with outlines capable of two alternative readings. The further development of Le Corbusier's painting can be anticipated at this juncture: from 1928 on he introduced – following Fernand Léger's example – the human figure, *objets trouvés*, and deep spatial effects into his still-life paintings. From 1932 on, the influence of Picasso becomes evident. In place of norms, that early celebration of the 'types' of modern life, the later paintings and graphic works took his own or traditional myths as subjects and had numerous points of intersection with contemporaneous architectural and urbanistic designs. In addition to canvases, Le Corbusier produced collages, tapestries, an important mural in the Pavillon Suisse of the Cité Universitaire in Paris, sculptures, as well as graphics. For a long time Le Corbusier's colour lithographs were an icon of the modern architectural office where, as a guarantee of good composition, his ⋆Modulor was also used. This was a system of proportions grounded on the golden section or the Fibonacci series using the human figures as its basis. The furniture he designed from 1929 on with Charlotte Perriand set standards of taste to an even more marked degree.

Le Corbusier's aesthetic influence is inseparably linked to his activity as a publicist, which began in 1920. As 'Le Corbusier' – the pseudonym being derived from the surname of his great-grandmother, Lecorbésier, which yielded, through the separation of the predicate, a punning reference suggested by his facial resemblance to a raven (corbeau) – he published that series of essays in the periodical *L'Esprit nouveau* which later appeared in book form (*Vers une architecture*, 1923) and achieved international recognition. Here he formulated the

Le Corbusier. Ville contemporaine (project, 1922)

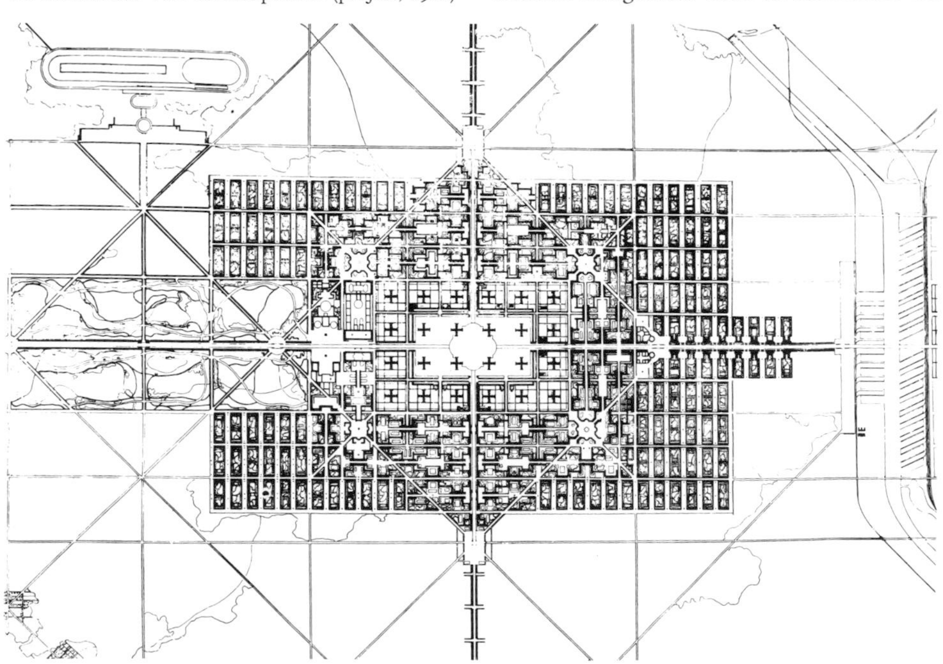

famous definition of architecture as 'the masterly, correct and magnificent play of masses brought together in light'. His comparisons with engineering constructions and with modern forms of transportation were formulated into such oft-misunderstood postulates as 'the house is a machine for living in' and that it should be as practically constructed as a typewriter. By this he meant not a mechanistic 'machine aesthetic' but rather complete rationality in plan, capacity for serial-production and function. A further enunciation of principles followed in 1926 (printed in Alfred Roth's *Zwei Wohnhäuser von Le Corbusier und Pierre Jeanneret*, Stuttgart 1927) with the 'Five points for a new architecture': the *pilotis*, roof terraces, free plan, continuous window strips and free façade composition were to be the essential elements of the new aesthetic (*Rationalism).

Of the other early programmatic writings, *Urbanisme* and *L'Art décoratif d'aujourd'hui* (both 1925) were assured of an equally strong impact thanks to their radical proposals. In 1930 the first volume of his collected works – theses, projects, and executed buildings – appeared; these were to grow to several volumes over the course of the following years. The resulting *Oeuvre complète* has been one of the most important source books of modern architecture.

The history of this influence derives as much from the demonstration models and city-planning projects which Le Corbusier, who from 1922 collaborated with his cousin Pierre Jeanneret, exhibited at the Paris Salon, as it did from his executed work. In 1922, he exhibited the Maison Citrohan – a simple box with supporting walls on the long sides, in a later version carried on *pilotis* – as well as the 'Ville contemporaine' for three million inhabitants. In 1925 the Esprit Nouveau Pavilion was intended as a prototype for a mass-produced living unit with a garden terrace to be incorporated into multi-storey apartment blocks (as in Le Corbusier's Plan Voisin for Paris). The executed work included the Villa Besnos in Vaucresson (1922), the Maisons La Roche and Jeanneret in Paris-Auteuil (1923), the Maison Cook in Boulogne-sur-Seine (1926), the Villa Stein at Garches (1927), the two houses at the Weißenhofsiedlung in Stuttgart (likewise

Le Corbusier. Plan Voisin for Paris (project, 1925): model

Le Corbusier. Houses at the Weißenhofsiedlung, Stuttgart (1927)

Le Corbusier. Second Maison Citrohan (project, 1922): model

Le Corbusier. Cité de Réfuge, Paris (1932–3)

Le Corbusier. Palace of the Soviets, Moscow (project, 1931)

Le Corbusier. Villa Savoye, Poissy (1929–31)

Le Corbusier. Pavillon Suisse, Cité Universitaire, Paris (1930–2)

1927), the Villa Savoye at Poissy (1929–31) and the Clarté apartment house in Geneva (1930–2). Characteristic of all these buildings – which have become monuments of modern architecture – are their general independence of terrain as well as a rich variety of interior and exterior spaces achieved by means of double-height rooms, gallery floors, bridges and ramps with views into the interior as well as 'framed' views looking out, all expressions of a genuine luxury in architecture which (as so expressively conveyed in the houses at Stuttgart) is conceived as a 'machine for living in', but not as the 'Existenzminimum' of a social housing design.

The same holds true in the architecture of his buildings for collective living, in which the enclosed rooms, or bedrooms as the case may be, are complemented by generously proportioned circulation areas and communal spaces which are treated as distinct architectural parts (Pavillon Suisse in the Cité Universitaire, Paris, 1930–2; Cité de Réfuge, Paris, 1932–3).

Le Corbusier also began to concern himself with the design of large-scale buildings. Thus he took part in the competitions for the Palace of the League of Nations in Geneva (1927) and for the Palace of the Soviets in Moscow (1931), and built the Centrosoyus Building in Moscow (1929–31). Especially impressive was the design for the great hall of the Palace of the Soviets, the roof of which was to be carried at the stage end by a great parabolic arch.

Le Corbusier. League of Nations Palace, Geneva (project, 1927)

As successors of the Centrosoyus came the projects for Carthesian skyscrapers (1938) and a skyscraper in Algiers (1938–42), and the construction of the Ministry of Health and Education in Rio de Janeiro (1936–43; executed by Lúcio *Costa, Oscar *Niemeyer and Affonso Eduardo *Reidy) and of the United Nations Building in New York (1947–50; carried out by Wallace K. *Harrison and Max *Abramovitz). These latter two buildings especially were prototypes for numerous office buildings throughout the world in the 1950s and 1960s.

The urban planning schemes which Le Corbusier worked out, first for Paris and then in the 1930s for several large North African and South American cities, proceeded from the assumption that an absolute authority over land and finances can ignore historical developments and democratic rights, that traffic takes priority, that the life of a person can be fulfilled by the planned ordering of places of production, administration, apartment houses and sports facilities, and finally that a modern metropolis of a million inhabitants requires a visibly monumental expression. These assumptions also formed the principles of the *Athens Charter, which resulted from the conclusions of the fourth congress of *CIAM in 1933. Much more humanistic visions of the future were presented in Le Corbusier's books *La Ville radieuse* (1935) and *Les Trois Établissements humains* (1945).

That Le Corbusier was hardly involved at all in the post-war reconstruction programme derived not so much from prejudice against his theses as from the attitude to restoration

Le Corbusier. Unité d'Habitation, Marseilles (1947–52)

adopted in Western Europe after World War II: the belief in a golden future, so dear to the 1920s, was not reintroduced in any field. Thus Le Corbusier's programmatic *Propos d'urbanisme* (1945) was seen as a renewed vision of a better world which did not respond to contemporary needs and hence seemed doubly anachronistic.

However, his post-war work was in no way inferior in its creative power to that of the pioneering years and was to be even more influential. The Unité d'Habitation at Marseilles (1947–52) masterfully accommodated in a single, variously articulated, block – 165 m (540 ft) long and 56 m (172 ft) high – a prodigious volume of space (337 apartments), the technical requirements (the living units are for example for reasons of sound-proofing inserted like individual cartons into the grid skeleton frame), the internal circulation and all urban daily requirements (shopping streets, community services, hotel, recreational landscape on the roof, which is as large as a stadium); moreover, it also provides – for some 1,800 residents – the very two-storey living units which since 1922 Le Corbusier had been elaborating as the modern habitat. Compared with Le Corbusier's own early horizontally extended housing at Pessac (1925), the vertical neighbourhood units which incorporated apartments in a single tower – these included the later schemes at Nantes-Rezé (1952–7), Berlin (1956–8), Meaux (1957–9), Briey-en-Forêt (1957–60) and Firminy-Vert (1962–8) – bear witness to their usefulness in mass housing. When compared with conventional apartment towers, they are of an incomparably greater sculptural power and experential richness; the analogy to an ocean liner is still perhaps the best.

Characteristic of Le Corbusier's later works is that they are no longer prototypes for a 'future architecture' and hence independent of any

Le Corbusier. Maisons Jaoul, Neuilly-sur-Seine (1952–6)

Le Corbusier. Monastery of Ste Marie-de-la-Tourette, Eveux-sur-l'Arbresle (1957–60)

specific site; rather they are unrepeatable, individual creations, even if many introduced 'motifs' that have since been widely imitated. Thus the pilgrimage church of Notre Dame-du-Haut at Ronchamp (1950–4) is a highly specific sculptural creation which derives from its place and socio-religious function and represents a wealth of novel general and particular aspects. In a different respect, this can also be claimed for the Maisons Jaoul at Neuilly-sur-Seine (1952–6), the monastery of Ste Marie-de-la-Tourette at Eveux-sur-l'Arbresle (1957–60), and the Carpenter Center for the Visual Arts at Harvard University in Cambridge, Mass. (1961–4).

Le Corbusier realized a complete synthesis of his early programmatic and pioneering buildings and his later sculptural-volumetric architecture in *India. His four buildings at Ahmedabad – the Museum (1955–6), the building of the Wool Weavers Association (1954–6), the Sarabhai House (1955–6) and the Shodhan Villa (1956) – combine the precision in plan and aesthetic of the Villas Stein and Savoye with a freedom which was a harbinger of the architecture of the second half of the century. In these buildings, a new richly-intoned language is created in which reinforced concrete is placed in dialogue with other building materials and with nature. On a rational engineering technology is now superimposed an 'inexpressible' (the word was coined by Le Corbusier to describe the feeling of space at Ronchamp) spatial and formal experience.

Le Corbusier's active role in Chandigarh, the new capital of the Indian state of Punjab (founded 1947), remained unfinished in terms of a 'Gesamtkunstwerk'. He was responsible only for the general plan (1950–1; with Maxwell *Fry and Jane *Drew) and the capitol area with its government buildings (1952–64), while the residential and commercial quarters were built by Indian architects. Le Corbusier achieved spatial creations of the highest quality in his own modern idiom which, however, in no way contradicts the historic architecture of India.

Le Corbusier's long period as a leading figure in modern architecture – for nearly half a century – was unique among architects of his time and is, finally, a reflection of his capacity to endow architecture with an expression which evokes the spirit of his epoch. In this sense he was at once the 'terrible simplificateur' in the tradition of the rationalist enlightenment and a creator of forms which will endure well beyond his time. MB

☐ Ozenfant, Amédée, and Jeanneret, Charles-Edouard, *Après le cubisme*, Paris 1918; Le Corbusier, *Vers une architecture* Paris 1923 (English ed.: *Towards a new Architecture*, London 1937); ——, *Urbanisme*, Paris 1925 (8th ed. published in translation as: *The City of Tomorrow and its Planning*, London 1929, and reissued in facsimile editions 1947, 1971); ——, *Précisions sur un état présent de l'architecture et de l'urbanisme*, Paris 1930; ——, *La Ville radieuse*, Paris 1935 (English ed.: *The Radiant City*, London and New York 1967); ——, *Quand les cathédrales étaient blanches. Voyage au pays des timides*, Paris 1937 (English ed.: *When the Cathedrals were white*, London 1947); ——, *Sur les quatre routes*, Paris 1941 (English ed.: *The Four Routes*, London 1947); ——, *Les Trois Etablissements humains*, Paris 1945; ——, *Propos d'urbanisme*, Paris 1946; —— and Pierrefeu, François de, *La Maison des hommes*, Paris 1942; Boesiger, W. (ed.), *Le Corbusier. Oeuvre complète* (8 vols.), Zurich 1930 ff.; Papadaki, S., *Le Corbusier. Architect, Painter, Writer*, New York 1948; Choay, Françoise, *Le Corbusier*, New York 1960; Besset, M., *Qui était Le Corbusier?*, Geneva 1968; Moos, S. von, *Le Corbusier: Elemente einer Synthese*, Freuenfeld 1968; Jencks, Charles, *Le Corbusier and the Tragic View of Architecture*, London 1973; *Le Corbusier Sketchbooks* (4 vols.), Cambridge, Mass. 1981–2.

Leonidov, Ivan Ilich, b. Vlasikh, near Kalinin, Russia, 1902, d. Moscow 1959. He worked first as a docker and farmhand, until his talent was first recognized by an icon painter in Tver'; this recognition enabled him in 1919 to join the Tver' art school. After developing his skill as a painter, he gained admission in 1921 to the VKHUTEMAS in Moscow, where he came under the influence of Alexander Vesnin and transferred from painting to architecture. He demonstrated his full mastery of the syntax of *Constructivism in 1926 with his student project for the *Izvestia* printing plant in Moscow. He began to break new ground with his final-year student project, a design for the Lenin Institute in Moscow, which was displayed at the first OSA (Association of Contemporary Architects) exhibition held in Moscow in 1927. With its glass-clad, free-standing structures and its elevated monorail, it envisaged a form of

Leonidov. Lenin Institute, Moscow (project, 1927): model

continuous open-ended regional development. L.'s mature vision was strongly influenced by the imagery of *Suprematism and it was no doubt this that led him to design a dynamic, yet non-rhetorical, curtain-walled architecture in the 1930 Palace of Culture projected for the site of the Simonov monastery in Moscow. In this characteristically simple yet powerful composition, he combined into a single complex a pyramidal sports hall-cum-winter garden; a hemispherical, transformable auditorium and an orthogonal research building. Above these glistening solids hovered an airship attached to a light steel-lattice mooring mast.

As with other Constructivists/Suprematists, L.'s style changed decisively after 1932, when elements drawn from traditional Russian iconography began to influence his later, somewhat baroque manner, as for example in the rather emblematic monumentality of his entry for the 1933 Narkomtiazprom competition. It is one of the tragedies of the pioneering period of the Modern Movement that L. was to realize only one notable work, namely, an extensively landscaped amphitheatre and ornamental stairway built for Ordjohikedze Sanatorium at Kislovodsk in 1932. KF

□ Magomedov, S. O. Khan, 'I. I. Leonidov 1902–1959', in: O. A. Shvidovsky (ed.), *Building in the USSR, 1917–1932*, London and New York 1971; Quilici, V., and Scolari, M. (eds.), *Ivan Leonidov*, Milan 1975; Koolhaas, R., and Oorthuys, G., *Ivan Leonidov*, New York 1981.

Lescaze, William, b. Geneva, 1896, d. New York, 1969. Studied under Karl *Moser at the Eidgenössische Technische Hochschule in Zurich. Worked in France until 1920 under Henri *Sauvage. He emigrated to the USA in 1920, and at first worked in Cleveland for Hubbell and Benes. In 1923 he went to New York, where he designed in a succession of styles, from the Collegiate Gothic of the Edgewood School, Greenwich, Conn., to the 1925 Paris Modern of his interiors for the Macy's Exposition of 1928. In 1929 he joined George *Howe to form the Howe and Lescaze partnership in New York.

To Howe's maturity and experience, L. brought an ability to handle newer modern forms. His own house in Manhattan (1934) was the first *International Style building of its kind in New York and may be profitably contrasted with Howe's Speizer House in Philadelphia (1935). The most significant product of this partnership was the Philadelphia Saving Fund Society (PSFS) Building (1929–32). After the dissolution of the firm, L. designed Unity House in the Pocono Mountains, Pa., and Williamsbridge Housing in Brooklyn, N.Y., an early modern housing development. His Longfellow Building in Washington, D.C., was the first International Style work in that city; it established a trend towards the exploitation of the cantilever that resulted in unrelieved piles of horizontal stripped windows.

After World War II, L. enjoyed tremendous success as a designer of commercial space in New York. His building at 711 Third Avenue is a restatement of the *parti* established at the PSFS Building.

□ Lescaze, William, *On Being an Architect*, New York 1942; Institute for Architecture and Urban Studies, catalogue 16: *William Lescaze*, New York 1982

Lethaby, William Richard, b. Barnstaple, Devon, 1857, d. 1931. Studied at the Royal Academy Schools in London. From 1877 worked under R. N. *Shaw, after 1889 in independent practice. L., who was strongly influenced by *Morris and *Webb, in both design and theory, created some of the most noteworthy and original buildings of the *Arts and Crafts movement, including Avon Tyrell in Hampshire (1891), the Eagle Insurance Co. Building in Birmingham (1899) and the church at Brockhampton, Herefordshire (1900–2). In his work Gothic Revival theory is developed and submitted to a regionally oriented symbolism. In 1894 he became the first Director of the Central School of Arts and Crafts in London, the first Architecture School with teaching workshops for the individual crafts and thus a prototype for the *Bauhaus. VML

☐ Lethaby, W. R., *Architecture, Mysticism and Myth*, London 1892; ——, *Form in Civilization*, Oxford 1957; Rubens, G., *William Richard Lethaby and His Work*, London 1983.

Lewerentz, Sigurd, b. Bjärtrå near Sundsvall, Sweden 1885, d. Lund 1975. After graduating from Gothenburg Technical College (1908) he worked in Germany under Bruno Möhring in Berlin (1908–10) and Theodor *Fischer (1909) and Richard *Riemerschmid in Munich (1910). He was one of the founders of the separatist Free School of Architecture in Stockholm in 1910, which aligned itself with the 'national realist' tendency (*Sweden). L. established his own practice in Stockholm (1911–17 with Torsten Stubelius; 1917–43 alone), moving subsequently to Ekilstuna (1943–58), Skanör (1958–70), and finally to Lund where he was an influential teacher. The early competition designs, such as that with *Asplund for Woodland Cemetery in Stockholm (1914), where L. was responsible for the landscape design, revealed the influence of the simplicity and poetic approach of *Tessenow's architecture. His late brick churches at Skarpnäck (1960) and Klippan (1966) continue the lyricism which announced a quiet critique of the functionalist tradition in European *Rationalism.

☐ Codrington, J., 'Sigurd Lewerentz 1885–1975', *Architectural Review*, no. 950, April 1976; Finnish Museum of Architecture, *Nordic Classicism*, Helsinki 1982.

Lewerentz. Church at Skarpnäck (1960)

Libera, Adalberto, b. Trento 1903, d. Rome 1963. After studying at the University of Rome, he joined *Gruppo 7 in 1927, the first official organization of Italian *Rationalism. In 1928 he organized the first 'Esposizione dell'architettura razionale'. As secretary of *M.I.A.R., launched in 1930, he was engaged in the polemical debate with the group of academic architects (who were very strong in Rome) and sought to have Rationalism adopted as the official architecture of Fascism. The attempt ended in defeat, despite efforts put forth for a compromise such as the Palazzo dei Ricevimenti e Congressi at the 'Esposizione Universale di Roma' (E.U.R.) projected in 1938. Numerous notable works of the 1930s include: above all, his contribution to the exhibition 'Mostra della Rivoluzione Fascista' (1932); houses at Ostia (1933); the Post Office in the Quartiere Aventino of Rome (1938; with Mario de Renzi); and the Malparte house on Capri (1938). After World War II, L.'s various works included the Olympic Village in Rome (1959; with others) VG

☐ Alieri, A., Clerici, M., Palpacelli, F., and Vaccaro, N. G., 'Adalberto Libera', *L'architettura – cronache e storia* (Rome), nos. 124–33, 1966; Aragon, Giulio, *Adalberto Libera*, Rome 1976.

Lissitzky, El (Eliezer Markovich), b. Polshinotz, near Smolensk 1890, d. Moscow 1941. Studied architecture first at the Technische Hochschule, Darmstadt, 1909–14. In 1915 he was awarded his architectural diploma in Moscow. The year 1919 saw his collaboration with *Malevich and the first 'Prouns'. He taught at the Moscow Academy in 1921, and in Germany and Switzerland, 1922–5; he returned to Russia in 1928. He worked with van

*Doesburg and *Mies van der Rohe and was a co-founder of *Constructivism. Simultaneously with Tatlin's project for a Memorial to the Third International, L.'s office designed a speaker's platform (1920) for Lenin in the form of a sloping steel structure of great expressiveness. In 1924–5, together with Mart *Stam, he designed the 'Cloud Props' project, an extensively cantilevered office block on immense piers. L. was the most important linking figure between Russian Constructivism and the Western European avant-garde of the 1920s. His futuristic dynamic conception was not without influence on the High-Tech architecture of the 1970s.

□ Richter, H., *El Lissitzky: Sieg über die Sonne. Zur Knust des Konstruktivismus*, Cologne 1958; Lissitzky-Küppers, S., *El Lissitzky. Life, Letters, Texts*, London and New York 1968; Frampton, Kenneth, 'The work and influence of El Lissitzky', *Architect's Year Book*, 12 (1968), pp. 253–68; Lissitzky, El, *Russia: An Architecture for World Revolution*, Cambridge, Mass. 1970; *El Lissitzky* (exhibition catalogue), Cologne 1976.

Lods, Marcel, b. Paris 1891, d. Paris 1978. Trained at the Ecole Nationale des Arts Décoratifs and the *Ecole des Beaux-Arts, Paris (diploma 1923), and taught at the latter 1948–64. Collaborated with Eugène *Beaudouin (1925–40); in private practice from 1945. L. was a member of *CIAM. He is best known for his pioneering work on prefabricated housing such as that in the Cité de la Muette at Drancy, and for his collaboration with Beaudouin on the Open Air School at Suresnes (1933) and with Beaudouin and Jean *Prouvé on the Maison du Peuple at Clichy (1939). After World War II he was charged with the reconstruction of one sector of the city of Rouen. His latter work includes the Maison des Sciences de l'Homme in Paris (1967, with Deponat and Beauclair).

□ Lods, Marcel, *Le Métier d'architecte*, Paris 1976.

Loos, Adolf, b. Brno 1870, d. Vienna 1933. An admirer equally of the logic of Roman architecture and of vernacular architecture, L. was one of the pioneers of the European Modern Movement. He was one of the first architects to react against the decorative trends of *Art Nouveau and to expound rationalist design theories.

The son of a stone-mason, L. attended classes at Reichenberg Polytechnic before studying architecture at the Technische Hochschule in Dresden. Upon completion of his studies, he was eager to broaden his outlook; in 1893 he made a journey to the *USA, where he remained for three years, working as a mason, a floor-layer, and even as a dish-washer. During this time he observed the innovations of the young *Chicago School: the expressive steel-frame structures William Le Baron Jenney introduced for office buildings, the austere blocks of Burnham and Root, and the uncompromising severity which *Sullivan manifested in his famous Guaranty Building (Buffalo, N.Y., 1894–5). It was Sullivan who, after providing American architecture with an original and personal style of floral surface decoration, wrote in 1892 in an essay entitled 'Ornament in Architecture': 'It would be greatly for our esthetic good if we should refrain entirely from the use of ornament for a period of years, in order that our thought might concentrate acutely upon the production of buildings well formed and comely in the nude.'

This reflection was to become the central point of L.'s aesthetic. On his return to Europe in 1896, he settled in Vienna, a cosmopolitan centre with a culture typified by elegance of thought and sophisticated manners. In this milieu, he showed himself forthwith to be an ardent and aggressive polemicist. In a first series of articles, published chiefly in the *Neue Freie Presse* in 1897 and 1898, he took up arms against the stylistic and aestheticizing tendencies preached by the painter Gustav Klimt and the architects *Olbrich and *Hoffmann who had founded the Secession movement in 1897. Basing himself partly on Sullivan's purist argument and partly on the rationalist doctrine which *Wagner had expounded to the Vienna Akademie der bildenden Künste in 1894, L. set out to show that the type of ornament inculcated by Art Nouveau was not suited to European culture; that a work divested of ornament is a sign of pure and lucid thought and a high degree of civilization; that good form must find its beauty in the degree of usefulness it expresses, and in the indissoluble unity of its parts; and that consequently all ornamentation must be systematically rejected.

L. was to resume and develop this thesis in a major essay published in 1908 entitled 'Ornament und Verbrechen' (Ornament and Crime). In order to help spread his theories, he had founded a Free School of Architecture in 1906.

Loos. Kärntner Bar, Vienna (1907)

Loos. House for Tristan Tzara, Paris (1926)

Among his most important works at this time were the renovation of the Villa Karma at Clarens, near Montreux (1906); the Kärntner Bar in Vienna (1907); the Steiner House, Vienna, of 1910, one of the first private houses to be built in reinforced concrete and a landmark in the architecture of this century (reshaping of plan, new method of condensing and articulating internal space, purity of the straight line, flat roof, horizontal fenestration, dominance of solids, cubic style); the commercial block on the Michaelerplatz, Vienna (1910), where the arrangement of the various levels looks forward to the complete expression of the 'volumetric plan' achieved in his Rufer House, Vienna (1922).

From 1920 to 1922 L. was in charge of municipal housing in Vienna, where he drew up some bold development schemes, such as the Heuberg model estate. In 1923 he settled in Paris, where he established contact with the leading figures of *Esprit Nouveau*. He also frequented Dadaist circles and built a house for Tristan Tzara (1926). After his return to Vienna in 1928, his buildings include: the Moller House at Pötzleinsdorf (1928); the Kuhner House at Payerbach (1930); and, also in 1930, the Müller House in Prague, which represents a highpoint in his oeuvre. It exerted a lasting influence on the next generation of architects, among them *Lurçat, *Mendelsohn, *Neutra and *Schindler. RLD

☐ Münz, L., and Künstler, G., *Adolf Loos: Pioneer of Modern Architecture*, London and New York 1966; Loos, A., *Spoken into the Void: collected essays*, Cambridge, Mass., and London 1982.

Lubetkin, Berthold, b. Tiflis, Georgia, Russia 1901. Studied principally in Moscow, Leningrad and Paris. After a brief collaboration with

Lubetkin. Highpoint I, Highgate, London (1933–5)

Jean Ginsburg in Paris 1927–30 (Apartment house at 25 avenue de Versailles, Paris; 1927), he established himself in London in 1931, where he was one of the founding members of the *Tecton group in the following year and a pioneering advocate of Continental modernism. In addition to his major architectural works – the penguin pool (1934) and other buildings at the Regent's Park and Whipsnade Zoos and the two north London apartment blocks Highpoint I (1933–5) and Highpoint II (1936–8) – L. worked on the planning of Peterlee New Town, after the dissolution of Tecton in 1948. In retirement since 1950, he was awarded the RIBA Gold Medal in 1982.
☐ Furneaux-Jordan, R., 'Lubetkin', *Architectural Review*, July 1955; Coe, Peter, and Reading, Malcolm, *Lubetkin and Tecton. Architecture and Social Commitment*, London and Bristol 1981.

Luckhardt, Hans, b. Berlin 1890, d. Bad Wiessee 1954. Studied at the Technische Hochschule in Karlsruhe. He was a member of the *Arbeitsrat für Kunst, the *Novembergruppe and later of the *Ring. From 1921 he worked in partnership with his brother Wassili *Luckhardt. In 1952 he was appointed a professor at the Hochschule für bildende Künste, Berlin.

Luckhardt, Wassili, b. Berlin 1889, d. Berlin 1972. Studied at the Technische Hochschule in Berlin-Charlottenburg. He was a member of the *Arbeitsrat für Kunst, the *Novembergruppe and later of the *Ring. He worked in partnership with his brother Hans *Luckhardt, 1921–54. After their first works in the spirit of *Expressionism – project for the Hygiene Museum in Dresden (1921), project for an office tower at the Friedrichstraße station in Berlin (1922) – the brothers turned in the mid-1920s to a consistent *Rationalism. In addition to their use of precise right-angles – as in their experimental housing in the Schorlemer Allee in Berlin (1927), houses on the Rupenhorn, Berlin (1928), the Berlin Pavilion at the 'Constructa' exhibition in Hanover (1951) – dynamically surging forms feature in their projects for the rearrangement of the Alexanderplatz in Berlin (1929), for the Medical College on the Burgberg in Preßburg (1933), and for the Freie Universität in Berlin-Dahlem (1952).
☐ Kultermann, Udo, *Wassili und Hans Luckhardt, Bauten und Entwürfe*, Tübingen 1958; Kliemann, H., *Wassili Luckhardt*, Tübingen 1973.

Lundy, Victor A., b. New York 1925. Studied at Harvard under *Gropius. His buildings include timber churches with large curved roofs (First Unitarian Church at Westport, Conn., 1961), and a motel with reinforced concrete awnings at different heights (Warm Mineral Springs Inn at Venice, Fla., 1958). He designed the exhibition pavilion of the U.S. Atomic Energy Commission, a 'pneumatic' structure, at Seattle (1962).

Lurçat, André, b. Bruyères, Vosges 1894, d. Sceaux 1970. Studied at the *Ecole des Beaux-Arts in Paris. In 1928 he was one of the founding members of *CIAM. His artists' studios, the Villa Seurat, in Paris (1925–6), together with the Villa Bomsel in Versailles (1926) and the Villa Guggenbuhl in Paris (1927), are among the pioneering works of the Modern Movement in *France. At the same time he drew up a number of other (unrealized) projects, at times radical, for dwelling houses. After his theoretical manifesto *Architecture* (Paris 1929) and the Hôtel Nord-Sud in Calvi (1930), which is a virtual homage to the intense Mediteranean light, L. became, with his Ecole Karl-Marx at Villejuif (1931–3), an advocate of the coalition of new architectural forms and the workers' movement. On the basis of this demonstration of architectural and social allegiances, L. was invited to Moscow in 1934, and remained there until 1937. There the 'Socialist Realist' debate renewed his awareness of such traditional values as monumentality and axiality, and this was reflected in his post-war buildings (mostly in Maubeuge and Saint-Denis) and in his ambitious essay *Formes, composition et lois d'harmonie* (Paris 1953–7). JLC
☐ 'André Lurçat', *Architecture, Mouvement, Continuité* (Paris), no. 40 (1976), pp. 5–38.

Lutyens, Sir Edwin (Landseer), b. London 1869, d. London 1944. When only twenty years old, he opened his own office in London, having worked for two years under the country-house architect Ernest George (where he met Herbert Baker, later his colleague in New Delhi). Influenced also by *Shaw and *Webb, he began his career with a series of often opulent country houses (in a style related to that of the *Arts and Crafts movement),

including Munstead Wood at Godalming, Surrey (1896), for Gertrude Jekyll, a garden designer who had created or rather revived the English cottage garden, as well as Deanery Garden at Sonning, Berks. (1899–1902). The creative freshness of these early houses soon gave way to a neo-classical language of forms as in Nashdom, a country house at Taplow, Bucks. (1905–9). The plan of New Delhi (1912) and the Viceroy's House (1912–30) are – along with the commercial buildings Britannic House (1920–4) and the Midland Bank headquarters in London (1924–39), as well as the British Embassy in Washington, D.C. (1925–8) – among the last great examples of the continuation of historicist design principles from the 19th century into the 20th. AM

□ Lutyens, E., 'What I Think of Modern Architecture', *Country Life*, vol. 69 (1931), pp. 775–7; Butler, A. S. G., with George Stewart and Christopher Hussey, *The Architecture of Sir Edwin Lutyens* (3 vols.), London 1950; Greenberg, Alan, 'Lutyens' Architecture Re-studied', *Perspecta* no. 12 (1969), New Haven, Conn., pp. 129–52; Inskip, Peter, *Edwin Lutyens*, London 1979; O'Neill, Daniel, *Edwin Lutyens: Country Houses*, London 1980; Gradidge, R., *Edwin Lutyens: Architecture Laureate*, London 1981; exhibition catalogue *Lutyens. The Work of the English Architect Sir Edwin Lutyens (1869–1944)*, London 1981.

Lutyens. Deanery Garden, Sonning, Berkshire (1899–1902)

Lyons, Eric Alfred, b. London 1912, d. London 1978. In the 1950s his schemes set a new standard for private-enterprise housing in *Great Britain, where he controlled the planning and landscaping of entire estates. His layouts feature simple buildings that display an eye for textures, and the highly repetitive use of structural elements and equipment in dispositions which largely avoid streets by creating courtyards and varying patterns of 'external enclosures'; this he considered to be the secret of urbanity. Flats at Ham Common, near Richmond; at Blackheath; and West Hill, Highgate (for the Soviet Trade Delegation). Houses, flats and maisonettes at Cambridge; housing for old people at Bognor Regis, with certain shared accommodation.

□ Furneaux-Jordan, Robert, 'SPAN: The Spec Builder as a Patron of Modern Architecture', *Architectural Review* (London), 125 (1959), pp. 102–20.

M

Mackay, David (John), b. Eastbourne, Sussex 1933. After studying in London at the Northern Polytechnic, he moved to Spain. Since 1962 he has worked in partnership with Josep *Martorell and Oriol *Bohigas. AM

☐ Mackay, D., *Contradictions in Living Environments*, London 1971; ——, *Wohnungsbau im Wandel*, Stuttgart 1977.

McKim, Mead & White. One of the largest and most prolific architectural firms in the *USA at the turn of the century, the New York-based office of McKim, Mead & White cultivated a sophisticated and urbane historicist (*historicism) vocabulary, first in elegant domestic designs and increasingly in monumental public architecture. The firm's early work was alternately imbued with the decorative and picturesque sensibilities of the youngest partner – Stanford White (b. New York 1853, d. New York 1906), who was closely associated with many of the period's leading artists – and by the controlled and austere monumental design of Charles Follen McKim (b. Chester County, Pa., 1847, d. New York 1909), whose training had been at the *Ecole des Beaux-Arts. The office, which produced some one thousand buildings by 1919, was disciplined by the organizational skills of William Rutherford Mead (b. Brattleboro, Vermont, 1846, d. New York 1928). The firm's earliest fame was won largely with large Shingle Style mansions and country clubs, such as the William G. Low House at Bristol, R.I. (1886–7), and the Newport Casino (1879–80), both of which had their roots in the planning and the picturesque sense of materials and craft of the domestic architecture of H. H. Richardson, in whose office McKim and White had met in the early 1870s. With the H. A. C. Taylor House in Newport, R.I. (1882–6), the firm heralded the revival of interest in American colonial architecture which marked the shift in style to a more rigorous order and classical conception of composition. This shift was paralleled by the use of Renaissance typologies and details in such urban residences as the Henry Villard Houses in New York (1882–5) and the consolidation of the planning techniques and classical imagery of the French Beaux-Arts tradition into a monumental American public architecture. Beginning with McKim's Boston Public Library (1887–98), a re-interpretation of Henri Labrouste's Bibliothèque Sainte-Geneviève (*France), the firm cultivated a new approach to urban architecture which came to present a counter-tradition to the *Chicago School. The triumph of neo-classical image-making in the 1893 World's Columbian Exposition assured the success of McKim, Mead & White's classical finesse which from the Rhode Island State Capitol at Providence (1891–1903) to Columbia University (1893–1902), Pennsylvania Station (1902–11) and the Brooklyn Museum (1893–1915), all in New York, created an image of urban America to be cultivated and reworked by the countless architects trained in the firm's offices (including such major figures as Cass Gilbert, Henry Bacon, and J. M. Carrère and Thomas Hastings). The publication of *A Monograph of the Work of McKim, Mead and White* (1915) was to have an influence in American architectural schools into the 1940s, as well as abroad. The enthusiasm of C. H. Reilly for their work was to have considerable echoes in English public and commercial architecture, particularly through the Liverpool University School of Architecture. Much disdained by the advocates of the *International Style, the urban and architectonic values of McKim, Mead & White's work have recently found new appreciation among a younger generation of American architects. BB

☐ *A Monograph of the Works of McKim, Mead and White, 1879–1915*, New York 1915 (reprinted 1973); Reilly, Charles H., *McKim, Mead, and White*, New York 1924; Baldwin, Charles; *Stanford White*, New York 1931; Scully, Vincent, *The Shingle Style*, New Haven, Conn. 1955; Roth, Leland M., *The Architecture of McKim, Mead & White, 1870–1920: A Building List*, New York 1978; ——, *McKim, Mead & White, Architects*, New York 1983 and London 1984.

Mackintosh, Charles Rennie, b. Glasgow 1868, d. London 1928. A resolute adversary of historic revivalism, M. was one of the most important precursors of 20th-century rationalist architecture. As the leader of the *Art Nouveau movement in Great Britain, the Scottish architect made a contribution of fundamental importance in reappraising the role of function in building, expressed in a style which draws often on ancient Celtic ornament and on the cultural traditions of Japan.

When he was barely sixteen, M. entered John Hutchinson's office as an articled pupil; from 1885 he attended evening classes at the Glasgow School of Art. In 1889 he was engaged as a draughtsman in the building firm of J. Honeyman and Keppie, where he remained until 1913 (from 1904 as a partner), and while there he met the architect J. Herbert McNair, his future brother-in-law. In 1890, he was awarded a scholarship which enabled him to make a study tour in France and Italy. Already in his first executed work, the corner tower of the Glasgow Herald Building (1894), M. revealed a rejection of academic traditions which was to be fundamental to his work. One year later, in December 1895, he participated in the opening exhibition of L'Art Nouveau in Paris with a number of posters which already displayed clearly the linear, symbolic style of the Glasgow School. In 1897 he won the competition for the new building of the Glasgow School of Art, erected between 1898 and 1909. In 1898 he drew up a bold scheme for a concert hall on a circular plan, covered by a parabolic dome, which was not however premiated at the Glasgow exhibition of 1901.

At the same time M. was involved in interior decoration and in furniture design. The pieces he designed are notable for their character, which is at once exquisite and austere, slender and taut, based on the straight line and the right-angle, and set off in light tones (ivory). The upswing of their slim parallels elongates their forms beyond any functional requirement, as M.'s aesthetic fancy turns to mannerism. This is the style he adopted when commissioned in 1897 to design the chain of Glasgow tea-rooms. The Buchanan Street Tea-room (1897–8) illustrated the curvilinear style of this first period (1894–1900) most completely: the walls were dominated by two-dimensional figures, tall and graceful, enclosed within a network of vertical lines and entwined by circular waves that evoked the manner of the painter Gustav Klimt. This style became known on the Continent especially after the exhibition of a suite of furniture at Munich in 1898, and through the contribution M. sent to Vienna for the annual exhibition of the Secession in 1900. The furniture and panels he showed in Vienna emphasized the close links between the Scottish trends and the Viennese School.

Mackintosh. Glasgow School of Art (1898–1907)

In the same year M. married a former student of the Glasgow School of Art, Margaret MacDonald, whose sister Frances had married Herbert McNair in 1899. These ties helped to knit together more closely a little group united since 1890 by similar professional and aesthetic interests, which had already won an international reputation under the name of 'The Four'. It was as the leader of this group that M. entered a competition in 1901, organized under the auspices of the *Zeitschrift für Innendekoration* of Darmstadt by its editor, A. Koch. The subject was a house for a connoisseur, including its interior decoration; M. was awarded second prize. His scheme envisaged a revolutionary use of space, with an arrangement of large, simple volumes distinctly cubic in appearance, stripped – in elevation – of any kind of ornament or moulding, and marked by an asymmetrical predominance of solids over voids: it was a harbinger of the purist style of *Loos.

In the country houses M. built in the environs of Glasgow (Windy Hill at Kilmacolm, 1899–

1901; Hill House at Helensburgh, 1902–3) he evoked the Scottish baronial tradition (angle towers with conical caps, huge double-pitch roofs, massive chimneys). The internal layouts of these houses evince great boldness in the handling of space. The hall of Hill House (1903) is a masterpiece where light, colour, openwork partitions, cage-type lamps and light furniture combine in a spatio-dynamic composition that anticipates Russian *Constructivism and Dutch *Stijl.

The superb library which M. built as an addition to the Glasgow School of Art (1907–9) shows similar stylistic trends. the straight line reigns supreme, and the subtle arrangement of horizontal beams and rectangular pillars which support the galleries punctuate space in a manner hitherto unknown, raising architecture to the level of poetic abstraction. Similar principles are at work, with equal effect, in M.'s Cranston Tea-room in Ingram Street (1907–11). Apart from this, in his short architectural career, the Scottish Pavilion (which M. built and furnished) at the Turin Exhibition of 1902 may also be noted.

He moved to London in 1913, where his activities were limited to designing furniture and printed fabrics. In 1920, he retired to Port-Vendres to devote himself exclusively to water-colour painting. RLD

□ Muthesius, Hermann, *Haus eines Kunstfreundes*, Darmstadt 1902; Pevsner, N., *Charles Rennie Mackintosh*, Milan 1950; Howarth, Thomas, *Charles Rennie Mackintosh and the Modern Movement*, London 1952; Macleod, Robert, *Charles Rennie Mackintosh*, London 1968; Billcliffe, Roger, *Architectural Sketches and Flower Drawings by Charles Rennie Mackintosh*, London 1977; ——, *Charles Rennie Mackintosh. The Complete Furniture, Furniture Drawings and Interior Designs*, Guildford and London 1978; Cooper, Jackie (ed.), *Mackintosh Architecture. The Complete Buildings and Selected Projects*, London 1978 (2nd ed. 1980).

Maillart, Robert, b. Berne 1872, d. Geneva 1940. After studying structural engineering from 1890 to 1894 at the Eidgenössiche Technische Hochschule (ETH) in Zurich, he worked in various engineering offices until he became an independent partner in the building firm of Maillart and Co., Zurich, in 1902. In 1911 he was appointed a lecturer at the ETH in Zurich.

Mackintosh. Library building, Glasgow School of Art (1907–9): exterior and reading room.

In 1912 he left Switzerland to build in Russia, whence he returned penniless after the October Revolution. In 1919 he started an engineering office in Geneva, followed in 1924 by others in Berne and Zurich.

M. built not only bridges but also designed the structural details for a large number of multi-storey buildings. The intrinsic character of his constructions shows up particularly clearly, however, in his bridges: these designs are the outcome of his ability to think through a problem in its entirety and to seek a specific solution to each situation based on his own specially developed methods of construction. In 1901 he built the first of his forty or so reinforced-concrete bridges, at Zuoz in the Engadine. It already displayed some of the essential features of that concept of his which did away with the old principle of separation between the functions of bearing and loading. All parts of a bridge were now integrated in their structural function, the roadway being no longer a load carried by the bridge vaults but incorporated as a structural element.

M.'s most important bridges are those built according to the principle he developed of the triply articulated box girder; they include the Rhine bridge at Tavanasa, Graubünden; the Rossgraben bridge near Schwarzenburg in the Canton of Berne (1932), 82 m (269 ft) long; and the overpass between Altendorf and Lachen, Canton Schwyz (1940), the last project personally supervised by Maillart. Another of his structural systems was the so-called stiffened bar arch which he used notably in the following: the Val Tschiel bridge (1925), and the curved Landquart railway bridge at Klosters (1930), both also in Graubünden; the Schwandbach bridge between Hinterfultigen and Schönentannen in the Canton of Berne (1933), also on a curve; and finally the Aire bridge at Lancy, Geneva, with an arch-span of 50 m (167 ft), designed in 1938 and built 1952–4. A number of his boldest bridge designs were never executed.

Among the multi-storey buildings for whose architectural form M.'s contribution was essentially responsible, the following may be mentioned: the entrance hall of a warehouse at Chiasso (1924–5); and the barrel-vaulted Cement Pavilion at the Swiss Provinces Exhibition, Zurich, 1939, a show building for the Swiss cement industry. His most important invention in the field of high structures was made in 1908 with mushroom slab construction, which he used for the first time on a large scale in 1910. In this method, columns, beams and floors are no longer treated as separate units as in timber or steel structures, but the column passes organically into the beamless floor slab.

Maillart. Bridge over the Thur, near Felsegg, St Gallen (1933)

Maillart. Cement Industry Pavilion, Swiss Provinces Exhibition, Zurich (1939)

Here again, a structural system that is economical in the use of materials permits flexibility in application and helps to ensure a light and elegant appearance. MS

□ Bill, Max, *Robert Maillart*, Zurich 1949 (3rd ed. 1962); Abel, John R., Billington, David P., and Mark, Robert (eds.), *The Maillart Papers*, Princeton, N.J. 1973.

Maki, Fumihiko, b. Tokyo 1928. Studied at Tokyo University, the Cranbrook Academy of Art, Bloomfield Hills, Mich., and at Harvard University. From 1954 to 1966 he worked in the New York offices of *Skidmore, Owings & Merrill, as well as under J. L. *Sert in Cambridge, Mass. In 1965 he opened his own office in Tokyo. Although he belonged to the group of young Japanese architects who launched *Metabolism in 1960, M. did not himself share in the utopian speculations of his associates *Kurokawa and *Kikutaki. His buildings – such as the campus of Rissho University in Kumagaya (1967–8), the Hillside Terrace Housing Complex in Tokyo (1969, 1973–8), the Kato Gakuen Elementary school in Numazu (1972), the Austrian Embassy in Tokyo (1976) or the National Museum of Modern Art in Kyoto (1978) – are characterized by a strongly sculptural, but nonetheless rationally cool, formal language, which occasionally recalls the work of his teacher, Sert. AM

□ Maki, Fumihiko, and others, *Metabolism 1960. Proposals for New Urbanism*, Tokyo 1960; Maki, Fumihiko, *Investigations in Collective Form*, St Louis, Mo. 1964; 'Fumihiko Maki', *Architectural Record* (New York), August 1976, pp. 67–80.

Malevich, Kasimir (Severinovich), b. near Kiev 1878, d. Leningrad 1935. Painter and sculptor. Studied at the School of Art in Kiev, and in 1902 moved to Moscow. In his early career he was strongly influenced by the painting of the Post-Impressionists, the Fauvists and later the Cubists (*Cubism). Between 1913 and 1915 he moved in the direction of *Suprematism: his picture *Black Square on White Ground* was first exhibited in 1915. In the 1920s he turned to sculpture and architecture; he worked with El *Lissitzky, visited the *Bauhaus and investigated compositional relationships and possibilities of simple cubes in his 'Architektona' and 'Planits', architectonic and sculpturally abstract constructions in wood. After 1930 he encountered increasing resistance in the Stalinist era (*Russia); finally he confined himself to figurative painting and constructing architectural models. VML

□ Malevich, K. S., *The Non-Objective World*, Chicago 1959; Andersen, Troels, *Malevich*, Amsterdam 1970; Zhadova, Larissa A., *Malevich: Suprematism and Revolution in Russian Art, 1910–1930*, London 1982.

Mallet-Stevens, Rob(ert), b. Paris 1886, d. Paris 1945. Studied at the Ecole Spéciale d'Architecture in Paris, where he himself taught from 1924. In 1929 he founded, together with *Chareau and others, the Union des Artistes Modernes. The leading exponent of the *Art Deco style in *France, he assimilated influences from Josef *Hoffmann and Charles Rennie *Mackintosh. In his buildings, notably the flats in the Rue Mallet-Stevens in Paris (1926–7), emphasis is laid on a Cubist type of formal image. GHa

□ *Rob Mallet-Stevens, architecte*, Brussels 1980; Delorme, Jean Claude, and Chair, Philippe, *L'Ecole de Paris. 10 architectes et leurs immeubles. 1905–1937*, Paris 1981, pp. 61–70.

Mangiarotti, Angelo, b. Milan 1921. Studied at the Milan Politecnico. In 1955 he entered into partnership with Bruno Morassutti, but since 1960 he has practised independently. For M. construction is the decisive determinant of architecture. The general appearance of his buildings suggests the influence of *Mies van der Rohe in their disciplined simplicity – M.

Mangiarotti. Mater Misericordiae church, Baranzate (with Morassutti; 1957)

was a visiting professor at the Illinois Institute of Technology in Chicago in 1953–4 – while the formal relationship of constructional elements to lines of static force reveals a kinship with the works of Pier Luigi *Nervi. His prefabricated structures, mostly of concrete, are never composed in an additive way of independent units, but rather are made up of elements which are related to one another and are so combined as to produce a unified form. M. has built notably the Mater Misericordiae church in Baranzate near Milan (1957, with Morassutti), an exhibition pavilion for the Fiera del Mare in Genoa (1963), a workshop hall for the Società Elmag at Lissone, near Monza (1964), as well as an administration and factory building at Cinisello Balsamo near Milan (1968). AM

☐ *Angelo Mangiarotti*, Tokyo 1965; 'Angelo Mangiarotti', *Architecture and Urbanism* (Tokyo), September 1974; Bona, Enrico D., *Angelo Mangiarotti. Il processo del costruire*, Milan 1980.

Markelius, Sven, b. Stockholm 1889, d. 1972. Studied in Stockholm at the Technical College and at the Academy of Fine Arts. Although influenced by *Le Corbusier, he never opposed the Scandinavian romantic tradition, with its own special conception of scale and space, but took account of it empirically in his own tempered modernism. He built flats and offices, and a concert hall at Hälsingborg (1934), and first won international recognition with his Swedish Pavilion at the New York World's Fair (1939). In his capacity as head of the town-planning department of the city of Stockholm (1944–54) he was responsible for the establishment of the satellite town of Vällingby (1953–9); this was notable for its remarkable variety of design and for a central pedestrian zone, the advantages of which were at that time not yet self-evident.

☐ Ray, Stefano, *Il contributo svedese all'architettura contemporanea e l'opera di Sven Markelius*, Rome 1969.

Markelius. Concert hall, Hälsingborg (1934)

MARS Group (Modern Architectural Research Group). Group of architects founded in London in 1933, which advocated the introduction of Continental theories of *Rationalism in *Great Britain. Among the founding members were the émigré architects Wells *Coates and Berthold *Lubetkin and the engineer Ove *Arup. The most noteworthy project of the group was their plan for the complete reconstruction of London on a linear model.

Martin, Sir (John) Leslie, b. Manchester 1908. Trained at the School of Architecture, University of Manchester, 1927–30, where he subsequently served as assistant lecturer, 1930–4; head of the School of Architecture, University of Hull, 1934–9; Professor and Head of the Department of Architecture, University of Cambridge, 1956–72. M. served as a co-editor (with the painter Ben Nicholson and the sculptor Naum Gabo) of the short-lived *Constructivist review *Circle* in 1937, one of the organs for the introduction of Continental modernism in England. He was principal assistant architect to the London, Midland and Scottish Railway, 1939–48. His best-known early work, the Royal Festival Hall, London (1951, with Robert Matthew, Peter Moro and Edwin Williams) dates from his period (1948–53) in the architecture department of the London County Council (he was chief architect 1953–6). From 1956 he conducted a private practice in Cambridge where he has built notably the Harvey Court Residential Building at Gonville and Caius College (1957–62; with Colin St John Wilson) and the Stone Building at Peterhouse (1960–4; also with Wilson). M.'s comprehensive planning approach and concern for materials and constructional methods have exercised considerable influence chiefly through the Centre for Land Use and Built Form Studies (now the Martin Centre) at Cambridge. BB

☐ Martin, Leslie, 'Notes on Developing Architecture', *Architectural Review*, no. 164 (1978), pp. 10–17.

Martorell (Codina), Josep (Maria), b. Barcelona 1925. Studied at the Escuela Tecnica Su-

Martorell. Santa Agueda holiday flats, Benicasim (1966–7)

perior de Arquitectura in Barcelona. In 1951 he formed a partnership with Oriol *Bohigas, which David *Mackay joined in 1962. In the context of architectural developments in Catalonia, Martorell, Bohigas and Mackay have played a leading role in theoretical matters as well as in their buildings. They maintain that a unified formal language of the type that the *International Style represented cannot be applied uniformly to various building tasks and situations, and they have thus developed a formally rich stylistic pluralism, which nonetheless has avoided a traditionalist regionalism. Among the most convincing examples of their work are the Santa Agueda holiday colony in Benicasim (1966–7), the Sant Jordi School in Pineda (1967–9) and the Bonanova apartment building in Barcelona (1970–3). AM

☐ 'Martorell, Bohigas, Mackay', *L'Architecture d'aujourd'hui* (Paris), no. 177, January–February 1975, pp. 74–89; *Martorell – Bohigas – Mackay: Arquitectura 1953–1978*, Madrid 1979.

May, Ernst, b. Frankfurt am Main 1886, d. Hamburg 1970. Studied at University College, London, and at the Technische Hochschule in Darmstadt, as well as that in Munich under Friedrich von Thiersch and Theodor *Fischer; in between he worked in the London city planning office of Raymond Unwin, 1910–12. He was City Planning Adviser in Frankfurt am Main, 1925–30, during which time he planned the housing estates for the 'New Frankfurt' in the context of an exemplary social democratic housing policy; these included Praunheim and Römerstadt (both 1927–30). In these, M. combined the urbanistic principles of the English satellite towns with the typologies and formal language of the rationalist *Neues Bauen. In execution he adopted the so-called 'montage' construction method, novel at the time; even the kitchens, the 'Frankfurter Küche' (design: Grete Schütte-Lihotzky), which were – from the functional point of view – radically reduced, were themselves prefabricated. From 1930 to 1933 M. was active in *Russia on large-scale urban planning; next, 1934–54, as a farmer and architect in Africa; and then, 1954–61, as director of the planning section of the 'Neue Heimat' community housing association in Hamburg. From 1957 he was a professor at the Technische Hochschule in Darmstadt, and from 1961 was municipal planning commissioner in Wiesbaden. VML

☐ Buekschmitt, J., *Ernst May: Bauten und Planungen*, Stuttgart 1963.

Maybeck, Bernard (Ralph), b. New York 1862, d. Berkeley, Cal. 1957. Studied at the *Ecole des Beaux-Arts in Paris, where he was much impressed by the restoration work of Viollet-le-Duc. From 1894 he had his own office in Berkeley, after 1902 in San Francisco; he retired from practice in 1938. Taught at the University of California at Berkeley and at the Mark Hopkins Institute of Art in San Francisco. M. was the earliest representative of the regionalist Bay Region Style, which William Wilson *Wurster was to bring to a restrained highpoint. Eclectic, especially Far Eastern motifs,

May. Römerstadt estate, Frankfurt am Main (1927–30)

Maybeck. First Church of Christ Scientist, Berkeley, Cal. (1910)

which have always played an important part in architecture on the West Coast of America even to this very day, were combined by M. with structural experiments such as the use of prefabricated units (First Church of Christ Scientist, with its expressive use of wooden construction, at Berkeley, 1910). He built private houses, clubs (Faculty Club of the University of California at Berkeley, 1902) and shops, and designed the Palace of Fine Arts for the 'Panama-Pacific Exposition', San Francisco (1915), in neo-classical style with romantic trappings.

□ McCoy, Esther, *Five California Architects*, New York 1960; Cardwell, Kenneth H., *Bernard Maybeck: Artisan, Architect, Artist*, Santa Barbara 1977.

Mayekawa, Kunio, b. Niigata-shi, Japan 1905. Studied at Tokyo University; worked first for *Le Corbusier in Paris, and independently from 1935. His investigations into the structural possibilities of reinforced concrete (stimulated by Pier Luigi *Nervi) led to buildings in a strongly sculptural idiom: City Hall, Kyoto (1958–60), Metropolitan Hall, Tokyo (1958–61). His apartment block at Harumi in Tokyo (1957) carries over Japanese domestic traditions into the dimensions of a modern skyscraper. In the office building for the Janome Sewing Machine Company in Tokyo (1965), the office floors are decoratively clad in expressively treated concrete elements placed in front of the façade to form a sun screen. M. had a considerable influence on younger Japanese architects; Kenzo *Tange, among others, has worked in collaboration with him.

□ Altherr, Alfred, *Drei japanische Architekten. Mayekawa, Tange, Sakakura*, Teufen and Stuttgart 1968.

Meier, Richard (Alan), b. Newark, N.J. 1934. Studied architecture at Cornell University. Worked successively with, among others, *Skidmore, Owings & Merrill and Marcel *Breuer in New York. Since 1963 he has been in practice independently in New York. His early built work is primarily domestic, including: the Meier House, Essex Fells, N.J. (1965); the Smith House, Darien, Conn. (1965–7); the Saltzman House, East Hampton, N.Y. (1967–9); and the Douglas House in Harbor Springs, Mich. (1971–3). He also did a number of studies for public buildings, but his first executed large-scale buildings were also housing: the Bell

Meier. Douglas House, Harbor Springs, Mich. (1971–3)

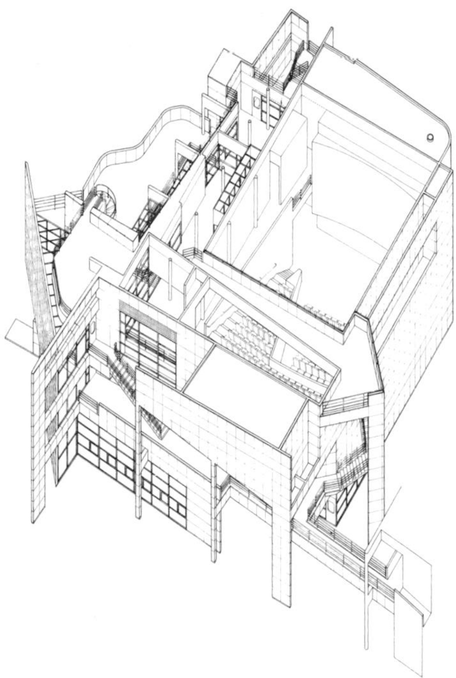

Meier. The Atheneum, New Harmony, Ind. (1975–9): axonometric projection

Laboratories in downtown New York converted into Westbeth artists' apartments; and Twin Parks housing in the Bronx (1969–74). A wider public notice accrued to him as the result of the *New York Five exhibition (1969) and book (1972). He was the most prolific builder in the group and the persistent use of white in his buildings is perhaps the main reason for the group's soubriquet 'white architects'. Well before the exhibition, M. began receiving public and industrial commissions. The Physical Education Center at Fredonia for New York State University dates from 1968–72. In 1971 began a whole series of projects for Olivetti, but these fell victim to a major change of company policy. In 1974 came the Atheneum at New Harmony, Ind., though the most important early public building, the Bronx Developmental Center in New York, was designed in 1970/1 and finished in 1976. The scheme for the Museum für Kunsthandwerk (arts and crafts) in Frankfurt won a closed competition in 1979 and was completed in 1984. That year M. was chosen to design the new Getty Museum in Los Angeles. Of the architects of his generation, M. is perhaps the most committed to the cultural context of his work and to a conscious mediation between public and private in an urban fabric, to which his entire formal language is devoted. JR

□ *Five Architects*, New York 1972; *Richard Meier. Architect*, New York 1976; *Richard Meier: Buildings and Projects 1965–1981*, Zurich 1982; *Richard Meier. Architect*, New York 1984.

Melnikov, Konstantin (Stepanovich), b. Moscow 1890, d. Moscow 1974. The first Soviet architect to achieve international repute, with his bold design for the Pavilion at the Paris 'Exposition internationale des arts décoratifs et industriels modernes' (1925). He was without a doubt the most individualistic of the young architects active after the Revolution. Starting with his projects for a workers' quarter in Moscow (1922) or the Moscow offices of the journal *Leningradskaya Pravda* (1923), his work was characterized by the architectural expression of movement within great dynamic forms.

His own house in Moscow (1927) was a singular building in the Russia of the 1920s, its design based on the intersection of two cylinders. The five workers' clubs he designed in Moscow (1927–9) each have a specific manifesto, revealing externally the auditoria and circulation spaces in an expression of continuous movement. M.'s radicalism and his rejection of the orthodoxies of the various organized avant gardes was expressed in his projects for the Christopher Columbus Lighthouse on Haiti (1929) and for the Palace of the Soviets in Moscow (1932). The two parking garages which he built in Moscow (1926 and 1929) increased his interest in the manipulation of movement in the city on a grand scale: his project for the People's Commissariat of Heavy Industry (1934) is the most striking example. In the ensuing years, his output – apart from interior refurbishment schemes – was confined to purely graphic expression. JLC

□ Starr, S. Frederick, *Melnikov. Solo Architect in a Mass Society*, Princeton, N.J. 1978.

Mendelsohn, Erich, b. Allenstein, East Prussia 1887, d. San Francisco 1953. Studied first at the Technische Hochschule in Berlin-Charlottenburg and then in Munich. He was initially influenced by *Expressionism, as is especially clear in his early typological sketches, which

Mendelsohn. Hat Factory for Friedrich Sternberg, Herrmann & Co., Luckenwalde (1921–3)

Mendelsohn. Cinema on the Kurfürstendamm, Berlin (1926–31)

distantly recall the works of Henry *van de Velde and Peter *Behrens. He even drew during his time in the army (1914–18) in Russia and on the Western front, producing sketches which, once translated into pen-and-ink drawings, were to win him considerable notice at a 1919 exhibition in Paul Cassirer's gallery in Berlin.

The machine-like aspects and the symbolic rendering of function by expressive and dynamic outline in these project drawings was carried over into his first major building: the Observatory and Astrophysics Laboratory at Potsdam, known as the Einstein Tower after its completion in 1921. Although the tower was of masonry construction, it had the formal and constructive appearance of reinforced-concrete. A whole series of other buildings soon followed, including: the Hat Factory for Friedrich Steinberg, Herrmann & Co. in Luckenwalde (1921–3); a two-family house in Berlin-Charlottenburg (1922), a commercial building in Gleiwitz (1923); and a machinery building for a textile factory in Wüstegiersdorf (also 1923). In addition during these years, he renovated the Rudolf Mosse House in Berlin (1921–3, with Richard J. *Neutra and R. P. Henning).

Especially decisive for the expression of his personal style were the two department store buildings for Schocken in Stuttgart (1926–8) and Chemnitz (1928–9). These are characterized simultaneously by a constructional discipline and by a flowing sense of line that is especially manifested in the band windows, which are cantilevered out from the structural members, and in the staircase towers. M. achieved an early highpoint in his nearly prototype-free formal inventiveness in the Woga complex in Berlin (1926–31). This included a cinema for an audience of 1,800 (its interior was to become a model for an entire series of large cinemas throughout the world), a cabaret, a café and apartments.

M. was Jewish, and chose to leave Germany in March 1933, travelling via Brussels to London, where in 1926 he shared an office with Serge *Chermayeff. The most famous of the handful of buildings he realized in *Great Britain is the De La Warr Pavilion at Bexhill-on-Sea (1935).

Already during his stay in England, which lasted until 1939, M. had commissions in Palestine where, in addition to private houses, he designed a hospital in Haifa (1937–8) and buildings for the Hebrew University in Jerusalem (1937–9). In 1939 he settled in Palestine (*Israel). Due to lack of employment, however, he emigrated in 1941 to the *USA, where he had made a study trip in 1924. In spite of his good introduction through an exhibition at the Museum of Modern Art in New York, he received practically no commissions and instead undertook extensive lecture tours. In 1945 he moved from New York to San Francisco, where he lived until his death. In the last six years of his life M. again enjoyed a period of considerable activity, principally designing religious buildings for Jewish communities (St Louis, Mo., 1946–50; Cleveland, Ohio, 1946–52; Grand Rapids, Mich., 1948–52; St Paul, Minn., 1950–4).

After his departure from Germany, M. never again attained the originality of his early work, and even in his native land he was followed by only second-class imitators rather than genuine

Mendelsohn. House on Pacific Heights, San Francisco (1950–1)

Metabolism. Sky House, Tokyo (1959), by Kiyonori Kikutake

disciples. The outstanding aspect of his German work was not only its freedom in the use and combination of reinforced-concrete, steel, glass, and masonry, but also and above all the powerfully sculptural treatment of volumetric composition. Functionalism plays a less evident role in his buildings than it does in those of the *Bauhaus circle and its architects; construction and function were rather subordinated to a dynamic overall form and an urbanistic conception of ensemble. PR

☐ Mendelsohn, E., *Amerika. Bilderbuch eines Architekten*, Berlin 1926; ——, *Rußland Europa Amerika*, Berlin 1929; *Erich Mendelsohn. Das Gesamtschaffen des Architekten*, Berlin 1930; Whittick, Arnold, *Erich Mendelsohn* (2nd, revised, ed.), London and New York 1956; Eckardt, Wolf von, *Erich Mendelsohn*, New York and London 1960; Zevi, Bruno, and Posener, Julius, *Erich Mendelsohn* (exhibition catalogue), Berlin 1968; Zevi, Bruno, *Erich Mendelsohn. Opera completa*, Milan 1970.

Metabolism. As a concept and as a group, Metabolism came into existence on the occasion of the Tokyo World Conference of Design in 1960 under the strong influence of Kenzo *Tange and his chief collaborator Takashi Asada. The original members included two young architects, Kiyonori *Kikutake and Kisho *Kurokawa, and the architectural critic Noboru Kawazoe; this group was later joined by the architects Masato Ohtaka and Fumihiko *Maki. Their activities ranged from regional planning and architecture to industrial design and various forms of propaganda, strongly affecting Japanese architecture of the 1960s and culminating in the Osaka World's Fair 1970.

Underlying most of the projects of the Metabolists was the pursuit of a dialectic syntheses of the public realm and private spaces; and in many cases these private spaces were expressed as minimal capsules produced by advanced mass-technology. Kurokawa's architecture best typified the Metabolist image, characterized by strikingly science-fiction-like forms. Kikutake's major concern centred on the concept of an archetype of spatial components – as represented by his own Sky House in Tokyo (1959) – while Ohtaka and especially Maki were developing the idea of what they called group form – as represented by Maki's design for the campus of Rissho University in Kumagaya (1967–8). A housing project submitted to the international competition of Peru (1968) was the last occasion in which the Metabolists acted as a group, and since the closing of the Osaka World's Fair, when the former optimism about the future of Metabolism began to fade away, their activities turned out to be more personal and multi-polar. Kurokawa's concern now concentrated on the co-existence of heterogeneous objects or concepts; in spite of the classicist-like appearance of his subsequent works, Kurokawa maintained that this approach was not an ideological shift but a development of his former Metabolist group-form theory, while Ohtaka adjusted his approach, turning in his designs to the use of a neo-vernacular style. HY

☐ Kawazoe, N., Kikutake, K., and Kurokawa, K., *Metabolism 1960. Proposals for New Urbanism*, Tokyo 1960; Kurokawa, K., *The Concept of Metabolism*, Tokyo 1972.

Mexico. The Revolution of 1910 and the turbulence of the following years broke the influence of the Paris *Ecole des Beaux-Arts which had prevailed over Mexican architecture since the mid-19th century and had largely replaced a tradition of dependency on the Spanish motherland. It also signalled the re-evaluation of the vernacular architecture of the country, especially that of the Spanish colonial period. Parallel to this development – but in marked opposition to it – many young architects, under the leadership and instruction of José *Villagrán García, including Juan Legorreta, Enrique Yañez and Enrique de la Mora, and independently of them Juan *O'Gorman, began, *c.* 1925, to plan their buildings on the principles of the Modern Movement, particularly in the area of hospitals and schools, as well as in workers' housing. At the same time a Mexican variant of *Art Deco served as a mediating style between these contradictory positions.

Metabolism. Rissho University, Kumagaya (1967–8), by Fumihiko Maki

A noteworthy regional style in housing developed in Guadalajara in the late 1920s. Luis *Barragán, Rafael Urzúa and Ignacio Díaz Morales went back to the simple local building forms of the early colonial period. For decades their buildings went unnoticed; today, however, they are considered exemplars of an abstract redefining of regional architecture.

Between 1930 and 1950 the principles of modernism established themsevles on a broader basis: in 1939 the Mexican government invited the former director of the *Bauhaus, Hannes *Meyer, to the country, where he paved the way for a new style of urban planning. The use of tower blocks for public housing began with the Presidente Alemán residential complex in Mexico City by Mario Pani, with 13-storey buildings for a total of 5,000 inhabitants (1947–50). Tall office buildings, which followed the international trend for glass curtain-wall façades, sprang up along the Paeso de la Reforma in Mexico City, as well as in the heart of the old city with the Torre Latinoamericano by Augusto Alvarez and Adolfo Zeevaert (1950).

A modern Mexican architecture with decidedly individual characteristics first appeared only *c.* 1950 and was most evident in one of the largest undertakings of the period, the University City in the southern part of the capital. After many years of planning (general site plan by Mario Pani and Enrique del Moral) the enormous complex – originally intended for 20,000 students – was realized in 1950–3, using the projects of nearly 100 architects and engineers. In spite of the numerous individual contributions, a certain overall conception did emerge. The contrasting of horizontal and vertical building volumes and extensive open spaces is not without reminiscences of Pre-Columbian urban layout. As in those prototypes, an integration of art and architecture was sought. The tall building block of the main library gave the painter-architect Juan O'Gorman the opportunity to clothe the façade in decorative mosaic; other buildings are treated with murals and strong sculptural reliefs with realistic subjects. The Olympic Stadium is exceptional in its harmony with the landscape: Its external conical shape conforms with that of an extinct volcano.

Also in the University City is Felix *Candela's first well-known shell construction,

Mexico. National Museum of Anthropology, Mexico City (1964), by Pedro Ramirez Vázquez

the Cosmic Ray Building (1951). In the following two decades Candela collaborated with various architects on similar constructions for market halls and factories; Candela also developed impressive spatial solutions for churches. A novel approach to plasticity in architecture was the result of his technical experiments.

As a continuation of his sculptural considerations, which, however, were always inseparable from the surrounding environment, the sculptor Mathias Goeritz built the Experimental Museum 'El Eco' in Mexico City in 1952 and thus suggested the trend towards an 'emotional' and 'minimal' architecture. The five functionless towers in the Ciudad Satélite suburb of Mexico City (1957, with Barragán) represented an especially influential formal solution.

The Pedregal sector was developed, beginning in 1948, on a lava field adjacent to the University City site. Barragán was responsible for the site plan, in which modern single-family houses were harmonized with a garden layout created by contrasting fields of raw lava with interconnected planted areas with flowering trees (architects: Francisco Artigas, Barragán, Max Cetto, Santiago Greenham and others). In this same area Juan O'Gorman created his own fantastic fairytale-like house (1953–6).

In the early 1960s the Nonoalco-Tlatelolco quarter of Mexico City was constructed for

Mexico. Ciudad Satélite, near Mexico City (1957), by Mathias Goeritz and Luis Barragán

Mexico. The architect's own house, San Angel (1953–6), by Juan O'Gorman

Mexico. Hotel Camino Real, Mexico City (1968), by Ricardo Legorrete

Mexico. Colegio de México, Mexico City (1975), by Teodoro González de Léon and Abraham Zablodovsky

70,000 residents to the plans of Mario Pani. The mix of different social classes was a primary aim in this project, in which buildings ranging from 4 to 22 storeys in height allowed half of the 95-hectare site to be left open and green.

Pedro Ramírez Vázquez' solution for the Anthropological Museum in Mexico City (1964), which is arranged around a rectangular patio, was both acclaimed and criticized. In its balance of open and closed surfaces this building fulfils the local requirements much more succesfully than the glass curtain-wall structure of the same architect's nearby Museum of Modern Art (1965).

A rejection of the *International Style – which persisted in José *Villagrán García and Juan Sordo Madaleno's Hotel Maria Isabel in Mexico City (1962) – is clearly evident in another Mexico City hotel, the Hotel Camino Real (1968) by Ricardo Legorrete, with its emphasis on the wall surfaces, attention to sunlight conditions and maximum privacy in the arrangement of the rooms.

The public buildings of the 1970s in Mexico City display a tendency to monumentality which is frequently characterized by the use of large supporting and infill elements. At the same time there has been increased attention to interior courts. Three buildings by Teodoro González de León and Abraham Zabludovsky are typical of this tendency: the Infonavit Administration Building (1973); the Colegio de México (1975); and the Rufino Tamayo Museum (1981), which is well integrated with its Chapultepec Park site. An even more pronounced monumentality is to be seen in the new Military Academy (Heroico Colegio Militar), which was designed by Augustín Hernández and Manuel González Rul.

Many of the basic theories of the new direction in Mexican architecture are to be found in the small oeuvre of Barragán. Although the sense of mysticism and weighty significance which characterize his simple volumes – both externally and internally – are difficult to imitate, his influence on the work of the younger generation of architects is unmistakable. HH

☐ Myers, I. E., *Mexico's Modern Architecture*, New York 1952; Cetto, Max L., *Moderne Architektur in Mexico*, Stuttgart 1961; Smith, Clive B., *Builders in the Sun. Five Mexican Architects*, New York 1967.

Mey, Johann Melchior van der, b. Delfshaven 1878, d. Beek, the Netherlands, 1949. His claim to a place in architectural history resides principally in the Scheepvaarthuis in Amsterdam (1911–16), the formal composition of which was largely to his design. This office building was an early expression of the aims of the School of *Amsterdam: integration of architecture and sculptural decoration, which is spread across the brick façade in a fantastic richness of detail; dramatic opening-up of the building by means of stair-hall which penetrates the building's corner site diagonally. The function of the steel-and-concrete building, which contained the administrative offices of six shipping companies, is expressed in the sculptural decoration based on the iconography of the sea and maritime trade. For this building he procured the collaboration of his slightly younger colleagues de *Klerk and *Kramer, whom he had met during his years in Eduard Cuyper's office and studio. He had left Cuyper in 1906, having won the Prix de Rome; he worked for the municipality of Amsterdam, 1909–12, designing several bridges. He collaborated in the large-scale housing programmes in Amsterdam West and South with a series of projects, including the Hoofdorpplein (1927–30). WP

Meyer, Adolf, b. Mechernich, Eifel 1881, d. on the island of Baltrum, in the North Sea 1929. Trained as a cabinet-maker. Attended the Art School at Düsseldorf and worked as an architect with *Behrens and Bruno Paul. He taught at the *Bauhaus 1919–25, and was city architect in Frankfurt 1926–29. He collaborated with *Gropius (Fagus Factory at Alfeld, 1911; and Jena Municipal Theatre, 1925), then built flats, schools, the planetarium of the Zeiss Works at Jena (1925–6), and designed municipal buildings in Frankfurt.

Meyer, Hannes, b. Basle 1889, d. Crocifisso di Savosa, Switzerland 1954. Trained in Basle as a mason and architectural draughtsman. Contemporaneously with his first works in architecture, he pursued further training in evening courses at the Kunstgewerbeschule, the Landwirtschaftsakademie and the Technische Hochschule in Berlin. From 1909 he was active in the movement for land reform and communal organization, for which he designed several buildings in an architectural language still classicist and traditional (Freidorf estate at Muttenz, near Basle, 1919–24). Around 1926 he embraced the Modern Movement's rationalism. In 1927 he was invited to become a teacher and master at the *Bauhaus in Dessau, where he succeeded *Gropius as Director (1928–30). He was active in the Soviet Union (*Russia), 1930–6, then in *Switzerland, and 1939–49 in *Mexico. He adamantly rejected an architecture based on aesthetic formalism, a position which led to conflicts with the other Bauhaus teachers, especially László Moholy-Nagy (*Hungarian Activism), the exponent of composition based principally on form. M.'s most important work is his competition project for the League of Nations Palace in Geneva (1926–7, with Hans Wittwer), a complex in an extreme Constructivist vocabulary which M. nonetheless refused to view in formal terms: 'This building is neither beautiful nor ugly. It asks to be evaluated as a constructive invention.' The Allgemeiner Deutscher Gewerkschaftsbund (United German Workers Union) Building at Bernau, near Berlin (1928–30, also with Wittwer), is elegantly adjusted to topographical conditions through the use of easily moved pavilions. GHa

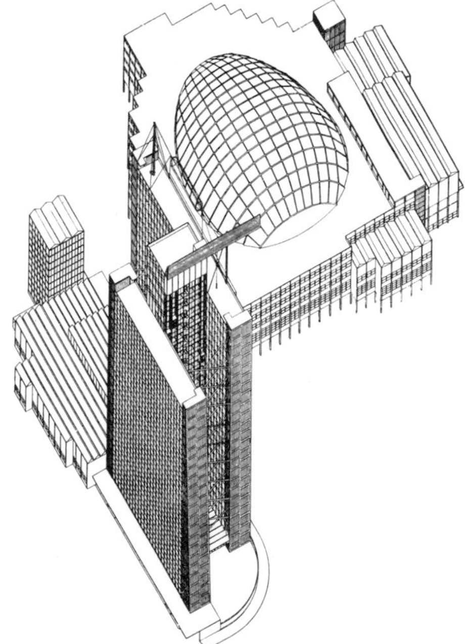

Meyer. League of Nations Palace, Geneva (project, with Hans Wittwer; 1926–7)

☐ Schnaidt, Claude, *Hannes Meyer. Bauten, Projekte und Schriften*, Teufen 1965.

M.I.A.R. (Movimento Italiano per l'Architettura Razionale). Italian ★Rationalism first came to wide attention through the first 'Esposizione dell'architettura razionale' which took place in 1928 in Rome and was organized by Adalberto ★Libera and the architectural critic Gaetano Minnucci. In addition to the members of the ★Gruppo 7 association, Luciano ★Baldessari, Mario ★Ridolfi and Alberto Sartoris were also included. In the same year, Gruppo 7 spawned a new movement, M.A.R. (Movimento Architettura Razionale), which – with Libera as its general secretary – united all of Italy's rationalist architects and architectural groups in four regional sections. Its most important task was the preparation of the 'Seconda esposizione dell'architettura razionale'. This took place in 1931, once again in Rome, and was the occasion for publishing a 'Manifesto per l'architettura razionale', with which Mussolini associated himself opportunistically. The polemical 'Tavolo degli orrori', which satirized the works of Armando Brasini, Gustavo Giovannoni and Marcello ★Piacentini, among others, led to a scandal: the M.I.A.R. was forced to adopt a compromise position in the otherwise tense cultural and political atmosphere of Fascism, with its continually ambivalent relationship to rationalist architecture. In the very same year the movement was disbanded. VML

☐ Giolli, Raffaello, *L'architettura razionale*, Bari 1972; Cennamo, Michele, *Materiali per l'analisi dell'architettura moderna, Il M.I.A.R.*, Naples 1976; Danesi, Silvia, and Patetta, Luciano (eds.), *Il razionalismo e l'architettura in Italia durante il fascismo*, Venice 1976.

Michelucci, Giovanni, b. Pistoia 1891. Studied at the Accademia delle Belle Arti in Florence. He was one of the architects of Santa Maria Novella Station in Florence (1933–6), the most important large-scale building of Italian ★Rationalism. On the one hand it is characterized by its bold, modernist architectural language, while on the other – due to its dignified marble cladding – it relates to the local classical tradition. In his later works M. turned to a strongly eclectic experimentation in a quest for the plastic qualities of a sculpturally conceived architecture. The church of San Giovanni

Michelucci. Church of San Giovanni Battista, near Florence (1960–3)

Battista, on the Autostrada del Sole (motorway) near Florence (1960–3), is a neo-expressionist (★Expressionism) collage, revealing a harsh juxtaposition of materials and forms.

☐ Borsi, Franco (ed.), *Giovanni Michelucci*, Florence 1966; Clemente, F., and Lugli, L., *Giovanni Michelucci: Il pensiero e l'opera*, Bologna 1966; Naldi, Fabio, *Giovanni Michelucci*, Florence 1978.

Mies van der Rohe, Ludwig, b. Aachen 1886, d. Chicago 1969. One of the four most influential architects of the 20th century – the others being Frank Lloyd ★Wright, ★Le Corbusier, and Walter ★Gropius – M. had no formal training in architecture. His initiation into building and the superb craftsmanship which his architecture possesses in such a high degree came initially from his father, a master-mason and stone-carver. In Aachen, he learned to draw as a designer for stucco decoration. In 1905 he went to Berlin, where he worked briefly for an architect who specialized in wooden structures. The better to master this material, he apprenticed himself for two years to Bruno Paul, a leading furniture designer. In 1908, M. joined Peter ★Behrens, at the time the most prolific architect in ★Germany.

The three years that M. spent with Behrens provided his most valuable training. In a sense Behrens' career anticipates that of Mies. On the one hand, as the designer for the Allgemeine Elektricitäts-Gesellschaft (AEG), Behrens designed not only the buildings of the German electrical combine but its products as well. More than any other architect of his generation, therefore, he anticipated the ideal of the architect as a comprehensive designer for the modern

Mies van der Rohe. Kröller House and gallery (project, 1912)

industrial society. But Behrens' factory production represented one aspect only of his oeuvre. He also brought the *neo-classicism of Karl Friedrich Schinkel to his architecture, and especially to his monumental commissions, although Schinkelesque neo-classicism occasionally appears in the severe masonry piers and simplified pediments of some of Behrens' factories as well. To create a modern architecture with a neo-classical severity of means, purity of form, perfection of proportions, elegance of detail and dignity of expression was also the underlying objective of M.'s career.

Initially, he was more overtly influenced by the neo-classical rather than by the industrial aspects of Behrens' work, in large part perhaps because he had served as the supervisor of construction for one of Behrens' monumental buildings, the German Embassy in St Petersburg (now Leningrad; 1911–12). Leaving Behrens in 1911, M. designed several houses in a neo-Schinkelesque style akin to Behrens' work. The most notable design of the group (and superior to the neo-classicism of his mentor) was a projected house and gallery for Mme Helene Kröller (1912). For the Kröller commission, M. went to Holland. There he came to know the work and philosophy of Hendrik Petrus *Berlage, who was the Dutch counterpart to Behrens. If Behrens was primarily concerned with form, Berlage derived his architectural philosophy from the 19th-century moralistic theory of the 'honest' expression of structure and materials, which was Gothic rather than classical in inspiration. Taken together, Behrens' emphasis on form, Berlage's on revealed structure and materials, and their joint desire for a new architecture were important influences on M.'s development.

His romantic neo-classicism continued up to the end of World War I. Now, his career in modern architecture was abruptly launched in a series of projects, from 1919 to 1924, which were astonishingly varied and original. They reflected the sense of liberation in post-war Berlin which suddenly felt the impact of native *Expressionism, of De *Stijl from Holland, of *Constructivism and *Suprematism from Russia. M. was active in this ferment, not only as a designer, but as a propagandist too. He was among the founders of the magazine *G* (for *Gestaltung*, creative force) which was devoted to modern art. He joined the *Novembergruppe; founded in 1918, and named after the month of the Republican Revolution, this organization, too, publicized the Modern Movement. Mies directed the architectural section from 1921 until 1925. It was principally in the annual exhibitions of the Novembergruppe that his early modern projects first appeared.

In two skyscraper projects, the first (1919) of triangular forms, the second (1920–1) of curved free forms, M. sought to dramatize the reflective qualities of glass in faceted shapes. In fact, the free-form curvature of the second of these skyscrapers was specifically determined by the shape which produced the greatest play of light over the building. A project for a reinforced-concrete office building (1922) was even more prophetic. Cantilevered slabs closed by a parapet permitted continuous inset window bands with the lightest of metal mullions. Although not widely known until much later, this project was among the first to feature ribbon windows, one of the standard motifs of modernist architecture. This stage in M.'s development is concluded by two projects for houses. One, in 1923, for a brick country house, used De Stijl principles. Brick panels in slab, **L** and **T** shapes, infilled where necessary with floor-to-roof window panels, modulated a spatial continuity through their arrangement in a tense asymmetrical equilibrium in space. For the first time in architecture, the wall by its placement and shape actually generated the plan. Although the design was schematic only, it nevertheless represented in a pure form the first truly architectural achievement employing De Stijl principles of composition, since earlier ventures had arbitrarily intermixed De Stijl with Cubist elements. The second project, for a concrete structure, involved a spreading structure in a pinwheel composition around a multi-terraced site. Both the horizontality of the house and the determination of the irregular mass in accordance with the major elements of the plan ran counter to the compact *prisme pur* enclosure of space which dominated the *International Style at the time. In this respect, M.'s concrete country house looked rather ahead to later developments of the International Style after 1930.

The latter half of the 1920s saw a few (very few) executed buildings in M.'s modern style. Notable among them were the Monument to Karl Liebknecht and Rosa Luxemburg in Berlin (1926; later demolished by the Nazis). A textured brick wall, faceted with horizontal, box-like projecting and receding elements, it was among the few significant memorials erected in the 20th century. Two brick houses – the Wolf House in Guben (1926) and the Hermann Lange House in Krefeld (1928) –

Mies van der Rohe. Reinforced-concrete office building (project, 1922)

Mies van der Rohe. Wolf House, Guben (1926)

reveal how far M. had come from his pre-war neo-Schinkelism, and how much his early neoclassicism continued to influence his work. Both possess a solidity and rootedness never associated with the International Style. The Wolf House is especially fine in the extension of the beautiful precision of the brick walls and in an abstract arrangement of brick terracing reminiscent of the Liebknecht-Luxemburg Monument.

His work at this time, however, is climaxed by two major works. One, the Weißenhofsiedlung in Stuttgart (1927), was a large-scale outdoor exhibition of housing of various types with designs by most of the leading modern European architects. Sponsored by the *Deutscher Werkbund and directed by Mies, this outdoor exhibition contained various temporary structures and no less than twenty-one permanent buildings, ranging from one-family villas to M.'s dominating apartment structure. An even more impressive work qualitatively, and indeed among the masterpieces of modern architecture, was M.'s German Pavilion for the International Exhibition in Barcelona (1928–9). It continued the De Stijl experiment of his project for a country house of 1923, but with a simplification of elements and a breadth of treatment far surpassing the complications of the earlier design. Over a portion of a raised podium, M. lightly supported a reinforced-concrete slab on chrome-plated steel columns of cross-shaped section. He placed vertical slabs of travertine and panels of glass of various kinds well under the spreading slab of the roof. Partially enclosing the roofed area, and partially sliding from under it, these panels in the right-angled asymmetrical arrangement loosely, but firmly, ordered the space while preserving its continuity. Two pools completed the complex: the larger on the open terrace; the smaller at right-angles to it at the opposite end of the podium. The smaller one was enclosed in a semi-court created by sliding the travertine panels from under the slab of the roof. The sculpture of a female figure by Georg Kolbe placed in the water serves as a discrete focal point within this scrupulously chaste pavilion, otherwise occupied only by some of M.'s furniture. It was in this pavilion that he displayed his famous 'Barcelona Chair'. Among the classics in modern furniture design, this was the culminating piece in a series of distinguished designs which he realized during the late 1920s. Although the pavilion received relatively little notice during the summer of its existence, the published record of the modest structure has since made it one of the most influential buildings of the 20th century.

Immediately after the Barcelona Pavilion, M. designed the most important house of his European career, the concrete-surfaced Tugendhat House at Brno, Czechoslovakia (1930). Built on a gentle slope, the house presented a closed one-storey front to the street, with two storeys to the rear. The continuous space of the lower living floor with its chrome-plated columns and free-standing panels (one a semicircle of Macassar ebony) recalled the treatment of the Barcelona Pavilion. Here an even richer display of M.'s furniture completed an elegance, every detail of which (down to the curtain tracks) was custom-designed.

The Tugendhat House was M.'s last important executed building in Europe. Among the projects of the early and mid-1930s, the designs for houses within walled courts are the most interesting. Although the surrounding brick walls occasionally opened on to a distant view, for the most part these houses were wholly bounded by their rectangular frame, while in one instance terraced houses of various sizes, separated by walls, were enclosed in a single rectilinear overall form. Inside the enclosure there was the usual Miesian spatial continuity, interrupted here and there by carefully placed glass walls and solid panels.

On Gropius's recommendation, M. succeeded Hannes *Meyer as Director of the *Bauhaus in 1930. By 1932, however, pressure from extreme right-wing factions caused him to move the school from Dessau to Berlin, where it had a brief and tenuous existence as a private institute until the Nazis forced its closure in 1933. The hostile political environment made it increasingly impossible to work in Germany and, in the summer of 1937, when just past fifty, M. emigrated to the *USA; there, in 1944, he became an American citizen.

In 1938 he had been invited to teach at the Illinois Institute of Technology (then the Armour Institute) in Chicago. His first major American commission, a campus plan and buildings for IIT (from 1940), immediately established the central theme of his American work: the exposed metal frame as it reticulated neutral rectangular volumes. He viewed the cleared site, which consisted of a number of city

Mies van der Rohe. Tugendhat House, Brno (1930)

Mies van der Rohe. Minerals and Metals Building, IIT, Chicago (1942)

Mies van der Rohe. Farnsworth House, Fox River, Ill. (1946–50)

blocks on Chicago's South Side, as an idealized space, much like the podium of the Barcelona Pavilion. On this he arranged rectangular and slab-shaped blocks in accord with a modular grid for the entire project, such that semi-courts and corridors of space were created in a manner analogous to (but more formal than) his use of slabs in the conditioning of interior space from the Barcelona Pavilion onward.

The revealed metal frame in his American buildings is rarely the structure itself, since fire regulations demand that most steel must be covered. Hence the visible 'structure' is more often symbolic of the reality beneath, much as pilasters symbolized columns in Renaissance buildings – except that M.'s pseudo-structure more convincingly resembles and more intimately relates to the real thing within. From the standard alphabet of the steelmaker's catalogue he welded mouldings as the metallurgical equivalent of the carved mouldings of the past. The careful proportioning of his frame, the graduation of components from heavy to light, the firm elegance of his profiling and the subtleties of transitions where corners occur or one material butts another: this intensity of effort and artistry expended on the image of the structure has been unexcelled and all but unmatched by his numerous followers.

Even as the first buildings were going up on the IIT campus, M. built a glass and metal house for Dr Edith Farnsworth in Fox River, Illinois (1946–50). Three floating slabs – a terrace slab, and behind it floor and roof slabs – are all lifted from the ground on metal **I**-beam supports. The welding of the supports to the sides of the slabs, as though magnetism kept the frame intact, enhances the floating quality of the spreading slabs. Smaller slabs, also seemingly floated, serve as stairs, from the ground to the terrace and from the terrace to the entrance porch of the rectangular glass-box living area. It is so apparently simple that the subtleties of this extraordinarily elegant frame are readily missed on casual inspection, as are the subtleties of a composition in which the evident asymmetry is countered by hidden symmetries.

The basic scheme of the Farnsworth House, the open pavilion, was used by M. on several

Mies van der Rohe. Crown Hall, IIT, Chicago (1952–6)

occasions, as in Crown Hall for the School of Architecture and Design at IIT (1952–6). Again apparently floating stairs lead to the floating terrace, and more stairs rise to the floor-slab, which is raised a few feet above the ground much as it had been in the Farnsworth House. Despite appearances, however, the Crown Hall floor-slab is conventionally supported from the basement beneath. Whereas the Farnsworth House was completely open beneath its floor-slab, the basement of Crown Hall is glazed. Again the openness of this space is enhanced by the suspended nature of the two slabs hanging or abutting (rather than resting) on their supports. Insofar as M. was concerned with space at all in his American work, it tended towards the centralized box of Crown Hall and not towards the further development of the subtly modulated spaces of his European work after the Barcelona Pavilion.

Enlarged again, the pavilion became the design for a Convention Hall project on the Chicago lake-front (1953). The roof-slab was intended to be a three-dimensional structure of interwoven trusses built on a cubic module of 9·10 m (30 ft) in each direction. Mies intended this heroic structural slab to span 219·50 m (720 ft) – or roughly two city blocks – so as to provide a colum-free interior space for a capacity audience of 50,000. Diagonal bracing extended from the outside edges of the three-dimensional ceiling trusses makes a two-dimensional truss of the exterior walls. This bracing would bring the entire structure down on low reinforced-concrete columns spaced 36·60 m (120 ft) apart.

The culmination of the series of pavilion buildings was the new National Gallery in West Berlin (1962–8). M. drew on a design for the administration building for the Bacardi firm in Santiago de Cuba, in which an immense coffered ceiling is supported on eight cruciform-

Mies van der Rohe. Convention Hall, Chicago (project, 1953)

Mies van der Rohe. New National Gallery, West Berlin (1962–8)

section supports, recessed far from the corners. A deeply recessed glass wall encloses an exhibition space subdivided only by several stage-like movable walls. Services and further exhibition space are housed in the pedestal storey, in front of which a sculpture court is arranged.

As the basic pavilion could be multiplied into a series of buildings, so could the skeletal skyscraper. M.'s two classic skyscrapers, Lake Shore Drive Apartments (1950–1) and the Seagram Building in New York (1954–8; with Philip Johnson), are in a sense exactly the same building creating different experiences, much as the Greek Temple of Poseidon at Paestum and the Parthenon in Athens are at once the same building and different buildings. Relative to one another, the Paestum-like severity of the Lake Shore Drive contrasts with the Parthenaic refinement of the Seagram Building. In the Lake Shore Drive Apartments, vertical blocks are set at right-angles to one another across a narrow interval of space. The complex possesses neither a true 'front' nor a true 'back'; the narrow side of one block is seen against the broad side of the other in a constantly changing relationship. The **I**-beam projections from the walls appear to close over the windows seen obliquely and open over those seen head-on; while moving so as to open those which closed we automatically close those which were open. The Seagram Building, on the other hand, reconciles the Lake Shore paradox of static elements in perpetual disequilibrium. The bronze building rises like a dense, dark cliff behind the absolute void of its entrance *plaza*. The axis of the *plaza* culminates in the formal grandeur of the entrance with its two-storey stilts each backed by the pylons of the elevator shafts. Whereas, in the window-grid of the Lake Shore Drive Apartments, horizontals con-

Mies van der Rohe. Seagram Building, New York (with Philip Johnson; 1954–8)

stantly challenge the verticals, this tension is reconciled in the Seagram Building by the clear affirmation of verticality. The perpetual tension of the first is reduced to a reconciliation of opposites. As M. extracted architecture from the brick or the **I**-beam considered as ultimate 'things in themselves', so he developed elemental building types to serve different purposes. His approach was narrow, but this very narrowness permitted his passionate integrity and purifying artistry to come to focus. In his greatest works, the concept of 'less is more' contains the paradoxical fulfilment of an ideal. WHJ

☐ Johnson, Philip, *Mies van der Rohe*, New York 1947 (2nd ed. 1953); Hilberseimer, L., *Mies van der Rohe*, Chicago 1956; Blake, Peter, *Mies van der Rohe. Architecture and Structure*, New York 1960; Drexler, Arthur, *Ludwig Mies van der Rohe*, New York 1960; Blaser, Werner, *Mies van der Rohe. Die Kunst der Struktur*, Zurich and Stuttgart 1965; Glaeser, Ludwig, *Ludwig Mies van der Rohe. Drawings from the Collection of the Museum of Modern Art* (exhibition catalogue), New York 1968; *Ludwig Mies van der Rohe* (exhibition catalogue), Berlin 1968; Speyer, James, and Koeper, Frederick, *Mies van der Rohe* (exhibition catalogue), Chicago 1968; Glaeser, L., *Ludwig Mies van der Rohe. Furniture and Furniture Drawings . . . Museum of Modern Art, New York* (exhibition catalogue), 1977.

Mills, Edward David, b. 1915. Studied at Polytechnic School of Architecture, London. In private practice since 1937; churches, schools, industrial buildings, research centres, flats and houses. Designed the British Industries Pavilion and the Britannia Inn at the Brussels International Exposition, 1958.

Modernisme arose in Catalonia and extended over a period of some forty years, from the eclectic revivals of the 1880s to the advent of 'Noucentisme', the cultural revival of Mediterranean classicism, just before World War I. It was composed of two distinct phenomena: National Romanticism and Progressivism. The former, known as 'La Renaixença', coincided with the recovery of the Catalan language after a century of repression. The literary and philosophical flourishing was a revival of popular rather than academic traditions, but in its nostalgic backwards glance 'La Renaixença' was an essentially conservative movement. Progressivism, which provided a balance to this conservatism, was largely the work of a small radical, non-conformist cultural group who tried to grapple with the realities and conflicts of the Industrial Revolution in ⋆Spain. It assimilated many European progressive currents, including Naturalism with its extension into the ⋆Arts and Crafts movement and ⋆Art Nouveau, as well as the belief that progress would result from science and technology. Fervent rationalists, the Progressivists sought to politicize their ambitions for a new society and were subsequently joined by the bourgeoisie who saw economic advantages in a liberal society better adjusted to modern social conditions and production, as opposed to the archaic establishment which prevailed in Madrid. Thus, unlike either Art Nouveau or the Arts and Crafts movement in England, 'Modernisme' lost its élite pedestal and became the instrument of one of the rare flourishings of popular cultural identity, albeit confined to the linguistic boundaries of the Catalan language.

The essential characteristics of 'Modernisme', of which over 1,000 examples still survive in Catalonia, may be summarized as: (1) the persistence of eclectic elements derived from the historical styles of the 19th century; (2) an enormous respect for materials, especially brick, and the exploitation of their constructive qualities as decorative elements; (3) the desire to design everything, from tile patterns and door knobs to lifts and furniture; (4) the use of double façades to act as a micro-climatic filter; (5) the use of applied decoration either independently of the architecture or as an integral part of it, intended to emphasize either the method of construction or the conceptual design. DM

☐ Bohigas, Oriol, *Reseña y catalógo de la arquitectura modernista*, Barcelona 1973; Marfany, Joan Lluis, *Aspectes del Modernisme*, Barcelona 1975.

Modulor. A proportional system relying on the golden section or the Fibonacci series, as the case may be, with the human body as its basis and intended to be used in calculating the proportions of building units. It was developed by ⋆Le Corbusier and his collaborators in 1942–8. The ideal body height is taken as 183 cm (6 ft), from which the initial dimensions of 226 cm (7 ft 5 in.), i.e. the height of a man standing upright with his hand raised, and 113 cm (3 ft $8\frac{1}{2}$ in.), the distance from the ground to the solar plexus, are

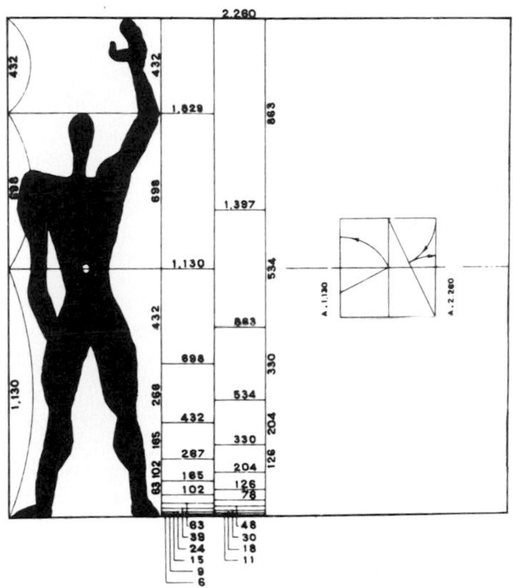

Modulor. Second version, based on a body height of 183 cm (6 ft)

derived. The measure of 113 cm yields a 'red series' (0·6 – 0·9 – 1·5 – 2·4 – 3·9 – 6·3 – 10·2 – 16·5 – 26·7 – 43·2 – 69·8 – 113·0 – 182·9, etc.) and the 226 cm a 'blue series' (1·1 – 1·8 – 3·0 – 4·8 – 7·8 – 12·6 – 20·4 – 33·0 – 53·4 – 86·3 – 139·7 – 226·0, etc.). In a first version of the Modulor a body height of 175 cm had been used, but this could not, in contrast to the later version, be converted to a convenient equivalent in the British system using feet and inches. AM

☐ Le Corbusier, *Le Modulor*, Paris 1948 (English translation: *The Modulor*, London 1954); ——, *Modulor 2*, Paris 1955 (English translation: *Modulor 2, 1955 . . .*, London 1958).

Moneo, José Rafael, b. Tudela, Navarra 1937. After studies at the Escuela de Arquitectura in Madrid, he entered the office of Jørn *Utzon in Hellebaek, Denmark. Later he spent two years at the Academia de España in Rome. In 1965 he established his own practice in Madrid. Since 1971 he has been a professor at the Escuela de Arquitectura in Barcelona. This combination of teaching and design lends a decidedly intellectual cast to his architecture. He is also one of the most active and highly regarded architectural critics in Spain. M. believes architecture to be an autonomous discipline seeking to find its legitimization in the classical tradition of proportion and composition. In design he combines this formal sense with an almost puritanical simplicity in the handling of materials. His preferred material, brick, is consciously used to 'humanize' his architecture and to soften the intellectualized abstraction of the design, a lesson perhaps derived from his Scandinavian experience, although certainly a well-established tradition in Madrid. His most notable buildings are: the Diestre factory in Saragossa (1963–7), where the refined profiles of the roof bays are etched into the brick skin; the Bankinter Building in Madrid (1975), a subtle extension to a small 18th-century palace; and the Town Hall in Logroño (1978), where his architecture plays an active role in preserving the vitality of the city. DM

☐ 'José Rafael Moneo', *Nueva Forma* (Madrid), January 1975.

Moore, Charles W(illard), b. Benton Harbor, Mich. 1925. Studied at the University of Michigan and at Princeton University. In 1962 he formed an association in Berkeley, Cal., with Donlyn Lyndon, William Turnbull and Richard Whitaker (MLTW), and continued this office, 1965–70, with William Turnbull in New Haven and San Francisco under the name MLTW/Moore-Turnbull. In 1970 he founded Charles W. Moore Associates in Essex, Conn., which was complemented in 1975 by a parallel working co-operative with William Grover and Robert Harper (Moore Grover Harper) in Essex, as well as a similar arrangement with John Ruble and Robert Yudell in Los Angeles, subsequently enlarged by the addition of the Urban Innovations Group of Los Angeles. He was a professor at the University of California at Berkeley, 1962–5, and at Yale University, 1965–75; since 1975 he has taught at the University of California in Los Angeles.

Together with his various partners, M. has created an extraordinarily diverse and typologically complex oeuvre. Among his most important early buildings are: his own house in Orinda, Cal. (1962), where he demonstrated for the first time the delimitation of the living zones by aedicule-like baldacchinos of wood; Condominium I at Sea Ranch, Sonoma County, Cal. (1964–5), where this theme was further developed in other forms; and the Athletic Club I at Sea Ranch (1966), which is presented in essence as a wind-screen that can be traversed. In 1966–8 he realized the Faculty Club of the University of California in Santa Barbara, since much altered, whose differentiated spaces provided the first evidence of theatrical effects in his work. In addition to a large number of typologically noteworthy single-family houses, such as the Klotz House in Westerly, R.I. (1967–70), M. was also able quite early on to build several housing estates which contradicted, in an almost paradigmatic way, the thesis that economical mass housing must of necessity be formless and uniform (Church Street South Moderate Income Housing in New Haven, Conn., 1966–9; Maplewood Terrace Low Income Housing in Middletown, Conn., 1970–1; Whitman Village Housing in Huntington, N.Y. 1971–5). In 1973–4 he built Kresge College of the University of California at Santa Cruz, which cited elements of the fora of antiquity to create a 'rural acropolis' (Moore) in its forest setting.

Among the most important works of recent years are: St Joseph's Fountain in the Piazza d'Italia in New Orleans (1975–8), a stage-like collage of antique set pieces with a strong folkloristic character; and the competition entry for a recreation and residential complex on the shore of Lake Tegel in Berlin (1980), in which the spectacularly used steamboat motif is accompanied by various quotations from Prussian classicism, 19th-century glass-and-iron architecture and regional construction.

M.'s most important contribution to contemporary architecture, one which has fallen on fertile ground in Europe, is his commitment to the adaptation of regionalist traits and the use of a language of signs that evoke 'memory'. It is fair to say that in the process his work is not entirely free of eclectic and mannerist elements. His theoretical approach to building for the 'impressive locality' touches not only the advocates of a regionally determined architecture, but also the current thinking within the school of *Rational architecture. FW

Moore. Kresge College, University of California, Santa Cruz (1973–4)

Moore. Condominium I, Sea Ranch, Cal. (Moore Grover Harper; 1964–5)

□ Moore, Charles, Allen, Gerald, and Lyndon, Donlyn, *The Place of Houses*, New York 1974; Futagawa, Yukio (ed.), *Houses by MLTW. Vol. One, 1959–1975*, Tokyo 1975; Moore, Charles, and Bloomer, K. C., *Body, Memory and Architecture*, New Haven, Conn. 1977; 'The Work of Charles W. Moore', *Architecture and Urbanism* (Tokyo), special number, May 1978; Allen, Gerald, *Charles Moore*, New York and London 1980.

Morandi, Riccardo, b. Rome 1902. Pier Luigi *Nervi apart, M. is the most interesting Italian exponent of reinforced-concrete structures. His international reputation is founded especially on: the bridge over the Maracaibo Lagoon in Venezuala (1957); the subterranean automobile showroom in Turin (1959); and the extraordinary viaduct at Polcevera, near Genoa (1965).

Morandi. Subterranean automobile showroom, Turin (1959)

His numerous later works include the terminal buildings at Rome's Fiumicino Airport (1970) and the bridge at Barranquilla, Colombia (1972). VG

☐ Boaga, Giorgio, and Boni, Benito, *Riccardo Morandi*, Milan 1962; Masini, Lara Vinca, *Riccardo Morandi*, Rome 1974.

Morris, William, b. Walthamstow, Essex 1834, d. Kelmscott, Oxon. 1896. Studied theology; architectural training under the Gothic Revivalist G. E. Street (where he met *Shaw and *Webb). Active as a painter in the Pre-Raphaelite circle around the brothers D. G. and Michael Rossetti, M. was greatly influenced by the architect A. W. N. Pugin and also by the critic and theorist John Ruskin in his passionate, romantically inspired quest to revive the spiritual and aesthetic principles of the Middle Ages, which he developed in opposition to the *eclecticism of his time and which he saw as intimately linked with progressive social ideals. For him, socialism was a conscious return to a life-style in which workmen took pleasure in their craft. In formal terms he stressed a need for 'honesty', sincerity and quality of craftsmanship. Although he was not himself responsible for any buildings, the Red House at Bexley Heath, Kent, which he commissioned from Webb in 1859, was a milestone in the English Domestic Revival. In 1861 M. founded the firm Morris, Marshall, Faulkner & Company, a production workshop for handicrafts, which was to be a nodal point of the reforming *Arts and Crafts movement. VML

☐ Morris, May (ed.), *The Collected Works of William Morris* (24 vols.), London 1910–15; Henderson, Philip, *William Morris, His Life, Work and Friends*, London 1967; Thompson, Paul, *The Works of William Morris*, London 1977.

Moser, Karl, b. Baden, Switzerland 1860, d. Zurich 1936. Studied at the Eidgenössiche Technische Hochschule in Zurich and then at the *Ecole des Beaux-Arts in Paris. He was active as an architect in Karlsruhe, 1887–1915, and was a professor at the Eidegenössische Techniche Hochschule in Zurich, 1915–28, during which time his pupils included many noted Swiss architects of later years. In 1928 he was elected the first President of *CIAM. Although his work was grounded in a restrained, classically oriented *historicism (Badischer Railway Station, Basle, 1912–13), M. created a pioneering work of modernism in *Switzerland with his reinforced-concrete St

Antonius Church in Basle (1926–7), a refined counterpart to *Perret's Notre Dame, Le Raincy, in France (1922–3).
☐ Kienzle, Hermann, *Karl Moser: 1860–1936*, Zurich 1937.

Murphy/Jahn. Architectural practice which has been known under various names in its nearly fifty-year history and today has a total staff of some 170 individuals; it is one of the leading architectural firms of Chicago, and has played a large role in forming the appearance of that city as we know it today.

The only surviving member of the office's original founders, C. F. Murphy, began his career in 1911 under the architect D. H. Burnham, who, along with John W. Root was one of the principal protagonists of the *Chicago School and had prepared in 1909 a much-acclaimed development plan for Chicago. After Burnham's death in 1912, Murphy became a partner in the office founded by Burnham's former partner Ernest R. Graham: Graham, Anderson, Probst and White. In 1937 Murphy and two other earlier partners of this firm, Alfred Shaw and Sigurd Naess, opened the office of Shaw, Naess & Murphy, and finally in 1959 the office of C. F. Murphy Associates. Helmut Jahn (b. Zindorf, near Nuremberg 1940) entered the office in 1967, having studied at the Technische Hochschule in Munich and under *Mies van der Rohe at the Illinois Institute of Technology. In 1973 he became partner, Vice-President and Director of the Design section; the renaming of the office as Murphy/Jahn followed in 1981.

In the 1960s under Jacques Brownson and Gene Summers (who had both studied at IIT), the office created some of the best work in Chicago in the image of the post-war Miesian idiom (Continental Insurance Building, 1962; O'Hare International Airport, 1963; Chicago Civic Center, 1965; extension to the First National Bank of Chicago, 1971; exhibition building, McCormick Place 1971).

With Jahn in charge of design, there was an increasing relaxation of the link to the model of Mies van der Rohe (Kemper Arena, Kansas City, 1974; sports hall of St Mary's College, Notre Dame, Ind., 1977; Rust-Oleum company headquarters, Vernon Hills, Ill., 1978; Xerox Center, Chicago, 1980; State of Illinois Center, Chicago, under construction); this trend has culminated in a rediscovery of *Art Deco (extension to the Chicago Board of Trade Building, and One South Wacker Building, Chicago, both under construction). PCvS
☐ *Architecture and Urbanism* (Tokyo), July 1978; 'New directions and new designs at C. F. Murphy Associates', *Architectural Record* (New York), July 1979, pp. 98–109; *Architecture and Urbanism* (Tokyo), April 1981, pp. 9–36; *Murphy/Jahn* (private publication), Chicago n.d.

Murphy. Chicago Civic Center (C. H. Murphy Associates; 1965)

Muthesius, Hermann, b. Groß-Neuhausen 1861, d. Berlin 1927. Studied at the Technische Hochschule in Berlin-Charlottenburg; worked in Wallot's office. Period in Japan in the Tokyo office of Ende & Böckmann; attaché at the German Embassy in London, 1896–1903, with a brief to study English architecture and design. Founder-member of the *Deutscher Werkbund in 1907. His 3-volume study *Das englische Haus* (Berlin 1904–5), by spreading a knowledge of the works of *Voysey and his contemporaries, stimulated a renaissance in domestic architecture on the Continent. The Cramer House in Berlin (1911–12) is an independent

essay, based on impressions of England, in its refined play with symmetry and asymmetry and carefully determined proportions.
☐ *Hermann Muthesius, 1861–1927* (exhibition catalogue), Berlin 1978.

N

neo-classicism. Although the word has been used to describe any number of departures in music (Les Six, Igor Stravinsky's compositions of the late 1920s and 1930s), in painting (Pablo Picasso, Giorgio de Chirico in the late 1920s, the Novecento movement in Italy), in literature (it has been applied to Paul Valéry, T. S. Eliot and Louis Aragon, as well as Jean Cocteau who actually called himself neo-classic), and even in physics (a return to certain forms of Newtonian description), it does not describe any clearly defined architectural phenomenon.

The term 'classicism' is taken by art historians to describe the movement towards greater restraint in the arts in the second half of the 18th century which was coupled with a renewed interest in antiquity, particularly Greek art. It originated in France and Italy, but soon extended to Britain, Germany and beyond. The unity and coherence of this movement was first challenged by Sigfried Giedion in *Spätbarocker und romantischer Klassizismus* (1922), which led to the adoption of the apparently contradictory term 'romantic classicism'. His analysis, though not timely, was necessary, since a return to a form of classicism characterized the first years of the 20th century.

To some extent this neo-classicism represented a reaction against a powerful attempt to create for the 20th century an 'unhistorical' style which marked some of the best work done in the last decade of the 19th, particularly that which goes under the name *Art Nouveau. In fact, the designers who led the reaction, Joseph Maria *Olbrich and Peter *Behrens, had been early Art Nouveau practitioners. Both of them adopted an increasingly severe style and within two or three years had transformed the floreated and curvilinear manner into a formal and geometrical one. This change happened so rapidly (between 1900 and 1904) that the new manner could only be developed by appeal to historical precedent. Both designers appealed to

neo-classicism. Exhibition pavilion of the Delmenhorster Linoleum Factory, Dresden (1906), by Peter Behrens

the German architecture of Napoleonic times This appeal recalled the greatness of the rising Prussian state and its nationalist reforming energies. Behrens gave this ethos its most effective embodiment in his work for the Allgemeine Elektricitäts-Gesellschaft (AEG), which included a new typeface for their publicity, the design of the manufactured objects, different electrical appliances and machinery and factory buildings. In this and in other work done at this time, Behrens insistently used deliberate references to classical architecture, as well as a tight proportional system.

In Britain motivation was less direct. The reaction against *Arts and Crafts freedom and whimsy took the form of a return to the 'vernacular', which was identified with 18th-century domestic building. At the same time, public building returned consciously to a reworking of certain 18th-century themes, though on a much larger scale, and often with large areas of unarticulated window-wall between the base and the crowning classical top dressing.

This use of textbook classical detail was much influenced by American example. After the Chicago World's Columbian Exposition of 1893 (called the 'White City' because of the mass of classical stucco buildings), it became the dominant mode of official and prestige building in the United States. The great man of Chicago at the time was Daniel Burnham, whose replanning of Washington and megalomaniac layout for Chicago became models of urban planning for a generation. The firm of McKim, Mead &

neo-classicism. Part of the site of the World's Columbian Exposition, Chicago (general plan by D. H. Burnham; 1893)

neo-classicism. Pennsylvania Station, New York (1906–10; demolished), by McKim, Mead & White

White, whose production included Boston Public Library (1888–92), the Pierpont Morgan Library in New York (1903) and Pennsylvania Station in New York (1906–10), provided the main monuments of the new U.S. opulent classicism which is very different from what goes under the name neo-classic in Europe.

Both were, however, dominated by the *Ecole des Beaux-Arts in Paris, whose leading teacher of theory, Julien Guadet, published a highly influential manual on architectonic composition in 1896. He taught a whole generation who passed through the Ecole a doctrine which, he told them, was immemorial and which had been taught with very little change since it was devised at the Ecole Polytechnique by J. N. L. Durand a century earlier. This generation included Auguste *Perret and Tony *Garnier. In spite of his personal friendship with Guadet, Perret rejected any adherence to the Ecole system. The reply to critics who noted similarities between Perret's work and French 'classical' architecture was that Perret had 're-invented' the classical trabeated system in concrete using wood prototypes, much as the Greeks had imitated wooden construction in their use of stone. Garnier's obsession with antiquity concentrated on the unitary order of the city, which he translated into his highly articulated vision of a Cité Industriélle, while its basic unit, the house, was consciously modelled on an antique prototype. As in Germany, the movement had begun with the turn of the century, though it became official when Perret wrested the commission for the Théâtre des Champs-Elysées from Henry *van de Velde *c.*

neo-classicism. *Chicago Tribune* competition entry (1922) by Adolf Loos

neo-classicism. Musée des Travaux Publics, Paris (1937), by Auguste Perret

1911, while Garnier began the Abattoirs de la Mouche in Lyons in 1909 – his first official job. Their new 'purged' and 'modern' classicism was quite different, sober and rational, as against the inflated academic style which also claimed 'classical' (mostly 17th- and 18th-century) precedent.

In Vienna, Josef *Hoffmann and a number of the pupils of Otto *Wagner (notably Josef Plečnik) employed simple, classical sobriety. Adolf *Loos used the classical orders as quotations and as a 'recall to order' rather than as optional ornamental features. He used marble Tuscan columns on the Goldman & Salatsch store on the Michaelerplatz in Vienna (1910) and one huge Doric column for the main office building in his design for the *Chicago Tribune* competition scheme (1922). He was explicitly opposed to the use of ornament and saw the orders as a defence against the 'ornamentalists' (who for him were Hoffmann and van de Velde). Karl Friedrich Schinkel, whom Loos quotes as the last of those who hold up the example of antiquity against the vagaries of 'ornamentalists', was an exemplar not only for the German-speaking lands, but for all northern Europe. Hack Kampmann and Carl Petersen in *Denmark, Gunnar *Asplund, Ivar Tengbom and Sigurd *Lewerentz in Sweden, even the early work of Erik *Bryggman and Alvar *Aalto were all marked by the teaching that went back to the tradition of Schinkel, which had been rooted in Finland by Carl Ludwig Engel.

*Le Corbusier had spent a short period in Behrens's office, but at the crucial time when Behrens was moving towards a strict design method, and had subsequently devised his regulating lines for arriving at a proportional scheme for every project. *Gropius, who remained longer with Behrens, and *Mies van der Rohe, who submitted to the same discipline, were individually influenced by their time in Behrens's office. Heinrich *Tessenow's formal discipline was coupled with a personal devotion to Schinkel, whose Neue Wache in Berlin he transformed into a World War I memorial; but also with an almost Ruskinian devotion to the crafts. His pupil Albert *Speer adopted not only Tessenow's lessons, but the rather more *osé* notions of Paul Schultze-Naumburg about the nature of a Teutonic architecture. However, his own works hardly rate the description 'neo-classical' in the sense in which it applies to Asplund or Loos. Nor does the term really apply to the work of the major inter-war Italian official architect, Marcello *Piacentini, whose rather heavy, pseudo-antique *eclecticism owes nothing to the shade of Schinkel or of his Italian contemporaries like Giuseppe Valadier or Antonio Selva. In fact it was the lessons and the Viennese example of Wagner and Hoffmann and even of Loos which worked more strongly on the most active architects of north Italy in the 1920s and 1930s. Gio *Ponti, Giuseppe De Finetti and Giovanni Muzio are more fitting representatives of such a tendency. Muzio particularly, because of his association with the painter Mario Sironi, is most closely related through the periodical *Valori Plastici* with de Chirico and some of the Parisian developments of the 1920s. But the Italian distinction, as between the anti-Fascist De Finetti and the committed Fascist Piacentini may serve as a caution against any facile identification of authoritarianism with classicism; around 1930, such an identification was all too easy. In 1927, the competition for the League of Nations Building in Geneva brought the disqualification of Le Corbusier's (arguably neo-classical) scheme in favour of a fivesome of much more

neo-classicism. Public Library, Stockholm (preliminary drawing, 1921), by Gunnar Asplund

neo-classicism. Casa della Meridiana, Milan (1924–5), by Giuseppe de Finetti

explicitly 'classical' or 'academic' projects which were conflated into a single executed one.

In *Russia, meanwhile, the experimental phase of Soviet construction was terminated by the victory of the VOPRA group at the June 1931 Communist Party congress when the new ideological stance of the party on 'proletarian classicism' was taken. Its first direct result was the winning of the competition for the new Palace of the Soviets in Moscow by the group led by Boris M. Jofan. This policy led to the employment of Ivan V. Zholtovsky and Ivan A. Fomin on many state projects, particularly the Moscow Metropolitan which became a showpiece of the new style, though its deliberate coarseness hardly puts it in the same class as the more refined neo-classicism of northern Europe.

Throughout the 1930s and 1940s (and even the 1950s and 1960s) the terms 'academic' and 'classical' were considered virtually synonymous and tarred with the mark of 'rhetoric' which somehow implied a concentration on the frivolous, the inessential, an avoidance of necessary tasks; in the latter part of the period, this necessity meant post-war reconstruction, and the requirements of mass production. Although several attempts to reconsider the problem of ornament were made in this context (particularly in the USA), it was taken for granted that any new ornament would be a-historical. However, the more important recall to order was rooted in a new *historicism.

Already in the 1950s, the work of certain historians concerned with primitive architecture (notably Sigfried Giedion) led to a rethinking of the basis of modernism. Other historians, such as Rudolf Wittkower and his pupil, Colin Rowe, pointed out, first in Britain, then in the USA, the historical roots of certain 'modern' manipulations. The value of type and norm was asserted against those of originality and the total rethinking of every programme which was current in the Modern Movement. This led first to a conflation of Miesian structural procedures with the atrophied remnants of Beaux-Arts axial planning, as in the work of Edward Durell Stone, Philip *Johnson, and even towards the end, of Mies van der Rohe himself. But this was not differentiated from the old modernity; a more thoroughgoing and consistent reaction is noticeable in the work of Louis *Kahn. Kahn's repeatable unit is often identified as a type formed so as to carry the maximum of historical reference.

By contrast, a later school of rationalist designers appeared in Italy in the 1970s (*Rational architecture). Grouped around Aldo *Rossi, it takes the opposite view: types are used (whatever their historical reference) because architecture has no relation whatever to ideology, and therefore the type, and in fact the building in which it appears, has no reference outside itself. This tendency was given its canonic showing at the XVth Milan Triennale in 1973. Since then there have been two notable departures from the canon. Michael *Graves, an exhibitor at that Triennale, has attempted a fusion of *Art Deco with a kind of neo-primitivist classicism; while Leon *Krier and Maurice Culot have developed a neo-Tessenowian appeal to the restoration of the building crafts and the permanence of the historically validated 'classical' type. JR

☐ Larsson, Lars Olof, 'Klassizismus in der Architektur des 20. Jahrhunderts', in: *Albert Speer. Architektur. Arbeiten 1933–1942*, Frankfurt am Main, Berlin and Vienna, 1978, pp. 151–75.

Neo-plasticism. Movement in European painting developed above all by Piet Mondrian after 1914, when he returned to Holland from Paris, having been active there in the circles of the Cubist painters (*Cubism). Mondrian adopted the name from the philosopher and mathematician M. H. J. Schoenmaekers; it refers to his central intention to reduce three-dimensional volumes to plans, which he considered the primary elements of plastic form. The basic theory of Neo-plasticism was set out in Mondrian's 'De Nieuwe Beelding in de Schilderkunst', published in 1917 in the first issue of *De Stijl*; the group De *Stijl adapted Mondrian's aesthetic to architecture. VML

Nervi, Pier Luigi, b. Sondrio, Lombardy 1891, d. Rome 1979. Graduated in engineering at Bologna University in 1913. From 1946 to 1961 he was professor of structural engineering in the Faculty of Architecture at Rome University.

This great builder ranked with *Freyssinet and *Maillart in his prodigious ability to derive beauty from the results of precise calculations, and form from the nature of his materials and techniques, which he made the instruments of his vision. He himself had many times postulated in his writings the principle that the process of creating form is identical, whether it is the work of technicians or of artists: the principle, that is, whereby the beauty of a structure, for example, is not just the outcome of calculations, but of an intuition as to what calculations to use, or with which it is to be identified.

The material that N. adopted was reinforced-concrete. His first structures (for a cinema in Naples) date from 1927. The idea was gaining ground (the source of much subsequent misunderstanding) that form must follow function, and it was this idea that brought N. the engineer into architecture forthwith. His first important work, the Communal Stadium at Florence (1930–2), consisting of nothing but exposed structural elements, was published straightaway in the most controversial journals as an example of modern architecture, which could be compared, in its dramatic exploitation of structure, with certain designs of *Le Corbusier, and which strikingly highlighted the expressive possibilities of the raw material, concrete.

With his designs for an aeroplane hangar at Orvieto (1935–8) and those at Orbetello and Torre del Lago (1940–3), N. concentrated his attention on a study of roofs built up from a network of load-bearing joists. These were to prove the object of constant and ever deeper research on his part, in an infinite variety prompted by his taste for creation and experiment. With the construction of these hangars (now destroyed), N. achieved a great step forward in the process of lightening his structures, as much for aesthetic as for technical reasons.

About 1940, he brought to a successful conclusion the studies and experiments he had been carrying out to obtain 'strength through form' in buildings, i.e. strength in surfaces alone; this is at once the most technically interesting and the most aesthetically satisfying of his achievements. He used this method for the great hall of the Exhibition Building in Turin (1948–9), which remains one of his masterpieces, although due to a misunderstanding on the part of those responsible for the actual construction an important internal detail, the form of the apse, was altered, thus depriving the structure of the significance which N.'s overall design had attained. The enormous building consists in effect of a single roof structure, made up of undulating prefabricated units.

A number of smaller buildings followed, based on the same principle of roofing in reinforced concrete which leaves the space below completely free; some are on a circular plan, such as the Casino at the Rome Lido (1950) and Banqueting Hall at Chianciano Terme (1950–2). At the same time N. was carrying out research on reinforced-concrete prefabrication, using small ferro-concrete moulds for on-site manufacture, in conjunction with a movable type of staging that he patented. This device permitted a great variety of designs based on a ribbed structure, making de *Baudot's boldest and most utopian designs now seem capable of realization. Another important invention in the technical field was N.'s system for the hydraulic pre-stressing of

Nervi. Communal Stadium, Florence (1930–2)

Nervi. Exhibition building, Turin (1948–9)

reinforced concrete. But none of these researches was an end in itself. The ever greater liberty which these technical improvements bestowed, by making work simpler and quicker, led Nervi to deeper researches of a quite different kind, e.g. on rhythm as an element of beauty. Examples include the Palazzetto dello Sport in Rome (1956–7, with Annibale Vitellozzi), and above all the conference hall of the UNESCO Building in Paris (1953–7; jointly with Breuer and Zehrfuss).

Like the Paris building's conference hall, the swelled surfaces of which are derived from mussels, insects or flower calyxes, the structure of the Pirelli skyscraper in Milan (1955–8, with Gio Ponti and others) is also derived from nature. This is the prototype of the building's sectional development, with its four main stanchions growing ever more slender towards the top (in a manner reminiscent of a tree), as might have been seen more clearly if a lighter cladding had been used. N.'s creative mastery of structure was also evident in the Centre National des Industries in Paris (1955, with Jean *Prouvé), in the circular exhibition building in Caracas (1956), in the Palazzo del Lavoro, Turin (1961), and the Papal audience chamber in the Vatican (1971). GV/AM

□ Nervi, Pier Luigi, *Arte o scienze del costruire?*, Rome 1954; ——, *Structures*, New York 1956; ——, *Aesthetics and Technology in Building*, Cambridge, Mass., 1965; Argan, G. C., *Pier Luigi Nervi*, Milan 1955; Joedicke, Jürgen, *The Works of Pier Luigi Nervi*, London 1957; Huxtable, Ada Louise, *Pier Luigi Nervi*, New York 1960; *Pier Luigi Nervi. Neue Strukturen*, Stuttgart 1962; Pica, Agnoldomenico, *Pier Luigi Nervi*, Rome 1969.

Nervi. Palazzetto dello Sport, Rome (with Annibale Vitellozzi; 1956–7)

Nervi. Palazzo del Lavoro, Turin (1961)

Netherlands. The reaction against the prevailing *historicism and *eclecticism of 19th-century Dutch architecture began *c.* 1890, notably with Petrus Josephus Hubertus *Cuypers, architect of the Rijksmuseum (1877–85) and the Central Station (1881–9) in Amsterdam; inspired by the French architect and theorist Viollet-le-Duc, Cuypers advocated a contemporary building style – albeit heavily indebted to Gothic prototypes – and a revival of craft traditions. Many notable architects were trained in his studio, including Hendrikus Theodorus Wijdeveld, Willem Kromhout and Karel Petrus Cornelius de Bazel; later on, each of these architects was to break with revivalist traditions in his own way. Although Cuypers paved the way, the real breakthrough to modern architecture is generally considered to be Hendrik Petrus *Berlage's Stock Exchange (1897–1903) in Amsterdam. Berlage's philosophy – the influence of which was spread by his various lectures, articles, and above all, by his steady building production – may be summarized as follows: rationality of construction, functional use of materials and simplicity of design. His Exchange symbolized a new architectural freedom and his ideas rapidly found ample expression both in villas and in public housing projects.

Soon, however, a younger generation of architects set itself against this 'rational' architecture. J. M. van der *Mey, Michel de *Klerk and P. L. *Kramer displayed their ideas in

Netherlands. The Scheepvaarthuis, Amsterdam (1911–16), by J. M. van der Mey and others

Netherlands. Villa Huis ten Bosch, Bosch en Duin (1915–16), by Robert van't Hoff

Amsterdam with the Scheepvaarthuis (1911–16); its exterior of exuberantly decorated brick was carried on a skeleton of reinforced concrete. The *Expressionist character of this architecture – known as the School of *Amsterdam – was widely followed and in the 1920s had a marked impact on the urban development of Amsterdam, where the socialist municipal council advocated the style's possibilities to lend dignity to workers' housing. The influence of the School of Amsterdam spread to towns like Groningen and Utrecht. For the most part, the style proved to be useful as façade architecture, for example in the 1920s in the Amsterdam South expansion scheme, based on a plan by Berlage. De Klerk and Kramer in particular realized masterpieces in this style; but after de Klerk's death the style lost much of its potency.

A number of architects followed the rationalist line established by Berlage, as seen in particular in the early work of Robert van't Hoff, for instance his Villa Huis ten Bosch in Bosch en Duin, Zeist (1915–16), inspired by the work of Frank Lloyd *Wright, as well as in the early work of Jan Wils. In 1917, both architects, together with *Rietveld, van *Eesteren, *Oud and others joined De *Stijl, a movement named after the magazine edited by Theo van *Doesburg which had proclaimed 'a new aesthetic consciousness' and aimed at 'logical relations between the consciousness of the age and its realization in everyday life'. These aspirations found expression in Rietveld's Schröder House in Utrecht (1924) and Oud's Café de Unie, Rotterdam (1924–5; destroyed in 1940).

In 1920 Oud and van Eesteren joined a group of progressive architects in Rotterdam, 'De Opbouw', which included, among others, Leendert Cornelius van der Vlugt, Johannes Bernardus van Loghem, Mart *Stam, Willem van Tijen and Marinus Jan Granpré Molière. For these architects, in Oud's words 'a good [in the sense of purely technological and practical] house is more important than a beautiful house'. They had an idealistic faith in new building techniques, preferred to work with the new building materials, steel, concrete and glass, and sincerely believed that their 'functional architecture' (*Functionalism) would contribute to a better future. Examples of this functionalist attitude are to be found especially in Rotterdam: Oud's municipal workers' housing De Kiefhoek (1925–7), the Bergpolder apartment block (1933–4) by van Tijen, van der Vlugt and *Brinkman, and the Van Nelle Tobacco Factory (1926–30) by Brinkman and van der Vlugt, with Stam as collaborating architect.

In Amsterdam few 'modern' designs were built during the 1920s, partly because the vetting committee favoured the Amsterdam School. In 1927, a number of progressive architects joined together in Amsterdam to form a new group: 'De 8'. They called themselves non-aesthetic, non-dramatic and non-romantic, and professed a preference for rationality of construction. To this group belonged, among others, Benjamin Merkelbach, Charles J. F. Karsten, A. Staal and Johannes *Duiker. Duiker soon received considerable acclaim for his Zonnestraal Sanatorium, Hilversum (1926–8, with Bernard Bijvoet), and the Open Air

Netherlands. Open Air School, Amsterdam (1928–30), by Johannes Duiker

School, Amsterdam (1928–30). By 1930 the two groups, 'De 8' and 'De Opbouw', were in close communication, and in 1932 they joined forces in the publication of the bi-monthly magazine *De 8 en Opbouw*.

There were frequent international contacts between architects, especially after the founding of *CIAM in 1928. Van Eesteren, who from 1930 served as president of CIAM, was a great promoter of the group's ideas in the Netherlands. After the *Athens Charter of 1933 had proposed new principles of town planning – light, air, interspacing and functional zoning – van Eesteren (who meanwhile had become head of the Town-planning Department of the City of Amsterdam) conceived the first expansion plan for Amsterdam (1934), based on these directives. This project was to serve as a model of modern town planning, although the disruption of World War II caused the realization of the greater part of it to be postponed until the 1950s.

In the 1930s the Modern Movement lost much of its initial impetus. Under the pressure of the economic crisis, there was a revival of traditionalism and a growing desire for spiritual, sometimes even religious, values. In 1932, the 'Groep 32' (A. Staal and P. Zanstra, amongst others) broke away from 'De 8 en Opbouw' and advocated a return to ornamentation in building.

Even stronger opposition to modern architecture came by the late 1920s from Granpré Molière, then professor at Delft Technical College. He sought principles of eternal beauty in architecture and took his inspiration from the maintenance of craft traditions and regional characteristics in Scandinavian and German architecture. He was the focus of the 'Delft School', which also included Johannes Fake Berghoef, Gijsbert Friedhoff and Samuel Josua van Embden.

The distinctions between the School of Amsterdam, Modernists and Traditionalists referred principally to the outward appearances of buildings. In the course of time, numerous architects fell under the sway of these various movements, some of whom achieved excellent results, such as Jan Frederick Staal in Amsterdam, and Willem Marinus *Dudok in Hilversum, whose most important work is the 'cubistic' Town Hall (1928–30) at Hilversum.

During World War II building activity practically came to a standstill. After the liberation reconstruction was slow to get under way, and at the outset it was principally the traditionalists who were able to put their ideas into practice.

In the area of Rotterdam devastated by bombing, however, reconstruction was based on a modernist redevelopment plan, presented

Netherlands. Town Hall, Hilversum (1928–30), by Willem Marinus Dudok

as early as 1946 by the head of the Town-planning Department, Cornelis van Traa. A rebuilt city centre with an entirely new street plan – corresponding only occasionally to the pre-war layout – was intended to provide a contemporary answer to the problems of the 20th century: zoning by functions, wide circulation corridors and ample open space. The main feature is the 'Lijnbaan' (1949–53), a shopping centre planned by van Traa, situated on a former residential site and characterized by zoning which keeps pedestrian and traffic circulation largely separate. Van den *Broek and *Bakema were the principal designers.

In the 1950s, the influence of the traditionalists waned and the modernist ideals of the 1930s again gained the upper hand. These were indeed pre-eminently suited to deal efficiently with the post-war housing shortage. In addition to the extension of existing towns and villages, entirely new towns arose, notably in the reclaimed land of the former Zuiderzee. The Wieringermeerpolder had already been reclaimed before the war, but at that time priority had been accorded to the development of separate small villages. After the war the new housing in the Noordoostpolder (reclaimed in 1942) was concentrated in fewer and larger towns. Although Emmeloord was built in traditional style, Nagele was designed by the group 'De 8', then the Dutch representative in CIAM, which had since been joined by Bakema and Aldo van *Eyck.

In the early 1960s, the authorities decided to stimulate industrialization and prefabrication in housing in order to tackle the persistent housing shortage. In Amsterdam this gave rise to the development of the new Bijlmermeer site, intended as the culmination of the CIAM ideas of the 1930s: high-rise blocks situated amidst green areas, with spacious ground-plans and complete zoning with division of pedestrian areas and traffic routes. When by the end of the 1960s construction was finally begun on the site, public opinion had turned against it. Mass media and activist groups in most large cities

Netherlands. The Lijnbaan shopping centre, Rotterdam (1953), by van den Broek and Bakema

Netherlands. Vredenburg Music Centre, Utrecht (1976–8), by Herman Hertzberger

vented their opposition to the impersonal and costly extension plans in general and pleaded for a re-evaluation of older residential districts: thus the notion of urban renewal was born in Holland.

From the early 1950s, architects within CIAM had been raising sharp criticisms of the Athens Charter's directives. A group of 'angry young men' protested against the one-sided analytical character of the congress meetings and in 1953 broke away to form Team X, aiming to give new meaning to the notion of urban identity. Their search for alternatives was clearly voiced in the Netherlands when, in 1959, van Eyck and Bakema (both members of Team X), with Herman *Hertzberger, became editors of *Forum*. In this magazine they propagated their ideas of habitability, identity, concern for individual needs, a sensibility to small scale as opposed to large (van Eyck: 'a house is a tiny city and a city is a large house') and demanded a humanized, more sensitive approach to structural problems.

The members of *Forum* were individualists. Van Eyck realized his ideas in the Amsterdam Burgerweeshuis (Orphanage, 1957–60), a large, complex structure consisting of a variety of small units, which earned him the reputation of being the father of Dutch *Structuralism; Bakema, on the other hand, sought to refine CIAM ideals. In his city-planning projects he used a mixture of building heights. Although his buildings were still quite large, he accentuated the expressive qualities of concrete. Hertzberger elaborated upon the idea of constructing large buildings out of small units of 'human scale' – as can be seen in the Centraal Beheer insurance office in Apeldoorn (1970–2) and also in the Vredenburg Music Centre in Utrecht (1976–8). Piet *Blom, who aired his ideas in the first issues of the new *Forum*, enlarged upon Structuralism in his own way by creating an 'urban roof : dwellings raised above the ground on stilts were to provide the stage for life in all its aspects. A typical example is the 'Kasbah' estate in Hengelo (1965–73).

Although the members of the *Forum* did not, with the exception of Bakema, build much themselves, the impact of their ideas was profound. A generation of younger architects, including Jan Verhoeven, Pietro Paolo Hammel and Henk Klunder were inspired by them. The emphasis on 'quality rather than quantity' was also adopted in 1968 by the Housing Minister, W. F. Schut, who decided to grant state subsidies for experiments in housing. The first realizations were housing projects in Hoevelaken (Verhoeven, 1968–75), Berkel Rodenrijs (Verhoeven, Hammel and others, 1973) and Spaarndam (Klunder, 1976).

Throughout the Netherlands, the renewal of old town quarters got started in the early 1970s; this was a joint action of renovation of old houses, slum clearance and the building of new dwellings, mostly respecting the existing street patterns. In addition, the new houses are generally carefully harmonized with their surroundings by height restrictions and use of appropriate building materials. An instructive example is the housing development in Zwolle (1977), built by van Eyck and Theo Bosch.

In the case of urban renewal, there has often been an element of user's participation. To be sure, there is nothing new about this. As early as 1961 Nicolaas John Habraken had advocated the participation of future users in the building of their dwellings, and as a result the Stichting Architecten Research (SAR) was founded in 1964. The SAR developed a method to permit the future occupants a say in planning both the floor-plans and in the design of their houses and their colour, and even in deciding the position of such details as windows and doors, all within given limits. An outstanding example of SAR housing is the site at Papendrecht (Frans van der Werf, 1978).

By 1980 the architecture of the Netherlands was rather diverse. In most new housing sites and also in the completely new town of Almere (Zuidelijke Ijsselmeer Polder) the building practices of the 1970s have continued: low-rise housing with a variety of 'individualistic' styles along winding streets. At the same time, however, many architects – particularly those not involved in the housing sector – have followed a line of their own, especially since *c.* 1978, when the architectural debate was given fresh momentum.

The tradition of the 1920s Moderns is continued in the work of such architects as: Petrus Hendrik van Rhijn and Bernard Antonie Johannes Spängberg, designers of the Amsterdam city railway (1977 on); and Willem Gerhard Quist, architect of the Berenplaat Waterworks (1960–5) on Beijerland, the Kralingen Waterworks near Rotterdam (1973–7) and the extension of the Rijksmuseum Kröller-Müller (1970–7), Otterlo.

Carel Weeber, an influential architect, has advocated a re-evaluation of the architectural and town-planning discipline, which seems to have been lost in the democratizing wave of the 1960s and 1970s. Examples of his work, such as the Arenaplan housing scheme in Alphen aan den Rijn (1976–80) and the Peperklip development (1980–2) in Rotterdam, reveal his predilection for distinct (mega-)structures. His dislike of nostalgic elements in housing is shared by many of his colleagues.

Since 1980 the polemicist/architect Rem *Koolhaas has exercized a great influence, especially on younger architects, with his theor-

Netherlands. Bijlmeer Station, Amsterdam (1977–80), by Spängberg and van Rhijn

ies of form and his focus on the dynamics of large cities.

A special place is occupied by Dom Hans van der Laan, a Benedictine monk, who had been a pupil of Granpré Molière in the 1920s. After World War II he set out to research basic architectural principles, and over the years has developed his own system of measurement and a theory of proportions. He set out his ideas in the book *Architectural Space* (1973), and they are reflected in the design of the conventual church (1960–7) at Lemiers, Vaals. HdH/IH

□ Broek, J. H. van den, *Gids voor Nederlandse architectuur/Guide to Dutch Architecture*, Rotterdam 1959; Vriend, J. J., *Architectuur van deze eeuw*, Amsterdam 1959; ——, *Reflexen, nederlands bouwen na 1945 / building in the netherlands / bauen in holland / l'architecture néerlandaise*, Amsterdam 1959; Grinberg, Donald I., *Housing in the Netherlands 1900–1940*, Delft 1977; Fanelli, Giovanni, *Moderne architectuur in Nederland 1900–1940*, 's Gravenhage 1978; Boasson, D., Milosévic, M., Ploeg, K. van der, and Taverne, Ed, *Kijkuit, omjeheen*, 's Gravenhage 1980; Casciato, M., Panzini, F., and Polano, S. (eds.), *Olanda 1870 bis 1940. Città, casa, architecttura*, Milan 1980; Haan, Hilde de, and Haagsma, Ids, *Wie is er bang voor nieuwbouw, Confrontatie met Nederlandse architecten*, Amsterdam 1981.

Neue Sachlichkeit (New Objectivity). Movement in European painting which, from *c.* 1920, developed as a reaction to Impressionism and above all *Expressionism. Its critical, socially engaged, realism is based on keen observation, extreme clarity of drawing and a determined ordering of all objects in a clear, at times stark, compositional frame. The term was coined by the art critic G. F. Hartlaub in 1924. One year later an exhibition of the 'Magical realists' was held in Mannheim under this rubric. Because of formal and ideological affinities the term 'Neue Sachlichkeit' soon came to be applied to modernist architecture (*Rationalism) and in particular to that of *Germany. VML

Neues Bauen. Term coined and widely used in German-speaking countries to denote 'avant-garde' architecture of the 1920s and 1930s. As early as May 1920, the exhibition of the *Arbeitsrat für Kunst bore this name. Hugo *Häring especially used the phrase in connection with his 'organhaftes Bauen' (*Organic architecture). The term – with its grammatical formation of a noun from an infinitive: *bauen* (to build) becomes *das Bauen* – emphasizes building process over final form; it later came to be used when referring to new architecture in general. WP

Neutra, Richard J(osef), b. Vienna 1892, d. Wuppertal, Germany 1970. Received his diploma from the Technische Hochschule, Vienna, in 1917. He met Adolf *Loos in 1910 and was influenced by the older architect's strictures against the use of ornament in architecture and by his admiration for American architectural design. In 1911, his interest in American architecture was broadened through the discovery of the work of Frank Lloyd *Wright, which had just been published in Europe. Many of the motifs that would dominate N.'s later architecture can be traced to this familiar and influential source.

Immediately after World War I, he worked in Switzerland, gaining experience in the fields of landscape and city planning. While employed in the Municipal Building Office, Luckenwalde, Germany, 1921, he met Erich *Mendelsohn, who was then building a hat factory there, and in the same year N. moved to Mendelsohn's office in Berlin. He moved to the USA in 1923, and for the next few years he worked alternately in Chicago, with the large commercial firm of Holabird and Roche, and at Taliesin, Spring Green, Wisconsin, with Frank Lloyd Wright. In 1925 he went to Los Angeles, beginning his practice in the office of another Vienna-born architect, Rudolph *Schindler. In

Neutra. Lovell House, Los Angeles (1927–9)

Neutra. Josef von Sternberg House, Los Angeles (1936)

Neutra. Kaufmann House, Palm Springs, Cal. (1946–7)

1927 the two men collaborated in a design project for the League of Nations competition.

In California, N.'s personal style rapidly came into focus. The key work in his early maturity was the rambling, quasi-picturesque Lovell House, Los Angeles (1927–9), built on a steep, challenging hillside site. Contemporary with *Le Corbusier's noted Villa Stein, Garches, France, and *Mies van der Rohe's Barcelona Pavilion, N.'s steel-framed Lovell House, with its slabs and balconies supported from above by steel cables, differs in certain structural details from these European masterworks, but is stylistically identical in terms of its thin, weightless forms which only partly enclose a series of fluidly juxtaposed interior spaces. In the 1930s N. developed a more pronounced personal idiom, using simple forms that were often realized in novel or unusual materials (the Josef von Sternberg House, Los Angeles, 1936). Always interested in large-scale planning, with implications of social welfare, Neutra found a wartime opportunity in the Channel Heights Housing Project, San Pedro, Cal. (1942–4), where out of necessity redwood was substituted for the more familiar materials of the machine age.

The apogee of N.'s career occurs in the immediate post-war era with the construction of the Kaufmann Desert House, Palm Springs (1946–7), and the Tremaine House, Santa Barbara (1947–8). Here the elegant restatements of the by now traditional International Style themes reach a striking degree of elegance and precision that is not present in the earlier work. In 1949, with an expanding practice, he formed a partnership with Robert E. Alexander which lasted until 1958 (to be followed by a partnership with his son, Dion Neutra, from 1965). In the last two decades of his life N. completed a series of major buildings whose quality, however, fails to match that of his earlier one-family houses. JMJ

□ Neutra, R., *Wie baut Amerika?*, Stuttgart 1927; ——, *Survival through Design*, New York 1954; Boesiger, W. (ed.), *Richard Neutra: Buildings and Projects* (3 vols.), Zurich 1951, 1959, 1966; McCoy, Esther, *Richard Neutra*, Ravensburg 1960; Hines, Thomas, *Richard Neutra and the Search for Modern Architecture*, New York 1982; Drexler, Arthur, *The Architecture of Richard Neutra*, New York 1982.

New Brutalism. New Brutalism gave conscious form to a mood that was widespread among younger architects in the 1950s, but in spite of the fact that it was expressed a sentiment that was felt in most parts of the Westernized world its origins can be pinpointed in space and time with some precision. Although Giedion was wrong in his etymology ('Brute + Alison'), he was right in identifying the Smithson family as the source of the term – either Alison *Smithson or the Smithsons' friend Guy Oddie (who used to call Peter *Smithson 'Brutus') was the first person to utter the phrase 'The New Brutalism', some time in the early summer of 1954.

New Brutalism. Hunstanton School, Norfolk (1949–54), by Alison and Peter Smithson

The basis was a mood of frustration brought on partly by the difficulties of building, especially in Britain, after World War II, and partly by disgust at the smugness of the compromising elders who were still able to build because they were well placed with the 'Establishment'. The stylistic preferences of these elders were known as 'The New Humanism' by the political Left, 'The New Empiricism' by the political Right. The New Brutalism as a phrase was intended as a mockery of both, but it drew attention to certain attributes of the architecture admired or designed by the Smithsons and their circle.

They set as a standard the uncompromising ruthlessness of *Mies van der Rohe and *Le Corbusier, their intellectual clarity, their honest presentation of structure and materials. At the same time, the younger architects sensed in the work of these masters a continuing tradition, an architecture that lay above and beyond styles and fashions – among the work of the past they admired the clarity and formality of Palladio, the heroic scale of the Anglo-Baroque architects Vanbrugh and Hawksmoor, and the clear-cut and massive forms of early 19th-century engineering structures.

But the architecture that emerged from these admirations was, in the beginning, purely Miesian. No doubt a streak of English puritanism accounts for this initial selection of a simple, elegant structural system, for it was applied to an absolute horror of any pretence or concealment; not only were structure and materials honestly expressed, but services as well. In the school at Hunstanton, Norfolk (1949–54), by the Smithsons – the first true Brutalist building – not only are steel and brick expressed with an honesty that goes even beyond the acceptable subterfuges of Mies, but pipe runs, electrical conduits, and other services are exposed to view. The austerity of this design was so remarkable that it attracted world-wide attention, and international comparisons were sought. Of these, Louis *Kahn's Yale University Art Gallery, New Haven, Conn. (1951–3), was in some ways more convincing than Mies' own work, because Kahn seemed equally preoccupied with the raw nature of the materials and concerned with the expression of the

New Brutalism. Park Hill, Sheffield (1961), by Jack Lynn and Ivor Smith

services. However, the original puritanical extremism of the English Brutalists rapidly began to merge with an international movement of different origins and only remotely comparable aims. This movement would be characterized by developments as diverse as the a-formal painting of Jackson Pollock and the a-formal planning of Le Corbusier's Chapel at Ronchamp, the *art brut* of Dubuffet and the *béton brut* of the Unité d'Habitation at Marseilles. Now, the Brutalism of the uncompromising exhibition of materials became allied to a Brutalism of form; the expressed symmetry of the Hunstanton School and the concealed symmetry of the Yale Art Gallery were abandoned in favour of a ruthless honesty in expressing functional spaces and their interrelationships. Even that adaptable rectangular geometry of *Rationalism was now cast aside in favour of modes of composition based on the topography of the site and the topology of internal circulation – as may be seen very clearly in the siting and planning of Park Hill, Sheffield, designed by Jack Lynn and Ivor Smith.

Once the Brutalism of a complex such as Park Hill is understood it becomes clear that the application of the term to such fashionably sentimental architecture as that of Leonardo Ricci is improper, as is any attempt to make 'Brutalists' out of – say – Juan *O'Gorman or Paolo *Soleri: Brutalism implied some sort of attempt to make manifest the moral imperatives that were built into modern architecture by the pioneers of the 19th century, and the use of shutter-patterned concrete or exposed steelwork was only a symptom of this intention. The fundamental aim of Brutalism at all times was to find a structural, spatial, organizational and material concept that was, in the Smithsons' eyes, 'necessary' in this metaphysical sense to some particular building, and then to express it with complete honesty in a form that would be a unique and memorable image. In the creation of this definitive image the other plastic arts provided, not an aesthetic, but an exemplar of method or a standard of comparison – thus the admirations of the Brutalists covered subjects as diverse as U.S. car-styling and the Ise shrines in Japan. Neither had any visible influence on Brutalist architecture, but both served as examples of images created out of the kind of necessary conditions the Brutalists believed to be fundamental, also, to the conception of buildings today. It was this insistence of the primacy of the given and necessary factors in the conception of a building that caused Sir John Summerson to compare the beliefs of the Brutalists to the Rigorism of Carlo Lodoli and other radical theorists of late 18th-century Italian Illuminism.

On this ground, a typical example of Brutalist building in Italy is the Istituto Marchiondi Spagliardi at Baggio, near Milan (1958–9) by Vittoriano Viganò, even though at first sight its departures from the common practices of the Modern Movement appear less extreme than those of the neo-Libertarian sentimentalists. Stylistically, the Istituto Marchiondi Spagliardi consciously echoes the ideas of the period of *l'architettura razionalista* (*Rational architecture) which provide an image that is entirely expressive of the stern reformative necessities that underlie the conception of this building.

Nevertheless, the building draws attention to the relationship of Brutalism to the traditions of architecture. For all its aggressive tone and uncompromising attitudes, Brutalism did not represent a radical departure from the traditional conception of architecture – it was in no way comparable to the technological extremism of Buckminster *Fuller, nor even to the methods of radical functional analysis developed in England by the Nuffield Trust. The most instructive comparisons to be made on this subject are with action-painting and *musique concrète*. Action-painting abandoned the last vestiges of formal composition but still accepted such 'outworn' traditions as the use of paint, canvas, and a rectangular format for the picture, all of which had been previously rejected at various times by modern painters; *musique concrète* abandoned the polite fictions of the sounds made by artificial musical instruments in favour of recordings of 'real noises', but it abandoned very little else of what had been left of the traditions of music by earlier modernist composers. Similarly the Brutalists, while abandoning fictitious surface for the 'reality' of steel and concrete and the concept of formal composition as necessary to the art of architecture, invariably practised and theorized within the basic traditions of architecture. RB

☐ Banham, Reyner, *The New Brutalism: Ethic or Aesthetic*, New York 1966.

New Brutalism. Istituto Marchiondi Spagliardi, Baggio, near Milan (1958–9), by Vittoriano Viganó

New Objectivity. *Neue Sachlichkeit.

New York Five. Designation for a circle of five architects, Peter *Eisenman, Michael *Graves, Charles *Gwathmey, John *Hejduk and Richard *Meier, whose work was the subject of an exhibition at the Museum of Modern Art, New York, held on the occasion of a 1969 meeting of the CASE group (Conference of Architects for the Study of the Environment). This formed the basis for the book *Five Architects* published in 1972. All the work displayed – without exception single-family houses and predominantly of wood, as in the first American houses of Walter *Gropius and Marcel *Breuer – represented a formal return, in some cases radical, to the *International Style of the 1920s and 1930s. *Le Corbusier was the principal point of departure, but direct references to *Rietveld and to *Terragni were also evident. Since the late 1970s the loose association has progressively dissolved as the five architects have pursued increasingly more distinct formal concerns. AM

☐ *Five Architects*, New York 1972.

Niemeyer, Oscar, b. Rio de Janeiro 1907. Graduated in 1934 from the Escola Nacional de

Belas-Artes, Rio de Janeiro, and a few years later stepped into a position of effective leadership when he succeeded Lúcio *Costa as head of the design team for the new Ministry of Education and Health building (1937–43).

N. was himself decisively influenced by *Le Corbusier, with whom he worked on the design for the Ministry of Education and Health during the master's short stay in Brazil, in 1936. He began by applying Le Corbusier's basic ideas, as in the Day Nursery, Rio de Janeiro (1937). Very soon, however, he began adding to such ideas an element of adaptation to local conditions, an imaginative and sometimes excessive, creative exuberance.

Disregarding the tenets of orthodox modernism whenever they seemed to him to run counter to his ideal of architecture as a great art of expression, N. has consistently striven for beauty and harmony, grace and elegance in an enriched formal vocabulary as the legitimate goals of architectural creation in opposition to merely technical and functional refinements. Unafraid of the curved line, for which he found good precedent in Brazilian Baroque architecture, he used it with an instinctive lyrical touch and an uninhibited spontaneity throughout his career – free-flowing and seemingly arbitrary in the earlier phases, subtly distilled and more intellectually sophisticated in his later work.

The group of buildings in Pampúlha (1942–4) is famous for its display of unusual forms, different yet kindred, its emphatic interplay of light and shade and its deliberate integration of architecture with painting and sculpture. The complex includes the Casino in which an ovoid prism is well joined to a crisply rectangular block; the circular Restaurant with its sun roof; the Yacht Club with its inverted double-slope roof; and the São Francisco Chapel with its parabolic shells.

In a series of projects N. explored the use of reinforced-concrete in the development of complex curved surfaces, such as the Duchen Factory (1950, with Helio Uchôa); here a block 300 m (984 ft) long is dramatized by a row of double-span curved rigid frames, spaced 10 m (33 ft) apart, In other buildings he emphasized the possibilities of long straight lines, in wide overhangs or in variously designed sloping supports, as in the School at Diamantina (1950).

The Parque Ibirapuéra exhibition buildings for the Fourth Centennial of the City of São Paulo (1951–4), which N. designed in collaboration with other architects, provide a rare instance of integrated planning of a group of permanent fair buildings over a wide area. N. unified the scheme by an irregular series of elevated pathways linking the various blocks: two low buildings, 140 m (460 ft) long, the Palace of Nations and the Palace of States, with their tilted concrete brackets; the three-storey Palace of Industry, 250 m (820 ft) long, with its various interior levels capriciously silhouetted by the outline of the mezzanine slab; and the dome-like Palace of the Arts, with its spectacular and almost surrealist interior.

N.'s crowning achievement was the design of all the main public buildings of Brasilia (1957–79). In Brasilia he designed most of the important buildings; in particular the Supreme Court,

Niemeyer. Yacht Club, Pampúlha (1943–4)

Niemeyer. Palace of Industry exhibition building, São Paulo (in collaboration; 1951–4)

Niemeyer. Congress Building and Ministries, Brasilia (1958)

the Presidential Palace, the Square of the Three Powers, the Congress Building and the National Theatre (all 1958). In these he was able not only to express the symbolic content of each job and of the whole, implicit in Lúcio Costa's sophisticated general plan, but also to achieve it within a restrained vocabulary, severely disciplined so as to lend special significance where necessary to one or another element in the general context: for example, the beautiful colonnade of the Palace of Dawn, the startling flower-like design for the Cathedral, the concave and convex dome of the Congress Building in contrast to the soaring twin towers and the horizontal expanse of the base block. Already in Brasilia there is evidence of a harking back to an individually expressed *neo-classicism, which in N.'s later work, such as the Mondadori Building in Milan (1968–75), was to be more pronounced. HEM/GHa

□ Niemeyer, Oscar, *Minha Experiencia en Brasilia*, Rio de Janeiro 1961; Papadaki, Stamo, *The Work of Oscar Niemeyer*, New York 1950; ——, *Oscar Niemeyer – Works in Progress*, New York 1956, ——, *Oscar Niemeyer*, New York 1960; Spade, Rupert, *Oscar Niemeyer*, London and New York, 1971; Sodre, Nelson W., *Oscar Niemeyer*, Rio de Janeiro 1978.

Novembergruppe. A loose association of radically minded artists, founded in Berlin in December 1918 at the instigation of the painters Max Pechstein and César Klein, and under the influence of the November revolution. Prominent members included the painters Lyonel Feininger, Wassily Kandinsky, Paul Klee and Ludwig Meidner, the architects Otto *Bartning, Alfred Gellhorn, Walter *Gropius, Hugo *Häring, Ludwig *Hilberseimer, Hans *Luckhardt, Wassili *Luckhardt, Erich *Mendelsohn, Ludwig *Mies van der Rohe, Bruno *Taut and Max *Taut, and the composer Hans Eisler.

Although the Novembergruppe shared many members with the *Arbeitsrat für Kunst, it was from the outset less politically ambitious and defined its radicalism in strictly artistic terms. An exhibition catalogue of 1919 declared: 'The Novembergruppe is a union of radical artists – radical in the rejection of previous forms of expression – radical in the use of new expressive techniques.'

The group was active in many fields. Between 1919 and 1932 it exhibited in Berlin on nineteen occasions. In 1920 an exhibition of graphics and watercolours was arranged in Rome in conjunction with Filippo Tommaso Marinetti, and a travelling exhibition visited Moscow and Japan in 1924. The group was also active in promoting new music and in supporting experimental films.

The Novembergruppe was officially banned by the National Socialist government in September 1933, but had already ceased to be active some two years previously. IBW

□ Kliemann, Helga, *Die Novembergruppe*, Berlin 1964; *Die Novembergruppe* (exhibition catalogue), Berlin 1977.

Noyes, Eliot, b. Boston, Mass. 1910, d. New Canaan, Conn. 1977. Architect and designer. Studied at Harvard Graduate School of Architecture, latterly under *Gropius and *Breuer. Much influenced by *Le Corbusier in his ideal of the integration of industrial design, architecture, sculpture and painting. Sometime director of the Department of International Design at the Museum of Modern Art, New York. His balloon house at Hobe Sound, Florida, was made by spraying concrete on to an immense inflated balloon, to produce a hemispherical shell. His houses all feature open plans subdivided by placement of furniture or fireplaces; the use of natural materials is also characteristic.

□ Noyes, Eliot, *Organic Design and Home Furnishing*, New York 1941; 'The Work of Eliot Noyes and Associates', *Industrial Design*, June 1966.

O

O'Gorman, Juan, b. Coyoacán, Mexico 1905, d. Mexico City 1982. Studied architecture at the National University of Mexico, and painting under Antonio Ruis, Ramón Alba Guedarrama and Diego Rivera. He was Director of the Town Planning Administration of Mexico City (1932–4) and afterwards ran his own practice. From 1932 to 1948 he was Professor of Architecture in the Architecture Section – of which he was a co-founder – of the National Polytechnic Institute of Mexico City. With his houses in San Angel, Mexico City (1929–30), he became one of the earliest Mexican adherents of the *International Style, from which he distanced himself in a guilt-ridden manifesto during the 1950s. The mosaics on the façade of the Main Library of the National University of Mexico in the new University City (1952–3), planned in collaboration with Gustavo Saavedra and Juan Martínez de Velasco, and above all his own house in San Angel (1953–6) are testaments to his radical shift towards an art of individual expression inspired by Mexican tradition. GHa

□ Smith, Clive B., *Builders in the Sun: Five Mexican Architects*, New York 1967.

Olbrich, Joseph Maria, b. Troppau 1867, d. Düsseldorf 1908. After attending the Staatsgewerbeschule (State School of Arts and Crafts) in Vienna, where Camillo Sitte was one of his teachers, and several years working in his native town, he studied under Carl von Hasenauer at the Akademie der bildenden Künste in Vienna, 1890–3. In his third year there he was awarded the Rome Prize, which enabled him to undertake a trip of several months from November 1893 through Italy to Tunis before entering Otto *Wagner's office. The collaboration with Wagner lasted until 1898 and thus fell within the period during which Wagner was working on the buildings of the Vienna Stadtbahn (metropolitan railway), on the design of which O. had a considerable influence. In 1897 he was one of the founders of the Wiener Secession, whose exhibition building (1897–8) he designed. In 1899 he was summoned to Darmstadt where, through the patronage of Grand Duke Ernst Ludwig of Hesse, he was given the opportunity of developing a synthesis of the *Arts and Crafts and Garden Cities (*Howard) movements in a great civic *Gesamtkunstwerk* (total work of art) in the spirit of *Art Nouveau. The artists' colony on the Mathildenhöhe at Darmstadt (1899–1901), on which other members of the artistic circle in Darmstadt, including *Behrens, also worked, was open to the public upon completion. As an 'exhibition', the buildings and their interior design constituted the exhibits and the ideal of a life-style permeated by art was advocated. In 1907 O. enlarged the colony around the Hochzeitsturm (Wedding Tower), which is one of the most

Olbrich. Wiener Secession exhibition building, Vienna (1897–8)

Olbrich. Wedding Tower on the Mathildenhöhe, Darmstadt (1907)

distinguished examples of civic adornment representative of the new architecture, as well as around the Art Gallery. In the Art Gallery building, as well as in the Tietz Department Store in Düsseldorf (1906), a tendency to more restrained forms and a shift towards *neo-classicism manifest themselves.

O.'s influence on later architecture resulted primarily from his Darmstadt buildings, which in certain respects anticipated the *Expressionism of subsequent years. GHa

☐ Olbrich, J. M., *Ideen*, Vienna 1899, 2nd ed. Leipzig 1904; ——, *Architektur*, 30 portfolios, Berlin 1901–14; Lux, Joseph August, *Joseph M. Olbrich*, Berlin 1919; *Joseph M. Olbrich. 1867–1908. Das Werk des Architekten* (exhibition catalogue), Darmstadt 1967; Schreyl, Karl Heinz, *Joseph Maria Olbrich: Die Zeichnungen in der Kunstbibliothek Berlin*, Berlin 1972; Latham, Ian, *Joseph Maria Olbrich*, London 1980.

organic architecture. As with most concepts used in architecture, the concept of an 'organic' style is borrowed from other fields and remains difficult to delimit once applied to architecture and building. It subsumes the harmonic relationship between the whole and the parts, but is also tied to natural processes such as birth, growth, and death.

The analogy between nature and architecture had already been given expression in the mid-18th century by the American sculptor Horatio Greenough. In his quest to overcome the aesthetic conceptions of his time which he rejected as eclectic, Greenough turned to nature as a source, for it offered the most diverse forms without reliance on pre-existing models. The correspondence of form and function which he claimed to recognize was conceived of as a God-given principle, rather than as the result of rational thought, as would later be argued.

While Greenough's speculations remained general, Louis *Sullivan, the most important architect of the *Chicago School, sought to

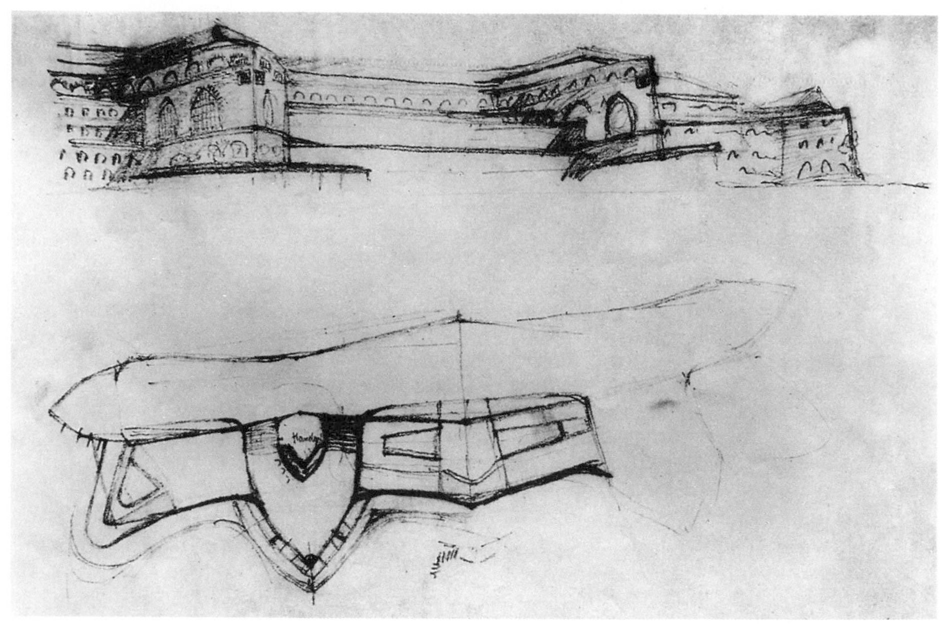

organic architecture. Main railway station, Leipzig (project, 1921), by Hugo Häring

extract the practical application for building. In an article of 1896, published under the title 'The tall office building artistically considered', he concluded, on the basis of observation of nature, 'that life is recognized in its expression, that form follows function'. From that he derived the principle: ' . . . that it is really the essence of every problem that it contains and suggests the solution.' Thus form is not understood as being based on previous knowledge or as something determined *a priori*, but as a search for something that is already latently present in the essence of the task at hand. The analogy of architecture with nature thus led to an ontologically (and not mechanistically) founded version of *Functionalism. It would seem critical to object that the interpretation of the essence of something is in itself always a subjective decision. However, Sullivan believed that this subjectivity did not derive from the individual's own ideas, but rather resided in the task.

Frank Lloyd *Wright expanded the philosophy of his 'lieber Meister', Sullivan, by insisting that form and function must be one; to convey this idea, he employed the phrase 'organic architecture'. For him the relationship of the parts to the whole was an essential feature: every part should have its own identity, but at the same time it should be inseparable from the whole. This was impressively manifested in his approach to spatial composition, for which the misleading term 'flowing space' was later used. Apart from the obvious fact that space itself does not move, but rather it is a matter of man who moves in space, Wright's spaces do not flow one into another without distinction. Rather they are divided one from another and linked together by small interposed spatial components. For Wright, each building was viewed as something special, in relation to the site on which it stood, and as part of the landscape of nature.

Hugo *Häring, with whom the concept of 'organ-like architecture' is linked, would certainly have been in agreement with all this. What distinguished him from Wright was not simply the fact that he was born later and lived in a different country, but also his rejection of what he described as the fairy-tale aspect of Wright's work – his preference for detail and ornament. Adolf *Loos's verdict, 'ornament is a crime', marks the watershed between Häring and Wright. Like Wright, however, Häring was convinced that it was a matter of searching for things and allowing their own form to develop; and, like Wright, he started from the premise that in nature 'the formal ordering of many things in space is in relation to a living development and to the fulfilment of tasks.' 'Thus if we want to discover form, we must be in harmony with nature'.

Similar ideas were espoused by two architects as different as Alvar *Aalto and Hans *Scharoun. It would certainly be incorrect to characterize Scharoun as a pupil of Häring but, at the level of principles and methods, they certainly had much in common. Häring built relatively little, while Scharoun was able to realize a whole series of major projects in the 1960s, including the Philharmonic Hall in Berlin, in which the space is conceived and designed in terms of a Häringesque view of the programme, or what Scharoun interpreted as the essence of the task. Aalto's work is different in many respects from that of Scharoun, but it too reveals certain points in common with Häring's way of thinking, such as the rejection of the determination of form by pure geometric volumes, the unorthodox use of natural materials and the careful attention to regional and topographical considerations. These were, moreover, characteristic of the second phase of modern architecture which began to develop at the beginning of the 1930s. Even Louis *Kahn could be cited, for he continually espoused the thesis that the form of a building must be developed from an understanding of the essence of the matter. Admittedly, Kahn saw this through the eyes of the *Ecole des Beaux-Arts and hence in his work the principle was reflected in a totally altered form.

Häring's reference to efficient forms in nature is to be explained by his particular point of view. For him nature was concerned not only with practical efficiency, as represented by the body of a greyhound, but also with distinguishing features such as a stag's antlers.

In our day, nature has also served as a model and an inspiration in other regards, and precisely where one would have least expected it: in the area of wide-span constructions, i.e. in the field of advanced technology. Here, the principle discovered in and borrowed from nature was that of achieving the maximum rigidity and endurance with the least amount of material. Already in the 1920s, with the reinforced-concrete shell structures of Franz Dischinger and Walter Bauersfeld, the comparison to an egg shell was evoked. By means of a double curvature in form and the use of a material of greater tensile and compressive strength, it is possible to achieve great spans combined with an exceptional thinness of construction. Most recently it has been Frei *Otto in Germany who developed new constructions by analogy with natural models. JJ

□ Greenough, Horatio, *Form and Function. Remarks on Art, Design and Architecture* (ed. Harold A. Small), Berkeley and Los Angeles 1947; Sullivan, Louis, 'The tall office building artistically considered', reissued in *Kindergarten Chats and other writings*, New York 1947; Wright, Frank Lloyd, *An Organic Architecture – The Architecture of Democracy*, London 1950; Lauterbach, Heinrich, and Joedicke, Jürgen (eds.), *Hugo Häring. Schriften, Entwürfe, Bauten*, Stuttgart 1965; *Natürlich bauen* (Proceedings of the Institut für leichte Flächentragwerke, IL 27), Stuttgart 1981.

organic architecture. The architect's own house, Helsinki (1934–6), by Aalto

organic architecture. Tent pavilion at the Bundesgartenschau, Cologne (1957), by Frei Otto

Otto, Frei, b. Siegmar, Saxony 1925. Studied at the Technische Universität in Berlin. In 1952 he established a studio in Berlin which was superseded in 1968 by his present studio at Warmbronn, near Stuttgart. Throughout his career he has kept his design and academic research activities separate; consequently, in 1957 he established the Entwicklungsstätte für den Leichtbau (EL) in Berlin, which was the forerunner of the Institut für leichte Flächentragwerke (IL), which he founded in 1964 at the Technische Hochschule in Stuttgart.

O. is a complex and, from some points of view, a somewhat contradictory figure; if at first he appears to be a rationalist in the tradition of the great 20th-century constructors and a structural determinist in his development of architectural form, this view is far from adequate since it ignores his rather typical German romanticism and his identification with nature which represents a further extension of this romanticism, As a fighter pilot in World War II, he was impressed by lightweight aircraft technology; also influential, though in a different way, are the Expressionist fantasies of Bruno *Taut, notably his crystalline temples and *Alpine Architektur* sketches. In a more general vein, he has admired greatly the work of Felix *Candela, R. Buckminster *Fuller and Walter Bird.

The modern tent, as distinct from tensile structures based on suspension-bridge technology, is largely O.'s creation. Traditional tents, long forgotten or maligned except as an exotic metaphor for the tabernacle or Crusader encampments, were revived by O. as a leading prototype for lightweight adaptable buildings. From the modern tent, with its efficient anticlastic shape, there stemmed a bewildering variety of structural types such as pre-stressed textile, cable-net and textile, and cable-net pavilions supported on masts or arches, grid shells, retractable or convertible roofs which combine features of both textile and steel-cable construction (the textile roof automatically extends or retracts along steel-cable supports), and pneumatic structures – in effect, air-supported tents.

The small Bundesgartenschau textile pavilions of the 1950s are amongst O.'s most lyrical and successful works – the riverside shelter and dance pavilions at Cologne (1957) and the small undulating star pavilions at Hamburg (1963)

Otto. Cable-net roofs at the Olympic Park, Munich (built by Behnisch & Partners; 1967–72)

impress by their integration of aesthetics and construction. Prior to 1963, his textile pavilions usually consisted of standard membrane elements arranged symmetrically in additive compositions. It was not until the mid-1960s, when he began working with Rolf Gutbrod, that O. began to explore picturesque asymmetrical roofscapes divided unevenly by interior low or high points. The Pavilion of the Federal Republic of Germany at Expo '67 in Montreal (1965–7) is the outstanding example of a freely formed roofscape suggestive of mountain scenery.

The restaurant pavilions at the Swiss National Exhibition of 1964 at Lausanne were O.'s first cable-nets. Previously all his roofs had been made of cotton canvas with modest spans of from 20 to 30 m (65–100 ft). The Lausanne pavilions were transitional membrane and cable-net constructions leading up to O.'s first truly large-scale cable-net roof, for the German Pavilion at Expo '67. With the completion of this structure, pre-stressed cable-net roofs came of age, and, for the first time, the constructional means used matched the structural demands of large-scale pre-stressed surface structures having a freely sculptured terrain. A new identity of form, structure and construction was now a possibility. The roofs of the main sports area in the Olympiapark in Munich (1967–72; built by Günter *Behnisch with O. as a consultant) realized a new scale in this type of development and led, moreover, to the pioneering of purely mathematical computer-based procedures for determining the cable-net patterns.

O. also exploited the inherent flexibility of textile structures by devising the convertible roof, in which variable geometry permits the roof membrane to be extended or retracted at will. A great many such roofs have been constructed in Germany, France and elsewhere, but none is so captivating as the roof for the Open Air Theatre at Bad Hersfeld (1967–8).

In the years after 1970 he concentrated his attention on the analysis of biological phenomena, developing his exploration and analysis of lightweight structures in nature. Because O. combined research into the optimum shapes for pre-stressed surface structures with the development of a new technological means for their realization, his innovations have proved of outstanding importance; indeed, it is in large part due to his efforts that the successful revival of the tent has come about, as well as the

Otto. Adaptable roof covering at the Open Air Theatre, Bad Hersfeld (1967–8)

creation of a new genre of 'modern tents' which exploit the advanced technological resources of the 20th century. PD

☐ Otto, F., *Structures: Traditional and Lightweight*, New Haven, Conn. 1961; ——, *Lightweight Structures*, 1963; Roland, Conrad, *Frei Otto: Tension Structures*, London and New York 1970; Glaeser, Ludwig, *The Work of Frei Otto* (exhibition catalogue), New York 1971; Drew, Philip, *Frei Otto: Form and Structure*, Boulder, Col. 1976.

Oud, Jacobus Johannes Pieter, b. Purmerend 1890, d. Wassenaar 1963. Educated at the Quellinus School of Arts and Crafts, the State School of Draughtsmanship in Amsterdam and Delft Technical College, which awarded him an honorary doctorate after World War II. He worked for Jan Stuyt and for P. J. H. *Cuypers, both in Amsterdam, for Theodor *Fischer in Munich, and for *Dudok in Leiden, before opening his own offices in Purmerend and Leiden. He was City Architect of Rotterdam, 1918–33, where he was responsible for the Spangen and Tussendijken housing estates (1920). From 1933 to 1954 he had an office in Rotterdam; thereafter he practised in Wassenaar.

Around 1916, he came into contact with Theo van *Doesburg, and was an active member of the new De *Stijl movement. Like most of his generation, O. was a great admirer of *Berlage, as his early works clearly show.

Oud. Housing scheme at, Hook of Holland (1924–7)

Oud. Shell Building, The Hague (1938–42)

Oud. Bio Children's Convalescent Home, near Arnhem (1952–60)

Berlage's honest handling of materials and structure was to influence O.'s *'Neue Sachlichkeit' approach, despite the obvious formal differences. O. was faced with the difficult task of translating De Stijl's often all too theoretical ideas into practical building terms. Examples of his De Stijl-type architecture include: the Café de Unie in Rotterdam (1924–5; destroyed 1940); a project for terraced housing on the promenade at Scheveningen (1917); and a design for a factory at Purmerend (1919). After a few years, O. broke with van Doesburg, who laid too much stress on the role of abstract painting in modern architecture. The housing schemes at Oud-Mathenesse (1922–4) and Kiefhoek, Rotterdam (1925–7), and at Hook of Holland (1924–7) demonstrate the transition to 'Neue Sachlichkeit'.

From *c.* 1935 onwards O. began to follow functionalist principles much more freely (Shell Building, The Hague, 1938–42). This defection led to rather harsh criticism, whereas – viewed in retrospect – this change of direction towards a more formalist academic design method seems to have been a harbinger of the increasing uncertainty that has been evident in architecture in recent years. However, the Bio-Children's Convalescent Home near Arnhem (1952–60) is clear evidence that the Shell Building belongs to an earlier creative phase. JJV/GHa

☐ Oud, J. J. P., *Holländische Architektur* (Bauhausbuch 10), Munich 1926; ——, *Mijn Weg in 'De Stijl'*, Rotterdam 1961; Hitchcock, Henry-Russell, *J. J. P. Oud*, Paris 1931; Veronesi, Giulia, *J. J. P. Oud*, Milan 1953; Fischer, Wend, *J. J. P. Oud: Bauten 1906–63* (exhibition catalogue), Munich 1965.

P

Pei, Ieoh Ming, b. Canton, China 1917. Studied at the Massachusetts Institute of Technology and at Harvard University. He was Director of Architecture at Webb and Knapp, Inc., in New York, 1948–55, since when he has had his own office in New York, designing administration buildings, department stores, urban planning projects. The Mile High Center in Denver, Col. (1956), dazzles with its façade composition of two intersecting systems: supports and beams clad in dark cast aluminium, air-conditioning units behind bright enamelled bands. With its emphasis on structural elements, this building is typical of the *International Style of the 1950s. The National Center for Atmospheric Research in Boulder, Col. (1967), the Everson Museum of Art in Syracuse, N.Y. (1968), and – to an even greater degree – the East Wing of the National Gallery of Art in Washington, D.C. (1971–8), bear witness to a turning towards a monumentality of simple stereometric forms.

☐ 'I. M. Pei & Partners: NCAR & Christian Science Church Center', *Global Architecture* (Tokyo), no. 41, 1961.

Peichl, Gustav, b. Vienna 1928. After attending the Staatsgewerbeschule in Vienna-Mödling and the Bundesgewerbeschule in Linz,

Pei. East Wing of the National Gallery of Art, Washington, D.C. (1971–8)

Peichl. Studios for Austrian State Radio (ÖRF), Salzburg (1968–72): central hall and aerial view

he studied under *Holzmeister at the Akademie der bildenden Künste in Vienna. In 1956 he opened his own office in Vienna; he was editor of the magazine *Bau*, 1967–70, and since 1973 he has taught at the Akademie in Vienna. Under the pseudonym 'Ironimus' he is also active as a caricaturist. Characteristic of P.'s architecture is a machine aesthetic, which is expressively handled in many cases and which derives especially from ship design. This is often paired with a Baroque-inspired axiality, as in the Rehabilitation Centre for the mentally retarded, Vienna-Meidling (1965–7), or in the Phosphate Elimination Works in Berlin-Tegel (1980 ff.). His use of a free overall form in which a basic type is adjusted to the particular situation by varying individual elements is seen in the regional studios of the Austrian State Radio (ÖRF) in Linz, Salzburg, Innsbruck, Dornbirn, Graz and Eisenstadt (1968–81), as well as in the Ground Signal Station at Aflenz, which blends into the landscape. AM

□ *Gustav Peichl. Bauten, Projekte, Meisterschule*, Vienna and Stuttgart 1981.

Pelli, Cesar, b. Tucuman, Argentina 1926. Studied at the University in Tucuman and at the University of Illinois at Urbana. From 1954 to 1964 he was Eero *Saarinen's partner; afterwards he went to Los Angeles where until 1968 he was chief designer in the firm Daniel, Mann, John & Mendenhall, and subsequently Design Partner in Gruen Associates until 1977. In that year he was appointed Dean of the Architecture School at Yale University in New Haven,

Conn., and at the same time opened his own office there. In the buildings which have attracted most public attention – the City Hall in San Bernardino, Cal. (1969) and the Pacific Design Center in Los Angeles (1971) – P. develops the late *International Style concept of a container architecture, which *Mies van der Rohe had postulated to the extent that the entire structure was to be sheathed in a skin of transparent and opaque glass with neither projecting mouldings nor any articulation of the interior spaces or subdivisions. In contrast to the all but expressionless exterior shell, homogeneous except for reflection effects and colour (a deep blue in the Pacific Design Center), highly effective 'disturbances' of the orthogonal structure of the building are introduced by step-backs, broken slopes, sudden protruding round forms, and sliced-off terminations at the ends of the building. These characteristics are still present in more recent projects, which are mostly bound to more traditional architectural concepts, such as the Hermann Park Towers in Houston, Texas (1979). In 1977 P. designed the tower addition and the rebuilding of the Museum of Modern Art in New York (1980–4). AM

☐ 'Cesar Pelli', *Architecture and Urbanism* (Tokyo), March 1971; 'Cesar Pelli', op. cit., November 1976; Pastier, John, *Cesar Pelli*, New York and London 1980; Frampton, Kenneth, *Cesar Pelli/Gruen Associates*, Tokyo 1981.

Peressutti, Enrico, b. Pinzano al Tagliamento (Udine) 1908, d. Milan 1973. Studied at the Milan Politecnico. In 1932 he was one of the founders of the Milan firm *BBPR.

Perret, Auguste, b. Brussels 1874, d. Paris 1954. As a neo-classicist (*neo-classicism) with a pronounced sensibility for modern technological requirements, he belonged to that tradition extending from Hennebique to de *Baudot which fostered significant changes in the methods used in reinforced-concrete construction. P.'s contribution marked both the endpoint of that earlier tradition and the beginning of a new one. In his active career spanning nearly fifty years as an architect/contractor and in his role as a teacher, he developed a formal language which, for all its variety, retains a strong cohesiveness. This is characterized in equal measure by the introduction of innovative constructional forms and by an allegiance to a traditional canon of forms. The influence of both Guadet's compositional teachings and Choisy's constructional theories is easily detected in P.'s own work, where tradition is upheld by inclusion in a new technological context.

The apartments in the Rue Franklin in Paris (1902–5) were P.'s first significant building after he left the *Ecole des Beaux-Arts and entered the family building enterprise. This building, which in ground-plan paved the way for *Le Corbusier's 'plan libre', celebrated in its elevation the possibility of an architectural renewal through the use of reinforced-concrete. The structural skeleton is emphasized and exploited for external effect. The walls, dissolved into ornamental surfaces, demonstrate clearly this distinction between frame and infill. Ornament derived from *Art Nouveau lends the infill panels a certain decorative force. P.'s next work, the garage in the Rue de Ponthieu, is far less dependent on decorative effects. Here, the structure of the façade is reduced to a strongly geometrical arrangement; an innovative awareness of materials is softened by a rhythmic sense of form. Only the portal and the large window above it are treated decoratively. By contrast, in the Théâtre des Champs-Elysées in Paris (1911–

Perret. Flats in the Rue Franklin, Paris (1902–5)

Perret. Notre Dame, Le Raincy, near Paris (1922–3)

13), originally planned by Henry van de ⋆Velde, the structural components are not strongly articulated and geometry is employed as a means to evoke a classical idiom.

The premises of P.'s pre-World War I work were chiefly two: to elevate the reinforced-concrete skeleton to the plane of architecture, and to adapt the Beaux-Arts aesthetic to new principles of frame and infill composition. The church of Notre Dame at Le Raincy, near Paris (1922–3), seems to contradict this. The outer walls, composed of prefabricated components, envelop the interior with a transparent mesh-work which, together with the vertical emphasis of the supporting members, evoke a Gothic cathedral. Nevertheless, even his post-war work bears witness to his pursuit of simplicity and clarity, in which a strengthening of the neo-classicist tendencies shown in the Théâtre des Champs-Elysées is unmistakable.

Typical of the tranquil-elegant style of these years are the competition designs for the Palace of the League of Nations in Geneva (1927) and for the Palace of the Soviets in Moscow (1931), as well as the Hôtel du Mobilier National (1934) and the Musée des Travaux Publics (1937) in Paris.

P.'s most important work after World War II was the reconstruction of Le Havre (1945–54), a model example of 20th-century neo-classical urban planning. NM

☐ Perret, Auguste, *Contribution à une théorie de l'architecture*, Paris 1952; Rogers, Ernesto Nathan, *Auguste Perret*, Milan 1955; Champigneulle, Bernard, *Auguste Perret*, Paris 1959; Collins, Peter, *Concrete: The Vision of a New Architecture; A Study of Auguste Perret and his partners*, London 1959; Ache, J. B. (ed.), *Perret* (exhibition catalogue), Paris 1959.

Piacentini, Marcello, b. Rome 1881, d. Rome 1960. Studied at the Accademia di San Luca in Rome, where he was active from 1906 as an independent architect. He was a professor at the Scuola Superiore di Architettura in Rome. Chief editor of *L'Architettura*, 1922–43.

Between 1910 and 1920 he established his professional reputation with a series of buildings which at once adhered to and surpassed the academic ⋆eclecticism of the day. Works such as the Villa Allegri in Rome (1915–17) document, for all their traditionalism, a courageous interest in modernistic experiments and represent, like Hermann ⋆Muthesius's villas in Berlin, the direct architectural expression of the cultivated bourgeoisie of the period.

With the Fascist seizure of power, P. suddenly became the leading exponent of the ominous and never clearly defined state architecture, the style of which oscillated between a reduced ⋆neo-classicism and the Novecento Italiano. His political opportunism won him numerous commissions. In 1926 he built the Hotel Ambasciatori in Rome; he remodelled the Piazza della Vittoria, 1927–32; in 1932 he completed the Via Regina Elena and, in con-

Piacentini. Hotel Ambasciatori, Rome (1926)

junction with Attilio Spaccarelli, the not surprisingly controversial Via della Consiliazione in Rome. The Città Universitaria, also in Rome, was built 1932–5; P. developed its monumentally conceived general plan and built the strongly axial, travertine-clad administration building. The monumental staircase, the pilasters at the entrance rising through several storeys with neither bases nor capitals, the expressive figurative relief sculpture in realist style, and the commemorative Latin frieze inscription are all characteristic features of Italian neo-classicism of the 1930s. From 1937 to 1942 Piacentini collaborated with Giuseppe Pagano, Luigi Piccinato, Ettore Rossi and Luigi Vietti in the planning of the centre of the satellite town EUR (Esposizione Universale di Roma) near Rome for the proposed international exhibition E42, which never took place because of the escalation of the war. The Via Roma in Turin dates from 1938, the Piazza della Vittoria in Genoa from 1942; and in 1959 P. worked with *Nervi on the Palazzo dello Sport in Rome.

P.'s influence on 20th-century Italian architecture was enormous, not only because of his considerable oeuvre, but also through his writings and activity as a teacher. While not a few of his works embrace the conventional and the commercial, his best works reveal an elegant synthesis of modernism and classical features which from a conservative position point the way to an Italian variant of the *International Style. VML

□ Piacentini, Marcello, *Architettura d'oggi*, Rome 1930; ——, *Volto di Roma*, Rome 1945; Pica, Agnoldomenico, *Architettura moderna in Italia*, Milan 1941; Portoghesi, Paolo, *L'eclettismo a Roma 1870–1922*, Rome 1969.

Piano, Renzo, b. Genoa 1937. Studied at the Milan Politecnico, where he himself subsequently taught, 1965–8. He was in partnership with Richard *Rogers, 1970–7, since when he has worked in association with the engineer Peter Rice. P., whose first works date from the mid-1960s, is concerned to achieve a technically determined architecture that is characterized as much by accommodation of the users' needs as by its aesthetic qualities. An example is the house at Garonne, near Alessandria (1969), which was erected and altered by the client

Piano. Centre National d'Art et de Culture Georges Pompidou, Paris (with Richard Rogers; 1971–7)

himself. P. collaborated with Rogers, 1971–7, on the Centre National d'Art et de Culture Georges Pompidou, the six-storey 'cultural machine' self-consciously inserted in the centre of Paris. The glass-enclosed internal spaces are, thanks to exposed spanning beams 48 m (157 ft 6 in.) long, entirely free of supports, allowing complete flexibility. The external appearance of the building is created entirely by the steel skeleton and the various service and vertical transportation elements painted in primary colours. This romantic-technical aesthetic recalls Antonio *Sant'Elia's visionary projects, as well as the graphic reveries of Russian *Constructivism and of the *Archigram group. In his later work P. continues the structural experiments of the Centre Pompidou, continually putting them at the service of social and participatory applications: experimental residential quarter in Corciano near Perugia (1978–82, with Peter Rice); 'district laboratory' for the urban renewal scheme in Otranto (1978, also with Rice); museum building for the Menil Collection in Houston, Texas (1981 ff.). VML

□ 'Piano + Rogers', *L'Architecture d'aujourd'hui*, (Paris), no. 170, November–December 1973, pp. 45–58; 'Renzo Piano. Projets et réalisations 1975–1981', op. cit., no. 219, February 1982, pp. 43–53.

Pietilä, Reima, b. Turku 1923. Studied at the Technical College in Helsinki. Since 1960 he has run his own office, with his wife Raili Pietilä (*née* Paatelainen), in Helsinki. He was a professor at the University in Oulu, 1972–9. Among the most important works of the partnership are the Kaleva church in Tampere (1966) and the Dipoli Students' Residence at Otaniemi, near Helsinki (1967). In the Kaleva church the wall shell curves inwards and narrow window strips create, with their vertical emphasis, a 'Gothic' effect, while at Dipoli the principal theme is the combination of one freely formed part constructed of random stone blocks, with another contrasting rectilinear part. In the Suvikumpu residential quarter in Tapiola (1966–9) life and rhythm is introduced into an apartment block by the use of varying floor heights and fenestration. The central buildings of Hervanta New Town, near Tampere (1979), create a constrast to the banal housing surrounding them. Even more than in their earlier work, this project carries meaning of a symbolic nature: in the shopping centre by reference to the covered-market architecture of the 19th century, in the Community and Leisure Centre by reference to old masonry and its natural surroundings. As they had always done in their work in Finland, the architects likewise pay great respect to local tradition in the Palace complex (1970–81) for the Emir of Kuwait, including the Chancellery, Cabinet Office and Foreign Ministry buildings. PS

□ *Architecture and Urbanism* (Tokyo), September 1974.

Poelzig, Hans, b. Berlin 1869, d. Berlin 1936. Studied at the Technische Hochschule in Berlin-Charlottenburg. He had his own office in Breslau, 1899–1916, and in addition he taught there, 1900–16, at the Kunst- und Kunstgewerbeschule (after 1911 the Akademie für Kunst und Kunstgewerbe), of which he was director from 1903. He was Municipal Architect in Dresden, 1916–20, and a professor at the Technische Hochschule there. In 1920 he became the head of a studio at the Prussian Akademie der Künste in Berlin, and in 1923 also professor at the Technische Hochschule in Berlin-Charlottenburg; among his pupils in Berlin were Egon *Eiermann, Julius Posener, Rudolf *Schwartz and Konrad *Wachsmann. His office building in Breslau (1911) anticipates a favourite motif of the 1920s, fenestration in horizontal strips. The water-tower at Posen (now Poznan; 1911), with its undisguised steel structure, resembles a hexagonal crystalline form; this was the first manifestation of P.'s architecture of *Expressionism. His designs just after World War I, including the project for the

Poelzig. Großes Schauspielhaus, Berlin (1918–19)

Poelzig. I.G. Farbenindustrie administration building, Frankfurt am Main (1928–31)

Salzburg Festival Theatre (1920–2), are of visionary imagination. The rebuilding of the Schumann Circus into Max Reinhardt's Großes Schauspielhaus, Berlin (1918–19), was based on these designs: the auditorium, a 'space cave' decorated with stalactite-shapes, was one of the most notable interiors of the Expressionist era. Towards the end of the 1920s, P. went over to buildings of a monumental straightforwardness, as in the I.G. Farbenindustrie administration block, Frankfurt am Main (1928–31).

☐ Heuss, Theodor, *Hans Poelzig, Lebensbild eines deutschen Baumeisters.* Tübingen 1939 and 1955; Posener, Julius (ed.), *Hans Poelzig: Gesammelte Schriften und Werke*, Berlin 1970.

Polk, Willis Jefferson, b. near Frankfort, Kentucky 1867, d. San Mateo, Cal. 1924. Pupil of *Maybeck. The Hallidie Building (San Francisco, 1918) by Polk and Co. is one of the first buildings with a fully glazed, non-loadbearing outer wall. It was a forerunner of the buildings of the Modern Movement on the American West Coast; its filigree floral decoration, however, is reminiscent of French *Art Nouveau and of *Sullivan's 'organic' ornament.

☐ Dillis, K. W., 'The Hallidie Building', *Journal of the Society of Architectural Historians*, 30 (1971), pp. 323–9; Longstreth, R. W., *A Matter of Taste: Willis Polk's Writings on Architecture in the Wave*, San Francisco 1979.

Pollini, Gino, b. Rovereto 1903. Studied at the Politecnico in Milan. He was a founder-member of *Gruppo 7. He has worked regularly in collaboration with Luigi *Figini.

Ponti, Gio, b. Milan 1891, d. 1979. Studied at the Politecnico, Milan, where he later taught (1936–61). The situation in which he found himself at the beginning of his career was characterized by the contradiction between the emerging *Rationalism in the circle of the *Gruppo 7 (founded 1926) and the ideas of the Novecento Italiano, largely based on neoclassicism and in which *Futurism was largely abandoned. P. represented an elegant 'modernistic' tendency, influenced by Otto *Wagner, which united classical motifs and rationalist clarity. In contrast to the other architects of his generation, who relied on the classical effects derived from the use of arches and columns, Ponti adhered in general to the tenets of the rationalist and functionalist school.

In 1928 he founded the journal *Domus*, one of the most important Italian architectural periodicals, which led the way in improving the taste

Ponti. Pirelli Skyscraper, Milan (in collaboration; 1956–8)

of the Italian public in interior design. In 1933, before he had discarded his neo-classicist leanings, he was appointed to the executive committee of the V Milan Triennale. Its great merit was that it drew the young 'rationalist' architects from Milan into the field of major international exhibitions.

P.'s long series of buildings began in 1923; but it was only in 1936, with the scheme for the Catholic Press Exhibition in the Vatican City, that he gave up the strict symmetry and conventions of neo-classicism. Also in 1936 he designed the first office block for the Montecatini Company in Milan (the second dates from 1951), in which he combined Novecento elements (e.g. maximum plastic evidence of volumes) with others of the rationalist system of aesthetics. In 1956–8 he realized his masterpiece in the Pirelli Skyscraper in Milan (with other architects and with *Nervi as structural engineer). With its bold structural skeleton, smooth, regular façades and tapering sides like a ship's bows, it was one of the first skyscrapers to abandon the rectangular block form customary up to that point. GV/GHa

☐ Ponti, Gio, *Amate l'architettura*, Milan 1957; Plaut, James S., *Espressione di Gio Ponti*, Milan 1954; Shapira, Nathan H. (ed.), *The Expression of Gio Ponti*, Minneapolis 1967.

Portman, John (Calvin) b. Walhalla, South Carolina 1924. Studied at the Georgia Institute of Technology in Atlanta. In 1953 he established an architectural office; the firm of John Portman & Associates was established in 1968. In many of his projects P. has also acted as the developer, and this has allowed him to determine not only the formal appearance, but also the programme of his buildings. He developed a new, highly successful hotel type, whose unmistakable trademark is the large interior court with shops, restaurants and places for strolling; these he has built mostly in depressed inner-city areas as an urban crystallization point. His best-known works are: the Peachtree Center in Atlanta, Ga., with its various buildings, including the Hyatt Regency Hotel (1967–71) and the Peachtree Plaza Hotel (1976); the Hyatt Regency Hotels at O'Hare Airport in

Portman. Hyatt Regency Hotel, San Francisco (John Portman & Associates; 1974)

Chicago (1971) and at the Embarcadero Center in San Francisco (1974); the Embarcadero Center itself (1976); the Bonaventure Hotel in Los Angeles (1977); and the Renaissance Center in Detroit (1977). AM

□ Portman, John, and Barnett, Jonathan, *The Architect as Developer*, New York 1976; 'John Portman. Peachtree Center, Bonaventure Hotel and Renaissance Center', *Global Architecture* (Tokyo), no. 57 (1981).

Portoghesi, Paolo, b. Rome 1931. Studied at the University of Rome; diploma 1957. From 1958 he had his own office in Rome, and since 1964 has been in partnership with Vittorio Gigliotti. He was a professor at the University of Rome, 1962–6, and subsequently at the Politecnico in Milan; since 1981 he has resumed teaching at the University of Rome. Chief editor of *Controspazio* since 1969 and editor of *Itaca* since 1977.

In the late 1950s P. was one of the first architects to turn away from *Rationalism and to orient himself strongly towards historical models. Paralleling his early architectural writings on Guarini and Borromini, he admitted into his own work traditions as diverse as oriental architecture, the Gothic, the Baroque, *Art Nouveau and romantic *eclecticism, which he combined with modernist forms and compositional elements to form creations as individual as they are unmistakable. Thus, the Casa Baldi near Rome (1959) presents a contradictory synthesis of the Baroque and De *Stijl. In the Casa Andreis in Scandriglia (1964–7), the Casa Papanice in Rome (1967) and the Church of the Sacra Famiglia in Salerno (1968–74) – all based on complex, circular geometries, – symbolic, historical, mathematical and technological considerations all contribute to a stimulating formal solution. At the same time P. investigated the aesthetic possibilities of inexpensive prefabricated building (Technical School in L'Aquila, 1969–78) and daring concrete vaulting structures (Islamic Centre and Mosque in Rome, begun 1976). Through his numerous writings and in his 'Prima mostra internazionale di architettura', an exhibition held at the 1980 Venice Biennale, he established himself as a leading intellectual spokesman of *Post-Modernism. VML

Portoghesi. Church of the Sacra Famiglia, Salerno (with Vittorio Gigliotti; 1968–74)

□ Portoghesi, Paolo, *Guarino Guarini*, Milan 1956; ——, *Borromini nella cultura europea*, Rome 1964; ——, *Le inibizioni dell'architettura moderna*, Rome 1974; ——, *After Modern Architecture*, Bari 1982; Norberg-Schulz, Christian, *Alla ricerca dell'architettura perduta: Le opere di Paolo Portoghesi e Vittorio Gigliotti*, Rome 1975; Moschini, F. (ed.), *Paolo Portoghesi. Progetti e disegni 1949–1979. Projects and drawings 1949–1979*, Florence 1979.

Post-Modernism. A term used in numerous disciplines to describe a style or theoretic point of view opposed to or superseding modernism. Repeatedly criticized as polemical or imprecise, Post-Modernism has nevertheless persisted as a major issue in many fields of artistic expression. In its most developed definition, the term may describe a world-view which rejects all of the Western world's verities: religious, rational or humanist.

In architecture this viewpoint has not been common, however, and thus, since the term came into widespread use in the mid-1970s, it has most commonly been employed to describe an eclectic style that uses elements of various periods, especially those of the classical tradition, often with ironic intent. Oft-cited examples are: the A T & T Building (1978–83) in New York by *Johnson and Burgee; the various residential designs of Robert *Stern; the Piazza d'Italia in New Orleans by Charles *Moore (1975–80); the Austrian Travel Bureau in Vienna by Hans *Hollein (1978); the Anti-

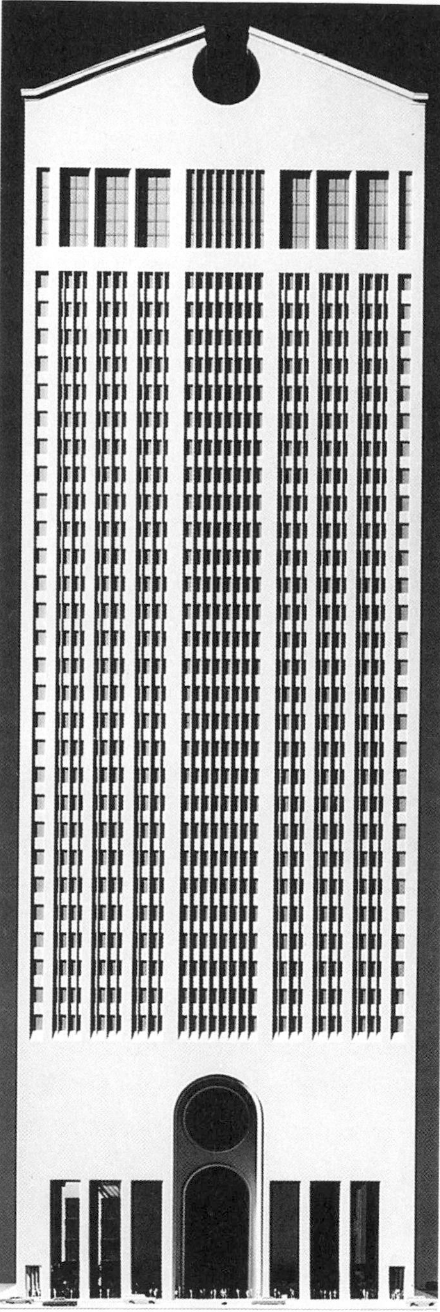

Post-Modernism. AT&T Building, New York (1978–83), by Johnson and Burgee (model)

Cruelty Society in Chicago by Stanley *Tigerman (1980); and, above all, the Public Services Building (1980–2) in Portland, Oregon, by Michael *Graves. Indeed, the pastel colours and oversized keystones of Graves's work are the most familiar hallmarks of 'post-modern' style.

Increasingly, however, in the early 1980s the term 'post-modern' has also been used more profoundly to describe a fundamental shift in assumptions about architecture and society. In this case the moral imperatives of modernism, i.e. that a building's form and appearance should result in some causative and logical way from the building programme, the nature of the material and constructional procedures, have been called into question and, as a result, often discarded.

The principal problem in using the term in this second sense arises from the fact that it does not resolve the ambiguities which have always been occasioned by the notion of 'modernism' itself. Indeed, efforts to define modernism started to proliferate at precisely the moment when a large number of people felt it belonged to the historical past. Several recent writers have distinguished between 'modernism' in the largest sense, referring to the Western Humanist tradition, and 'modernity', referring to the more specific ideals and goals of such avant-garde artists of the early 20th century as Stravinsky, Pound, Eliot, Picasso and *Le Corbusier. In the first case Post-Modernism would be a reaction to the scientific, rational, man-centred culture developed in Western Europe and America over the last several centuries. In certain respects this position represents a logical extension of 20th-century modernism, pushing it to the point where it calls into question the very assumptions on which it initially rested. Such a radical position is best exemplified in the early work of the composer John Cage and a number of writers and literary critics. In architecture perhaps only the work of Peter *Eisenman approaches this point of view. Eisenman's work is an extension of modernism, especially abstract painting and sculpture, in that he attempts to create an autonomous architecture, one which does not derive its rationale and meaning from anything external to itself. The forms he uses are meant to be devoid of all conventional meanings and are used only as raw materials for a set of manipulations based on analogies to linguistic structure. Eisenman has described his method as working with syntax rather than semantics, that is with the way the words or elements are put together rather than with their inherent meaning. Although these manipulations are rigidly regulated according to rules, the choice of the rules themselves is admittedly arbitrary and thus constitutes a break with modernism. The specific forms may appear to be unchanged, but all notions of social or aesthetic utopianism are gone, as well as the beliefs in the universality of simple geometry and primary colours and other moral imperatives that had formerly guided the work of the modernists.

The second alternative, Post-Modernism as an opposition to 'Modern Movement' or 'Modernity', implies a more or less decisive break with the major goals of 20th-century avant garde, and a re-integration with the ideals of the pre-modernist era. This conception of Post-Modernism, by far the more common, is associated primarily with American architects such as Michael *Graves, Charles *Moore, Robert *Stern and others. It is usually described by its proponents as an attempt to restore meaning to architecture by the re-introduction of conventional architectural elements, and to be more pluralistic by enlarging the repertory of styles and forms available to the designer. However, the break is by no means a clean one since modernist style, stripped of its underlying ideologies, is admitted as one of the historical styles. Critics charge that this stance fostered an architecture devoid of all meaningful rules, one which merely follows fashions and traffics with the mass-market. Proponents, on the other hand, claim that through historic reference and adaptability they are restoring the continuity of the built environment and reinforcing the sense of specific places which they feel modernists denied or even destroyed. A small but growing minority of architects, such as Raymond Erith and Quinlan Terry in *Great Britain or Allan Greenberg in the *USA, advocate the use of classical elements, to be employed in a much more straightforward, literal fashion (*neo-classicism).

Because the term Post-Modernism has only been applied to architecture since the mid-1970s and since its definition is still greatly contested, it is difficult to sketch its history. This problem is compounded by the fact that for many post-modernists the very notion of a linear, cause-and-effect history is suspect. There does, however, seem to be some consensus about some

Post-Modernism. Piazza d'Italia, New Orleans (1975–80), by Charles Moore

important episodes in the development of anti-modern and post-modern theory and practice. Despite the numerous attitudes over a long period which may be isolated as precursors, it was only in the 1960s that an overtly anti-modernist polemic came to the fore. One of the earliest and most sustained attacks originated outside the architectural profession in the form of reactions to the programmes of urban renewal. A classic example was Jane Jacob's influential *Death and Life of Great American Cities* (1961).

From within the profession several Americans established themselves early on as critics of modernist practice. Charles Moore, in both teaching and a series of architectural projects, sought an architecture based on anthropomorphic forms, historical memory and even a degree of whimsy. Philip Johnson, in a series of widely publicized lectures, undermined some of the most basic assumptions of avant-garde 20th-century architecture in asserting the primacy of art, intuition and beauty over functionalist and rationalist concerns.

Finally, Robert *Venturi challenged modernist practice and ideas in *Complexity and Contradiction in Architecture* (1966), in which he argued for a more complex and vital architecture, opening the door for the simultaneous use of elements derived from history and from the vernacular. He celebrated ambiguity and irony, qualities not commonly even acknowledged by modernists as elements of architectural expression. The influence of his wife, the planner Denise Scott Brown, and of the sociologist Herbert Gans was conspicuous in his second book, *Learning from Las Vegas* (1972). In this book, the outgrowth of a Yale seminar, the Venturis and Steven Izenour turned to the popular, even raucous, American landscape for sources and focused especially on the commercial roadside 'strip'. They argued that the large signs of the Las Vegas casinos were appropriate architectural forms for an automobile-oriented culture. By extension, they posited the notion that the simple shed with applied decorations was a more reasonable model for many kinds of buildings than the heroic work of the modernists who, in forbidding decoration, had rendered the entire structure decorative. Although the Venturis always considered themselves modernists, their reliance on 'taste' rather than on modernist moral imperatives allowed their followers to view them as father figures of Post-Modernism.

In Europe the situation was quite different. For the most part the European avant garde has castigated Post-Modernism as American, consumer-oriented 'kitsch'. There does, however, exist an important anti-modernist strain that has a number of things in common with Post-Modernism. During the 1960s the writings and teaching of Aldo *Rossi first brought to light ideas that have been developed under the banner of *Rationalist architecture. In his *Architettura della città* (1966) Rossi argued against the generation of new forms by the use of functional and structural necessities and argued instead for forms created by analogy with the buildings of the traditional European city centre, with its clearly defined public and private spaces. These forms he supposed to be based on archetypes latent in the city dwellers' collective memory.

A popularization and codification of Rationalist views, although without Rossi's intensely personal poetry, was provided by Rob *Krier in his *Stadtraum in Theorie und Praxis* (1975). The European Rationalists, while definitely anti-modernist, can only with difficulty be considered Post-Modernists since they have, for the most part, merely substituted one set of moral imperatives for another. The new basis of thought has been the left-wing political tradition that earlier had nourished many of the modernists. In recent years the cross-fertilization of American and European ideas has created interesting hybrids. Europeans like Paolo *Portoghesi have championed American Post-Modernism while Americans such as the group of architects and the Institute for Architecture and Urban Studies in New York have translated and published the writings of the Rationalists. Europeans have undeniably been influenced by American practice, while the Americans have appropriated Rationalist forms and used them widely, almost always stripped of their entire theoretical basis. The result has been a tremendous proliferation of approaches and styles. In the case of the housing projects of Ricardo *Bofill at Saint-Quentin-en-Yvelines in France (1981) or the works of Arquitectonica in Miami or many Japanese works, it is hard to know whether modern or post-modern, European or American, influences are most important.

Concurrently with the early writings of Venturi and Rossi came a number of other events that shook the basis of modernist practice. By enthusiastically accepting elements from low culture, Pop artists such as Claes Oldenburg effected a blurring of the traditional distinction which such modernist critics as Clement Greenberg had insisted upon as the necessary protection of the avant garde from mass-consumption 'kitsch'. Hans *Hollein in Austria and SITE (*Wines) in the USA exemplify this tendency in architecture. The recent growth of research and interest in architectural history has had a similar effect. By devoting serious attention to previously maligned or overlooked figures, for example, *Lutyens or the German Expressionists (*Expressionism) of the 1920s, historians documented the diversity of modernism. By focusing on such subjects as the *Ecole des Beaux-Arts, they tacitly condoned the original targets of the modernist polemic. Recent works by Colin Rowe, notably his *Collage City* (with Fred Koetler, 1977), and David Watkins' notable *Morality and Architecture* (1977) have attempted to expose the contradictions and fallacies of modernism itself.

In a wider intellectual sphere, semeiology had a profoundly corrosive effect on modernist assumptions, since it increasingly suggested that, far from being universal, almost all meanings inherent in cultural activities were conventional and culturally bound. Although its implications for buildings were widely discussed in the early 1970s, the direct transfer of such ideas to architectural practice, for example Peter Eisenman's attempt to use ideas from the study of language in his work, was problematic.

By the mid-1970s a spate of popular books, such as Peter Blake's *Form Follows Fiasco* (1977) or Brent Brolin's *Failure of Modern Architecture* (1978), diffused the post-modern critique and announced the death of modernism by cataloguing all of its alleged crimes. A somewhat later example, Tom Wolfe's *From Bauhaus to Our House* (1980), has found a wide public. Charles Jencks' *Language of Post-Modern Architecture* (1977) provided the first influential attempt to define and codify Post-Modernism. In colourful and highly polemical prose, Jencks argued that modernists were interested in 'univalent', post-modernists in 'multi-valent', or 'double-coded', imagery; modernists in universal truths, post-modernists in history and local context; modernists in technology and structure, post-modernists in the vernacular, the metaphorical and in a new kind of ambiguous space. Despite these clear-cut simplifying definitions, Jencks' book was little more than a catalogue of stylistic categories.

In the last few years, a more searching exploration of Post-Modernism has begun, notably in articles by Robert Stern and Jorge Silvetti in the first volume of the *Harvard Architectural Review* (1980), in the essays in the catalogue of the 1980 Venice Biennale, *Architecture 1980: The Presence of the Past*, and in the anthology *The Anti-Aesthetic, Essays on Post-Modern Culture* (1983). Recently, several efforts have been made to erect a theory of architecture based on convention and choice rather than on principle of universal validity. The most notable of these is perhaps William Hubbard's *Complicity and Convention: Steps toward an Architecture of Convention* (1980). The rise of a younger generation of architects trained by such influential figures as Stern and Graves suggests the possibility for the creation of a set of architectural forms proper to the Post-Modernist point of view. RBr

☐ Jencks, C., *The Language of Post-Modern Architecture*, London 1977; ——, *Late-Modern Architecture and Other Essays*, London 1980; *Harvard Architectural Review*, vol. 1, 1980; Pommer, R., 'Some Architectural Ideologies after the Fall', *Art Journal* (New York), Fall 1980; Portoghesi, P., *After Modern Architecture*, New York 1982; Foster, Hal (ed.), *The Anti-Aesthetic, Essays on Post-Modern Culture*, New York 1983; Klotz, Heinrich (ed.), *Die Revision der Moderne: Postmoderne Architektur 1960–1980* (exhibition catalogue), Munich 1984; Klotz, H., *Moderne und Postmoderne. Architektur der Gegenwart 1960–1980*, Wiesbaden 1984.

Powell and Moya. Sir Philip Powell and John Hidalgo Moya studied at the Architectural Association School, London, and in 1946, two years after graduating, founded their partnership to carry out the Pimlico Housing Scheme (now Churchill Gardens, 1946–62), London, which they had won (in competition against sixty-four other entrants) with a design that proved a significant landmark in the attempt to establish a post-war vernacular. Their work includes the vertical feature ('Skylon') at the *Festival of Britain, London, 1951; Mayfield Comprehensive School, Putney (1956; 'subtle, elegant, humane' – Ian Nairn); Princess Margaret Hospital, Swindon (1972); hexagonal theatre with arena stage, Chichester (1961); Cripps Buildings, St John's College, Cambridge (1967); and the Museum of London, in the Barbican redevelopement (1976).

Prouvé, Jean, b. 1901 Nancy, d. 1984 Nancy. Trained 1917–20 (under Emile Robert) as an art metal worker in Nancy, where his father, Victor Prouvé, was one of the leading figures of the local *Art Nouveau. Early on, he was given important furnishing commissions which soon brought him into contact with the architectural avant garde of *France.

Around 1930, P. developed a system of replaceable wall components, the first of its kind, as the basis of an easily erected housing prototype of light-metal construction on stanchions. Through a refined balancing of the requirements of statics, materials and production, he developed a formal language most closely related (even in furniture) to the automobile industry. In all his designs there is a clear distinction between supporting and enclosing elements. He was one of the first to make the principle of the curtain wall technically feasible (1934) and subsequently a pioneer in its practical application (Club House on the Buc airfield, 1938; architects Eugène *Beaudouin and Marcel Lods).

The Maison du Peuple at Clichy (1937–9, architects Beaudouin and Lods) is one of the pioneering works of modern technologically oriented architecture, with its projecting steel

Prouvé. Spa building, Evian (with Maurice Novarina; 1957)

Prouvé. Curtain-wall façade on the Lycée at Bagnols-sur-Cèze (with Badani and Roux-Dorlut; 1958)

construction, skin of large expanses of glass, and assembly-line wall-units of sheet metal and integral glazing. In his construction and production workshops at Maxéville near Nancy, which he directed personally until opening his own consulting firm in Paris in 1954, P. introduced innumerable collaborators to his work and methods. His self-set programme was to meet the challenge of an architecture based on industrially fabricated components which were lightweight for both easy transport and straightforward on-site erection. he strove to create buildings which would give full expression to the dynamic and freedom which he felt must characterize a mass-culture served by machine production.

P.'s most convincing constructions consist of several types: roof structures resting on steel supports and asymmetrical jib arms stabilized by tensile cables (temporary school building at Villejuif, 1953; Spa building, Evian, 1957, architect Maurice Novarina); steel space-frames for roofing large surfaces (Congress Hall, Grenoble, 1967; Total service stations, 1968); and curtain-wall designs distinghuished by elegant details. P.'s curtain-wall façades are to be found on numerous French school buildings, and also on an apartment block in Paris (1953; architect Lionel Mirabaud), on the Institute buildings of the Free University in Berlin-Dahlem (1963, 1967–79; architects *Candilis, *Josic and

Prouvé. Houses at Meudon-Bellevue (1959)

Prouvé. Prefabricated houses (Sahara type) under construction (1958)

*Woods, together with Manfred Schiedhelm), as well as on an office tower at La Défense, near Paris (1967; architects Jean de Mailly and Jacques Depussé). Especially noteworthy are P.'s prefabricated houses (development at Meudon-Bellevue, 1949; prototype for Abbé Pierre with prefabricated concrete units as the core, 1956; Sahara types, 1958), for their function and spatial effect are as unified as if taken from the same mould, while his social vision of a new equitable industrial age is also given convincing form. MB

□ 'Jean Prouvé', *Architecture* (Brussels), nos. 11/12, 1964; *Jean Prouvé* (exhibition catalogue), Paris 1964; Huber, B., and Steinegger, J. C., (eds.), *Jean Prouvé. Architektur aus der Fabrik*, Zurich 1971; Clayssen, Dominique, *Jean Prouvé: L'Idée Constructive*, Paris, 1983.

Purism. The first exhibit of the purist movement took place in 1918 in the Galerie Thomas in Paris. The catalogue contained a manifesto under the revealing title 'Après le cubisme' ('After Cubism') signed by the painter Amédée Ozenfant and the painter, sculptor, and architect Charles-Edouard Jeanneret, later known as *Le Corbusier. After brusquely declaring the bankruptcy of *Cubism, they announced a new art, which was to be developed through an economy of means, collaboration with technology, and pure geometry. The impersonalness and cool restraint in no way negated the poetry of their strongly composed pictures of simple, mechanically built-up figurative elements. The purist aesthetic which, like that of the *Bauhaus, strove for association with standardization and industrial production, was propagated between 1920 and 1925 in the pages of the periodical *L'Esprit nouveau*. In the person of Le Corbusier it was introduced into architecture and urban planning. VML

R

Rainer, Roland, b. Klagenfurt 1910. Trained at the Technische Hochschule in Vienna. Began teaching 1953; from 1956 he directed a master class at the Akademie der bildenden Künste, Vienna. He was Planning Director for the City of Vienna, 1958–63. In conscious opposition to the fortification-like Viennese apartment blocks of the 1920s, R. strongly advocated the concept of 'articulated and decentralized' garden cities, which he was first able to realize in the prefabricated Veitingergasse housing estate in Vienna (1953–4, with Carl Auböck). Further important examples of his influence on town planning are the Mauerberg estate in Vienna (1964) and Puchenau garden city, near Linz (first building phase 1969, second 1975). The city halls of Vienna (1958), Bremen (1964) and Ludwigshafen (1965) are characterized by strong sculptural effects derived from an adroit manipulation of construction itself. AM

□ Göderitz, J., Rainer, R., and Hoffmann, H., *Die gegliederte und aufgelockerte Stadt*, Tübingen 1957; Rainer, R. *Livable Environments*, Zurich 1972; ——, *Für eine lebensgerechtere Stadt*, Vienna 1974; Kamm, Peter, *Roland Rainer: Bauten, Schriften und Projekte*, Tübingen 1973.

Rainer. City Hall, Bremen (1964)

Rational architecture. Students' Residence, Chieti (1976; 1979–84), by Giorgio Grassi and Antonio Monastiroli

Rational architecture. Movement in contemporary architecture launched by Aldo *Rossi, which postulates a rational and executable solution of the problems of design grounded on the logical ordering of cities and architectural types.

The concept of Rational architecture, which Rossi had already sketched out in theoretical terms in 1966 in *L'architettura della città*, was explicitly developed in the book *Architettura razionale* by Rossi and others, published in 1973 on the occasion of the XVth Milan Triennale. Rational architecture combines the rationalistic architectural theory of the Renaissance, Enlightenment classicism and the thought of the 1920s and considers architecture as an independent science which contains within itself its natural laws and thus its formal legitimacy. These natural laws can be reworked through the study of the City of Types. The city is viewed primarily as an historical place and the type as a historically immutable primary element of architecture which cannot be further reduced. A theoretically and politically contemplated search should overcome the alienation of man and architecture: thus the principle of functionalism is rejected in favour of formalism, which sets itself against production by the division of labour in an effort to restore a desired unity. Among the most important buildings of Rational architecture figure Rossi's apartment block in the Gallaratese 2 complex in Milan's Monte Amiata housing estate (1969, 1970–3) and the Students' Residence in Chieti by *Grassi (1976, 1979 ff.).

Rational architecture. An apartment building in the Gallaratese 2 complex, Milan (1969; 1970–3), by Aldo Rossi

Architects who share intellectual sympathies with Rational architecture include: Mario *Botta, J. P. *Kleihues, Léon *Krier, Rob *Krier, Bruno Minardi, Franco Purini, Bruno *Reichlin, Fabio *Reinhart, Luigi Snozzi, Salvador Tarrago y Cid and O. M. *Ungers. VML

□ Rossi, Aldo, *L'architettura della città*, Padua 1966 (English ed.: *The Architecture of the City*, Cambridge, Mass. 1982); Grassi, Giorgio, *La costruzione logica dell'architettura*, Venice 1967; Bonfanti, E., Bonicalzi, R., Braghieri, G., Raggi, F., Rossi, A., Scolari, M., and Vitale, D., *Architettura razionale*, Milan 1973; *Rational Architecture/Architecture Rationelle*, Brussels 1978.

Rationalism. Architectural movement of the first half of the 20th century, whose common intellectual position consisted in the pursuit of the most rational possible solution to design problems. Although it comprised an aspect of *Functionalism, it encompassed wider philosophical, political, social, economic, stylistic and symbolic questions.

The intellectual principles of Rationalism go back to a tradition which is as old as architectural theory itself. Vitruvius had already established in his work *De Architectura* that architecture is a science that can be comprehended rationally. This formulation was taken up and further developed in the architectural treatises of the Renaissance. Progressive art theory of the 18th-century opposed the Baroque beauty of illusionism with the classic beauty of truth and reason. With the works of J. N. L. Durand, E. E. Viollet-le-Duc, Gottfried Semper, Auguste Choisy, and Julien Guadet, the intellectual legacy of this 'architecture of the Enlightenment' was continued throughout the 19th century with new emphasis and principles.

Twentieth-century Rationalism derived less from a special, unified theoretical work as from a common belief that the most varied problems posed by the real world could be resolved by reason. In that respect it represented a reaction to *historicism and a contrast to *Art Nouveau and *Expressionism.

It was not by chance that the ideological superstructure of the new movement extended from the sceptical humanistic socialism of a Ludwig *Mies van der Rohe to the radical communism of a Hannes *Meyer. The belief in a better society in a better world was the driving force underlying the quest for a better architecture; this was not to be individualistic, but rather collective; its expression was not to be confined to individual buildings but rather to multiple architectural and urbanistic operations; it was to be not only national, but international (*International Style).

From these premises were derived the five following (here simplified) principles which were characteristic of Rationalism:

(1) The concept of urban planning, architecture, and industrial design as the means for fostering social progress and democratic education. To design was thus no longer viewed as an individual search for form but primarily as a social and ethical activity.

(2) The maxim of economy which was applied as much to land use as to building itself. The desire to create dwellings for everyone led, of necessity in the economically unsettled 1920s and 1930s, to the 'apartment for the minimal existence' (*Existenzminimum*): rational use of plots, inexpensive building methods, minimalized ground-plans, a severe and ornament-free formal language.

(3) The systematic reference to industrial technologies, standardization and prefabrication for all levels of environmental design from city planning to industrial design. At the same time there arose the paradox that the building industry was not prepared for such a radical conversion and continued for the most part with conventional production. Nonetheless, individual objects were so designed that they *could* be mass-produced, if one had the ability or desire to do so. Even when in reality it did not enter the question, series production (or its theory) influenced the formal vocabulary of Rationalism, which consequently produced metaphors of industrialization.

(4) Priority to be given to urban planning over architecture. In the face of the drastic housing shortage, solutions on a massive scale seemed more important than individual operations – hence the flourishing of housing estates (*Siedlungen*).

(5) The rationality of architectural form, which was seen as the methodically developed result of objective requirements, above all of a political, social, economic, functional or constructional type. Form thus seemed – at least in part – a logical entity, which would not remain subject to the whims of individuals but was rather collectively controllable. The aesthetic question was, at least in theory, pushed into the background; research into the feasibility of the process of formal invention was, in the first place, founded on ethical considerations.

In spite of all protest to the contrary, Rationalism quickly evolved into a thoroughgoing and unified style with a typical and definable language of forms; and in spite of all protest to the contrary, it became in the first instance an artistic movement. It was above all at the *Bauhaus that the trends of the artistic avant garde of the early 20th century converged as in a crucible and in turn enriched Rationalist architecture. The comparatively new materials steel, concrete and glass were composed in buildings with clear, closed and, for the most part, white-

Rationalism. AEG Turbine Factory, Berlin (1908–9) by Behrens

Rationalism. Fagus Factory, Alfeld an der Leine (1910–11), by Gropius

Rationalism. *Chicago Tribune* Tower (competition project, 1922) by Gropius and Meyer

painted surfaces, with crisply-cut openings, expansive glazing, and rectangular volumes; houses were designed on the basis of hygienic considerations, ground-plans rationalized and dissolved into 'flowing space continua', and the separation of interior and exterior space was to a great extent abolished; constructional and functional parts were for the most part made visible, historical elements and decorations were eliminated, and finally the notion of the façade having a privileged appearance gave way to an equal treatment of all parts of the building.

Among the earliest works of the 20th-century architectural Rationalism are buildings by Auguste ⋆Perret, especially his flats in the Rue Franklin in Paris (1902–3), and Peter ⋆Behrens, such as the AEG Turbine Factory in Berlin (1908–9). Primacy must, however, be accorded to those by Adolf ⋆Loos; his Steiner House in Vienna (1910) constituted an emblem of budding Rationalism that was as revolutionary as it was impressive. In addition there were the urbanistic visions of Tony ⋆Garnier and Antonio ⋆Sant'Elia. Numerous noteworthy contributions were made by Soviet ⋆Constructivism and the Dutch De ⋆Stijl group.

The architecture of the second generation of progressive architects of the 20th century – above all ⋆Le Corbusier, ⋆Gropius (who already in 1910–11 had created a pioneering work of Rationalism in the Fagus Factory at Alfeld an der Leine), Mies van der Rohe and J. J. P. ⋆Oud

– represents a synthesis of the social and aesthetic advances that were characteristic of the third decade of the century; these had for the most part been given their earliest expression in chiefly unexecuted projects drawn up immediately after World War I. Mies van der Rohe's designs for tall buildings of steel and glass (1919 and 1920–1), Gropius's *Chicago Tribune* Tower entry (1922; with Adolf *Meyer) and that for the 'redents', the distantly-spaced skyscrapers on a cruciform ground-plan in Le Corbusier's 'Ville contemporaine' project (also 1922), were all much indebted to the earlier architectural achievements of the *Chicago School.

One of the first decisive realizations of the ideals of mature architectural Rationalism was the jewellery shop which Gerrit *Rietveld designed in the Kalverstraat in Amsterdam (1921). Parallel to this were Le Corbusier's projects for the Maison Citrohan (1920–2) and Mies van der Rohe's designs for a country house in brick (1922) and an office building in concrete (1923). Larger works of 'classic' Rationalism followed: the Bauhaus at Dessau (1925–6) by Gropius, the Maison Cook (1926) and Maison Stein (1927) by Le Corbusier, the housing estate at Hoek van Holland (1924–7) by Oud, the housing estate for the Reichsforschungsgesellschaft (Imperial Research Association) at Dessau-Törten (1926–7) by Gropius, the Dammerstock quarter in Karlsruhe (1927–8), the great Siemensstadt housing estate in Berlin (1929–30), Mies van der Rohe's German Pavilion at the World's Fair in Barcelona (1929), his Tugendhat House in Brno (1930), as well as the Villa Savoye at Poissy (1929–31) by Le Corbusier.

Rationalism. Maison Stein, Garches (1927), by Le Corbusier

Despite Frank Lloyd *Wright's influence from the beginning of the century onward on

Rationalism. German Pavilion at the World's Fair, Barcelona (1929), by Mies van der Rohe

younger architects, even outside the *USA (especially in the *Netherlands and in *Germany), the new style was of French, Dutch, and German origin. Before the end of the 1920s it had scarcely gained a foothold in other European countries or in the USA. Even in the original countries it advanced only with difficulties; continually opposed by the advocates of traditionalism, it achieved only an extremely limited amount of built work. An important stage in the battle for general recognition was that architectural avant-garde manifesto, the Weißenhofsiedlung (estate) of 1927, which was built in Stuttgart on the occasion of an exhibition 'Die Wohnung', prepared by the *Deutscher Werkbund; this served to unify the efforts which up till then had been essentially disparate and individual, and at the same time demonstrated agreement as to formal intentions. The *CIAM (Congrès Internationaux d'Architecture Moderne), which were to become the most important theoretical backbone of the movement, were launched a year later. Thus Rationalism, despite incessant internal and external confrontations, achieved a considerable expansion in both Europe and the USA in the early 1930s. Yet shortly afterwards, the political and cultural situation in Germany, *Italy, and the USSR (*Russia) interrupted its development in these countries; soon World War II would halt nearly all building activity.

After the war the Rationalist movement experienced a return which was as quantitatively overwhelming as it was qualitatively dubious: the 'classic' period lay in the past. Its philosophical, political and social assumptions were no longer valid; its protagonists had grown old. The few noteworthy buildings which were produced as stragglers within the original Rationalist tradition – of which the highpoint is Mies van der Rohe's Neue Nationalgalerie in Berlin (1962–8) – remained isolated and balanced, for all their aesthetic qualities, on the edge of obsolescence. Having become entangled in the profound contradiction of the 'economic miracle' and the 'energy crisis', the avant garde now directed its attention to new proposals. VML

☐ Guadet, Julien, *Eléments et théorie de l'architecture: Cours professé à l'Ecole Nationale et Spéciale des Beaux-Arts* (4 vols.), Paris n.d. [1901–4]; Gropius, W., *Internationale Architektur*, Munich 1925 (new impression Mainz 1965); Hilberseimer, L., *Großstadtbauten*, Hanover 1925; ——, *Großstadtarchitektur*, Stuttgart 1928; —— (ed.), *Internationale neue Baukunst*, Stuttgart 1927; Behne, Adolf, *Der moderne Zweckbau*, Munich 1926 (reprinted Berlin, Frankfurt am Main and Vienna 1964); Meyer, Peter, *Moderne Architektur und Tradition*, Zurich 1927; Platz, Gustav Adolf, *Die Baukunst der neuesten Zeit*, Berlin 1927; Moholy-Nagy, L., *The New Vision: From Material to Architecture*, London 1939; Hilberseimer, L., *The New City*, Chicago 1944; ——, *The New Regional Pattern*, Chicago 1949; Watkin, D. J., *Morality and Architecture*, Oxford 1979.

Reichlin, Bruno, b. Bellinzona, Switzerland 1941. Studied at the Eidgenössische Technische Hochschule (ETH) in Zurich; diploma 1967. He worked under Giovanni Klauss König at the University of Florence, 1969–70, and since 1970 has been active as a designer jointly with Fabio *Reinhart. Both men worked under Aldo *Rossi at the ETH in Zurich, 1972–4. In 1973–4 they built the Casa Tonini at Torricella, which alludes to the Palladian villa type, simultaneously alienating the type and submitting it to reinterpretation. They continued the villa theme in the Casa Sartori at Riveo (1976–7), where quotations of classical elements occur in the most extremely reduced form. Their concept of architecture as a graphic system has even found expression in several renovations (Office of the Magistrate in Sornico, 1975–7; restoration of the church in San Carlo, 1975–9). In 1976 the partnership was expanded to include two new members: Marie-Claude Bétrix and Eraldo Consolascio. AH

Reichlin. Casa Tonini, Torricella (with Fabio Reinhart; 1973–4)

☐ Steinmann, Martin, and Boga, Thomas (eds.), *Tendenzen. Neuere Architektur im Tessin* (exhibition catalogue), Zurich 1975, pp. 41–5, 76, 130–1; *Architecture and Urbanism* (Tokyo), Sept. 1976, pp. 35–44; Nicolin, Pierluigi, 'Architettura intrinseca. Opere di Bruno Reichlin e Fabio Reinhart', *Lotus International* (Milan), no. 22 (1979), pp. 94ff.; Schweizerischer Werkbund (ed.), *Bruno Reichlin, Fabio Reinhart, Marie-Claude Bétrix, Eraldo Consolascio 1970–1979* (portfolio of 22 loose sheets), Basle 1979.

Reidy, Affonso Eduardo, b. Paris 1900, d. Rio de Janeiro 1964. Studied at the Escola Nacional de Belas Artes, Rio de Janeiro, where he later served in 1930–1 as assistant to the Professor of Architectural Design, *Warchavchik. In 1931 he himself became Professor of Architectural Composition and in 1954 Professor of Urban Planning at the Federal University in Rio de Janeiro. In 1936 he joined the team of young architects responsible (with *Le Corbusier as consulting architect) for the Ministry of Education Building. In the Pedregulho Housing Estate, Rio de Janeiro (1947–52), with its apartment block, 260 m (850 ft) long, following the winding contour of the hillside, are included a school, gymnasium, clinic, laundry and shops. Access is by bridges to the middle level of the building. The Communal Theatre in Rio de Janeiro (1950) features a precise and pleasant application of the inverted double-slope roof. R.'s most significant work, the Museum of Modern Art in Rio de Janeiro (1954–9), combines an exhibition building and a 1,000-seat theatre; the former is notable for its rows of concrete ribs enclosing and supporting the roof and floor slab and for the then novel method employed to combine natural daylight with artificial lighting.

R.'s architecture is characterized by considerable formal and structural freedom, but never, as is sometimes the case in *Niemeyer's work, oversteps the boundary of 'art for art's sake'. HEM/GHa

☐ Frank, Klaus, *The Works of Affonso Eduardo Reidy*, New York 1960.

Reinhart, Fabio, b. Bellinzona, Switzerland 1942. Studied at the Eidgenössische Technische Hochschule in Zurich. Since 1970 he has worked with Bruno *Reichlin, and like Reichlin was an assistant under *Rossi at the Zurich school, 1972–4.

Reidy. Pedregulho estate, Rio de Janeiro (1947–52)

Revell. Office building, Helsinki (with Keijo Petäjä; 1952)

Revell. City Hall, Toronto (in collaboration; 1958–64)

Revell, Viljo (Gabriel), b. Vaasa 1910. d. Helsinki 1964. Studied at the Technical College in Helsinki. His Crystal Palace in Helsinki (1935, with N. Kokko and H. Riihimäki), a bazaar building which also incorporated a cinema, was in the spirit of the early Modern Movement. The Rehabilitation Centre for War Invalids in Liperi (1948) borrows from *Wright in addition to bearing witness to northern European Romanticism of the 1940s. The office building he designed with Keijo Petäjä in Helsinki (1949, 1950–2) was a harbinger of the *International Style in Finnish architecture. The Meilahti state school in Helsinki (1952–3, with Osmo Sipari) is a study in the composition of freely disposed volumes. In 1958 he won, in conjunction with Heikki Castren, Bengt Lundsten and Seppo Valjus, first prize in the competition for a new City Hall in Toronto (completed 1964), in which two curved office towers embrace a discus-shaped assembly hall. In addition to his activity as an independent architect, R. has played an important role in the reconstruction programme launched in 1942 by the Finnish Architects' Association (until 1949). In that effort he was especially concerned with questions of rationalization, standardization and prefabrication. PS

□ Ålander, Kyösti (ed.), *Viljo Revell. Works and Projects*, New York 1966; Hertzen, Heikki von, and Speiregen, Paul D., *Building a New Town: Finland's New Garden City, Tapiola*, Cambridge, Mass. 1973.

Ridolfi, Mario, b. Rome 1904. Studied at the University of Rome; diploma 1929. Subsequently, he worked in collaboration with Adalberto *Libera. From 1930 he was a member of the *M.I.A.R. In 1933 he travelled to Germany, where he was strongly influenced by *Gropius, *Mies van der Rohe, *Mendelsohn and Bruno *Taut. After World War II he worked in collaboration with the engineer W. Frankl. R.'s first important building, the Post Office in the Quartiere Nomentano in Rome (1932), combined elements of *Rationalism and *Expressionism and of 'magical realism' and thus anticipated the crisis of the 'aesthetic of reason'. With the Palazzina in the Via di Villa Massimo in Rome (1937), R. adopted a decidedly rationalist position. Nonetheless, after 1945 he altered his position fundamentally: in

1946 he published, together with G. Carcaprina, that popularly, even pluralistically inclined *Manuale dell'architetto*, which was to leave such a strong imprint on Roman architecture of the immediate post-war years. In 1950 he directed, together with Lodovico Quaroni, a group of young architects, including Carlo *Aymonino and Mario Fiorentino, in the planning and execution of the INA-Casa in the Tiburtino quarter of Rome; with its irregular, 'spontaneous' structure and traditionalist buildings, this was to become an emblem of Italian neo-realism. At about the same time, 1950–4, he realized the Casa a Torre in the Viale Etiopia, Rome, an example of unequivocally urban and standardized architecture freed from the romantic nostalgia of the Tiburtino project.

R. later found himself increasingly isolated within the development of architectural ideas, not the least because of his stubborn refusal to follow an avant garde which seemed to him socially irrelevant. He concentrated on refining his own architectural language, which was characterized by correctness of construction, emphasis on 'poor' materials, extremely coarse (but by no means anti-technological) handwork, and physical and psychological functionality. This introverted approach was very clearly evident in small buildings such as the Kindergartens for the Canton Vesco neighbourhood at Ivrea (1960) and at Poggibonsi (1960–1) or the Casa Lina in Terni (1966). VML

□ Canella, Guido, and Rossi, Aldo, 'Architetti italiani: M. Ridolfi', *Comunità* (Milan), no. 41 (1956); Cellini, F., D'Amato, C., and Valeriani, E., *L'Architettura di Ridolfi e Frankl*, Rome 1979.

Riemerschmid, Richard, b. Munich 1868, d. Munich 1957. After studying painting, he turned first, under the influence of William *Morris and the *Arts and Crafts movement, to designing furniture, rugs, fabrics and glass, and finally to architecture *c.* 1900. He was a founding member of the Munich Vereinigten Werkstätten für Kunst and Handwerk (Associated workshops for art and handicraft) in 1897, and of the *Deutscher Werkbund, of which he was chairman, 1920–6. He was Director of the Kunstgewerbeschule, Munich, 1912–24, and from 1926 of the Werkschulen in Cologne. His most important work is the Chamber Theatre in the Munich Schauspielhaus (1901, with Max Littmann). R. also drew up the plans for the Garden City of Hellerau, near Dresden (begun 1909), where he designed the workshops (1910). These bear witness to a tendency towards a classically inspired style. AM

Rietveld, Gerrit (Thomas), b. Utrecht 1888, d. Utrecht 1964. After apprenticeship from 1899 to 1906 in his father's joinery shop and work as a draughtsman in a jewellery studio, R. opened his own cabinet-making business in Utrecht in 1911. In 1918, chiefly through the agency of Robert van't Hoff, he came into contact with the founders of De *Stijl, of which movement he remained a member until 1931, and which inspired him in furniture designs which were conceived primarily as spatial compositions (Red-Blue armchair, 1918; Berlin armchair, 1923).

In 1921 he began a collaboration with the interior decorator Truus Schröder-Schräder, with whom he built the Rietveld-Schröder House in Utrecht in 1924, the programmatic architectural expression of De Stijl. Here the use of a lightweight steel skeleton made possible a flexible, continuous interior space without enclosed rooms, and even the boundaries between inner and outer space are minimized. Also with Truus Schröder-Schräder, he built terrace houses in the Erasmuslaan in Utrecht (1934), and the Vreeburg Cinema, Utrecht (1936). R.'s post-World War II designs include: the Netherlands Pavilion at the Venice Biennale (1954); the sculpture pavilion in the Sonsbeek Park in Arnhem (1954, re-erected at Otterlo, 1965); and

Rietveld. Rietveld-Schröder House, Utrecht (with Truus Schröder-Schräder; 1924)

the Rijksmuseum Vincent van Gogh, Amsterdam (1963–72, with J. van Dillen and J. van Tricht). JJV/GHa

☐ Brown, Theodore M. *The Work of Gerrit Rietveld, Architect*, Cambridge and Utrecht 1958; Buffinga, A., *Gerrit Thomas Rietveld*, Amsterdam 1971; Baroni, D., *The Furniture of Gerrit T. Rietveld*, Woodbury, N.Y. 1978.

Ring, Der (The Ring). Berlin architectural association founded 1923–4 as 'Zehnerring' (Ring of Ten), in order to represent the interests of the *Neues Bauen. The group was renamed 'Der Ring' in 1926 and expanded; its members were Otto *Bartning, Walter Curt Behrendt, Peter *Behrens, Richard Döcker, Walter *Gropius, Hugo *Haring (general secretary of the association), Otto *Haesler, Ludwig *Hilberseimer, Artur Korn, Carl Krayl, Hans *Luckhardt, Wassili *Luckhardt, Ernst *May, Erich *Mendelsohn, Adolf Meyer, Ludwig *Mies van der Rohe, Bernhard Pankok, Hans *Poelzig, Adolf Rading, Hans *Scharoun, Walter Schilbach, Karl Schneider, Hans Soeder, Bruno *Taut, Max *Taut, Heinrich *Tessenow and Martin *Wagner. The common goal was 'to serve the international movement which is striving with conscious rejection of past-enshrined forms to solve the building problems of our time with the means of contemporary technology, and to prepare the ground for the new architecture of the new scientific and social epoque.' When the involvement of the modernist core of the Ring – those associated with Mies van der Rohe in the construction of the Weißenhofsiedlung in Stuttgart (1927) – gave rise to a dispute with Paul *Bonatz and Paul Schmitthenner, these two representatives of the 'Stuttgart School' decided to launch a traditionally oriented counter-group, the *'Block'. The Ring was disbanded in 1933 under the political pressure of National Socialism. VML

☐ Lane, Barbara Miller, *Architecture and Politics in Germany, 1918–1945*, Cambridge, Mass. 1968.

Roche, (Eamonn) Kevin, b. Dublin 1922. After studying at the National University of Ireland in Dublin, he entered the offices of Michael Scott and Partners in Dublin and then that of Maxwell *Fry and Jane *Drew in London, before going to the *USA in 1948. He entered Eero *Saarinen's office in 1951, where he became head partner responsible for design in 1954.

After Saarinen died in 1961, R. took over the office together with John *Dinkeloo and transferred its operations from Bloomfield Hills and Birmingham, Michigan, to Hamden, Conn. From 1966 until Dinkeloo's death in 1981, the firm operated under the name Kevin Roche John Dinkeloo and Associates; it then became Kevin Roche and Associates. In their buildings Roche and Dinkeloo combined the abstract

Roche. Oakland Museum, Oakland, Cal. (Kevin Roche John Dinkeloo and Associates; 1961–8)

Roche. Ford Foundation Building, New York (Kevin Roche John Dinkeloo and Associates; 1963–8)

geometry of *Mies van der Rohe with powerful structural expression and a pronounced corporeality developed from the specific situation. Their Oakland Museum in Oakland, Cal. (1961–8), one of their first works after taking over Saarinen's office, brought them considerable attention, not only for its success as a museum but also on account of their extremely skilful creation of public space. Even more highly acclaimed was the Ford Foundation Building in New York (1963–8), with its greenhouse-like interior court opening up new perspectives for the penetration of interior and exterior space. Among the most important of Roche and Dinkeloo's other works are: the headquarters of the Knights of Columbus (1965–9) in New Haven, Conn.; the extension of the Metropolitan Museum of Art in New York (1967–78); the administration building of the Cummins Engine Company in Columbus, Ind. (1972–9); and the project for the Fiat company headquarters, Turin (1973). AM

□ Drew, Philip, *The Third Generation: the changing meaning of architecture*, New York 1972; Cook, J. W., and Klotz, H., *Conversations with Architects*, New York 1973; Futagawa, Yukio (ed.), *Kevin Roche John Dinkeloo and Associates, 1962–1975*, Tokyo. Fribourg and Stuttgart 1975.

Rogers, Ernesto Nathan, b. Trieste 1909, d. Gardone, Italy 1969. Studied at the Politecnico in Milan, where he himself taught from 1962 (from 1964 as a professor). A founding member in 1932 in Milan of the office of *BBPR, he distinguished himself not only as a practising architect, but also as an architectural publicist.

Rogers, Richard. Lloyds Building, London (1979–84)

He was a co-editor of *Quadrante*, 1933–6, and edited *Domus*, 1946–7; he also edited *Casabella-continuità*, 1953–64, and under his direction it became one of the most important architectural journals in Europe. AM

□ Rogers, E. N., *Esperienze dell'architettura*, Turin 1958; ——, *Editoriali de architettura*, Turin 1968.

Rogers, Richard, b. Florence 1933 (of British parents). Educated at the Architectural Association School in London and at Yale University, his first experiments in architecture were made as a member of Team 4 (comprising also Norman *Foster, Wendy Foster and Su Rogers). The Reliance Controls Ltd Factory at Swindon (1967) became well known as an example of industrial architecture which was both a neat package and a structural tour-de-force. The use of external diagonal braces was the main characteristic of the latter aspect, and it may well be attributed to Rogers, since after splitting with Foster (who has concentrated on the neat package), R. has become increasingly devoted to the architecture produced by structural tours-de-force. Of these the Centre National d'Art et de Culture Georges Pompidou in Paris (1971–7, with Renzo *Piano) is the most famous. The designs for Lloyds in the City of London and that for Inmos at Newport, South Wales, both continue to gain their principal effect from the display of structure and service elements on the exterior. R. (like Foster) has therefore become a principal proponent of a 'true' functionalist architecture (*Functionalism), going beyond Louis *Kahn in the analysis of form and mechanism, in an attempt to eliminate the arbitrary and wilful character of façade-making. RM

□ 'Richard Rogers: Interview with Dennis Sharp', *Building* (London), April 1979; *Richard Rogers and Partners. An Architectural Monograph*, London 1983.

Rossi, Aldo, b. Milan 1931. Studied at the Politecnico in Milan; diploma 1959. He worked for *Casabella-continuità*, 1959–64, and was professor at the Milan Politecnico, 1969–72; he was a guest professor at the Eidgenössische Technische Hochschule at Zurich, 1972–4. Since 1974 he has again been professor in Milan and has also taught at the Istituto Universitario di Architettura in Venice since 1976.

The founder and principal exponent of *Rational architecture, R. developed his own architectural position in the circles around Ernesto Nathan *Rogers. His first designs dating from 1960 display simultaneously the influence of the Modern Movement of the 1920s and that of the Novecento Italiano, and combine the classicist visions of an Etienne-Louis Boullée with the rationally determined rigorism of a *Loos. The 1965 project (in part realized) for the Town Hall Square in Segrate recalls Giorgio de Chirico's 'Pittura metafisica', with its extremely sparse fountains of elementary geometrical shapes, its broad steps and herm-like column stumps. The same metaphysical atmosphere pervades the four-storey block of flats of ivory-coloured stuccoed reinforced concrete which R. built (1970–3) as part of the Gallaratese 2 residential complex, realized under the direction of Carlo *Aymonino in Milan's Monte Amiata housing estate. The narrow building, at one point pierced entirely, is freed from the ground so that a continuous colonnade is established on two levels from one to two storeys in height. The formal language is radically ascetic in its reduction to a few typical elements. It is derived from a critical-historical involvement with traditional urban architecture which, R. feels, contains the elementary rules that determine all architecture – from the single dwelling to large-scale planning. R. himself explains: 'In my house designs, I refer to the basic types of living which the architecture of the city has formed through a long process. On the basis of this analogy every corridor is a street, every court a city square, and a building reproduces the places of the city.' In 1971 he designed, in collaboration with Gianni Braghieri, the project for the new San Cataldo cemetery in Modena, an axial, complex composition formed of repetitive passageways and monumental geometries; the project was redesigned in 1973 and 1976, and construction finally began in 1980. Meanwhile, he had designed the school in Falagnano Olana (1972) and a project for a house in Borgo Ticino (1973). For the 'Prima mostra internazionale di architettura' at the 1980 Venice Biennale, R. created the 'Teatro del mondo', a small floating theatre of steel and wood, which recalls the 16th-century tradition of ephemeral architecture.

Rossi. San Cataldo cemetery, Modena (with Gianni Braghieri; 1971–6; 1980–5)

He underpins his work as an architect with a noteworthy theory, the principles of which he formulated in 1966 in *L'Architettura della città*. That so few of his projects have been realized is due largely to their subversive power and their uncompromising nature. There is hardly an architect in the late 20th century who has been so controversial and the subject of such intensive discussion. VML

□ Rossi, Aldo, *L'architettura della città*, Padua 1966 (English ed.: *The Architecture of the City*, Cambridge, Mass. 1982); ——, *Scritti scelti sull'architettura e la città*, Milan 1975; ——, *A Scientific Autobiography*, Cambridge, Mass. 1981 (paperback ed. 1984); 'Aldo Rossi', *Architecture and Urbanism* (Tokyo), no. 65 (1976); Moschini, Francesco (ed.), *Aldo Rossi: projects and drawings, 1962–1979*, New York 1979; Braghieri, Gianni, *Aldo Rossi*, Bologna and Barcelona 1981; Institute for Architecture and Urban Studies, New York, *Aldo Rossi in America 1976 to 1979* (exhibition catalogue), New York 1979.

Rudolph, Paul, b. Elkton, Kentucky, 1918. Studied at the Alabama Polytechnic Institute in Auburn and under *Gropius and *Breuer at Harvard University. In 1948 he entered into partnership with Ralph Twitchell in Sarasota, Fla. In 1952 he opened his own office, and was Dean of the Yale School of Architecture in New Haven, Conn., 1958–62. Since 1965 he has lived in New York.

R.'s early buildings in Florida, including the Healy Guest House (1948–9) and the Hook House (1951–2) in Sarasota, as well as the Walker Guest House (1952–3) on Sanibel Island and the somewhat later Riverview High School in Sarasota (1957–8) all bear witness to the formal austerity of the *Bauhaus, although

Rudolph. Art and Architecture Building, Yale University, New Haven, Conn. (1958–64)

already softened by an unorthodox delight in constructive experimentation. The Mary Cooper Jewett Arts Center, Wellesley College, Wellesley, Mass. (1955–8), is the first announcement of R.'s turning towards a 'new freedom' in its details, which harmonize with the surrounding collegiate neo-Gothic architecture and especially with its expressively composed stair hall. This 'new freedom' which left modernism behind was a trend that influenced numerous architects working in America at the time, including *Breuer, *Johnson, and Eero *Saarinen.

A definitive turning to an architecture of form for form's sake in manifested most clearly in the Sarasota High School in Florida (1958–9), as well as the Art and Architecture Building at Yale University, New Haven (1958–64), a concrete 'sculpture' which evokes reminiscences of *Wright's Larkin Building in Buffalo, N.Y. (1904–5), and forms a provocative contrast to its anonymous surroundings. The Milam House at Jacksonville, Fla. (1960–2), recalls De *Stijl in the framework of its façade overlooking the beach. The Parking Garage on Temple Street in New Haven (1959–63) stands apart; here R. succeeded – as hardly anywhere else – in achieving an intimate unity of function, construction, and sculptural expression. The Married Students' Residence Complex at Yale University (1960–1) displays marked regionalist tendencies, surprising in R.'s work. The combination of brick walls and continuous concrete bands recalls *Le Corbusier's Maisons Jaoul at Neuilly-sur-Seine (1952–6), as well as *Stirling and Gowan's houses at Ham Common (1955–8), while the intimate arrangement of forms, the shadowed, terraced complex, harmonizes entirely with the topographical conditions.

After the Yale Art and Architecture Building R.'s most ambitious building is certainly the State Service Center in the Government Center of Boston (1962, 1967–72), where terraced flat wings and a strongly articulated tower are arranged around a public square in a composition which pays homage to the Campio in Siena.

Since the mid-1970s R. has distinguished himself increasingly in urban planning work, such as the projects for Stafford Harbor, Va., a resort on the Potomac River (1966), in which the construction accentuates the rolling landscape, and for the Graphic Arts Center in New York (1967), which is terraced over the Hudson as a series of supporting and enclosing towers on which are suspended separate three-dimensional elements. AM

☐ Moholy-Nagy, Sibyl, *Introduction to the Architecture of Paul Rudolph*, New York 1970;

Rudolph. Graphic Arts Center, New York (project, 1967)

Spade, Rupert, *Paul Rudolph*, London and New York 1971; 'Paul Rudolph', *Architecture and Urbanism* (special number), Tokyo, July 1977.

Russia. Russian architecture of the period around 1900 was characterized by a style allied to the widespread international *Art Nouveau, and known in Russia as 'modern style'. This modern style had three principal features: the reworking of elements from the Russian vernacular; the stylization of motifs from nature; and the earliest experiments in Russia with the new technology of steel-frame construction, mostly in conjunction with brick. The exponents of this style conceived of themselves as the opponents of the *eclecticism of the late 19th century. In general they upheld a common ideal in the search for the new and beautiful form, especially in façade composition. In this two principal types of decoration were introduced: on the one hand, a largely sculptural treatment of the essential structural elements and, on the other, a largely graphic incorporation of painting or majolica panels with no functional rationale. Further characteristics of 'modern style' design were functionally appropriate ground-plans, since buildings were now planned from the inside out, as well as a break with the strict axiality which had predominated in earlier styles. Fedor Osipovich Shekhtel (1859–1926) was the best-known architect working in this style. The majority of buildings of this period, however, took as their prototypes old Russian architecture, that is the native architectural tradition which had been ousted by the introduction of *neo-classicism at the end of the 18th century. The most striking example of this was the Kazan Railway Station in Moscow (1913–41) by Alexei V. Shchusev (1873–1949) – a miniature city within the city, having as its principal accent a tower modelled on one of the towers of the citadel at Kazan.

Although the 'modern style' remained aloof from eclecticism, there were affinities between the two approaches, in their emphasis on decoration and in their propensity for stylization and lyrical interpretation. In opposition to it, a new variant of Russian neo-classicism developed *c.* 1910; this viewed the 'modern style' as merely the logical consequence of eclecticism. The fundamentally rational position of neo-classicism in the aesthetic expression of constructive legitimacy, its tendency to clarify, its handsomeness, and its moderate decoration made it the ideal link between cultural heritage and modern building tasks. The key to understanding the subsequent academic architecture of Soviet Russia lies in the period between the abortive revolution of 1905 and the Bolshevik Revolution of October 1917. The centre of the new neo-classicist movement was St Petersburg, a city whose appearance had become firmly established in the earlier neo-classical period, *c.* 1800. Interest in the city's own historical form was aroused by the 200th anniversary of the foundation of St Petersburg, celebrated in 1903, and the first highpoint came in 1911 with the 'Exhibition of the History of Architecture and the Arts and Crafts' held in the St Petersburg Academy of Fine Arts, itself an early neo-classical building. Ivan Fomin, who designed the exhibition, was – like most of the architects who then set the tone in Russia – a graduate of the architectural faculty of the

Russia. Building for the newspaper *Utro Rossii*, Moscow (1907), by Fedor O. Shekhtel

Academy. Ivan Zholtovsky, who by this time was already working in Moscow and who was a lifelong admirer and interpreter of Italian Renaissance architecture, had also studied there. Many of the young graduates of the St Petersburg Academy saw themselves as the true renewers of Russian architecture in the name of neo-classicism; but World War I destroyed all hopes for a new flowering of that architecture for which St Petersburg seemed to have been waiting for decades.

After the October Revolution all art schools in Russia were turned into 'Free State Art Workshops' (the VKHUTEMAS, which was comparable to the *Bauhaus in Germany, was launched in Moscow in 1920). Although new construction was out of the question at this time, numerous architectural competitions were held. In the fine arts proponents of *Constructivism and *Suprematism had indeed come to the fore, but architecture remained dominated by the academicians. Thus for example, Zholtovsky was appointed director of the architecture section within NARKOMPROS (People's Commissariat for Architectural Science) and Shchusev was awarded the commission for reconstructing the new capital city, Moscow ('New Moscow'). In Petrograd, the former St Petersburg, all planning was co-ordinated by the Director of the Municipal Museum, Lev Ilin, a graduate of the Academy of Fine Arts; the chief considerations were the preservation of the neo-classical basis of the old capital and the restoration of areas destroyed during revolutionary skirmishes. Thus, the revolutionary architecture of Soviet Russia, if one takes that to mean the architecture which came out of the Revolution itself, was an academic architecture. Fomin began the development of his 'red Doric' in the competition for the Palace of the Workers (1919), a large cultural and sports centre in Petrograd, and he continued this style in the 1920s. Moreover, in this early post-revolutionary phase the design of communal housing, industrial complexes and public institutions was oriented towards historical prototypes. An exception to this was to be found in the fantastic architectural models produced by the SCHIVSKULPTARCH group (Group for the synthesis of painting, sculpture and architecture) formed around the architect Nikolai A. Ladovsky in Moscow.

It was only during the period of the 'New Economic Policy' (1921–7), in which the economy gradually became stabilized, that a modern Soviet architecture was first formulated. In conjunction with the competition for the Palace of Labour in Moscow (1923), which was never to be realized, the brothers Alexander, Leonid, and Victor Vesnin developed a project for a building in reinforced concrete. Konstantin *Melnikov's Soviet Pavilion at the 'Exposition internationale des arts décoratifs et industriels modernes' in Paris in 1925 gave the impression abroad that his bold design was representative of Soviet architecture in general. In fact its influence began to spread only after 1925 and then for a short period in which it determined the building styles of the country. Even so, this period was characterized by numerous opposing factions. The OSA (Association of Contemporary Architects) brought the Constructivists together under Alexander Vesnin and Moisei Ginzburg, who sought a functional justification in building. The ASNOVA (Union of Modern Architects), under Janos Matza and Nikolai Ladovsky, was most concerned with the effects of architectural form on the human psyche; the MAO (Moscow Architecture Society), under Leonid Vesnin and Alexei Shchusev, was a group of modernist and academic architects; and finally the OACH (Society of Artist-Architects), whose members were the academicians

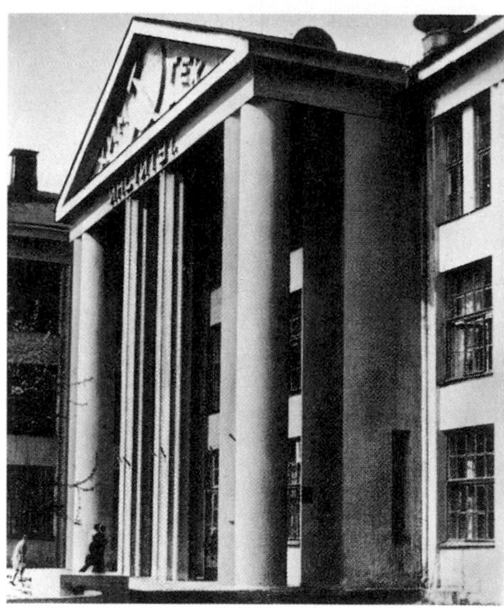

Russia. Polytechnic Institute, Ivanovo-Vosnessensk (1927–32), by Ivan Fomin

of the Academy of Fine Arts in Leningrad (the former Petrograd and St Petersburg) under Leonti Benua. In 1929 there was formed yet another group, VOPRA (Syndicate of Unions of Proletarian Architects), led by Janos Matza and Karo Alabjan; this group spoke out strongly against all other associations and finally contributed to their dissolution in 1932, when they were replaced by a single Union of Architects of the USSR under the direction of Alabjan, Ginzburg, Zholtovsky, Ladovsky and others.

The period of the first Five-Year Plan (1928–32) coincides with the heyday of these various factions in modern architecture, which was dominated by the Constructivists. In urban planning of the period two concepts vied with one another: on the one hand, the Urbanists proposed the rearrangement of all cities into units of 50,000 inhabitants each; on the other hand, the Disurbanists proposed the dissolution of the cities, which would be replaced by long, interconnected linear settlements. The leading Urbanists were L. Sabsovich and the Vesnin brothers; the major exponents of Disurbanization were M. Okhitovich, Ginzburg and Ivan *Leonidov. The designs advocated by both groups made little practical sense in this stormy phase of industrialization, with its urgent demands for the creation of new industrial districts, and in 1930 the pragmatic Ernst *May and his team in Frankfurt am Main were called to Moscow.

In Moscow, the centre of modern architecture, the 1928 competition for the Lenin State Library had already brought the Leningrad academicians Vladimir Gelfreikh and Vladimir A. Shehuko into rivalry with the Vesnin brothers. In the competition for the Palace of the Soviets in Moscow, which extended from 1930 to 1934, workers' designs were also submitted which had nothing to do with Constructivist design and which in their monumentality and symbolic content had a decisive effect on architecture in the ensuing years. From 1930 onwards, the question of how buildings should look in a socialist society came to be voiced more and more strongly in architectural circles. Soon there was a widespread feeling that a primary fulfilment of function requirements was not enough; rather, emotive qualities had equally to be taken into account. The complete break with the architectural values of the past was interpreted as a typical symptom of the inevitable demise of a now obsolete bourgeois culture.

The three principal dictates of socialist realism – the typical, the spirit of the party, and the spirit of the people – were not readily translated from the realms of literature and the fine arts to that of architecture. In broad terms, it meant time and again for architecture a socialist content and a nationalist form, brought to realization by the use of the newest building techniques. At the first General Congress of the Union of Soviet Architects in 1937 all architects were enjoined in this regard to take account of local particularities in each building design, to study the riches of vernacular art, as well as to embrace the classical qualities of clarity and simplicity in composition. At the congress criticisms were voiced once again concerning the poverty of Constructivist architecture and in the same context the growing eclecticism in Soviet architecture was deplored. A synthesis of the arts was sought, in which architects, painters and sculptors would work together on each project. At the same time, new rationalized building methods were developed, including prefabrication. The Moscow Academy of Architecture was founded in 1933 and within it, in 1935, a section devoted to monumental painting. In 1935 the first general plan for Moscow was approved; this, in its adherence to the ring-form structure of the city, took up once again ideas from the 'New Moscow' project of the early 1920s. The largest undertakings of the general plan were the Moscow

Russia. Underground station (Mayakovskaya), Moscow (1938), by Alexander Dushkin

Russia. Railway station in Pushkin (1950–2) by Yevgeni Levinson and Igor Fomin

Russia. Apartment building on Smolensk Square, Moscow (1947–9), by Ivan Zholtovsky

underground system and the Moscow-Volga Canal. In the individual Soviet republics architects sought to unite the use of traditional forms and ornament with new materials; all these various attempts were illustrated in one place in the form of pavilions at the Moscow Agricultural Exhibition of 1939. With the outbreak of war all building operations were halted in threatened areas, with the exception of the Moscow underground; the Moscow workshops were dissolved and the architects were evacuated to the Asian regions of the Soviet Union.

Beginning in 1943, the first plans for the reconstruction of destroyed cities were prepared; in these it was generally proposed to restore the original aspects of the cities, and to harmonize new buildings – especially those in old Russian towns – with the existing urban fabric, both in scale and in external appearance. In the large cities, such as Kiev, monumental axial avenues were to be laid out. In Moscow work on the Palace of the Soviets was not resumed after the war, but rather in 1947, on the occasion of the 800th anniversary of the city's foundation, eight skyscrapers were projected, of which seven were built in the following years. Such tower accents recurred on a smaller scale in most Soviet cities, with the exception of Leningrad where the distant view of the old buildings was carefully preserved.

Post-war Soviet architecture set out to reflect, in its emotional content, the victory over the Fascist aggressors. Late in 1954, at an architectural congress in Moscow, Nikita S. Khruschchev criticized high building costs and the search for decoration. In 1955 the Party Congress decided that architectural practices of past years were to be branded as a distortion of the cultural heritage and that the comprehensive industrialization and mechanization of

Russia. Sport Palace, Tbilisi (1960–2), by V. Meshishvili and Y. Kazradze

building operations were to be treated as a national priority. Scientific research was to replace traditional architectural composition. The second competition for the Palace of the Soviets (1957–9) reflected clearly both this rejection of academic styles and the shift towards modern architecture; once again, however, the project never came to fruition. In 1958 the Soviet Union chose to be represented at the Brussels World's Fair by a pavilion of glass and steel. In the next two decades, standardization in housing, using a variety of methods, dominated the scene. In the 1970s architects resumed their intense collaboration with artists and at the same time architectural details of the 1930s made a fresh appearance. In the various Soviet republics, local architectural approaches were developed from the expressive means of national traditions. CB

□ Kopp, Anatole, *Town and Revolution*, New York 1970; Lissitzky, El, *Russia: an architecture for world revolution*, Cambridge, Mass. 1970; Vogt, Adolf Max, *Russische und französische Revolutionsarchitektur. 1917/1789*, Cologne 1974; Senkevitch, A., *Soviet Architecture 1917–1962; a biographical guide to source material*, Charlottesville, Va. 1974; DeMichelis, M., and Pasini, E., *La città sovietica 1925–1937*, Venice 1976; Cohen, J.-L., DeMichelis, M., and Tafuri, M., *URSS 1917–1978: La città, l'architettura. La ville, l'architecture*, Rome and Paris 1979; Borngräber, C., *Architettura accademica in URSS 1919–1959*, Milan 1984.

S

Saarinen, Eero, b. Kirkkonummi, Finland 1910, d. Ann Arbor, Michigan 1961. The son of Eliel *Saarinen, he moved to the *USA in 1923 with his parents. He studied sculpture at the Académie de la Grande Chaumière in Paris, 1929–30, and architecture at Yale University in New Haven, Conn., 1930–4. After several trips to Europe he entered his father's office in Ann Arbor, Mich., in 1937 (1941–7 in partnership with his father and J. Robert Swanson, from 1947 with his father alone). From 1950 he directed his own office in Birmingham, Mich., under the name Eero Saarinen and Associates.

Eero Saarinen, whose first works were done *c.* 1938 in collaboration with his father, first won individual attention in 1948 with his competition design for the Jefferson National Expansion Memorial near St Louis. The elegant parabolic arch, 192 m (625 ft) high, drew

Saarinen, Eero and Eliel. General Motors Technical Center, Warren, Mich. (1948–56)

directly on an unrealized project by Adalberto *Libera for the entrance to the 'Esposizione Universale di Roma' (EUR) of 1942, and was finally built in 1963 as 'Gateway Arch'. Together with his father and the architectural firm Smith, Hinchman and Gryllis, he built the General Motors Technical Center in Warren, Mich., a composition of rectangular steel-and-glass buildings reminiscent of *Mies van der Rohe's Illinois Institute of Technology in Chicago (1940 ff.), but harmoniously arranged around a central artificial lake.

However, this geometrical and technological purism was but an episode in S.'s development, which formed the prelude to an *eclecticism as experimental as it was manneristic. Like Philip *Johnson or Paul *Rudolph, S. turned to a bewildering stylistic pluralism, whose richness of individual sculptural forms goes back to his early interest in sculpture. The sculptural concrete shell of the Kresge Auditorium and the romantic masonry cylinder of the Chapel at the Massachusetts Institute of Technology in Cambridge were built in 1953–5. In 1955–60 he collaborated with the architectural group Yorke, Rosenberg and Mardall on the monumental and academic United States Embassy in London. The organically curved roof structure of the David S. Ingalls Ice Hockey Rink of Yale University in New Haven, Conn., was realized in 1956–8, and the TWA Terminal Building at Idewild (today JFK International) Airport, with its strongly sculptural, symbolic-allegorical features, was built 1956–62. The technologically outspoken John Deere & Co. Administration Center in Moline, Ill., was built 1957–63. Finally, in 1958–63, came the elegant, expressive Terminal Building of Dulles International Airport, near Washington, D.C.

This continual striving for new forms, unhampered by ideological convictions, yielded a series of highly subjective creations, for the most part dramatically staged and not infrequently displaying S.'s technical virtuosity; the heterogeneity of his work defies any categorization. This is equally true of his work in product design (e.g. the plywood chair of 1940, in conjunction with Charles *Eames). An uninterrupted flirtation with the unusual and the spectacular was not conducive to forming a school. Nonetheless, such noteworthy architects as *Pelli, *Roche and *Dinkeloo all had their start in S.'s office. VML

☐ Temko, Allan, *Eero Saarinen*, New York and London 1962; Spade, Rupert, *Eero*

Saarinen, Eero TWA Terminal Building, John F. Kennedy Airport, New York (Eero Saarinen and Associates; 1956–62)

Saarinen, London and New York 1971; Kuhner, Robert A., *Eero Saarinen: His Life and Work*, Monticello, Ill. 1975.

Saarinen, (Gottlieb) Eliel, b. Rantasalmi, Finland 1873, d. Bloomfield Hills, Mich. 1950. In Helsinki he studied painting and architecture simultaneously, 1893–7, at the University and the Polytechnic, respectively. He was active in independent practice from 1896 to 1923 (1896–1905 in partnership with Herman Gesellius and Armas Lindgren, 1905–7 with Gesellius only). In 1923 he emigrated to the *USA, where he had his own office in Evanston, Ill., 1923–4, and from 1924 in Ann Arbor, Mich. (1937–41 in collaboration with his son Eero *Saarinen; he and his son were joined by J. Robert Swanson in partnership, 1941–7, after which he again practised with his son alone). From 1924 he taught at the Architecture School of the University of Michigan at Ann Arbor, and was its Director, 1925–32, and President, 1932–50. From 1948 he was also Director of the Graduate Department of Architecture and Urban Planning at the Cranbrook Academy of Art in Bloomfield Hills.

Saarinen, Eliel, Hvitträsk Studio House, Kirkkonummi, near Helsinki (with Gesellius and Lindgren; 1902)

Saarinen, Eliel. Cranbrook School for Boys, Bloomfield Hills, Mich. (1926–30)

Shortly before the turn of the century, S. moved in the circle of young Finnish artists which included the composer Jean Sibelius, the painter Akseli Gallén-Kallela and the architects Herman Gesellius, Armas Lindgren and, somewhat apart, Lars Sonck. He distinguished himself in his earliest works in that National Romantic style which began to establish itself in *Finland as a 'patriotic' reaction against 'imperialist' *neo-classicism and drew notably on the legacy of the Gothic Revival, the *Arts and Crafts movement and the Neo-romanesque of H. H. Richardson. The Finnish Pavilion at the Paris Exposition Universelle of 1900, which S. designed in conjunction with Gesellius and Lindgren, employed a version of this style enriched by oriental motifs. The Hvitträsk Studio House at Kirkkonummi, near Helsinki (1902), also built in collaboration with Gesellius and Lindgren, continued – in its external appearance – in that tradition and developed a style with overtones of *Art Nouveau. The interior represented a new interpretation of Gallén-Kallela's own studio house in Ruovesi (1895), and was executed to a high standard of craftsmanship. This building marked Finland's entry into the field of experimentation in domestic design begun earlier by *Webb and *Shaw in England and continued at that time by *Hoffmann, *Mackintosh and *Wright; a specific sense of national identity was not, however, sacrificed.

Gesellius, Lindgren and Saarinen did not simply build Hvitträsk together, they also lived and worked there. This romantic idyll came to an abrupt end in 1904 when S.'s individually prepared design was awarded first prize in the Helsinki Central Station competition. His winning design would be altered several times before the building was finally erected in 1910–14. With its elegantly articulated masonry masses, its functional organization, its equally sensitive and expressive use of materials, and its streamlined detailing, this was to become a model of its type; its influence is clearly seen in, among others, the Stuttgart Central Station (1914–28) by Paul *Bonatz and Friedrich Eugen Scholer.

The urban scheme which S. drew up in 1910–15 for Munkkiniemi-Haaga, near Helsinki, was distinguished for its care, thoroughness and complexity. Evidence of his continuing involvement with urban problems, which he saw as being closely related to architecture, can be seen in his plans for Budapest, 1912; Canberra, 1912; and Greater Helsinki, 1917–18.

With his project – historically aware, but by no means historicist – for the *Chicago Tribune* Tower (1922), S. won second prize in an international competition which attracted worldwide attention, and thus became known in the USA. When George and Ellen Scripps Booth founded the Cranbrook Academy of Art in Bloomfield Hills, S. was appointed architect of the entire complex; he built the Cranbrook School for Boys, 1926–30, the Kingswood School for Girls, 1929–30, and the Institute of Science, 1931–3; the Museum and Library followed in 1940–3. In this task he collaborated with his wife, the sculptress and weaver Louise (Loja) Gesellius, as well as with the Swedish sculptor Carl Milles. He combined architecture and sculpture with the same enthusiasm that Wright had shown in his Prairie Houses, yet a new element at Cranbrook was the overriding urbanistic concept which gave rise to a whole that was one of the most organically and harmoniously designed complexes in all 20th-century architecture. The formal language evolved from a romantic picturesque *eclecticism into a dignified reductivism.

In his rich and varied œuvre S. never renounced his own romantic origins; their traces are even to be detected in the work he carried out after 1937 with his son Eero. Progressively, though without ever embracing the radicalism of the avant garde, S. became one of the most important advocates of the Positivist heritage of the 19th century, a heritage which he introduced independently into the architecture of the 20th. VML

☐ Saarinen, Eliel, *The Cranbrook Development*, Bloomfield Hills, Mich. 1931; ——, *Search for Form*, New York 1939; ——, *The City: Its Growth, Its Decay, Its Future*, New York 1943; Christ-Janer, Albert, *Eliel Saarinen*, Chicago, London and Toronto 1948; Hausen, Marika, 'Gesellius – Lindgren – Saarinen', *Arkkitehti* (Helsinki), no. 9, 1967.

Safdie, Moshe, b. Haifa 1938. Studied at McGill University in Montreal. He worked with van Ginkel and Associates in Montreal and with Louis *Kahn in Philadelphia before establishing his own practice in Montreal in 1964. In 1975 he became professor and Director of the Desert Architecture and Environment Department at Ben Gurion University in Beersheva, Israel; since 1978 he has been a professor at Harvard University. His first major work, the 'Habitat' at Montreal's Expo '67, brought him instant fame. Although far from being a pioneer work in the use of prefabricated concrete systems, it succeeded in dramatizing that approach, and in articulating, in appropriate architectural form, that assembly of 'building blocks' which *Gropius had adumbrated, in his own 'Baukasten im Großen', in a theoretical project of 1923. It also lifted the concept of the prefabricated concrete-box unit from a utilitarian technique to the level of emotive architecture. In his later work he went on consistently to use technology and geometry not only as a discipline, but as a means to transform pragmatic purposes to poetic ends, as can be seen especially in two projects in Jerusalem, the Yeshivat Porat Yosef Rabbinical College (1971–9) and the Mamilla project (1972). These reflect the cubic geometry of the country's indigenous architecture, but in S.'s hands they acquire a breadth of scale, if not of size, which

Safdie. 'Habitat', Expo '67, Montreal (1967)

transforms vernacular forms into a more monumental mould – a characteristic which is perhaps the principal heritage of his earlier association with Kahn. GHe

☐ Safdie, Moshe, *Beyond Habitat*, Cambridge, Mass. 1970; ——, *For Everyone a Garden*, Cambridge, Mass. 1974; Drew, Philip, *The Third Generation: the changing meaning of architecture*, New York 1972.

Salvisberg, Otto, b. Konz, near Berne 1882, d. Arosa 1940. After training at the Technikum in Biel and working under Friedrich von Thiersch and Karl Hocheder in Munich, as well as under Robert Curjel and Karl *Moser in Karlsruhe, S. went to Berlin in 1908 and was active there until the 1930s.

The expressionistically inclined Lindenhaus (1912–13), the picturesquely informal Winkler House (1912) and the emphatically regular

Salvisberg. The Lory-Spital, Berne (with O. Brechbühl; 1926–9)

Neutze House (also 1912) bear witness to a phase of stylistic searching. Around 1926 S. turned to the Modern Movement, to which he remained faithful, although with considerable reflection. He was responsible for several structures in the 'Uncle Tom' housing estate (1926–31), built under the direction of Bruno *Taut, and designed the balcony house over the Aroser Allee in the 'Weiße Stadt' (White City) in Berlin-Reinickendorf (1929–30). In 1930 he was offered a position at the Eidgenössische Technische Hochschule in Zurich. The Loryspital in Berne (1926–9, with O. Brechbühl), a horizontally layered building with expansive glass façade towards the south, received almost instant recognitition. The Institute Building of the University of Berne (1930, likewise with Brechbühl), a 180 m (590 ft) long complex with repetitive rows of fenestration, whose flat front is given rhythm by the bold projection of four curved auditoria, is exemplary of S.'s striving to suffuse pure functionalism with effective dramatization. FJ

☐ Wertheim, Paul (ed.), *Neuere Arbeiten von O. R. Salvisberg*, Berlin 1927; Salvisberg, O. R., *Zeitfragen der Architektur. Die ETH dem SIA zur Jahrhundertfeier*, Zurich 1937; 'Otto R. Salvisberg 1882–1940' *Werk. Archithese* (Niederteufen), October 1977, pp. 3–54.

Samonà, Giuseppe, b. Palermo 1898. Studied at the University of Palermo. From 1922 he was active as an architect in Messina, and since 1958 in Rome in collaboration with Giuseppina and Alberto Samonà. He was Director of the Istituto Universitario di Architettura in Venice, 1945–71. His work, for all its rigour, is not without its expressionistic and eclectic moments. Early on, it was oriented towards the diverse forms and the traditionalist craftsmanship of Frank Lloyd *Wright, without however denying its objective-functionalist principles. Whilst his Post Office building, built 1933–6 in the Quartiere Appio in Rome, was still entirely within the spirit of Italian *Rationalism, the influence of *organic architecture was already evident in his project of 1938–40 for a Villa at Baia, near Naples. The bold design proposed for the extension of the Parliament Building in Rome (1967) was at once a homage to *Wright, *Le Corbusier and Russian *Constructivism. In the head office of the Banco d'Italia in Padua (1968), one of S.'s most important works, respect for the place, historical awareness and artistic individuality are united in a highly distinctive manner. VML

☐ Lovero, Pasquale, *Giuseppe Samonà, L'unità architettura urbanistica. Scritti e progetti 1929–73*, Milan 1975; Aymonino, C., Ciucci, G., Co, F. dal, and Tafuri, M., *Giuseppe Samonà. Cinquant'anni di architettura* (exhibition catalogue), Rome 1975.

Sant'Elia. Study (1913)

Sant'Elia, Antonio, b. Como 1888, d. near Monfalcone 1916. In 1905 he received a diploma from the school of architecture in Como; from 1911 he studied at the Accademia di Brera in Milan and at the Scuola di Belle Arti in Bologna, where he received his diploma in 1912.

Strongly influenced by the Stile Liberty architects Raimondo *D'Aronco and Giuseppe *Sommaruga, as well as by the Viennese Secession group (and especially by J. M. *Olbrich), S. had begun his career in 1911 with a small villa in *Art Nouveau style near Como, built for the industrialist Romeo Longatti. In the years immediately afterwards he worked principally in Milan and took part, for instance, in the competition for the cemetery in Monza (1912) with an exotic-eclectic design. He first developed an independent style of his own during this period: as in the case of Adolf *Loos, this occurred under the influence of North American skyscraper cities, but whereas Loos – as a result of his trip to the *USA of nearly twenty years earlier – was indebted above all to the realistic and rationally determined aspects of this architectural culture, the young S. was fascinated more by the romantic aspect. In 1913 he began his grand project for the Città Nuova. He produced simplified perspective drawings and visionary sketches for a utopian metropolis of the future: terraced skyscrapers with exposed steel frames at the upper levels and detached lift shafts; grandiose circulation arteries, with lanes criss-crossing at various levels; slender bridges, of steel or concrete, to link the shafts, apartment blocks and roads; bold, monumental and abruptly truncated building volumes intended as abstract studies in form, without clearly stated functions. Several of these virtuoso drawings – in no way free from expressionistic moments and still betraying the influence of the Viennese school – were exhibited in February 1914 in the 'Prima mostra annuale della Federazione degli architetti italiani', organized in Milan by the Association of Lombard Architects. Several months later, also in Milan, a large selection of his drawings was shown in the first exhibition of the Nuove Tendenze group, a recently formed association which counted Mario *Chiattone and Marcello Nizzoli, as well as S., among its members. The catalogue contained a spirited declaration rejecting the past, honouring the new world of technology and proclaiming a revolutionary architecture; it was signed by S. Both the drawings and the text attracted much attention, notably that of Filippo Tommaso Marinetti, leader of the then five-year-old Futurist movement (*Futurism): shortly thereafter S. was recruited, without resistance, into the ranks of this activist group of artists, and Marinetti edited S.'s earlier declaration for publication in the periodical *Lacerba* as the manifesto 'L'Architettura futurista', his changes consisting principally of the insertion of the adjective 'futurist' at every possible juncture.

S. did not have much time to contemplate his relationship with Marinetti: with Italy's entry into the war in 1915 he found himself in the front line, and he was killed the following year. He left behind nearly 300 drawings of an uncommon visionary power. Little of this came to fruition, apart from a few buildings from his Liberty period and the memorial to the war dead in Como (this was designed, after one of S.'s own sketches, by Enrico Prampolini and completed in 1933 by Attilio and Giuseppe *Terragni). However, S.'s radical, and therefore largely isolated, images were essential in smoothing the way for *Rationalism. *Le Corbusier's 'Ville contemporaine' of 1922, for instance, would be unthinkable without the Città Nuova of 1913–14. In *Italy itself, S.'s work prepared the way for that mixture of classical and rational feeling, which led, on the one hand, to the Novecento Italiano and, on the other, to Terragni, in whom his ideas found their most virtuoso and independent interpreter. VML

☐ Argan, Giulio Carlo, 'Il pensiero critico di Antonio Sant'Elia', *L'Arte* (Rome), September 1930; Sartoris, Alberto, *Antonio Sant'Elia*, Milan 1930; Dottori, Gherardo, *Sant'Elia e la nuova architettura*, Rome 1933; Mariani, Leonardo, 'Disegni inediti di Sant'Elia', *L'Architettura* (Rome), July/August 1955 and January/February 1956; Apollonio, Umbro, *Antonio Sant'Elia*, Milan 1958; Caramel, L., and Longatti, A., *Antonio Sant'Elia* (exhibition catalogue), Como 1962; Badaloni, Pier Giorgio, *Il futurismo: Antonio Sant'Elia e la nuova dimensione umana*, Rome 1970.

Sauvage, (Frédéric) Henri, b. Rouen 1873, d. Paris 1932. Studied at the *Ecole des Beaux-Arts in Paris. He worked in Paris in partnership with Charles Sarazin, 1898–1912, and from 1919 he ran his own office. In 1928 he taught at the Ecole des Arts Décoratifs in Paris, and then, 1929–31, at the Ecole des Beaux-Arts. After beginning in *Art Nouveau style – his Villa Majorelle in Nancy (1898) is considered one of the most important works of the 'École de Nancy' – S. later evolved into one of the principal exponents of the early Modern Movement in *France. In 1903 he and Sarazin founded the Société Anonyme de Logements Hygiéniques à Bon Marché, for which S. subsequently realized numerous buildings, models of their kind in terms of living standards in multiple dwellings. These included the apartment blocks in the Rue Vavin (1912) and the Rue des Amiraux (1922), both in Paris, where he developed the idea of progressively stepped-back terraces, which he had first sketched as early as 1909. The Magasins Decré in Nantes (1931), destroyed during World War II, bore witness in its open display of a steel skeleton and

Sauvage. Apartment building in the Rue Vavin, Paris (1912)

its complete transparency and eschewal of all ornament, to a shift in Sauvage's late work to a more radical Modern Movement approach. AM
☐ *Henri Sauvage. 1873–1932*, Brussels 1978; Delorme, Jean Claude, and Chair, Philippe, *L'Ecole de Paris. 10 architectes et leurs immeubles. 1905–1937*, Paris 1981, pp. 41–60.

Scarpa, Carlo, b. Venice 1906, d. Tokyo 1978. Studied at the Accademia di Belle Arti in Venice, in which city he practised as an independent architect from 1927. He was Director of the Istituto Universitario di Architettura in Venice, 1972–8.

S., who remained indebted to the Gothic-Byzantine tradition of his native city throughout his career, was equally influenced by Frank Lloyd *Wright and the De *Stijl movement. In addition, he never denied his deep spiritual connection with *Art Nouveau and especially with *Olbrich and *Mackintosh. His first work in the late 1920s and early 1930s consisted of elegant interiors and exhibition installations. Major recognition came first in 1953–4 with the renovation of the Galleria Nazionale della Sicilia in the Palazzo Abbatellis in Palermo, which is one in a series of museum restorations which were as sensitive as they were creative: Accademia, Venice (1952); Museo Correr, Venice (1953–60); six rooms in the Uffizi, Florence (1956; in conjunction with Ignazio *Gardella and Giovanni *Michelucci); the annexe to the neo-classical Gipsoteca Canoviana at Possegno, near Treviso (1956–7); Galleria Querini Stampalia, Venice (1961–3); and finally and most noteworthy, the commission for the interior design of the Museo Castelvecchio, Verona (1964). In these works, S.'s refined inventive power unfurls itself in dramatic settings, bold material juxtapositions, and exquisite, mannered and over-emphasized details. Thus the dialogue between old and new is founded as much on clear legible contrasts as it is on empathetic borrowing and transitions.

Likewise in S.'s designs for new buildings, his sure sense of scale, his preference for noble materials and refined decoration, as well as his commanding precision, are given full expression. The Villa Zoppàs in Conegliano was built in 1948; the Olivetti Store in Venice of 1957–8 is a sensuously precious spatial composition around a monumental central pier. The Casa Veritti in Udine (1955–61) already displays openly S.'s preference for complex volumetric penetrations which reached a highpoint in 1961 in the Padiglione del Veneto at the 'Italia '61' exhibition in Turin: a chamfered interior is inscribed within the perfect square of the ground-plan, within which curved elements are embedded. The Brion cemetery at San Vito d'Altivole, near Treviso, was built in 1970–2, a subtle composition of heterogeneous, formally luxurious, architectural *objets trouvés* as an aesthetic, sublimated celebration of death. In 1973–5 S. realized his last major work – the new building for the Banco Popolare di Verona.

Among his best-known (and most significant) exhibition designs, which in some cases produced new 'ways of seeing' the display, were the Paul Klee exhibition at the 1948 Venice Biennale (S. acted as an advisor there from 1941 on), the Piet Mondrian exhibition in the Galleria d'Arte Moderna in Rome in 1956, the Frank Lloyd Wright Exhibition at the XIIth Triennale in Milan (1960), and the Erich Mendelsohn Exhibition at the Venice Biennale of the same year.

Scarpa. Brion cemetery, San Vito d'Altivole, near Treviso (1970–2)

The importance of S.'s work for the architecture of the present century resides in his conservatism. In the 1950s and 1960s – a period in which technology and progress were generally in the forefront – he demonstrated in his quiet work a commitment to workmanship, a respect for the past and an understanding of architecture as a sculptural, integral art. His individualism did not foster a school, but such independent personalities as Bruno Morassutti and Gino *Valle were formed in his circle, and his work has evident noteworthy parallels with that of Louis *Kahn and Hans *Hollein. VML
□ Los, Sergio, *Carlo Scarpa – Architetto poeta*, Venice 1967; Brusatin, Manlio, 'Carlo Scarpa Architetto Veneziano', *Contraspazio* (Bari), nos. 3/4, 1972; Pozza, Neri (ed.), *Carlo Scarpa* (exhibition catalogue). Vicenza 1974; Kahn, Louis, and Cantacuzino, Sheban, *Carlo Scarpa* (exhibition catalogue), London 1974; Yokoyama, T., and Toyota, H., 'Carlo Scarpa', *Space Design* (Tokyo), June 1977; *Progressive Architecture*, 62 (1981), no. 5, entire issue; *Carlo Scarpa et le musée de Vérone* (exhibition catalogue), Institut Culturel Italien, Paris 1983.

Scharoun, Hans, b. Bremen 1893, d. Berlin 1972. Like Hugo *Häring, to whom he felt himself allied, S. advocated in both his architecture and his writings the idea of an 'organ-like building' (*organic architecture), which, in the spirit of new beginnings of the 1920s, represented an alternative to *Rationalism as propounded by *Le Corbusier in particular. But unlike Häring, who died in 1958, S. had a very active building career in the post-war years. His projects and executed works reveal a conception of building which starts from the essence of the programme and seeks to give expression to it in formal and spatial composition.

After his school years in Bremerhaven, S. studied at the Technische Hochschule in Berlin-Charlottenburg (1912–14). Even when he was still a high school student, his extraordinary talent as a draughtsman was already evident. An early drawing of a church (1910) bears an inscription, the essence of which would come to characterize his later work: 'An independent architect should not be directed by sensations, but rather by reflections.'

In 1915–18 he was the director of an architectural advisory council concerned with reconstruction in East Prussia, and subsequently, 1919–25, he worked as an independent architect in Insterburg, East Prussia. He was involved in the *Gläserne Kette, which Bruno *Taut had launched, and from 1926 was a member of Der *Ring. From this period date residential buildings (Kamswyken estate near Insterburg, 1920), competition entries (Friedrichstraße office block, Berlin, 1922), and a series of utopian sketches, which take up the dominant contemporary theme of the communal centre and the city crown ('Stadtkrone') and are closely related to *Expressionism. As a member of the Ring, S. built a house (1927) in the Weißenhofsiedlung in Stuttgart. He served as a professor at the Staatliche Akademie für Kunst und Kunstgewerbe in Breslau, 1925–32. He built a residential hall with communal services in the basement for the *Deutscher Werkbund exhibition 'Wohnung und Werkraum' (Living and Work Space) in Breslau (1929). He was also responsible for the general development plan for the huge Siemensstadt housing estate (1929–30), the residential development of the Jungfernheideweg and the Mäckeritzstraße, all in Berlin. Also involved in the execution of the Siemensstadt project were Otto *Bartning, Fred Forbat, Walter *Gropius, Hugo *Häring and Paul Rudolf Henning.

In the 1930s, during the Nazi regime, S. was restricted to building private houses: the Schminke House in Löbau, Saxony (1933), a glass-and-steel construction with extensive terraces; the Mattern House at Bornim, near Potsdam (1934); the House for Dr Baensch in Berlin-Spandau (1935); and the Moll House in Berlin-Grunewald (1937). During this period of enforced calm he produced numerous sketch designs and watercolours reflecting ideas that would prove fruitful later on.

After the war S. was at first Director of the Building and Housing Department for Greater Berlin (1945–6) and in 1946 he drew up, together with the 'Planungskollektiv' (Planning Collective) work group, a plan for the reconstruction of the devastated city. In the same year he was appointed to a chair in urban planning at the Technische Universität in Berlin, where he taught until 1958 and was an

Scharoun. Residential hall at the Deutscher Werkbund exhibition, Breslau (1929)

Scharoun. Schminke House, Löbau (1933)

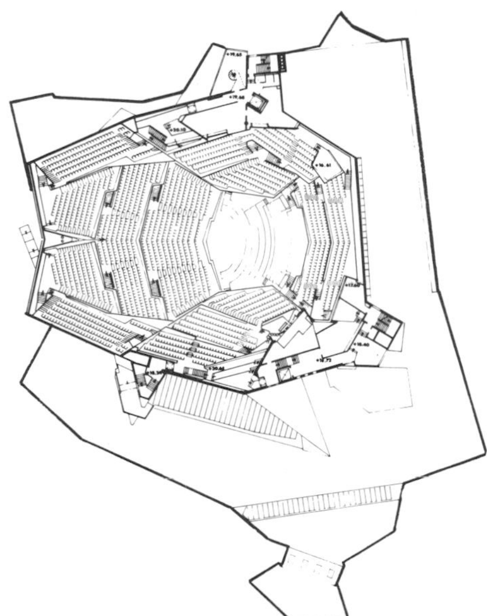

Scharoun. Philharmonic Hall, Berlin (1956–63): plan and exterior view

important influence for an entire generation of young architects. He was also Director of the Institut für Bauwesen of the Deutsche Akademie der Wissenschaft in (East) Berlin, 1947–50.

A series of major projects and prize-winning competition designs were produced in the 1950s: for the Liederhalle in Stuttgart (1949); for the Amerika-Gedenkbibliothek (America Memorial Library) in Berlin (1951); for the Convalescent Home in Berlin-Tiergarten (1952); for the Nationaltheater in Mannheim (1953); and for the Staatstheater in Kassel (1953–5). None of these was built, however, not even his proposal for a Volksschule (elementary school) in Darmstadt (1951), representing an entirely new approach to the organization of educational buildings. What was built in this period were residential buildings which in layout and design represented alternatives to *Le Corbusier's Unité d'Habitation: the tower group 'Romeo and Juliet' in Stuttgart-Zuffenhausen (1954–9) and the tower block 'Salute' in Stuttgart-Möhringen (1961–3), as well as the farmstead dwellings of the Charlottenburg-Nord development in Berlin (1956–61) directly adjacent to the great Siemensstadt estate of three decades earlier. There were also two school buildings, which took up the theme proposed for Darmstadt of organization by age groups: the Geschwister-Scholl Gymnasium (secondary school) in Lünen (1956–62) and the Haupt- und Grundschule (junior school) in Marl (1960).

The most important of S.'s late buildings is probably the Philharmonic Hall in Berlin (competition 1956; completed 1963). It is enlivened by the tension of foyers at various levels with often surprising vistas, while within the auditorium attention is focused on the orchestra. From the idea of 'music at the centre' S. developed a small and easily observed area of composed space; the determinants of his search for form were neither aesthetic not formal, but rather the notion of movement in space, and of happenings within space.

The opportunities previously denied to S. due to adverse political conditions presented themselves only in the later stages of his career, resulting in an impressive series of important buildings: the German Embassy in Brasilia (1970); the German Maritime Museum in Bremerhaven (1970–5); apartment towers in Berlin-Reinickendorf (1970) and Böblingen (1971); the Municipal Theatre in Wolfsburg (1965–73); and the Staatsbibliothek Preußischer Kulturbesitz in Berlin (1964, 1967–78), sited directly adjacent to the Philharmonic Hall and completed after S.'s death by his former partner Edgar Wisniewski. JJ

□ Pfankuch, P., (ed.), *Hans Scharoun. Bauten, Entwürfe, Texte*, Berlin 1974; Jones, Peter Blundell, *Hans Scharoun*, London and Bedford, 1978.

Schindler, Rudolph M(ichael), b. Vienna 1887, d. Los Angeles 1953. Studied at the Akademie der bildenden Künste in Vienna under Otto *Wagner, whose late style, with its harbingers of Continental *Rationalism, was to have a lasting effect on him. In 1914 he went to Chicago, where he entered *Wright's office in 1917. Sent by Wright in 1920 to supervise construction of the Barnsdall complex near Los Angeles, he opened his own office there in 1921 and continued in practice there until his death. He had a loose collaboration in 1925–6 with *Neutra, whom he had already met as a student in Vienna. S.'s most important building is the Lovell Beach House at Newport Beach, Cal. (1925–6), which can be seen as an independent American parallel to De *Stijl in its expressive articulation of structure and the play of horizontal and vertical as well as of space and void.

□ McCoy, Esther, *Five California Architects*, New York 1960; *R. M. Schindler* (exhibition catalogue), Santa Barbara, Cal. 1967; Gebhard, David, *Schindler*, New York 1972.

Schwarz, Rudolf, b. Strasbourg 1897, d. Cologne 1961. Studied in Berlin at the Technische Hochschule and, under *Poelzig, at the Preußische Akademie der Künste. He was successively Director of the Kunstgewerbeschule in Aachen, 1927–34, Director of Town Planning in Cologne, 1946–52, and Professor of Town Planning at the Kunstakademie in Düsseldorf, 1953–61. His ecclesiastical buildings form an important contribution to Roman Catholic church design in the 20th century: he sought to bring congregation and altar into a much stronger relationship through simple formal means, drawing equally on tradition and on modernist design requirements for large internal spaces. Among his most typical designs are the Fronleichnamskirche in Aachen (1928–30, with Hans Schwippert), St Anna, Düren (1951–6), and St Michael, Frankfurt am Main (1953–4). AM

□ Hammond, Peter (ed.), *Towards a Church Architecture*, London 1962; Schwarz, Maria, and Conrads, Ulrich, *Rudolf Schwarz, Wegweisung der Technik und andere Schriften zum neuen Bauen, 1921–1961*, Wiesbaden 1979; Sundermann, Manfred (ed.), *Rudolf Schwarz* (exhibition catalogue), Bonn 1981.

Segal, Walter, b. Ascona, Switzerland, 1907. He emigrated to England in 1936 and subsequently became a British citizen. His architectural education included phases at the Technical College in Delft and the Technische Hochschule in Berlin, as well as at the Eidgenössische Technische Hochschule in Zurich. This background, together with the fact that his studies occurred in the years 1927–32, has ensured that he was from the beginning an active member of the Modern Movement, and that his sympathies have remained with *Functionalism ever since. His own work, however, has always been marked by an energetic empiricism, with a constant concern for constructional method and cost control, and this has freed it from stylistic crudity and pre-ordained formalism. For the same reason, perhaps, very large commissions have eluded him, and he typifies the small intensive private practice, which works through personal attention at all levels, and which produces a result closely matched to social need. It is from this basic standpoint that his recent work on 'Self-build' housing must be judged. RM

□ Segal, Walter, *Home and Environment*, London 1948; ——, 'An Architect's Approach to Architecture', *JRIBA* (London), July 1977; McKean, John Maule, *Walter Segal*, Stuttgart and Zurich 1980.

Seidler, Harry, b. Vienna 1923. Studied at the University of Manitoba in Winnipeg and at Harvard University under *Gropius and *Breuer. Before settling in 1948 in Sydney, he worked briefly under Breuer in New York and under *Niemeyer in Rio de Janeiro. His houses of the early 1950s reveal him as a disciple of his teacher Breuer's 'lyrical' rationalism of those same years, which led away from the *International Style in its incorporation of natural building materials such as wood and rubble, as well as its adjustment to the nature of the landscape. When S. received his first large-scale commissions *c.* 1960, his style began to reflect a classically inspired formal discipline. Examples are: the Australia Square Tower in Sydney (1960–7); the Commonwealth Trade Group Office in Barton, Canberra (1970–5); and the Australian Embassy in Paris (1973–7). AM

☐ *Harry Seidler, 1955/63*, Sydney, Paris and Stuttgart 1963; Blake, Peter, *The Work of Harry Seidler*, Sydney, New York and Stuttgart 1973.

Sert, Josep Lluís, b. Barcelona 1902, d. Barcelona 1983. Studied at the Escuela Superior de Arquitectura in Barcelona, then worked under *Le Corbusier and Pierre Jeanneret in Paris, 1929–31. He was in independent practice in Barcelona, 1929–37, and there – with Sixt Yllescas – founded the group GATCPAC in 1930. He was in Paris, 1937–9, and emigrated to the *USA in 1939; he was President of *CIAM, 1947–56. S. was Professor of Urban Planning at Yale University, New Haven, Conn., 1944–5, and later became Dean of the Graduate School of Design at Harvard University, Cambridge, Mass., 1953–69. His design for the Spanish Pavilion at the Paris Exposition Universelle of 1937 revealed him as an advocate of the *International Style. His designs for the Fondation Maeght in Saint-Paul-de-Vence (1959–64) and the Fundación Joan Miró in Barcelona (1972–5) manifest a more plastic and spatially enriched architecture, the meridional tendency to utilize the play of light and shade being expressed in a personal manner. GHa

☐ Borràs, Maria Lluisa (ed.), *Sert: Mediterranean Architecture*, Boston 1975.

Sert. Fondation Maeght, Saint-Paul-de-Vence (1959–64)

Shaw, Richard Norman, b. Edinburgh 1831, d. London 1912. Studied under William Burn and at the Royal Academy in London before entering the offices of Anthony Salvin and then of G. E. Street, where he succeeded Philip *Webb. His early work was in the neo-Gothic style (church at Bingley, Yorks., 1864–8), which he increasingly simplified and refined; he had a strong influence on the entire *Arts and Crafts movement. His house architecture in the 'Old English Manorial' and 'Queen Anne' styles had a formative effect on English and American domestic design and through *Muthesius was later much appreciated in Germany. Among the most important buildings of his mature period are New Zealand Chambers in the City of London (1872; demolished), Lowther Lodge in Kensington (1873; today Royal Geographical Society), as well as the extremely elegant Old Swan House in Chelsea (1873). Contemporary with Old Swan House are his designs for the first English garden suburb, Bedford Park, Middlesex, west of London. In the last decade of the 19th century, he turned to a powerful *neo-classicism (Chesters, Northumberland, 1891; Piccadilly Hotel, London, 1905). He did not shy away from exploiting new materials discreetly and to advantage: indeed, behind its classical façade Portland House, London (1907–8), represents one of the first major uses of reinforced concrete in English architecture. VML/BB

☐ Saint, A., *Richard Norman Shaw*, London 1976; Girouard, Mark, *Sweetness and Light*, London 1977.

Sheppard, Richard Herbert, b. 1910. Studied at the Architectural Association School of Architecture, London; in private practice since 1938, latterly in partnership with Geoffrey Robson and others. Wide range of buildings, especially educational ones; awarded RIBA Bronze Medal for Harrowfield Boys' School, Harold Hill, Essex (1954). Winner of the limited competition for Churchill College, Cambridge (1959), with a design featuring twenty courts grouped informally round a library and clerestory-lit reading room in the centre. Students' hall of residence, Imperial College, London; pithead, Dudley Colliery, Northumberland.

□ 'The Work of Richard Sheppard, Robson and Partners, *Architectural Design*, July 1957.

Shinohara, Kazuo, b. 1925 Numazu, Japan. After graduation from the Tokyo Institute of Technology, he taught there, and has been a professor since 1970. His earlier works were marked by a concern for 'Japanese character'. However, this was expressed not by individual shapes but by a more basic form of spatial composition which resulted in intensive expression of symbolic objects, as was represented by the free-standing column in the House in White in Tokyo (1966). This approach towards symbolic form was made more abstract and geometric in the 1970s, a process in which his buildings largely lost their Japanese associations in terms of appearance. The Unfinished House in Tokyo (1970) could be considered a typical product of this period. The house in Uehara (1975) was another turning point, in which S. applied more realism and a greater degree of expression. HY

□ *Kazuo Shinohara: 16 Houses and Architectural Theory*, Tokyo 1971; *Kazuo Shinohara II: 11 Houses and Architectural Theory*, Tokyo 1976; 'Kazuo Shinohara', *SD* (Tokyo), January 1979.

Shinohara. House in Uehara (1975)

Sirén. Chapel of the Technical College, Otaniemi (1957)

Sirén, Heikki, b. Helsinki 1918. After studying at the Technical College in Helsinki, he joined the practice of his father Johann Sigfrid Sirén, before opening his own office in Helsinki in 1948 in partnership with his wife Kaija *Sirén. Their buildings are among the best examples of a specific Scandinavian modernism which had its origins in the 1930s and owed much to the formal issues of the preceding neo-classical style (*neo-classicism). Characteristic are a grand simplicity in spatial arrangement and an emphatic restraint in formal development, as exemplified in the Parliament Building by Johann Sigfrid Sirén, completed in 1931. Among the most important works of the Siréns are the Chapel of the Technical College at Otaniemi (1957), the Otsonpesä terrace-housing development in Tapiola (1959) and the Brucknerhaus (concert hall) in Linz (1974). AM

□ *Kaijo + Heikki Sirén, Architekten*, Helsinki and Stuttgart 1977.

Sirén, Kaija, b. Kotka, Finland 1920. Studied at the Technical College in Helsinki. Since 1948 she has worked in partnership with her husband Heikki *Sirén.

SITE. Multi-disciplinary group – an organization launched in 1969 by James *Wines.

Siza (Vieira), Alvaro (Joaquim de Melo), b. 1933 Matosinhos, near Oporto, Portugal. Studied at the Escola Superior de Belas-Artes do Porto. He worked with Fernando Tavora, founder of the 'Oporto School', before starting his own practice in 1958. Most of his modest early commissions were designed for the community of Matosinhos and were works which came to realization with characteristic slowness – as much due to the building capacity of the region as to the personality of the architect. His unusual sensitivity towards both the existing local topography and the temporality of the work was manifest from the outset from his Boa Nova seaside restaurant (1958–63) to the two swimming pools he built in Matosinhos and Leça da Palmeira, erected between 1958 and 1966. This degree of sensitivity to the *genius loci* also characterized a series of houses he built between 1967 and 1977, above all the Alcino Cardoso House in Moledo do Minho (1971) and the Beires House in Povoa do Varzim (1973–6). These residences embody characteristic features of his style, the former showing how new elements may be introduced into the site as though they were parts of a pre-existing scheme, the latter displaying a delicacy of detailing which is at once modern and traditional.

S.'s affinity for Alvar *Aalto's heteroclitic method is perhaps most evident in the branch of the Pinto e Sotto Maior Bank in Oliveira de Azemeis (1971–4), although here, as in his other organic compositions, the plastic irregularity of the volume and mass is always tempered by symmetrical components drawn from the tradition of Italian Rationalism.

S.'s career as a public architect has been closely linked to the chequered fortunes of the Portuguese Revolution of April 1974. This is most clearly manifest in the Bouça (1973–7) and São Victor (1974–7) housing complexes in Oporto, both built as urban infill under the auspices of the residential housing associations which were set up by the state and bore the acronym SAAL, as an integral part of the Portuguese 'new deal'. Despite the limited

Siza. São Victor housing, Oporto (1974–7)

success of these collective endeavours, S.'s continuing importance in the current architectural debate derives from his ability to demonstrate, through the extraordinary vitality of his art, the validity of critical regionalism in pointing the way to a cultural approach. KF
☐ 'Alvaro Siza, projets et réalisations, 1970–80', *L'Architecture d'aujourd'hui* (Paris), no. 211 (October 1980); 'Alvaro Siza', *Architecture and Urbanism* (Tokyo), December 1980.

Skidmore, Owings & Merrill (SOM). In 1936 Louis Skidmore (1897–1962) and Nathaniel Owings (1903–84) founded a joint office in Chicago, to which was added a second office in New York one year later; in 1939 John Merrill (1896–1975) joined the partnership.

From the beginning, the office was organized on novel principles taken over from the office organization of the American business world. Teamwork and individual responsibility along with appropriate motivation of employees on the one hand were combined with anonymity of the individual and a strictly economic working method on the other. While the early years were largely taken up with the establishment of the firm's structure and its further branch offices, the breakthrough to international recognition as an architectural practice came with Lever House, New York (1952). This 21-storey office building, which unified an entire series of new compositional elements into a single solution, was to set a trend in North American

Skidmore, Owings & Merrill. Connecticut General Life Insurance Co. administration building, Bloomfield, Conn. (1957)

architecture. Noteworthy is the organization of the building masses as a base and a distinct, cubic, rectangular tower slab with a light, largely transparent, outer skin. An entire series of similar projects by SOM followed, throughout America, in which the architects' responses – undoctrinaire, but formally brilliant and at the time especially well-adapted to each client's functional requirements – lifted these buildings well above the majority of their countless imitators.

SOM not only took up influences from the *International Style, *Mies van der Rohe and the early *Le Corbusier, but has also decisively influenced the architecture of the *USA since the 1950s in its own right. It was SOM who developed the new building type of the company headquarters as a flat building complex in a park-like landscape setting, and brought it to its masterful perfection. Examples are the administration building of the Connecticut General Life Insurance Company in Bloomfield, Conn. (1957), the Upjohn Company in Kalamazoo, Mich. (1961), the United Airlines Building in Des Plaines, Ill. (1962), the American Can Co. in Greenwich, Conn. (1970), as well as the Weyerhaeuser Company in Tacoma, Wash. (1971).

The Chicago office took up the tradition of architecture determined by construction which had flourished in that city (*Chicago School). In the Inland Steel Co. Building in Chicago (1958) SOM interpreted this tradition with an independent handwriting that also showed the influence of Mies van der Rohe's first Chicago works. But, while Mies soon developed a method in which the structural frame was kept behind the façade articulation, SOM exposed the structure and gave it full expression, developing a whole series of new treatments for façades. This must also be attributed to the fact that from the beginning engineers – such as Myron Goldsmith and Fazlur Khan – were included in the design teams and were represented as partners. The archetype of the skeleton construction was realized in the office building of the Business Men's Assurance Co. of America in Kansas City, Mo. (1963). It was also in the Chicago office that the building systems were originally developed which first made buildings of great height economically feasible. The 'tube construction', worked out by Fazlur Khan, in which the external supporting components of a skyscraper constituted a self-supporting tubework, led – in such reinforced-concrete constructions as the Brunswick Building in Chicago (1965) and the One Shell Plaza Building in Houston (1971), as well as in such steel-frame constructions as the John Hancock Center (1970) and the 450m high (1,500 ft) Sears Tower (1974), both in Chicago – to highly impressive technical and formal results. The Hancock Center was also the first large-scale multifunctional complex, a type which incorporated residences, offices and shops in a single building. In the early 1960s, Walter Netsch in Chicago developed what he named the 'field theory' design system, which was especially applicable to university buildings and hospitals. The field theory was an early attempt to break away from a strict rectilinear design schema by strong differentiation in plan and elevation. It was a logical and consistent system. Since its opening, the San Francisco office has pursued in many of its works formally diverse compositional solutions developed from the interior spaces outward. In these the latent regionalism of the American West Coast is given reflection. The recently founded office in the oil capital, Houston, has seen a very dynamic development, like the city itself whose skyline is today largely dominated by various SOM buildings.

Inspired by *Roche and *Dinkeloo's Ford Foundation Building in New York, SOM has, in the last few years, designed a number of buildings with atrium interior halls in the form of covered spaces with plantings and public facilities. These have given a new dimension to office building in America. Examples are the Fourth Financial Center in Wichita, Kan. (1974), the First Wisconsin Plaza Building in Madison, Wis. (also 1974), and the 33 West Monroe Building in Chicago (1980).

SOM has also been responsible for a series of large building complexes outside the USA, especially in Islamic countries. Among them, the National Commercial Bank Building in Jeddah, Saudi Arabia (1982), established a new scale for office towers in hot climatic zones, and the Haj Terminal at King Abdul Aziz International Airport at Jeddah is the largest tent-roof construction in the world.

Skidmore, Owings & Merrill. National Commercial Bank, Jeddah (1982)

SOM's strength has always been the capacity for original, but trend-setting and formally brilliant solutions. In the process a monumental note has often arisen which is obvious and convincing since it is stamped with a belief in the fundamental value and dynamism of American tradition.

Supported by its pre-eminent organization, SOM has successfully created for itself (by a considerable margin) a leading position among the architecture and engineering offices both in the USA and throughout the world: in 1980, the value of SOM's commissions reached the level of $95 million, of which some eighty per cent related to administration and commercial buildings. In the same year the firm comprised 2,063 employees, including 1,036 architects and 363 engineers. The majority of the first great generation of architects and engineers at SOM – Gordon Bunshaft and Roy Allen in New York; Bruce Graham, Myron Goldsmith and Walter Netsch in Chicago; Edward Bassett in San Francisco – were in retirement by the 1980s. However, a large number of younger talents have found an assured place in all of SOM's offices over the years, so that continuity and

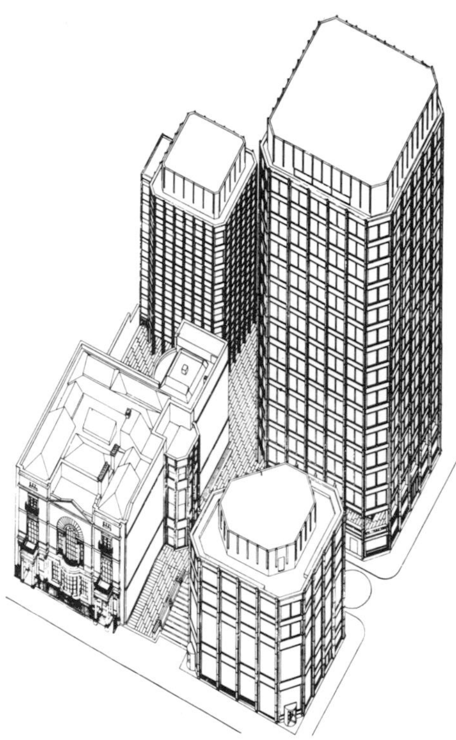

Smithson. Economist Building, London (1964)

Smithson. Robin Hood Gardens estate, London (1972)

identity of the organization are certain to be maintained. OWG

□ Danz, Ernst, *Architecture of Skidmore, Owings & Merrill 1950–1962*, New York 1962 and London 1963; Drexler, A., and Menges, A., *Architecture of Skidmore, Owings & Merrill 1963–1973*, New York 1974; Bush-Brown, Albert, *Architecture of Skidmore, Owings & Merrill: Architecture and Urbanism 1973–1983*, London and New York 1984; Woodward, Christopher, *Skidmore, Owings & Merrill*, London and New York, 1970; Owings, N. A., *The Spaces in Between, an Architect's Journey*, Boston 1973.

Smithson, Alison, b. Sheffield 1928. After studying at the University of Durham, in 1950 she opened, together with her husband Peter *Smithson, an office in London. She was a member of the Independent Group, whose discussions of the dependency of art on modern technology and the subculture of the masses played an important part in the development of Pop Art. She was also a member of the radical Team X within *CIAM.

The Smithsons' importance in post-war architecture derives equally from their buildings and their formulation of the theoretical principles of *New Brutalism. The building which launched this movement, the Hunstanton School in Norfolk (1949–54), a steel skeleton with glass-and-brick infill, is allied with the work of *Mies van der Rohe in

its formal strength and its emphasis of construction, but rejects the classical proportions and perfectionistic details of his work. Other significant buildings by the Smithsons are the Economist Building in London (1964), whose spatial composition creates an urban setting of singular quality; and the Robin Hood Gardens housing estate in London (1972), where they sought, by building corridor-streets above ground level and including two-storey dwellings, to retain for the intended occupants something of the familiar atmosphere of the streets of terraced houses which they had previously occupied. AM

☐ Smithson, A. and P., *Uppercase*, London 1960 (revised ed.: *Urban Structuring*, London and New York 1967); ——, *Without Rhetoric: An Architectural Aesthetic*, London and Cambridge, Mass. 1973; Smithson, A. (ed.), *Team X Primer*, London 1965; McKean, John M., 'The Smithsons: A Profile', *Building Design*, May 1977.

Smithson, Peter (Denham), b. Stockton-on-Tees, Co. Durham 1923. Studied at the University of Durham and the Royal Academy Schools in London. Since 1950 he has worked in partnership with his wife Alison *Smithson. He also was a member of the Independent Group and of Team X (*CIAM).

☐ See preceding entry.

Soleri, Paolo, b. Turin 1919. After completing his studies at the Politecnico in Turin, he joined Frank Lloyd *Wright at Taliesin West, 1947–8. In 1949 he collaborated with Mark Mills on the Dome House in Cave Creek, Arizona, which is roofed by two intersecting domes. He returned to Italy, 1950–5, where he built the expressive and bizarre Ceramica Artistica Solimene factory at Vietri sul Mare, near Salerno (1953). Since 1955 he has been involved almost exclusively with the design of alternative urban planning models and in 1956 founded the Cosanti Foundation in Scottsdale, Arizona, to pursue that end. By 1970 he had designed thirty 'Arcologies' (a term coined from architecture and ecology) – a series of high-density, fantastically unreal megastructures for up to six million inhabitants, conceived as the antithesis to the dissolving metropolis of the automobile era. The thirteenth of these Arcologies, Arcosani, originally projected for 1,500 inhabitants, has been under construction since 1970 in the desert some 125 km (80 miles) north of Scottsdale. AM

Soleri. Dome House, Cave Creek, Arizona (with Mark Mills; 1949)

☐ Soleri, Paolo, *Arcology: The City in the Image of Man*, Cambridge, Mass., and London 1969; ——, *The Sketchbooks of Paolo Soleri*, Cambridge, Mass. 1971; *Paolo Soleri: Architectural Drawings* (exhibition catalogue), New York 1981.

SOM. *Skidmore, Owings & Merrill.

Sommaruga, Giuseppe, b. Milan 1867, d. Milan 1917. Studied architecture at the Accademia di Brera, Milan. He was the main exponent of Italian *Art Nouveau, together with *D'Aronco, *Basile and Pietro Fenoglio. He employed floral Art Nouveau details, particularly in his decorative friezes, which contrast with the bare masonry. Notable works include the Palazzo Castiglioni, Milan (1900–3), and the Mausoleum Faccanoni, Sarnico (1907).

☐ Villard, Ugo Monneret de, *L'architettura di Giuseppe Sommaruga*, Milan 1908; Pevsner, N., and Richards, J. M. (eds.), *The Anti-Rationalists*, London 1973.

Sostres (Maluquer), Josep Maria, b. La Seu d'Urgell, Spain 1915. Becaue of a previous childhood illness, he could not complete his architectural studies at the Escuela Superior de Arquitectura in Barcelona until he was thirty years old. This delay provided an opportunity to widen his studies and interests to include architectural history, poetry, and painting as well, all of which made his an architecture of the broadest cultural scope at precisely that moment when, under the Franco dictatorship, Spanish architecture found itself at an exceptionally low ebb. To combat this situation S. and a small group of architects in Barcelona formed 'Grup R' in 1952 to revive the ideals and purposes of the early Modern Movement, which had fallen victim to the civil war. S. was the theoretical spokesman of the group. In addition, his interest in history spurred him to launch the group 'Amigos de Gaudí' long before *Gaudí's architecture had received wide recognition. He has been teaching architectural history at the Escuela Superior de Arquitectura in Barcelona since 1957. In private practice since 1947, S. has built little; yet, with a fine sensibility and through his synthesis of the vocabulary of the Modern Movement, he has been enormously influential. Among his most important works are: the Casa Augusti in Sitges (1955); the Casa M.M.I. in Barcelona (1958); the Hotel Maria Victoria in Puigcerdà (1957); and the *El Noticiero Universal* Newspaper Building in Barcelona (1965), which recalls the discipline of Giuseppe *Terragni and is outstanding in its show of respect for the context of the street. DM

☐ Domènech, Luis, 'Josep Maria Sostres', *Arquitecturas bis* (Barcelona), May 1974; 'Josep Maria Sostres', *2C Construccion de la Ciudad* (Barcelona), August 1975.

South Africa. The four provinces that were joined together in 1910 to form the Union of South Africa had differing colonial histories and, in consequence, different patterns of architectural development – the only one of note being that of the Cape of Good Hope, where a Dutch vernacular was cultivated in the 18th and 19th centuries, with some sharpening of expression provided by the French refugee L. M. Thibault (1750–1815). This local tradition was further expanded and enriched at the end of the century with the arrival of Herbert Baker who was to build Groot Schuur, Cecil Rhodes' official residence, and later the Rhodes Memorial, both near Cape Town. Thereafter, the focus of all architectural activity was in the Transvaal province, in Pretoria, where Baker was to build the Union Buildings, and most notably in Johannesburg, where Baker and his pupils J. M. Salomon and Gordon Leith were to set the tone in the years that followed for all public and private building of any distinction. On the rocky ridge to the north of this mining town Baker and his followers set up an array of noteworthy houses composed with random rubble and contrasting white-washed walls and classical elements that introduced an Italianate style altogether appropriate to the setting and climate. Sir Edwin *Lutyens, too, contributed to the establishment of this easy and expansive classicism, designing the World War I memorial (in the zoo) and the art gallery (awkwardly sited on a railway cutting and incorrectly orientated), both in Johannesburg. With the advent of modernism, however, this earlier tradition was to be rudely rejected.

The introduction of modernism was brought about, virtually unaided, by Rex Martienssen, who travelled to Europe, first in 1925 and thereafter on repeated occasions, making direct contact with *Le Corbusier and Fernand Léger and returning with paintings and drawings by them. In 1931, Martienssen joined the staff of the School of Architecture of the University of the Witwatersrand, Johannesburg, and became joint editor of the *South African Architectural Record*, both of which he now used most determinedly and brilliantly to further his propaganda aims. Between 1932 and 1939 a handful of houses in a Corbusian idiom of an extraordinary finesse were erected in Johannesburg by Martienssen and his associates, notably Norman Hanson, Gordon McIntosh and John Fassler (an earlier enthusiast of Cape Dutch architecture who was later to attempt an Auguste *Perret revival). Other European influences were brought to bear on this development, notably by Kurt Jonas, who had studied law in Berlin, and was concerned with collective rather than individual expression, and Gordon Pabst, also from Berlin, who pursued a singularly individualistic course. Ultimately, though, the style that all these men were cultivating was found too harsh and uncongenial and after World War II (Martienssen having died of 'flu in 1942 while on a military training course) it was Americanism, both in the form of Brazilian modernism and the sprawling Californian ranch-house style, that came to dominate architectural design. Even *Bauhaus graduates such as Stefan Ahrendts succumbed completely to this vogue. For office developments the model was provided also by America, by the work of *Skidmore, Owings & Merrill. This change to a more relaxed and eclectic modernism had to a certain extent been anticipated by one of the earlier exponents of European modernism,

Douglass Cowin, born in South Africa, but trained at Liverpool University, where American inspiration had long been cultivated. Cowin, though a designer of no great distinction, set the style for textured and coloured bricks contrasted with white- or cream-painted frames and panels of plaster that dominated during the 1950s. The ubiquitous exponent of this fashion was Harold Le Roith, responsible for a number of apartment blocks in Johannesburg. Since then the evolution of architecture in South Africa has followed, quite faithfully, international trends, with only one touch of individualism, that displayed by Amancio Guedes, a graduate of the University of the Witwatersrand and Professor of Architecture there since 1975, but most of whose work is to be found in Mozambique. RMi

Spain. Modern architecture in Spain may be dated to the appearance of *Modernisme, a uniquely Catalan phenomenon, which was more than simply the local version of *Art Nouveau, as it has often been considered. Nonetheless, it was, like its counterparts in other countries, an outgrowth of mid-19th-century Romanticism and the nostalgic revival of medieval culture. The Catalans considered that the roots of their cultural and national identity lay in the Middle Ages. At the same time a revival of the national language, Catalan, helped spread this movement to a wide populace. Thus, although Modernisme was related to the English *Arts and Crafts movement of William *Morris, known through trade connections with Great Britain, the Catalans did not find their efforts restricted to a culture of the élite. One cause was the relatively late development of the Industrial Revolution in Spain, which was financed by commercial exploitation of Cuba. The Victorian-minded bourgeoisie was especially eager to catch up with and to surpass their European rivals in scientific and cultural endeavours as well. In addition, the feeling of a Catalan national rebirth or 'Renaixença' made it imperative that the initiative be populist, which indeed it was. This served the interests of the newly enriched classes well, for by casting social problems in medieval terms the workers' attention was essentially directed away from revolutionary notions and towards patriotism. Thus 'Modernisme' was one of those rare moments when high and low culture coincide in a free popular style understood and enjoyed by all. This accounts for the style's extraordinary dynamism and its geographic and temporal expansion. 'Modernisme' was practised by a great number of artists and manifested not only in architecture but also in decoration, crafts, music, painting and literature as well.

During its years of formation 'Modernisme' in architecture was highly eclectic (*eclecticism), and even its mature monuments do not shed this character, as in Antonio *Gaudí's first building, the Casa Vicens (1878–80), or in Josep Vilaseca's Taller Vidal (1879–84) and Triumphal Arch (1888), all in Barcelona. Three major creative strands, each associated with an outstanding architect, may be distinguished in Catalan 'Modernisme', Gaudí's mature work is the clearest expression of the rich experimentation with Baroque spatial and surface effects, decorative images drawn from nature, and the almost abusive manipulation of structure to achieve these ends. In the finest works, such as the chapel of the Colonia Güell in Santa Coloma de Cervelló (1898–1914), Gaudí abandoned the detailed early style of the Palau Güell in Barcelona (1885–9) for a more impassioned and totally sculptural expression. Francesc Berenguer, Joan Rubió and Josep Maria Jujol (church in Vistabella, Tarragona, 1918–23) also represent this tendency. Lluís Domènech i Montaner pursued a more rational approach, probing the real necessities of each programme and producing buildings of real brilliance in the

Spain. Palau de la Música, Barcelona (1904–8), by Lluís Domenech i Montaner

Palau de la Música (1904–8) and the Hospital de Sant Pau y de la Santa Cruz (1902–10), both in Barcelona. Jeroni Granell and Antoni Gallissà could be classified as belonging to this more rationalist stream; however, Domènech's influence lay less in his work *per se* than in the analytical process of his design and his organizational ability to work with teams. Together with his teaching, this teamwork prepared the way for the rationalist undercurrent of 'Noucentisme' in the 1920s and for rationalist modernism itself in the 1930s. The third strain was epitomized by Josep Puig i Cadafalch, who based his architecture on his own historical researches. Although his work has a strong air of gothic revivalism, he was able to transform this historical vocabulary into something of great personal and domestic charm (buildings for the Casaramona factory in Barcelona, 1912). It is interesting to note that *Gropius met Puig in Barcelona in the early years of the first decade of this century and confessed to being strongly influenced by Puig's insistence on the necessity of reviving the arts and crafts by means of schools of industrial design. Unlike William Morris, however, Puig accepted industry, which was, of course, a basis of Catalan 'Modernisme'. From 1911 onwards the free inspiration of 'Modernisme' based on nature and gothic functionalism receded and gave way to the classical order of a Mediterranean urbanity. This Mediterranean classicism was divided between the archaeological approach (church of Montserrat by Nicolau Rubió, finished by Raimon Durán, 1920–40, both of whom also designed modernist buildings) and the early Rationalism of Francesco Folguera and the brothers Ramón and Antonio Puig Gairalt.

In Madrid the eclectic architectural tradition of the 19th century continued undisturbed well into the 20th, although becoming increasingly more regional in character and historically informed. A certain controlled monumentalism was introduced by Antonio Palacios (Central Post Office in Madrid, 1903–18); but it was via the traditional regional use of brick that a revival of inherent architectural qualities was eventually to be manifested. The best representative was Antonio Flórez, who combined the severity of *Schinkel (Concepción-Arenal School in Madrid, 1923–9) with a free expression of functions and materials within a historical vocabulary drawn in part from H. H. *Richardson (Menéndez y Pelayo School, 1923–9, and students' residence in the Calle del Pinar, 1911–13, both in Madrid). Flórez was followed by Fernando García Mercadal who, after a four-year tour throughout Europe (1923–7), returned to Spain and gave a major impetus to the Modern Movement with his 'Rincón de Goya' in Saragossa (1927; destroyed). Others were also feeling their way tentatively to a modernist approach, including: Secundino Zuazo (Casa de las Flores apartment building, 1930–2, and the Frontón Recoletos, 1935, with the engineer Eduardo *Torroja, both in Madrid); Rafael Bergamín (house for the Marqués de Villora, 1927–8, and nurses' residence, 1933, both in Madrid); and Castro Fernández Shaw (petrol service station in Madrid, 1927), whose projects were closer to *Art Deco and Streamlined Modern than to the purity of the Modern Movement pioneers.

Spain. Casa del Barco, Madrid (1933–6), by Rafael Bergamín

The International Exhibition in Barcelona in 1929, although famous especially for the German Pavilion by *Mies van der Rohe, reflected for the most part the monumental pomposity of the dictatorship of José Antonio Primo de Rivera. Also notable, however, were the Art Deco fountains by Carlos Buigas, the gardens by the French architect Jean Forestier and the reconstructed vernacular buildings, brilliantly laid out in the village 'El Pueblo Español' by Francesco Folguera and Ramón Raventós (with the painter Xavier Nogués and the writer Miquel Utrillo). It was one of the purest responses to Camillo Sitte's *City Planning according to artistic principles*. In 1930 Josep Lluís *Sert and Sixt Yllescas founded in Barcelona the

GATCPAC (Grup d'Artistes i Tècnics Catalans per el Progrés de l'Arquitectura Contemporànea). In the same year an 'E' was substituted for 'C', whereby GATEPAC became the Spanish section of CIRPAC (Comité International pour la Résolution des Problèmes de l'Architecture Contemporaine) at a meeting in Saragossa (*CIAM): GATEPAC organized exhibitions and lectures; and at the 1932 meeting of CIRPAC in Barcelona a pre-draft of the famous *Athens Charter was drawn up. The group also edited the magazine *AC*, which published articles on rationalist architecture and, together with *Le Corbusier, it produced the famous Plan Macia (1932–4) for the urban reform of Barcelona. Notable buildings of that time are the Nautical Club in San Sebastián (1930) by José Manuel de Aizpúrua and Joaquín Labayen, and the Dispensari Antituberculoso in Barcelona (1934–6) by *Sert, Juan Bautista Subirana and Josep Torres Clavé.

The Civil War (1936–9) put an end to Modern Movement architecture, but a slow revival began in the 1950s. Under the auspices of the Instituto Nacional de Colonización whole new villages were built; in these, tradition inspired some very picturesque solutions, as at Esquivel, Seville (1948) by Alejandro de la Sota and Vegaviana, and Cáceres (1954–8) by José Luis Fernández del Amo. In 1952 José Antonio Coderch and Manuel Valls designed their 'Casa Ugalde' in Caldes de Estrac, Barcelona, where surrealist formal effects were deliberately sought in a desperate rejection of the social and cultural realities of the moment. In order to come to terms with these realities, a group of architects in Barcelona formed in 1952 'Grup R', which went back to the point where GATCPAC had begun twenty years earlier. On the one hand there was an admitted influence from Italian neo-realism and British *New Brutalism (workers' housing development in Calle Pallars in Barcelona by Josep *Martorell and Oriol *Bohigas, 1960), while on the other hand there existed a genuine intention to revive the traditions of the early Modern Movement, which had been so violently obliterated in Spain by the Fascist regime. Josep Maria *Sostres experimented with the forms of De *Stijl in his Casa M.M.I. in Barcelona (1958), Antoni Moragas with the Nordic architecture of *Aalto in his Cinema Fémina in Barcelona (1950–2), Joseph Antonio Coderch with the elegant *International Style of *Neutra in his many villas, and Guillermo Giráldez, Pedro López and Javier Subias with the severity of *Mies van der Rohe in their Law Faculty Building in Barcelona (1958).

Madrid architects were influenced either by American architecture's geometrical play of forms, as in the work of José Antonio Corrales and Ramón Vázquez Molezún (School in Herrera de Pisuerga, Palencia, 1955; Spanish Pavilion at the World's Fair, Brussels, 1957–8), and Javier Carvajal and José Maria García de Paredas (Church in Vitoria, 1958–9), or, in the field of housing, by the approach of the London County Council (*Great Britain), as in the work of José Luis Romany, Francisco Sáenz de Oiza and Manuel Sierra (Batan neighbourhood, Madrid, 1955–61) or that of José Luis de Iñíguez Onzoño and Antonio Vázquez de Castro (Cañorroto neighbourhood, Madrid, 1957–9).

In the 1960s architects found that, with the economic boom, their influence had, with a few notable exceptions, become almost negligible. The 'Grup R' dwindled, to be replaced by the more academic 'Pequeño Congreso', which was active throughout the whole country and under whose auspices sixty or seventy architects met in a different place every six months to discuss buildings, projects and related themes. Meanwhile, clear regional differences began to

Spain. Housing in the Calle Pallars, Barcelona (1960), by Martorell and Bohigas

become evident. In the Basque country Luis Peña summarized in his domestic buildings the traditional architectural vocabulary without, however, renouncing the Modern Movement. In Catalonia, Martorell, Bohigas and *Mackay, Clotet and Tusquets (*Studio PER) as well as *Bofill looked back to the resources of 'Modernisme' and re-interpreted its design elements in an appropriate language. Madrid, as the capital, struggled with novelty and with big business, which produced one of the most outstanding buildings in Sáenz de Oiza's Torres Blancas (1961–8). Although the subtleties of José Rafael Moneo (Diestre factory in Saragossa, 1964–7) and Federico Correa and Alfonso Milà (Montesa factory, Barcelona, 1963–4) seemed to signal architectural stability for the 1970s, this was not forthcoming.

The economic collapse of the 1970s diminished building opportunities and encouraged architectural theorizing. Even those buildings which were realized were largely important for their theoretical significance (Belvedere Georgina in Llofriu, Gerona, 1972, by Clotet and Tusquets; Walden 7 in Sant Just Desvern, Barcelona, 1970–5, by Bofill). Following the death of Franco, the advent of a fragile democracy has seen the prerogative in architecture being switched from the private to the public sector. A representative of this tendency is Luís Peña who, in addition to other works, has created some very remarkable public squares in his Basque homeland. DM

☐ Flores, Carlos, *Arquitectura española contemporánea*, Madrid 1961; Bohigas, Oriol, *La arquitectura española de la Segunda República*, Barcelona 1978.

Spain. The Barrio Gaudí quarter, Reus, Tarragona (Taller de Arquitectura; 1964–7)

Spain. Torres Blancas, Madrid (1961–8), by Sáenz de Oiza

Speer, Albert, b. Mannheim 1905, d. London 1981. Studied at the Technische Hochschule first in Munich and then in Berlin, and served as assistant under his Berlin teacher *Tessenow until 1931. He gained Hitler's attention with the redecoration of the NSDAP Headquarters in Berlin (1932) and was given an official position under the Third Reich. After the completion of his colossal plans for the Zeppelin field and parade grounds at Nuremberg (1934–7), he was promoted to Generalbauinspektor (Head of architectural works) for the capital city, Berlin. There, he built the new Chancellery (1938–9) and planned, among other unrealized state buildings, the Great Assembly Hall (Große Halle; 1938) and the Führerpalais (1939), as well as the 'North-South Axis' (1936–7) which was to connect the Great Hall in the Tiergarten to a new projected Southern Railway Station. Impressed by S.'s organizational talents, Hitler appointed him in 1942 Minister for Armaments and Munitions (from 1943 Minister for Mobilization and War Production); after the war S. served a twenty-year term in the Allied prison, Spandau, in Berlin.

S. cultivated a dry reductivist *neo-classicism, which increasingly sacrificed any ideas of quality to an ever-growing megalomania manifested in projects on a vast scale. As a more or less apolitical showman, he quickly fell under the spell engendered by the seemingly limitless possibilities of his official position and increasingly lost his grasp on reality. FJ

□ Speer, Albert, *Inside the Third Reich: Memoirs*, New York 1970; ——, *Spandau: The Secret Diaries*, New York 1976; ——, *Infiltration*, New York 1981; Larsson, Lars Olof, *Die Neugestaltung der Reichshauptstadt. Albert Speers Generalbebauungsplan für Berlin*, Stuttgart 1978; *Albert Speer Architektur. Arbeiten 1933–1942*, Frankfurt am Main, Berlin and Vienna 1978.

Spence, Sir Basil (Urwin), b. Bombay (of English parents) 1907, d. Eye, Suffolk, 1976. Studied architecture in Edinburgh and London, worked under *Lutyens and Rowland Andersen before forming a partnership with Partner and Kinnenmouth in Edinburgh. Moved to London, and there established Sir Basil Spence and Partners. S. is no doubt best known for the rebuilding of Coventry Cathedral (1954–62), won in competition in 1950; he also designed the Sea and Ships Pavilion for the *Festival of Britain (1951). He subsequently had an extremely active career in housing and university buildings. His latter work, such as the British Embassy in Rome (1971) and the Knights-

Speer. Große Halle, Berlin (project, 1938)

Spence. Coventry Cathedral (1954–62)

bridge Barracks, London (1970), continued to display that monumental approach to architecture, inherited ultimately from Lutyens, which kept his work at the centre of considerable controversy.

Stam, Mart(inus Adrianus), b. Purmerend, Holland, 1899. Throughout most of his career he worked in collaboration with other architects, such as *Poelzig and Max *Taut (1922), *Brinkman and van der Vlugt (1925–8), and Ernst *May (1930–4). On the initiative of Hannes *Meyer, he was invited to teach at the *Bauhaus in Dessau in 1928–9. After World War II he served briefly as a professor at the Art Academies in Dresden and East Berlin. In the 1920s and 1930s he was among the leading members of the left wing of the avant garde which strove to create a socialist society, and, with other like-minded colleagues, he offered his services to the recently established Soviet Union (*Russia), where he was primarily active as May's assistant in city planning matters. His radical political engagement was an expression of his rejection of the role of artistic intuition in architectural creation as advocated by the group De *Stijl, as well as the emphasis on scientific-analytical experimentation as propounded by Hannes Meyer. Working with El *Lissitzky, S. was involved in one of the most important works of *Constructivism, the 'Cloud Props' project (1924–5). Several years later he collaborated with Brinkman and van der Vlugt on the design of the Van Nelle Tobacco Factory in Rotterdam (1926–30), a pioneering work of modernist industrial architecture. Among S.'s independent designs are the tubular steel chair for the Thonet company (1926) and his terrace houses at the Weißenhofsiedlung in Stuttgart (1927). AM

☐ Dorthuys, G., *Mart Stam*, London 1970.

Steffann, Emil, b. Bethel (Bielefeld) 1899, d. Mehlem/Rhine 1968. After a private apprenticeship under Professor Münch of the Baugewerkschule in Lübeck and volunteer work under the Municipal Building Director of Lübeck, Pieper, S. built his first modest houses and met Rudolf *Schwarz, with whom he formed a lasting friendship. In 1941 S. was part of a team responsible for the reconstruction of villages in Lorraine, and built, among others, the emergency church (disguised as a communal barn) at Bust. He was in charge of housing projects for the Archdiocese of Cologne, 1947–9, and his work as an independent architect began with the reconstruction of the Franciscan monastery in Cologne (1950). Subsequently he designed over forty ecclesiastical buildings, including the St Elizabeth parish centre in Oplanden (1953–8) and the Carthusian monastery of Marienau, near Seibranz (1962–4, with Gisberth Hülsmann). He cultivated the clear expressive strength of simple, naturally occurring materials, sensible construction, and an elementary, easily perceived spatial organization. FJ

☐ 'Erinnerung an Emil Steffann. Von einer inneren Organisation der Räume', *Bauwelt* (Berlin), 70, no. 19, 18 May 1979, pp. 766–87;

Stam. Terrace houses at the Weißenhofsiedlung, Stuttgart (1927)

Steffann. The Carthusian Marienau monastery near Seibranz (with Gisberth Hülsmann; 1962–4)

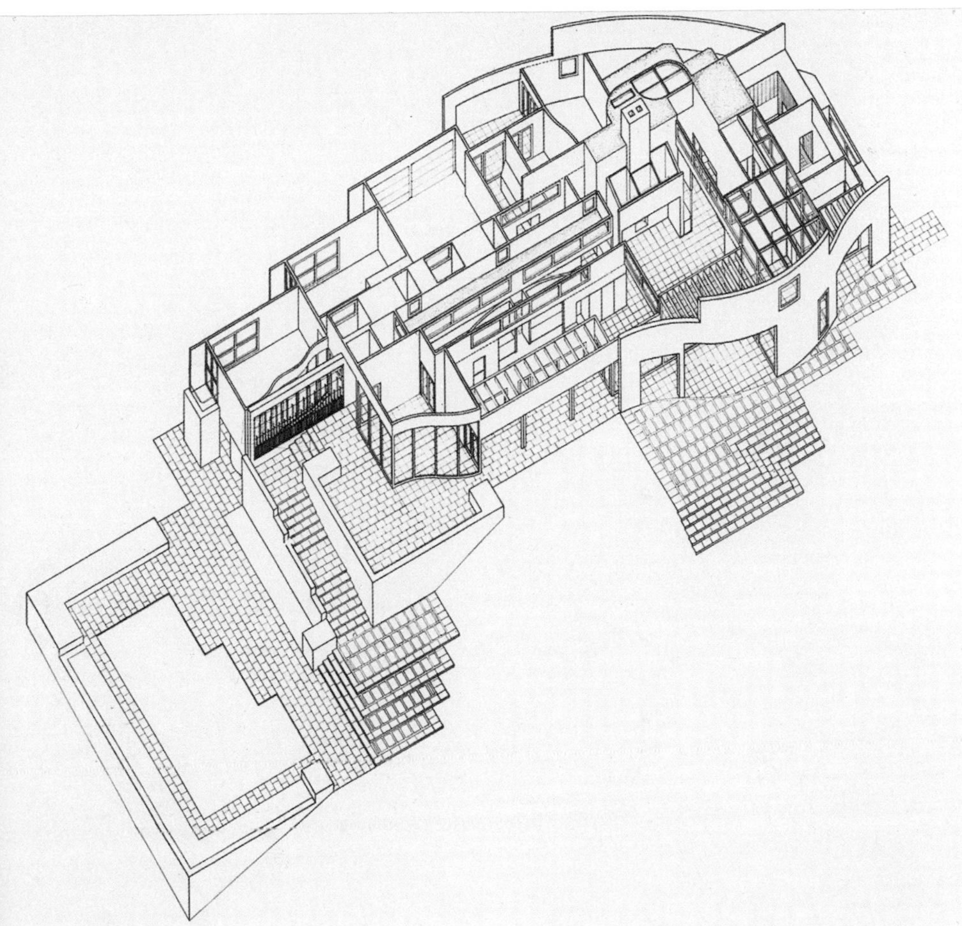

Stern. Ehrman House, Armonk, N.Y. (1975)

Hülsmann, G., Sundermann, M., and Weisner, U., *Emil Steffann* (exhibition catalogue), Bielefeld 1980; 'Emil Steffann 1899–1968', *Bauen + Wohnen* (Munich), 36 (1981), no. 10, pp. 9–16.

Stern, Robert A. M., b. New York 1939. After study at Columbia University, New York, and at Yale University, he worked briefly in Richard *Meier's office. He was subsequently active as a planner for New York City until 1969 when he opened an office in association with John S. Hagmann. Since 1977 he has directed his own office in New York and been a professor at Columbia University. S. is one of the leading figures of *Post-Modernism, to which he has also contributed essential theoretical statements, beginning with the issue 9/10 of the Yale architectural journal *Perspecta* (1965), which he edited and which constitutes one of the first manifestos of Post-Modernism. In opposition to the abstraction and technological orientation which he criticizes in the *International Style, S. advocates an architecture that is 'associational', 'perceptional' and 'grounded in culture'. This is to be achieved by a return to history and through a consciously eclectic collage and superimposition of established forms which are endowed with new meaning. His best-known works as an architect include: the Lang House in Washington, Conn. (1974); the Ehrman House in Armonk, N.Y. (1975); the project for the Roosevelt Island development (competition entry, 1975); and the project undertaken for the retail stores chain Best Products (1979). AM

☐ Stern, Robert A. M., *New Directions in American Architecture*, New York 1969; 'The Work of Robert A. M. Stern and John S. Hagmann', *Architecture and Urbanism* (Tokyo), October 1975; *Robert Stern*, London 1981; Arnell, Peter, and Bickford, Ted (eds.), *Robert A. M. Stern. Buildings and Projects 1965–1980*, New York 1981.

Stijl, De. The group of artists known as 'De Stijl' was formed in Leiden in 1917 around the magazine of the same name. Its founding members were: the painter and architect Theo van *Doesburg; the architects Jacobus Johannes Pieter *Oud, Jan Wils and Robert van't Hoff; the poet Antony Kok; the painters Bart van der Leck, Piet Mondrian, Vilmos Huszar and Gino Severini; and the sculptor Georges Vantongerloo. Van der Leck left the group very early on, followed by van't Hoff in 1919. Also in 1919, the architect Gerrit *Rietveld joined the group.

Strongly influenced by *Cubism, the new group developed a much more radical position than its prototype. In the light of the philosophical background of Dutch Calvinism, it subscribed to such ethical principles as truth, objectivity, order, clarity and simplicity; it was opposed to tradition, and became closely involved with the social and economic conditions of the time. De Stijl rejected an individual, in favour of an objective-universalist, view of the world. Its abstract formal language, freed entirely from natural models, was taken over directly from *Neo-plasticism: straight lines and immaculate surfaces which met and intersected at right-angles; the use of primary colours – red, blue and yellow – contrasted with white, black and grey; the pure cube, treated not as a static or closed form, but rather dynamically de-composed, free of boundaries, and expressed as a part of continuous space.

De Stijl's involvement with architecture was considerable from the outset. The group was

Stijl, De. The Huis ter Heide, near Utrecht (1916), by Robert van't Hoff

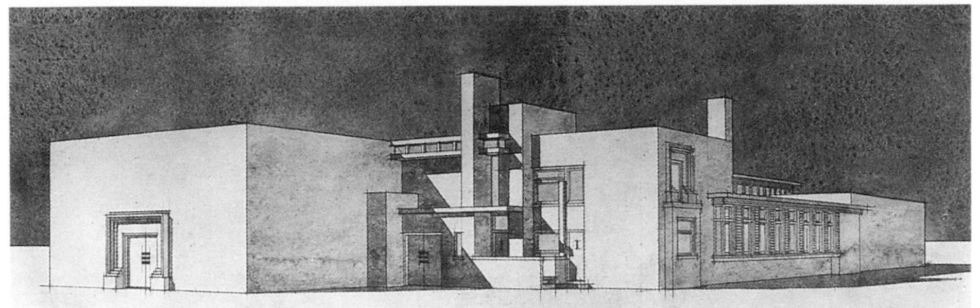

under the direct influence of *Berlage, who served as a link to one of the multifarious sources of the name they had adopted: it was Berlage's customary abbreviation for Gottfried *Semper's materialist architectural treatise *Der Stil in den technischen und tektonischen Künsten* of 1860. It was also through Berlage that De Stijl's members came to admire the work of Frank Lloyd *Wright. Paradoxically, they shared this interest (as well as the link to Berlage) with their most ardent opponents, the School of *Amsterdam, to whose quaint expressiveness they reacted with the most rigid asceticism.

With its first manifesto of 1918, De Stijl formulated for the first time a consistent artistic theory. Among the earliest concrete architectural works in the De Stijl circle were the houses which van't Hoff built between 1914 and 1916 at Huis ter Heide, near Utrecht, with strong and direct borrowings from Wright, as well as Oud's 1919 project for a distillery at Purmerend. In addition there were Rietveld's furniture designs, which reached a programmatic and aesthetic highpoint with his Red-Blue armchair of 1918.

A new phase of De Stijl began *c.* 1921. Kok, Oud, Vantongerloo, and Wils left the group to follow their own artistic pursuits. Their places were subsequently filled by the painter and film-maker Hans Richter, the architects Cor van *Eesteren and Frederick *Kiesler, the painter and architect El *Lissitzky, the painter César Domela, the poet Hugo Ball, and the sculptor, painter and poet Hans Arp. It was through Richter's agency that van Doesburg travelled to Germany, a trip which resulted in his being invited to the *Bauhaus by Walter *Gropius. His brief stay there in 1921 was to have profound consequences for the future orientation of the school. Through Lissitzky, who two years earlier had collaborated closely

Stijl, De. Distillery at Purmerend (project, 1919) by Oud, and (*below*) axonometric studies for a house (1923) by Theo van Doesburg and Cor van Eesteren

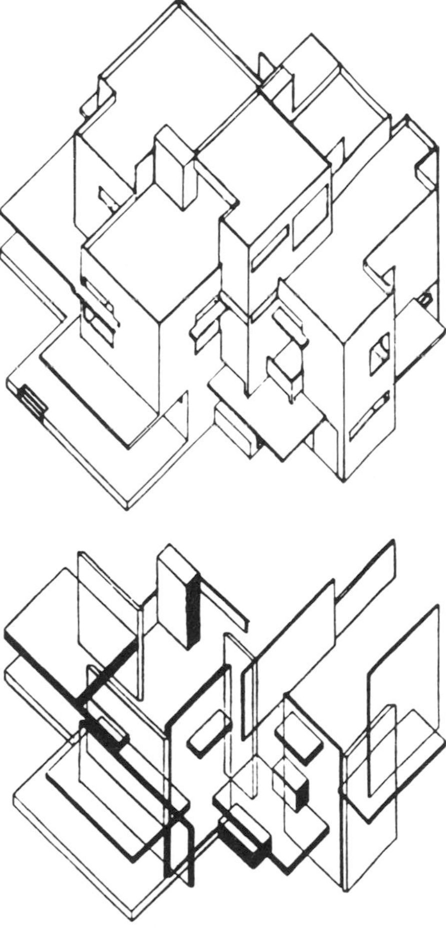

with Kasimir *Malevich, the influence of *Suprematism and of Russian *Constructivism was especially strong within De Stijl.

Impressed by Lissitzky's 'Proun' compositions, van Doesburg and van Eesteren developed *c.* 1923 their own axonometric studies for neo-plasticist houses, which were exhibited the same year in Paris at the Galerie 'L'Effort Moderne'. Immediately afterwards Rietveld translated van Doesburg's theses of 'Tot een beeldende architectuur' (1924) into the reality of the Schröder House, Utrecht, which he built in collaboration with, and for, Truus Schröder-Schräder. It was the single most spectacular building of De Stijl.

Van Doesburg's introduction of the diagonal in his paintings and the subsequent dispute with Mondrian, who left the group in 1925, introduced the third and last phase of De Stijl. In the meantime, van Doesburg and van Eesteren had come under the sway of Lissitzky's technological and social interests; they formulated their ideas in an essay of 1924: 'Vers une construction collective'. This phase had its architectural highpoint in the Café L'Aubette in Strasbourg (1926–8) which Van Doesburg renovated in collaboration with Hans Arp and Sophie Taeuber-Arp. Here the diagonal was the formal determinant. In any case the café was to be the last neo-plasticist work of any significance; in subsequent years De Stijl came increasingly under the influence of *Neue Sachlichkeit and the Modern Movement (van Doesburg's own house at Meudon-Val-Fleury, France, 1929–30). With van Doesburg's death in 1931, the group lost its mainstay and consequently disbanded; in the following year publication of its journal ceased.

The De Stijl movement lasted scarcely fourteen years and relied chiefly on three personalities: van Doesburg, Mondrian and Rietveld. Yet its innovative potential was so great that it influenced many late architectural developments in the 20th century: from Ludwig *Mies van der Rohe to figures as diverse and even opposed in the contemporary architectural spectrum as Peter *Eisenman and Paolo *Portoghesi. VML

□ *De Stijl, Internationaal Maandblad voor Nieuwe Kunst, Wetenschap en Kultuur*, Leiden 1917–31; *De Stijl* (exhibition catalogue), Amsterdam 1951; Zevi, Bruno, *Poetica dell' architettura neoplastica*, Milan 1953; Jaffé, H. L. C., *De Stijl 1917–1931. The Dutch Contribution to Modern Art*, Amsterdam 1956; Overy, Paul, *De Stijl*, London 1969; *De Stijl: 1917–31. Visions of Utopia* (exhibition catalogue), New York 1982.

Stirling, James, b. Glasgow 1926. Studied architecture at Liverpool University. His father was a marine engineer and this might account for his love of tight, ship-shape modern design; while the presence of Colin Rowe as a fellow-student may help to explain the classical and humanist tendencies seen in his later work.

In 1953 S. began to work for *Lyons, Israel and Ellis in London, where he met James Gowan. They commenced practice together in 1956 and soon became known for a series of buildings which, though uncompromisingly modern, owed little to the then predominant *International Style. The principal works of the partnership were: houses at Ham Common (1955–8); competition for Churchill College, Cambridge (1958); project for Selwyn College, Cambridge (1959); and Leicester University Engineering Building (1959–63), which achieved world-wide fame both for its dramatic contrast of red bricks and greenhouse glazing and for the audacity of its formal precision.

From 1963 to 1971 Stirling practised alone. To this period belong many original designs,

Stirling. Flats at Ham Common (Stirling and Gowan; 1955–8)

Stirling. Leicester University Engineering Building (Stirling and Gowan; 1959–63)

including the Cambridge University History Faculty Building (1964–7); residential units for students at St Andrews University (1964–8); the projects for Dorman Long Headquarters in Middlesbrough (1965); the Florey Building for Queen's College, Oxford (1966–71); housing for Runcorn New Town (1967–76); the Olivetti Training School at Haslemere (1969–72); and projects for Siemens AG in Munich (1969) and for Derby Civic Centre (1970). In the two last projects Leon *Krier was assistant, and his hand may be detected in drawings made between 1968 and 1970. Almost ten years were to pass before S. again received an important British commission – for the extension of the Tate Gallery in London (1980; now under construction).

From 1971 Stirling was in partnership with his associate Michael Wilford. Their more important work includes: projects for the Olivetti headquarters at Milton Keynes (1971) and for an Arts Centre at St Andrews University (1971); competition designs for the Kunstsammlung Nordrhein-Westfalen in Düsseldorf and the Wallraf-Richartz Museum in Cologne (both 1975); extensions to the Staatsgalerie Stuttgart (1977; opened 1984); and a new building for the Württembergisches Staatstheater in Stuttgart.

After taking part in a competition for Lower Manhattan in 1968 and serving as a visiting critic and professor at Yale University School of Architecture from 1960, S. became well-known in the USA. As a result he received numerous commissions, including: an extension to the School of Architecture, Rice

Stirling. Housing in Runcorn New Town (1967–76)

University, in Houston (1979–81); the new wing of the Fogg Art Museum, Harvard University, Cambridge, Mass. (1979); and the Chemistry Department, Columbia University, New York (1981).

Some critics have seen Stirling's work after 1970 as taking on an increasingly formalist tendency. Works such as the Staatsgalerie Stuttgart and the Tate Gallery extensions have been referred to as 'post-modern' (*Post-Modernism). Close examination will, however, show the underlying unity of all his work, although there is certainly an important shift, somewhat analagous to the shift in *Le Corbusier's late work with Ronchamp, in that, compared with his earlier buildings, a freer rein is given to expressive gestures. S. is always consciously experimental in his use equally of eclectic reference and formal structures. In freely admitting the wilful nature of all artistic creation, he has liberated himself from the false determinism which plagued so much architectural production after 1945. The element of 'historicity' in his work is no less self-conscious and wilful than was the element of 'modernity' in his early work. It is this candour and lack of preconception which makes his work so important; the unpredictability of S.'s response to the demands of each commission ensures a continuation of interest on the part of the younger generation in any new work by him. RM

□ Stirling, J., *James Stirling. Buildings and Projects 1950–74*, London and New York 1975; Arnell, Peter, and Bickford, Ted (eds.), *James Stirling. Buildings and Projects 1950–82*, New York 1983.

Structuralism. Term introduced by the architectural critic Arnulf Lüchinger for the new Dutch architecture which centred on Aldo van *Eyck and the magazine *Forum*, which van Eyck edited 1959–63, together with *Bakema, *Hertzberger and others. The term suggests a historical as well as doctrinal relationship to the researches of the ethnological structuralist Claude Lévi-Strauss, who in the 1960s postulated a-historical basic structures underlying all cultural processes, and sought to establish such primordial models of relationships. Structuralist architecture likewise proceeds from a base of underlying 'objective' formal structures; these 'Archeforms' determine the entire history of architecture. In this sense, design is nothing but the creative search for archetypal solutions. The structuralist architects opposed both the

Structuralism. Detail of layout for student residences (project, 1925) by Le Corbusier

Structuralism. Municipal Orphanage, Amsterdam (1957–60), by Aldo van Eyck

neutrality of the Modern Movement, as it allowed a much too undefined and sterile freedom of choice to users, and the formal richness of *Expressionism, which was seen as being too emotionally charged and subjective. As an alternative, they proposed a multifarious order, a 'labyrinthine clarity': within a disciplined, non-hierarchical, but nonetheless stimulating architectural framework, each user would be accorded an individual choice.

The architectural principles of Structuralism can be traced to several early designs by *Le Corbusier, such as his 1925 project for student residences composed like a carpet on an orderly and regular circulation network. Such ideas also appeared in several of Louis *Kahn's works, as well as in those of Alison and Peter *Smithson: Structuralism as a movement, however, grew directly out of the debate between *CIAM and Team X. Among its most important advocates, in addition to van Eyck (Municipal Orphanage in Amsterdam, 1957–60), are Herman Hertzberger (Administration Building of the Centraal Beheer Insurance Company in Apeldoorn, 1970–2) and Piet *Blom ('Kasbah' housing estate in Hengelo, 1965–73). VML

☐ Eyck, Aldo van, 'CIAM 6, Bridgwater: Statement against Rationalism, 1947', in: Giedion, Sigfried, *A Decade of Modern Architecture*, Zurich 1954; Lüchinger, Arnulf, 'Strukturalismus – eine neue Strömung in der Architektur', *Bauen + Wohnen* (Munich), 31 (1976), no. 1, pp. 5–40; ——, *Strukturalismus in Architektur und Städtebau*, Stuttgart 1980.

Stubbins, Hugh, b. Powderly, Ala. 1912. Became *Gropius' assistant at Harvard Graduate School of Design in 1939. Private houses, schools, office blocks, churches. The stage of the Loeb Theatre at Harvard (1957–60) can be changed from a proscenium type to an arena. The Congress Hall in Berlin, which was erected for the Interbau Exhibition of 1957, comprises auditorium, conference rooms, exhibition hall and theatre. Its saddle-shaped roof, whose weight is partly carried by walls and internal columns, partly by two anchors, is a bold feat of engineering. More recently much acclaimed for his Citicorp Building in New York City.

Studio PER. Umbrella partnership established in Barcelona in 1965 and comprising two distinct and separate architectural practices. Lluís Clotet (b. Barcelona 1941) and Oscar Tusquets (b. Barcelona 1941) form one practice, while Pep Bonet (b. Barcelona 1941) and Christian Cirici (b. Barcelona 1941) form the other. What is common to both practices is a bellicose attitude towards established norms, which they express both in critical texts and in architecture. This aggressiveness is matched, however, by a meticulous care in detailing (which all four learned from Federico Correa) their often exquisitely designed buildings. Both practices favour a minimal architecture in which effect is derived from simplicity.

Clotet and Tusquets are the more prolific, with several outstanding buildings already to their credit, including the Casa Penina in Cardedeu (1968), which challenged established attitudes towards the suburban house by its triangular plan and excavated enclaves for privacy. The Belvedere 'Georgina', a weekend house in Llofriu (1972), is an ironic 'Post-Modern' (*Post-Modernism) garden pavilion in the form of a temple to that very motor car which makes the modern weekend possible, while the Casa Vittoria in Pantelleria, Italy (1974), re-interprets the spatial role of the column in defining the adjacent external spaces.

In contrast, Bonet and Cirici are more restrained in their architecture, which emphasizes to a greater extent the constructional process, often exploited to achieve poetic interior spatial effects. Their best works are: the Profitos furniture factory in Polinya (1973), notable for its radical handling of volumes; the Tokyo housing block in Barcelona (1974), with its *Aalto-inspired detailing; and Bonet's own house at Vilamajor (1976), evoking industrial constructions. DM

☐ 'Studio PER', *Architecture and Urbanism* (Tokyo), no. 4, 1977.

Sullivan, Louis (Henry), b. Boston 1856, d. Chicago 1924. His training was brief and unsystematic. At sixteen he began his studies at the Massachusetts Institute of Technology in Cambridge, but left after only one year; he then spent a brief period in the Philadelphia office of Frank Furness and soon thereafter followed his parents to Chicago. There, he worked for several months in the office of William Le Baron Jenney, the most important architect of the time in the city (*Chicago School). In 1874 he went to the *Ecole des Beaux-Arts in Paris, but returned to Chicago in 1876, thus concluding his formal training.

In 1879 S. began his collaboration with the engineer Dankmar *Adler and in 1881 became his partner. In their first years together, both indulged in the same decorative *eclecticism that was practised by most of their colleagues. It was under the influence of the buildings of H. H. Richardson, especially the Marshall Field Wholesale Store in Chicago (1885–7), that their architecture took a new direction. Examples are the Selz, Schwab & Co. Factory (1887), notable for the simplicity of its brickwork, and the strong reminiscences of Roman architecture evident in the freestone-clad Walker Warehouse (1889), both in Chicago. In the latter S. united several storeys by continuous pilasters combined with round arches – a motif which he was subsequently to use in nearly all his multistorey buildings.

In 1889 S. and Adler completed the Auditorium Building in Chicago. Its various functions (a theatre to seat more than 4,000 people, a hotel and office building) and its complexity were a challenge both to Adler's technical-scientific talents and to S.'s architectonic-artistic skills. In spite of ingenious technical details and a decoration as rich as it was fantastic, the building reveals the excessive demands of the programme, especially in the lack of unity in its façade, whose numerous compositional motifs were not adequate to express the overwhelming volumes. S. was much more successful in his following works, in which he was able to find forms better suited to the unusual proportions of new skeletal constructions. He abandoned the classical horizontal division of the façade, and expressed the stack of identical, and for the most part functionally neutral, floors by means of a vertical articulation (Wainwright Building, St Louis, 1890–1; Schiller Building, Chicago, 1892; Stock Exchange, Chicago, 1894; Guaranty Building, Buffalo, 1895). In the place of historicist reminiscences he employed – whenever the client's budget permitted – an orna-

Sullivan. Auditorium Building, Chicago (with Adler; 1887–9)

ment based on plant forms either confined to single members or extending over the whole façade.

After the split with Adler, S.'s commissions increased considerably, despite personal problems which in the event were to enhance their architectural quality. In 1899 and 1903–4 he built his most important work, the Schlesinger and Mayer (today Carson Pirie Scott & Co.) Department Store in Chicago. Instead of accentuating the vertical constructional elements, he now took the skeleton-determined floor heights and upright supports as the basis of his composition. While he emphasized this system in the upper storeys by means of a cladding of white terracotta and deeply recessed windows, he overlaid the two lower storeys with a rich, energetic ornamental pattern.

S. varied the formal possibilities of representing the type of construction in two commissions to design façades for existing buildings, that of the Bayard Building in New York (1898) and the Gage Building in Chicago (1898–9). Unfortunately, the limited nature of his later commissions provided him with no opportunity to pursue further the radical tendency of the façade of his Chicago department store. Buildings like the National Farmers Bank in Owatonna, Minn. (1907–8), are rendered impressive by their unity of volume and form and through the strength of their detail and ornament.

Sullivan. Guaranty Building, Buffalo, N.Y. (1894–5)

Sullivan. The former Schlesinger and Mayer department store (Carson Pirie Scott & Co.), Chicago (1899–1904), in its original form

The long path from the first skeleton buildings clad with historicizing façades to those buildings in which 'the structural dimensions provide the real basis for the artistic formation of the exterior' – words which could just as easily have been uttered by *Mies van der Rohe – is a reflection of S.'s conviction that art must be founded on scientific method. No building of the 19th century reflected this thought as clearly as did his Schlesinger and Mayer Department Store. Opposed to this is the conception of S. as a protagonist of *organic architecture. But the organic aspect – in the sense of form derived from nature – of his buildings was confined to surface ornament, whose extraordinary richness in many cases seems a disconcerting contradiction of the aesthetic objectivity of the structural requirements, His oft-cited and oft-misunderstood maxim that form should follow function was not seen by S. as the point of departure for an organic architecture in the manner of Frank Lloyd *Wright or Hugo *Häring. It derived much more from an emphatic rejection of any autonomous form in building which failed to take account of function and construction. PCvS

☐ Sprague, Paul, *The Drawings of Louis Henry Sullivan*, Princeton, N.J. 1979.

Superstudio. Experimental architectural group founded in 1966 by Adolfo Natalini and Cristiano Toraldo di Francia; later Piero Frassinelli joined the group, as did Alessandro and Roberto Magris, and Alessandro Poli was associated with Superstudio, 1970–2. The group was dissolved in 1978. Its members were active as teachers (from 1973), principally at the University in Florence.

Superstudio won notice in the late 1960s with projects that fall between architecture and fine art, in a manner similar to Hans *Hollein's work. They deliberately contrast 'negative' utopias – as intellectually provocative, fundamentally lyrical, metaphors with a Marxist cast – with the hollow functionalist (*Functionalism) practice of the post-war years and with the overly-zealous and overly-confident and optimistic activism of such technologically avant-garde groups as *Archigram. The project 'Il monumento continuo' of 1969 consists of an endless framework which expands over the earth's entire surface area and represents a cynical critique of contemporary abstract planning euphoria. The proposal to submerge all of Florence by blocking the Arno and leaving only the dome of the cathedral to emerge slightly as an attraction for aquatic tourists (1972) was an ironic commentary on the 'Save the Historic Centres' campaign.

The exhibition 'Fragments from a personal museum' (1973) suggested nihilistic alternative models for a 'radical architecture' by means of enigmatic surrealistic graphics.

In 1978 Superstudio recognized that its subversively intended critique of capitalistic architecture was having no effect and hence abandoned collaborative production. The defiant symbolism of the disbanded group has continued to have echoes in Adolfo Natalini's projects (e.g. for a building on the Römerberg in Frankfurt am Main, 1979). VML

Superstudio. Design for a building on the Römerberg, Frankfurt am Main (project by Adolfo Natalini; 1979)

☐ Superstudio, 'Drei Warnungen vor einer mystischen Wiedergeburt des Urbanismus', *Archithese* (Niederteufen), no. 1 (1972); ——, *Italia vostra, Salvataggi di centri storici*, Florence 1972; Masini, Lara Vinca (ed.), *Topologia e morfogenesi, Utopia e crisi dell'antinatura. Momenti delle intenzioni architettoniche in Italia*, Venice 1978.

Suprematism. A term coined by Kasimir *Malevich for a purely abstract art of the type first seen in his canvas *Black Square on White Ground* (1913). For Malevich, Suprematism meant the 'supremacy of pure sensation in the fine arts'. The simple formal elements in his paintings were later also applied to abstract architectonic compositions, which have considerable affinities with the contemporary work of the De *Stijl group.

Sweden. In 1900 Sweden was a mainly agrarian country with a population of *c.* 5 million. Although industrialization was imminent, only around a quarter of the population were employed in industry (including mining and forestry). Not until *c.* 1930 did the urban population surpass the rural one.

The transition of the dominant roles in society from officialdom and the aristocracy to the liberal/middle classes created new tasks for architects. The private sphere now became important. The painter Carl Larsson (*The House in the Sun*) played a leading role in this domestic movement and was widely followed by a burgeoning architectural profession engaged in designing both private homes and buildings for this new economic sphere. Meanwhile, the style of public buildings maintained old traditions.

Two attempts to create a more deliberately 'contemporary style' stand out amidst the general, more or less eclectic, production of the first decade of the century. One trend was modernist, taking inspiration from the schools of Vienna (*Wagner) and *Chicago and manifesting itself especially in bank and office buildings as well as schools in central Stockholm and a few other places. Notable architects were Ernst Stenhammar, Gustaf Wickman, Georg Nilsson and Carl Bergsten. This development came to an end towards 1912.

The other tendency, 'national realist' in character, was inspired by the English *Arts and Crafts movement, but also involved a continuation of themes already established in Sweden in the early 1890s by architects such as Ferdinand Boberg, whose massive four-square architecture was inspired by H. H. Richardson. The preference for the massive block was now combined with a strong interest in craft techniques and what were pointedly called 'genuine' materials. Attention was increasingly focused on the Swedish vernacular tradition as a source for architectural inspiration. Spearheaded by a group of leading architects, mostly living in Stockholm, this trend had as its leading exponents such men as Carl Westman and Ragnar Östberg (villas, official buildings), Erik Lallerstedt (railway stations, churches, houses), and Lars Israel Wahlman (Engelbrekt church in Stockholm). Stockholm's City Hall by Östberg (1911–23) is generally regarded as the belated culmination of this epoch, although it is primarily a very personal work, even heralding the *neo-classicism of the following years in its spatial treatment.

The first modern attempt to apply principles of architectural design to the industrial environment was the state-built hydro-electric power station and accompanying canals and locks, built at Trollhättan to Erik Josephson's designs in 1906–16. As municipal architect for the town of Västerås in the 1910s and 1920s, Erik Hahr won considerable acclaim for his sensitive redevelopment of a medieval town consisting of timbered buildings into a modern industrial town, while preserving a sense of continuity with the past. The model industrial settlement of Bergslagsbyn at Borlänge, built in 1915–21 by *Almqvist, reflects the influence of Raymond Unwin's planning principles. Nearby, at Forshuvudfors, Almqvist built the first of his famous hydro-electric power stations (1921), which signalled a departure from the vernacular tradition.

Sweden. Elementary School, Eksjö (1908–10), by Georg Nilsson

Sweden. Galerie Liljevalch, Stockholm (1916), by Carl Bergsten

Sweden. Housing in Gothenburg (1922–3) by Arvid Fuhre

In the first decade of the century, Per Olof Hallman in Stockholm and Albert Lilienberg in Gothenburg designed numerous residential quarters much influenced by Camillo Sitte's principles. At the same time the concept of the apartment building forming a peripheral enclosure to a large verdant central court brought an important reform of the closed urban block structure. Among the finest examples are those by Arvid Fuhre, built in Gothenburg in the 1920s.

Neo-classical tendencies first appeared soon after 1900 and predominated in the 1920s. This neo-classicism was primarily a Scandinavian and Northern European style, distinct from the tradition of the *Ecole des Beaux-Arts. Its products were frequently on a small scale, reflecting an interest in rationalizing the small house through a combination of intellectual analysis and an increased sensibility to the handling of space and materials. Together with the preceding 'national realist' stage, it marked an artistic highpoint in the quality of design in 20th-century Swedish architecture. The most important architects were: Ivar Tengbom (who worked mainly for large business concerns – Headquarters of the Stockholm Private Bank, 1915; and of the Swedish Match Company, 1928); Gunnar *Asplund, the artistic leader, whose formal language was widely imitated; and his more intellectual, rationalist friend Sigurd *Lewerentz. Asplund and Lewerentz collaborated on the winning competition design (1914) for the Stockholm South Cemetery, for which each man would later build a noteworthy chapel in the 1920s. Elsewhere in the country, fine neo-classicist designs were realized in Gothenburg and by such municipal architects as Gunnar Leche in Uppsala and Gunnar Wetterling in Gävle.

Striving towards a rationalist mastery of design problems, Almqvist gained the distinction of becoming the 'first Swedish functionalist' by the mid-1920s, achieving international recognition with his hydro-electric power stations near Hammarfors and near Krångfors (1925–8). It fell to Asplund, in his brilliant designs for the 1930 Stockholm Exhibition, to open symbolically the 'New Era' in a distinguished and convincing manner, and he remained the artistic leader until his death in 1940.

The work of the Co-operative Society's architects' office (founded 1924) under Eskil Sundahl was, however, much more typical of Swedish architecture of the 1930s and 1940s, an era of social-democratic rule and of ambitious and progressive public building policies – inhibited, however, by limited resources. Characteristic were new building types such as co-operative retail stores and inexpensive restaurants, tourist hotels in mountain and island resorts, and low-rise apartment houses, free-standing in green surroundings. Untouched by World War II, Swedish architecture enjoyed an uninterrupted development in which small-scale projects, a social awareness and careful design combined to yield one of the most convincing manifestations of the 'new architecture' anywhere.

During the 1940s the somewhat schematic character of early Swedish modernism was

Sweden. Rosta estate, Örebro (1948–52), by Sven Backström and Leif Reinius

Sweden. Vällingby, near Stockholm (1953–5), by Sven Backström and Leif Reinius

softened by the influx of Anglo-Saxon ideas with sociological overtones. In an effort to foster community groups, 'neighbourhood units' were incorporated in town-planning schemes. Often, architects returned to the courtyard-type housing of the 1920s, although it was now more loosely composed to suit suburban settings. An important variation of the tall apartment block, a type which had been first introduced in Stockholm *c.* 1940 (Sven *Markelius was Director of the City Planning office, 1944–54), was the 'star-house' pioneered by Sven Backström and Leif Reinius, both leading housing architects (Gröndal estate in Stockholm, 1946–51, and Rosta estate in Örebro, 1948–52). Classicizing tendencies were kept alive throughout the 1940s in the work of the Nils Ahrbom and Helge Zimdal and the Nils Tesch and L. M. Giertz partnerships.

The traditional basis of architecture underwent a significant change *c.* 1960, thanks to the effects of economic recovery and prosperity – an increase in the number of motor vehicles, a restructuring of retail trade, and the widespread use of prefabrication in construction. The architectural profession responded to these new socio-economic forces with 'production-adapted design' and comprehensive planning. The result was, however, an increasing professional uncertainty, as traditional building skills and knowledge were neglected and the last vestiges of classicist architecture, still kept alive by a few of the older generation of municipal architects, were swept away. For a while, church architecture offered a sanctuary where creative design experienced a St Martin's summer. Most remarkable perhaps was the late flowering of the elderly Lewerentz in his churches at Skarpnäck (1960) and Klippan (1966). Peter Celsing (b. 1920) was almost alone among the younger generation in employing the 'grand manner' in his architecture (churches at Vällingby, Gothenburg, Uppsala, etc.; Cultural Centre with temporary Parliament Building, Stockholm).

Architectural activity in the decade 1965–75 was dominated by the government's housing programme, which called for one million new dwelling units to be constructed in ten years. Although this was a great achievement in terms of quantity, the designs did not establish a high standard of quality. The established techniques of the Modern Movement were merely applied on a colossal scale which none of the architects fully mastered; rather, crudely structured patterns were simply multiplied to accommodate the great number of units required. By the early 1970s many units remained unoccupied and the emphasis was rapidly switched to the production of small houses, which had not been built in Sweden for many years. Again, however, the method was mere repetition of a simple pattern.

The popular reaction to this wholesale restructuring of the environment was a renewed interest in the nation's historical heritage which was being so rapidly sacrificed. Simultaneously, the position of the architectural profession was also weakened, with stricter building regulations affecting a number of practical design factors; however, numerous other aspects of design, notably the urban environment, remained uncontrolled. Architects had increasingly less control over the construction industry and witnessed an increase in the non-architect-designed building market. Swedish architecture, which – despite the absence of outstanding achievements – had been characterized by a generally high standard during the years of the country's 'middle way' (1930s to early 1950s – steering a middle course between capitalism and socialism), now plummeted to a point of near-nadir. Only a few architects maintained a distinguished level, notably the English-born Ralph *Erskine, who more than any other architect remained true to the social approach of the 1940s, gradually achieving international fame for his housing schemes (Nya Bruket at Sandviken and, in England, Byker at Newcastle-upon-Tyne). Another very competent designer was Carl Nyrén who, in banks and churches, showed a consistent skill in his handling of scale and materials.

Sweden. The Nya Bruket estate, Sandviken, near Gävle (1972–80), by Ralph Erskine

The situation of Swedish architecture by the early 1980s was rather unsettled. The role of the architect in the overall building market was on the decline. Although conscious of the unresolved problems posed by a rapidly maturing industrial society, they had failed to achieve a renewal of either architectural theory or practice. The especially strong rationalist tradition in Sweden had resulted in a certain impregnability in the face of post-war innovations abroad, but it has also engendered a sort of 'Oedipus complex' among younger architects. Although the situation is in a state of flux, a lively debate has arisen in recent years; the chief concerns are to persuade the country of the absolute need not just for good architecture, but also for the development of the means to bring it to realization. BL

□ Ahlberg, Hakon, *Swedish Architecture of the Twentieth Century*, London 1925; Svenska Arkitekters Riksförbund SAR (ed.), *New Swedish Architecture*, Stockholm 1939, ——, *Swedish Housing of the 'Forties*, Stockholm 1950; Hulten, B., *Building Modern Sweden*, Harmondsworth 1951; SAR (ed.), *New Architecture in Sweden*, Stockholm 1961; Kidder Smith, G. E., *Sweden Builds*, New York 1957; Råberg, Per G., *Funktionalistiskt genombrott*, Stockholm 1972.

Switzerland. The adoption of a new constitution in September 1848, which provided for a central federal govenment and local control of the various cantons, raised the question of a political and cultural national identity for the first time. A new national spirit sought to establish as valid prototypes for a 'Swiss architecture' the country's farming villages and small towns. As a result, numerous regional buildings were designed in a self-consciously native, traditional style. These included local railway stations, post offices, kiosks, inns, banqueting halls and exhibition pavilions. The 'Swiss vil-

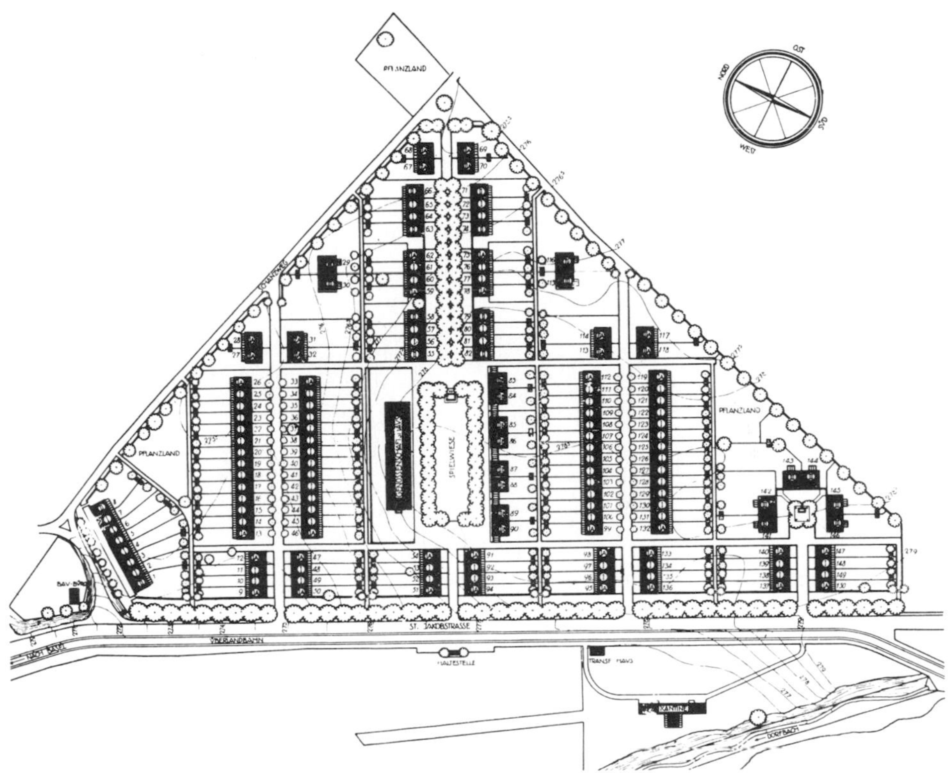

Switzerland. Freidorf estate, Muttenz, near Basle (1919–24), by Hannes Meyer

lages' at the federal exhibitions of 1883 and 1896 were typical expressions of this folklorism. The larger cities and their public buildings remained untouched by this late romantic patriotism, further averted by the growing influence of the rational and internationally inclined professors at the Eidgenössisches Polytechnikum, founded in Zurich in 1855.

Between this native romanticism and the academic approach favoured by Gottfried Semper at the 'Bauschule' of the Polytechnikum, there was no place for a local *Art Nouveau at the turn of the century. In Switzerland that style appeared only in conjunction with an existing *historicism or in very much altered variations. In spite of its adherence to historical forms, Swiss architecture of the years 1900–14 did not reject an involvement with the constructive possibilities and functional requirements of the period. The Oscar Weber Department Store (1910) in Zurich by Otto Pfleghard and Max Haefeli developed the neo-Gothic in a very inventive and influential manner, which recalls the skeletal pier constructions widely used by contemporary German department store architects. Likewise, the northern Renaissance style employed in the Peterhof Office Building, Zurich (1913–14), by Otto and Werner Pfister emphasized the verticality of the ferro-concrete skeleton. In his Badischer Railway Station in Basle (1912–13) Karl *Moser surpassed the historicism of the 19th century in the tense composition of his building masses and his synthesis of Secessionist (*Austria) and neo-classical forms.

The Union of Swiss Architects (Bund Schweizer Architekten), founded in 1908, was represented at the Swiss Provinces Exhibition held in 1914 in Berne by a pavilion in a Biedermeier/neo-classical style inspired by German models; *neo-classicism was reduced to a bourgeois scale, or a 'Compromise between Versailles and the Garden City' (Jacques

Switzerland. Colnaghi House, Riehen (1927), by Hans Schmidt and Paul Artaria

Gubler). The title of Paul Mebes' book *Um 1800* ('Around 1800', 1908) provided an oft-cited motto for this harking back to the early 19th century; by this was meant not just a formal principle, but also a social attitude. In 1912 the Basle architect Hans Bernoulli returned from Berlin to his native city. During an earlier trip to England he had visited Hampstead Garden Suburb and was now firmly convinced that the small terrace house was the best housing type. In 1914, on the eve of World War I, he built the first estate of nineteen terrace houses in Basle. Although neutral Switzerland was not directly affected by the war, the lack of building commissions was such that by the end of the war there was a severe housing shortage. Most architects joined Bernoulli in arguing for a standardized small house.

The first large undertaking of the sort was the Freidorf estate at Muttenz, near Basle (1919–24), by Hannes *Meyer. This was a 'village-like commune' for 150 families with different house types 'with good bourgeois proportions' (Meyer). Between 1924 and 1930 several communal estates were built in Basle, the most important of these – including 'Im Vogelsang' (1924) – being by Bernoulli. The buildings respected traditional types – e.g. in their axial symmetry and small windows – and were constructed by small firms. Early modernism in Swiss housing was manifested not in its technical-formal aspect, but its socio-political implications.

New possibilities first opened up in the second half of the 1920s with the development of the building industry. It was a decisive factor in the penetration of the *'Neues Bauen'. The main influences came not from *Germany, whose contemporary *Expressionism did not elicit the interest of Swiss architects, but rather from Holland (*Netherlands). The initial interest was not in formal, but rather in technical problems: in 1924 Mart *Stam, Hans Schmidt and El *Lissitzky founded the journal *ABC*, which appeared at irregular intervals until 1928. Its 'Contributions to Building' were the most radical manifestos of a rational, and thus industrialized, architecture, to date. The earliest example of 'Neues Bauen' in Switzerland was Rudolf Steiger's Sandreuter house at Riehen, near Basle (1924), which is indebted to the early houses of Frank Lloyd *Wright in its combination of a wooden frame construction with reinforced-concrete and brick, as well as in its shed roof. Subsequently, numerous houses consistently employing the new formal language were constructed in and around Basle in 1928–9, including the Colnaghi House at Riehen

(1927) by Paul Artaria and Hans Schmidt – the first steel-skeleton construction – and, by the same architects, a residence for single women in Basle (1929). In and around Zurich it was especially Max Ernst Haefeli who broke away from traditional housing types, as in the model houses in the Wasserwerkstrasse built for the exhibition 'das neue heim' (1928). The first modern ecclesiastic building in Switzerland was realized in 1926–7 by Karl *Moser: the church of St Antonius in Basle, with side-aisles in exposed concrete, whose cubic masses abandon *Perret's classicist reminiscences at Le Raincy.

The 'Congrès Internationaux d'Architecture Moderne' (*CIAM) were founded in 1928 at La Sarraz, where *Le Corbusier's programme for a first assessment of the position of modern architecture was attempted. Some twenty-five architects from eight countries accepted the invitation. Although the attempt to create an influential international institution did not succeed, this first congress held in Switzerland benefited from the contribution made by local architects and laid the groundwork for the discussions in subsequent years.

The Weißenhofsiedlung (1927) in Stuttgart, planned by the *Deutscher Werkbund, was

Switzerland. Church of St Antonius, Basle (1926–7), by Karl Moser

Switzerland. Residence for single women, Basle (1929), by Paul Artaria and Hans Schmidt

followed with especial comradely interest by the allied Swiss Werkbund. Swiss architects were involved in the interior design of several model houses and Alfred Roth was the site architect for the two houses by Le Corbusier. In 1930 the Swiss Werkbund organized the 'Erste Schweizerische Wohnausstellung Basel', in which thirteen architects from throughout Switzerland were involved in building the model housing estate. Thanks to the use of standardized building parts and industrial assemblage, the sixty terrace houses were quickly and cheaply erected. The 'WOBA' was the first social housing estate realized by the architects of the 'Neues Bauen' in Switzerland. The Werkbund's Neubühl estate in Zurich followed with 200 units, whose nine varied types were conceived with higher aspirations; although standardized elements were also used here, the prefabrication aspect was less comprehensive (Paul Artaria and Hans Schmidt, Max Ernst Haefeli, Carl Hubacher, Rudolf Steiger, Werner M. Moser, Emil Roth, 1930–2).

About this time modernism had successfully made its mark, not least thanks to a number of buildings whose moderate approach made the movement readily acceptable. It was no coincidence that Otto Rudolf *Salvisberg, who returned from Berlin in 1929 to take up a professorship at the Eidgenössische Technische Hochschule in Zurich, was no adherent of the militant avant garde. On the contrary, he championed a modern *aesthetic* of architecture. His most important buildings – the Loryspital

Switzerland. The Werkbund's Neubühl estate at Zurich-Wollishofen (1930–2)

in Berne (1926–9), the Elfenau mothers' and infants' home in Berne (1929–30) and the office building for Hoffmann-La Roche AG in Basle (1936–40) – reveal an elegance which bears witness to Salvisberg's search for style through their 'calm objectivity' (*sanfte Sachlichkeit*: Julius Posener).

German and Italian totalitarianism was experienced not only as political but also as a cultural pressure. Many believed they could resist it by a return to regionalism; a problematic attempt to combine native tradition and modernism led to the so-called 'Heimatstil'. Monumentalizing forms, as in the concrete neo-classicism of the University of Fribourg (1941) by Denis Honegger and Fernand Durand, remained the exception. In contrast to Germany, the continuity of 'Neues Bauen' was never entirely interrupted in Switzerland; examples are buildings of Alfred Roth, Otto H. Senn and Hermann Bauer, such as Bauer's primary school on the Bruderholz in Basle (1938–9), a typological pioneer that was the first school to employ the pavilion system.

Shortage of materials and reduced manpower severely restricted building activity during World War II. Especially notable are several wooden buildings which are free of all nostalgic vernacularism: the Gwad housing estate near Wädenswil (1943–4) by Hans Fischli, and single-family houses by Paul Artaria, Max *Bill, and Ernst Egeler.

Immediately after the war, in an improved economic climate, many buildings were designed as responses to a philosophy of constructional economy and functionalism. The architects who distinguished themselves were those who tried to develop classic modernism further: Werner M. Moser, Roth, Senn and Rudolf Steiger.

However, the influences of a younger generation of architects was soon to be felt. Ernst *Gisel's Park Theatre in Grenchen (1949–55) was the first of an important series of cultural buildings, schools, churches and houses by an architect with an individual style, uncommitted to any established movement.

Architects sought to clothe the countryside in new-style terraced estates clinging to the landscape. The best-known was the Halen estate near Berne, built in 1959–61 by *Atelier 5. The concrete architecture of Atelier 5 comes close to the style of *New Brutalism. Swiss architecture of the 1960s was played out between the two extreme positions represented by Atelier 5's Boiler Factory in Thun (1958–9) and Franz Füeg's contemporary Metal Construction Workshops in Kleinlützel. Füeg belonged, with Alfons Barth, Fritz *Haller, Max Schlup and Hans Zaugg, to the so-called 'Solothurner School', whose approach was nearest to that of *Mies van der Rohe, without being directly dependent on his work. The idea of an architecture which unites the puritan aesthetic with claims to objective validity underlies the strong orthogonal composition, modular organization and crystalline transparency, as well as the most extreme reduction to essentials allied to technical perfection seen in their works. Examples are the church in Meggen by Füeg (1966) and the

Switzerland. Higher Technical Training Centre, Brugg-Windisch (1961–6), by Fritz Haller

Higher Technical Training Centre in Brugg-Windisch by Haller (1961–6).

Walter Maria *Förderer represented an opposite point of view in his advocacy of architecture as an individual artistic creation. His buildings are expressive, sculptural forms – from the Commercial High School in St Gallen (1957–63) to the Church Centre in Hérémence (1963–71), which formed the highpoint of his plastic treatment of space. Claude Paillard's Saatlen church in Zurich-Schwamendingen (1961–4) is composed of closed cubic forms, while his Municipal Theatre in St Gallen (1964–8) consists of a series of stepped prisms. Openly Baroque effects are achieved in the curved, intersecting spatial boundaries of the collegiate church in Sarnen (1964–6) by Joachim Naef and Ernst and Gottlieb Studer. Experimental ideas in the handling of space were especially evident in the new churches of this period, notably in the numerous works of Justus Dahinden (for example the Herz-Jesu-Kirche in Buchs, 1963–5). Restrictive building codes provided the impetus for the pyramidal form of Dahinden's Administration Building for Ferrolegeringar AG in Zurich (1967–70).

The optimistic building boom of the 1960s was succeeded by a reflective critique, originating – surprisingly – in the Ticino region. Several younger architects reacted against the spread of characterless commercial buildings within the confines of a small country like Switzerland. From the outset, the 'Ticino School' represented no single direction; what united its members was a radical rejection of current orthodoxy, the reconsideration of classic modernism, and a heightened historical awareness. Early on, Aurelio Galfetti adapted Le Corbusier's ideas to Ticinese topography (Casa Rotalinti, Bellinzona, 1961); Tita Carloni incorporated elements from factory buildings in his school at Stabio (1968–74); Luigi Snozzi united the repertoire of classical Rationalism with that of traditional Ticinese houses (Casa Cavalli in Verscio, 1976); Mario *Botta's buildings stood out in strong contrast with the surrounding banal architecture (Casa Bianchi in Riva San Vitale, 1971–2; School in Morbio Inferiore, 1972–7); through their elemental forms and relationship to the landscape they succeeded in creating a sense of 'place'. Livio Vacchini's schools in Losone (1973–7) and Locarno (1972–9) also constitute focal points in otherwise formless built environments. Bruno

Switzerland. Commercial High School, St Gallen (1957–63), by Walter Maria Förderer (with Rolf Georg Otto and Hans Zwimpfer)

Switzerland. Casa Cavalli, Verscio, Ticino (1976), by Luigi Snozzi

*Reichlin and Fabio *Reinhart's Casa Tonini in Torricella (1972–4) and Casa Sartori in Riveo (1976–7) tackle the problem of the villa type with a critically reworked 'Palladianism'; an affinity to the theories of Italian *Rational architecture is unmistakable.

To the north of the Alps this tendency can still be detected, most convincingly in the medical training centre in Altdorf (1977–9) by Joachim Naef and Ernst and Gottlieb Studer. Here everything is reduced to an elementary. almost box-like stereometry, whose forms have an almost emblematic quality, e.g. the triangular 'pediment' motif in the corridors or the line of round windows on a columnar portico. A round window is similarly employed in the house at Oberwil (1979–80) by Jacques Herzog and Pierre de Meuron as an 'autonomous element', a motif which distances the building from its environment. The entrance wing of the Museum of Contemporary Art in Basle (1976–9) by Wilfried and Katharina Steib has a pronounced angularity which sets it off from the adjacent older structures.

Most recently, several architects have come to prominence with buildings that are consciously restricted in their use of elements considered 'usual' in domestic design: they respect regional traits without romantic intrusions. Thus, roofs, windows and doors, for instance, are inconspicuous in their simplicity, and simple construction makes judicious use of trusted local materials. Yet this architecture is anything but a display of primitivism; Michael Alder's residential designs (Ziefen, 1969–70; Rodersdorf, 1979; Gempen, 1979) are, in their studied anonymity, a sign of circumspect and careful work on the house type in its original sense of being a functional place to live in. Ivano Gianola's Ticenese buildings (Novazzano, 1973–4; Castel San Pietro, 1979–80) also reflect a similar approach. The housing estates by the Metron group ('Chlepfes', near Appenzell, 1973–4; Brugg-Windisch, 1977 and 1981) are also examples of a new-found simplicity, which in the face of present-day problems seems increasingly appropriate. AH

☐ Bill, Max, *Modern Swiss Architecture, 1925–1945*, Basle 1949; Kidder Smith, G. E., *Switzerland builds*, New York and London 1950; Volkart, Hans, *Schweizer Architektur*, Ravensburg 1951; Altherr, Alfred, *Neue Schweizer Architektur*, Teufen and Stuttgart 1965; Bachmann, J., and von Moos, S., *New Directions in Swiss Architecture*, London 1969; Burckhardt, Lucius and Annemarie, and Peverelli, Diego, *Moderne Architektur in der Schweiz seit 1900*, Winterthur 1969; Birkner, Othmar, *Bauen + Wohnen in der Schweiz 1850–1920*, Zurich 1975; Gubler, Jacques, *Nationalisme et internationalisme dans l'architecture moderne de la Suisse*, Lausanne 1975; Steinmann, M., and Boga, T. (eds.), *Tendenzen. Neuere Architektur im Tessin* (exhibition catalogue), Zurich 1975; Adler, F., Girsberger, H., and Riege, O., *Architekturführer Schweiz*, 2nd ed., Zurich 1978; Blaser, Werner, *Architecture 70/80 in Switzerland* (exhibition catalogue), Basle, Boston, Mass., and Stuttgart 1981.

T

TAC (The Architects Collaborative). Founded in 1945, TAC is an architectural association in which Walter *Gropius joined with architects of the younger generation (Norman Fletcher, John Harkness, Sarah Harkness, Robert McMillan, Louis McMillen, and Benjamin Thompson). Gropius here realized his conception of 'teamwork by individualists' in such large TAC schemes as the Harvard Graduate Center, Cambridge, Mass. (1949), the U.S. Embassy in Athens (1956), the Johns-Manville Co. World Headquarters in Jefferson County, Col. (1976), and the project for Baghdad University.

☐ *The Architects Collaborative 1945–1965*, Teufen 1966; *TAC 1945–1972*, Barcelona 1972; 'The Architects Collaborative: Recent Works', *Architecture and Urbanism* (Tokyo), July 1978.

Tange, Kenzo, b. Osaka 1913. Studied at Tokyo University, where he served as an associate professor, 1946–63, and then as professor until 1972. After graduation he joined the office of Kunio *Mayekawa, a former member of *Le Corbusier's staff. For T., Le Corbusier's exceptionally poetic expression was something more than mere articulation of the *International Style. During the war, when T. was taking part in a graduate programme at Tokyo University, after having resigned from Mayekawa's office, he won first prize in two separate competitions, one for a Monument on Mount Fuji (1941) and the other for a Cultural Centre in Bangkok. In these competitions he demonstrated an extraordinary capacity to combine dynamic large-scale town-planning methods with explicit symbolic forms, which are derived from traditional Japanese architectural styles.

Tange. Peace Centre, Hiroshima (1949–56): Community Centre and Museum

In the period immediately after the war, T. concentrated on city planning. In 1949 he won first prize in the competition for the Hiroshima Peace Centre, which was conceived as the new city core after the city had been largely devastated by the atomic bomb. Aside from a few previously constructed temporary structures, this project was T.'s first major building, and he was invited to present it to the *CIAM of 1951 in relation to its theme 'The Core of the City'.

This presentation virtually served as T.'s international debut. However, in addition to the universality of the design's general conception, it is possible to find in this project the same tendency which had formed the basis of his unrealized competitions during the war. Although the overt nationalistic elements present in the earlier competition designs were no longer present, the two buildings of the Peace Centre clearly demonstrate how his sensibility, inspired by traditional Japanese architecture, was incorporated into the dynamic urban composition. In the following years, T. designed a number of public buildings which showed the same characteristics. He also developed the full potential of structural form based on the most modern technology, thus establishing himself both as a leading figure in the Modern Movement and as the prime mover in the search for a new Japanese national architecture. In fact, in the controversy over what form a national architecture should take in the post-war Japanese democracy, T. maintained that the new style should synthesize the two opposite poles of ancient art and civilization in Japan: the Yayoi culture (in a sense similar to Nietzsche's concept of Apollo in the Greek tragedy) and the Jomon culture (Nietzsche's Dionysius). The Kagawa Prefectural Office Building (1955–8) and the Tokyo Metropolitan Hall (1952–7) were represented in the spirit of Yayoi tradition and the Sogetsu Kaikan Hall in Tokyo (1956–8, demolished) and the Sports Arena in Takamatsu (1962–4) in the spirit of the Jomon tradition. In the 1960s T. produced quite dynamic images in the design of public buildings and also in his urban design projects. These projects were again based on the syntheses of extraordinarily symbolic forms, in a manner which testifies to T.'s revulsion against 'boring modern architecture' (he even reversed the axiom of *Functionalism, by stating that 'only the beautiful can be functional'), and on the systematic method of composition as represented by urban core-systems and the concept of components (*Metabolism). The Tokyo National Gymnasium (1964) and the Yamanashi Press & Broadcasting

Tange. Kagawa Prefectural Office Building, Takamatsu (1955–8)

Centre (1966) are among the most notable products of this period.

In the late 1960s he drew up numerous proposals for projects overseas, and he continued to make these overtures during the 1970s, a period in which architectural activity in his homeland had suffered a decline. However, in these international projects, the Japanese sensibility which characterized his former works had virtually faded away, and his work is now approaching the language of the so-called 'late modern' architecture in the USA and Europe. HY

☐ Boyd, Robin, *Kenzo Tange*, New York 1962; Altheri, Alfred, *Three Japanese Architects*, Teufen 1968; Kultermann, Udo, *Kenzo Tange 1946–69*, New York 1970; 'Kenzo Tange and URTEC, Urbanists and Architects', *The Japan Architect* (Tokyo), 234, vol. 51 (1976), nos. 8/9.

Tange. Tokyo National Gymnasium (1964)

Tatlin, Vladimir E., b. Kharkov 1885, d. Moscow 1953. Studied art in Moscow, 1909–11. Under the influence of *Cubism and *Futurism, he bcame one of the leading advocates of *Constructivism in *Russia after 1913. Following abstract compositions in glass, metal and wood, he designed a project for a gigantic Monument to the Third International (1920): within a steel construction 300 m (1,300 ft) high were to be suspended transparent glass assembly halls which would express their various political functions through the speed of their revolutions. He termed such syntheses of steel frame and electrification 'political sculpture', and saw it as a celebration of the Socialism of the future. In the 1920s he designed furniture and other household objects which reveal a greater concern for everyday reality. GHa

☐ Andersen, Troels, *Vladimir Tatlin* (exhibition catalogue), Stockholm 1968; Milner, John, *Vladimir Tatlin and the Russian Avant-Garde*, New Haven, Conn. 1983.

Taut, Bruno, b. Königsberg 1880, d. Istanbul 1938. Trained at the Baugewerksschule in

Taut, Bruno. The Hufeisensiedlung ('Horse-shoe' estate), Berlin-Neukölln (with Martin Wagner; 1925–30)

Königsberg. Worked in the office of Bruno Möhring in Berlin in 1903 and 1904–8 with Theodor *Fischer in Stuttgart. From 1909 he was in practice in partnership with Franz Hoffmann, and 1914–31 with his brother Max *Taut in Berlin. Early works included a turbine house at Wetter/Ruhr (1908), a convalescent home in Bad Harzburg (1909–10), and several apartment houses in Berlin. In 1912 he was appointed advisory architect to the Deutsche Gartenstadtgesellschaft and designed garden suburbs in Magdeburg (1913–14 and 1921) and in Falkenburg, near Berlin (1913–14). His Monument des Eisens at the Internationale Baufachausstellung of 1913 in Leipzig and the Glashaus at the Werkbund-Ausstellung of 1914 in Cologne both brought him considerable critical notice, and the latter brought him into contact with the glass fantasist Paul Scheerbart, whose ideas influenced him strongly.

A committed pacifist, he worked during World War I on his polemical tracts, later published as *Die Stadtkrone* and *Alpine Architektur*. In November 1918 he signed the programme of the Politischer Rat geistiger Arbeiter and was a founder-member of the *Arbeitsrat für Kunst and of the *Novembergruppe. In the immediate post-war years he was the undisputed leader of the utopian tendency in German architecture of *Expressionism and exerted great influence through the Arbeitsrat für Kunst, the *Gläserne Kette, and the magazine *Frühlicht*. The utopian phase was short-lived, however, and a growing commitment to *Rationalism developed after 1920.

He was city architect in Magdeburg, 1921–3, and introduced a controversial programme of coloured façade restoration; 1924–32 he was architectural adviser to GEHAG (Gemeinnützige Heimstätten-, Spar- und Bau-Aktiengesellschaft) and was responsible for many large-scale estates in Berlin. This gave him the opportunity to apply his theories on functional and labour-saving design, which were modelled on the Taylor system. The results count among the century's most important achievements in mass housing. Typical housing estates include the 'Hufeisensiedlung' (1925–30, with Martin Wagner) and the 'Uncle Tom's Cabin' scheme (1926–31). T. was professor of architecture at the Technische Hochschule in Berlin, 1930–2, and was elected to the Prussian Academy of Arts in 1931. In 1932–3 he made a working visit to the USSR.

After his enforced emigration in 1933, he lived for three years in Japan, was employed by the Crafts Research Institute in Sendai, and wrote on Japanese art and culture. In 1936 he was appointed professor at the Academy of Arts in Istanbul. He designed schools in Ankara, Izmir and Trabzon, and university buildings in Ankara, as well as his own house in Ortaköy. IBW

□ Taut, Bruno, *Die Stadtkrone*, Jena 1919; ——, *Alpine Architektur*, Hagen 1919; ——, *Die Auflösung der Städte*, Hagen 1920; ——, *Die neue Wohnung*, Leipzig 1924; ——, *Die neue Baukunst in Europa und Amerika*, Stuttgart 1929; ——, *Architekturlehre*, Istanbul 1937; Junghanns, Kurt, *Bruno Taut 1880–1938*, Berlin (East) 1970; *Bruno Taut 1880–1938* (exhibition catalogue), Berlin 1980; Whyte, Iain Boyd, *Bruno Taut and the Architecture of Activism*, Cambridge 1982.

Taut, Max, b. Königsberg 1884, d. Berlin 1967. Trained at the Baugewerksschule in Königsberg, and was employed, 1906–11, in the office of Hermann Billing in Karlsruhe. From 1911 he had his own practice in Berlin (in partnership with Franz Hoffmann, 1914–50, and with his brother Bruno *Taut, 1914–31). Prior to World War I, T.'s commissions included schools at Finsterwalde (1911–12) and Nauen (1913–15), the Koswig textile factory at Finsterwalde (1913), and a prize-winning pavilion at the Internationale Baufachausstellung of 1913 in Leipzig. In 1918 he became a founder-member of the *Arbeitsrat für Kunst, the

★Novembergruppe, and subsequently of the ★Ring. Although he was a member of the ★Gläserne Kette group, his drawings from this period shunned the extremes of fantasy and reflected the interest in concrete construction which had already appeared in his pre-war work. Two office blocks in Berlin, for the Allgemeiner Deutscher Gewerkschaftsbund (1922–3) and for the Verband der Deutschen Buchdrucker (1922–5, with Mart ★Stam), were pioneering examples of concrete-frame construction and seminal buildings in the development of the ★Neue Sachlichkeit movement in architecture. Unable to practice in the years 1933–45, T. re-emerged in 1945 as a leading figure in West German architecture. He was a professor at the Hochschule für bildende Künste in West Berlin, 1945–54. His principal late work was in housing. Major works include: the Reuter-Siedlung in Bonn (1949–52); extension of his brother's 'Hufeisensiedlung' in Berlin-Neukölln (1954); and the August-Thyssen-Siedlung, Duisburg (1955–64) IBW

□ Taut, Max, *Bauten und Pläne*, Berlin 1927; ——, *Berlin im Aufbau*, Berlin 1946; *Max Taut* (exhibition catalogue), Berlin 1964.

Tecton. Group of architects founded in London in 1932 by ★Lubetkin together with Anthony Chitty (left 1936), Lindsey Drake, Michael Dugdale (left 1934), Valentine Harding (left 1936), Godfrey Samuel (left 1935) and Frances Skinner. In 1946, Denys ★Lasdun became a partner. The group, which was the most important representative of the ★International Style in ★Great Britain, was disbanded in 1948. It became known especially for its fantastically shaped buildings for the London Zoo (1932–7) which recall the Russian Constructivist sculptures of Naum Gabo and Antoine Pevsner; the Highpoint I (1933–5) and Highpoint II (1936–8) flats at Highgate in London; and the Finsbury Health Centre in London (1935–8). AM

Tecton. Finsbury Health Centre, London (1935–8)

□ Coe, Peter, and Reading, Malcolm, *Lubetkin and Tecton. Architecture and Social Commitment*, London and Bristol 1981.

Terragni, Giuseppe, b. Meda near Milan 1904, d. Como 1941. Attended the technical school in Como, 1917–21, then studied at Milan Politecnico, 1921–6; ran his own office (together with his brother Attilio), 1927–39.

He was one of the most important and independent protagonists of Italian ★Rationalism, in which he played a decisive role from the beginning. His work is emblematic of the contradictory process by which the architecture of the early 20th century in ★Italy freed itself from provincial ★eclecticism and attached itself to the European modernist movement without abandoning the strong imprint of classical principles: in fact it developed in an intermediate zone, as fascinating as it was precarious, between revolutionary renewal and conservative tradition.

The first work which brought the young architect to notice was a project for a gasworks, which he designed in 1927 and exhibited in the same year at the Monza Biennale. Several months earlier, T. had been one of the seven founding members of ★Gruppo 7. Thus he already found himself immersed in the polemic which was unleashed around Italian Rationalism. The confrontation was especially piquant as both the young rationalist challengers (who banded together in 1930 in the ★M.I.A.R.), as well as the established academic opposition (under the spiritual leadership of Marcello ★Piacentini), were supporters of Fascism and both strove to win Mussolini's favour.

In 1927–8, against bitter opposition, T. built the five-storey block of flats 'Novocomum' in Como. Both its provocative sleekness and its bold corner solution with the dramatic superimposition of a semicircular glazed part combined with a fully rectilinear volume led to heated discussions. Although the building

Terragni. Novocomum flats, Como (1927–8)

Terragni. Casa del Fascio, Como (1932–6)

already clearly shows T.'s hand, it is, like his earlier projects, by no means free of dependence on Russian *Constructivism. His masterpiece is the Casa del Fascio in Como (1932–6); this administration building, which had as one of its primary aims its function as an elegant set-piece for Fascist mass rallies, is a lightly modified classical palazzo type centred on a glass-roofed interior court. The building forms a harmonically proportioned, white marble-clad cube completely devoid of ornament; it reveals in part its similarly-clad – and thus dematerialized – constructional skeleton. Solid and void, which complement each other in terms of light and shade, are markedly and effectively contrasted in the four differently-handled façades.

In 1933 he contributed the Artist's House on a Lake at the First Milan Triennale (in collaboration with other architects). In 1936–7 the Casa Bianca, which shows the influence of *Mies van der Rohe, was built in Seveso. Also dating from 1937 are two stylistically diverse works – evidence of T.'s creative complexity: the project for the Danteum in Rome (with Pietro Lingeri), a profoundly intellectual, metaphysical creation, and the Antonio Sant'Elia kindergarten in Como, an elegant building in the style of international Rationalism. The Casa del Fascio in Lissone was built in collaboration with Antonio Carminati in 1938–9, and in 1939–40 he realized his last important work, the Casa Giuliani Frigerio in Como.

T.'s independent œuvre, which absorbed the best aspects of the poetry of the Novecento Italiano, as well as of Giorgio de Chirico's 'Pittura metafisica', and reworked them into an uncommonly consistent 'third way' between academic *neo-classicism and orthodox Rationalism, represents a highpoint within the development of Italy's modern architecture. In that respect, T. can be compared with *Sant'Elia. His crystalline architectural language, full of hidden semantic implications, his obsessive concern with 'form as form' and its geometrical legitimacies, as well as his respect for the historic tradition of architecture – characteristic of Italian Rationalism – would find their continuation in the 1960s in the *Rational architecture developed by Aldo *Rossi. In addition, his œuvre was to have a significant influence on the work of the *New York Five, and above all on that of Peter *Eisenman. VML

□ Labio, Mario, *Giuseppe Terragni*, Milan 1947; Veronesi, Giulia, *Difficoltà politiche dell'architettura in Italia 1920–1940*, Milan 1953; 'Omaggio a Giuseppe Terragni', *L'Architettura – cronache e storia* (Milan), no. 153, July 1968; Mantero, E., *Giuseppe Terragni e la città del razionalismo italiano*, Bari 1969; Zevi, Bruno (ed.), *Giuseppe Terragni*, Bologna 1980; Schumacher, Thomas, 'From Gruppo 7 to the Danteum: A Critical Introduction to Terragni's *Relazione sul Danteum*', *Oppositions*, 9, pp. 89–107.

Tessenow, Heinrich, b. Rostock 1876, d. Berlin 1950. Attended the Städtische Bauschule in Neustadt (Mecklenburg), 1896, and the Royal Saxon Baugewerkschule in Leipzig,

Tessenow. Training Centre for rhythmic gymnastics (Jacques-Dalcroze-Institut), Hellerau, near Dresden (1910–11)

1897; studied under Karl Hocheder and Friedrich von Thiersch at the Technische Hochschule in Munich, 1901–2. He taught at the Städtische Baugewerkschule in Sternberg, 1902–3, and that in Lüchow; in 1904 he taught under Paul Schultze-Naumburg at the Kunstschule in Saaleck, and was Director of the Baugewerkschule in Trier, 1905–9. From 1910 he was active in Hellerau without an official position, then became a professor at the K.K. Kunstgewerbeschule in Vienna, 1913–18. From 1918 he was again in Hellerau, before becoming head of the architecture section of the Akademie der bildenden Künste in Vienna, 1920–6. From 1926 to 1941 and again from 1946 he was professor at the Technische Hochschule in Berlin. T.'s early work still bears witness in its intellectual foundations to the *Arts and Crafts movement, but already from 1905 an increasing striving for simplicity is evident (single-family terrace houses for the Neu-Dölau development near Halle an der Saale). Formal elements which would come to typify his later work surfaced here: prismatically carved house forms, smooth surfaces, pitched roofs, terraced treeless and semi-open areas leading to the entrances, and delicately mullioned windows.

The first houses were erected in 1909–11 in Hellerau Garden City, where in addition *Riemerschmid, *Fischer, *Muthesius and Schumacher also worked. At the same time T. also built the Training Centre for rhythmic gymnastics (Jacques-Dalcroze-Institut) in Hellerau – an axial, symmetrical layout on a nearly square ground-plan, whose rigorous, classically inspired formal language forgoes all solemnity. In 1925–7 he collaborated with Oskar Kramer on the Sächsische Landesschule in the Dresden suburb of Klotzsche, a strongly articulated complex which derives its expressive effects from a rhythmic placing of similar,

Tessenow. Heinrich-Schütz School, Kassel (1927–30)

economical architectural elements. In the Heinrich-Schütz School in Kassel and the covered swimming pool in the Gartenstraße in Berlin (both 1927–30), T. moved closer to contemporary *Rationalism.

The elegant remodelling of Schinkel's Neue Wache (Guardhouse) in Berlin as a memorial to victims of World War I dates from 1930–1. After 1933 T.'s success was hindered by the rise of National Socialism; his former pupil *Speer did not even once manage to procure a commission for him.

T. was somewhat of an outsider in the architecture of the first half of the century, already so hard to classify. His conscious traditionalism was never without regional and classicist traits and, both in his care to unite his buildings with the terrain and in his attention to human scale, he had much in common with *Häring's 'organic architecture'. All avant-garde experimentation is foreign to his work; but so too is all popularizing nostalgia. His influence, exercised both through buildings and by his simple theoretic writings, was at once unspectacular and wide-ranging. Among those he influenced was *Le Corbusier, when he was in contact with the circle of the *Deutscher Werkbund: Le Corbusier's Villa Jeanneret, built two years later in La Chaux-de-Fonds, bears witness to this influence. T.'s pupils, properly speaking, include the Austrian Franz Schuster, who built a multi-family dwelling in Ernst *May's Römerstadt in Frankfurt am Main in 1927; finally, his sedate and strong architectural spirit has been kept alive in the work of such protagonists of *Rational architecture as Giorgio *Grassi. VML

☐ Tessenow, H., *Zimmermannsarbeiten*, Freiburg 1907; ——, *Hausbau und dergleichen*, Berlin 1916; ——, *Handwerk und Kleinstadt*, Berlin 1919; Grassi, G., 'Architettura come mestiere' (foreword to Tessenow, H., *Osservazioni sul costruire*), Milan 1974; Wangerin, Gerda, and Weiss, Gerhard, *Heinrich Tessenow. Ein Baumeister 1876–1950. Leben, Lehre, Werk*, Essen 1976.

The Architects Collaborative. *TAC.

Tigerman, Stanley, b. Chicago 1930. Studied at the Massachusetts Institute of Technology in Cambridge, at the Institute of Design in Chicago, and – interrupted by a break of several

Tigerman. Daisy House, Porter, Ind. (Stanley Tigerman and Associates; 1977)

years which included a period working in the office of *Skidmore, Owings & Merrill – at Yale University (under *Rudolph). He was head designer, 1961–2, under Harry M. Weese in Chicago, where he subsequently entered into partnership with Norman Koglin. Finally in 1964 he opened, in Chicago, his present office: Stanley Tigerman and Associates. He was a professor at the University of Illinois at Chicago Circle, 1965–71. In the 1960s he designed immense megastructures of steel space-frames, such as Instant City (1968), which bears witness to the influence of *Mies van der Rohe in its crystalline sharpness, as well as to that of Walter Netsch, his former superior at SOM. The rationalist style tending to abstraction is also prominent in the vacation house constructed in a former barn in Burlington, Wis. (1970–3), which is one of the most ingenious examples of the adaptation of an old building to new uses. T.'s most recent works are expressions of the attempt, in a partly ironic and shocking way, to explore the metaphorical possibilities of architecture (*Post-Modernism), an example of which can be seen in the Daisy House at Porter, Ind. (1977), built for the proprietor of a strip-tease club; this house, with its phallic overtones, is reminiscent of Ledoux's project for an Oikema. AM

☐ Tigerman, Stanley, *Versus. An American Architect's Alternatives*, New York 1981; *Seven Chicago Architects* (exhibition catalogue), Chicago 1976.

Torroja (y Miret), Eduardo, b. Madrid 1899, d. Madrid 1961. Studied civil engineering in Madrid until 1923, when he began his own practice. He was director of the Instituto Técnico de la Construcción y del Cemento (now Instituto Eduardo Torroja), which is today one of the leading test laboratories for building construction methods.

Torroja. Grandstands at the Zarzuela racecourse, near Madrid (1935)

His first major work was the Tempul aqueduct over the river Guadalete, where the longitudinal girders were pre-stressed. He became known internationally through his roof for Algeciras Market Hall (1933); here the concrete shell roof, resting on eight external supports, has a diameter of 47·50 m (156 ft). For the Zarzuela racecourse near Madrid (1935) he designed a system of fluted grandstand roofs with a very extensive cantilever, counterbalanced by vertical tie rods behind the stanchions. In the same year he built the shell roof of the Frontón Recoletos (destroyed in the Spanish Civil War), whose form derived from the penetration of two barrel vaults of different dimensions running parallel to each other. An example of T.'s ingenious treatment of steel as a structural material is the roof of the Las Corts football stadium in Barcelona (1943); projecting 25 m (82 ft), the roof features a sinuous outline.

T. stands out as one of the great creators of architectural form in the 20th century. As his many works built in Europe, Africa and America strikingly demonstrate, he possessed great imaginative powers, capable of posing unusual problems and devising unexpected solutions for them, together with an immense technical capacity for putting them into practice. In contrast to the usual mathematically minded type of engineer, he asserted from the outset the rights of the imagination. For him calculations only served to show whether an idea would in fact work in practice. AC-P/GHa

☐ Torroja, Eduardo, *Philosophy of Structure*,

Berkeley, Cal. 1958; ——, *The Structures of Eduardo Torroja*, New York 1958; Cassinello, Fernando, 'Eduardo Torroja', *Cuadernos de Arquitectura* (Barcelona), August 1961.

U

Ungers, Oswald Mathias, b. Kaiseresch, Eifel, 1926. Studied under Egon *Eiermann at the Technische Hochschule in Karlsruhe. In 1950 he opened his own office in Cologne. He was a professor at the Technische Universität in Berlin, 1963–8, and since 1969 has taught at Cornell University. After completing a significant number of residential projects, including his own house in Cologne (1959) and apartment blocks in the Märkisches Viertel of Berlin (1964–6), U.'s building activity came to an abrupt halt in the mid-1960s. His subsequent involvement with architecture was for a time exclusively on paper, and included a great number of important competition projects (Students' Residence Hall in Enschede, 1964; Staatliche Museen in the Tiergarten, Berlin, 1965; reorganization scheme for the Tiergarten, 1973; Wallraf-Richartz Museum in Cologne, 1975; residential development in the Ritterstraße, Marburg, 1976).

Towards the end of the 1970s, U. – who had in the meantime achieved an international reputation – once again had opportunities to build (residence on the Goethepark in Berlin, 1980–2; Frankfurt Congress Hall, 1980– ; Badische Landesbibliothek, Karlsruhe, 1979–). With *Kleihues, he is one of the most important German practitioners of a new rationalistic architecture (*Rational architecture), in which he undertakes radical typological experiments, in line with those carried on for many years by Aldo *Rossi, but also combined with romantic conceptions in part inspired by Karl Friedrich Schinkel. FW

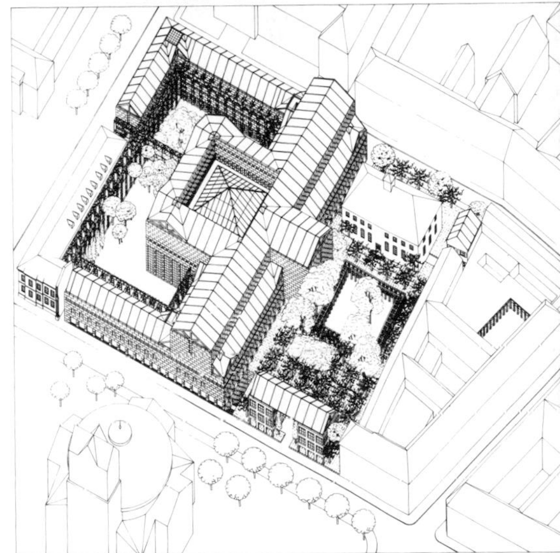

Ungers. The architect's own house, Köln-Mungersdorf (1959)

Ungers. Badische Landesbibliothek, Karlsruhe

□ Ungers, O. M. and L., *Kommunen in der Neuen Welt 1740–1971*, Cologne 1972; Gregotti, Vittorio, 'Oswald Mathias Ungers', *Lotus* (Milan), nos. 11/12 (1976), pp. 14–41; 'Ungers', *Das Kunstwerk* (Stuttgart), 32 (1979), nos. 2/3, pp. 132–41; 'Architekt O. M. Ungers', *Deutsche Bauzeitung* (Stuttgart), no. 10 (1979), pp. 15–44; Frampton, Kenneth (ed.), *O. M. Ungers: Works in Progress* (exhibition catalogue), New York 1981; Ungers, O. M., *Architecture as Theme*, Milan 1982.

USA. For a long time after the discovery of the 'new world' by Europeans, North American architecture was directly shaped by European movements and tendencies. During the colonial period the major influences were at first Dutch and then above all English (Georgian style). With the Declaration of Independence of the

USA. Pierpont Morgan Library, New York (1902–3), by McKim, Mead & White

United States of America (1776) and the victory over the British, the Greek Revival style began to gain favour, and hence French neo-classical (*neo-classicism) influences in particular became important. During the 19th century neo-classical and romantic neo-Gothic styles developed simultaneously; among the most important architects of the period were Benjamin Latrobe, Thomas Jefferson, Robert Mills, Alexander Jackson Davis, James Renwick and Richard Upjohn. Towards mid-century, under the influence of the English *Arts and Crafts movement, the neo-medieval tendency was strengthened (Victorian style).

While the USA had up to that point played a subordinate, even passive role in architecture, this situation was to change dramatically in the last thirty years of the 19th century, with the appearance of an outstanding personality: H. H. Richardson. Even though he absorbed impulses from European architectural experiences (he studied at the *Ecole des Beaux-Arts in Paris and was influenced by Joseph-Auguste Vaudremer's tempered use of Romanesque forms), he reworked them into a fully independent style, which was subsequently to be influential in Europe (especially in Scandinavia). His massive, closed neo-Romanesque buildings unite historicist and rationalist traits with a discipline as powerful as it was stringent. Its influence is felt in, among others, the Shingle Style, which was used for country houses between 1870 and 1890. The smoothness and free ground-plans of these houses also reflect the reform ideas of R. N. *Shaw; but the external walls were not clad, as in Shaw's work, in clay tiles but rather in wooden shingles.

Richardson's influence was to prove far more extensive, however, notably on the clear formal language developed in the buildings of the *Chicago School (and thereby on the works of Dankmar *Adler, Daniel Hudson Burnham, John Wellborn Root, William Holabird and Martin Roche, and Richard E. Schmidt), and was particularly important for Louis *Sullivan's development. In this regard, Richardson can be considered at once the father figure of American *organic architecture and of American modernism.

Around the turn of the century, architecture in the USA was divided into two principal trends. On the one hand, the neo-classical tradition enjoyed an extensive 'come-back', having been given prominence in the academically composed 'White City' of the 'World's Columbian Exposition' in Chicago (1893, general plan by D. H. Burnham). This represented a reaction to the individualist designs of the early rationalist Chicago School. An especial flourishing of this style was seen in the numerous elegant buildings of the East Coast firm of *McKim, Mead & White, who were principally active in New York and designed numerous buildings in which they employed the Italian Renaissance, Neo-Palladian, Beaux-Arts and Colonial Revival modes. On the other hand, a romantic position – whose development reached back, via Sullivan and the strongly expressive 'heresies' of Frank Furness, to the American version of the Gothic Revival – developed with much vigour. On the West Coast the organic ideal survived with particular strength, as did the moral reforming of the Arts and Crafts and the tradition of exquisite craftsmanship associated with *Art Nouveau in the sublimely refined œuvre of the brothers *Greene as well as in the robust, exotically effervescent early Bay Region Style of Bernard *Maybeck.

The figure of Frank Lloyd *Wright towers above all others. A pupil of Sullivan, he adopted, after uncertain beginnings, a decidedly anti-classical approach, although the best of his work never denies the rational discipline he had imbibed from his 'lieber Meister'. The revolutionary concept of his Prairie Houses, which he built between 1894 and 1909 in the Chicago suburbs, quickly became known in Europe, thanks to *Berlage and to two publications of Wright's work (1910, 1911) by Wasmuth, the Berlin architectural publisher. They were to exercise an influence on nascent

USA. Palace of Fine Arts, San Francisco (1915), by Bernard Maybeck

USA. Robie House, Chicago (1908–9), by Frank Lloyd Wright

*Rationalism and above all on the Dutch group De *Stijl. But even the School of *Amsterdam, the Dutch school largely influenced by *Expressionism, was to exploit the horizontal overhangs, the flow of internal spaces and the expressive use of materials in Wright's work. In the USA, however, Wright at first, like the late Sullivan (National Farmers Bank in Owatonna, Minn. 1907–8), received relatively little attention. At the same time, within the two major movements of neo-classicism and neo-Romanticism, appeared the largely independent works of Henry Bacon, Cass Gilbert, Irving *Gill, Bertram Goodhue, George *Howe, Richard Morris Hunt and James Gamble Rogers. The contribution of Albert *Kahn stood apart from these conventional architectural practices. His firm rapidly specialized in large-scale industrial buildings, and continued the trend of large American architectural offices, like McKim, Mead & White, but with some novel characteristics: his utilitarian, rough buildings are for practical purposes unwitting predecessors of modernism.

USA. *Daily News* Building, New York (1929–30), by Raymond Hood

But the breakthrough for Rationalism in America was still several years off. While the 1920s represent a highpoint for the architectural avant garde in Europe, American political isolationism left the country all but untouched by these dramatic cultural developments. The most important international competition of the period, that for the *Chicago Tribune* Tower (1922) was not won by one of the modernist entries submitted from Europe (Bernard Bijvoet and Johannes *Duiker, *Gropius and Adolf Meyer, Ludwig *Hilberseimer, Clemens *Holzmeister, Adolf *Loos, Bruno *Taut and Max *Taut all entered), but rather by the reduced neo-Gothic design of Raymond *Hood and John Mead Howells. Eliel *Saarinen was awarded second prize for a moderately traditionalist design; a year later, he settled in the USA and thus contributed to that series of successful emigrations from Europe which was to increase significantly in the 1930s. Richard *Neutra emigrated in the same year, ten years after his compatriot and fellow-student Rudolph *Schindler. Their early works, in which the influence of Wright was combined with that of Otto *Wagner and Adolf Loos, were the first in the late 1920s to introduce the *International Style to the USA.

In the meantime, the modernist aesthetic had gained ground on the East Coast and above all in New York. The *Art Deco style, thanks to its restrained modernism and its talent for unproblematic mediation between various artistic positions, was fashioned into an independent architectural position. Within the 'New York School' arose the fundamentally symbolic aspirations of Harvey Wiley Corbett, Jacques André Fouilhoux, Jacques Ely-Kahn and William Van Alen. They were still frivolously celebrating the light-hearted 'jazz age' on the eve of the Great Depression of 1929, while Hugh Ferriss produced shadowy expressionist visions in his renderings. The immanent frivolity of the new 'fashion' made it easy for an architect such as Raymond *Hood to make the transition in seven years from the elegant *historicism of 1922 to a sheer, expressive modernism in the *Daily News* Building, New York (1929–30).

USA. The National Gallery of Art, Washington, D.C. (1937–40), by John Russell Pope

In the 1930s the impact of European (and particularly German) immigrants favoured the final triumph of the International Style, which had already passed an important milestone with the PSFS (Philadelphia Saving Fund Society) Building in Philadelphia (1929–32) by George Howe and William *Lescaze. In 1937 Gropius, *Mies van der Rohe, and Marcel *Breuer arrived in the USA, in 1938 Martin *Wagner, and three years later Erich *Mendelsohn. At Harvard University Gropius continued his teaching activity (begun at the *Bauhaus), and he was soon followed by Wagner and Breuer; Mies van der Rohe played an analogous role at the Armour Institute of Technology (later Illinois Institute of Technology) in Chicago. Their influence on the East Coast was decisive and to some extent reached the proportions of a cultural imperialism. Its first manifestation was seen in the single-family houses that Gropius and Breuer built in the Boston region. Later, with their cool, perfect, autonomous stereometry, Mies van der Rohe's buildings were to become the prototype of a new American architecture. The cultural invasion was so strong that even Wright, for all his independent and anti-European feelings, could not avoid responding in his own work: he built the Kaufmann House ('Fallingwater') in 1936–9 near Mill Run, Pa., as a creative synthesis of organic and European rationalist architectural elements.

The West Coast saw a quieter and more continuous development. Here William Wilson *Wurster, Harwell Hamilton Harris and John Yeon continued to pursue independently the heritage of Maybeck and thus introduced a new era of the Bay Region Style, characterized by elegance and restraint. At the same time, Schindler and Neutra refined their version of the International Style, while Wright, after the apotheosis of Fallingwater, turned to new experiments with fortress-like closed houses, in which Richardson's original forms were given new life.

Amidst all this, of course, the classicist tradition persisted without interruption. It was, above all John Russell Pope who preserved it in a new version notable for its purity and orthodoxy.

Konrad *Wachsmann arrived in North America in 1941, where his radical technologically oriented experiments were in line with those which R. Buckminster *Fuller had pursued as early as the 1920s and which were to lead in the 1950s and 1960s to large geodesic dome constructions. Immediately after World War II, especially in the work of Mies van der Rohe and Philip *Johnson, a synthesis of neo-classicism and the International Style was achieved; in this the technology and aesthetic of the industrial era was put to the service of a 'new classicism' (Farnsworth House, Plano, Ill. 1945–50; Johnson House, New Canaan, Conn. 1947–9). The structural perfection and tectonic elegance of these houses had their counterpart on the other side of the country in the refined structures of Charles ★Eames and, slightly later, of Craig ★Ellwood.

The reductivist clarity of the work of Mies van der Rohe and Johnson was easy to imitate and to copy by industrialized methods, so that it rapidly developed into a fashion, especially for office and industrial buildings. The architectural firm of ★Skidmore, Owings & Merrill (SOM) – successors to the high-quality economic potential of McKim, Mead & White and inheritors of Albert Kahn's utilitarianism – adopted the metal-and-glass formula and played out its multifarious possibilities in countless buildings. Various other large architectural offices pursued a similar path, including those of Wallace K. ★Harrison and Max ★Abramovitz, I. M. ★Pei, and Eero ★Saarinen (son of the Finnish architectural pioneer). In sharp contrast to this geometric discipline, Wright – in his late work – resorted to a confusion of forms beyond measure; this taste for the bizarre and the exotic was to live on in the work of Bruce ★Goff and Paolo ★Soleri.

The exhaustion of the creative potential of the restricted language of the late International Style was predictable; it had begun already in the mid-1950s. The search for new means of expression led to a spirit of ready experimentation and eclectic mannerism which investigated and employed classical forms side by side with the romantic overtones that Alvar ★Aalto had once again brought into prominence in the dramatically curved slab of his Senior Students' Dormitory (Baker House) at the Massachusetts Institute of Technology in Cambridge (1947–8). This superficial play with transient 'costumes' which were subject to rapid change, in accordance with the laws of advertising, was soon embraced and adopted by Eero Saarinen, among others.

Saarinen announced a 'sculptural' style to succeed the purist approach and, moreover, did not shy away from naive figurative metaphors. Edward Durell Stone reintroduced decorative perforated walls of bricks and ashlar or metal gratings, while Minoru ★Yamasaki indulged in a luxurious and brittle historicism with a neo-Gothic slant. Finally, even Paul ★Rudolph, albeit with restraint, revealed his inclination towards the use of heterogeneous and rich idioms ('the new freedom'). Philip Johnson had been, anyway, one of the first to abandon the type of asceticism imported from Europe in favour of a new and unorthodox historicism. Even at SOM there was a clearly heard reaction to this shift in taste, to the extent that the filigree-like curtain-wall façades, which had almost become a trademark of the firm, were abandoned in favour of a heavy classicist monumentality. Meanwhile, the later American works of Mies van der Rohe, as well as ★Le Corbusier's Carpenter Center for the Visual Arts in Cambridge, Mass. (1961–4), remained in their unshakable consistency untouched by the feverish searching after novelty for its own sake.

USA. The architect's own house, New York (1956), by Edward Durell Stone

The reaction to the ever-expanding ramblings through the realm of possible architectural forms, as ephemeral as it was arbitrary, was led by a personality who, like Richardson in his time, was trained within the Beaux-Arts tradition: Louis I. ★Kahn. Now, however, he extended these lessons in so single-minded a manner that his influence spread far beyond America's borders – to Europe itself. Kahn took as his starting point Mies's aesthetic, but he interpreted it much more in terms of handicraft and roughness. In his architectural stance he combined fundamental beliefs of Richardson, Sullivan and Wright, and realized a sort of 'fulfilment' of the previous hundred years of North American architecture. His craving for the solid, ordering principles of a powerful tradition led him to an involvement with historical models and archetypes, which he combined into elegant, festive compositions in which a strong sense of geometric discipline is retained.

Kahn's work, as consistent as it was pioneering, remained largely isolated and decidedly atypical in the context of American architecture; yet the 1960s brought – not least through his slogan 'back to order' – a generalized calming down. Eero Saarinen turned in his late work to a measured technological expressionism; and Kevin *Roche and John *Dinkeloo, who took over his office, continued – in a more disciplined way – this tradition. Their experiments in the field of large glazed halls (Ford Foundation Building, New York, 1963–8) were taken up by John *Portman and translated into an urban scale. At SOM, Walter Netsch introduced, with his 'field theory', an attempt to move away from strictly rectilinear design. Johnson continued with the production of classical monumental architecture, but now endowed with far greater ceremonial character and fortress-like articulation. At the same time, on the West Coast, Charles W. *Moore,

USA. National Football Foundation Hall of Fame, New Brunswick, N.J. (project, 1966), by Venturi and Rauch

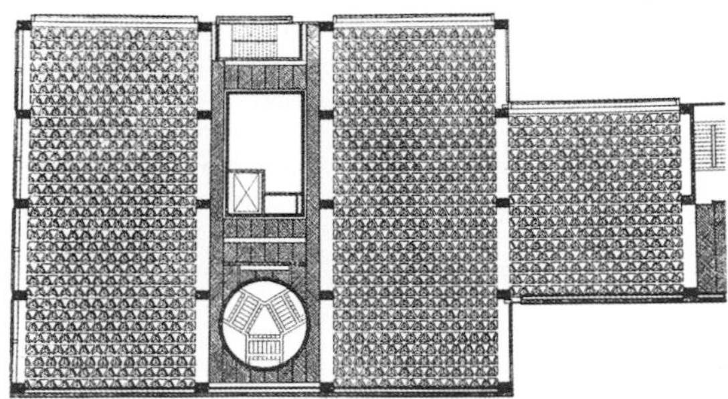

USA. Yale University Art Gallery, New Haven. Conn. (1951–3), by Louis Kahn

together with Donlyn Lyndon, William Turnbull and Richard Whitaker, continued in the unbroken tradition of the Bay Region Style with simple, high-quality buildings wholly alien to the tone of the East Coast.

In another direction, the work of Robert *Venturi aimed, in the wake of the Pop Art of the 1960s, to make the aesthetic potential of American everyday culture useful to architecture. In the context of an anti-classical and anti-European polemic – which was not without parallels to that begun sixty years earlier by Wright – Venturi abandoned the modernist maxim of the unity of interior and exterior, of form and function, of beauty and usefulness, which he mockingly compared with the 'Duck' (in reference to a duck-shaped café on Long Island). Instead he advocated the 'decorated shed' design principle, which considered the separation of function and decoration. In his buildings, which are so designed as to be distinguished only with difficulty from the usual type of American commercial architecture, he realized the theoretical postulates that he had summarized and published in 1966 under the title *Complexity and Contradiction in Architecture*.

Displaying an equally strong intellectual stamp were the roughly contemporary ideas developed by the *New York Five – Peter *Eisenman, Michael *Graves, Charles *Gwathmey, John *Hejduk and Richard *Meier – but these were totally incompatible with the views held by Venturi's circle. While Venturi strove for a 'non-straightforward architecture', the Five advocated metaphysical clarity: it was not by chance that they concentrated their efforts on the elaboration of the formal language of Le

Corbusier and of Giuseppe *Terragni. Their purism thus hardly expressed – any more than did Venturi's preference for the hybrid and impure – a social, functional, or technological obligation. Rather, in the first instance it was an extreme cult of form to which they paid homage in an uncommonly elegant series of buildings, almost without exception with a snow-white exterior.

The contrast between the 'Whites' and the 'Greys', between the classically oriented new 'New York School' and the romantic 'Philadelphia School', sharpened increasingly during the 1970s. The circle around Venturi, to which Moore grew closer and which was joined by Robert A. M. *Stern, John S. Hagmann, Stanley *Tigerman and James *Wines and the SITE group, turned ever more decisively to a radical eclecticism, which was unified under the rubric of *'Post-Modernism'. Frank O. *Gehry assumed a special position in that group with his collages of discard material, which evoked memories of hippie settlements. The circle around the New York Five, to which Raimund Abraham was linked by poetic visions, held fast to its purism. Only Graves would gradually abandon the position of the Whites and slide towards the Greys' position.

Simultaneously at SOM, at first undisturbed by such confrontations, bold structural experimentation continued, culminating in 1974 in the Sears Building – 450 m (1,500 ft) high – in Chicago. Johnson, who in the meantime had begun working again in the glass-and-steel tradition, was the first of the great 'establishment' figures to react to the romanticism of the Greys and translate their post-modern formal language into the scale of the super-skyscraper. SOM and even C. F. Murphy Associates (renamed *Murphy/Jahn in 1981), who had still carried on the technological aesthetic of Mies van der Rohe's work in the 1960s, followed suit.

Finally, there are many architects on the contemporary scene who play a fairly independent role, separate from the debate between Whites and Greys. They include: Diana Agrest and Mario Gandelsonas, who, under the influence of Rem *Koolhaas, have been chiefly concerned with a new evaluation of the skyscraper type; Emilio Ambasz, who practises a 'hidden' and background architecture by the use of a few basic components; Romaldo Giurgola, who employs symbolic monumental forms in a self-effacing manner; Hugh Hardy, whose vocabulary ranges from technological expressiveness to restrained traditionalism; Daniel Libeskind, who – in his drawings, using the formal language of the avant garde of the 1920s – recreates the chaos of Piranesi's visionary works; and finally Cesar *Pelli, who has made a name through his novel use of glazed outer skins. VML

USA. Pacific Design Center, Los Angeles, Cal. (1971), by Cesar Pelli and Gruen Associates

USA. Sears Tower, Chicago, Ill. (1972–4), by Skidmore, Owings & Merrill

□ Tallmadge, Thomas E., *The Story of Architecture in America*, New York 1927, rev. ed.

1936; Kimball, Fiske, *American Architecture*, New York 1928; Mock, E. B., *Built in USA 1932–44*, New York 1944; Fitch, James Marston, *American building. The historical forces that shaped it*, Boston and London 1947, rev. ed. 1966; Hitchcock, Henry-Russell, and Drexler, Arthur, *Built in USA: Post-war architecture*, New York 1952; Mumford, Lewis, *Roots of Contemporary American Architecture*, New York and London 1952; McCallum, Ian, *Architecture USA*, London and New York 1959; 'America', *Zodiac* (Milan), no. 8 (1961); Burchard, John, and Bush-Brown, Albert, *The Architecture of America. A Social & Cultural History*, Boston and Toronto 1961; Stern, Robert A. M., *New directions in American Architecture*, New York 1969; Hunt, William Dudley, *Encyclopedia of American Architecture*, New York 1980; Diamonstein, Barbaralee, *American Architecture Now*, New York 1980; Whiffen, O. Marcus, and Koeper, Frederick, *American Architecture 1607–1976*, Cambridge, Mass. 1981.

Utzon, Jørn, b. Copenhagen 1918. The most original architectural talent in Danish modern architecture, U. showed early on an attraction for the *organic architecture of Frank Lloyd *Wright and Alvar *Aalto. The influence of

Utzon. Sydney Opera House (1956–73): exterior and longitudinal elevation

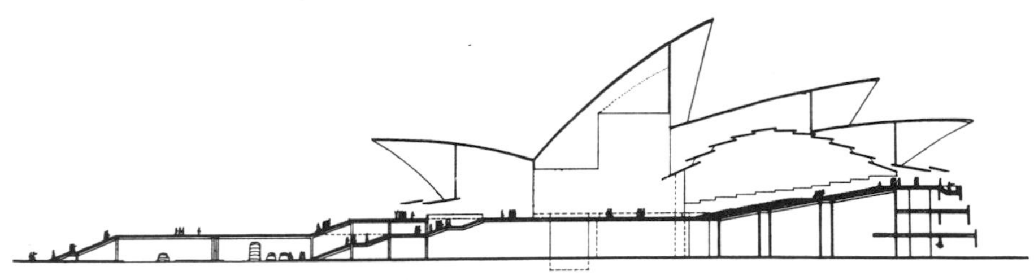

Aalto was strengthened subsequently by a period of several months working in his Helsinki studio in 1946.

After studying at the Academy of Fine Arts in Copenhagen, 1937–42, where Kay *Fisker and Steen Eiler Rasmussen were his teachers, U. worked for three years under *Asplund in Stockholm.

In 1952 he built his own house in Hellebaek. The open ground-plan and free arrangement of space was at that point something entirely new in Danish architecture. Shortly thereafter, in 1952–3, he built a house in Holte in which a concrete construction elevates the timber-clad building one storey above the ground.

In 1956 he won first prize in an international competition for the new Opera House in Sydney, which was built on a mole jutting into the city's harbour. The Opera House, Concert Hall and Foyers, with their shell roofs up to 60 m (197 ft) high, stand above an extensive artificial platform which in turn serves as the cover for the lower levels with experimental theatre, access for vehicles and auxiliary rooms. The shells were erected on a daring and original constructive principle developed by U. in collaboration with Ove *Arup. Unfortunately, U. was not able to stamp the interiors with his personal style as well; he found himself forced in 1966, after repeated interference with his work, to leave the completion to others.

In a number of projects dating from 1958 onwards, U. varied the idea of raised platforms or bastions (Secondary school at Helsingør, 1958; Pavilion complex for the Copenhagen World's Fair, 1959; Theatre in Zurich, 1964). Contemporaneously with these dynamic and imaginative projects, two residential complexes were built in North Zeeland; the Kingo Houses in Helsingør (1956–60) and the houses in Fredensborg (1962–3). In both cases he composed 'chains' of housing units grouped around central courts, with the individual chains following the contours of the site.

The Sydney Opera House led U. to an intensive study of the problems of industrialized building, in which he strove to avoid the usual clichés. He has worked with the principles of an additive architecture consisting mainly of concrete prefabricated components which yield richly interchangeable compositions. Examples are the projects for the town centre of Farum (1966) and for a school centre in Herning (1969), as well as the 'Expansiva' building system (1969). Among his most visionary works is his project for a Museum in Silkeborg (1963), which goes back to a suggestion made by the painter Asger Jorn. The major part of the sculptural building complex was to be sunken so that a hollow space would be created in the centre, thereby offering visitors a highly diversified spatial experience. The church in Bagsværd, near Copenhagen (completed 1976), has a high interior which is lit by skylights arranged along the external walls. U.'s most recent work is the Parliament Building in Kuwait, for which he submitted the winning design in an international competition. TF

☐ Utzon, Jørn, 'Additive Architecture', *Arkitektur* (Copenhagen), 14 (1970), no. 1; Drew, Philip, *The Third Generation: the changing meaning of architecture*, New York 1972.

V

Vago, Pierre, b. Budapest 1910. At the age of eighteen he came to Paris to study under Auguste *Perret at the Ecole Spéciale d'Architecture. While still a student, in 1932, he became editor-in-chief of the journal *l'Architecture d'aujourd'hui*. In private practice from 1934, he designed a prefabricated all-metal house, exhibited at the Exposition de l'Habitation of that year. Town planning, schools, housing (in Berlin 1957, with apartment-units one-and-a-half storeys high), churches (Basilica of St Pius X at Lourdes, 1958, with *Freyssinet as engineer).

Valle, Gino, b. Udine 1923. Studied at the Istituto Universitario di Architettura in Venice and at Harvard University. In 1948 he entered the office of his father Provino Valle in Udine, which he later took over with his brother Nani. Since 1977 he has been a professor at the school of architecture in Venice. He seeks to invest his buildings with heightened significance through a strict fulfilment of functional requirements. A typical example from his main field of activity, industrial buildings, is the Zanussi administration building in Pordenone (1961). While he has shown himself to be a consistent adherent of *Rationalism, this building is also related to *New Brutalism. In buildings of other types, he has at times had recourse to regional traditions, as is clearly manifested in the double house in Udine (1965–6). AM

□ 'Gino Valle', *Zodiac* (Milan), no. 20 (1970), pp. 82–115.

Van de Velde, Henry, b. Antwerp 1863, d. Zurich 1957. The apostle in theory and practice of functional aesthetics and 'pure form', between 1900 and 1925 he exerted a decisive influence on architecture and the applied arts, particularly in *Germany. He had been attracted to music, literature and painting before turning to architecture. In 1881 he became a student at the Académie des Beaux-Arts at Antwerp, where he attended the painting classes; he continued his studies with Carolus Duran in Paris, 1884–5. He made contact with the Impressionist painters and Symbolist poets, and was particularly impressed by Georges Seurat, whose pointilliste technique seemed to embody a spatial concept capable of opening up new prospects in architecture. Returning to Antwerp, he took part (1886) in founding the cultural circle named 'Als ik Kan' (after van Eyck's motto) and, a year later, 'L'art indépendant', an association of young neo-Impressionist painters. From 1889 onwards he took part in the international activities of the famous avant-gardist Brussels group known as 'Les Vingt', where he became interested in the synthetical art and flowing hand of Gauguin, the English *Arts and Crafts movement, and the socially oriented work of William *Morris. About 1890 he became associated with the journal *Van Nu en Straks*, for which he devised a revolutionary layout, new typography and woodcut ornaments in a style derived from Gauguin.

In 1895 (two years after *Horta's Hôtel Tassel), he built his own home, 'Bloemenwerf', at Uccle near Brussels. It is designed as an organic whole and completely fitted out (joinery, hardware, furniture, carpets, curtains, dinner service, glasses, silver) in a uniform style reflecting English inspiration. Characteristic features include a return to a rational style that 'frankly and proudly' displays the processes of manufacture in all fields, an uncompromising logic in the use of materials, and a rejection of all ornament inspired by nature and all historic detailing. But his renewed awareness of structural function still retained sentimental overtones. His thinking was influenced by German romanticism. 'Whether it was a matter of the works of German, Austrian or Dutch artists', he wrote later, 'we were all more attached than we thought to a kind of romanticism which would not allow us to consider form "without ornament", we were too much painters, too much wedded to literature, to glimpse the necessity of abandoning ornament and decoration . . . the temptations and subconscious insinuations of romanticism prompted us to bend and twist our structural schemes and present them as ornaments acting as structural elements, or as structures imbued with the rhythm of a linear ornament.'

The fact remains that V.'s cult of linear ornament, of the undulating line, was strengthened by his enthusiastic adherence to the neo-romantic theory of empathy, formulated by Theodor Lipps in 1903. The originality of his designs soon caught the attention of the art historian Julius Meier-Graefe and the art dealer Samuel Bing, who helped to ensure their international popularity. In 1895 Bing invited V. to fit out four rooms of a shop he was opening in Paris under the name of 'L'Art Nouveau'. His robust and curvilinear furniture aroused much enthusiasm at the Dresden Exhibition of Applied Arts in 1897.

Henceforth, V.'s path was clear: he would make his career in Germany. Before he left Belgium (1899), Meier-Graefe commissioned him to do the interior decoration of the Maison Moderne he had founded in Paris, and introduced him to the group in Berlin associated with the newspaper *Pan*. There he also won

Van de Velde. School of Applied Arts, Weimar (1906)

many commissions (Hohenzollern Craftwork Shop, 1899; Haby's barber shop, 1901; premises for the Habana Tobacco Co., 1900). During the winter of 1900–1, he undertook a lecture tour in Germany, during which he explained his artistic principles (these were published in Leipzig in 1902 under the title *Kunstgewerbliche Laienpredigten*). At the instance of Karl Ernst Osthaus, he undertook the interior decoration of the Folkwang Museum at Hagen (1900–2). The strong modelling and curved ornamentation of this building are typical of Art Nouveau, and mark the culminating point of the first phase of V.'s career, which closes with the retiring room he designed for the Dresden Exhibition of Applied Arts in 1906.

The second phase, from 1906 to 1914, is opened by the foundation and building of the Weimar School of Applied Arts, thanks to V.'s influence with the Grand Duke of Saxe-Weimar, to whose court he had been attached since 1901 as artistic counsellor, charged with raising the level of design in local industry. Here he found an ideal field for exercising his vocation as a teacher. He introduced a new system of instruction based on the development of spontaneous feeling and a constant recourse to each student's powers of invention, avoiding the use of models from the past and the study of historic styles. These methods gave rise to new forms, which German industry was not slow to adopt.

The design of the Weimar school buildings clearly expresses the development of V.'s architectural thought. Although traditional building methods are employed, a surer sense of space and volume is evinced. Plastic expression is

Van de Velde. Werkbund Theatre, Cologne (1914): general view and detail of entrance with decoration by H. Obrist

emphasized, just as it was a feature of the heavy roof, with its original profiling, of the Werkbund Theatre in Cologne (since destroyed). Built for the Werkbund Exhibition of 1914, it was laid out on a symmetrical plan, with a heavy traditional shell. Although of original appearance, it embodied numerous innovations that provided a brilliant answer to the requirements of the dramatic art of its day: auditorium in the shape of an amphitheatre, independent proscenium, circular horizon, and, in particular, a tripartite stage. V., who was friendly with Gordon Craig and Max Reinhardt, had already in 1910–11 drawn up the first plans for the Théâtre des Champs-Elysées, Paris; this theatre was subsequently realized, in an altered form, by Auguste *Perret.

He moved to Switzerland in 1917, and in 1921 he went to Holland, where he was commissioned by the Kröller-Müller family to design a museum, which he ultimately built, to a modified plan, at Otterlo (1937–54). This building is a work of great simplicity and harmony, free of all rhetorical effects; it is perfectly adapted to its site and function (one level throughout, main and secondary circulation, top lighting, etc.).

V. returned to Belgium in 1925. With the support of the Minister C. Huysmans, he was given the opportunity once more of carrying out the experiments he had conducted at Weimar: in 1926 he founded the Institut des Arts Décoratifs. He was the principal of this school until 1935; in addition, he occupied the chair of architecture at the University of Ghent from 1926 to 1936. RLD

□ van de Velde, H., *Déblaiement d'art*, Brussels 1894; ——, *Aperçus en vue d'une synthèse d'art*, Brussels 1895; ——, *Vom neuen Stil*, Leipzig 1907; ——, *Geschichte meines Lebens*, Munich 1962; Mesnil, J., *Henry van de Velde et le Théâtre des Champs-Elysées*, Brussels 1914; Osthaus, Karl Ernst, *Henry van de Velde. Leben und Schaffen des Künstlers*, Hagen 1920; Casteels, Maurice, *Henry van de Velde*, Brussels 1932; 'Henry van de Velde', special issue of *La Cité* (Brussels), 1933, nos. 5/6; Teirlinck, Herman, *Henry van de Velde*, Brussels 1959; Hammacher, A. M., *Die Welt Henry van de Veldes*, Cologne 1967; Hüter, K.-H., *Henry van de Velde. Sein Werk bis zum Ende seiner Tätigkeit in Deutschland*, Berlin (East) 1967.

Venturi, Robert, b. Philadelphia 1925. Studied at Princeton University. He worked in various offices, including those of Eero *Saarinen and Louis I. *Kahn until 1958, in which year he established his own architectural firm with several partners in Philadelphia. In 1964 he formed a partnership with John Rauch, which was expanded in 1967 to include Denise Scott Brown (Venturi's wife). Currently, Steven Izenour and David Vaughan are also associated with the firm. Over the years they have realized such paradigmatic buildings as: the Guild House Retirement Home, Philadelphia (1960–3); the Vanna Venturi House, Chestnut Hill, Pa. (1962); the Humanities Building of the State University of New York at Purchase (1968–73); the Dixwell Fire Station in New Haven, Conn. (1970–4); the Peter Brant House, Greenwich, Conn. (1971–3); Franklin Court in Philadelphia (1972–5); the addition to the Allen Art Museum of Oberlin College, Oberlin, Ohio (1973–6); the Faculty Club of the Pennsylvania State University (1974); and the Basco Showroom on the outskirts of Philadelphia (1979). All of these illustrate, in often highly diverse statements, V.'s determination to translate into architectural terms such elements of perceptive psychology as ambiguity, memory, and contradictoriness.

Venturi. Guild House Retirement Home, Philadelphia, Pa. (1960–3)

V. came to worldwide attention less through his built œuvre, however, than through his writings on architectural theory. In 1966 he published *Complexity and Contradiction in Architecture*, in which he analyzed, in most original ways, the continuous play with multiple meanings and contradictions in the history of Western architecture. In 1972 he published, together with Denise Scott Brown and Steven Izenour, the book *Learning from Las Vegas*. Here he made it clear that it was no longer a matter of denying formal qualities in the supposed ugliness of the American everyday environment. Instead he proposed to acknowledge them as artistic stimuli in architectural design (*Post-Modernism). FW

□ Venturi, R., *Complexity and Contradiction in Architecture*, New York 1966 and London 1977; Venturi, R., Scott Brown, D., and Izenour, S., *Learning from Las Vegas*, Cambridge, Mass. 1972; Maxwell, Robert, and Stern, Robert A. M., *Venturi and Rauch*, London 1978; Moos, Stanislaus von, and Weinberg-Staber, M. (eds.), *Architektur in Alltag Amerikas. Venturi und Rauch*, Zurich 1979.

Villagrán García, José, b. Mexico City 1901. Studied at the Architecture School of the Academia de San Carlos in Mexico City (today the Architecture School of the National University of Mexico). He himself taught there for more than a quarter of a century and thus exercised a pronounced influence over the younger architectural generation in Mexico. Inspired by *Le Corbusier and *Gropius, he became one of the most important proponents of the Modern Movement in his country, which, however, he advocated more convincingly in his teaching than in his own architecture. Among other works, he designed the Architecture School and the Art Museum of the National University of Mexico in the new University City (1951, with Alfonso Liceaga and Xavier García Lascurain). AM

☐ Villagrán García, José, *Problemas en la formacion del arquitecto*, Mexico City 1964; 'José Villagrán García', *Arquitectura* (Mexico City), September 1956.

Villanueva, Carlos Raúl, b. Croydon, England 1900, d. Caracas 1975. Studied at the *Ecole des Beaux-Arts in Paris, and in 1929 opened his own office in Caracas. From 1929 to 1939 he served as architect to the Venezuelan Ministry of Public Works, and from 1940 to 1960 he was consulting architect to the Banco Obrero in Caracas. In 1944 he founded the faculty of architecture at the University of Venezuela in Caracas, at which he subsequently taught.

As was typical among architects of his generation, throughout Latin America, V.'s early work was an attempt to renew the traditions of local colonial architecture. Quite soon, however, he came to a deep understanding of the new ways of thought in architecture and devoted himself with a missionary zeal to the spread of modernist architecture in his own land. To the inspiration received from the great masters of his time he added characteristic personal elements: a dynamic and spontaneous quality in structural design, forcefully expressed in exposed concrete; a catholicity of taste reflected in extensive collaboration with many painters and sculptors, as well as in a daring use of polychromy; and a feeling for large-scale composition. Of V.'s most important work, the buildings for the University City of Caracas, the Stadium (1950–2), with its daringly cantilevered marquees, built in shell concrete, with exposed ribs, and the Auditorium (Aula Magna) and the Covered Plaza (Plaza Cubierta) of 1952 are the best known. The Aula Magna has a clean white curved ceiling against which float a large number of variously coloured and shaped panels designed by Alexander Calder (with Robert Newman as acoustics specialist); these have a twofold function, aesthetic and acoustic. The austerity of the exterior, emphatically expressing the structural framework, is compensated by the lightness and airiness of the Plaza Cubierta, the large semi-enclosed foyer, highlighted by a décor conceived by Arp, Léger, Vasarely and others.

Of V.'s huge housing projects, necessitated by the rapid growth of Caracas, at least two must be mentioned as examples: the 'Dos de Diciembre' estate (1943–5), with 2,366 dwellings for 12,700 people – designed in collaboration with José Manuel Mijares, José Hoffman and Carlos Branco; and the 'El Paraiso' (1954) complex, with duplex units in a four-storey and a sixteen-storey building. The frank expression of the structure distinguishes these buildings, like most of his work, from the mainstream of the *International Style and lends his œuvre an uncompromising, dynamic spirit. HEM/GHa

☐ Hitchcock, Henry-Russell, *Latin-American Architecture since 1945*, New York 1955; Moholy-Nagy, Sibyl, *Carlos Raúl Villanueva*, New York 1964.

Voysey, Charles Francis Annesley, b. Hessle, Yorkshire 1857, d. Winchester 1941. Worked under Thomas Seddon and in collaboration with George Devey before opening his own architectural office in 1882. Under the influence of the *Arts and Crafts movement and especially of *Morris, V. became one of the most important figures of the English Domestic

Voysey. Broadleys, Windermere (1898–9)

Wachsmann. Cellular construction system (1950–3)

Revival. Above all, he designed country houses which drew on the rural architectural traditions of the Tudor and Stuart periods, but which adopted a new free ordering of internal spaces (Perrycroft at Coewall, 1893; Norney at Shackleford, 1897; The Orchard at Chorley Wood, Herts., 1899). His elegant interiors were influenced by Arthur Mackmurdo and rivalled those of C. R. *Mackintosh. V.'s undoctrinaire response to functional requirements and his simple formal language contributed to opening the way for the early phase of modernism in England. VML

☐ Voysey, C. F. A., *Reason as the Basis of Art*, London 1906; Gebhard, David, *Charles F. A. Voysey. Architect*, Los Angeles 1975; Brandon-Jones, John, *C. F. A. Voysey, Architect and Designer, 1857–1941*, London 1978.

W

Wachsmann, Konrad, b. Frankfurt an der Oder 1901, d. Los Angeles 1981. Wachsmann was a pioneer of industrialized building in theory, practice and teaching. He always advocated that the scientific and technical resources of mass production should be applied to the processes of building, and he held a corresponding structural and aesthetic conception of architecture. He came straight from building in timber to the problems of prefabrication. Trained as joiner and carpenter, W. was a student at the Academies of Art at Dresden (under Heinrich *Tessenow) and Berlin (under Hans *Poelzig). From 1926 to 1929 he worked as chief architect for the firm of Christoph & Unmack, the largest manufacturers of timber buildings in Europe at the time. In 1932 he was awarded the Rome Prize by the German Academy in Rome. In the years following, which he spent in Rome, he was occupied with building blocks of flats in reinforced concrete.

Emigrating to the United States, he founded a partnership with Walter *Gropius, which lasted from 1941 to 1948; from it emerged the General Panel Corporation, the first fully-automated factory for the production of prefabricated building components. In 1950, he was appointed Professor of Design at the Illinois Institute of Technology in Chicago and director of the Department of Advanced Building Research.

His research concentrated on the basic character of universal elements in building construction which can be mass produced. His starting point was 'modular co-ordination', which governed the relationship of the various building components to each other. These components should be as simple as possible and capable of as many different combinations as possible. A 'universal module', identical with the 'planning module' comprised all the modular categories (material, performance, construction, installation, etc.).

W.'s research found a practical application above all in the General Panel System, which was made up of prefabricated timber units (1943–5). In the 1940s he was commissioned by the U.S. Air Force to develop the 'Mobilar Structure', a system for the construction of aircraft hangars to any required size by the addition of tubular steel struts. He made a special study of the nature of the connections and joints of cellular structures such as Buckminster *Fuller's geodesic domes or Le Ricolais's space structures, built up from similar elements.

W. was concerned equally with a technical and scientific building procedure that utilized mass-production methods and with a corresponding understanding of structure in architecture. Time and time again, his apparently utopian projects anticipated future realities, and stimulated discussion – beyond the limits of architecture – of spiritual problems in a technological age. MS/GHa

□ Wachsmann, K., *Aspekte*, Wiesbaden 1961; ——, *The Turning Point in Building*, New York 1961.

Wagner, Martin, b. Königsberg 1885, d. Cambridge, Mass. 1957. Studied at the Technische Hochschule, first in Berlin-Charlottenburg and then in Dresden. Member of the architectural group Der *Ring. He was Municipal Architect in Berlin, 1926–33; there he collaborated closely with *Gropius, *Häring, *Mies van der Rohe, *Poelzig, and *Scharoun. He emigrated to Turkey in 1935, and from there to the *USA; he taught at Harvard University, 1938–50.

Under the Weimar Republic, he was one of the most important advocates of a state architectural policy that would seek to unite socialist ideals with post-war reality. The Lindenhof housing estate, built to his plans in Berlin-Schöneberg (1918–21), anticipates the most important elements of his urban planning of later years: buildings on the periphery that were closed on the street side, broad courtyards, a centre as a meeting place and unified composition of buildings. This was a concept that the subsequently elaborated with Bruno *Taut in the large Britz housing estate ('Hufeisensiedlung', or 'Horseshoe estate') in Berlin-Neukölln (1925–30).

Wagner, Otto, b. Penzing, near Vienna 1841, d. Vienna 1918. A precursor of 20th-century architecture and town planning, he was the founder of the 'Vienna School', the most notable members of which were *Loos, *Hoffmann and *Olbrich. W. played a role in *Austria equivalent to that of *Sullivan in the United States, *van de Velde in Belgium and *Berlage in the Netherlands. Perhaps more than that of any other architect, his work reflects the great changes in taste that were taking place at the turn of the century.

He began his studies in 1857 at the Technische Hochschule in Vienna. He spent some time in 1860 at the Berlin Bauakademie and completed his training at the school of architecture of the Akademie der bildenden Künste, Vienna, 1861–3. The first phase of his career is marked by a historicist approach to design. He adopted a form of classicism derived from the Tuscan and Florentine High Renaissance: closed plans that were lucid, logical and severely geometrical. His work earned him such a reputation that he was commissioned in 1890 to draw up a scheme for the complete replanning of the City of Vienna. Of this, the only proposal to be realized was the construction (1894–7) of the Stadtbahn, or metropolitan railway network.

In 1894 he was appointed head of a special class in architecture at the Vienna Akademie. This year also marked the opening of a second phase in the development of his work (1894–1901), characterized simultaneously by a rationalist conception of architecture and a delight in the floral ornament of contemporary *Art Nouveau. While van de Velde was opening his famous campaign in Brussels to purify the formal language of architecture (*Déblaiement d'art*, 1894), W. put forward in his inaugural lecture at the Vienna Akademie a doctrine that has become famous under the title of *Moderne Architektur*. In his view, the new architecture must take the requirements of modern life as its point of departure, and find adequate forms to express them. Two years after Sullivan's plea (*Ornament in Architecture*, 1892), and three years before the first statements of Loos, W. was extolling horizontal lines, flat roofs, and a reductivist style that would draw its powers of expression from a strict respect for structural principles and the 'truthful' use of materials.

The Stadtbahn station in the Karlsplatz (1888–9) is typical of this transitional period. The use of a steel frame, in accordance with French models, would – in keeping with W.'s own theoretical requirements – have demanded the abandonment of all purely decorative features; in the event, however, the building is embellished with floral ornamentation. He thus sought a compromise between doctrinal demands and aesthetic form.

W. went on to adopt a more radical attitude in full conformity with the principles he defended. The Post Office Savings Bank in Vienna (1904–6) dominates the third and last phase of his career; the economy of its trape-

Wagner, Otto. Post Office Savings Bank, Vienna (1904–6): façade and banking hall

zoidal plan, developing harmoniously around a central hall, the feeling for monumentality, the flexible handling of space, the complete eschewal of ornament and the perfect integration of steel and glass combine to make this building an unmistakable landmark in the history of modern architecture. RLD

☐ Wagner, Otto, *Moderne Architektur*, Vienna 1896 (4th ed.: *Die Baukunst unserer Zeit*, Vienna 1914); Lux, Joseph August, *Otto Wagner*, Munich 1914; Tietze, Hans, *Otto Wagner*, Vienna 1922; *Otto Wagner. Das Werk des Architekten* (exhibition catalogue), Vienna 1963; Geretsegger, H., and Peintner, M., *Otto Wagner, 1841–1918. The Expanding City and the Beginning of Modern Architecture*, New York 1979.

Warchavchik, Gregori, b. Odessa 1896, d. São Paulo 1972. After studying at the University in Odessa and at the Istituto Reale Superiore de Belle Arti in Rome, he worked for several years under Marcello *Piacentini. In 1923 he went to Brazil, where he at first practised in São Paulo, and then, 1931–3, with Lúcio *Costa in Rio de Janeiro. Finally, after 1934, he settled in São Paulo. From 1931 he was a professor at the Escola Nacional de Belas Artes in Rio de Janeiro. His 'Manifesto on Modern Architecture', published in 1925, served as the point of departure for the Modern Movement in Brazil.

His own house in São Paulo (1927–8), with its strong cubistic symmetrical composition, is of an elegant *Art Deco design; the houses he built in the 1930s belong to the pioneering works of the *International Style in Latin America.

☐ Warchavchik, Gregori, 'Acerca de arquitectura moderna', *Correio de Manha* (Rio de Janeiro), 1 November 1925; *Gregori Warchavchik* (exhibition catalogue), São Paulo 1975.

Webb, Philip (Speakman), b. Oxford 1831, d. Worth, Sussex, 1915. He was at first an assistant in G. E. Street's office, where he met William *Morris, with whom he later collaborated closely, notably as a designer for the firm of Morris, Marshall, Faulkner & Company, founded in 1861. W. built town and country houses, in which medieval stylistic elements are merged with 18th-century reminiscences in unconventional compositions. His early Red House (1859), built for Morris at Bexley Heath, Kent, is – with its free, asymmetrical ground-plan, its unity of interior and exterior and its unpretentious façades of red brick – one of the first attempts at a renewal of domestic design within the Gothic Revival.

☐ Lethaby, W. R., *Philip Webb and his Work*, Oxford 1935; Brandon-Jones, John, 'Philip Webb' in Ferriday, Peter (ed.), *Victorian Architecture*, London 1964; Macleod, Robert, *Style and Society*, London 1971.

Williams, Sir (Evan) Owen, b. Tottenham, London 1890, d. London 1969. After studying at the University of London, he worked initially as an engineer and constructor; in the 1930s he created some of the most significant buildings of modern architecture in *Great Britain through his use of new construction techniques. The Boots' Factory at Beeston, Notts. (1930–2) – in which the mushroom-pier support system developed by Robert *Maillart was used for the first time in Britain – and the Pioneer Health Centre in Peckham, London (1934–6), are noteworthy examples of an engineer's architecture which is both constructionally and formally successful.

☐ Gold, Michael, 'Sir Owen Williams, K.B.E.', *Zodiac* (Milan), no. 18 (1968), pp. 11–30; Rosenberg, S., Chalk, W., and Mullin, S., 'Sir Owen Williams', *Architectural Design*, July 1969.

Wines, James, b. Oak Park, Illinois, 1932. He worked first for more than a decade as a sculptor before launching the multi-disciplinary organization SITE (Sculpture in the Environment) in New York in 1969. In 1973 he took on Alison Sky, Emilio Sousa and Michelle Stone as partners. Since 1975 he has been a professor at the New Jersey School of Architecture, New-

Wines. Tilt Showroom, Towson, Md. (1976–8)

ark. The SITE group seeks a union of art and architecture which will direct architecture away from orthodox '*Functionalism', a programme characterized by W. himself as 'De-architecture'. They are especially known for their work for the retail stores chain Best Products, including the Peeling Project in Richmond, Va. (1971–2), the Indeterminate Façade in Houston (1974–5) and the Tilt Showroom in Towson, Md. (1976–8), in all of which the observer is meant to be shocked by some eccentric detail. AM

☐ SITE, *SITE Projects and Theories*, Bari 1978; ——, *SITE. Architecture as Art*, London 1980.

Woods, Shadrach, b. Yonkers, N.Y. 1923, d. New York 1973. After studies in engineering in New York and literature in Dublin, he entered *Le Corbusier's office in Paris in 1948. There he met Georges *Candilis, with whom he collaborated until 1967: from 1951 to 1955 as his partner in the African office of ATBAT (Atelier des Bâtisseurs) in Casablanca; from 1955 to 1963 in Paris where, joined by Alexis *Josic, they opened the office of Candilis/Josic/Woods; and after 1963 again with Candilis alone. In 1968 he became a professor at Harvard University, and from 1970 he had his own office in New York. Like Candilis and Josic, his reputation rests principally upon the group's collaborative planning of the new town Toulouse le Mirail (competition 1962, realized 1964–77). AM

☐ Woods, Shadrach, *Stadtplanung geht uns alle an*, Stuttgart 1968; see also under Candilis.

Wright, Frank Lloyd, b. Richland Center, Wisconsin 1867, d. Phoenix, Arizona 1959. Studied engineering 1885–7 at the University of Wisconsin in Madison and worked at the same time for Allen D. Conover. Subsequently he practised for a short time in the studio of John Lyman Silsbee, who introduced him to the principles of the Shingle Style. In addition to these brief professional experiences, visits to his grandfather's farm near Spring Green, Wis., were influential in his early years in stimulating a special love of nature.

In 1888 W. entered the office of Louis *Sullivan and Dankmar *Adler, where he played a large role in the design of houses (Charnley House, Chicago, 1892). At the same time he absorbed many principles from the teaching of his 'Lieber Meister', as he called Sullivan: the naive philosophy of the American 'founding fathers', the ultra-individualism of the writer Henry David Thoreau and the naturalism of Thomas Jefferson. He derived further theoretic inspiration from his reading of Ruskin (*Arts and Crafts) and Viollet-le-Duc (*France). He found architectural models in the works of the East Coast masters H. H. Richardson, Bruce Price, as well as *McKim, Mead & White.

Three other formative influences deserve mention: the fascination and poetry of additive and interlocking forms aroused by childhood acquaintance with Froebel kindergarten toys; the attraction of the open ground-plans and crafted finish of Shingle Style houses; and the exoticism of traditional Japanese architecture as represented by the reconstruction of the Ho-o-den Temple as the Japanese Pavilion at the World's Columbian Exposition held in Chicago in 1893.

The result of W.'s love of nature was his decision to abandon the big city in favour of the suburbs. In Oak Park, an upper-class green oasis in the suburbs of Chicago, he established a studio in 1889. In his first commissions he paid homage to the single-family house as the basis of a new, individualistic democracy for the 'Happy Few'. After hesitant attempts to adjust to the Beaux-Arts (*Ecole des Beaux-Arts) style (design for the Milwaukee Library, 1893), he opted definitively for an anti-classical and anti-European approach and followed instead the 'organic' ideal as a sign of American cultural independence (*organic architecture). He left Sullivan and Adler in 1893 and entered into partnership with Cecil Corwen; three years later he set up an independent practice in Oak Park. The Winslow House in River Forest, Ill. (1894), still bears witness to the classical residue of his dependence on Sullivan, but already the typical characteristics of W.'s own early style are manifested: the overhanging roofs, the emphasis placed on horizontals, and the asymmetrically resolved building composition. Thus was launched that series of Prairie Houses which would receive its definitive formal language in two projects published in February 1901 in the *Ladies' Home Journal* (A Home in a Prairie Town; A Small House with Lots of Room in it). It was an independent type of single-family house set in green surroundings, which was oriented towards the North American farmhouse in its noble simplicity, its avoidance of purely representational and non-functional space, and its

Wright. Willitts House, Highland Park, Ill. (1902)

free articulation of the farmhouse tradition. For the further development of this elegant *Gesamtkunstwerk*, W. always sought out a qualified team of artists and technicians.

The Willitts House in Highland Park, Ill. (1902), was typical of the Prairie Houses. The ground-plan is cruciform, designed around a central chimney; internal living spaces are individually shaped but flow freely one into another. The asymmetrical wings of the building reach out like arms and unite house and nature on ideal axes.

In the Martin House in Buffalo, N.Y. (1904), W. introduced a forerunner of the horizontal bands of windows which became a prominent feature in his later houses. He used them as a dominant formal element in the Tomek House in Riverside, Ill. (1907). The Coonley House (1907–11), also in Riverside, is a complex image in which the ceilings of the rooms are inclined, matching the shallow slope of the roof.

Wright. Larkin Building, Buffalo, N.Y. (1904–5)

The Robie House in Chicago (1907–9) marks the climax and finale of the series of Prairie Houses. As it was no longer a case of a building set in an open site, but rather of a city house (albeit with a large garden for the time), the axis of the ground-plan, composed with grandeur, follows that of the adjacent street. The aesthetic effect derives principally from the play between the axially composed building volumes with two bay windows on the street façade and the appended side wings which challenge this symmetry.

During the same period as the Prairie Houses were built, W. realized the Larkin Building in Buffalo, N.Y. (1904–5; demolished 1949). In the city, that contact with nature which only seemed feasible in an open site was abandoned: the office building was instead oriented inward. A central space, lit from above by a skylight, was surrounded by four-storey galleries. The cubic exterior was articulated simply as a puristic, monumental block, to which four projecting and completely closed corner towers housing the staircases were appended. The towers also served as ventilation shafts for the extraction of cool or stale air: the Larkin Building was one of the first office buildings equipped with climatic control. The Unitarian Church in Oak Park, Ill. (1905–7), is a reinforced-concrete building in a heavy, monumental manner, somewhat Egyptianizing in its expressive language.

In 1909 W., who had moved his office back to Chicago in 1897, conceded that the dream of a democracy based on individual dwellings in the romanticized indigence of the suburbs could not be realized. He left his wife and six children and travelled to Europe with Mrs Cheney (the wife of a former client) as his mistress. There, they stayed principally at Fiesole in Italy. In 1910, a major exhibition of his work was held in Berlin, and in 1910 and 1911 the publisher Ernst Wasmuth published two portfolios which, along with the early propagandistic activity of H. P. *Berlage, were to exercise a decisive influence on European architecture. This influence can even be detected in the work of such independently minded personalities as *Gropius – whose model factory at the Cologne Werkbund exhibition of 1914 reveals clearly a direct dependence on the Park Inn Hotel in Mason City, Iowa (1909–10) – and even *Mies van der Rohe, whose 1923 design for a brick house was a purified form of the Prairie House type. After his return to the USA, W. founded in 1911 the Spring Green Cooperative in the solitude of Wisconsin, in order to make a fresh start; he began with the construction of his own house, Taliesin, its name being adopted from the eponymous Druidic bard. Midway Gardens in Chicago (1913) bore witness to an almost expressionistic search to discover the various possibilities of forms and building materials. This open-air restaurant and pleasure ground, which, in its sculptural décor, anticipated Art Deco, was demolished in 1929 during the Prohibition era.

In 1914 Mrs Cheney (who had reverted to her maiden name of Borthwick) died tragically in a fire at Taliesin; shaken and isolated, W. now devoted himself entirely to the rebuilding of his house. The financial difficulties involved in this provoked him to undertake the Imperial Hotel in Tokyo (1915–22, with Antonin Raymond), which was to be especially acclaimed for its technical refinements and its earthquake-proof supporting structure (attributed to the engineer Paul Mueller). W.'s stay in Japan – lasting, with interruptions, six years – combined with his personal crisis resulted in a decisive shift in terms of his architectural style.

This shift was already evident in the Barnsdall House in Los Angeles (1917–20), which turned the experience of the Prairie House on end: here, massive, closed building volumes, set under a heavy roof slab and decorated with motifs derived from Mayan art, were compactly grouped around an inner courtyard. This fortress-like, introverted complex aimed to establish a clear break with the natural setting and to dominate the surrouding landscape. The

Wright. Unity Church, Oak Park, Ill. (1905–7)

Wright. Millard House ('La Miniatura'), Pasadena, Cal. (1921–3)

Millard House ('La Miniatura'), built in 1921–3 in Pasadena on similar principles, was the first instance of W.'s use of the 'textile block' – a technique he had himself invented. The prefabricated concrete components, either solid or perforated, were employed in a manner that denied any differentiation between interior and exterior and allowed for a covering of vines or other climbing plants on the surfaces.

Taliesin burned down for a second time in 1925 and again in 1927. W. calmly rebuilt it and gathered around him a mystically inspired sect. In 1928 he built the Ocatillo Desert Camp near Chandler, Arizona, as a temporary settlement, a base from which to penetrate subsequently even further into the desert.

W.'s masterpiece, in which he realized a creative synthesis of organic architecture and

Wright. Kaufmann House ('Fallingwater'), near Mill Run, Pa. (1935–9)

Cubist and rationalist influences, was the Kaufmann House ('Fallingwater'), near Mill Run, Pa. (1935–9). This luxurious building is set on and over a stream at the point where it breaks into a waterfall. The focal point of the arrangement is, as in the Prairie Houses, the chimney and hearth; built on the solid rock they are – like all the building's vertical supporting elements – made of freestone. Attached to this plane are orthogonally superimposed horizontal levels, parallel surfaces of smooth concrete, which extend into nature and seem almost to bridge the small valley. A lively, complex play of interlocking spatial penetrations is developed, which makes radical use of the possibilities of reinforced concrete. The dialectic between interior space and the landscape is resolved through subtle transition points in this unique poetry.

If Fallingwater represents W.'s ideal solution for life in nature, one year later he began the administration building of the chemical company S. C. Johnson & Sons in Racine, Wis. (1936–9), which was to give form to his notion of work in the city. Once again – as in all of his urban projects – it provided an inward-turned image, with no visual connection to the exterior; the complex is lit by skylights and strips of glass tubes set high in the walls. Free-standing, mushroom-shaped reinforced-concrete supports, which are set on joints and resolved as huge circular plates at ceiling level, subdivide the vast office space. The later laboratory tower (1944–50) stood out above this strongly composed complex.

From 1937 on, W. built Taliesin West, his winter residence in the desert region of Paradise Valley, near Scottsdale, Arizona. An artificial piece of nature is created in the obliquely angled geometric composition of limestone and wood gathered on the site, a technique already tested in the Ocatillo Desert Camp. The massive 'desert concrete' walls, the open timber-framed structure and the tent-like roofing serve to unite surroundings and house as well as interior and exterior. The whole complex has remained a permanent building site, based on the concept of an architecture in a constant state of 'becoming'.

In the meantime, W. had begun, with the Willey House in Minneapolis (1934), his series of Usonian Houses: small, free-standing single houses for 'true Usonians' (Americans), often with walls of clapboards and flat roofs covered with wooden slats – a building type which proved startlingly various and imaginative in form, despite its low costs. Times had changed since the Prairie Houses. W. held fast to the two central principles: 'for every individual an individual style' and 'for every place an appropriate formal language', but he abandoned the cruciform grouping of spaces around the hearth in favour of a freer and more economic planning. He replaced the usual closed kitchen with working zones attached to the living spaces and generally skylit, and incorporated all the rooms, including the bedrooms, into the continuum of the house. The Usonian Houses developed from strongly orthogonal ground-plans via various geometric structures and finally to a confusion beyond measure of united, interpenetrating and sliding forms: W. used them as

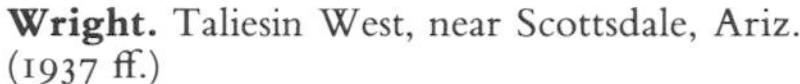

Wright. Taliesin West, near Scottsdale, Ariz. (1937 ff.)

Wright. S. C. Johnson & Son, Racine, Wis.: interior of administration building (1936–9), and general view of the complex showing the later laboratory tower (1944–50)

Wright. Solomon R. Guggenheim Museum, New York (1943–6, 1956–9)

a medium for formal experimentation. Among the most important are the Jacobs House in Madison (1936), the Sturges House in Brentwood Heights, Cal. (1939), and the Miller House in Charles City, Iowa (1946).

The spiral motif had first appeared in his work in 1925, in the project for the Gordon Strong Planetarium on Sugar Loaf Mountain, Maryland – a sort of science-fiction ziggurat intended to serve as a pilgrimage site for nature worshippers. In the Solomon R. Guggenheim Museum in New York (1943–6, 1956–9) the theme which he had elaborated many years earlier was finally realized. Its principal feature is a gallery within a white, spiral-formed and gently tapering funnel; visitors are carried to the top by lift and can then descend the internal spiral ramp on foot in order to view the pictures displayed on the walls.

The Price Tower in Bartlesville, Okla., was built in 1953–6; this nineteen-storey tower of offices and apartments harks back to earlier projects for tall buildings (Buildings for the National Insurance Company in Chicago, 1924; St Mark's Tower, New York, 1929) and strives for a new formal definition of the skyscraper. In addition to various projects in which the ageing architect increasingly indulged his fascination with the extravagant and the exotic (including the Marin County Civic Center in San Rafael, Cal., 1957–66), he built the Beth Sholom Synagogue in Elkins Park, Pa., in 1958–9. Over a ground-plan in the form of a triangle expanded to a hexagon rises a

Wright. Price Tower, Bartlesville, Okla. (1953–6)

sharply angled 'tent' of steel, glass, and plastic, which evokes associations with Indian wigwams and reflects the colour of the sky.

Despite his unyielding individualism, in his work W. did not confine himself to the angle or to the individual architectural composition, but concerned himself as well with urbanistic visions. When he fled the USA in 1909, he had already experienced the misery of an overcrowded capitalist metropolis such as Chicago ('where one sells everything and above all sells one's self'), as well as that of the isolated surrogate for nature as represented by the most elegant suburbs. The alternatives which he sought were expressed in his 1932 project for Broadacre City, which went back to a 1915 suggestion (Model Development for Chicago) and was to receive its definitive statement in 1958 as Living City, in which Ebenezer *Howard's Garden City was united with a Utopia. This was rooted in the ideas of Jean-

Wright. Marin County Civic Center, San Rafael, Cal. (1957–66)

Wright. Beth Sholom Synagogue, Elkins Park, Pa. (1958–9)

Jacques Rousseau, as well as in early anarchism, and acquired the scale of a vast landscape: an area of four square miles (over 1,000 hectares) was to be urbanized, with at least 4,000 m^2 of land allocated to each family. The development, which was enclosed by a street network based on the grid principle, was planned according to contemporary needs and financial requirements. The industrial sector lay in the outer zone, directly adjacent to the railway. Living City, which W. worked out in abstraction from the actual urban planning problems of the America of the Roosevelt era, is an architectural expression of his personal craving for a liberal and egalitarian community. The place of freedom and social harmony coincided thus with the greatest possible mobility: the automobile would be the tool and the symbol of individual freedom and would thus inform the structure of the development.

Although W. himself believed in the chimera of his horizontal, freely extended, 'landscape city', he also followed the opposite concept of locating housing in concentrated clusters surrounded by expansive undisturbed green zones. In 1956 he came to the vision of 'Illinois' for Chicago. Stimulated by the first successes in the production of atomic energy, he designed a narrow, towering, variously articulated, mile-high skyscraper for 130,000 inhabitants; its 528 floors were to be served by 56 atomic-powered lifts and countless escalators.

In an active career spanning more than sixty years, W. developed a hitherto unknown diversity of architectural forms and ideas. His astounding capacity for self-renewal had, however, nothing in common with capricious *eclecticism: just as Mies van der Rohe embodied the European myth of the Enlightenment, so W. developed in his tireless search for forms 'the American myth of the pioneer, who must always seek the new in order to find changed relationships in himself'.

W. was too stamped by his own individuality in his architectural language to serve directly as the inspiration for a school of disciples. His stimulus was more fruitful, however, in the most varied architectural movements (from *Expressionism to *Rationalism), the most diverse groups (from the School of *Amsterdam to De *Stijl) and the most varied architects. This resulted from the fact that he conducted, alongside his intensive building activity, an equally intensive activity as a publicist. He gave countless lectures, confided his thoughts on architecture in many books with considerable emphasis, and published the better part of his work. In addition, his pupils have spread the ideas of organic architecture throughout the world. VML

□ Gutheim, Frederick (ed.), *Frank Lloyd Wright on Architecture: Selected Writings 1894–1940*, Hitchcock, Henry-Russell, *In the Nature of Materials, 1887–1941: The Buildings of Frank Lloyd Wright*, New York 1942; Zevi, Bruno, *Frank Lloyd Wright*, Milan 1947; Scully, Vincent, *Frank Lloyd Wright*, New York and London 1960; Storrer, William Allin, *The Architecture of Frank Lloyd Wright: A Complete Catalog*, Cambridge, Mass. 1974; Gutheim, Frederick (ed.), *In the Cause of Architecture: Essays by Frank Lloyd Wright for the Architectural Review 1908–1952*, New York 1975; Sweeney, Robert L., *Frank Lloyd Wright: An Annotated Bibliography*, Los Angeles 1978; Twombly, Robert C., *Frank Lloyd Wright: His Life and Architecture*, New York 1979.

Wurster, William Wilson, b. Stockton, Cal. 1895, d. 1973. Studied at the University of California. In independent practice from 1926; in 1945 he joined Theodore Bernardi and Donn Emmons in partnership. Influenced by *Maybeck, W. was an exponent of the 'Bay Region Style', the Californian variant of Regionalism. He became known for his town and country houses, which are distinguished by their modesty, adaptation to environment and consideration of locally prevailing social, economic and climatic conditions. An early example of this 'everyday-architecture', which is more concerned with function than form, is the Gregory Farmhouse, near Santa Cruz, Cal. (1927), and a characteristic later example the Reynolds House in San Francisco (1946), an unpretentious, elongated wooden building, freely articulated and with a gently sloping hip roof.

□ 'Profilo di un architetto americano: William Wilson Wurster', *Architettura* (Rome), May 1957; Peters, Richard C., 'L'architetto William Wilson Wurster', *Casabella* (Milan), April 1960.

Y

Yamasaki, Minoru, b. Seattle 1912. Studied at the Universities of Washington (Seattle) and New York. Worked in the offices of the Empire State Building architects Shreve, Lamb and Harmon; with *Harrison, Fouilhoux and *Abramovitz; and with the stream-line designer Raymond Loewy. He achieved international notice, together with George Hellmuth and Joseph Leinweber, his partners at the time, for the Lambert Airport at St Louis, Mo. (1953–6), whose reception halls consist of a series of intersecting barrel vaults.

A characteristic feature of his style is the dissolution of the wall into an apparently textile-like fabric, which serves to disguise the structural members: umbrella walls made of profilated blocks, as at the American Concrete Institute (1958) in Detroit; metal grilles in the Reynolds Metals Regional Sales Office at Southfields, Mich. (1959). The impression of contrived elegance which is typical of Y.'s later designs is most strikingly evident in the World Trade Center, New York (1966–73, with Emery Roth & Sons), where the façades are dissolved by a superimposed linearity, of neo-Gothic inspiration, which disguises the shape and mass of the twin towers.

□ Yamasaki, M., *A Life in Architecture*, New York 1979.

Yorke, Francis Reginald Stevens, b. 1906, d. 1962. Studied at Birmingham University School of Architecture. Founder-member of the MARS Group (British section of *CIAM) and pioneer of modernism in *Great Britain, with his reinforced-concrete houses at Gidea Park, Essex (1933, with W. *Holford, G. Stephenson and A. Adam) and house at Nast Hyde, Hatfield (1935). In partnership with Marcel *Breuer, 1935–7, and from 1944 with Eugene Rosenberg and Cyril Mardall, which firm was responsible for many important projects, including schools at Stevenage (1947–9), Oldbury, and Pool Hill, Salop. (1955–7); academic buildings in London, Merthyr Tydfil and Leeds; housing at Stevenage, Harlow and in the Hansa district of Berlin; hospitals in Londonderry, Crawley and Hull; a department

Yamasaki. Reynolds Metals Regional Sales Office, Southfield, Mich. (1959)

store in Sheffield, and Gatwick Airport, Sussex. He was the editor of the annual volume *Specification* from 1935 to the time of his death, and was the author of standard works on modern houses and (with Sir Frederick *Gibberd) modern flats. HM

Yoshizaka, Takamasa, b. Tokyo 1917, d. Tokyo 1980. Studied at Waseda University in Tokyo, where he was active as a teacher until his death. As the son of a diplomat, he experienced early exposure to foreign cultures, and this enabled him to develop a cosmopolitan world-view. His experience in Europe in his youth and his study of *Le Corbusier's work (he worked in his studio in Paris 1950–2) were later combined in unique fashion with his heritage of pan-Asian thought. He was not only an architect and regional planner but also an organizer of many private institutions and the author of many fine essays. The influence of Le Corbusier was reflected quite clearly in his architectural works, but this influence came exclusively from the brutalistic (*New Brutalism) and vernacular-oriented period of his former teacher's later work. Among Y.'s most representative works are the Villa Coucou in Tokyo (1957) and the Gozu Hall (1961). HY

☐ 'Takamasa Yoshizaka 1917–1981', *Kenchiku Bunka* (Tokyo), May 1981.

Z

Zanuso, Marco, b. Milan 1916. Studied at the Milan Politecnico; diploma 1939. His buildings include the Olivetti Factory in São Paulo, Brazil (1956–8), a scheme consisting of 'honey-comb' cells covered with a roof of thin shell vaults.

Zehrfuss, Bernard (Louis), b. Angers 1911. Studied at the *Ecole des Beaux-Arts in Paris. He worked in Tunisia, 1943–8, and from 1948 had his own office in Paris. His buildings include: the Renault Factory at Flins (1952); the UNESCO Building in Paris (1953–8, with *Breuer and *Nervi); the Centre National des Industries et Techniques, Paris (1958, with Robert Camelot and Jean de Mailly); and the Musée de la Civilisation Gallo-Romaine in Lyons (1975).

Sources of illustrations

Illustrations are identified by page number and, wherever necessary, by an indication of position on a page (*a* = above, *b* = below, *c* = centre, *l* = left, *r* = right). Items not listed were supplied either by courtesy of the architect(s) or from the archives of Verlag Gerd Hatje, Stuttgart.

Friedrich Achleitner, Vienna 26*a*; A.C.L., Brussels 20*a*, 42*a*; Acme Photo 130; Michel Aertsen, Rio de Janeiro 51*r*; Akademie der Künste, Berlin 34*a*, 144, 254, 301*bl*; Amerika Haus, Cologne 367*a*, 368*l*; Annan, Glasgow 207; *The Architects' Journal* 71*r* (photo S. W. Newbery), 320; *The Architectural Review* 135*r*, 203*b*, (photos de Burgh Galwey) 71*a*, 247, (photos Dell and Wainwright) 131*b*, 340, (photo S. W. Newbery) 132*a*, (photos Henk Snoek) 127*a*, 315*b*; Architext, Amsterdam 46*b*, 85*l*, 240, 244, 322*b*; A.U.A. Documentation, Bagnolet (photo F. Derdour) 109*r*; courtesy, Australian Tourist Commission 353*a*; Morley Baer, Monterey, Cal. 230; Öffentliche Basler Denkmalpflege 332; courtesy, Behnisch & Partners 256; Denkmalpflege der Stadt Bern 295*b*; Therese Beyeler 143*l*; Bombelli 169; Christian Borngräber, Berlin 287–91; Brecht-Einzig Ltd 136, 321; British Architectural Library/RIBA 131*a*, 132*b*, 135*a*, 358; F. Català-Roca, Barcelona 313; Chevojon, Paris 34*b*, 298; Chicago Architectural Photo Co. 66–7, 325*a*; C.I.M.T., Paris 272*bl*; E. Claesson 329; *Country Life* 159*a*; Charles Phelps Cushing 234; Dandelet, San Anselmo 369*r*; Dominique Devie 18*a*, 107*c*; Dino, Milan 265*b*; John Donat, London 103; Michael Drummond, Montreal 59*a*; J. Ecuyer, La Chaux-de-Fonds 193; Hans Finsler, Zurich 54*a*; Fotogramma, Milan 249; Bildarchiv Foto Marburg 19*a*, 151, 170, 215*l*, 264, 265*a*, 356; Frankfurt am Main, Stadtarchiv 212*b*; Reinhard Friedrich, Berlin 124; Claude Gaspari 303; G. Gasparini, Genoa 172*a*; Marcel Gautherot, Rio de Janeiro 50*al*/*bl*, 52*b*, 279; Alexandre Georges, Pomona, N.Y. 182*a*, 227*b*, 266; Foto Atelier Gerlach, Vienna 27*r*, 28*a*, 87*l*, 203*al*; G. Gherardi-A. Fiorelli, Rome 239*a*; Ghizzoni di Scotti, Como 168*b*, 296; Marianne Goeritz 218*al*; Julien Graux, Paris 109*l*; Manfred Hanisch, Essen 48; Hedrich-Blessing, Chicago 163, 222, 224*l*, 226, 232, 268, 276*b*, 365*a*, 366; Lucien Hervé, Paris 107*b*, 197*r*, 198*l*, 261; Historisches Museum der Stadt Wien 26*b*; HNK Architectural Photography, Chicago 343; Hochschule für Architektur und Bauwesen, Weimar 157; courtesy, Hoechst AG 41; Jesper Hørn, Copenhagen 80*a*; Franz Hubmann, Vienna 152; courtesy, Institut für leichte Flächentragwerke, Stuttgart 127*b*, 255*b*, 257; Karl E. Jacobs, Berlin 140*r*; Jens Jansen, Stuttgart 295*a*; *The Japan Architect* (photos Masao Arai) 165*a*, 192*b*, 304*a*; Pierre Joly-Véra Cardot, Bures-sur-Yvette 62*b*; Keren-Or, Haifa 167*a*; A. F. Kersting 23, 134; Foto-Kessler, Berlin 227*a*; courtesy, KLM 76; Balthazar Korab 181, 371; Kunsthistorisches Institut, Bonn 233; Landesbildstelle, Berlin 215*r*, 339; Landesbildstelle Württemberg, Stuttgart 49*b*, 82, 316*l*; Erwin Lang, Los Angeles 61; Björn Linn 327*a*, 328, 330; André Martin 141; MAS, Barcelona 118, 119*b*; Angelo Masina, Bologna 12*l*; F. Maurer, Zurich 128; Metropolitan Opera Association, New York 145*a*; Joseph W. Molitor, Ossining, N.Y. 286*a*; David Moore, Sydney 60; Bernhard Moosbrugger, Basle 333*b*, 334*b*; José Moscardi, São Paulo 53, 250; Museum of Finnish Architecture, Helsinki 99*a*, 101*b*, 284, (photos H. Havas) 11, 12*a*, 100, 280*l*, (photo Martti I. Jaatinen) 101*a*, (photo E. Mäkinen) 10, (photo Pietinen) 304*b*, (photo Roos) 99*b*, (photo A. Salokorpi) 98*b*, (photo E. H. Staf) 98*a*, (photo Jussi Tiainen) 102*b*, (photos Welin) 9, 255*a*; (photo V. A. Vahlström) 57; The Museum of Modern Art, New York 94*al*, 123*b*, 223; National Buildings Record, London 133*a*; courtesy, National Film Board of Canada 58; courtesy, National Gallery of Art, Washington, D.C. 259; National Monuments Record, London 22, 97; Hermann Ohlsen, Bremen 273; van Ojen, The Hague 258*a*; Openbare Werken, Rotterdam 242; Österreichische Nationalbibliothek, Vienna 87*r*, 361; Artur Pfau, Mannheim 126*a*; courtesy, the Pierpont Morgan Library, New York 346; Renes, Arnhem 258*b*; Retoria, Tokyo (photos Yukio Futagawa) 33, 63*b*, 120, 180*b*, 299; Rijksdienst voor de Monumentenzorg, Zeist 241*b*, 281, 318; Roger-Viollet, Paris 89, 262*a*; Jean Roubier 110*b*; Ruhr Universität, Bochum 18*b*; Armando Salas Portugal, Mexico City 218*ar*, 219*a*; Sandak, Inc. 153*b*, 348; Oscar Savio, Rome 14; Ali Schafler, Korneuburg 260*a*; Shokokusha, Tokyo 337*a*; Julius Shulman, Los Angeles 85*r*, 219*r*, 246, 309; Hans Sibbelee, Amsterdam 190; Francesca Signorini, Perugia 96; Skomark Associates, Philadelphia 357; R. Spreng, Basle 209*r*; George H. Steuer 225; Stiftung Preussischer Kulturbesitz 253*a*; Ed. Stoecklein 278; Dr Franz Stoedtner, Düsseldorf 19*b*, 40*a*, 93, 139, 154, 200; Ezra Stoller Associates 55, 164, 182*b*, 213*b*, 286*b*, 306–7, 352*a*, 365*b*; Ateljé Sundahl, Nacka (photo C. G. Rosenberg) 24*b*; Jerzy Surwille 29; Yutaka Suzuki, Tokyo 31*b*; courtesy, Swedish Tourist Traffic Association 211; H. Tempest Ltd, Nottingham 248; Foto Teuwen, Basle 333*a*; Monika Uhlig, Cologne 175*b*; Gerhard Ullmann, Berlin 188*a*, 263; United States Information Service, Bonn-Bad Godesberg 292, 293*a*, 325*l*, 367*c*/*b*, 368*r*; Vasari, Rome 171*a*; Jan Versnel, Amsterdam 45*a*; Jürgen Wagner 126*b*; Gunnar Wåhlen, Stockholm 327*b*; Jørgen Watz, Lyngby 78*r*, 79*c*/*b*; A. Winkler, Munich 25, 108; Arno Wrubel, Düsseldorf 125.

Index

Figures in **bold** type indicate main entries; those in *italics* refer to illustrations.